BRITAIN AT BAY
1938–1941

BRITAIN AT BAY

The Epic Story of the Second World War,

1938–1941

ALAN ALLPORT

ALFRED A. KNOPF

NEW YORK

2020

THIS IS A BORZOI BOOK PUBLISHED BY ALFRED A. KNOPF

Copyright © 2020 by Alan Allport

All rights reserved. Published in the United States by Alfred A. Knopf, a division of
Penguin Random House LLC, New York, and distributed in Canada by Random House
of Canada, a division of Penguin Random House Ltd., Toronto. Originally published in
hardcover in Great Britain by Profile Books Ltd, London, in 2020.

www.aaknopf.com

Knopf, Borzoi Books, and the colophon are registered trademarks of
Penguin Random House LLC.

Library of Congress Cataloging-in-Publication Data
Names: Allport, Alan, [date] author.
Title: Britain at Bay : the epic story of the Second World War, 1938–1941 /
Alan Allport.
Other titles: Epic story of the Second World War, 1938–1941
Description: First edition. | New York : Alfred A. Knopf, 2020. | Includes bibliographical
references and index.
Identifiers: LCCN 2020028530 (print) | LCCN 2020028531 (ebook) |
ISBN 9780451494740 (hardback) | ISBN 9780451494757 (ebook)
Subjects: LCSH: World War, 1939–1945—Great Britain. | Great Britain—Politics
and government—1936–1945. | Great Britain—Social conditions—20th century. |
World War, 1939–1945—Campaigns—Great Britain. | World War, 1939–1945—Social
aspects—Great Britain.
Classification: LCC D759 .A635 2020 (print) | LCC D759 (ebook) |
DDC 940.53/41—dc23
LC record available at https://lccn.loc.gov/2020028530
LC ebook record available at https://lccn.loc.gov/2020028531

Front-of-jacket images: (details, left to right) Winston Churchill & Neville
Chamberlain, 1940. Granger; RAF Hawker Hurricanes, 1940, U.K. (detail).
Universal Art Archive / Alamy; Children to be evacuated at Eastbourne, Sussex,
1939 (detail). Bentley Archive / Popperfoto / Getty Images.

Jacket design by Jenny Carrow

Manufactured in the United States of America

First American Edition

Deo gratias Anglia redde pro victoria

Dedicated to the fifteen passengers and crew members of the steam merchant *Alphacca* who died when she was torpedoed off Cape Palmas, Liberia, on 4 April 1942.

Contents

LIST OF ILLUSTRATIONS

1. The wreckage in Broadgate, Coventry, 25 August 1939, after an Irish Republican Army (IRA) bomb. Photo: Central Press/Stringer/Getty
2. A British Army armoured car patrols the streets of Belfast in July 1935. Photo: R. Lock/Stringer/Getty
3. A factory worker at the Singer Motors works in Coventry. Photo: Fox Photos/Stringer/Getty
4. British troops blow up houses in the village of Miar, near Haifa, during the 'Arab Revolt' in British Mandate Palestine. Photo: Fox Photos/Stringer/Getty
5. Neville Chamberlain, British chancellor of the exchequer 1931–37 and prime minister 1937–40. Photo: Fox Photos/Stringer/Getty
6. British foreign secretary Austen Chamberlain. Photo: AFP/Stringer/Getty
7. Chamberlain shakes hands with Adolf Hitler at the conclusion of the Munich Conference in September 1938. Photo: Historical/Contributor/Corbis
8. Neville Chamberlain with Winston Churchill in 1939. Photo: Hulton Deutsch / Getty
9. The battleship HMS *Prince of Wales* is launched, 3 May 1939. Photo: Central Press/Stringer/Getty
10. A French battleship in the harbour of Mers-el-Kébir, in north-western Algeria, burns on 3 July 1940 after being attacked by British warships. Photo: Central Press/Stringer/Getty
11. Evacuee children from London arrive in the coastal town of Eastbourne September 1939. Photo: Bentley Archive/Popperfoto/Getty
12. From the left: Chief of the British Imperial General Staff Sir Edmund Ironside; General Alphonse Georges, commander of the French northeastern front; Winston Churchill; General Maurice Gamelin, commander-in-chief of the French armed forces; and Lord Gort,

commander of the British Expeditionary Force in France. Photo: Keystone/Getty

LIST OF MAPS

FOREWORD

This book, the first of two parts, is an attempt to understand how Britain fought the Second World War: how it became involved in it in the first place, how it fought it, why it was ultimately on the winning side and what the war did to its institutions, its culture and its society. It is a version of the story that omits the well-loved but misleading clichés that have traditionally infused it. In doing this, it becomes a story that is more interesting, more valuable, more important than ever. Britain's war can be understood, broadly, as a tale of two parts.

The first part, which this volume is concerned with, is a story mostly about defeat – diplomatic defeat followed by military defeat after military defeat. What it tries to explain is how a country that got so many things catastrophically wrong in the early years of the conflict managed not just to hold out against Hitler but, by the second anniversary of the war's outbreak in September 1941, to have apparently halted the rout, and even, perhaps, to be constructing a plausible theory of victory. It ends on a note of cautious hope. The second part will show how such hopes eventually became realities, and how the British people rallied themselves as part of a powerful global alliance to defeat Nazism, fascism and Japanese militarism – and what the cost of that victory would turn out in the end to be.

A NOTE ON MONEY

Throughout the period discussed in this book, the currency system used in the United Kingdom was based on pounds, shillings and pence, written as '£ s. d.' – for example, £3 10s. 6d. There were twelve pence in a shilling and twenty shillings in a pound.

After Britain abandoned the Gold Standard in 1931, the exchange rate between the pound and US dollar fluctuated for the rest of the decade. Between 1934 and 1938 £1 averaged around $5. Balance of payment pressures in the final year of peace owing to rearmament saw the pound fall to $4.60, and at the outbreak of war in September 1939 it briefly reached a low of $3.99. In March 1940 the pound was pegged at $4.03, and it remained at that fixed rate until it was devalued in 1949.

It is impossible to apply a one-size-fits-all conversion of 1930s and 1940s wages and prices into modern terms because the costs of goods and services have inflated at different rates in the intervening years. As a rough guide, a male manual worker in 1938 might have expected to earn about £3 10s. a week (working an average forty-eight hours). A woman's pay was typically half that of a man. Working-class wages rose significantly during the war, but so also did the cost of living, cancelling out to some extent the benefit. Middle-class income was calculated in terms of annual salary rather than weekly earnings. An annual salary over £250 excluded the recipient from participation in the national unemployment insurance scheme and was regarded in the 1930s as a benchmark dividing the working and middle classes. A senior white-collar worker – for example, the branch manager of an important regional office – might earn £1,000 a year or more.

A newly built terraced house in the London area cost about £400 in the mid-1930s. The same house in 2020 would cost around £800,000.

To get a sense of how state expenditure translates into modern terms, compare the United Kingdom's total central government spending in 1935 of £732 million with the 2020 figure of £667 billion (911 times greater). It can also be useful to consider cost in terms of function. The unit cost of a Supermarine Spitfire Mark I in the late 1930s was around £9,500. The unit cost of the combat aircraft that performs the same role for the RAF today, the Eurofighter Typhoon, is approximately £110 million, or 11,500 times greater.

PART ONE

THE BRITISH WAY AND PURPOSE

1

SHIRE FOLK

In November 1949 Major Warren Lewis, brother of C. S. Lewis, wrote what was probably the first ever review of J. R. R. Tolkien's novel *The Lord of the Rings*. The manuscript he had read was in an inchoate state. It did not even have a title. But this 'New Hobbit', the long-awaited sequel to Tolkien's 1937 children's story of that name, had captivated Lewis immediately. 'Golly, what a book! The inexhaustible fertility of the man's imagination amazes me,' Lewis enthused in his diary. He was struck by Tolkien's mastery of description, his poignant characterisations and the unflagging energy of the narrative. This, he felt, was 'a great book of its kind'.

Lewis wondered, though, if critics would interpret *The Lord of the Rings* as a political satire about contemporary Europe, rather than as the timeless mythopoeic fantasy that Tolkien had intended to write. 'By accident, a great deal of it can be read topically,' Lewis thought, 'the Shire standing for England, Rohan for France, Gondor the Germany of the future, Sauron for Stalin.' He even wondered if the 'egregious' Lewis Silkin, the minister of town and country planning in Clement Attlee's Labour government, would be identified as the vandal wizard Saruman, destroyer of the novel's pastoral idyll, the Shire.[1]

None of this would have pleased Tolkien. In 1965, in the foreword to the second edition of *The Lord of the Rings*, he explicitly rejected the idea that his story was intended as an allegory of any historical event, most of all the recent great war against Nazism. 'The real war does not resemble the legendary war in its process or its conclusion,' Tolkien insisted. Even so, for all such protestations, Lewis had clearly been on to something back in 1949. He had realised that Tolkien's future audience was going to see associations between events in Middle Earth and those in their own world. But then Tolkien himself, in his 1965 foreword, conceded that the absence of any deliberately embedded allegory did not preclude his readers' right to interpret the text as they saw fit. *The Lord of the Rings* might not serve as an allegory. But it had what he called 'applicability'.[2]

Tolkien had, after all, never made any secret of the fact that the Shire, the setting of the first four and final two chapters of *The Lord of the Rings*, was modelled on the rural Warwickshire he half-remembered from his childhood in the 1890s.[3] Even the Shire's location, on the north-western edge of Middle Earth, correlated with the usual placement of the British Isles on the map of Europe. The Shire, with its drystone walls, hay wains, country alehouses and sheriffs, was an affectionate parody of the pre-industrial 'Deep England' already central to conservative (especially Catholic conservative) conceptions of English identity at the beginning of the twentieth century, through the writings of authors such as G. K. Chesterton, H. J. Massingham and H. V. Morton.[4]

And the Shire's diminutive inhabitants, hobbits – 'charming, absurd, helpless hobbits', as Gandalf the Wizard calls them – corresponded very neatly with the gentle and unassuming self-image that the English people had adopted for themselves in the years after the First World War.[5] They had not always seen themselves as such meek creatures. The brash, bumptious ogre John Bull, the personification of English virtues who had symbolised the age of High Britannic Imperialism and gunboat diplomacy, was no hobbit. But, after the slaughter of the Western Front, the English were weary of John Bull's aggressive theatricality. Now they saw themselves exemplified by the 'Little Man' – 'small, kindly, bewildered, modest, obstinate, and very loveable', as the writer and MP Harold Nicolson described him, and most famously depicted by the cartoonist Sidney Strube, in the *Daily Express*, with bowler hat, umbrella, bow tie, high collar, pince-nez glasses and bushy white moustache.[6] Strube's Little Man offered an Englishman for a new, milder, altogether more quotidian age.

Writing in 1934, the conservative historian Arthur Bryant argued that this modern Little Englishman was a 'stolid, tolerant, good-humoured, reliable kind of person, so strong withal (because he is so much at peace with himself) so gentle'.[7] W. R. Inge, a former dean of St Paul's Cathedral, said of him that he was 'humane; cruelty excites him to violent indignation. He is a bad hater, and has a short memory for injuries.' His chief vices were intemperance ('in eating more than drinking') and a 'disinclination for hard and steady work'. But he made up for these faults by 'a peculiar sense of humour [...] preserving him from fierce and cruel fanaticisms'.[8] Tolkien, writing a few years later, would describe his hobbits as 'an unobtrusive but very ancient people' who loved 'peace and quiet and good tilled earth', whose faces 'were as a rule good-natured rather than beautiful, broad, bright-eyed, red-cheeked' and who found pleasure mainly in 'eating and drinking' and 'simple jests'.[9] Clearly, the English were the close cousins of these artless, introverted and complacent people of the Shire.

Too complacent, perhaps. Tolkien's affection for his hobbits was unreserved. But *The Lord of the Rings* can be understood, among other things, as a warning about the dangers of languorous detachment from the evils of the world. Frodo Baggins, the novel's protagonist, is, like all hobbits, a confirmed believer in Splendid Isolation at the beginning of Tolkien's story. Frodo's initial preference is to turn away from the threat emerging from Mordor rather than openly to confront it: to hide away the dangerous magical ring that he possesses, to speak nothing of it and to hope that the storm will pass by his sleepy homeland and that better times will follow. Gandalf, frustrated at this guileless wishful thinking, must chivvy him into action, force Frodo to accept that, whether he likes it or not, the destructive forces that threaten to overwhelm Middle Earth will not spare the Shire simply because it appears harmless.

Whether Tolkien recognised these parallels with the conflict against Nazi Germany is unclear. As a pessimistic cultural conservative, he had a complex attitude towards the Second World War. He was ambivalent about its outcome. He felt that it had been fought with a machine-age ugliness that would in time merely 'breed new Saurons, and slowly turn men and elves into orcs'.[10] His political views had never been straightforward. During the Munich crisis in 1938, Tolkien expressed more suspicion of atheistic Russia than of Germany.[11] Despite his origins in colonial South Africa, he was a Little Englander who had no interest in fighting to defend a British Empire he abhorred.[12] But his personal detestation of Hitler – in part because of the violence the Nazi leader had done to the reputation of northern European mythology – was persistent and sincere.

From its first publication in 1954 *The Lord of the Rings* was interpreted by many of its readers as a warning about the perils of good people failing to act in the face of a malign existential threat.[13] After all, how could a British audience that had lived through the Appeasement era of the 1930s and the terrible events that followed it not find in Tolkien's story something uncannily familiar? Here was a tale about the people of a small and peripheral land, happy in their isolation and primitive democracy, perhaps a little too incurious about events beyond their frontiers, suddenly being faced with a monstrous, militaristic terror from the east, one that they had previously overlooked or else dismissed as none of their concern. A terror to which they would only respond at the last moment; a terror which, as a result, came very close to sweeping away their gentle, parochial civilisation once and for all, and which they were ultimately able to triumph over only because of their unassuming strength of character. To the readers of the 1950s, the applicability of this story to the events of Munich, Dunkirk and the Blitz must have seemed to jump off the page.[14]

By 1954, Tolkien's story was one the British had told themselves about the Second World War many times over already. As early as the winter of 1939, in his Penguin Special paperback *Why Britain Is at War*, Harold Nicolson had insisted that 'the British people are by nature peaceful and kindly', a nation of hobbits who

> desire nothing on Earth except to retain their liberties, to enjoy their pleasures, and to go about their business in a tranquil frame of mind. They have no ambition for honour and glory, and they regard wars, and even victories, as silly, ugly, wasteful things. They are not either warriors or heroes until they are forced to; they are sensible and gentle men and women.

'Somewhat indolent by temperament', this 'sleepy, decent and most pacific race' had regrettably ignored Nazi Germany's ambitions for too long, Nicolson admitted, for 'only by dire necessity' could they ever be 'stirred to do unpleasant things'. But in the end they had been provoked once too often. Hitler, Nicolson declared, would now discover to his cost the conviction and tenacity of the mild-mannered islanders whom he had so rashly underestimated.[15]

Why Britain Is at War was published in the sleepy first months of the conflict. In June 1940, when the Allied armies on the continent collapsed in the face of the German *Blitzkrieg*, France fell and Britain seemed on the brink of invasion and defeat, the left-wing novelist J. B. Priestley mobilised the same myth to even more influential effect in his series of 'Postscript' broadcasts on the BBC. Priestley described to his listeners how the 'kindness, humour and courage' of the British people would inevitably overcome the 'half-crazy, haunted, fearful minds' set against them.[16] Most famously, he drew on the story of the commercial paddle-steamers conscripted into service to rescue the troops trapped on the Dunkirk beaches as a way of epitomising what the war was about, and how it would be won. It was a war,

Priestley declared, of people from an 'innocent foolish world' of pork pies and sandcastles, Pierrots and amusement arcades, who had found themselves pitted against madness and machine-age tyranny; of civilians performing feats of unexpected courage 'so absurd and yet so grand and gallant that you hardly know whether to laugh or to cry when you read about them'.[17]

Priestley did more than just rally a confused and frightened nation in June 1940. He helped to teach the British how to understand what was happening to them as a 'People's War' of humble, essentially civilian-minded heroes like the Little Man depicted by Strube. His version of Dunkirk was one of 'little ships' crewed by stout-hearted amateurs saving their country's army when all else had failed, rather than the professional Royal Navy, which actually rescued most of the trapped soldiers. Priestley's influence is undiminished eighty years later. Christopher Nolan's 2017 blockbuster *Dunkirk* is basically one of Priestley's Postscripts illustrated with twenty-first-century special effects. Its central character is not some brawny uniformed Achilles but the mild-mannered, middle-class, middle-aged Mr Dawson (Mark Rylance), the skipper of a diminutive pleasure yacht, a Dorset Frodo sailing into battle in knitted pullover, armed with nothing more martial than a hot, sweet cup of tea.

What writers such as Nicolson and Priestley had begun, Winston Churchill continued and confirmed in his six-volume *The Second World War*, a history which, after its completion in 1954 (the same year that the first volume of *The Lord of the Rings* was published), would become the most influential narrative of the conflict in the English-speaking world. The moral Churchill offers for Britain's war is of a Shire Folk almost undone 'through their unwisdom, carelessness, and good nature' in allowing Hitler to rearm and conquer the West. Churchill cast himself in the early chapters of his first volume, *The Gathering Storm*, published in 1948, as a Gandalfian seer whose warnings about the threat from Germany in the 1930s had been ignored almost until it was too late. 'Poor England! Leading her free, careless life from day to day [... behaving] as though all the world was as easy, uncalculating, and well-meaning as herself.'[18]

What made the Shire Folk narrative so persuasive to the British, whether it was told by a man of the left such as Priestley or a conservative patriarch like Churchill, was that it explained the nation's early wartime failures, as well its subsequent successes. Those failures and successes were products of the same unchanging national characteristics. The British had been gulled into almost catastrophic carelessness in the 1930s by the cunning of their enemies. But what the Germans, in their hubris, had failed to guess at were the inner reserves of fortitude such a modest island race possessed – a stubborn unwillingness to be bullied, and an indomitable pluck even in the face of as grotesque and triumphant a Moloch as Hitler. The Shire Folk, it turned out, were a people of brilliant 'muddlers-through', inspired amateurs in an emergency:

> Ease and peace had left this people still curiously tough. They were, if it came to it, difficult to daunt or to kill; and they were, perhaps, so unwearyingly fond of good things not least because they could, when put to it, do without them, and could survive rough handling [...] in a way that astonished those who did not know them well and looked no further than their bellies and their well-fed faces.[19]

That was Tolkien describing his hobbits. But it could just as easily have been Churchill writing about Dunkirk, or the Battle of Britain, or the U-boat war in the Atlantic.

It is not difficult to see why the British found this appealing. To be sure, it portrayed them as a people with shortcomings – dangerous shortcomings of naivety and unworldliness that had almost ruined them. But *attractive* shortcomings all the same. Perhaps, the Shire Folk myth suggested, they should have been more aware of what was going on abroad during the 1930s. Perhaps they should have been more cognisant of the terrible possibilities of Nazism, more urgent in their response to German rearmament. But there was nothing shameful about preferring peace to war. There was nothing inexcusable about being too good-hearted to understand the totalitarian mind. They had done the right thing in the end. Besides, foolish and incompetent (and conveniently dead) leaders had encouraged them in their early follies. Attlee's left and Churchill's right could agree on that. This was a myth that had something to offer everyone, no matter what their politics.

It was – is – all the same, a myth. To call it a myth does not mean that there is no truth to it at all. Like all myths that endure, it has succeeded precisely because it includes much that is true. But it also includes much that is true but deceptive, and much that is only half-true, and much that is not true at all. If we want to really understand the British experience of the Second World War, we need to acknowledge the Shire Folk myth, salute it and then set it aside. Because the British people who fought and defeated Hitler from 1939 to 1945 were not nearly as innocent as hobbits. Nor as unprepared for the viciousness of total war. Nor anything like as nice.

2

ULSTER *KRISTALLNACHT*

The manager of Astley's hardware shop was standing a few feet away from his front window when the explosion happened. He remembered afterwards 'a loud boom and a terrific inrush of air which threw me to the ground. The front door and the whole of the structure and windows were blown inwards.' The blast tossed cars across Broadgate, Coventry's main shopping promenade. It left the pavement ankle-deep in shattered glass and scattered children's toys and women's handbags a quarter of a mile in every direction. Passing trams and buses were punctured with flying shrapnel. Once the sound of the explosion had reverberated away, the screams and whimpers of the injured became audible. Rescuers, gingerly making their way through the rubble, could see bodies lying in the brick dust as the smoke began to clear.[1]

Sixty people, it turned out, had been wounded, most of them by lacerating glass and clumps of debris. 'I have never experienced anything like it, absolute chaos,' wrote one survivor, Joan Thornton. 'The falling glass did more damage than anything.'[2] Three of the wounded died of their injuries at the scene, one of them a fifteen-year-old boy. Another two people were found dead, having been killed instantly by the blast. One of them, twenty-one-year-old Elsie Ansell, was so badly disfigured that she could be identified only by her engagement ring. Five days after the explosion she was buried, in her wedding dress, in the grounds of St Barbara's in Earlsdon, the church in which she had been expecting to marry. Four days after her funeral, Britain declared war on Germany.

The smack of detonation; the rain of crystal scythes and timber and masonry; the doleful search for survivors afterwards; the reckoning with the dead. For six years the British would have to get used to this grim procession of events, not least in the city of Coventry, doomed for destruction by the Luftwaffe. But what happened in Broadgate on 25 August 1939 was not an air raid; indeed, it had nothing to do with the Germans at all. The

explosive device that blew up Astley's front windows arrived by an altogether less complex delivery system than a Heinkel or a Dornier bomber. It
was left on the kerbside in the front basket of an errand boy's bicycle. The
man who left it there, later identified as Joby O'Sullivan, was making his way
by train to Holyhead and the mail-boat to Dublin when the bomb went off.
The British authorities never caught him. But five of his accomplices were
apprehended soon after the bombing, and in the winter of 1939 they were
tried at Warwick Assizes for murder. Two of them, James McCormack and
Peter Barnes, were convicted and hanged at Winson Green Prison in Birmingham in February 1940 – the last two members of the Irish Republic
Army (IRA) to be executed in Great Britain.[3]

Why did the IRA blow up Broadgate? We don't know. It may have
been deliberate. It may have been a mistake. It was not a one-off attack,
however. It was merely the bloodiest incident yet in a campaign – the
'S-Plan' – which had been going on since January 1939. The S-Plan was the
most violent terrorist campaign that the British mainland had experienced
since the late nineteenth century, and one that would not be matched in its
ferocity until the pub and motorway bombings of the 1970s.

The IRA bombed Broadgate to try to cajole and frighten the British
state into handing over to the government in Dublin the six counties of
Northern Ireland, which had remained part of the United Kingdom after
the rest of Ireland had achieved quasi-independence in 1922. The S-Plan
involved hundreds of incendiary and high-explosive attacks across England's major cities at a rate of almost one every day. Coventry had been
a target several times already before the Broadgate explosion. Telephone
cables had been destroyed, bombs placed in shop letterboxes, sticks of gelignite sent to the city's main post office and, in one of the campaign's more
quixotic touches, four municipal public lavatories blown up.

Other English cities had suffered in much the same way. Hotels,
cinemas, banks, power stations, postal sorting offices, gas mains and
aqueducts had all been targeted. One of the walls of Walton Gaol in Liverpool had been blown up in a failed attempt to set off a prison break.
London Tube stations had been bombed. An attempt to destroy Hammersmith Bridge had been narrowly foiled by the actions of a passer-by,
who subsequently received an MBE for his valorous efforts. There were
rumours of planned attacks on Buckingham Palace, Windsor Castle and
the Houses of Parliament. The Broadgate victims were not the S-Plan's
first fatalities. A Manchester fish porter and a passenger waiting in the

left-luggage area of London's King's Cross station had both been killed a few weeks earlier.

For the police, 1939 was a frustrating year of trying to guess where the IRA might strike next. Vehicles passing through the Rotherhithe and Blackwall tunnels under the Thames had been searched for explosives. The Grand Union Canal in Paddington basin was drained in a laborious and, as it turned out, fruitless search for dumped weapons. Road blocks had been set up around Birmingham and the city's main police station girdled by a thick steel mesh. A radiologist had written to the *Daily Telegraph* proposing a novel security measure: perhaps, he suggested, luggage at train stations ought to be X-rayed to see whether there were weapons or explosives in it (the idea was not taken up). The home secretary, Sir Samuel Hoare, told his Cabinet colleagues that they were faced with a most serious terrorist threat, 'a highly organised secret society which incites and ruthlessly enforces fanatical obedience'.[4]

In a way, the whole S-Plan campaign had been a kind of dress rehearsal, albeit on a vastly less lethal scale, for the sort of ordeal that the Luftwaffe was going to dole out to the British people during the Second World War – and, equally, that RAF Bomber Command was going to dole out to the German people. Terrorism, like strategic bombing, was a method of asymmetrical warfare. It was an attempt to strike at an enemy obliquely rather than head-on. Its goal, at least in part, was to break the adversary's morale: to 'subjugate the obdurate will of our inveterate and powerful opponent', as the main planning document setting out the S-Plan put it.[5]

The IRA campaign, like the German and British strategic bombing campaigns, began with a formal renunciation of any attempt deliberately to kill civilians. All targets were to be strictly economic and industrial in nature – 'precision strikes' against the means of enemy production only. As it progressed, however, there was greater and greater temptation to set such fine distinctions aside. By April 1939 the IRA, having suffered a series of embarrassing failures, and frustrated by the British government's lack of response, warned that its 'conditional' restraint against the taking of innocent life might now be withdrawn.[6] The bomb that blew up Broadgate may have been an expression of this new ruthlessness. Later it was suggested that the real target may have been Coventry's main power station, and that the bomb had been accidentally left in the city's shopping district because O'Sullivan panicked and abandoned it half-way through his mission.[7] We don't know. Either way, to take a powerful explosive device into a busy street risked killing many people. Precision strikes were always a good deal easier to perform on paper than in practice, for airmen as well as terrorists. Fatalities – intentional or collateral – were hard to avoid.

The S-Plan anticipated the strategic bombing campaigns of the Second World War in another way too: it failed. The IRA could not, in the end, terrify an entire people into submission any more than the Luftwaffe or the RAF could. Shedding blood only made the victims more determined to resist. The Broadgate bombing was, as it turned out, the beginning of the end of the S-Plan. The campaign meandered on for seven months after the outbreak of the European war, but it attracted less and less attention from the police and the public, who by then had other, more urgent things on their minds. The last bomb definitely attributable to the IRA blew up a rubbish heap in London in the spring of 1940. Hardly anyone noticed. The S-Plan's author, Jim O'Donovan, wrote afterwards that it had been 'hastily conceived, scheduled to a premature start, with ill-equipped and inadequately trained personnel, too few men and too little money'. This would not have been a bad summary of the strategic bombing efforts of the Germans and the British during the first two years of the war.[8]

*

Coventry's Broadgate was blown up by the IRA, not the German air force. But Nazi complicity in the S-Plan was strongly suspected by the British public in 1939. In a speech to the House of Commons outlining the government's response to the terrorist campaign, Samuel Hoare hinted that the IRA's activities were being 'closely watched and actively stimulated' by what he called 'foreign organisations'. Josiah Wedgwood, a Labour backbencher, developed the theme. The attacks were evidence that members of 'the physical force party of the Fascist world' were acting in conspiratorial unison. The IRA was merely one small part of 'the whole Fascist movement against liberty, democracy and freedom'.[9] Hoare, for his part, was careful not to spell out exactly what he meant by 'foreign organisations'. He was probably referring to Irish-American IRA sympathisers rather than the Germans. But he did not correct Wedgwood.[10]

The link between the IRA and the Nazis was understandable enough. It was no secret in the late summer of 1939 that Britain and Germany were edging towards war. In the circumstances it seemed highly plausible that Hitler might have co-opted a domestic terrorist group like the IRA to harm and distract his enemies. Some witnesses to the Broadgate bombing interviewed by the police were convinced that they had seen aircraft in the sky moments before the explosion, and that they had actually been attacked by the Luftwaffe. Such threats had been conflated before. When, back in May, the IRA had set off a magnesium bomb in a Paramount cinema in Birmingham, there had been pandemonium inside the auditorium as members of the audience panicked, thinking that the long-dreaded German aerial Blitz had begun. 'Keep calm – it's only the Irish again,' someone shouted to reassure the crowd (whether they added 'and carry on' is unknown).[11]

The IRA *did* try to get the Germans to co-operate with them in 1939. But they did not get very far. Jim O'Donovan made three trips to Germany that year to try to persuade officials of Hitler's military intelligence, the Abwehr, to provide support to the Irish terrorist effort in Britain. But the Germans were unimpressed by O'Donovan's organisation, regarding it, with good reason, as amateurish, ineffective and riddled with informers. They offered encouragement and some token material assistance, but little else. The relationship between Irish radicalism and continental totalitarianism was mostly fantasy.[12]

But it was appealing fantasy, all the same, because it underscored for the British the *foreignness* of IRA violence to their own way of life. By the 1930s the British were heavily invested in the Little Man conception of themselves. Key to this was the idea of their nation as a uniquely gentle, domesticated and consensual place, a 'peaceable kingdom' in which belligerence was rare, moderation the norm and reasonableness celebrated.[13] The Broadgate bombing represented everything that was supposedly inimical to British civilisation in the 1930s: a resort to terror rather than persuasion; an indifference to the suffering of innocents; a contempt for constitutional process. Britain, according to the Little Man view of the world, was an offshore haven of tranquillity, mercifully detached by geography from the cruel and quarrelsome mainland of Europe. The techniques of political terror commonplace on the continent – pogroms, purges, assassinations – were unknown on the English-speaking side of the Channel. 'Our methods,' the military commentator J. F. C. Fuller pointed out, 'are not of the stiletto, the bomb, and the cup of bad coffee.' Thinking of the collapse of parliamentary democracy across Europe in 1935, the historian J. E. Neale sought consolation in his own nation's exceptionalism. 'We may thank God,' he said, 'we are not as other men are.'[14]

Some of this was true. The Great Britain of the 1930s had a stable and moderate political system, no small thing in an age of totalitarianism. Its three main political parties all sought to govern from the centre rather than the margins and did not challenge the validity of election results even in defeat. Extremists who rejected this constitutional order, like the Communists and Blackshirts, could boast noisy antics which got a lot of press attention and a handful of well-placed sympathisers, but so far as the masses were concerned they never occupied anything more than a tiny and contemptible niche in political life. The violence of their street marches and protests only underscored how foreign and marginal their ideas were.[15]

In a broader sense, too, the two decades following the First World War represented probably the greatest single period of civil peace in all English history, before or since. Rates of recorded violent crime were at an all-time low. Twenty-four prisons were closed for lack of inmates.[16] According to George Orwell, the 'gentle manners' of the English people were one of the characteristics that differentiated them most obviously from other Europeans between the wars. 'In no country inhabited by white men,' he suggested, 'is it easier to shove people off the pavement.'[17] Even the era's occasional moments of political turbulence apparently underscored the idea of the peaceable kingdom. The General Strike of 1926 was remembered afterwards as an exhibition of British self-control and good-humoured tolerance. Instead of battering one another with truncheons and broken bottles, the police and the picketers had, it was said, played football in the streets.[18] The English, thought Stanley Baldwin, were the 'kindest people in the world'.[19]

This portrait of the peaceable kingdom left out a lot of awkward details, however. The British state did not organise *putsches* against its citizens. But it did hang them and whip them with enthusiasm. Countless acts of everyday violence in inter-war Britain were excluded from the official record, either because they were never reported or because investigating them was not considered to be within the proper purview of government. Husbands could beat and rape their wives in the 1930s with an impunity we would find shocking today. Much working-class violence was occluded from middle-class view except on rare, horrifying occasions. Gladys Langford, a London schoolteacher on a visit to Bath on Easter Monday 1938, was disgusted to find herself caught up in a 'fearsome fight [...] the combatants came out of a doorway like projectiles from a cannon's mouth; one with a bloody nose fell in a heap almost at my feet, the other pounced on him and pummelled him'. On the train home to London, 'packed with sots', football hooligans hurled empty bottles through the carriage windows.[20]

The British police did not always exhibit the cheerful restraint that popular tradition would suggest, especially when pitted against left-wing protesters. In 1931 a crowd of 20,000 unemployed demonstrators in Manchester was attacked by mounted constables bearing truncheons. The following year, angry policemen conducted a night-time reign of terror in working-class Birkenhead following street protests over the Means Test. 'Batons were wielded to good effect,' the local newspaper noted, with fifty marchers left 'screaming and shouting on the road'.[21]

Above all, to make the idea of the peaceable kingdom work, you had to ignore an awful lot of places under British rule that did not resemble England, especially rural southern England, one bit. This was most true of the overseas Empire, of course. But you did not have to travel all the way to Calcutta or Cape Town to see a very different kind of British attitude towards violence from the one on normal display in the Home Counties. All you had to do was take the ferry from Stranraer in Dumfries and Galloway and cross the twenty miles of the North Channel to Belfast.

Mainland Britons before the Second World War had little consciousness of Northern Ireland. Few thought of it as part of their own homeland. Neville Chamberlain notoriously described the conflict between the Sudeten Germans and the Czechs as 'a quarrel in a faraway country between people of whom we know nothing'. He could just as easily have called the sectarian divide within Northern Ireland a quarrel in a nearby province between people of whom we know even less. The British state was not in any great hurry to talk about Ulster, a policy of official absent-mindedness that continued into the war itself. Between 1942 and 1944 the Army Educational Corps produced a series of eighteen 'British Way and Purpose' pamphlets. These were intended to facilitate discussion in military units in problems of contemporary citizenship and to help soldiers better appreciate what it was they were fighting for. The pamphlets ranged widely in topic, from the mechanics of parliamentary democracy to the development of the colonial empire to housing, health and education reform in the post-war British state. In all its 600 pages the main text mentioned Northern Ireland exactly twice. Neither of these passing references suggested that there was anything in the least bit unusual or challenging about the six counties of Ulster. They were a non-problem so far as the British Way and Purpose were concerned.[22]

So when Northern Ireland's brutality suddenly erupted in the middle of an English high street, as it did in Coventry on 25 August 1939, the mainland masses were unsurprisingly shocked. It was a violence that was freakishly, unintelligibly alien to them. Yet the province of Northern Ireland was just as much a legally constituted part of the United Kingdom as Yorkshire or Surrey. Ulster's violence was every bit as British as red pillar boxes and fish and chips.

Looking at the state of the UK on the eve of the Second World War from the perspective of Belfast, rather than London, offers a very different picture of the Britain of the 1930s than the one we usually imagine. Northern Ireland was no peaceable kingdom, no land of constitutional moderation and open-minded forbearance, no country of Shire Folk innocently whiling away the last years of peace. At the territorial margins of the United Kingdom in 1939 there existed an older, fiercer, crueller, altogether more messianic Britishness than the kind that could be found in Godalming or Shrewsbury.

*

From the vantage point of the early twenty-first century, at a time when the United Kingdom as a multi-regional polity seems fractured and fissuring, the late 1930s look like a period of exceptional national harmony. At no time before or since in the UK's history had so many people been so comfortable thinking of themselves, first and foremost, as British. Welsh and Scottish nationalist consciousnesses, often driven in the past by religious discord, were at a low ebb. In Wales much of the pre-war passion of the separatist movement had receded with the disestablishment of the Anglican Church and the breaking up of big English-owned estates. Scotland too had won full independence in spiritual matters from England, leading to the reunion of the United Free Church with the Church of Scotland in 1929.

Parliamentary politics encouraged cohesion. The major British political parties competed nationwide for seats. The Conservatives won two-thirds of Scotland's constituencies in the 1931 election. Labour dominated in Wales, but neither Welsh nor Scottish socialists had any time for parochial identity politics; they saw the future in strictly British terms. Plaid Cymru and the Scottish National Party between the wars became absorbed with medieval obscurantism and an unhealthy taste for continental fascism, neither of which was calculated to impress the sober middle classes of Cardiff or Edinburgh.[23] In any case, the terrible slaughter of the

First World War had bequeathed a legacy of shared sacrifice that Britons from all parts of the UK could embrace as a unitary tragedy.

Ireland had always been the greatest challenge to the cohesive integrity of the British state. The fate of Ireland had preoccupied Westminster before the First World War. By the summer of 1914 it had seemed that it might drag the entire United Kingdom into civil war until the outbreak of an even greater crisis on the continent. But the creation of the Irish Free State in 1922 had uncoupled Irish politics from British life. By the late 1930s most Britons had come to terms with the idea that the Irish were a fundamentally different people from themselves. Few people in mainland Great Britain regretted any longer the fissuring of the Free State from the rest of the UK.[24]

But the split had not been complete. Northern Ireland, made up of six of Ulster's historic Protestant-majority counties, had chosen to remain part of the United Kingdom rather than join the Catholic-dominated Free State. No one quite knew whether this was a permanent arrangement or not. Neither the government in London nor in Dublin liked it much. But neither had any urgent desire to change the status quo. Éamon de Valera, the Free State's prime minister, had a romantic attachment to the idea of Irish unification, but he was busy constructing an Irish-language-speaking clerico-peasant state in the south, and he was well aware that this project would be horribly complicated by the intrusion of 800,000 truculent Presbyterians thrown into the mix. The British government paid lip-service to the idea of Ulster's innate Britishness and treated the IRA's demands to withdraw from the province with scorn, but it had little enthusiasm for Northern Ireland remaining permanently part of the UK. Eventually 'there would have to be a united Ireland,' mused Neville Chamberlain, 'just as there was a united Canada'.[25] Only the fear of reigniting the passions of 1914 prevented it.[26]

So Northern Ireland persisted, a province of 1.2 million people, two-thirds of them Protestant, one-third Catholic. It was the most economically depressed region in the whole of the UK. At no point during the 1930s did Ulster's official unemployment rate fall below 22 per cent, and since this figure excluded agricultural and uninsured workers, the real rate was probably closer to one in three. The post-1931 slump hit the region particularly hard. In 1932 and 1933 Harland and Wolff, the great Belfast shipyard which had constructed the *Titanic*, built no vessels at all. Northern Ireland's poverty remained at a Victorian level of indigence. According to a survey of a working-class Belfast housing estate in 1938, one third of families were living in circumstances of extreme economic distress. A report into the city's housing stock described 'damp, moldering walls, many of them bulging, rickety stairs, broken floors, crumbling ceilings ...[with] some of the houses mere hovels, the people living in indescribable filth and squalor'. Infant mortality rates were much worse than anywhere on the mainland. There were twice as many cases of death by tuberculosis among Northern Ireland's children as England's.[27]

Overseeing this misery was a local government of such corruption, cronyism and geriatric indifference to the welfare of its own people that it would have been the great national scandal of the 1930s if only more Britons had been aware of its outrages. Viscount Craigavon, Northern Ireland's prime minister for the first nineteen years of the province's existence, was sixty-eight in 1939. He had become incapable through ill-health of more than an hour's work a day but refused to retire. Under his distracted and capricious leadership, Northern Ireland's political life stultified. Only twelve individual ministers served under Craigavon throughout the whole inter-war period. With little pressure on them to perform good governance, the result was systemic negligence, corruption and a taste for costly symbolic vanities shocking in a province so poor. When the Treasury in London baulked at the cost of the grandiose parliamentary building at Stormont that Ulster's government wanted built, Craigavon ordered that over £30,000 of Northern Ireland's own public moneys should be spent on the project rather than economise on the design. Welfare in Belfast was in the hands of the Board of Guardians, a group whose members made little secret of the fact that they considered the whole concept of poor relief a conspiracy to cheat honest middle-class rate-payers of their money. Appearing before the Guardians was described by one of their terrified and humiliated wards as 'like being brought into the Star Chamber'.[28]

On the British mainland, behaviour like this would have provoked protest and resistance. But Craigavon and the other leaders of his ruling Ulster Unionist Party (UUP) could always rely on Northern Ireland's sectarian hatreds to dampen any dangerous stirrings of class-based politics. Ulster's Protestants were constantly reminded by the UUP that they were a people under siege, with the threat coming partly from de Valera's Papist hordes to the south, but even more so from the Catholic community within Northern Ireland itself. Ulster's Catholics – heretical, unassimilable and fundamentally disloyal, according to the UUP – were said to represent an existential threat to the Northern Irish state and the Protestant religion, the two things being held as inseparable. If Catholics could not actually be expelled from Northern Ireland, then they needed at least to be continually monitored, controlled and, when necessary, subjugated.

The existence of the IRA supplied a useful base of evidence for this claim of Catholic disloyalty. IRA terrorists killed three police officers of the Royal Ulster Constabulary (RUC) in 1933. When King George VI and Queen Elizabeth visited Ulster in July 1937, IRA members blew up several customs posts in protest.[29] Still, these sporadic outrages from a tiny extremist group hardly justified the Unionist state's 'outlandish paranoia' about the supposedly murderous intentions of hundreds of thousands of Catholics.[30] Certainly, many Northern Irish Catholics had concluded by the 1930s that they had little stake in the province's future. But this was hardly surprising, given that their own government refused to acknowledge a legitimate part for them in the political process.

Instead of the 'normal' class-based politics of the peaceable kingdom on the mainland, then, what existed in Ulster in the 1930s was a 'continental'-style system of two ethno-religious societies living side by side in conditions of permanent alienation and distrust. Protestants and Catholics did not just worship at their own churches. They also had their own schools, newspapers, shops and sports leagues.[31] It was not an equal division. The Protestant majority enjoyed the imprimatur of the state, with all the benefits that flowed from that.[32] In matters of housing, education and public employment Northern Ireland's Catholics were systematically afforded second-class citizenship. Only one in ten of the province's civil servants was Catholic, and almost all of them were low-ranking functionaries barely trusted by their own superiors. In 1934 Dawson Bates, Northern Ireland's minister of home affairs, refused to make phone calls from his office until his Catholic telephonist was replaced.[33] Electoral boundaries were carefully gerrymandered to ensure the perpetuation of a *Herrenvolk* majority. Though Catholic voters outnumbered Protestants overall by 2,000 in (London)derry, for instance, the city's municipal corporation was kept in safe Unionist hands by twelve seats to eight.

These inequities extended into the private economy. Belfast's most important employers – Harland and Wolff, the Short aircraft factory and Mackie's textile machinery works – were all notorious for preferring to hire Protestants. Basil Brooke, Craigavon's minister of agriculture and the man who would subsequently become Northern Ireland's longest-serving prime minister, publicly declared in March 1934 (with Craigavon's approval) that no good Protestant should employ a Catholic. 'I am an Orangeman first and a Member of Parliament afterwards,' Brooke observed to his constituents.[34] This was almost exactly a year after the Nazis had declared a boycott of Jewish businesses across Germany.

Enforcing state authority within Northern Ireland fell to the full-time RUC and its notorious reserve paramilitary, known as the 'B-Specials'. Both organisations drew their recruits almost entirely from the Protestant community, and especially from secretive fringe groups such as the Ulster Protestant League. Police power in Northern Ireland was very different in character from elsewhere in the UK, owing to the Civil Authorities (Special Powers) Act, or SPA. The SPA was originally passed in the emergency conditions of 1922 at the end of the Irish War of Independence. Its powers had only been supposed to last one year, but it was found to be so useful that it was annually renewed by Stormont up to 1933, and made permanent thereafter.

Using the authority granted to it by the SPA, Northern Ireland's government could impose curfews, prohibit public gatherings and protest marches, ban newspapers, arrest members of the public wearing uniforms or bearing items associated with proscribed organisations, search for and seize contraband goods, indefinitely detain those suspected of 'subversive activity' or exclude them from entering Northern Ireland, punish anyone making a report 'intended or likely to cause disaffection to His Majesty' and, in broad terms, 'take all such steps and issue all such orders as may be necessary for preserving the peace and maintaining order'.[35] In December 1938 the SPA was used to introduce internment without trial for suspected IRA men. Some of these detainees were taken to a prison hulk called the *Al Rawdah*, moored off Killyleagh, into which they were packed in bronchitic squalor for five months. The SPA granted Craigavon's executive virtually unlimited domestic powers of control and surveillance, which were directed specifically at an ethno-religious minority regarded as a parasitical and disloyal enemy within. The SPA formed, in the words of a National Council for Civil Liberties (NCCL) report in 1936, 'the basis for a legal dictatorship'.[36] W. J. Stewart, a progressive Unionist critical of the UUP, described Northern Ireland's government in the 1930s as 'more completely in control of the six counties than either Hitler or Mussolini in their own countries'.[37]

State proscriptions against the Catholic community created an atmosphere in which Protestants felt licensed to administer extra-legal mob violence of their own – and Craigavon's government proved willing to turn a blind eye to such behaviour so long as it did not get out of hand. In September 1934 a Protestant crowd ran rampant in Catholic Belfast, wrecking forty homes and killing a disabled man by battering his head in with a concrete slab. This, however, was merely a prelude to the Orange marching season the following summer, the most violent single period in Belfast's inter-war history.[38] During two nights of rioting in May 1935 the RUC brought up an armoured car equipped with a machine-gun to fire on alleged IRA snipers in the city's Lancaster and Little Patrick Streets. An uneasy calm followed. But this was broken again on 12 July, the anniversary of the 1690 Battle of the Boyne and the great carnival day of Protestant Ulster. Thousands of working-class Orangemen returning from their triumphal marches through the city centre that evening got into stone-throwing street brawls with local Catholics. Shots were fired. One witness later recalled a Protestant marcher standing coolly at the top of Lancaster Street firing a revolver repeatedly at nearby Catholic houses. 'It looked so harmless in action,' he remembered:

> The reports of the shots so faint, the small puffs of smoke so innocent that it was incredible that this was an instrument of death. Even more fantastic was the fact that nobody except myself seemed to be paying particular attention to him – not even the two policemen standing within two yards of him.[39]

For over a week Belfast burned. On 22 July mobs carrying sticks and iron bars congregated outside factory gates throughout the city, shouting about what they were going to do to any Catholics they found inside. As factory employees emerged to go home, the mobs laid into them. Men were viciously beaten. Girls were slashed with razor blades. By this point, even the Craigavon authorities were becoming alarmed at the possibility of losing control of the city. Ulster's prime minister appealed for the British Army to intervene to restore order and put a general curfew into place. The violence ended. In all, nine people had been killed, many hundreds more injured, 430 Catholic homes destroyed and 2,241 Catholics forced to flee their Protestant-majority districts.[40]

The 1935 riots were the most serious breakdown of law and order in the United Kingdom throughout the whole decade. Nothing on their scale took place in Northern Ireland again until the 1960s. Briefly, they caught the attention of the British public on the mainland, a very unwelcome thing so far as the Craigavon government was concerned. But from Stormont's point of view, such 'nights of broken glass' served two useful purposes. They reminded Ulster's Catholic minority of its vulnerability, and they diverted the frustrations of working-class Protestants away from the failures of the Northern Irish state to alleviate their poverty and misery. In any case, the British public's curiosity did not last long. There was no enthusiasm in Whitehall to inquire deeply into the circumstances of what had happened. In August 1935 Daniel Mageean, the Catholic bishop of Down and Connor, asked the British prime minister, Stanley Baldwin, to investigate the Craigavon government's use of its executive powers. Baldwin was entitled to do so under the 1920 Government of Ireland Act. Mageean received a one-sentence reply from the prime minister's office: Mr Baldwin was 'at present absent from London'. He never heard anything more on the subject again.[41]

*

By the late 1930s at least half a million people living in mainland Great Britain were Irish-born. More were arriving all the time, drawn by the high wages in Britain's thriving light engineering industries. Between 1931 and 1937 the rate of migration to Great Britain from Ireland increased five-fold.[42] Millions more Britons were descended from Irish immigrants or had married into diasporic families, some of which had crossed the Irish Sea over two centuries earlier.

Theirs was, overall, a story of successful assimilation. Yet latent suspicions lingered, always ready to be provoked under the right circumstances. The Irish, it was whispered in Britain, were constitutionally inclined to violence. Their fecundity and fecklessness were said to be at odds with sober Anglo-Saxon values. They sponged off Britain's taxpayers by demanding public assistance ('it has been truly said that Ireland has discovered how to make England pay for its poor', the *Times* suggested archly in 1936[43]). A Catholic's real loyalty was surely to Rome rather than to the British Crown. The Irish spoke differently. They dressed differently. They behaved differently. Many English people in the 1930s continued to think of the Irish, deep down, as 'duplicitous peasants'.[44]

In some parts of Britain, such as Liverpool and Glasgow, there still existed a tradition of sectarianism which defied the general British drift towards secular tolerance in matters of religion. Fighting between Orange summer marchers and local Catholics was a constant feature of life in Glasgow's Bridgeton, Gorbals and Govan districts throughout the 1930s.[45] Liverpool's inter-war working-class vote was as split on religious lines as Belfast's. The Liverpool Protestant Party, led by an Orange Order chaplain, played an important part in the city's right-of-centre politics. Violence between the two communities in Liverpool, though never on Ulster's scale, was sporadic between the wars.[46]

The S-Plan attacks in 1939 provoked a fresh burst of Liverpool's belligerent nativism. In January 1939 city councillor David Rowan organised a meeting of 1,500 people at Picton Hall to demand that the police keep closer surveillance on members of Liverpool's Irish community. Rowan's argument combined economic resentments with fears of terrorist violence. Several men were brought on stage to complain about losing their jobs to Irish immigrants. 'In two or three years, instead of Liverpool being called Liverpool, it'll be called Dublin,' Rowan cried, to shouts of 'shame!' from the crowd.[47] Vigilante attacks against young working-class Irishmen suspected of being S-Plan terrorists took place across the city throughout 1939. In late July, James Terry, a young fitter's labourer from Co. Waterford, was attacked inside a Liverpool cinema when a woman, seeing him light a match, screamed: 'He's an IRA man!' Terry fled the building, being badly beaten on the way. When the police arrived, they found him perched on top of a fire engine, surrounded by an angry mob: 'For God's sake, get me out of this!' he shouted. His life was saved, but the hapless Terry found himself in front of a city magistrate the following day on a public mischief charge, accused of causing a panic.

Such incidents were not confined to Liverpool. On 24 June IRA bombs went off outside four banks in central London, including the Piccadilly branch of Lloyds. After the blast in Piccadilly, the crowd on the street attacked a young man who had happened to be seen running near the site of the explosion; it was said afterwards that he had 'looked Irish'. He was pummelled with fists and umbrellas, with accompanying cries of 'Stop him, kill him, lynch him!' The Broadgate killings made the final week of August 1939 in Coventry especially fraught. Thousands of the city's factory workers held a one-day strike meeting at which they demanded that Coventry employers immediately fire all Irish workers, and that the police allow native workers to 'assist' in the 'interrogation' of those thought responsible for the bombing. At Dartmoor Prison, where a number of convicted IRA men were being held, eleven Irish prisoners were hospitalised that week after being beaten up by English inmates.[48]

The police responded to the bombing campaign in different ways, some constabularies taking great pains to distinguish IRA terrorists from the Irish community at large, some less so. Newspaper stories from the Spanish Civil War had been full of reports about seditious 'Fifth Columnists', and the possibility that Irish migrants might be providing sanctuaries for IRA men did not seem completely fantastical. In London the Metropolitan Police asked hotel and boarding-house staff to provide details about any new visitors with Irish addresses or accents. The public was encouraged to report sightings of Irishmen 'idling' during daylight hours on the streets of the capital. S-Plan attacks provoked panicky and legally dubious police work. After the Piccadilly bombing constables 'dashed through the crowd haphazardly', as one witness later put it, rounding up dozens of men with Irish brogues. The whole operation was conducted with such a lack of basic procedure that all of the detained men had to be released later in the day for want of evidence – including a couple of suspects who, it turned out later, really had been involved in planting the bomb.

*

The Britain that went to war in 1939 was, arguably, a much more unified country than it is today. The Second World War would strengthen its unities further still. It is natural, eighty years later, to feel pangs of nostalgia about such cohesion. It is understandable to wonder where the self-confidence and sense of place that the British once seemed to possess has gone. But these feelings should be treated with caution. National unity came at a price. Creating a sense of inclusiveness for the many meant excluding the few.

'Britishness' was not an uncomplicated idea in the 1930s. The people of the United Kingdom did not fight the Second World War with any single and unambiguously agreed notion of who they were, what they were defending or what it was they were hoping to accomplish from the conflict. To many brave and industrious Ulstermen and -women the war was about defending an uncompromising Protestantism that saw little distinction between the threats of continental fascism and continental Popery – 'Ulster is nobody's Czechoslovakia', Craigavon insisted to Westminster politicians who he suspected might be planning to cut a deal with Dublin over the fate of the province.[49] To most mainland Britons such a *Herrenvolk* conception of Britishness was mystifying and appalling – or it would have been if they had known it existed (an Englishman travelling to Ulster for the first time felt like he was 'arriving in a kind of political lunatic asylum,' thought the Unionist J. W. Nixon).[50]

Northern Ireland maintained a stable constitutional relationship with the rest of the United Kingdom in the 1930s only because most people chose to turn a blind eye to its policy of apartheid. On the eve of the war with Nazi Germany, hundreds of thousands of British citizens were being treated as enemy aliens in their own country because of the fact of their religion. Many British politicians on the mainland must have known this to be the case, and they may not have much liked it. But they also knew that to deal with the issue would risk a serious challenge to domestic order at a time of gathering international crisis. It is understandable that no one in Westminster wanted to provoke a confrontation with Stormont with the menace of Hitler looming, but the price was systematic injustice. It is not a decision to get sentimental about now.

The war was going to be a stress-test of how committed people in the United Kingdom were to civil liberty as a core principle of Britishness. Winston Churchill recognised the challenge that a war against a major power like Germany would present to this principle on the first day of the war, as the Commons was introducing emergency measures that would drastically roll back traditional limits on state power. 'Perhaps it might seem a paradox that a war undertaken in the name of liberty and right should require, as a necessary part of its processes, the surrender for the time being of so many [...] dearly valued liberties and rights,' he said:

> In these last few days the House of Commons has been voting dozens of Bills which hand over to the executive our most dearly valued traditional liberties. We are sure that these liberties will be in hands which will not abuse them, which will use them for no class or party interests, which will cherish and guard them, and we look forward to the day, surely and confidently we look forward to the day, when our liberties and rights will be restored to us.

Earlier in 1939, the S-Plan terrorist campaign had provoked a similar kind of test, on a smaller scale, of how far the British were willing to compromise their traditional civil liberties in the name of public safety. In July 1939 the home secretary had introduced the Prevention of Violence (Temporary Provisions) Act to the Commons, a remarkable piece of legislation rushed through Parliament at breakneck speed, largely forgotten in the subsequent hubbub of war but something that ought to be better remembered than it is. The Prevention of Violence Act granted the home secretary the authority to prohibit anyone who had been resident in Great Britain for less than twenty years from entering or re-entering the country if it was believed that they were 'concerned in the preparation or instigation [...] of acts of violence designed to influence public opinion or Government policy with respect to Irish affairs'. He could expel such persons from the United Kingdom and detain them for up to five days prior to that expulsion. The Act allowed, for the first time in history, a political appointee to imprison, deport and exile British subjects without reference to the courts. It also empowered the police, under certain circumstances, to conduct searches and seizures of suspects' property without obtaining a judicial warrant first. British subjects – as all Irishmen and -women still legally were in 1939, even those living in the Free State – had never been subject to such peacetime restrictions before.

Hoare insisted to Parliament that the new Act was a 'temporary measure to meet a passing emergency' which would remain on the statute books for no longer than two years.[51] Some MPs were not convinced. They saw it as an attack on Britain's culture of democracy. 'We are proud that this is a free country,' argued William Wedgwood Benn (father of Tony and grandfather of Hilary). 'Our people hold their heads a little higher because they believe they enjoy a measure of freedom [...] I do not think public opinion will be assisted by giving the Home Secretary power to turn us all into ticket-of-leave men, if he so wishes.'[52] In return, supporters of the Act regarded these objections as a sop to terrorists. 'What about King's Cross?' demanded Sir Joseph Nall, Tory MP for Manchester Hulme. 'What about the people who are being maimed and killed?' It was much better, he argued, 'to deport a dozen innocent persons than to allow one innocent person to be killed'.[53] The Prevention of Violence Act passed into law.

Even before the Second World War broke out, then, fears of terrorism had already caused the government drastically to revise traditional assumptions about the freedoms of the individual British citizen. The Prevention of Violence Act was a first step in the creeping Hibernicisation of British law during the twentieth century, a process in which restrictions on civil liberty originally applied in 'troubled' Ireland were progressively transferred to the rest of the United Kingdom as well. In time, an indefinite state of emergency would become the new normal. There is a direct evolutionary line that can be traced from the Broadgate attack in 1939 to HM Prison Belmarsh, Britain's own Guantánamo Bay, today: from Hoare's temporary action against a 'limited number of misguided individuals' to the national security state that Britain has now become.

To be sure, the government in the summer of 1939 did not go as far as it might have wished. Hoare would have liked to have the power to intern suspects without trial in Great Britain, just as the Stormont government could in Northern Ireland – 'public opinion is moving in favor of more drastic powers,' he told his Cabinet colleagues when deliberating the Act. But he recognised that getting such a drastic peacetime infringement of habeas corpus through Parliament would be difficult.[54] He forswore any such intention in the Commons debate, arguing that internment would too much resemble 'the system of concentration camps' in Germany.[55] Hoare used the lesser powers granted him by the Prevention of Violence Act sparingly. By December 1939 only about 200 orders had been served by the Home Office against individual suspects, three-quarters of them expulsion orders.

But one of the reasons Hoare did not demand even greater powers was that he did not have to. De Valera was determined to crush the IRA, an organisation that he felt was a threat to his own monopoly of power in the Irish Free State. He had no qualms about using extraordinary legal authority to do it. In June 1939 the Dublin parliament introduced its own Offences Against the State Act, a far more draconian piece of legislation than anything Samuel Hoare would request in Westminster. De Valera's government was permitted to intern without trial anyone suspected of being an IRA member or sympathiser, and to prosecute them in special criminal courts which did not need to observe the normal rules of prosecutorial evidence. It was this, not the Prevention of Violence Act, which had really brought the IRA to heel by the autumn of 1939.

Britain, for all its faults, was a very different kind of country from the European dictatorships in the late 1930s. Its people had every right to regard those differences as precious and ennobling. But sometimes the only reason that the British government was able to treat its citizens with moderation was because other governments elsewhere were willing to behave far less liberally towards *their* citizens. That was true of the IRA threat in 1939. It would be equally true of the battle against Nazi Germany two years later once the totalitarian Soviet Union became Britain's ally. The British at war had the luxury of remaining 'free' because others did not.

3

A DIFFERENT KIND OF NATION

Mention 'Thirties Britain' today and you will generally evoke two strikingly contrasting images. One is of a patrician world of aristocrats and servants, a *Downton Abbey* vision of the pre-war past, all Rolls-Royces and village fêtes and chambermaids, in which the British ruling class continued to enjoy much the same leisured authority and power it had possessed for all the previous 900 years. The other image is of the 1930s as the 'devil's decade' – of Auden's 'Smokeless chimneys, damaged bridges, rotting wharves and choked canals', of squalor, poverty and discontent, of the unemployed marching in futile anger and despair hundreds of miles from the slums of Jarrow to London to protest to Parliament against their plight. *Brideshead Revisited* and *The Road to Wigan Pier*, the Eton boating song and the Means Test: these are our historical signposts for understanding the decade before the Second World War.

Both these worlds certainly existed. If – in around, say, 1935 – you had driven from York north-east along the A64 towards Scarborough, then at some point between Kirkham Abbey and Malton you would have seen, to your north, the great country house of Castle Howard, the residence of the Hon. Geoffrey William Algernon Howard, fifth son of the ninth earl of Carlisle. This Baroque and Palladian fantasy, surrounded by an estate of almost 10,000 acres of woodland and elegantly manicured park, still radiated all the traditional confidence of the British aristocracy.[1] Inside was one of the finest privately maintained art collections in the world. Classical statuary, busts and urns appropriated during eighteenth-century Grand Tours of the continent stood in the corridors. There was the marble altar from the Temple of the Oracle at Delphi, which Admiral Nelson had seized from the French in Naples, Georgian furniture by John Linnell, over a dozen Canalettos, other works by Holbein, Ricci, Pellegrini, Gainsborough and Reynolds, and the magnificent Burne-Jones stained-glass windows of the chapel. From this palace of mannered patrician leisure Geoffrey Howard, lord lieutenant of the North Riding, local justice of the peace, could look out over the Vale of York and feel, with a calm equanimity, that he was its greatest citizen.

On the face of it, the status of the British aristocracy seemed as settled in 1935 as it had been since William the Conqueror's invasion in 1066. The leading ranks of the Conservative Party were still full of titled men in 1935. Prime minister Stanley Baldwin's foreign secretary, Anthony Eden, was the younger son of a seventh baronet. The man who would succeed Eden at the Foreign Office, Lord Halifax, was a viscount whose grandfather had been the earl of Devon and whose great-grandfather was Earl Grey (of the tea and the Reform Act), and who had himself grown up shooting and riding to hounds on his family's magnificent estates in Yorkshire. Baldwin had a marquess (Lawrence Dundas) at the India Office and a viscount (Philip Cunliffe-Lister) at the Air Ministry. He would appoint a colonial secretary (William Ormsby-Gore) who had a baron for a father and a tenth marquess for a grandfather. In 1938 two sons of the seventeenth earl of Derby, the great patrician ruler of Lancashire, would serve alongside one another in Cabinet.

Beyond the highest ranks of political office, titled men of the landed gentry such as the Hon. Geoffrey Howard continued to hold key positions in government, the civil service, the law, the church and the armed forces. Grandees such as the earl of Sandwich and the marquess of Bath reigned as uncrowned kings of Huntingdonshire and Wiltshire, just as their great-grandfathers had done a century before. The network of aristocratic prestige and patronage in the shires through offices such as lord lieutenant, master of foxhounds, chairman of quarter sessions, justice of the peace, colonel of the yeomanry and chairman or conveyor of the local county council remained thickly woven in 1935. The nobility continued to serve as landlords to their tenant farmers, as sponsors of Commons seats, as conferrers of clerical livelihoods.[2]

Fifteen miles south-west of Castle Howard, meanwhile, in the city of York, there was a very different kind of Britain in 1935. York was not especially disadvantaged by the standards of the decade, yet more than three in ten of its 55,000 working-class residents were living in households too poor to provide what the British Medical Association regarded as the bare minimum standard for a healthy diet. Individual cases of blight and poverty, compiled by the city's famous social statistician Seebohm Rowntree, told the story. One family of eight, he recorded, was packed into two bedrooms, their 'extremely dark and unhealthy' kitchen equipped only with a defective oven. Another family of nine was in a sink-less house with no clean water supply, their five girls, aged seven to sixteen, sleeping in the same room as the parents. Another family of five was living in a Corporation house so persistently damp that every resident was suffering from chronic respiratory illness. A seventy-two-year-old widow was living alone, sleeping on a sofa in a one-room hovel, with just 3s. 3d. a week to spare for food. A second widow, forty-six, with a thirteen-year-old daughter ill from diphtheria, was in a house with a badly leaking roof. 'We see,' commented Rowntree, 'how far the standard of living of many workers falls short of any standard which could be regarded, even for the time being, as satisfactory.' For forty years Rowntree had investigated the causes of York's poverty. There was, he reflected, something deeply disquieting about the fact 'that in a country so rich as England, over 30% of the workers in a typical provincial city should have incomes so small that it is beyond their means to live even at [a] stringently economical level'.[3]

Britain in the mid-1930s remained a country of staggering want and inequality. Two-thirds of income earners brought in a weekly wage of less than £2 10s., an amount that was barely half the minimum considered necessary for a family of four to live decently.[4] More than a million families were too poor to pay rent on the open market for proper housing with electricity, running water and an indoor toilet. Only one in ten working-class adolescents was in secondary school education. One in five families had no meaningful possessions to speak of, other than pawn tickets and debts.[5] Britons lived in such scenes of misery as 'Rusty Lane' (Grice Street) in West Bromwich, a street that J. B. Priestley described in his 1933 state-of-the-nation travelogue *English Journey* as 'a picture of grimy desolation' that mocked all the pomp and pretensions of government, making them look 'a miserable farce'.[6]

Yet looking at 1930s Britain only from the vantage points of Castle Howard and York's squalid tenements obscures as much as it reveals. In truth, the foundation of British aristocratic power had experienced an irreversible weakening in the first decades of the twentieth century, and it was never going to be the same again. The traditional model of gentlemanly estate management had become untenable for many aristocrats because of the decline in the capital value of land, a fall in agricultural prices and steep hikes on death duties – especially devastating given the number of titled young men who had died in the trenches of the First World War. By 1937 one in three of the families listed in *Burke's Landed Gentry* had sold all the land they had, and many others were barely hanging on.[7] 'A silent revolution', as Joseph Kenworthy, tenth Baron Strabolgi, put it, had wiped out the basis of the traditional ruling elite's wealth in just a generation or two.[8]

The grandees had had to adapt as best they could. Their country houses were let or handed over to the National Trust, the London mansions they had occupied for 'the season' given up. Family heirlooms, works of art and libraries disappeared under the auctioneer's hammer. Even those aristocrats who managed to survive had to trim their budgets drastically. By 1931 the full-time staff at Castle Howard had been reduced from twelve servants to four; the east wing of the house was closed off to save electricity and heating bills; the meat budget was cut to a shilling a day; and China tea made way for 'servant's' (Indian) tea instead.[9] Some landlords reinvested their wealth in the stock market and became *rentiers*, directing their children towards careers in business and the higher professions. Others decamped between the wars to Rhodesia or Kenya, where patrician fantasies could still be played out on the cheap amid the flame trees and the jacarandas. A few of the most embittered drifted into far-right politics. Lord Tavistock, the future duke of Bedford, was an enthusiastic early Mosleyite, and one of the founders of the pro-Nazi and anti-Semitic British People's Party, which boasted a distinguished slew of aristocratic patrons.

As for the Devil's Decade: while millions of British people remained shockingly poor in the mid-1930s, and the economic slump brought on by the Wall Street Crash had dumped new miseries onto cotton, coal, steel and shipbuilding towns across the country, the fact remained that the United Kingdom overall was far more prosperous than it had been a generation earlier. Real wages for manual workers had almost doubled since 1914.[10] The Victorian workhouse had given way to state emoluments to cover sickness, old age and unemployment. To our eyes, there does not seem anything very extravagant about 1930s Britain's narrowly circumscribed, erratically distributed and often cruel and humiliating social welfare system. Yet at that time it was probably the most generous system of its type in the world.

Seebohm Rowntree, for all his regret about York's continuing poverty, noted with satisfaction that the overall economic condition of the city's working class was 30 per cent better than it had been at the time of his first study in 1899. 'Working hours are shorter,' he pointed out: 'housing is immeasurably better, health is better, education is better.' A key factor in this improvement had been 'the remarkable growth in social services' in the intervening years.[11] Infant mortality rates had halved in England and Wales since the turn of the century.[12] People were eating better, enjoying more leisure time and living in healthier homes. During the 1930s the public authorities demolished over 339,000 slum properties and found 1.4 million people better accommodation.[13] West Bromwich's Conservative MP pointed out to Priestley after the publication of *English Journey* that one in six of his town's residents had been rehoused in better dwellings.[14]

Indeed, not very far away from West Bromwich, in those areas of the English Midlands and south in which the factories of the 'new' domestic consumer economy were being built, a very different kind of Britain was coming into existence in the 1930s, even if it is one that has been largely lost from our sight today. Take, for example, Coventry, which, were it not for the distorting filter of the Second World War, might be remembered today as the archetypical site of 1930s Britain rather than Jarrow or a patrician stately home. When J. B. Priestley visited Coventry in 1933 during the writing of his *English Journey*, much of the picture-postcard cathedral city of cobbled lanes, alleyways and gabled Elizabethan terraces still existed. But that Coventry had already begun disappearing. By the late 1930s municipal developers had already ripped out much of the medieval street pattern (Butcher Row, Ironmonger Row, Trinity Lane, the Bull Ring) just north of Broadgate in order to create spacious thoroughfares for automobile traffic.[15]

Coventry in the 1930s was fast becoming a city of chrome and stainless steel and petrol fumes, a city of factories – some still in the cluttered metropolitan hub, but many more in the spacious new industrial estates being constructed in a fat prosperous ring around the city. It was Britain's inter-war Motown, a city of Alvis and Armstrong Siddeley, BSA and Daimler, Lea-Francis and Morris, Standard and Triumph. Of GEC telephones, Courtaulds synthetic textiles, Armstrong Whitworth bombers and VHF radios for the Forces. Coventry in the 1930s, in short, was prosperous, self-consciously modern, rudely democratic and unsentimental about its own past.

Its factories demanded new inputs of capital and labour – labour especially. Coventry's population in the 1930s expanded seven times faster than that of the rest of the country. This was an urban expansion that had not been seen in Britain since the age of steam and iron a hundred years earlier. On the eve of the Second World War, about 10,000 new workers and their families were arriving every year. Coventry sucked in migrants from the impoverished areas of the Scottish midlands and south Wales and

Ireland and northern England. The victims of the IRA Broadgate bombing reflected this nomadic character. One of the dead was from Montgomery-shire, another from Port Talbot.

Coventry factory work was tiring, dirty and monotonous. Trade unions were banned by the car companies, lay-offs in slack periods, especially in the winter months, common. But there were plenty of jobs to be had and plenty of hours to be accumulated on the clock. And the pay was excellent – as much as £4 or £5 a week even for an unskilled worker at a time when the average industrial wage was still under £3 a week. Coventry's factory employees had the highest discretionary purchasing power in Britain and the city, for its size, the highest level of working-class house owner-occu-pation. Better-paid workers who did not own their homes outright were able to find comfortable places to live on the excellent new council estates in Radford and Stoke Heath, Hen Lane and Cheylesmore. According to a municipal public health meeting in 1938, Coventry was 'the healthiest place in the world', thanks to its state-of-the-art medical facilities, such as the new infectious diseases hospital in Whitley.

Retail luxuries were plentiful. One in five Coventrians had access to a car – an extraordinary figure for the 1930s. The city had almost as many radio showrooms as butchers. Brand-new palaces of consumption such as the Owen Owen department store and the Rex Cinema, with its Wurlitzer and tropical aviary, offered prosperous working-class residents an accent on personal service never known before.[16] Thirty years later, city workers could still recall their youthful delight at being 'received like royalty' by shop assistants. With money to spare, Coventry's largest companies were able to extend a patrician hand to their workforces too. GEC had its own golf course, a social club with 4,000 members and a company dance hall with a soda and ice cream buffet and an illuminated fountain.[17]

These privileges were not unique to Coventry. They could be found also in Oxford, Luton, Dagenham, Brentford and other towns lucky enough to be the sites of Britain's new light engineering economy. They formed the new world which Priestley described, one of 'giant cinemas and dance-halls and cafes, bungalows with tiny garages, cocktail bars, Woolworths, motor-coaches, wireless, hiking, and factory girls looking like actresses'.[18] Orwell was also quick to recognise the importance of this strange new liminal ter-ritory. To him it was a place epitomised by 'tinned food, *Picture Post*, the radio and the internal combustion engine'.[19] We tend to associate this sort of mass consumer affluence with the 1950s at the earliest. But that's only because the austerity of the wartime and post-war era obscured the way it had already been firmly in place, in the most fortunate parts of the country anyway, twenty years earlier.

*

The true masters of 1930s Britain were the middle class. Lord Halifax and the Stanley brothers added a decorative lustre to the Cabinet rooms of the 1930s. But it was middle-class men like Baldwin and his successor as prime minister in 1937, Neville Chamberlain – the first an ironmonger's son, the second a scion of a great West Midlands screw-making dynasty – who held the power now. Both Baldwin and Chamberlain came from wealth and privilege, to be sure. The former had attended Harrow and Trinity College, Cambridge, the latter Rugby School. But neither would have ever been confused for a gentleman of the old landed order. Nor would they have welcomed such an error. 'I come from the middle classes,' Chamberlain boasted, 'and I am proud of the ability, the shrewdness, the industry and providence, the thrift by which they are distinguished.'[20] Representatives of the fading aristocracy might privately sneer that Chamberlain, as Lord Londonderry put it, was a mere 'Birmingham tradesman'. They might decry, like Lord Cecil, the vulgar *parvenus*, commercial *arrivistes* and 'middle-class monsters' of Baldwin's Cabinet.[21] The new rulers of Britain were nonchalant. They saw their own rise very differently. So far as they were concerned, they were introducing a new and much-needed seriousness, sobriety and no-nonsense, businesslike energy to national life.

The middle class, far more than the aristocracy, represented the presiding conscience of Britain in the 1930s. Its men and women constituted the moral backbone of the nation, setting the standards of dress, accent, behaviour and taste. As the newspapers like the *Daily Express* and the *Daily Mail*, which pandered to their conceits, were never slow to point out, the middle class was the bulwark of modern Britain, the 'constitutional class' which worked hardest and most selflessly, gave the most and received the least in return. No other class was so conscious of its own identity, so aware of its enemies or so well organised politically and as determined to act in its own interests. Middle-class power was mobilised partly through its informal networks – the dance and drama and motoring and sports clubs, the ratepayers' unions and women's guilds, all ostensibly 'non-political' but committed all the same to preserving a particular way of life.[22] Its formal political expression came in the shape of the Conservative Party, the traditional landlords' lobby which in the space of a couple of generations had adapted itself entirely to middle-class ambitions. The 'office boys' its patrician leader Lord Salisbury had mocked forty years earlier had become the Tory base, and a formidable one at that.

Lincolnshire grocer Alfred Roberts, forty-three in 1935, exemplified all the confidence, authority and mores of middle-class Britain between the wars. Roberts had left school at thirteen and had moved to the market town of Grantham to become a shop manager just before the First World War. Within six years he had saved up enough capital to buy his own small retail business. Despite working sixty or more hours a week in his shop, he was nonetheless a tireless and enthusiastic civic volunteer – Methodist lay preacher, part-time justice of the peace, president of the Rotary Club and the Chamber of Commerce, chairman of the National Savings Movement group and Workers' Education Association, school governor, town councilman, chairman of the Borough Finance Committee, alderman and ultimately mayor of Grantham. This was an age in which far more of the basic machinery of government was conducted at the local level than today; men such as Alderman Roberts were essential to its efficient functioning and major figures of prestige and authority in their own right.

Roberts stuck to a philosophy of simple Smilesian virtue: of self-help, hard work, autodidacticism, self-denial and Wesleyan rigour.[23] Many years later, his younger daughter, Margaret, writing under her married name of Thatcher, recalled the Grantham shop's mahogany spice drawers and black lacquered tea canisters, and her father's 'practical, serious, and intensely religious' philosophy of life:

> Those who had worked hard, accumulated a nest egg, and achieved a precarious respectability lived on a knife-edge, and feared them if some accident hit them, or if they relaxed their standards of thrift and diligence, they might be plunged into debt and poverty [...] so the emphasis [was] on hard work. In my family we were never idle – partly because idleness was a sin, partly because there was so much work to be done, and partly no doubt because we were just that sort of people.[24]

Roberts's politics were not overtly partisan. Although he volunteered on behalf of Grantham's Conservative Party candidates at election time, he sat on the town council as an independent. His allegiance, as he saw it, was not to any particular party but to the ratepayers of Grantham. And the essential task of local government, he believed, was to keep taxes as low as possible and public expenditure concomitantly limited. Roberts viewed this as a matter of ethics as much as of economics. There was, he believed, an inherent moral hazard in levying taxes on hard-working burghers to pay for social services for the idle. 'The people who don't pay the rates are sponging on those who do,' he complained in 1937.[25] Roberts did not dispute that those who had been fortunate in life had an obligation to the poor. But that obligation ought properly to be discharged through voluntary charitable work rather than a compulsorily funded state dole. There appears to have been a strong belief in his household that a truly respectable poor, worthy of assistance, was also a polite and deferential one – hence young Margaret's satisfaction at seeing the children of the unemployed 'neatly turned out' and appropriately grateful for anything they received.[26]

In one respect Alderman Roberts was untypical of the 1930s middle class, because he took his own rhetoric about self-denial seriously. His wife, Beatrice, made all the children's clothes. The family had no hot running water indoors, nor modern conveniences such as a refrigerator or a washing machine, though they certainly could have afforded them.[27] Even within the austere circles of Methodist Grantham, this was considered a bit extreme. For most middle-class Britons the 1930s were years of conspicuous consumption. Steady wages, falling prices and low unemployment for non-manual workers meant solid real income gains. For much of the period, even a married man with two children earning the healthy sum of £400 a year paid no income tax at all; a man on £500 only paid £8 a year. 'Cheap money' policies ensured that mortgage interest remained low. State subventions in grammar school funding kept secondary school education affordable.

The middle class were the great beneficiaries of the boom in home building and domestic goods production between the wars. Theirs was a world of privately owned semi-detached houses in ribbon developments and garden suburbs, of Morris Minors and Austin 7s, of telephones, bank accounts and annual holidays to Bexhill and Clevedon, or Brittany and the Black Forest for the slightly better off and more adventurous. Of after-dinner drinks and whist; and perhaps, too, a resident domestic maid or a nanny (one in twenty households had at least one live-in servant).[28] Much of Britain's economic recovery after the slump of the early 1930s was founded on the willingness of the middle class to splurge on domestic luxuries. If everyone had behaved as abstemiously as Alfred Roberts, the revival would have been much slower.

The success of the middle class in mobilising its own resources in defence of its political goals and in dominating the national ideological narrative of the era can be seen in the triumph of Stanley Baldwin's party throughout the decade, even if this specifically Conservative triumph was partly obscured under the veneer of a coalition 'National Government'. The National Government had been created at the height of the post-Wall Street Crash economic crisis in August 1931, after the previous minority Labour Party administration led by Ramsay MacDonald, which had been in office since 1929, had collapsed in a dispute over spending cuts. King George V had persuaded MacDonald to stay on as prime minister in a new coalition with Conservative and Liberal MPs. This had meant MacDonald severing ties with most members of his own party, which promptly declared him a traitor and expelled him. But when the new coalition presented itself to the electorate in October, it achieved the greatest landslide in British history, winning two-thirds of the popular vote and 554 out of 615 seats in the Commons. Most of these victories were by Conservative Party members: Baldwin, though in principle only deputy prime minister, was the true leader of the National Government coalition, and quite content to leave the increasingly sick and distracted MacDonald nominally in charge for the time being while he made the real policy decisions. He finally became prime minister in his own right in June 1935.

That November, Baldwin repeated his electoral feat of four years earlier when National Government rule was confirmed in a second general election. Though the coalition could not fully match the scale of the 1931 rout, 431 of its candidates, including 388 Conservatives, were returned to Westminster, with Labour winning just 154 seats. With National candidates having received over 53 per cent of the popular vote, Baldwin could claim an indisputable people's mandate. The Conservative-dominated coalition was clearly going to be able to maintain power quite comfortably until it was time to hold a new election in 1939 or 1940.[29] 'All the omens are for four years of quiet stable government,' thought Tory MP Leo Amery. He anticipated a 'monotonously uneventful parliament'.[30]

The National Government victory in 1935 transcended Great Britain's regional divides. Its candidates won an absolute majority of votes in England, Scotland and Wales. Its crushing 71 per cent triumph in prosperous rural counties such as Kent, Surrey and Sussex was not especially surprising. What might strike people today as more unlikely was its success in industrial working-class areas which – until the 2019 election swept away such assumptions anyway – we think of as traditional Labour strongholds. Baldwin's coalition won absolute majorities in London, Edinburgh, Manchester, Birmingham, Liverpool, Newcastle, Leeds and Bradford. Towns like Salford, Sunderland, Oldham and Blackburn fell exclusively to National candidates. Urban constituencies such as East Ham North, Cardiff South, Glasgow Pollock and Camberwell North-West all returned Conservatives in 1935. The incumbent Tory MP in Jarrow only lost his re-election bid by a couple of thousand votes.[31] This was Jarrow – the town that more than any other had come to epitomise the bleakness and anger of the Depression. Yet in 1935 almost 47 per cent of its electorate voted for Baldwin's man.

The National Government could never have achieved this by relying on the support of the middle class alone. There were simply not enough middle-class voters. Even by a generous definition, only about one in five Britons could have been called middle-class in 1935. Baldwin's most important political achievement in the 1930s was to persuade enough working-class voters – half of them, roughly – that their interests coincided with those of men like Alfred Roberts.[32] This was no mean feat at a time when 15 per cent of the nation's insured workers, most of them manual labourers, were on the dole.[33]

He was able to take advantage of the ambivalent attitude that the manual workers of the booming new economy had about their place in the class structure in the 1930s. The employees of companies like Morris Motors and GEC, non-unionised and prospering under the National Government's direction, did not feel any particular solidarity with the cotton weavers and coal miners of the beleaguered north. If (as they saw it) Lancashire and Tyneside's workers, egged on by fanatical shop stewards, had fecklessly priced themselves out of their own jobs, then that was their problem, not Coventry's.[34] Labour and the trade unions, by this view, spoke for the selfish sectional interests of one strain of the working class alone. Baldwin insisted that he preached not perpetual class conflict but social concord and sustainable, incremental progress for all. 'There is only one thing which I feel is worth giving one's whole strength to,' he proposed, 'and that is the binding together of all classes of people in an effort to make life in this country better in every sense of the word.'[35]

And by 1935 Baldwin had a good case that the National Government had delivered good government. It had inherited a disastrous situation from Labour in 1931, with almost 3 million insured workers on the dole, the state unemployment fund bankrupt, a £114 million trade deficit, business confidence in collapse and sterling in free fall. By 1935 the situation looked far better. Unemployment had been roughly halved. The pound had stabilised. The economy was clearly reviving. The export trade was strengthening, consumption and investment growing. Whether all these things had happened because of decisions the National Government had made or simply because the world economic situation had improved since 1931 is debatable. The point is that they had happened on the coalition's watch. Real wages had risen. The cost of living had fallen. Taxes had been cut. The government had overseen the construction of one million new houses. A programme of modest rearmament was under way. Under the circumstances, Baldwin's claim in his election manifesto that 'we have emerged from the depths of depression to a condition of steadily returning prosperity' seemed perfectly plausible. Even G. D. H. Cole, the Fabian socialist and no friend to the Tories, admitted in 1938 that the National Government had shown 'a good deal of skill [in] pulling Great Britain successfully through the greatest depression in history'.[36]

To the factory hands of Coventry's car and telephone and textile works, who wanted plentiful work, generous wages, clean and comfortable homes, decent healthcare and schools, cheap entertainment and, in general, a better life than their parents had enjoyed – all things that the Conservatives seemed to be delivering in 1935, and without the need for any revolutionary innovations in government – the avuncular pipe-smoking, peacemaking Stanley Baldwin was a safe bet. Their Woolworths Britain rallied to him in 1935. All but one of Warwickshire's sixteen parliamentary constituencies returned coalition MPs.

All this would seem like a great puzzle ten years later, in the immediate aftermath of the Second World War, when Labour's Clement Attlee was almost as triumphant with the voters as Baldwin had been. Attlee's radical programme of post-war social and economic reconstruction, involving large-scale nationalisation of industry and the creation of a comprehensive welfare state system, including the National Health Service (NHS), was a repudiation of much that the National Government of the 1930s had stood for. And it was tremendously popular. Why, then, had many of the same voters who had put Attlee into Downing Street supported very different policies back in 1935?

For writers like Priestley and Orwell, the answer was simple: what had happened in 1931 and 1935 was an act of collective absent-mindedness, a regrettable lapse of judgement rather than an expression of the people's true will. They dismissed the prosperity of the pre-war years. Britain in the 1930s had been 'a stony wilderness of world depression and despair', according to Priestley, tolerated only because 'the nation's mind was elsewhere, withdrawn, more than half asleep, charmed and lulled by politicians with a good bedside manner'.[37] Everyone, as Orwell put it, had done 'the wrong thing in perfect unison' in the 1930s.[38] Britain had been engaged in a sort of national sleepwalk which its people had only been shocked out of by the cathartic jolt of military defeat in 1940.[39]

No one at the end of the war was interested in much defending the National Government from such accusations. Labour had no incentive to do so. Few Conservatives saw much point doing it either. Winston Churchill had not served in the National Government in peacetime and had no investment in its reputation. Many of his junior colleagues had served in it, but they could see which way the wind was blowing, and they chose to forget about or minimise the parts they had played in Baldwin's administrations. The idea that voters ten years earlier had simply been too guileless to understand the folly of what they were doing was an explanation of events that suited the Shire Folk myth nicely.

But if we want to really understand what Britain was like before the Second World War, we must evaluate the National Government's success on its own terms, not in the patronising, teleological terms of 1945. There was nothing inevitable about its decline into ignominy. If war had not broken out in 1939, then it's highly likely that Neville Chamberlain, who had succeeded Baldwin as prime minister in the spring of 1937, would have won another comfortable general election victory in 1940. The Conservative-led coalition would have continued to dominate British politics into the new decade, uninfluenced by any drastic leftward shift in the public mood occasioned by military defeat and the demands of total war. Baldwin and Chamberlain's policy prescriptions and values, not those of Keynes's *General Theory* and the Beveridge Report, would have continued to shape the national debate in the 1940s. There would have been no 'Revolution of 1945', no nationalisations of British industrial sectors and probably no NHS either, or at least not the NHS in the form we know today. By 1945 the Tories, perhaps under the leadership of a dynamic younger figure such as R. A. Butler, might have been looking at their fourth successive election win. Churchill, by this point seventy years old, and not in good health, would have been retreating into dignified retirement from the Commons back benches, his lifetime goal of reaching the premiership having ultimately eluded him. Clement Attlee would have become just another of the Labour Party's string of forgotten disappointments.

The war did not just transform lives. It also transformed values: especially views about the scope and ethics of state action. Undergirding the Baldwinian achievement in the 1930s was a philosophy of government that was confident, coherent, popular and, by its own lights, progressive. The fact that it was a philosophy that did not survive Dunkirk does not detract from this. Millions of people went to war in 1939 to defend a particular idea of British civilisation, epitomised by the values of the National Government, which they regarded as compassionate, efficient and just. A lot of them, as Priestley and Orwell suggested, would change their minds about it during the war, and come to embrace different ideas about the future of the country. But not all of them would. Those who did not change their minds would return home at war's end to a new and very different Britain which they neither recognised nor much liked.

*

The 1935 election was important in an international sense as well as a domestic one. Liberal government was dying in Europe as the British voted. Parliamentary regimes in Italy, Germany, Austria, Spain and Poland had succumbed to anarchy or dictatorship. France, which had just gone through six changes of prime minister in two years, was hardly an advertisement for stable leadership or the peaceful resolution of policy differences. In February 1934 the French police had shot dead fifteen protesters in a political riot in the Place de la Concorde. French politicians risked more than verbal brickbats. The socialist leader and future prime minister Léon Blum had already been threatened with violence by his opponents many times and would be almost beaten to death by far-right thugs in early 1936.[40] Britain, by contrast, seemed a haven of stability on the margins of the troubled continent. To Baldwin's supporters in the press, the election result in 1935 was a victory not just for the prime minister and his coalition but for the British people and the British constitution too. The non-violent continuity of representative government was a triumph of liberal verities. 'The British people have given unchallengeable proof of their steadiness to the world,' the *Times* acclaimed after the result came in.[41] Mr Baldwin's mandate, declared the *Daily Express*, made him 'the strongest democratic leader in the world'.[42]

Baldwin himself could not quite decide what he thought about democracy, however. The very idea of it was rather new. The 1935 general election was only the third to be conducted under what we would now consider the basic criterion of democratic practice – which is to say, the participation of the entire adult population. Women had received the vote on the same terms as men only as recently as 1928. And British men had only enjoyed full democratic liberties since 1918. In 1910, only 58 per cent of the adult male population had had the right to vote. France had first introduced universal male suffrage in 1848, Germany in 1871. In this respect, Britain had been a distinct laggard. When Baldwin had first entered Parliament in 1908, only 7 million people could vote in a country of 45 million. Most Britons on the eve of the Second World War had come to maturity in a country that was not technically democratic at all. Democracy had 'arrived at a gallop', as the prime minister put it.[43]

Democracy, according to historian Richard Weight, was 'what Britain primarily meant to most of its inhabitants and its allies abroad' during the Second World War.[44] It's a claim that seems self-evident enough on the face of it. Yet the country's wartime leaders did not speak very much about democracy as a particularly British national characteristic. In his radio address of 3 September 1939, announcing the declaration of war against Germany, Neville Chamberlain described 'the evil things that we shall be fighting against – brute force, bad faith, injustice, oppression and persecution'. But he did not invoke democracy as an alternative to them. King George VI did not mention democracy in his own radio speech later the same day. Nor did Winston Churchill in his remarks to the Commons on the outbreak of war. Churchill, in fact, made rather fewer references to it than we might expect. He only used the word once in Parliament in all of 1940. The significance of democracy to British collective identity did not necessarily seem obvious to everyone at the time. In 600 pages and twenty-seven chapters about *The Character of England* in 1947, the book's authors mentioned democracy in passing twice – in the section on recreation and games.[45]

The fact was that not everyone was convinced that the recent advent of mass democracy had been such a good idea. The extension of the franchise to the masses had been accompanied by high unemployment at home and a diminution of British power overseas. Perhaps this was not a coincidence.

Perhaps the participation of the masses in decision-making was inimical to good government. Parliamentary democracy might be a failing experiment, not suited to the complex technical decisions that had to be made to run an advanced industrial state. Baldwin felt that he and the Conservatives were in a 'race for life' to educate the electorate in its responsibilities before demagoguery could take hold.[46]

Concerns about democracy came from some unexpected quarters. One could have predicted that a grandee like Baron Wemyss would grumble that 'when every crossing sweeper has a voice in matters, it is quite impossible for any government to rule'.[47] But even Harold Nicolson, a 'National Labour' MP loyal to MacDonald, privately distinguished his sympathy for Britain's poor from any confidence in their ability to govern. 'I hate uneducated people having power,' he admitted in his diary: 'I fear "the People" means nothing to me except ugliness.'[48]

Winston Churchill's views about democracy were surprisingly complicated. He worried that the granting of universal suffrage had diluted the influence in political life of the 'strongest and wisest' members of the community. Churchill felt that state policy towards India and the European dictators in the 1930s was distorted by the need to appeal to the masses. He suggested at one point that the franchise laws ought to be changed to give extra votes to heads of households.[49] Even when he was in a more generous mood, Churchill's conception of democracy did not include much room for the practical involvement of the masses in the decisions that affected their lives. 'My idea of it,' Churchill suggested in a speech to the Commons in late 1944,

> is that the plain, humble, common man, just the ordinary man who keeps a wife and family, and goes off to fight for his country when it is in trouble, goes to the poll at the appropriate time, and puts his cross on the ballot-paper showing the candidate he wishes to be elected to Parliament [...] and then elected representatives meet together and decide what government, or even, in times of stress, what form of government, they wish to have in their country.[50]

This was a description of rule by consent, not a project of active citizenship. To voters from more assertive revolutionary traditions, such as the United States, it could seem anaemic and uninspired, passive acquiescence in elite power rather than shared governance.

Scepticism about democracy in the 1930s was felt particularly strongly among those who opposed the National Government's appeasement of Hitler and Mussolini. This is a point that has been forgotten nowadays because we sympathise so completely with the anti-appeasers. We envision them as champions of the people against the Establishment elite, people who held full confidence in the wisdom of the ordinary man and woman. This assumption explains the remarkable scene in the 2017 Churchill biopic *Darkest Hour* in which the prime minister, wavering briefly in his determination to resist Hitler, descends into a London Underground station to receive a much-needed pep talk from stout-minded common folk.

But this scene, a fantastic invention, entirely distorts the relationship between diplomacy and democracy in the 1930s. To many of Chamberlain's critics, the ordinary man and woman were precisely the problem. After all, Appeasement was a hugely popular policy. It was a product of democracy. To those who opposed it, the proud tradition of muscular British resistance to foreign dictatorship was being undermined by politicians pandering to the facile pacifism of the masses. Foreign policy had 'got tangled up with vote-catching', complained the anti-Nazi diplomat Sir Robert Vansittart. This resentment was targeted especially towards women, who were imagined as hysterical, peace-at-any-price dupes. Enfranchising women had 'brought nothing but degradation and dishonour to politics', thought MP Richard Law, who gave one of the bitterest Commons speeches against the Munich agreement in 1938. To Nicolson, also a staunch anti-appeaser, 'historians of our decline will say that we were done the moment we gave women the vote.'[51]

Much of the support for Appeasement was driven by a fear of democracy too. The National Government's middle-class base could not rest easy even after the victory of 1935. Middle-class Tories imagined their world to be under siege from an ever-growing band of enemies: sinister plutocrats (inevitably foreign and Jewish), grasping trade unionists, Bolshevik-minded socialists and insolent, overpaid manual workers.[52] According to Charles Masterman, the 'standard[s] of civilisation' and 'agreeable manners and ways' of suburban London were threatened by 'those great masses of humanity', swinish and destructive, lurking just on the other side of the privet hedges, 'always prepared seemingly to engulf it'.[53]

Middle-class propriety in the 1930s was performative. It rested on fragile and expensive foundations: the mortgaged private home, grammar school education for the children, the doctor not on the free, state-subsidised panel. For many 'black coated' workers on modest incomes not much different from those of skilled manual labourers – retailers and clerks, teachers and insurance agents, small businessmen, minor civil servants – maintaining a respectable middle-class standard of life was a precarious business, requiring constant vigilance and sacrifice. Marriages had to be delayed, families restricted to one, or at most two, children. With no welfare safety net to rely on (either because they were excluded from it by the Means Test or because of the offence to propriety that relying on it would have represented) they were always haunted by the spectre of financial and social ruin.

Such middle-class Britons remembered the grim days immediately after the First World War, when high income taxes and inflated prices had seemingly doomed the salaried and *rentier* classes to the status of a 'New Poor'. The early 1920s were a time when demobilised ex-officers tramped back and forth across the country as commercial salesmen, living out of suitcases in dingy boarding houses, working for pitiable commissions; when respectable burghers shivered in their drawing rooms for want of coal; when impudent shop stewards preached Red Revolution while factory workers with fat wage packets packed the pubs. The panic had not lasted. Deflationary Conservative policies and mass industrial unemployment had helped to restore the social status quo by the mid-1920s. But the middle class had not forgotten. They had learned that their primacy was delicate, never to be taken for granted.[54]

And by the late 1930s the shadow of war appeared to be threatening it once again. Britain was having to rearm in the face of the militaristic challenges of Germany, Italy and Japan. Rearmament had disturbing economic and social implications.[55] It meant, for one thing, a rapid rise in government spending and revenue. Defence spending was, as *The Economist* put it, 'the greatest public works programme ever devised in time of formal peace'.[56] Between 1935 and 1938 public expenditure rose by 17.6 per cent. To match this growth in outlay, an increasingly large share of the nation's personal income had to be siphoned off in the form of taxes, national insurance and health contributions.[57]

The burden of rearmament spending was not distributed evenly across the classes. It was middle-class income taxes that were paying for armaments factories – factories that would then employ mostly working-class labourers. Rearmament was, in that sense, a process of wealth transfer from one class to another. Between 1938 and 1940 manual working wages in Britain increased by 30 per cent while middle-class salaries remained virtually unchanged.[58] As Tory back-bench MP Michael Beaumont complained, the burden of paying for collective security for the nation was falling 'on one class of the community exclusively'.[59]

The income gap between the middle and working classes was narrowing. As it did, so too did the respectability gap. A 'jaunty equality' was beginning to threaten the traditional prestige of white-collar civilisation.[60] When that chronicler of suburban England John Betjeman wished 'friendly bombs' to fall on Slough in 1937, he was expressing a timely middle-class snobbery about 'air-conditioned, bright canteens' and factory hands' wives who had the temerity to dye their hair blonde – in other words, about Woolworth Britain's troubling lack of deference. The masses were growing conscious of their own power. What would be the result in the long term?

The Conservative leadership was not unaware of this danger. In April 1938 the chancellor of the exchequer, Sir John Simon, warned the Cabinet that the growth of rearmament spending could not continue for much longer 'unless we turned ourselves into a different kind of nation' – one that abandoned for ever the liberal-capitalist axioms of balanced budgets, low taxation, minimal inflation and non-state interference in wage and price levels.[61] Expanding the military-manufacturing sector any further would necessitate drastic new government powers. Millions of workers in the munitions factories would become government employees in all but name. Their demands would have to be appeased in the name of industrial peace. Militant Britain would become a centralised Jacobin state, socialist in practice if not in principle.

'Any war,' wrote Oliver Harvey, Lord Halifax's principal private secretary at the Foreign Office, 'will bring vast and unknown social changes – win or lose.'[62] The British middle class seem to have understood this too. By the late 1930s attempts to deter Germany militarily were already transforming the country in ways it disliked. If war ever broke out, the transformation would be even faster. The First World War had shattered Britain's aristocracy and, for a short time, had seemed likely to destroy the middle class too. A Second World War would surely finish the job. 'If war comes,' the *Observer*'s editor, James Garvin, warned in September 1938, 'all forms of property will be taxed nigh to extinction under the defusive name of "Conscription of Wealth".'[63]

When we consider why Britons like Garvin were attracted to the National Government's Appeasement policy in the late 1930s, it's important to remember that, as far as many of them were concerned, it was not just the international balance of power that was at stake. The cost of another world war would be measured not just in lives, terrible though that would be. War would also accelerate the rise of a new kind of egalitarian democracy, which they thought would be coarse, unprincipled – and irreversible. They knew that any such conflict would be a 'People's War'. And they hated the idea.

4

THE SCHOOL OF EMPIRE

The soldiers did not go to al-Bassa to make arrests. They went to make a point.

We can never know what went through the minds of the villagers as they watched the riflemen and the armoured cars approaching on that Wednesday morning. Perhaps some of them had heard the explosion the night before, knew about the warnings that the local headmen, the *mukhtars*, had received from the British military authorities, knew what had happened in other villages under the same confused and angry circumstances, guessed what was going to happen next.

The previous night, a 15-hundredweight patrol lorry belonging to the 2nd Battalion of the Royal Ulster Rifles (RUR) had been destroyed in a roadside bomb attack. The makeshift land mine, made of oxygen cylinders filled with gelignite – what we would now call an 'improvised explosive device', or IED – had killed two of the riflemen on board the lorry instantly, and mortally wounded two others, including a young lieutenant. They were not the battalion's first casualties since it had arrived in Palestine almost a year earlier. For months the Ulstermen had been fighting a frustrating war of shadows against Arab insurgents – 'oozl-barts', they called them – in Samaria and Galilee and along the Syrian border. There had been night raids and ambushes and wild goose chases after snipers and smugglers and bomb-makers. Plenty of Arabs had been killed, and some Ulstermen too. But the patrolmen's murder had been an unprecedented provocation. The British troops were already bored, and bitter, and tired of being shot at and blown up by ghostly figures who disappeared into the anonymity of the villages during the day. Now they were furious.

The 2nd RUR Battalion's commander, Lieutenant-Colonel Gerald Whitfield, had made it clear to the local *mukhtars* that any further acts of terrorism against his men would result in immediate punitive measures directed at whichever Arab community happened to be closest to the site of the attack. The RUR lorry had been near al-Bassa, a little mixed Muslim-Christian community of about 2,000 people in the sub-district of Acre. The farmers of al-Bassa grew olives and pomegranates, figs and apples. The village had two churches, a mosque, shops, coffee houses and a public elementary school for boys. A Dutch visitor in 1851 had remarked on the 'inexpressible charm' of its green pastures, which he called 'truly refreshing to the eye'.[1] There was no evidence to suggest that anyone from al-Bassa had taken part in the destruction of the Ulstermen's lorry, or had known about it in advance. But that was not why the soldiers were going there on that Wednesday morning, 7 September 1938, anyway. They were going to make a point.

We don't know for certain what happened when they got there. We rarely do in cases like these.[2] Witnesses on both sides conflate details and confuse timelines. Sometimes they are too traumatised to remember clearly what was done to them. Sometimes they have good reason to keep quiet about what they did. The official record tends to be bland and unhelpful. Regimental histories are invariably silent. But we have some idea what went on in al-Bassa that day. The riflemen began searching and looting the village's houses and shops. The residents were gathered together in the main street and beaten with sticks and rifle butts. Four of them were shot. Then, about 100 of them were taken to a nearby military stockade, where the British officer in command selected four men from the group – it is not clear why he chose those particular men – and made them undress, place their bare feet on cacti and thorns, and kneel. They were then whipped until they fainted. Pieces of flesh, it was said, 'flew from their bodies'. Afterwards, the villagers were transported to a second military camp.

While all this was going on, back in al-Bassa, armoured cars of the 11th Hussars (Prince Albert's Own) Regiment, who had accompanied the Ulstermen on their punitive expedition, were machine-gunning every building in the village. The walls were systematically peppered with .303 bullets – 'We blew the lot,' said one trooper afterwards.[3] This went on for about twenty minutes. Then the riflemen moved in with lighted braziers. 'We set the houses on fire,' recalled Desmond Woods, one of the junior officers of the 2nd Battalion's 'C' Company, which took part in the operation. 'We burnt the village to the ground.'[4] Then the soldiers left. It was about one o'clock in the afternoon.

When did they come back? It may have been the following day, or the day after that. We don't know for sure. But they did come back, and we know what happened when they did, because somebody who came with them took photographs.[5] The day the soldiers returned to al-Bassa they selected about fifty of the residents and marched them down the road to the point where the original bomb attack had taken place. Once they were there, about twenty of the villagers were told to get onto a bus. A few of them panicked, tried to run and were shot. Once enough of them had been herded on board, the Arab driver was ordered to set off down the road. We don't know if he had seen the Royal Engineers sappers burying the land mine directly in front of the vehicle. What we do know is that when the bus's front wheels touched the mine, it was torn apart in a huge explosion. Many of the passengers were killed instantly. The survivors who had watched all this were ordered to collect the mangled remains which had been thrown across the roadside, dig a pit and shove them into it. Constable Ricke, one of the Palestine Police officers who had come along to watch, took photographs as the villagers performed the interment. Another policeman, Raymond Cafferata, wrote to his wife a few days later: 'You remember reading of an Arab bus blown up on the frontier road just after Paddy was killed? Well, the Ulsters did it – a forty-two-seater full of Arabs.'[6] We don't know how many of the villagers were killed on these two visits to al-Bassa. Twenty seems a conservative estimate. It may have been more.

'It paid dividends,' Desmond Woods reflected on the battalion's destruction of al-Bassa many years later. 'But of course, you can't do those sorts of things today.'[7]

*

You couldn't do those sorts of things then, either. Not openly, anyway. Nobody in September 1938 was under any illusion about what you called deliberately blowing up a bus packed with unarmed civilians. You called it what it was – which is to say, murder. But soldiers and policemen weren't supposed to steal money from civilians either. Nor were they supposed to loot and gratuitously destroy their property, beat them unconscious with rifle butts and pick-axe helves, shoot them 'trying to escape' or deliberately run them over with lorries. They were not supposed to place hostages in wire cages without food or water in the hot Levantine sun for days at a time until the prisoners died of heat exhaustion and dehydration. They were not supposed to use what were euphemistically known as 'Turkish methods' against detainees being held for interrogation – water-boarding them, electrocuting them, tearing hair from their faces and heads, pulling out their fingernails, beating them with rubber truncheons and nail-studded clubs, crippling them, sodomising them. Yet it's attested that all these things happened at one time or another in Palestine during the Arab Revolt from 1936 to 1939.[8] And that British soldiers and policeman and civil officials either gave the nod to such things being done or did them themselves.

Which is not to say that such things were the norm. Incidents like al-Bassa were outrageous precisely because they were unusual. On the whole, the British Army and the various colonial *gendarmeries* that worked alongside it in the 1920s and 1930s behaved fairly well – certainly with a good deal more self-restraint than the security forces of other imperial states. There is nothing in the British record in Palestine to compare with the devastating violence of the Rif War in Spanish Morocco, for instance, or the Italian pacification of Libya, both of which involved killing on a vastly greater scale. Many British soldiers behaved impeccably in Palestine during the Arab Revolt. The men of the 2nd Battalion of the Cameronians (Scottish Rifles), for instance, were praised by local people for their good-humoured moderation during a tour of duty in 1937.[9] The Coldstream Guards and Royal Northumberland Fusiliers received similar plaudits the following year in Jerusalem.[10] Abuses were usually the product of spite and frustration rather than premeditated brutality. 'At times tempers flared,' admitted Bertie Pond, who went to Palestine as the regimental sergeant-major of the 2nd Queen's Own Royal West Kent Regiment in 1938:

> Soldiers would see Arab atrocities, and there were some of their mates killed and on occasion, they, the troops became bloody angry. In the heat of an action, when a prisoner is brought in, you see your friend near you – you think 'shoot the bastard' and I know of one or two occasions where this happened. But it is a source of great pride to all, as a British soldier, that you can count such incidents on the fingers of one hand and that after such an incident, the unit itself, however much they had been provoked, felt ashamed.[11]

No British commanding officer was ever responsible for the kinds of indiscriminate slaughter that the Spanish and the Italians committed in Morocco and Libya, and he would not have got away with it if he had been. The fate of Reginald Dyer, the brigadier-general who was compelled to retire in disgrace after ordering the killing of as many as 1,000 protesters at Amritsar in 1919, weighed heavily on every commanding officer's mind in the 1930s. Nobody wanted to be the next Dyer. Even the Anglican bishop of Jerusalem, Francis Graham Brown, a fierce critic of military excesses in Palestine, thought that the worst incidents were not officially sanctioned by the army authorities, and were privately regretted – though not, he noted, officially condemned.[12]

All the same, the reality of keeping order in a global empire, even an 'empire of liberty' such as Britain's, meant sometimes doing very ugly things. It is easy to sentimentalise the British Empire's twilight years – to dwell on the quaint absurdities of late-period imperialism, the *sola topees* and *pukka memsahibs* and cold baths and gin-and-tonics on the veranda. But there is no getting away from the fact that the British Empire's survival, like that of all empires, ultimately rested on the willingness of hard-faced men to commit violence in its name. Someone had to be prepared to do things such as beat a teenage detainee with a tent mallet and a pick-axe handle so viciously that one of his eyes was knocked out of its socket and left hanging by a thin thread of gristle.[13] Or smash out the brains of an uncooperative protester with a rifle butt.[14] All the Empire's liberal intentions and genteel appurtenances could not alter that.

The British Empire in the 1930s was admired, even by its critics, for its progressive achievements. There were lots of things to admire. But, on the brink of world war, its existence greatly complicated Britain's claim to special moral authority. And to win that war, the imperial motherland would have to make some ruthless compromises with its own values.

*

It is difficult, now, to remember just what a permanent fixture the British Empire once seemed. It was still one of the great facts of the world in the 1930s: impossible to miss, older than anyone could remember and apparently indestructible. London was not just the capital city of the United Kingdom but the epicentre of a vast intercontinental estate of 14 million square miles (36 million square kilometres) of territory, one quarter of the world's land surface. The Empire had been there for so long, had endured and outlasted so many threats to its survival, was taken so completely for granted, that it was hard for people to imagine it ever going away. 'The Empire is not only our master hope, it is our greatest heritage,' Stanley Baldwin had said in 1925:

It is something infinitely precious which we hold in trust from our forefathers and for our children. To be worthy of that trust, we cannot merely be passive admirers of its achievement and its promise. We must all, in our several degrees, be active learners in the school of Empire.[15]

Yet few Britons spent much time thinking about it. They were, as Bernard Porter has called them, absent-minded imperialists. 'I frankly despair,' wrote a civil service official in 1923, 'of making the great heart of England take any intelligent interest in the colonies.'[16] This was not for want of trying by Empire boosters. The years between the wars saw a great wave of imperial-minded propaganda – the marketing of 24 May as 'Empire Day', recognised as a holiday by most schools and accompanied by a glut of imperial-themed BBC programming; the organisation of two British Empire exhibitions, one in Wembley in 1924, the other in Glasgow in 1938; the Empire Marketing Board's attempts to get consumers to think globally.[17] The *Daily Express*'s red crusader first appeared on the newspaper's masthead in 1933 to promote the campaigns of its proprietor, Lord Beaverbrook, for Empire tariff reform. The inaugural performance of William Walton's *Crown Imperial* march was at the coronation of George VI in 1937.

But none of this made any deep imprint in the popular consciousness. The idea of Empire just did not sit well with the new, dominant Shire Folk conception of Britishness, which emphasised parochialism, domesticity and meek ambition. This is why Britons found it so easy to forget about the Empire altogether during their 'finest hour' of 1940. After the fall of France they accepted, indeed embraced, the idea that they were fighting on alone against the Nazis. This was pure fiction. The Empire was a crucial source of manpower and *matériel* keeping the British war effort going in 1940. The belief in 'aloneness' was, however, compelling. Consciousness of Empire only complicated that belief, so it was sloughed off.[18]

Those who did think about Empire between the wars had to answer two questions. One was whether the Empire still represented a net asset to British power or whether it had become a distraction and a deficit. To imperial promoters, the answer was self-evident. The Conservative MP Leo Amery, for whom the British colonies were a lifelong *idée fixe*, wrote in his 1935 book *The Forward View* that it 'hardly needs arguing' that the Empire contained all the material conditions necessary to make it 'one of the great world units of the future'.[19] Neville Chamberlain agreed: Britain shorn of its empire would be a 'fourth-rate power', he declared in 1937.[20]

Possessing the pink bits on the map certainly made Britain a very different sort of European country from, say, Poland, which it otherwise might have resembled in terms of land mass and population size. Measured by area, resources and human capital, the British Empire appeared to compare favourably even with the sprawling hinterland empires of the United States and the Soviet Union. Its total population of 491 million in 1931 dwarfed that of the 161 million of the USSR and America's 122 million. Even its white population, though significantly smaller at 71.5 million (about two-thirds of it in the United Kingdom), was not so far off the United States' 109 million, and larger anyway than Germany's.

The Empire's climatic, mineralogical and biological diversity meant that it contained within its borders an impressive proportion of the world's food and raw materials: 23 per cent of its wheat, 50 per cent of its rice, 60 per cent of its rubber, 50 per cent of its chrome, 46 per cent of its tin and 70 per cent of its gold. Four in ten of all the world's cattle grazed on British land. So did 36 per cent of its sheep.[21] The Empire's scattered littoral character meant that most of the globe's strategic marine choke points – both ends of the Mediterranean, the Cape of Good Hope, the Strait of Malacca – were in British hands. Plus, the Empire's plentiful natural harbours provided the Royal Navy with a worldwide network of fuelling stations for its warships.

All this represented power – power that Britain had recently mobilised to great effect. During the First World War, the Empire had contributed almost 3 million men in uniform to supplement the 5 million mobilised by the United Kingdom itself. Millions more contracted labourers, drafted from the colonies, had sweated behind the front lines. The Empire's physical and financial contributions to the war effort had been considerable. Military expenditure by the Government of India (funded entirely by Indian taxpayers) had risen six-fold by the end of the war to £140 million. The Raj had sent millions of tons of wheat and war *matériel* to the British and Allied home fronts.[22]

Moreover, since the war, Britain's economic relationship with its Empire had grown much more interconnected. In 1914 just 25 per cent of Britain's import trade and 36 per cent of its export trade had taken place within the Empire. By the late 1930s these proportions had swelled to 39.5 per cent and 49 per cent respectively.[23] The First World War and the economic uncertainty that had followed it had brought an end to the Victorian old order of *laissez-faire* in which people, products and capital had been able to move across national borders with little or no restriction. Now the world's markets were being divided up by high tariff walls. In 1932 the United Kingdom had formally abandoned free trade in favour of imperial preference – the once shocking idea of turning the Empire into an autarkic trading bloc, a vast British *Zollverein* girded by protectionist barriers, had become a reality. Henceforth, as Amery put it, 'the creative energies of the markets of the Empire' could be 'directed in the main to mutual development, instead of being dissipated upon an unreciprocating world'.[24]

These were the most obvious benefits of Empire. There were more intangible returns too. Controlling a large proportion of the world afforded the United Kingdom a self-confidence and prestige that it would otherwise not have enjoyed. In 1939 the folds of the Union Jack smacked smartly against flagstaffs all the way from the Eastern Mediterranean to Brisbane, from the Great Rift Valley to the Yucatán peninsula. The viceroy of India, reigning quasi-regally from within the awesome red and cream sandstone walls of his palace in Delhi, was a colonel from Linlithgowshire. The king of Egypt, heir to the Pharaohs, received his instructions from a former Foreign Office clerk. Great tracts of mangrove swamp and rainforest the size of Yorkshire and Wales were the responsibility of plump-faced youths from minor public schools. Albert Frederick Arthur George Windsor was not only the world's greatest Christian king but also the world's greatest Hindu king, and Sikh king, and Muslim king. Such facts could not help but awe the United Kingdom's rivals a little. To Adolf Hitler, it was simply 'the greatest power on Earth'.[25]

Yet not all of this was as good as it sounded. Agglomerating Britain's overseas territories into one made the Empire look a lot like the United States and the USSR on paper; but in reality, it did not resemble either of them one bit. The Soviet Union and America were contiguous land masses enjoying all the advantages of territorial unity and interior lines of communication. The British Empire was a randomly dispersed marine archipelago in which people and resources were arbitrarily separated by thousands of miles of ocean. It was all vulnerable frontier, no deep hinterland into which an imperial army could retreat to safety in an emergency.[26] During the First World War this had not mattered too much, since the fighting had been concentrated so overwhelmingly on the Western Front. Hardly any of Britain's colonies had been exposed to any risk of invasion. But by the

1930s Japan and Italy, formerly allies, represented new threats in the Mediterranean and East Asia. Britain could not simultaneously defend these areas and the homeland too. The Empire's geographical liabilities had been exposed.

The Empire's population was certainly enormous. But the aggregate total of its subjects obscured the vastly unequal way in which wealth, education and opportunities were distributed among them. Seventeen out of twenty of the imperial populace lived in India and the tropics, almost all of them penurious, illiterate peasants scratching a living at a medieval level of subsistence. The Empire's poverty and underdevelopment greatly limited the United Kingdom's ability to mobilise its resources. Most of it was quite incapable of defending itself.

The exceptions to this were the white settler peoples in Australia, New Zealand, Canada, Newfoundland, South Africa and the plantation colonies of east and central Africa – migrants who had built imitation Britains across the globe, expropriating or exterminating the local populations along the way. Here were prosperous, well-educated communities, some with nascent industrial economies. Most of them maintained a deeply felt, if somewhat imprecise, allegiance to the Empire and the global 'British race'. There was no shortage of platitudinous assurances of comity at the various Imperial Conferences that took place between Dominion statesmen between the wars. But the very fact that those conferences were necessary at all demonstrates that imperial decision-making was no longer concentrated exclusively in London. Dominion opinion now had to be considered in Britain's foreign policymaking, a great complication to its diplomacy. Neville Chamberlain knew as he travelled to Munich in September 1938 that if Britain went to war to defend Czechoslovakia, there was no guarantee that Canada and Australia would automatically follow suit. Defence expenditure in the United Kingdom as a percentage of national income was over five times that of Canada and Australia.[27] Ottawa and Canberra expected to be consulted on military matters; they did not expect to pay for the privilege. The British taxpayer had to pick up the cost of keeping the Empire secure.

The problem that Britain faced in the 1930s was that the conditions that had once made its imperial ambitions relatively effortless and cost-efficient no longer applied to anything like the same degree. Britain's inward turn towards imperial trade reflected economic weakness, not vigorous autarkic health. The Empire it had built was a curate's egg. A few bits of it were very valuable indeed; a lot of it had occasional, if limited, worth; and great swathes of it were no use at all, and represented nothing but a wearying, yet undiscardable burden to the Mother Country.

*

Then there was the question of what it was all about. What did the British Empire stand for by the 1930s? When people said they 'believed' in it, were even willing to die for it, what did they mean? Did they believe in the superiority of the Anglo-Saxon racial stock? The truth of the Protestant faith? Western civilisation? British ideals and institutions? Was the Empire's purpose to secure the power of the metropole? To serve as a model for international peace and co-operation? To hold back the forces of barbarism? There were people who believed in some or all of these things. A lot depended on what the Empire of their own imagination was – what kind of mental images the word conjured up when they thought about it. Flinders Street in Melbourne represented a very different kind of Empire from the Serengeti Plain. Thinking about Empire as a Caribbean shanty town was not the same as thinking about it as an Imperial Airways flying boat, or as the New Guinea Highlands, or as the Royal Calcutta Turf Club.

The nineteenth century had been a century of empire-building: of exploration, conquest and great moral crusades, such as the suppression of the slave trade. The new century was a century of empire management: worthy, but dull. Imperialism had entered its prosaic age. The Victorians had celebrated their bellicosity in gleeful and unapologetically bloodthirsty terms appropriate to an age of Social Darwinist triumphalism. Many imperialists continued to nurse the same feelings in the 1930s. Across the white communities of the Empire, there were plenty of people who still adhered unembarrassedly to the view that the British race's world-historical task was to rule other, less fortunate races – benevolently, to be sure, but with a firm hand, and with no complicating nonsense about one day transferring power from imperial master to native subject. In 1937 Churchill spoke unblushingly of the right of 'a stronger race, a higher grade of race' to replace other, lesser, peoples.[28] Lord Halifax believed that there was nothing 'unnatural nor immoral' about the idea of superior and inferior races.[29] Anthony Eden spoke of 'reasserting white-race authority' in East Asia.[30]

The problem was that such views were becoming increasingly impolite by the 1930s. And they were embarrassing at a time when the British government was trying to claim the moral high ground in its dealings with Hitler. There were some uncomfortable parallels between the blood-and-soil rhetoric of National Socialism and the language of Anglo-Saxon empire. Hitler had always lathered praise on the white supremacism that underpinned British rule in Africa and Asia. 'The Englishman has always understood,' he wrote in 1920, 'that he must be master, and not brother.'[31] When the Nazi court philosopher Alfred Rosenberg suggested in 1933 that Germany's new anti-Semitic laws were not incompatible with Anglophone traditions because 'the British Empire too is based on a racially defined claim of dominance', he struck a sensitive nerve.[32] The Canadian poet Wilfrid Campbell had proclaimed in 1914 that 'to serve Empire and race' was the 'great thought, great hope and desire'. This had been received well enough at the time. By the 1930s it had started to sound a little too much like a quotation from *Mein Kampf*.[33]

The British denied, of course, that the parallel was fair. 'Enemy propaganda has always striven to represent Britain as grabbing land all over the globe, stealing other people's "possessions", exploiting them exclusively for our own benefit, repressing them by force [...] the truth is in reality quite the reverse,' insisted Major W. E. Simnett in *The British Way and Purpose*:

> We no longer regard the Colonial Empire as a 'possession', but as a trust or responsibility. 'Imperialism' in the less reputable sense of that term is dead [...] it has been superseded by the principle of trusteeship for colonial peoples, in which the interests and welfare of the native peoples are regarded as paramount.[34]

Empire by the 1930s had been rebranded to suit the age of Shire Folk: conquest and annexation were out, benign guardianship in. In an era in which the signature values had become the self-determination of peoples and international concord, it was necessary to think of the Empire as a mild and benevolent force in world affairs, a guarantor of progress and stability.[35] It was to be understood as a kind of grand philanthropic gesture, distributing valuable knowledge (sacred and profane) and the benefits of industrial civilisation to the darkest and most benighted corners of the world – a mission school here, an irrigation scheme or institute of tropical medicine there.

Above all, the British Empire by the 1930s was an instrument of peace in a disorderly and unhappy world, 'a great force for good,' according to Baldwin.[36] 'Our business in the years to come,' wrote historian Arthur

Bryant, 'is not so much to govern, as in the past, as to give the world a lead in the business of living wisely and peacefully and nobly.'[37] And to educate its peoples towards happy and responsible self-government. Empire's official mission statement was now to put itself out of business one day – even if that day was a long way off.

On the whole, the British people between the wars had no quarrel with this new way of thinking about their Empire. It suited their milder, more amiable conception of themselves. They rarely thought about Empire much at all. But in so far as they did think about it, most of them were convinced that it was a good thing, that its subject peoples were much the happier for its existence and that the rest of the world looked upon it – and them – with envy and admiration.[38]

Yet, as we have seen, governing an empire was always going to be an exercise in violence. Its dirty work would go on just as it had always gone on, no matter how much this jarred with the idea of enlightened trusteeship. But by the 1930s this was a greater problem than it had once been, because the British had convinced themselves that brutality was inimical to their character – 'frightfulness,' Churchill said, was not 'a remedy known to the British pharmacopoeia' – and because twentieth-century mass communications were making it harder and harder to keep such brutality quiet.[39] If the only way to keep the Empire stable was to betray the values of the imperial centre, then people might start to wonder whether there was any point to keeping it at all.

*

Nowhere epitomised the contradictions of Empire between the wars so vividly as Palestine. There were plenty of other imperial canker sores – in India, Burma, Afghanistan, Egypt – but Palestine was a troubled colony like no other, the graveyard of proconsular reputations, where experienced civil servants saw their careers and sound constitutions ruined. 'One works all day and half the night and gets nowhere in the long run,' complained William Battershill, chief secretary to the British Palestine government. 'One is tempted to say: *how long, O Lord, how long?*'[40]

Edward Keith-Roach, governor of Jerusalem, had to take a rest cure abroad for several months in the mid-1930s because the stress and overwork of his job had almost caused him to go blind.[41] Armed assassins were discovered in the gardens adjoining his offices several times; a time bomb once went off under his sitting room window. He had to be accompanied by three policemen carrying pistols at all times. 'I began,' he recalled, 'to hate never being alone by day and hearing the tramp, tramp, tramp of sentries during the nights.'[42] The High Commissioner from 1931 to 1937, Arthur Wauchope, was driven into early retirement by what appears to have been a mental breakdown caused by the pressure of his job. 'Wauchope loves every stone of this country,' Lieutenant-General Sir John Dill wrote of him. 'He has worked himself to the bone for it – and it has let him down.'[43]

Palestine was not, strictly speaking, an imperial territory at all but rather a 'League of Nations Mandate', held in what was supposed to be temporary trust on behalf of that international organisation. For most day-to-day purposes this did not make much difference. The League's supervision was never very exacting. Wauchope's fine, white-stoned Government House building in Jerusalem, designed by Austen Harrison, looked much the same as any other High Commissioner's residence around the world.[44] In the happy early days of the British presence, the expatriate community arranged tea parties and tennis matches and productions of Gilbert and Sullivan, while across the cactus fields of the Jordan Valley riders in exquisite hunting pink chased down jackals as if they were pursuing foxes across Wiltshire. Wauchope held a hunt ball each Lent, with foxhounds parading around the ballroom of Government House.[45]

The new taxonomy of Empire was significant all the same. The British had captured Palestine from the Ottomans in 1918 and held onto it afterwards because it was useful. It formed a territorial bridge linking Egypt and the Suez Canal with India. It acted as a refuelling hub for imperial air communications between Europe and the East. The port of Haifa was a valuable Levantine naval base for the Royal Navy and the terminus of an oil pipeline running from Kirkuk and Mosul which supplied the Mediterranean Fleet based in Malta. These were the iron facts of imperial grand strategy.

But they were not used as the justification for the Mandate. The British were officially in Palestine to do good. Upon the assumption of control in 1920, a flood of imperial officials, professionals and proselytisers arrived – civil servants, soldiers, policemen, teachers, doctors, engineers, businessmen, missionaries – many of them straight from India and Africa, and bearing all of the worthy, self-assured assumptions about a civilising mission that they had first acquired in the Serengeti and Peshawar. Schools and hospitals were built, bridges constructed, marshes drained, irrigation systems dug. By the time the British left in 1948, the life-expectancy of the typical Palestinian peasant (*fellah*) had risen by fifteen years. Rates of infection for malaria, trachoma, smallpox, typhoid and other infectious diseases had plummeted. Most Arab boys were receiving at least a few years of formal schooling. Tireless and largely forgotten altruists of Empire had achieved these things, and more besides.[46]

Whose land would Palestine be, though, ultimately? In 1917 Arthur Balfour, then foreign secretary, had made a public commitment to the worldwide Zionist movement that if Palestine was liberated from the Ottomans, it could become the site of a 'national home' for the Jews within the British Empire. Precisely what that commitment meant, for the Mandate's majority Arab population as much as the people of the Jewish *Yishuv* (or community) themselves, Balfour did not make clear. And it became no clearer in the years after the First World War.

Leo Amery, the secretary-of-state for the colonies from 1924 to 1929, thought that Jewish immigrants to Palestine, with their 'robust physique and virile appearance' and Western mores, might create a quasi-British civilisation in the wilderness that one day could become a fully participating imperial dominion.[47] 'Our ultimate end,' he wrote in his diary at the time, 'is clearly to make Palestine the centre of a western influence, using the Jews as we have used the Scots, to carry the English ideal through the Middle East.'[48] Others were less convinced. Lord Robert Cecil warned that 'there is not going to be any great catch in [Palestine ...] we shall simply keep the peace between the Arabs and the Jews. We are not going to get anything out of it. Whoever goes there will have a poor time.'[49]

Even optimists like Amery assumed that the process of dominion-building would be slow. The number of Jews migrating from central and eastern Europe was not very great throughout the 1920s – in 1928, barely 2,000 arrived. All that changed with Hitler's ascent to power in Germany. Over 30,000 Jews came to Palestine in 1933. By 1935 it was twice that. Jews, who had constituted 16 per cent of the Mandate's population in 1931, now made up over a quarter of its people.[50] The concomitant wave of land purchases from Arabs (many of them absentee brokers who did not consult their own tenants during the negotiations) greatly disturbed the fragile balance of ethnic-commercial power.[51] Angry displaced *fellahin* drifted to the urban slums, which proved fertile ground for militant indoctrination. By the beginning of 1936, with armed gangs of unemployed Arabs taking to the Samarian countryside to conduct sabotage and banditry against Jewish settlers and the British authorities, the warnings of Lord Robert Cecil were looking ominously prescient. The Arab Revolt had begun.[52]

*

The British were caught totally unprepared. All the troops in Palestine that they had at their immediate disposal in early 1936 were two battalions of infantry and a few RAF armoured car squadrons – about 1,500 men all told. This modest force was quite inadequate to deal with a national *intifada*. Large-scale military force – always the last and least desirable option so far as the economy-minded British were concerned – had to be deployed. Troops were rushed from Egypt and Malta. By September 1936 there were 20,000 of them in place, including an entire division of twelve infantry battalions under the command of Lieutenant-General Sir John Dill, the future Chief of the Imperial General Staff (CIGS).

For about a year the violence subsided. The War Office withdrew most of the troops. Then it suddenly flared up again, more viciously than ever. By early 1938 the British were losing control of large parts of Samaria and Galilee. Administrators were forced to travel with armed guards for fear of assassination. No country road was safe from land mines or snipers.[53] 'Sitting at home by the fire in England,' colonial policeman Sydney Burr wrote to his parents,

> You cannot visualise a country only the size of Wales, under British rule, where there is absolutely no law and order. Police and troops are powerless, and our only object out here seems to be clearing up the mess after the crime has been committed.[54]

The United Kingdom was engaged in the most serious counter-insurgency crisis since the Irish War of Independence. This had become Neville Chamberlain's Middle Eastern War on Terror, a conflict in which 262 British soldiers and policemen would ultimately be killed – one-and-half times as many as during the fighting in Iraq from 2003 to 2011. The counter-insurgency challenge was prodigious. Palestine had towns, cities and soft targets aplenty – roads, railways, telegraph lines, the airport at Lydda, the crucial oil pipeline at Haifa. Arab tactics reflected this. Rather than attempt any large-scale, open-field engagements against British units which they were bound to lose, they chose instead to make hit-and-run attacks – sniping, bombing, arson – that were minor in their individual effects but which collectively disrupted the normal rhythm of administration across the country. This was an insurgency of a distinctively modern kind.

Terror was the rebels' watchword: not just terror against the British and the Jewish *Yishuv* but terror too against fellow Arabs who showed insufficient enthusiasm for the cause. The insurgents understood that controlling the local community was key to the outcome of the campaign. They operated a shadow government paralleling that of the Mandate authorities, demanding taxes in cash or kind from villagers and enforcing a quasi-legal system of their own (complete with courtrooms accessorised with stolen typewriters and judicial wigs).[55] All Arabs were expected to co-operate with the insurgents on pain of severe punishment. Townsmen were warned to stop wearing their traditional urban headgear, the *tarboosh*, and to adopt the rural cloth *keffiyah* instead, to make it easier for guerrilla fighters to slip anonymously in and out of the Mandate's built-up areas.[56] By the autumn of 1938, as the Royal Ulster Regiment went on its rampage in al-Bassa, British authority over much of Palestine had more or less disintegrated. General Sir Edmund Ironside, visiting Palestine at the behest of the War Office, reported to London that 'civil government has completely broken down'.[57] William Battershill agreed: 'The gangs rule the country.'[58]

The spectacle of Palestine's native people rising up to confront British imperial power had excited the sympathies of people across the Arab and Islamic world. The Empire counted 50 million Muslims among its subjects, most of them in what is today Pakistan.[59] The prospect of a substantial portion of the global *Ummah* rising up in sympathy with the Palestinians did not bear thinking about. As a Government of India report warned: if Britain did not bring the Arab Rising to a quick end, 'the Moslems of India will look upon Britain as the enemy of Islam.'[60] All of this was going on as Britain appeared to be simultaneously teetering towards war with Hitler and Mussolini. Troops might be needed in Europe at any moment. The tiny British garrison in Egypt was threatened by much larger, unfriendly, Italian forces in Libya and Abyssinia.

In London, Henry Pownall, the Army's Director of Military Intelligence and Operations, was sunk in gloom as he reflected on the situation. The Colonial Office was screaming for reinforcements for the Mandate which the War Office dared not send. The Arab Revolt was proving not just impossible to suppress but threatening to spread anti-imperial disaffection across the whole of the Middle East as well. 'God,' he wrote in his diary, 'what a mess we have made of the whole of this Palestine affair!'[61]

*

The Munich agreement with Nazi Germany on 30 September 1938 and its purchase, for the time being, of peace in Europe created a window of opportunity to resolve the Palestine crisis once and for all. Chamberlain was determined to use it. The equivalent of two infantry divisions were immediately rushed to the Mandate, an unprecedented military deployment of 25,000 men. This was the Palestine 'surge' – an attempt to use sheer weight of numbers to overwhelm and crush the Arab rebels.

A new ruthlessness born of urgency imposed itself on British efforts. The Old City of Jerusalem, which had largely fallen out of the authorities' control earlier in the year, was retaken by force. Civil control of the Mandate was effectively handed over to the military. Strict security measures were introduced: a rural curfew, ID cards and permits for road and rail travel, arrests, convictions and summary executions of any Arabs suspected of involvement in the uprising. Bands of irregulars operating in the countryside were hunted down and apprehended or killed. 'Loyal' Arab units were armed to defend pro-government villages.

Experts in imperial coercion were brought in. Sir Charles Tegart, formerly of the Calcutta Police, supervised the construction of an eighteen-foot concertina wire fence along Palestine's northern border to prevent arms smuggling from French Syria. He ordered, too, the building of dozens of 'Tegart forts', reinforced concrete police and military posts, some of which remain in use by the Israeli authorities today. Tegart was an enthusiastic believer in collective punishment and the establishment, copying the practices of the North-West Frontier, of a list of 'good' and 'bad' Arab villages – the former to be rewarded with government subsidies, the latter to be fined and, if necessary, burned.[62] He created 'Arab Interrogation Centres' in which detainees were systematically tortured, although the existence of these had to be kept a secret from many of his own colleagues. When Keith-Roach found out that Tegart's 'Turkish methods' were being used in Jerusalem, he successfully demanded that that particular centre be closed down.[63]

Many British units exercised restraint during counter-insurgency operations. But the fact was that their rules of engagement were sufficiently ambiguous to allow almost any kind of conduct. The 1929 *Manual of Military Law* forbade soldiers to mistreat civilians, but also indicated that 'any degree of force' was theoretically allowable in the face of an armed insurrection, and that actions that would 'inflict suffering upon innocent individuals' were not only permissible but 'indispensable as a last resource' to compel acquiescence. Both the *Manual* and the 1937 Palestine Defence Order in Council were explicit that collective punishments and 'retribution' against local communities – even those which had no connection to any particular offence against the security forces – were acceptable methods of keeping public order. What the Royal Ulster Rifles did in al-Bassa was a moral atrocity and embarrassing enough for the authorities to try to hush it up, but it was probably quite legal. Given how vaguely the battalion's officers had been authorised to do whatever they felt was necessary to keep the peace, at a pinch they could have argued that blowing up a bus packed full of civilians was within their rights.[64]

The essential rule was not to get caught red-handed doing anything too barbarous. No British soldier doling out rough justice to one of the 'oozl-barts' had to fear the attentions of social media in 1938. 'Running over an Arab is the same as a dog in England except we do not report it,' Sydney Burr confessed matter-of-factly to his parents in a letter home.[65]

The Palestine authorities did their best to keep information about what was going on in the Mandate as far from British eyes as possible. Newspaper reporters were excluded from the areas of greatest violence.[66] Britons on the spot who asked too many awkward questions were chastised for their disloyalty. When a local welfare officer, Miss Nixon, complained about soldiers stealing and beating up Arabs and destroying their tents, she was warned that it 'was not her business to make these investigations'.[67] In March 1939 Clarence Buxton, the assistant district commissioner for Beersheba, sent a report to Battershill warning that the crisis in Palestine could not be resolved 'by a competition in terrorism'. The Army, he claimed, was using tactics – including the use of hostages as 'human mine exploders' at the front of convoys and trains – that were often indistinguishable from those of the rebels themselves. 'Buxton intends to persist in obstructing instead of co-operating,' the colonel of the 2nd Highland Light Infantry fumed when he saw this.[68] Given the intense moral pressure to display imperial solidarity, most Britons who suspected that nasty things were going on in their name chose to ignore them.

Those who did not got few answers. When Bishop Francis Graham Brown heard rumours that something appalling had happened at al-Bassa, he went to see the village for himself. He was sufficiently shocked by what he saw to arrange an interview with the local divisional commander, Major-General Bernard Montgomery, who had just taken over as the senior British Army officer in northern Palestine. Monty, though the son of a bishop himself, was not in one of his more loquacious moods the day he met Brown. 'I shall shoot them,' is all he would say of the local Arabs in response to the bishop's questions. Brown left the meeting feeling 'absolutely bewildered'. 'The man,' he said of Montgomery, 'is blood mad.'[69]

*

By the spring of 1939 the new ferocity shown by British forces had begun to show results.[70] An official military report boasted with satisfaction that most of Palestine's hinterland was once again under government control.[71] The Revolt had run its course. A few diehard insurgents continued to operate, but by the outbreak of war in Europe in September the British had successfully reasserted their authority across the Mandate.

Nobody in London was under any illusion that Palestine had returned to lasting stability. The surge had been no more than a temporary demonstration of imperial power. The War Office needed those troops elsewhere now. Imperial prestige had demanded that the Arab rebels be crushed. But with the end of the Revolt it was time to revisit the whole question of Palestine's future. At the heart of the issue was Jewish immigration and Britain's continued commitment to the Balfour Declaration. Unless the Palestinians themselves could be satisfied on this point, Sir Miles Lampson, the British ambassador in Egypt, warned the Cabinet: 'if war comes, we shall have to take on the Arabs as well as the Italians and Germans. What would our position then be in the Near East? I shudder to think.'[72]

Facing such a grim prospect, Chamberlain was blunt. 'If we must offend one side, let us offend the Jews rather than the Arabs,' he told the Cabinet.[73] Charles Bateman, Lampson's deputy in Cairo, wrote: 'I can't see any justification for the loss of a single British soldier in the faction fight between those damned Semites.' As for the Jews: 'let us be practical,' he continued:

> They are anybody's game these days [...] we have not done badly by them so far and they should be made to realise that crying for the moon won't get them anywhere – especially if we are the only friends they have left in the world.[74]

In May 1939 the government published a White Paper on Palestine which proposed to heavily restrict Jewish immigration for the next five years, and bring it virtually to an end thereafter. The news was greeted with anger and dismay in the international Jewish community. In London, Moshe Shertok, head of the Palestine Jewish Agency's political department, was approached by an Oxford undergraduate who wanted permission to murder Neville Chamberlain on the floor of the House of Commons before killing herself.[75] The Irgun, a radical breakaway faction of the main Jewish paramilitary defence force, the Haganah, began terrorist operations of its own against the British authorities. But these were extreme responses. The British had calculated correctly. Mainstream Jewish organisations, for all their frustration, felt themselves in no position to mount any resistance to an empire that, at that moment, was one of the few things standing between themselves and Nazi Germany.

In addition to hundreds of British lives, the Arab Revolt resulted in the deaths of over 300 Palestinian Jews and at least 5,000 Arabs.[76] It demonstrated, in a thousand quotidian ways, all of the squalor and cruelty that inevitably end up accompanying a 'police action' led by bored and frustrated colonial troops stranded in the midst of a sullen and hostile local population. It was a nasty, unrewarding war of shadows, fought in sidestreets with cudgels and pick-axe helves and broken bottles as often as rifles.

It had shown that the Shire Folk could be ruthless when necessary – ruthless in the way with which they had crushed the Arabs, but ruthless too in the way they had then coolly betrayed the Mandate's Jews. By sharply limiting any further migration to Palestine, the 1939 White Paper closed off one of the last remaining escape routes for the Jews of central and eastern Europe in the final months before Hitler's conquests and genocidal fantasies made flight impossible. Such was the pitiless moral calculus essential to the maintenance of empire.

PART TWO

UMBRELLA MAN

5

GUILTY MAN

On 5 July 1940 a slender, 125-page book called *Guilty Men*, probably the most influential polemic ever published in Britain, appeared on the streets of London. Written over four frenetic days on the roof of the London *Evening Standard* offices in Fleet Street, *Guilty Men* was a collaboration by three journalists – Michael Foot, Frank Owen and Peter Howard – who assumed the collective pen-name 'Cato'. It was an instant scandal and an instant success. Many respectable retailers and distributors, including W. H. Smith, refused to handle it. The publisher Victor Gollancz had it sold in Soho on street barrows (some purchasers, probably led to believe that it was a sex manual by its title, must have been in for a disappointment). But it went through twenty-two impressions in its first three months and ended up selling 217,000 copies.[1]

Guilty Men was an odd book. Its erratic style and lack of narrative coherence betrayed its hasty creation and the heterogeneous talents and loyalties of its three authors. They are usually today described as 'a trio of left-wing journalists', but that label only really matches Foot, who eventually became an ill-fated leader of the Labour Party. Frank Owen was more of an old-fashioned South Wales Liberal than a left-winger, while Peter Howard, a former England rugby international, was hard to pin down ideologically. He had already drifted from Mosley's early crypto-fascism to *Sunday Express* conservatism, and within a few months of contributing to *Guilty Men* he had become a leading figure in Frank Buchman's evangelical 'Moral Rearmament' movement. In 1941 Howard published another book, *Innocent Men*, which to some extent repudiated his views of a year earlier.

People who know *Guilty Men* only by its reputation can be surprised at its content. The book is a concerted attack on British foreign policy of the 1930s, but a selective one. It slams Britain's treatment of Czechoslovakia in 1938 as a moral disgrace but is contemptuous of Poland, the country Britain did ultimately go to war to protect from Nazi Germany, dismissing it as a 'peasant nation' run by a 'degenerate crew'.[2] It portrays David Lloyd George as a lost hero of the 1930s, even though he had described Hitler in 1936 as 'the greatest living German'. It is (to put it mildly) less than honest about the Labour Party's record on pre-war rearmament. Its snobbish asides about the social origins of Horace Wilson, the permanent secretary of the Treasury, have not aged well.

Still, it is a remarkable piece of journalism, with a clear and devastating central message. The book begins with a powerful (if overwrought) account of the misery and chaos of the Dunkirk evacuation in the final days of May 1940. It describes the heroism of British soldiers armed only with rifles and bayonets having to fight Nazi tanks and dive-bombers. Only Shire Folk ingenuity and courage, it explains, saved the army from destruction. But 'Cato's main theme is not military but political, a story of the pre-war period rather than the war itself – namely, how Britain's soldiers, as he puts it, 'were doomed *before* they took the field'.[3] Doomed, he explains, by the lassitude, naivety and cowardice of the leaders of the 1930s National Government, who failed, despite all the evidence staring them in the face, to understand the danger posed by Hitler and to make adequate preparations to confront him.

Guilty Men is an angry book. But it ends confidently. The shock of military catastrophe would, 'Cato' suggested, provoke a national revival. Past mistakes would be recognised, discredited former leaders finally brought to account. *Guilty Men* concludes with an enthusiastic paean to the man who was then the newly appointed prime minister, Winston Churchill, demanding that 'the men who are now repairing the breeches in our walls should not carry along with them those who let the walls fall into ruin [...] let the guilty men retire.'[4]

In the course of his polemic 'Cato' takes a swipe at many villains. Some of them are comic, others criminal or contemptible. There are the two conniving mediocrities Stanley Baldwin and Ramsay MacDonald, divided by formal party allegiance yet united, 'Cato' claims, in their determination to prevent anyone with more energy or vision than themselves coming to power. There is the consummate political survivor Sir Samuel Hoare, always in some office or other, never achieving anything no matter where he is. There is the 'bum-faced evangelical' Sir Thomas Inskip, whose selection as minister for the co-ordination of defence in 1936 'Cato' describes as the most extraordinary political appointment since Caligula made his horse a consul – a gibe, often attributed to Churchill, that *Guilty Men* popularised for the first time.

But the chief scoundrel, the wicked uncle of this grim fairy tale, is Neville Chamberlain, MacDonald's and then Baldwin's chancellor of the exchequer from 1931 to 1937, and prime minister thereafter until the fateful month of May 1940. More than half of *Guilty Men* is devoted to the events of Chamberlain's three-year premiership. Our image of him as a starched, corvine man-with-an-umbrella owes much to 'Cato'. *Guilty Men* immortalised several of Chamberlain's most unfortunate phrases, particularly his claim, just a few days before the German invasion of Norway in April 1940, that Hitler had 'missed the bus' and lost his chance for a quick victory against the Allies.

Above all, *Guilty Men* established Chamberlain in the popular mind as the most consequential and disastrous leader of the Shire Folk: the stubborn, foolish patriarch who gulled his sleepy people into believing that all would be well if they simply did nothing about Hitler in the 1930s. 'Cato' solidified a narrative that would compel and endure long after the war itself. As the historian David Dutton puts it:

> [Chamberlain], it was, above any other single individual, who stood charged with incompetence and deception, diplomatic misjudgements and military miscalculations. Chamberlain, it was, who had been blind to his duty, failing to prepare the country in the face of an obvious danger and stifling the voices of those who had been presumed to speak the truth.[5]

At the time of *Guilty Men*'s publication in July 1940, Chamberlain, though no longer prime minister, was still lord president of the council, a member of Churchill's War Cabinet and leader of the Conservative Party – one of the most powerful men in the country, and a politician whose ambitions were not necessarily finished. The purpose of writing *Guilty Men* was, then, in part, to make a revival of Chamberlain's fortunes impossible. This turned out to be unnecessary. Just a few weeks after the book was released, Chamberlain discovered that he was suffering from an incurable bowel cancer which would kill him before the end of 1940. Too ill to continue serving in the War Cabinet, he resigned in early October. By then, the shadows of *Guilty Men* were already evident. Chamberlain complained in his diary that the press reports on his departure from public life were 'short, cold, [and] for the most part deprecatory', with not one showing 'the slightest sign of sympathy for the man'.[6]

Yet Chamberlain maintained confident to the end that history would redeem him. It's not clear if he ever read *Guilty Men* in the last few months of his life, but he was aware of its general thesis, and it was one that he felt would not endure. 'Even if nothing further were to be published giving the true story of the past two years, I should not fear the historians' verdict,' he wrote in his final days.[7]

Perhaps it is a mercy that he felt this way, because few politicians can have misjudged their own posthumous reputations so spectacularly. By the end of the Second World War, Neville Chamberlain was a figure whom people either pitied or detested depending on their generosity of spirit. In *The Gathering Storm*, Churchill described him as 'upright, competent, well-meaning', an effective party leader, talented administrator and honest patriot. But he also assailed Chamberlain as a politician with 'a lack of all sense of proportion' whose arrogance and narrow-mindedness prevented him from seeing the folly of his actions. In the end, Churchill suggests, his predecessor as prime minister proved incapable of mastering the situation he found himself in:

> His all-pervading hope was to go down to history as the Great Peace-maker; and for this he was prepared to strive continually in the teeth of facts, and face great risks for himself and his country. Unhappily, he ran into tides the force of which he could not measure, and met hurricanes from which he did not flinch, but with which he could not cope.[8]

Others were less polite still. In his 1948 *Diplomatic Prelude*, the historian Lewis Namier described Chamberlain as 'ignorant and self-opinionated', with 'the capacity to deceive himself as much as was required'.[9] A. L. Rowse called him a 'vain old fool'.[10] There were some attempts to push back. Keith Feiling's official biography, published in 1946, attempted a modest, dignified rehabilitation of the dead prime minister. A few of Chamberlain's former protégés, such as Quintin Hogg, spoke in his (highly qualified) defence, describing him as a tragic but noble figure. It made no difference. The *Guilty Men* interpretation of Chamberlain's career was virtually unassailable by the late 1940s, even – perhaps especially – within the Conservative Party which he had once led. The Tories had discreetly excised him from their own history 'rather like a disgraced Bolshevik'.[11]

Even today, after more than half a century of academic revisionism and debate about the rights and wrongs of Appeasement, the popular view of Neville Chamberlain and of his role in the outbreak of the Second World War remains largely the same as the one first drafted by 'Cato' in the summer of 1940.[12] The American historian Victor Davis Hanson's recent description is typical: Chamberlain was a 'well-intentioned *naïf* [...] taken in for years by Hitler's lies', a man whose 'pathetic' and 'weird' diary entries reveal him to have been fundamentally incapable of understanding the timeless problems of diplomacy and strategy. Worse, his decision not to confront Hitler in 1938 over the annexation of Austria or the Czech crisis 'made more likely a European war in 1939 that would eventually lead to the deaths of sixty million over the next six years'.[13]

It is hard to imagine a more serious charge being levied against a twentieth-century statesman. Chamberlain is blamed, essentially, for everything that happened between 1939 and 1945 – for the devastating global military conflict, for the Holocaust, everything. What would such a proud man think if he knew that his name had become a byword for political incompetence and cowardice? That his attempts to deal with Hitler by peaceful diplomacy had become the most reviled acts in the history of foreign policy?

To understand the origins of the Second World War, it is necessary to consider this most 'miserably ending' of all British prime ministers. For he is easily the most misunderstood leader the United Kingdom ever had.[14]

6

THE BONES OF A BRITISH GRENADIER

'I went to see the King of the Hellenes on Friday,' Neville Chamberlain wrote to his sister Ida on 13 November 1938. This was six weeks after signing the Munich Treaty with Hitler, the agreement that had prevented the outbreak of European war, albeit at the cost of Czechoslovakia's dismemberment, and made the British prime minister one of the most famous men in the world. 'While I was talking to him,' Chamberlain continued:

> my secretary talked to his chamberlain, who related the following tale. Just before he left Greece, he met an old peasant woman who asked whether he would be seeing Mr Chamberlain. On being told that this was possible, she showed him a cross which, like most Greek peasants, she was wearing round her neck. In the cross was a tiny hole for the reception of a relic of the True Cross (of which there is apparently an unlimited supply to be obtained). You see, she said, I haven't filled up my hole. Now when you go to London I want you to get for me a little bit of Mr Chamberlain's umbrella to put in my cross.[1]

No one capable of rising to the rank of prime minister has ever been encumbered by a great deal of modesty. But to revel in a comparison to Christ might strike the proudest statesman – even a Unitarian freethinker with a bust of Darwin on his mantelpiece – as dangerously hubristic, if not actually blasphemous. This is not something that seems to have troubled Arthur Neville Chamberlain. His letters to his spinster sisters Ida and Hilda reveal a man perfectly content to be thought of as the saviour of mankind, unburdened by any evidence of irony or hesitation.

'Countless letters continue to pour in expressing in most moving accents the writers' heartfelt relief and gratitude,' he had told Ida a few weeks earlier. Presents were arriving at Downing Street every day. 'It's most embarrassing!' wrote Chamberlain, not actually showing much embarrassment.[2]

He had, he noted, received among this cornucopia of gifts two cases of fine German Rhenish wine, flies and salmon rods (it was well known that he was a keen recreational angler), watches and tweed cloth for sporting suits and socks. Thousands of flowers had been sent by Dutch devotees. He had numberless, reverent admirers across the world. The Hungarian masses, he had been told, regarded him and his wife, Annie, as 'their father and mother'.[3] On a celebratory trip to Paris, Chamberlain told Hilda that he had wound the window of his car down and told the driver to go slowly 'so that the people might have some chance of looking at me'.[4] In Rome, 'all wanted to express their gratitude and appreciation, many of them saying "you don't know how we *love* you." [...] every soul I passed saluted, took off their hats, clapped their hands, and shouted "*Viva*" and "*Chamberlain*".'[5] He was, he believed, now 'the most popular man in Germany', Hitler not excepted.[6]

Sometimes, the more you learn about a famous person, particularly if you get to glimpse something of their private character and feelings, the harder it is not to sympathise with them on some basic human level, regardless of what you might think of what they did. Neville Chamberlain is not one of those people. The more you learn about the private man, the harder it is to find anything to like about him at all. Chamberlain's letters to his sisters are a wearisome chronicle of conceit and disdain. Humourless, pedantic, prickly and tediously self-absorbed, his writing lacks any of the glimpses of raw, vivid humanity that one sees in Churchill even at his most disagreeable moments. A great hater, Chamberlain seems to have been incapable of putting himself into anyone else's shoes or of demonstrating any imaginative consideration for the inner lives of other human beings. Even his desire to do good in his domestic political career, while sincere enough, was founded on a haughty upper-middle-class assumption that he knew how to organise working people's lives better than they did themselves.

Chamberlain was certainly intelligent, and he was by no means the provincial ignoramus some of his opponents mocked in caricature. He had travelled more than most politicians, was one of the few men in high office who had ever studied engineering and the physical sciences, and had an extensive knowledge of natural history, the great love of his private life. Nor was he a cultural philistine. He adored Beethoven and could hold his own in an academic discussion of Shakespeare. For all this, though, Neville Chamberlain never exhibited any real intellectual curiosity. He was vain, mean, casually bigoted, boring, ungrateful, spiteful, obstinate and friendless. Egotistical but also insecure and thin-skinned, he cultivated close relations with the Fleet Street barons and lobby correspondents and gloried in favourable newspaper reports about himself, yet complained bitterly that the press was always attacking him.[7] One of his biographers, Nick Smart, describes him as 'an unpleasant man, a nasty piece of work'.[8] Hitler, according to a British intelligence report, privately referred to him as an *Arschloch* ('arsehole'). It is hard not to think that the *Führer*, for once, may have had a point.[9]

Even Chamberlain's political allies could see his unattractive qualities clearly enough. His older half-brother Austen wrote of him in 1924 that 'N's manner freezes people [...] everyone respects him and he makes no friends.'[10] Leo Amery, a fellow Birmingham MP and Cabinet colleague, described him as 'a schoolmaster and a rather autocratic and a somewhat narrow-minded one at that'.[11] Amery was not the only contemporary to be reminded of a priggish academician when in Chamberlain's company. When asked to become parliamentary secretary to the Ministry of Health in 1937, Liberal National MP Robert Bernays remembered his interview with the prime minister as being 'awful [...] it was like a headmaster telling a boy that he had so pleased him for the last few terms that he had decided to make him house prefect'.[12] Arthur Balfour said that he 'seemed to have a heart like stone'.[13] R. A. Butler, one of Chamberlain's most devoted supporters, described him as 'clear and upright but inelastic', resembling in his manner a Stuart king.[14] Even Chamberlain himself, in an unusual moment of self-awareness, once confessed to Hilda that he had been taken aback by how 'pompous [...] and unspeakably repellent' he came across in newsreel footage.[15]

Yet many people today assume, partly because of his advocacy of peaceful negotiation with Hitler and partly, perhaps, because of his appearance and manner – his frail, ovine voice, his resemblance to a meek and rather put-upon clerk – that Neville Chamberlain was a weak and timid politician.[16] This is certainly not how his contemporaries saw him. Arthur Salter, who sat as an independent Member of Parliament for Oxford University in the late 1930s, thought Chamberlain was 'a man, not of straw, but of iron – tough, sound and true throughout; inelastic but unimpressionable; not to be molten to another shape by any but the fiercest of fires'.[17]

Despite being almost seventy years old when he became prime minister, Chamberlain had a remarkable physical constitution and could work long hours without showing any sign of fatigue. His mastery of detail was well known. So too was his intimidating style. His bark, said Sir Robert Vansittart, the permanent Foreign Office under-secretary, was as bad as his bite.[18] One of the great ironies of Chamberlain's career is that, when he replaced Baldwin as prime minister, his fellow Tories were delighted by the thought that this was the end to the appeasement of the Labour opposition. Churchill crowed that Chamberlain would turn the Conservatives from a 'flock of sheep' into a 'pack of wolves'.[19]

This confidence turned out to be well placed. Chamberlain was combative, even brutal, with the shadow front bench in a way that the lethargic, affable Baldwin had never been. 'His instinctive attitude towards a critic was to resist and bear down, not to conciliate and compromise,' thought Arthur Salter. 'An opponent must be crushed.'[20] The Conservative chief whip David Margesson wrote that Chamberlain's 'cold intellect' and taste for sarcasm was a shock to Attlee and Greenwood after his predecessor's consensus-seeking. 'He beat them up in argument.' Butler likened his approach to politics to that of dropping a ton of bricks on his opponents.[21] He dismissed the Opposition bench as 'dirt'.[22] Labour MPs, for their part, hated him. Attlee and Greenwood never forgave Chamberlain for his acerbic jibes on the Commons floor. When the time came for revenge in May 1940, they revelled in it.

Chamberlain was just as dominant over his National Government colleagues. He brooked no dissent in Cabinet. 'Once he has given his opinion, there is no more to be said,' noted Margesson.[23] He assumed a leading role in the Cabinet long before he became prime minister. 'I have become a sort of acting P.M.,' he boasted immodestly but accurately enough in 1935.[24] Anthony Eden, his first foreign secretary, and later one of Chamberlain's most passionate critics, looked forward to the transfer of power in 1937 because the new leader had 'the makings of a really great Prime Minister'.[25] His dynamism contrasted sharply with Baldwin's languorous approach to office. Amery wrote in his diary in July 1937 that under its new leader the government would 'go progressively from strength to strength'.[26]

Chamberlain re-injected vitriol into party politics. But, like Churchill, he was not really an orthodox Tory. Indeed, when he accepted the party's offer of leadership in 1937, he went out of his way to distance himself from 'you Conservatives', as he called his fellow MPs. The Chamberlains were liberals, even radicals, by tradition. Neville and Austen's father, Joseph, was a magnetic populist who had captivated the masses (and split two political parties with his opposition to Irish home rule and his support for tariff reform) in the final years of Queen Victoria's reign. Neville's allegiance to the Conservative Party was circumstantial. He described the Conservative brand as 'odious' on one occasion, and mused about creating an entirely new party of the centre-right. His confidence in the power of the state to implement lasting social progress was more Fabian than Tory.[27] During his first stint in ministerial office in the 1920s, he joked that he and Samuel Hoare were the two socialists in the Conservative government.[28]

Chamberlain was never, in fact, fully happy thinking of himself as a politician at all. For a man destined to become prime minister, his entry into national parliamentary politics came amazingly late. He took a seat in the Commons for the first time a month before his fiftieth birthday, having spent most of his adult life up to that point in industrial management and local government in his native Birmingham.[29] Neville Chamberlain is exactly the kind of leader people wish for when they say that they want to see a businessman from the 'real world' running the country, rather than the world of career politics. Chamberlain saw himself as a down-to-earth pragmatist bringing bluff commercial know-how to statecraft. He believed he had a special relationship with the masses and could speak to their hopes and fears over the heads of the political elite and the media chattering class.[30]

This distaste for politics-as-usual had a dark side. Chamberlain's preference was always to seize the initiative. He found the structural inertia of democratic lawmaking frustrating. Like other businessmen who have turned to politics, he seems to have envied Hitler and Mussolini's freedom to act without tiresome constitutional restrictions. He had, Eden noted, 'a certain fondness for dictators, whose efficiency appealed to him'.[31] Chamberlain was not above behaving ruthlessly, even illegally, to get his way. He had no compunction about bypassing and misleading his own ministers. He employed the mysterious and sinister Sir Joseph Ball, Director of the Conservative Research Department and former MI5 man, to spy on the Opposition, tap the phones and bug the houses of his rivals and rubbish his enemies in Ball's grotesque anti-Semitic journal *Truth*.[32]

Chamberlain's enemies mocked his origins in the provincial middle class. He was, they suggested, a jumped-up provincial mayor, a Brummagem mediocrity ignorant of the world, better suited to planning municipal sewage works than great matters of state. Many accounts of Chamberlain cite Austen's jibe (originally recorded in Eden's memoirs) that 'you must remember that you don't know anything about foreign affairs.' They rarely add that this was an off-the-cuff joke at a dinner party, not a carefully considered fraternal character analysis.[33] In fact, no less a person than Churchill suggested to Baldwin in 1928 that Chamberlain would make a good foreign secretary.[34] Eden initially welcomed Chamberlain's promotion to prime minister because he took a far greater interest in diplomatic affairs than Baldwin had ever done.[35]

To be sure, Chamberlain would have preferred to become prime minister at a time when he could concentrate his energies on the domestic issues that mattered most to him, especially local government services reform. In 1937 he accepted that that was not to be, and that, like it or not, foreign policy would dominate his premiership. He was determined, however, to end the drift that had characterised British diplomacy under Baldwin. Chamberlain wanted Britain to stop lurching from crisis to crisis and, instead, for the government to negotiate a once-and-for-all settlement of European affairs. He was convinced that a man with business experience like himself was especially well placed to do this.

High diplomacy, for Chamberlain, was the art of the deal. He saw himself as a fixer who could get anyone to say 'yes' given enough time. His years in the world of commerce had made him, he believed, an acute judge of character and a sharp negotiator. His theatrical descent by aeroplane on Hitler's Berghof in September 1938 to meet with the German dictator face to face was entirely characteristic of this personal, media-driven approach to crisis management, one that showed an acute consciousness of the power of words and images in the new age of cinema and radio. Chamberlain 'attached great importance to the dramatic side of the visit' when recounting it to his Cabinet colleagues afterwards, since, as he put it, 'a new technique of diplomacy relying on personal contacts' was now required in the modern age.[36] Appeasement was part business, part public spectacle.

In much of this, he and Churchill were like-minded. Both men saw themselves as mavericks rising above the petty squabbling of party faction. Neither of them had any shortage of self-confidence, although they were sometimes afflicted by crippling private moods of gloom. Both were convinced that they had a special gift for dealing man to man with foreign dictators – Hitler in Chamberlain's case, Stalin in Churchill's. Each of them was sure that he, and he alone, could save his country. Chamberlain and Churchill's eventual fates were very different. Their basic approaches to statecraft, though, were far less so.

*

Chamberlain hated war. This is one way in which he and the man who succeeded him as prime minister really were different. Churchill, the former
cavalry subaltern, never entirely shed a romantic childhood fascination with
battle. The thought of war, he admitted a little shamefacedly, excited him.
Chamberlain could never understand this. He was every bit the Victorian
Cobdenite, a man who found war incomprehensible and cruel, a barbaric
folly that disrupted the virtues of free commerce and liberal progress. Flying
over London on his way back from meeting Hitler for the second time in
September 1938, Chamberlain recalled looking out of the window of his
aircraft and imagining with repulsion a German bomber following much
the same course over the thousands of defenceless houses below.

Like so many other Europeans of his generation, Chamberlain had been
profoundly shaken by the horror of the First World War, during which his
beloved cousin Norman, who had served alongside him on Birmingham
city council, had been killed in Flanders. When he contemplated the possibility of another war with Germany, Chamberlain said his thoughts were
frequently with 'the seven million of young men who were cut off in their
prime, the thirteen million who were maimed and mutilated, the misery
and the suffering of the mothers and fathers' of the previous conflict. 'In
war there are no winners, but all are losers,' he affirmed.[37] As prime minister,
Chamberlain was determined to do everything he possibly could to make
sure that Britain never took part in such a grotesque slaughter again.

His convictions about the follies of war were not just emotional,
however. They also reflected a clear-eyed belief that war by the 1930s had
become antithetical to the interests of the British state. Another world
war on the scale of the first would be disastrous for British imperial power,
no matter which side ultimately won. Britain's commercial and trading
network was the largest in the world, its commitment to global capitalism
greater than that of any other nation. It had, then, far more to lose than any
other nation from the disruption of that network through war. Chamberlain desired peace not just because it was the right thing to do, but because,
as a British chiefs of staff report put it, 'it is in our imperial interests, having
an exceedingly vulnerable empire, not to go to war.'[38] His determination to
prevent conflict with Germany was founded on a hard-headed understanding of national advantage.

This did not mean that Chamberlain was a pacifist. He called armed conflict between nations 'a nightmare', but he always accepted that there were some circumstances in which he might have to take Britain to war.[39] There were, he said, 'certain vital interests of this country for which, if they were menaced, we should fight', regardless of what the final cost might be.[40] We know Chamberlain meant this because, of course, ultimately, he acted on it. It is a curious fact that he and his French counterpart Édouard Daladier are today reviled as having been 'soft' on Hitler in the 1930s even though they were almost the only two democratic politicians who ever declared war on Nazi Germany as a matter of principle.

The question for Chamberlain – and really, this is the question that lies at the heart of the origins of the Second World War – was not whether Britain should ever go to war but, rather, what specifically were the interests so 'vital' that the country would have no choice but to do so. Chamberlain sketched a few of these out: the defence of British territory and the imperial lines of communication; the preservation of British 'liberties' and the British way of life; the prevention of any other nation dominating the world and so endangering these things.[41] Few of his countrymen and -women at the time would have found anything to quarrel over in such a list.

The problem, though, was translating such general principles into practical policy. A direct military attack on the Empire was one thing, the rise of a state like Nazi Germany, still only posing a potential threat in the future, quite another. At what point could you say for certain that someone like Hitler represented a definite menace to British interests, as opposed to merely (and reasonably) reasserting the rights of his own people? Ignoring a critical danger for too long would be disastrous. But so too would be launching a hasty, unnecessary, speciously rationalised war.

What weighed heavily on Chamberlain's mind was the thought that, if he plunged Britain into a needless war, he would be responsible not only for the deaths of millions of people but also for the likely collapse of an imperial polity that he believed to be essential to world prosperity and civilisation. He could, he wrote, 'never forget that the ultimate decision, the Yes or No which may decide the fate not only of all this generation, but of the British Empire itself, rests with me'.[42] It infuriated him that, from his point of view, his critics looked at this responsibility so glibly. He was disdainful of MPs who brayed from the Commons benches that the government should 'take a firm line' on such or such a diplomatic issue without, at the same time, having the clarity or courage of mind to state clearly what 'taking a firm line' could mean.[43] Such people were beneath contempt so far as Chamberlain was concerned. It was for men such as himself, men who understood the awful stakes involved, to make the decisions.

*

Great Britain in the first half of the twentieth century commanded a global maritime empire. It was also, at the narrowest point of the English Channel, just twenty miles from the continental mainland. It was part of Europe, yet also not part of it. The British had never been quite able to decide what their role in European affairs ought to be. The temptation to retreat into imperial isolation, to turn a stout back to the sordid and malignant quarrels going on on the other side of *la Manche*, had always been strong. Chamberlain disliked foreigners as much as any British prime minister before or since. He especially disliked the French. France's leftist coalition government, the 'Popular Front', epitomised to his mind all the fragility, corruption and decadence of the Third Republic. Given the choice, Chamberlain would have gladly abandoned the French, and Europeans in general, to their own truculent ends. His premiership turned out to be an unhappy education in the ineluctable demands of geography.

When he became prime minister in 1937, Chamberlain inherited, among other things, a British military commitment to France. Admittedly, it was not much of a commitment by that point. Its formal language was so vague, its loopholes so capacious, that it required the British government to do almost nothing if it didn't want to. It had been professionally neglected for a long time. The British and French chiefs of staff had held no serious conversations about strategy for years. All the same, it was a commitment that would never entirely go away, because no matter how disagreeable the thought of it might be, it was nonetheless founded on a fundamental matter of national self-interest. For good or ill, Britain's fate and France's were bound up with one another.

Britain had, after all, gone to war in August 1914 to prevent France from being overwhelmed by Germany. It had been such a controversial decision at the time that it had had to be dressed up as a quite different kind of decision, a decision to protect *Belgium*. By invading Belgium, and so breaching the 1839 treaty guaranteeing its neutrality, the Germans had done Britain's Liberal government of the time a great favour by providing a convenient alternative *casus belli*. But the fact remained that, even if Germany had scrupulously adhered to international law in August 1914,

Britain would probably have had to go to war anyway. What choice would it have had? If France had had to face Germany on the Western Front alone, it would probably have been defeated. Britain could not have stood by with disinterest at the prospect of this. By conquering France, Germany would have gained hegemony over all Atlantic Europe. It would have been disastrous for Britain's long-term security. It would have been an affront to the British tradition of trying to maintain a continental balance of power.

France, thanks in good part to its cross-Channel alliance, had emerged victorious from the war. But grim actuarial logic was working against it by 1919. Over 1.4 million Frenchmen had been killed defending *la mère patrie*. Tens of thousands of square miles of prime French agricultural and industrial land had been devastated by the German occupiers. France by 1919 was even less capable of defending itself against a German invasion than it had been five years earlier. 'France victorious must grow accustomed to being a lesser power,' the diplomat Jules Cambon reflected ruefully.[44] The Germans were temporarily hobbled by the restrictions imposed on them by the Treaty of Versailles. Their army was limited to a 100,000-man self-defence force, the Rhineland border region demilitarised, reparations payments levied. But these were ephemeral weaknesses. No treaty provision could ever correct France's fundamental inferiority in strength. 'As soon as the first shock of defeat has passed away,' Arthur Balfour warned in March 1919, 'Germany will organise herself for revenge [...] no manipulation of the Rhine frontier is going to make France anything more than a second-rate power.'[45]

In order to allay these fears for its future, Britain and the United States had agreed during the Versailles negotiations to enter a permanent three-power alliance guaranteeing France's borders. The guarantee was signed a few hours before the main treaty on 28 June 1919. But the British prime minister, David Lloyd George, had never had any sincere belief in this alliance. He had therefore slipped in a small but mischievous amendment to the guarantee's language at the last minute. British participation would come into effect only once the US Senate had ratified its part in the three-power agreement. That November the Senate so decisively rejected the main Treaty of Versailles that the guarantee to France was not even brought up for discussion. Lloyd George, and Britain, were off the hook. France had been left with nothing.[46]

This did not sit well with Austen Chamberlain, Neville's half-brother, who was serving as Lloyd George's chancellor of the exchequer while the

Versailles talks were going on. During his youth Austen had spent time studying in Paris and Berlin, and those adolescent encounters had left him a lifelong Francophile and an equally passionate Germanophobe. In 1924 he became foreign secretary in a new Tory administration led by Stanley Baldwin. The French, Austen argued to his Cabinet colleagues, lived 'in nightmare horror of Germany'.[47] He saw, then, the revival of Anglo-French co-operation as the 'cardinal object' of British foreign policy in Europe. This was not simply a question of feeling sorry for the French; it was a matter of urgent British self-interest. Britain, Austen argued, could no more tolerate seeing France fall to the Germans now than it had been able to back in 1914. That intervention had been so hasty as almost to fail; it was time to accept the inevitability of Britain's continental commitment and to plan for it properly.

He was not alone in this. As the chiefs of staff put it in a memorandum to the Committee of Imperial Defence at the time:

> For us it is only incidentally a question of French security; essentially it is a matter of British security [...] the true strategic frontier of Great Britain is the Rhine; her security depends entirely upon the present frontiers of France, Belgium and Holland being maintained and remaining in friendly hands. The great guiding principle of the German General Staff in making plans for a future war will be, as in the last war, to try to defeat her enemies in detail. Any line of policy which permitted Germany (with or without allies) first to swallow up France, and then to deal with Great Britain would be fatal strategically.[48]

A firm British promise to defend the frontier would, by relieving France's anxieties, encourage it to seek a new *rapprochement* with its enemy to the east which, ideally, would render the balance-of-power problem moot. At the very least, it would deter Germany from attacking again. 'If we withdraw from Europe,' Austen warned, 'I say without hesitation that the chance of permanent peace is gone.'[49]

But when the issue came up in Cabinet and the Committee of Imperial Defence, he faced a solid front of resistance. Arthur Balfour and Lord Curzon, both former foreign secretaries themselves, and Winston Churchill, Baldwin's chancellor of the exchequer, all voiced their objections to any peacetime Anglo-French alliance. Churchill was particularly implacable.

Though a lifelong Francophile, like Austen, it was, he said, a 'tremendous risk' to consider any cross-Channel military guarantee. Churchill refused to accept the idea that Britain's fate was bound up with that of France at all. France, he believed, 'could be left to stew in her own juice without having any bad effect on anybody or anything'.[50]

And it was Churchill, not Austen Chamberlain, who represented the popular mood on this matter. Britain in the early 1920s was enjoying a spate of France-bashing not seen for at least a generation. It was one that transcended class and party. While a supercilious ex-viceroy like Curzon might scoff that 'the French are not the sort of people you go tiger hunting with', leftist intellectuals like E. D. Morel and H. N. Brailsford were equally convinced that France was returning to its Bonapartist tradition of belligerent empire-building.[51] When French troops were sent to occupy the Ruhr industrial basin in 1923 to punish the Weimar Republic for its failure to pay reparations, Curzon had suggested they were seeking 'the domination of the European continent', while Ramsay MacDonald called it evidence of the 'historical craving' of the French for military hegemony.[52] H. G. Wells decried Paris's 'aggression' and 'reckless greed'.[53] Germany's fundamentally greater strength was easy to forget in this orgy of fashionable Francophobia. It did not represent an atmosphere conducive to forging a deeper politico-military union. The left-liberal *New Statesman* described the pre-war understanding with France as 'a fly-blown idol' best consigned to the rubbish heap.[54]

In any case, anyone in the 1920s proposing a continental commitment had to argue against the tens of thousands of names being inscribed on the memorials to the missing at Thiepval on the Somme and at Ypres's Menin Gate. And these names represented just a fraction of the nation's three-quarters of a million dead, most of them buried somewhere on the Western Front. Britain's intervention on France's behalf in 1914, and its unprecedented construction of a mass land army afterwards, had swung the balance of the war in the Allies' favour. But it had also triggered a slaughter so terrible as to mock the very worth of that sacrifice. The 1914 Liberal government had committed the nation 'to following the dictates of a Continental strategy which drew us willy-nilly into a policy foreign to our traditions', as the military commentator B. H. (Basil) Liddell Hart put it: 'It was heroic, but was it necessary? It was magnificent, but was it war? [...] [did] it even benefit our allies in the long run? Did we sacrifice our security, our mortgage on the future, for a gesture?'[55] Even the army's inter-war chiefs of the Imperial General Staff could not answer that question. It is hardly surprising that politicians, answerable to the grief-stricken public, shrank from it too.

Austen, then, got nowhere with his plans for a fully fledged Anglo-French alliance. What he had to settle for instead was a far more attenuated multinational guarantee, the form of which had been originally proposed by German foreign minister Gustav Stresemann. This was negotiated in Locarno, on the Swiss shore of Lake Maggiore, in October 1925. Under the terms of this 'Locarno Treaty', Germany, France and Belgium all pledged to recognise the existing frontiers of western Europe. Britain and Italy would act as guarantor powers which would intervene militarily should that pledge ever be broken.

Whatever private misgivings Austen may have felt about the limitations of Locarno compared with his original design, he suppressed them on the day the treaty was signed, 16 October 1925, his sixty-second birthday. It was an emotional event. Austen, Stresemann and the chief French negotiator, Aristide Briand, embraced tearfully. Back in Britain, Locarno was praised as a breakthrough for peace. Balfour called it the final day of the First World War. Austen returned home in triumph to receive a Garter knighthood and, the following year, the Nobel Peace Prize.[56]

Britain had made a continental commitment. But a commitment to do what, exactly? Locarno obligated it to intervene if Germany ever attacked France again, but the treaty equally obligated Britain to intervene militarily *against* France if that country ever attacked Germany. It was never going to be easy for the British armed forces to plan for another continental war if they did not know which side they would be on until the last moment. More important in practice, though, was that any British intervention in a Franco-German conflict would only take place if 'flagrant' and 'unprovoked aggression' had occurred. It was up to the British government itself to decide if this had happened.[57] Britain could simply ignore its Locarno obligations if it wanted to.

The result was that after Locarno there was even less pressure than before to make realistic preparations for military intervention on the continent. The year following the signing of the Treaty, the chiefs of staff observed to the Foreign Office that, if war broke out in Europe, Britain would only be able to send two under-strength *ad hoc* divisions across the Channel, a pathetically ineffectual expeditionary force even by the standards of 1914. The United Kingdom was incapable of honouring its

Locarno responsibilities even if it wanted to. The Empire neither could nor would help. The Dominion governments made it clear that they had no interest in contributing to such a force.[58]

Few politicians were perturbed by any of this. Locarno's terms were so loosely drafted that there was no reason to see any urgency in Britain's lack of military strength. Indeed, that lack of strength was to everyone's advantage: a large, expensive continental-style military build-up would have provoked a huge political row at a time when the Treasury was demanding financial prudence. Churchill persuaded the Cabinet in 1928 to make the 'ten-year rule' which had been operating informally since the end of the First World War – an assumption that Britain would not be involved in a major continental conflict for at least a decade – a standing annual assumption. Defence spending in the wake of Locarno fell, not rose. It would continue to fall until a year after Hitler came to power.

What Locarno really represented, then, was a confirmation of the isolationist strategy Britain had pursued ever since it had abandoned the idea of a peacetime Anglo-French alliance in 1919. The Locarno guarantee to France was a sop to cross-Channel anxieties, a gesture that Britain had neither the desire nor the means to deliver on. Politicians such as Baldwin would insist sententiously now and again that 'when you think of the defence of England [...] you think of the Rhine. That is where our frontier lies.'[59] No one, including Baldwin himself, took such rhetoric seriously. The chiefs of staff pressed occasionally for a more realistic attitude towards the responsibilities that Britain had taken on as a result of Locarno, but never did so with any real energy or conviction. There was no political support for such thinking. Almost everyone who seriously considered the matter in the 1920s accepted that, in certain dire circumstances, Britain might have to intervene militarily to help France. Hardly anyone who accepted this was also willing to recognise its policy consequences, because to do so would have required facing some unpopular choices.

*

What about eastern Europe? Britain's commitment to France was limited enough. It was non-existent east of the Rhine. Even Austen Chamberlain saw no reason for his country to get involved in Germany's quarrels with new post-Versailles states such as Poland and Czechoslovakia. 'In Western Europe we are a partner,' he declared. 'In Eastern Europe our role should be rather that of a disinterested *amicus curiae*.'[60] The fate of the disputed 'Polish Corridor', the strip of Pomeranian territory awarded to Poland by the Versailles peacemakers in 1919 which now divided East Prussia from the rest of Germany, was one, he said, 'for which no British government ever will or ever can risk the bones of a British grenadier'.[61] Indeed, Austen hoped that Locarno would encourage the Weimar Republic to divert its irredentist energies towards its eastern borders.

France could not be so complacent. In 1914 the French had relied not just on the hope of British support but also, even more urgently, on their alliance with Tsarist Russia. The withdrawal of the Bolshevik USSR from conventional European diplomacy since the Revolution of 1917 had robbed the French of a vital strategic ally against Germany.

Post-war France had signed alliances with Poland in 1921 and Czecho-slovakia in 1924 to try to build a compensating 'little Entente' to the east that would restrain German revisionist ambitions. These alliances had unpleasant implications for the British. Nothing about them formally involved Britain. But what if war broke out between Germany and France over some quarrel originating in Warsaw or Prague? British politicians felt that the outbreak of the First World War had taught them not to get dragged into far-off conflicts that were none of Britain's business. As Sir John Simon put it, 1914 stood out as a 'dreadful warning' to keep out of eastern troubles at all costs.[62] But even the most hard-bitten Francophobe in the Cabinet knew deep down that if a day ever came when France was in danger of being militarily overwhelmed by Germany, Britain would have to intervene whether it wanted to or not. In such a catastrophic scenario, British grenadiers might have to die for Danzig after all.

Most statesmen dealt with this dilemma by not thinking about it too much. Austen Chamberlain left the Foreign Office for good in 1929 after four post-Locarno years of dignified languor. His Francophilia departed with him. Ramsay MacDonald, who took over as prime minister that year and stayed in 10 Downing Street until 1935, believed that France was 'steeped in the militarist mind' and fundamentally untrustworthy.[63] His colleagues in the National Government, Tory and Labour alike, largely agreed with him. The rise to power of the Nazis in Germany in 1933 shook none of this detachment. Indeed, it only seemed to make Britain's deci-sion to avoid a continental commitment all the wiser. The week after Hitler became German chancellor, the liberal *Daily News* opined that 'the best thing we have done was to refuse a military guarantee of safety to France.'[64]

Churchill said that Britain's aim should be to 'live our life in our island without being drawn again into the perils of the continent of Europe'.[65]

The Germans were delighted by this show of indifference. Leopold von Hoesch, Berlin's ambassador in London from 1932 to 1936, commented acerbically to one of his colleagues that anti-Nazis in Britain who were 'up in arms against Germany on account of her domestic politics and her alleged war spirit and militarism' nonetheless quailed at the thought of making any gesture of support to France.[66]

Even Hitler's open defiance of Locarno changed nothing. In March 1936 his army crossed into the demilitarised Rhineland, an explicit violation of the pledge Germany had made eleven years earlier. Alfred Duff Cooper, secretary of state for war, travelled to Paris to discuss how to respond. In a speech afterwards, he proposed that France and Britain had permanent entangling interests which Hitler's actions were placing in danger. It was a vague enough statement of cross-Channel solidarity. But it provoked a blunt rebuttal from the Labour Party leader, Clement Attlee, who accused Duff Cooper of positing the existence of a Franco-British military alliance. Sir John Simon reassured the Commons that no such alliance existed. There was merely an 'understanding' between the two powers. Britain had no interest in Locarno either.[67] Hugh Dalton, Labour's senior spokesman on foreign policy, blamed the French for what had happened.[68] Charles Corbin, the French ambassador in London, observed wearily to his masters in Paris that the word 'alliance' now exerted 'a veritable terror' in British politicians' minds.[69]

*

There was another potential way of dealing with the Franco-German problem that embraced neither imperial isolationism nor old-style balance-of-power diplomacy. It was 'collective security' through the League of Nations, the Geneva-based organisation that had been established after the First World War as a forum for the arbitration of inter-state grievances. The League was enormously popular in Britain throughout the inter-war years. Even politicians who privately had no real faith in it had to pay lip-service to its moral authority. All three parties in the 1935 general election lauded collective security through the League, the Conservatives describing it as 'the keystone of British foreign policy'.

Collective security was a hugely attractive phrase. But its exact meaning became less and less clear the more you thought about it. Harold Nicolson, though a staunch supporter of the League himself, pointed out the public's confusion about this in 1935. He had received a letter from one of his constituents demanding that Nicolson support the idea of collective security through the League while also 'opposing any entanglements in Europe'. This, Nicolson suggested, was 'self-contradictory nonsense'. To his dismay, few of the audience members to whom he told this story could see why.[70]

The problem was reflected in a tension between Articles Eight and Sixteen of the League of Nations' Covenant. Article Eight declared that all member states should try to reduce their own national armaments to the lowest possible level. Collective security was meant to be based on 'a belief in the power of world opinion and in pacific means of settling disputes' rather than on violence.[71] But Article Sixteen declared that, if moral appeals and economic sanctions failed, the League's members were treaty-bound to supply military forces to punish any country that attacked another. Presumably, if such military action was required, the most powerful members of the League, such as Britain, would be expected to take the lead. But that would mean a potentially limitless commitment to intervention anywhere across the globe. Taking collective security seriously would mean *more* foreign entanglements for Britain, not fewer. It would need *stronger* armed forces than it already possessed, not weaker.[72]

If collective security was ever to mean anything beyond pious hopes, then, the leading member states of the League ought to be spending more on defence. Yet it was League supporters in Britain who were among the loudest calling for the government to reduce its existing armament budget. Neville Chamberlain regarded this paradox with scorn. The League's popularity meant that in public he had to go through ritual pieties of praise for it. Privately, he was contemptuous of it and its supporters. Collective security was 'a palpable sham', he said in August 1936. League advocates were 'cranks', woolly-headed idealists who shrank from facing up to the consequences of their demands.[73]

The League's half-baked reaction to Italy's invasion of Abyssinia in October 1935 exemplified for Chamberlain everything that was wrong with collective security. The League's lobbying movement in Britain, the League of Nations Union (LNU), responded to Mussolini's attack on Abyssinia with an exhortation that 'the whole force of the League should be used to stop the war'. But it remained silent as to whether that might require countries such as Britain to attack Italian troops or ships. Indeed, even as LNU members demanded action against Italy, they also continued to decry the government's modest efforts to increase defence spending.

Two weeks after Mussolini's invasion, the League headquarters in Geneva announced a series of financial and raw material embargos against Italy – but not, crucially, one on coal or oil imports, which would have been futile anyway because the Italians could always turn to a non-member state like the USA to supply these.[74] To Sir Robert Vansittart, League sanctions were 'the worst of all worlds'. They lacked any coercive potency that might save Abyssinia. But they also alienated Italy at the very moment when the British and French governments were trying to woo Mussolini away from a pact with Hitler.[75]

The Italian dictator's forces, unhindered by the League's actions, marched into the Abyssinian capital, Addis Ababa, in May 1936. The war was effectively over. In June, Chamberlain made world headlines by describing any continuation of the sanctions against Italy as 'the very midsummer of madness'. Maintaining punitive measures when Abyssinia was already conquered was not only futile, he argued, but injurious to the greater cause of peace as well. League sanctions were making it impossible for the British and French to sit down with the Italians to discuss a lasting settlement of Mediterranean affairs.

Chamberlain had spoken publicly without first seeking approval from the foreign secretary, Anthony Eden. He had to apologise. But his view prevailed. Churchill agreed with Chamberlain that the sanctions were pointless. Even his brother Austen, who had been a staunch advocate of sanctions the previous year, now changed his mind. A week after the 'midsummer of madness' speech the British Cabinet agreed to ask Geneva to suspend the sanctions.[76] On 15 July the League agreed.

The following year, Chamberlain, now prime minister, asked in the Commons: 'What is the use of repeating parrot-like that we believe in the League?' His task, he said, was to 'find practical means of restoring peace to the world'.[77] He would waste no more energy on follies such as collective security. He would defend British interests his own way.

7

THE STUPIDEST THING THAT
HAS EVER BEEN DONE

On 13 August 1935 the Conservative MP and former colonial secretary Leo Amery met Adolf Hitler at his Alpine villa in Obersalzberg, Bavaria. 'Hitler, in a plain grey flannel suit met me on the veranda,' recalled Amery in his memoirs after the war:

> We sat and talked for the better part of two hours [...] his attitude was not unpleasantly boastful [...] he was, no doubt, treating me to the same reasonable stuff with which he was to fill up Lloyd George and Lord Lothian and even guileless old [George] Lansbury [...] while I found him shrewder than I expected, he certainly did not strike me as of outstanding intellect, still less as possessing a peculiarly impressive or hypnotic personality. In spite of his efforts to be agreeable I found him unattractive and above all, commonplace – my first impression was that both his appearance and his manner were those of a shop-walker.[1]

This was Amery's version of events in 1955. His impressions of Hitler at the time, recorded in his diary, were less filtered by hindsight. He and Hitler had talked, Amery wrote, of Europe's general political problems; Amery had been struck by the German leader's 'vigorous commonsense'. He liked Hitler's

> directness and eagerness to let his hearer know all his mind. Intellectually he has a grip on economic essentials and on many political ones too, even if it is crude at times and coloured by deep personal prejudice. A bigger man, on the whole, than I had expected [...] we got on well together I think, owing to the fundamental similarities of many of our ideas.

They had, however, carefully avoided talking about controversial subjects –
Austria, constitutional rights in Germany, colonial matters and, of course,
the Jews.[2]

There was nothing discreditable about Amery's decision to meet with
Hitler in 1935. It took place at the instigation of Joachim von Ribbentrop,
soon to be a short-lived and disastrous German ambassador in London,
who sounded Amery out while he was on a sightseeing visit to southern
Germany. Plenty of other British politicians made the profane pilgrimage
to Obersalzberg in the 1930s. Doing the rounds of the dictators while on
holiday in Europe was common enough among Conservative MPs: Duff
Cooper met Mussolini at Easter 1934 and found he was 'quite in agreement'
with the Italian leader on disarmament, declaring him 'humorous, and completely lacking in pose'.[3] While still an undergraduate at Balliol, Somerset
de Chair, later a Tory MP and later still Jacob Rees-Mogg's father-in-law,
had an audience with *Il Duce* and found him to be 'amiability himself [...]
no one who like myself, has come under the direct influence of the great
dictator's personality can fail to have the profoundest admiration not only
for the man himself, but for the machine of which he is the very soul.'[4]
Churchill almost met Hitler in 1932.

Nor is there anything particularly unusual about Amery's first impressions of the German leader, coloured as they were with much the same
mixture of curiosity, cautious admiration and condescension that British
visitors of a certain class tended to experience when meeting him. When
Lord Halifax was first ushered into Hitler's presence in November 1937, he
mistook him for a footman and almost handed him his coat and hat.

All the same, the meeting is noteworthy for two reasons. One is that
Amery was Jewish through his Hungarian mother, Elisabeth Johanna
Leitner. To what extent, if any, he identified with his maternal family's
faith is unclear (and has been the subject of much speculation, inevitably
inconclusive, by historians). But he was certainly aware of it, and it was
known, though rarely discussed, by his friends and colleagues.[5] The other
reason is that Amery would eventually become one the most famous of
the 'anti-appeasers' who challenged Chamberlain's attempts to compromise
with Hitler in the late 1930s. He was one of just a few Conservatives to
remain in their seats, stony-faced, when Chamberlain made his celebrated
announcement in the House on 28 September 1938 that Hitler had agreed
to a conference in Munich to resolve the Czech crisis. In the two years that
followed, Amery made a pair of critical interventions in Commons debates

for which he is still famous: the first to goad Chamberlain into declaring war on Germany after the invasion of Poland, the second, eight months later, helping to provoke the prime minister's final downfall.

Yet in August 1935 this resolute opponent of appeasement had still not made up his mind about Hitler. Nor would he for at least another two-and-a-half years.[6] Certainly, Amery's visit to Obersalzberg was long before Hitler's most egregious breaches of international law – the annexation of the Rhineland, the *Anschluss* with Austria, the seizure of the Sudetenland, the march on Prague. Still, it is worth considering what had already happened in Germany by August 1935. Hitler's Third Reich was a one-party police state operating under a series of emergency decrees which had suspended the rule of law and all restrictions on executive power. The process of *Gleichschaltung*, or the systematic elimination of all non-Nazi organisations from public life, was well under way. Tens of thousands of prisoners were in torment in the regime's first, crude, brutal concentration camps. Germany's Jews had been excluded from the civil service, universities and professional life; they were shortly to be formally stripped of their Reich citizenship. Extra-judicial violence with the open connivance of the state was common practice. Germany had withdrawn from the League of Nations. Hitler, in violation of the Treaty of Versailles, had decreed the reintroduction of conscription and the creation of a Luftwaffe in order to pursue, by force if necessary, a policy of territorial irredentism. This was the same man with whom Amery could say he shared 'fundamentally similar' ideas.

Amery was hardly the only British politician who was slow to appreciate the depths of Hitler's nihilistic fantasies. The point is that we misunderstand the origins of the Second World War if we think of British politics in the late 1930s as a battleground contested between two clearly defined camps, one of 'appeasers' and one of 'anti-appeasers'. No two discrete groups ever existed. Chamberlain's foreign policy always had its critics and its supporters. But they were not always the same people from month to month, and the reasons for support or criticism were not always the same.[7]

Most politicians and public figures who took a position on appeasement, for or against, agreed about far more than they disagreed. They wanted to avoid another war. But they accepted that there were certain vital interests for which Britain might have to fight, no matter what. Many of them saw Germany as the greatest long-term threat to British security, but they conceded that the Germans had some reasonable complaints about the Versailles settlement that ought to be addressed. Most of them were appalled by the Nazis' treatment of political opponents and Jews, but they felt that this was ultimately an internal German matter. A lot of them found Hitler vulgar, foolish and possibly dangerous. But they assumed that, beneath his braggadocio, he was a normal politician who would respond to rational incentives and deterrents. Most of them, certainly after 1937 anyway, felt that Britain needed to rearm to confront the challenges of an increasingly dangerous world. But they did not wish to impair the country's long-term financial health in the process. Differences, then, were largely a matter of emphasis and timing rather than fundamental attitudes: the means of getting to the right end, not what the end itself ought to be.

Those people who opposed Chamberlain during the appeasement years could never fully agree on what an alternative foreign policy should look like.[8] Some of them sought collective security through the League of Nations, some favoured alliances with Europe's democracies, some saw a case for an expedient alignment with fascist Italy or communist Russia, while others spurned the thought of foreign partnerships entirely and preferred a rearmed British Empire to remain aloof from continental affairs. Some proposed several of these things at one time or another, only to drop them later on. Personal rivalries complicated the picture too. Amery was said to be 'intellectually contemptuous' of Anthony Eden, even though both were critics of Chamberlain by 1938.[9] Eden's supporters in turn distrusted Churchill and the rest of the 'Winston brigade', as Harold Nicolson put it.[10]

Amery's foreign policy views were *sui generis*. He was probably the most unfaltering imperial isolationist in high politics, one of the hard Brexiters of his day. As early as 1915 he had already outlined his views on the continental commitment, and they remained largely unchanged for the next quarter of a century:

> We are not a part of Europe, even if the most important unit of the British community lies off the European coast. This war against a German domination in Europe was only necessary because we had failed to make ourselves sufficiently strong and united as an Empire to be able to afford to disregard the European balance.[11]

In this, he and Neville Chamberlain were temperamentally allied. While still chancellor in 1936, Chamberlain wrote to Amery saying, 'I think you know that limitation of commitments in Europe is the policy which commends itself to me.'[12] Both men feared the possibility of getting 'tied up' in alliance with France and Russia.[13] The only European state Amery had any time for at all was fascist Italy. Mussolini's charisma seems to have had the same effect on Amery as on Cooper and de Chair. Listening to *Il Duce* address troops in Venice in August 1936, Amery was struck by 'the perfect elocution and the simplicity of the skill with which he struck all the notes to which he wished his audience to respond'.[14] Two years later, meeting with Mussolini in the Palazzo Venezia in Rome, Amery rhapsodised: 'He has grown greatly in personality I felt and his dark eyes with the whites showing all round, set in his powerful brown face are very impressive.'[15]

As for Nazi Germany, Amery saw little reason for Britain to do anything about Hitler's early provocations. He thought it 'futile' to object to the remilitarisation of the Rhineland in 1936, predicting that 'the whole thing is likely to fizzle out in talk'.[16] Even as his opinion of Hitler soured he remained unconvinced that Britain ought to interfere in the politics of central or eastern Europe. Amery considered the fate of the Czech Sudetenland none of Britain's business, and saw advantages to accommodating Hitler's ambitions in *Volksdeutsche* lands outside the Third Reich.[17] Though by the end of the Czech crisis Amery had become highly critical of Chamberlain, this had little to do with any matter of principle. He simply felt that the prime minister, having inserted himself into the dispute, had lost credibility by backing down at the last minute. If he had not been willing to fight over the fate of the Sudetenland, he should not have got involved in the first place.

Churchill's record during the 1930s was similarly more complicated than his hagiographers suggest. Although Churchill's war memoirs would later portray him as a consistent opponent of international aggression, in fact he showed no real interest in Japan's predatory behaviour towards Republican China until 1937. He was ambivalent at best about Mussolini's invasion of Abyssinia; even *The Gathering Storm* refers to the victim nation as a 'wild land of tyranny, slavery and tribal war'.[18] Churchill agreed with Chamberlain about the 'midsummer madness' of continuing sanctions against Italy after the conquest of Addis Ababa.[19] Until 1938, Churchill's sympathies in the Spanish Civil War were mostly pro-Franco.[20]

His early attitude towards Nazi Germany was also not straightforward. Far from demanding a vigorous military response to the German remilitarisation of the Rhineland in 1936, he counselled caution and restraint.[21]

Churchill's public statements about Hitler remained ambiguous until surprisingly late. It was, he said in a 1937 article for the *News of the World*, a
'mystery of the future' whether the German leader would be pronounced 'a
monster or a hero [...] whether he will rank in Valhalla with Pericles, with
Augustus and with Washington, or welter in the inferno of human scorn'. In
a piece for the *Evening Standard* the same year Churchill argued that 'one
may dislike Hitler's system and yet admire his patriotic achievement. If our
country were defeated, I hope we should find a champion as indomitable.'[22]
(Compare this with Neville Chamberlain's statement three years earlier that
'[I] hate Nazism and all its works with a greater loathing than ever.'[23])

Even once Churchill had sized up Hitler as a definite menace, he still
left open the possibility of meeting the Nazi leader half-way. In late July 1938
he was arguing that the Czechs needed to make 'every concession compat-
ible with the sovereignty and integrity of their state' over the Sudetenland
issue.[24] Churchill warned them not to be 'obstinate' and 'obdurate'.[25] In
terms of practical alternatives to appeasement, Churchill chopped and
changed. He adopted the language of collective security briefly in 1936, but
he never showed any real interest or confidence in the League of Nations.
He took up the idea of alliances with France and the USSR in 1938, but
remained hostile to the idea of a British expeditionary force being sent to
the continent in time of war – a necessary precondition for a meaningful
alliance with either state.[26]

Churchill's views in the 1930s were not always as fundamentally different from Chamberlain's as myth suggests. The two men got on much
better than might be imagined. ('I can't help liking Winston, even though I
think him nearly always wrong,' Chamberlain once said.[27]) Churchill's real
bête noire was Baldwin, not Chamberlain. Once the former had withdrawn
into ennobled retirement in the spring of 1937, Churchill's relations with
the National Government improved quite a bit. Some of this, to be sure,
was down to expediency. Churchill never gave up hope of being offered a
ministerial position in Chamberlain's Cabinet, and so he tempered his criticisms accordingly. All the same, he genuinely admired the prime minister's
efforts to increase armament spending, even if he did not feel they went
far enough. Churchill and Chamberlain only really fell out badly in the
six months following the Munich settlement. For the rest of the time their
relationship was one of cautious mutual respect.[28]

It's important, then, not to think of Chamberlain's opponents in 1938
and 1939 as a harmonious chorus denouncing appeasement with one voice.

Churchill, Amery, Eden and other critics of appeasement were just as unsure what was going to happen next as everyone else, just as confused about how to deal with a leader as unprecedented and capricious as Hitler, just as hesitant when faced with choosing between principle and convenience, honour and self-interest. Lord Halifax described the situation in the late 1930s as 'groping in the dark like a blind man trying to find his way across a bog, with everybody shouting from the banks different information as to where the next quagmire is!'[29] Things that might seem obvious now were far from obvious then. What to us is the past, unalterable and fated, was to them still the future, full of possibility, confusion and doubt.

*

When Chamberlain became prime minister in May 1937, Britain's relations with Nazi Germany were going through a quiet spell. Hitler had shocked the world by remilitarising the Rhineland fourteen months earlier. But since then, the *Führer* had retreated into enigmatic silence on foreign affairs. All the same, it was clear that the international system that had developed in the 1920s was finished. No one really believed in the sanctity of the Versailles Treaty any longer. Collective security through the League of Nations had failed to save Abyssinia. Germany apparently no longer recognised the restrictions of Locarno. Something else would have to take the old system's place if peace and stability were to be re-established.

For years Chamberlain had sat in Cabinet meetings in which the British government dithered over what to do about Hitler. Now, with Baldwin gone, he held the 'wonderful power' of the premiership, and he revelled in its possibilities. He had achieved the pinnacle of power that neither his father nor his elder brother (who had died two months earlier) had ever reached. This might have filled even a humble man with a sense of hubris, and Neville Chamberlain was not a humble man. As chancellor of the exchequer 'I could hardly move a pebble,' he gloried in a letter to Ida. 'Now I have only to raise a finger and the whole of Europe is changed!'[30]

Chamberlain was convinced that if he seized the initiative and made direct contact with the European dictators, he could negotiate a comprehensive deal that would bring the years of uncertainty to an end. This would mean a heavy engagement with European politics in the short term. But the aim was always, in the end, to withdraw from continental problems. Chamberlain remained a thoroughgoing imperial isolationist. The point was to negotiate a settlement in central Europe that would allow Britain to refocus its energies on its vital global concerns, particularly in the Mediterranean and the Far East.

To make such a settlement, however, Chamberlain would first have to reorganise the existing diplomatic establishment more to his liking. Anthony Eden, the foreign secretary, was an obstacle. Eden's views about Hitler were not very different from Chamberlain's. Both of them found the German dictator personally appalling. But they were not opposed in principle to peaceful German expansion in central and eastern Europe, which they regarded as tertiary to British interests. Eden, though, was implacably hostile to fascist Italy. This was a problem for Chamberlain because he wanted to woo Mussolini into an Anglo-Italian agreement to oppose any German annexation of Austria. By February 1938 Chamberlain had decided that his foreign secretary must 'yield or go'.[31] He went.

After the war, in *The Gathering Storm*, Churchill would present Eden's resignation as a disaster for the anti-appeasement cause and a grievous personal blow. 'Sleep deserted me' on the night Eden left the Foreign Office, Churchill claimed. 'I lay in my bed consumed by emotions of sorrow and fear.'[32] But by 1948 Eden was Churchill's own deputy leader of the Conservative Party. In fact, ten years earlier, Churchill had shown no such dramatic concern. Indeed, he had been one of the first Conservative MPs to sign a petition expressing continued support for the government after Eden's departure.[33] Eden and Churchill were never close. Churchill resented his exclusion from Eden's inner circle in the 1930s; he was still complaining about it years later.[34]

Chamberlain replaced Eden with the Yorkshire squire Edward Wood, Viscount Halifax, who had previously been lord president of the council. Halifax was a gentleman by genealogy and temperament to his admirers – 'deeply religious, almost a mystic, not perhaps very practical minded but a great moral strength'.[35] To less appreciative observers he came across as an insufferably pious Anglo-Catholic bore. Lord Beaverbrook, owner of the *Daily Express*, called him 'a sort of Jesus in long boots'. Halifax had served as Viceroy of India from 1926 to 1931, where he had successfully negotiated terms with Gandhi, and was, perhaps, regarded as a good man for dealing with gnomic mystics like Hitler.[36] Not that Halifax's abilities necessarily mattered so far as Chamberlain was concerned, for he privately declared that he 'intended to be his own foreign secretary' from now on.[37]

Eden's resignation, in the end, made no difference diplomatically.

Unbeknown to the British government, Mussolini had already made a secret agreement with Hitler to acquiesce in the German takeover of Austria. This *Anschluss* with the Third Reich took place on 12 March 1938. It was the first of Germany's 'flower wars', in which invading troops were bombarded with bouquets by the ecstatic local *Volksdeutsche*. In Vienna an 'avalanche of terror' engulfed the city's Jewish population; jeering mobs beat up passing Jews, spat on them and forced them to scrub pro-independence slogans off the pavements on their hands and knees.[38] Chamberlain called it 'all very disheartening and discouraging'. He complained that the 'wretched Germans' had spoiled his weekend getaway at Chequers.[39]

After the *Anschluss*, international attention shifted north-eastwards to Czechoslovakia and the matter of the German-speaking minority in the Sudetenland border region. On 24 April, Konrad Henlein, leader of the pro-Nazi Sudeten German Party (SdP), made a speech in Carlsbad demanding that the Prague government grant political autonomy to the region's *Volksdeutsche* community. This 'Carlsbad Memorandum' would serve as the catalyst for the crisis to come. Hitler had already secretly ordered his general staff to make contingency plans for a possible invasion of Czechoslovakia later in the year. Such a war would have potentially catastrophic implications for European peace. Czechoslovakia was not only a member state of the League of Nations and the last surviving democracy east of the Rhine, but it also had military alliances with France and the USSR.

From the first, Chamberlain had no fundamental interest in the rights or wrongs of the Sudeten question either way.[40] Czechoslovakia would always be, to him, 'a faraway country' full of querulous foreigners whose problems were of no ultimate concern to the British Empire. His only concern was that the issue was an obstacle to a comprehensive European peace settlement. Such a view reflects badly on him in hindsight, but it was not particularly unusual at the time. Most British politicians, including many of the leading anti-appeasers, were lukewarm at best about the principles involved in the Sudetenland question. On the day the Germans marched into Austria, Amery wrote in his diary that 'I am inclined to think that the best hope of peace now lies in telling Germany that if she touches Czechoslovakia we are in it too.'[41] But a week later, having thought it over, he was less sure:

> The more doubtful I have become, partly because we shall not get
> Dominion or home public opinion sufficiently united, even more

because geography is against us and with Austria gone, we cannot prevent the steady economic squeeze on Czechoslovakia or the increase of domestic trouble fomented from Germany.[42]

Henlein, a shrewd actor who could play the reasonable moderate to a tee when he had to, visited London that spring and charmed Churchill, who emerged from their meeting convinced that the Sudeten leader was an honest man whom Prague could and must do business with.[43] In fact, Henlein had long been on Berlin's covert payroll, and he understood perfectly well that his real job, if Hitler so chose, was to manufacture a suitable provocation for war. The Sudetenlanders would 'always demand so much that we cannot be satisfied', he secretly assured the German leader.[44]

Chamberlain's first intervention in Czech affairs was modest enough, but superficially triumphant. It's now largely forgotten that there were *two* war scares over the Sudetenland in 1938. The first happened on the weekend of 21–22 May, when British and French foreign intelligence agents reported that the Germans were concentrating their forces on the Czech border as a possible first move in a surprise military attack. The Czechs, alerted to the danger, mobilised their army. Halifax told Sir Nevile Henderson, the British ambassador in Berlin, to deliver a note to the German government warning them that if France became involved in a war over Czechoslovakia, then Britain 'could not guarantee' that it would not also intervene.

In fact, there was no planned invasion. Preparations for war had barely begun. The puzzled Germans issued a denial, and by Monday the scare was over. But Chamberlain (who had once again had a weekend fishing trip ruined) was convinced that 'British firmness' had stayed Hitler's hand.[45] Nor was he alone. Amery thought that 'Neville has succeeded in doing the very thing Grey failed to do in 1914, namely make Germany realise the danger of precipitate action.'[46] If anything, the opposite was true. Hitler was infuriated by press reports that he had backed down in the face of Halifax's vague remonstrance.[47] Case Green, the invasion plan, had always been speculative up to this point. Now the *Führer* determined to attack Czechoslovakia no later than 1 October.[48] 'Standing firm' had not deterred Hitler at all, but rather spurred him to greater belligerence.

Britain's 'success' during the May war scare had had just the opposite effect on Chamberlain. Impressed by his own statesmanship, the prime minister was now keen to get further involved in the Sudetenland issue. But he wanted the Germans to find his intentions more ambiguous than before.

The British government was henceforth to maintain a studiously aloof position, hoping to impress neutrals with its objectivity as well as keeping Germany and France guessing about its plans. The Germans, Chamberlain's reasoning went, would have to be more cautious if they could never know for sure whether Britain would intervene on France's side in a war for Czechoslovakia. The French, similarly, could not strike too aggressive a pose if they were not completely confident of British assistance.[49] At no point that summer did the British government ever unambiguously guarantee France military assistance in the event of war. This, of course, was to reproduce precisely what Amery had called Grey's big mistake in 1914.

The conflict between Prague, Henlein's Sudetenlanders and Berlin simmered on. Chamberlain dispatched a superannuated former Cabinet minister, Lord Runciman, to report on the rights and wrongs of the Sudeten issue. Runciman, who tried to turn down the offer twice, complained that the government was 'pushing me out in a dinghy in mid-Atlantic', a remark that captured well his feelings about his mission to Czechoslovakia, if not its geography.[50] On 4 September, under pressure from London and Paris, the Czech president, Edvard Beneš, offered Henlein the 'Fourth Plan', a set of constitutional reforms that yielded most of the demands of the Carlsbad Memorandum. This was a futile concession, though, because Henlein was not interested in a peaceful resolution. On 12 September, Hitler made a much-anticipated speech at the climax of the annual Nuremberg Party Rally, a rant full of invective against Beneš and the Czechs. This was the cue for a series of SdP-choreographed riots the following day. Prague declared martial law and partly mobilised the Czech army. The crisis appeared to be spiralling out of control.

For the past month Chamberlain had been mulling over an emergency option he called 'Plan Z'. Now he decided to try it. He sent a message to Hitler offering to fly to Germany to discuss the crisis man-to-man. The *Führer*, suspicious but unable to snub such a proposal from so distinguished a statesman as the British prime minister, accepted. Chamberlain left Heston aerodrome in Hounslow (now largely buried under the M4) on the morning of 15 September. Amery thought it 'courageous'.[51] Churchill called it 'the stupidest thing that has ever been done'.[52]

'His hair is brown, not black, his eyes blue, his expression rather disagreeable,' Chamberlain wrote to Ida of Hitler after he returned to England:

Altogether he looks entirely undistinguished. You would never notice

him in a crowd and take him for the house painter he once was [...
but] in spite of the hardness and ruthlessness I thought I saw in his
face I got the impression that here was a man who could be relied
upon when he had given his word.[53]

There were 'no signs of insanity but many of excitement,' he told his Cabinet
colleagues. Hitler would occasionally meander off the point and embark on
one of his tirades. Overall though, Chamberlain thought,

> it was impossible not to be impressed with the power of the man.
> He was extremely determined; he had thought out what he wanted
> and he meant to get it and he would not brook opposition beyond
> a certain point. Further [... I] formed the opinion that Herr Hitler's
> objectives were strictly limited.[54]

Chamberlain spent several hours with Hitler at the Obersalzberg
Berghof. The prime minister did not really get what he wanted, which was
the start of a comprehensive discussion about Anglo-German relations.
The two men did, however, sketch out the basis of a peaceful solution to
the crisis in Czechoslovakia. This would require, Hitler insisted, that the
Czechs first concede the principle of ceding the Sudetenland to the Third
Reich if such a move were to be ratified by plebiscite. Chamberlain, as indifferent as ever to where the Sudetenland finally ended up ('I don't care two
hoots,' he told Ida), was open to floating the idea to the Cabinet if it meant
resolving the Czech issue once and for all.[55] The meeting ended cordially.

Back in London, Chamberlain's colleagues heard the proposal without
enthusiasm but with a sense of gathering fatalism. 'I should have thought it
was quite clear that we have to go to the limit to try to satisfy what Hitler
said were his claims, on the ground that as he put them, they were not
entirely unjustifiable,' wrote Alexander Cadogan, the permanent under-
secretary at the Foreign Office:

> If he goes beyond them, he will have gone beyond our limit, and there
> will be nothing to be done but to oppose them. Our moral position
> will be all the stronger for having strained to the utmost to give him
> satisfaction, and his position before the world [...] will be all the
> worse.[56]

On 18 September, Daladier and the French delegation glumly agreed to the plan too. It was relayed to the Czechs by the British and French ministers to Prague, who descended on Beneš like, as he put it later, 'two angels of death'.[57] Beneš was outraged: ceding the Sudetenland would do unprecedented violence to Czechoslovakia's sovereignty. The angels of death were unmoved. Prague, they warned, would be on its own if it rejected the plan. On 21 September the Czechs capitulated.

Chamberlain flew back to Germany the following morning, having apparently settled all but the mundane details of how the plebiscite and any subsequent territorial transfers would be managed. He was in for a nasty shock when he met Hitler at the Rheinhotel Dreesen in Bad Godesberg. The *Führer* declared that he would not recognise any plebiscite unless German troops had physically occupied the Sudetenland first. Moreover, if this did not happen by 26 September, he would invade Czechoslovakia. Chamberlain was aghast. A later meeting produced a 'concessionary' movement of the deadline to 1 October (which was no concession at all: Germany was in no position to act militarily until then anyway), but no more.

Chamberlain called Halifax from Germany, saying that Hitler's new demands 'would not do'.[58] However, when Cadogan heard the prime minister recount his mission to his senior colleagues back in London on the afternoon of 24 September, he realised with gathering horror that Chamberlain was now 'quite calmly for total surrender [...] Hitler has evidently hypnotised him'.[59] Chamberlain accepted that the Nazi leader had gone well beyond what had been initially agreed at the *Berghof*, but he argued that it was worth conceding to his new ultimatum if it meant being able to make progress on a general European settlement. He had, he felt, made a favourable impression on Hitler that he could exploit in the future.

Chamberlain had previously enjoyed almost total mastery of his Cabinet. But this concession was one too many. Before leaving for Bad Godesberg, his colleagues had asked him to break off negotiations immediately if Hitler made any new demands. Now Halifax, after a sleepless night wrestling with his conscience, could bear it no longer. He told the prime minister that the new German requirement was unacceptable. The Cabinet rallied around the foreign secretary. Such open mutiny was a 'horrible blow' to a man as thin-skinned as Chamberlain. He briefly considered resigning in anger.[60] But Halifax was implacable. Hitler was now resorting to 'unadulterated blackmail'.[61] Daladier too made it clear, once he heard the results of the meeting, that France could not accept these new terms. Chamberlain, for the second time in four days, had no choice but to accede to an ultimatum.

On Monday, 26 September, Halifax, without the prime minister's authorisation (and to his great irritation), made a press statement declaring that if France honoured its treaty commitment to the Czechs, Britain would enter the war too.[62] The following evening, Chamberlain made his famous BBC broadcast warning the public that the apocalypse might be nigh. 'How horrible, fantastic, incredible it is, that we should be digging trenches and trying on gas-masks here, because of a quarrel in a faraway country between people of whom we know nothing,' he told a stunned nation. Air Raid Precautions (ARP) and other civil defence measures had already begun across Britain the previous weekend. On 28 September the Royal Navy mobilised. 'Now we are in for it, unprepared as usual,' Amery wrote in his diary:

> I am by no means an optimist for the outcome. Czechoslovakia may hold out for months and Germany break down internally. Or it may collapse in a week and we may find ourselves besieged in Hong Kong, and Singapore, driven out of Egypt and Palestine, with most of London and our chief munitions works in ruins.[63]

Had Hitler wished it, the Second World War would have broken out that first weekend of October 1938. It was his choice to make. At the very last moment he lost his nerve. He began to fear that the German people were not really in any mood for war. Britain and France appeared to be serious about standing by the Czechs. Second thoughts crept in. On the morning of 28 September, Hitler received a message from London proposing a multi-power conference in Germany to resolve the crisis. After a cantankerous meeting with his lieutenants, several of whom, including Goebbels and Göring, were also starting to get cold feet, Hitler agreed to the offer. The news from Berlin was delivered to Chamberlain as he was addressing the Commons that evening. A great roar rose up from both sides of the House as MPs heard of the eleventh-hour breakthrough. Even Churchill strode up and shook Chamberlain by the hand.[64]

The resulting conference in Munich's *Führerbau* on 29 September 1938 was one of the most slapdash affairs in diplomatic history. It lasted from lunchtime till the early hours of the following morning with no agenda and no proper minutes. Minor functionaries wandered randomly back and forth between the rooms, grazing on the buffet. The seating plan had not been organised. Interpreters had not been assigned. There were no note-pads or sharpened pencils. When Hitler tried to sign the final document, he discovered there was no ink.

The agreement that finally emerged was a modest tweaking of the demands made at Bad Godesberg. Instead of an immediate German mili-tary occupation, the Czechs would have until 10 October to withdraw. An international commission would supervise the transition, the plebiscites and any subsequent movements of population. On paper, Hitler's con-cessions were significant; in practice, much would depend on the spirit in which the Germans subsequently behaved. Chamberlain and Daladier signed. The Czechs, of course, were not present.

The following morning, the prime minister talked with Hitler in the latter's private apartment. Chamberlain produced a piece of paper that he had drawn up earlier at the British delegation hotel. It cited the agreement that had just been signed as symbolic of the determination of Britain and Germany never to go to war again. Hitler glanced at it briefly and signed it. Chamberlain tucked it away in his pocket. This, far more than the Sude-tenland agreement, was, he felt, his real prize.

Exhausted, the prime minister flew back to Heston on 30 September to be greeted by an ecstatic crowd. He flourished the piece of paper and read its contents aloud before heading off to Buckingham Palace through London streets packed with cheering people ('they were lined from one end to the other [...] shouting themselves hoarse, leaping on the running board, banging on the windows and thrusting their hands into the car to be shaken'[65]). At the Palace he appeared on the balcony with the king and the royal family. Later that evening, back in Downing Street preparing to speak to the crowd outside, someone suggested to Chamberlain that he quote Disraeli's remark, following the 1878 Congress of Berlin, that he had returned from Germany with 'peace with honour'. The prime minister, according to one witness, 'coldly disdained such a piece of theatricality'. 'I don't do that sort of thing', he said. But a few minutes later he found himself saying:

> My good friends, this is the second time in our history that there has come from Germany to Downing Street peace with honour. I believe it is peace for our time.

Chamberlain was never lucky with words. He probably regretted these ones immediately. A week later he tried to excuse them as 'a moment of some emotion, after a long and exhausting day'. It was already too late.[66]

8

TO MAKE GENTLE THE
LIFE OF THE WORLD

Whatever we might think about what happened at the Munich conference, so far as its two protagonists were concerned, one of them, Chamberlain, had won, and the other, Hitler, had lost. Neither man greatly cared one way or the other about what had happened to the Sudetenland. The real question at Munich had been: war or peace? Chamberlain, through his own force of will, had demanded peace, and he had secured it. He had exposed Hitler's aggressive bluster as fraud. It was obvious by the scenes of wild relief on Munich's streets as the conference broke up and the British prime minister headed back to the airport that ordinary Germans had no appetite for war at that moment. Chamberlain had refused to take the easy option of violence; he had held back Armageddon by his own sheer moral courage. The *Führer* had been chastened. Now, Chamberlain hoped, he could press this psychological advantage by organising a comprehensive settlement of Europe's remaining grievances.

Hitler, for his part, had been uncharacteristically mute and sullen throughout the whole conference. He was getting almost everything he ostensibly wanted for almost no cost. But the Sudetenland was not really what he wanted at all. Hitler wanted war. He lived in the mental world of the *fin de siècle*, of imperial German writers like von Treitschke and von Bernhardi, for whom war was the supreme expression of the living spirit, the ennobling stimulus necessary for the healthy progress of race and nation. War, for Hitler, was a pure good for its own sake, the 'essence of human activity'.[1] Yet he had baulked at the opportunity to begin a war because of a last-minute failure of nerve – something that was especially humiliating once he concluded (probably wrongly) that Britain and France would not, in the end, have intervened to save Czechoslovakia. Hitler had been forced to haggle over policy details like one of the bourgeois politicians he so despised. Chamberlain, that 'desiccated stick' who had duped him out of his cheap, easy little war, had been hailed by the German masses as a hero. After the conference, Hitler swore to himself, there would be no more Munichs. The next time Ares beckoned, he would neither flinch nor falter.

Chamberlain came back from Munich ebullient. His mood did not last. In the weeks that followed the conference it became clear that the agreement over the Sudetenland had not brought about a fresh start for Anglo-German relations after all. In a speech on 9 October, Hitler complained about Britain's haughty, interfering 'airs'. Germany, he said, would no longer tolerate 'the tutelage of governesses'.[2] Chamberlain was vexed by the German leader's refusal 'to make the slightest gesture of friendliness' towards him, insinuating in a letter to Hilda that Hitler was jealous because of Chamberlain's own enormous popularity throughout Germany.[3]

Meanwhile, the occupation of the Sudetenland was carried out with malignant glee.[4] Roger Makins, one of the Foreign Office officials assigned to the international commission to oversee the transfer, reported to London in mid-October that he and his colleagues had been 'able to do little more than watch the constriction of the rabbit by the boa'. Czechoslovakia, henceforth, would be 'little more than a German colony'.[5] On 9 November the *Kristallnacht* pogrom, by far the largest and most vicious orgy of state-sanctioned violence against Germany's Jews yet, shocked the world. Chamberlain called it a barbarity, though he was chiefly irritated about the fact that it made his job more difficult. It was probably intended to. *Kristallnacht* was the Nazis' response to the millions of Germans who had shown themselves to be so distressingly keen on peace back in September. It was meant as a reminder to them of who their enemies were.[6]

By the end of 1938 Munich was looking more and more like a false dawn. It had not brought about the diplomatic breakthrough that the prime minister had wanted. It had also exposed the fragility of the Anglo-French relationship. Throughout the autumn crisis Chamberlain had treated the French premier, Édouard Daladier, with scarcely concealed disdain. Daladier had not been consulted on the Runciman mission. Nor had he been told beforehand about Plan Z. At Munich the two leaders had been on such bad terms they barely spoke to one another. Chamberlain did not see fit to consult Daladier about the private agreement he signed with Hitler at the end of the conference. Nor did relations improve afterwards. During their visit to Paris in November, Chamberlain and Halifax bluntly reminded the French that Britain had no interest in assuming any serious continental commitment. The largest theoretical expeditionary force that could be sent across the Channel would be made up of two ill-equipped divisions.[7] Military co-operation was virtually non-existent. Sir Hugh Dowding, Air Officer Commanding-in-Chief (AOC-in-C) of RAF Fighter Command, was warned by the Air Ministry not to discuss any war plans with the French, and to tell them nothing about British military organisation, aircraft performance, production figures or service strengths.[8] The French, it was strongly implied, were supplicants who ought to be grateful for any help they received at all.

By December 1939, however, Halifax was having second thoughts about the wisdom of this. He warned a Committee of Imperial Defence meeting that 'a time might come when the French would cease to be enthusiastic about their relations with Great Britain if they were left with the impression that it was they who must bear the brunt of the fighting and slaughter on land.'[9] There was a risk that, if pushed too far, a demoralised France might withdraw into a purely defensive posture behind its fortified borders – a move that would have dangerous implications for British security. At Munich the French had been forced to abandon their alliance with the Czechs to appease the British. True, they had not really wanted to honour that alliance. But the point was that they had now lost the Czechs' thirty-four divisions, one of their few reliable counterweights to German power. As Halifax went on, there was 'some slight danger that, if Germany attempted to come to an agreement with France for her to stand aside while Germany attacked us, they might be tempted to accept'.[10]

This concern took on a more urgent form when reports of a possible surprise German attack on the Netherlands began reaching the Foreign Office in January 1939. There was nothing to it – British intelligence was confounded by dozens of such spurious rumours. But it provoked an urgent reassessment of strategy. Britain could not allow the Low Countries to fall into German hands. A Nazi-controlled Belgium or Netherlands would be a perfect forward base for an air attack on the British Isles. But Britain could not defend the Low Countries alone without French assistance. And the French were going to demand more than a token military effort from the British if they did so. As the military attaché in Paris pointed out:

> There is always latent in France the view that Britain is quite willing to fight her battles on the continent with French soldiers [...] They recognise freely the financial effort which is inherent in the possession of

a fleet and an air force like ours, but they go on to state that a financial effort in the circumstances of today is not enough. They say that what is required is an *effort du sang*.[11]

The chiefs of staff agreed. 'It is difficult to say how the security of the United Kingdom could be maintained if France were forced to capitulate,' they wrote to the Cabinet. The defence of Britain might therefore 'have to include a share in the land defence of French territory'. Chamberlain tried to make the counter-argument that the French would find the RAF's strategic bombing capability a more useful contribution to their security than any British land army. But this overlooked the psychology of alliance politics in a democratic age. The prime minister was ultimately forced to concede the point. Staff talks were arranged between the British and French armies. The Cabinet agreed that a properly equipped field force would be prepared for continental war.[12] In the Commons on 6 February, Chamberlain made a direct public commitment to the cross-Channel alliance. 'Any threat to the vital interests of France from whatever quarter it came must,' he said, 'evoke the immediate co-operation of this country.'[13] Twenty years of strategic isolationism were over – for the moment.

While this was going on, the German grip on what remained of Czechoslovakia tightened. The Prague government was told to abandon the League of Nations, to demobilise its army, to hand over its gold reserves to Berlin and to adopt the same anti-Jewish laws as the Third Reich.[14] Slovakian secessionists were incited to revolt. The Hungarians, already rewarded with territorial gains the previous November, were encouraged to demand still more pickings. On 14 March, Slovakia declared independence. That evening, President Emil Hácha, who had replaced Beneš after Munich, was summoned to Hitler's Chancellery and bullied to the point of cardiac arrest into 'requesting' a German protectorate of Bohemia and Moravia. German troops entered Prague the following morning.

Czechoslovakia had disintegrated without any of its citizens firing a shot in its defence. This did not speak well of its viability as a state. Perhaps what this showed was that it had not been wise to create it at Versailles in the first place, still less ever to consider fighting for it. The Nazis had seized the valuable Škoda armament works and engorged themselves on the Czechs' currency and bullion reserves. But was this such a blow to British security that it was worth going to war over? Even Amery suggested after Munich that the 'liquidation' of entanglements with Czechoslovakia was the one good thing to come out of the agreement.[15] The *Daily Express* lamented Prague's fate, but reminded its readers that the 'distant regions on the Danube lie quite outside our bailiwick'.[16]

Still, Hitler had promised at Munich that he had no more territorial demands. He had now defied all the norms of the international community, plus a solemn agreement made with the British government. Even if it had not been wise to get involved in the Czech question, the fact was that Chamberlain had done so, and by doing so he had invested a good deal of his country's reputation in its outcome. Britain's right to be taken seriously was at stake. That, surely, was a vital national interest.

The prime minister made a statement to the Commons on the afternoon of 15 March. It was natural, he said, that he should 'bitterly regret' what had happened to Czechoslovakia. But, he went on, 'though one may have to suffer checks and disappointments from time to time, the object which we have in mind is of too great significance to the happiness of mankind for us lightly to give it up.' The House was not impressed. Chamberlain, as Labour MP David Grenfell chided, seemed to possess a 'remarkable state of detachment' about what had just happened.[17] He was 'pushing understatement to the point of irony', the *Daily Telegraph* concurred.[18]

Two days later, either recognising that he had hit the wrong note or with a gathering sense of his own indignation, Chamberlain gave a more forceful response in a speech in his native Birmingham. 'Is this the last attack upon a small State, or is it to be followed by others?' the prime minister asked:

> Is this, in fact, a step in the direction of an attempt to dominate the world by force? [...] no greater mistake could be made than to suppose that, because it believes war to be a senseless and cruel thing, this nation has so lost its fibre that it will not take part to the utmost of its power in resisting such a challenge if it ever were made.

Three things had changed since Munich that help to explain Chamberlain's more belligerent response to Hitler in March 1939. The first was that the chiefs of staff's Joint Intelligence Committee (JIC) had begun to offer the Cabinet more optimistic assessments of Britain's military situation. The JIC was now more confident that Britain would be able to withstand an initial German aerial onslaught thanks to early-warning radar and the fast monoplane fighters going into service with the RAF. Moreover it now believed that Britain, in alliance with France, would enjoy better staying power than Germany over the course of a war lasting three or more years. The JIC appreciation still recommended avoiding any major conflict until at least 1940, when the situation would be more favourable still. But its new advice stiffened the resolve of Cabinet members who wanted to take a tougher line with Hitler.[19]

The second thing was Halifax's growing independence from Chamberlain. The prime minister had never really been able to reassert his old dominance over the Cabinet after the rebellion over the Bad Godesberg memorandum. Halifax, unlike Chamberlain, had never regarded Munich as anything other than a necessary capitulation. Perhaps prodded by his High Church conscience, he was clearly running out of patience with the policy of mollifying Hitler, and in this he spoke for the wider Cabinet too. On 18 March, Halifax told Chamberlain that it was no longer a matter of eastern Europe or western Europe. The real matter was 'Germany's attempt to obtain world domination'.[20] He was not blind to the difficulties ahead. A war fought in defence of Poland or Romania would be 'devastating'; the independence of neither state was of any inherent vital interest to Britain, or possible to guarantee in practice anyway. But it would still be better than 'doing nothing'.[21]

The third thing that had changed was a growing sense among Cabinet members that the public now wanted a tougher line towards Germany. It is hard to know if there was any substance to this. There were no Twitter feeds to monitor in 1939, no big data clouds for policy quants to scrutinise. Opinion polling was in its infancy. The by-election results after Munich were mixed. In November 1938 the Conservative candidate in Bridgwater, Somerset, was defeated by an Independent anti-appeasement challenger. But the following month in Kinross and Western Perthshire, Katharine Stewart-Murray, the duchess of Atholl, who had resigned her seat and the Conservative whip to protest against the Munich deal, failed to be re-elected, defeated by a National government candidate.[22]

Politicians who sought to divine 'what the country wanted' tended to base their conclusions on such dubious indicators as newspaper leader columns, letters received from constituents or conversations with chauffeurs and groundskeepers. They tended, in other words, to discover what they wanted to discover. All the same, by March 1939 several members of Chamberlain's government had concluded that the public was tired of conciliating the Nazis. The country, thought Halifax's principal private secretary, Oliver Harvey, had been 'undoubtedly stirred' by events in Prague.[23] It was time for the British lion, its honour compromised at Munich, to show a little bite.[24]

All of this helps to explain Chamberlain's sudden and remarkable decision to offer an unconditional guarantee of support to Poland on 31 March 1939. The replacement of the Czech question by the Polish question had come about almost accidentally. Back in late October 1938, Joachim von Ribbentrop, Germany's foreign minister, had invited the Polish ambassador, Józef Lipski, to a meeting to discuss the future of the corridor dividing East Prussia from the Reich hinterland. Ribbentrop suggested that the *Volksdeutsche* city of Danzig, which adjoined East Prussia, a League of Nations protectorate since 1919, ought to be returned to Germany, and an *Autobahn* and rail link built across the Polish territorial corridor which could re-establish land communications between the two unattached parts of the Reich.

Lipski, under instructions from Józef Beck, his country's foreign minister, firmly declined the proposal. In January, Beck himself was asked to Berlin to meet with Hitler, where the proposal was made again, though this time in far less diplomatic tones. The Poles, suspecting that they were being sized up as the next Czechoslovakia, remained intransigent. By late March the Nazi press was loudly declaiming about 'atrocities' committed against the German ethnic population in western Poland. Hitler had already ordered his general staff to prepare operational plans for a full-scale war against the Poles in the autumn.[25]

The fate of Danzig specifically, and the Republic of Poland more generally, was Britain's proximate reason for going to war in September 1939. They were much less worthy causes than anything that had been a stake at Munich. Danzig and the Polish Corridor had been German since 1871 and territories of the Kingdom of Prussia for a century before that. Most Danzigers were enthusiastic about reabsorption back into Germany. Halifax thought Danzig's status as a League of Nations free city 'a most foolish provision' of Versailles.[26] The British Ambassador in Warsaw warned London that Danzig was 'a bad wicket on which to make a stand'.[27] The Conservative MP Cuthbert Headlam thought the idea of going to war over Danzig 'grotesque and wicked'.[28]

Nor was the Polish Republic a very noble object of sympathy. Whatever Czechoslovakia's problems, it had at least been a reasonably functional democratic state. Poland had been a military dictatorship in all but name since 1933. Its parliamentary elections were rigged, its opposition politicians routinely hounded. The government maintained its own concentration camp for alleged enemies of the state. Anti-Semitism, much of it officially sanctioned, flourished enthusiastically in Polish public life. It was the Poles who had first floated the idea of exiling unwanted Jews to Madagascar, later a Nazi flight of fancy. Despite owing its own existence to Versailles, Poland was no respecter of the post-war settlement. It had territorial designs extending all the way to the Black Sea. In October 1938, in a moment of brazen opportunism after the Munich conference, it had seized the town of Teschen from Czechoslovakia. The Warsaw government, Daladier thought, had displayed a predatory, 'cormorant', attitude towards its victimised neighbour. Relations between the Poles and British and French diplomats in early 1939 were cool, at best.[29]

Nonetheless, this was the state to which Britain, along with France, offered a guarantee of support on the last day of March 1939. Other guarantees to Romania and Greece were to follow shortly afterwards. But it was the Polish guarantee that really mattered, because it was Polish territory that Hitler had immediate designs on. Chamberlain was as studiously indifferent about the rights and wrongs of Danzig and the corridor as he had been about the Sudetenland. The purpose of the guarantee was not to prevent any future change to Poland's frontiers. It said nothing about defending every square inch of Polish territory. It did not preclude further negotiations between Berlin and Warsaw over the fate of Danzig. The British would be the ones to decide whether Poland's independence had been jeopardised, not the Poles themselves.[30]

Nor was the guarantee a realistic strategic commitment. Warsaw was a thousand miles from London. If war broke out, the Poles could not possibly be given any direct military assistance. The guarantee's point, as Sir Nevile Henderson told the Germans in May, was to establish that 'making brute force the sole arbiter in international affairs' was no longer acceptable.[31] It was, said Chamberlain, 'not perhaps very material' precisely what Britain was guaranteeing. He was doing it 'not in order to save a particular victim, but in order to pull down the bully' by calling his bluff.[32] There was a good deal of cynicism to that, especially given what might happen to an overly emboldened Poland if it decided to defy Nazi negotiations on the strength of Britain and France's pledges. But then, Chamberlain honestly thought the Nazis would decline the challenge.

By giving Poland his guarantee, the British prime minister had not given up on appeasement. There could be no further conciliation for the time being, thanks to the Nazis' duplicitous stupidity over Czechoslovakia. But perhaps Hitler would see sense or be toppled by more reasonable men among the Nazi coterie. Then conciliation might begin again. The Polish guarantee was a warning, an opportunity for Berlin to reflect on and learn from.

The tragedy of what followed was that Chamberlain and Hitler had drawn exactly opposite conclusions from the Sudeten crisis the previous year. The British prime minister was convinced that Hitler would back down from war over Poland, as he had backed down on 28 September 1938 by agreeing to talk. 'Hitler now realises that he can't grab anything else without a major war and has decided therefore to put Danzig in cold storage,' Chamberlain wrote to his sister on 30 July before heading off for a lengthy salmon-fishing holiday in Scotland.[33]

Hitler, though, felt he had taken the measure of the 'little worms' he had met at Munich. He did not really want a war with Britain and France at that moment, with his great rearmament programmes still uncompleted, but he was convinced that they would do anything to avoid one too. They would betray the Poles in the end, just as they had betrayed the Czechs.[34] They would make 'extremely theatrical anti-German gestures', he told the Italian foreign minister Count Ciano, but it would all amount to nothing in the end.[35] On 23 August the Molotov–Ribbentrop Pact with the USSR provided Hitler with a guarantee of his own, one that ensured he would not have to worry about an extended eastern front once he had defeated the Poles. That would ensure that the British and French would stay out. And if they did not? Well ... he was willing to take that risk. He would not be cheated of his splendid little war this time.[36]

The last two weeks of August 1939 played out much as the last two weeks of the previous September: with hysterical denunciations in the German press of the enemy's 'provocations', with cynical offers of mediation by the ever reasonable Mussolini, with warnings to Hitler delivered by sober-looking British and French diplomats in suits and hats, and with rambling tirades from the *Führer* in response. All that was different was the climax. At dawn on Friday, 1 September, German troops and armoured vehicles crossed into Danzig and over Poland's western frontier as the Luftwaffe roamed the Polish skies, bombing and strafing. Later the same morning, the Polish ambassador to the court of St James's met with Halifax and asked when the British would announce their declaration of war. He was told: immediately.

Chamberlain took the guarantee to Poland seriously. On 22 August he had sent a personal letter to Hitler spelling out unambiguously that an attack on that country would mean war with Britain.[37] Three days later, Britain and Poland signed a fully fledged military alliance. When the Cabinet met on the morning of 1 September, Chamberlain was clear with his colleagues that there could be 'no possible question where our duty lay'.[38] Yet during the final hours of peace the prime minister managed, somehow, to put on a dithering performance which confirmed the darkest suspicions of every anti-appeaser in Britain that he was going to abandon Poland to its fate.

The problem lay in part with the French. In the interests of cross-Channel solidarity, Chamberlain thought it politically desirable for the two countries to declare war on Germany simultaneously. He did not wish it to seem to the French people that Britain was pushing its ally into anything. But the government in Paris insisted it could not sanction an ultimatum to Germany until the French parliament had met on Saturday, 2 September. So Chamberlain only offered a generalised warning to Hitler when he spoke in the House of Commons that Friday evening. The following morning, Chamberlain announced he would make a further statement in the House within hours. But Daladier's foreign minister Georges Bonnet, who was still seeking a last-minute settlement with Berlin and stalling for time, telephoned to say that no French ultimatum was as yet forthcoming, and it would anyway have to have at least a two-day expiry period. Chamberlain cancelled his planned parliamentary statement, then rescheduled it for the evening. Rumours began to spread in the Commons lobbies.

Chamberlain arrived at a packed and unsettled House of Commons on the evening of 2 September, as a violent thunderstorm over London provided an appropriately apocalyptic backdrop. In a 'flat, embarrassed voice', he spoke in vague terms of the crisis, without giving any clear indication of when, if at all, the Germans would be handed an ultimatum. MPs on all sides were stunned. 'For two days, the wretched Poles had been bombed and massacred,' recalled Amery, who, according to the Labour member Hugh Dalton, had sat 'red-faced and speechless with fury' as Chamberlain droned on. 'Was all this havering the prelude to another Munich?' Amery wondered:

> It was essential that someone should do what he had failed to do, or been unable, to do [...] that was to voice the feelings of the House and of the whole country. Arthur Greenwood rose to speak for the

Opposition. I dreaded a purely partisan speech, and called out to him across the floor of the House: '*Speak for England*.'[39]

Greenwood, a well-liked mediocrity whose dipsomania ruined what otherwise might have been a great parliamentary career, rose to Amery's challenge. 'I am gravely disturbed,' he told the House:

> An act of aggression took place 38 hours ago. The moment that act of aggression took place one of the most important treaties of modern times automatically came into operation [...] I wonder how long we are prepared to vacillate at a time when Britain and all that Britain stands for, and human civilisation, are in peril. We must march with the French.

Chamberlain responded as best he could that 'the government is in a some-what difficult position'. But it was clear that he could not hold back his own party, let alone the opposition, much longer. After the session, Cabinet members led by Sir John Simon confronted Chamberlain in what the prime minister called afterwards 'a sort of mutiny'. Stung by and indignant at this disloyalty, but out of other options, Chamberlain phoned Daladier to tell him that the British were going to go ahead with an ultimatum the follow-ing morning no matter what the French did.

At nine o'clock on Sunday, 3 September 1939, Sir Nevile Henderson presented a note to the German government in Berlin. It informed them that if they did not indicate within two hours that they were immediately going to withdraw their troops from Poland, Britain would declare war. At a quarter past eleven in London, with no word from Germany, Cham-berlain broadcast on the BBC. Britain was going to fight for Danzig. Did Chamberlain reflect, as he was speaking, that this was exactly the cause which Austen had once declared was not worth the bones of a single British grenadier? We don't know. What we do know is that the broadcast itself – replete with self-exculpation, resentment, charmless conceit and a sincere horror at the evils that were about to be unleashed – was quintessential Neville Chamberlain.

> You can imagine what a bitter blow it is to me that all my long struggle to win peace has failed. Yet I cannot believe that there is anything more or anything different that I could have done and that would have been more successful.

*

Within a week Chamberlain had recovered some of his old confidence. 'I have a feeling that [peace] won't be so very long,' he wrote to Ida on 10 September. Chamberlain believed that Hitler had wanted to find a solution to the Danzig crisis right up to the final days. 'But at the last moment some brainstorm took possession of him – maybe Ribbentrop stirred it up – and once he had set his machine in motion he couldn't stop it.'[40] It was all a great mystery. The one thing Chamberlain was sure about was that he himself was beyond reproach. He had done everything that was humanly possible to prevent the war. There was nothing he would choose now to have done differently then.

There is a good deal of pathos in the spectacular trajectory of Neville Chamberlain's rise and fall. From those days of glory in the immediate aftermath of Munich, when he was as well known around the world as Charlie Chaplin and Gandhi, and special assistants had to be drafted in to handle the tens of thousands of congratulatory letters arriving daily in Downing Street, and Harry Roy's Tiger Ragamuffins played 'God Bless You, Mr. Chamberlain' and *Coeur de Filet Neville Chamberlain* was served in the grill room at the Dorchester, to today, when Birmingham City Council can barely bring itself to recognise the existence of its famous son.[41]

But Chamberlain's insufferableness makes it very hard to sympathise with him. The fact is that he was terrible at doing many things he was convinced he could do wonderfully. He was a dreadful judge of character. He fundamentally misunderstood Hitler from their first meeting. He was an appalling negotiator, far too susceptible to having his head turned by cheap praise, something the *Führer* caught on to immediately. After the flight to the *Berghof* in September 1938, Chamberlain's head was filled with unctuous insincerities passed along by Nazi officials. Hitler, he was told, had been 'very favourably impressed' by the prime minister: 'I have had a conversation with a *man*.'[42] Flatter Chamberlain, Hitler realised, and he would believe almost anything you wanted him to.[43]

Chamberlain made the fundamental error of 'mistaking personal cordiality for similarity of aim'.[44] His unwillingness to subject his beliefs to any kind of critical self-inquiry meant that, once he had decided something, he was incapable of seeing other things that were staring him in the face. 'His mind,' as one of his colleagues said, 'once made up, was ringed round by a barrier so hard and so unimaginative that no argument could penetrate it.'[45] It was a cognitive weakness that was to have appalling consequences for himself and his country.

Chamberlain botched the Sudetenland negotiations in 1938. There was, and remains, a perfectly reasonable case that Britain should never have got involved in them in the first place. The Nazis cynically exploited the demands of the *Sudetendeutsche*. But those demands were, in and of themselves, valid enough on the Wilsonian grounds of national self-determination. Even Jan Masaryk, the Czech ambassador in London, conceded after Munich that his country would have been better off if the Sudetenland had never been part of it.[46] Standing aside and leaving the Czechs to their fate in 1938 would not have been without costs. Czechoslovakia would, presumably, have been invaded by the Germans – though whether Hitler's nascent armed forces would, in an all-out war, have found the Czechs such easy pickings is a question we can never answer. The conquest of Czechoslovakia would have been a triumph for a dictatorship that was willing to wage aggressive war in violation of the spirit and letter of the League of Nations Covenant. But Czechoslovakia's fate did not represent an existential concern to the British Empire any more than the fate of any small central European state.

Still, Neville Chamberlain chose to get involved in the Czech question. Once he had done so, British prestige was inextricably bound up in its outcome. In a letter he wrote to the prime minister shortly before Munich, Amery argued that 'much might have been said for a policy of deliberate abstention from the whole European conflict'. But, he continued, 'after all our intervention [...] we [cannot] possibly shirk our responsibility now.'[47] The problem was that Chamberlain never thought that Czechoslovakia was worth fighting for. He had, then, ignored his own advice to his colleagues that 'no State, certainly no democratic State, ought to make a threat of war unless it [is] both ready to carry it out and prepared to do so.'[48]

At Munich this irresponsibility was laid bare as Chamberlain made little secret of the fact that he was willing to agree to almost any sacrifice by the Czechs, however shameful and debilitating, if it would extract him from a commitment to war he clearly regretted. There was some truth to Churchill's spiky accusation afterwards that '£1 was demanded at the pistol's point. When it was given, £2 were demanded at the pistol's point. Finally, the dictator consented to take £1 17s. 6d. and the rest in promises of good will for the future.'[49] Hitler never took the 'little worm' in Downing Street seriously again. The German leader completely misread Britain's conviction in the Danzig crisis the following year. But it was an understandable mistake, given what he had seen at Munich.

Chamberlain, then, had no one but himself to blame for his failure. But his desire not to go to war over the Sudetenland in September 1938 was sensible. Historians have been arguing ever since about whether the Czech crisis was the best moment for the British and French to confront Hitler militarily. If the western Allies had opened hostilities against the Third Reich before Hitler's rearmament was completed, and before he had obtained Czechoslovakia's financial and industrial resources, would Germany have collapsed relatively quickly and the Second World War have been concluded in a matter of months, rather than years? Could the tens of millions of deaths on the battlefields and in the Holocaust have all been avoided? Some historians later claimed that Chamberlain made a grave miscalculation in 1938. Williamson Murray, for instance, argued that the results of an earlier war 'would have been inevitable and would have led to the eventual collapse of the Nazi regime at considerably less cost than the war that broke out the following September'.[50]

This may be true. But two things should be said about such counter-factual speculations. One is that Hitler ultimately concluded that September 1938 had been Germany's lost chance to go to war and win.[51] In one of his final statements in the Berlin bunker in April 1945, as he awaited final defeat, Hitler opined that Munich had represented 'a unique opportunity of easily and swiftly winning a war that was in any case inevitable. Although we ourselves were not fully prepared, we were nevertheless better prepared than the enemy.'[52] Hitler's opinion on the matter is hardly definitive. But it is at least worth taking into account.

The other thing is that even if September 1938 was, in hindsight, the best moment for Britain and France to go to war, that has no moral bearing on Chamberlain's behaviour at the time because he was told, clearly and persistently, by his professional military advisers that it was not so. In what Halifax called an 'extremely melancholy document' in March, the chiefs of staff had asserted that Czechoslovakia would be swiftly overrun no matter what Britain did.[53] France had no ability to launch an effective attack on Germany's western frontier defences.[54] The British military attaché in Moscow warned London not to expect any decisive contribution from the USSR, even if Stalin decided to honour his alliance with the Czechs, which was far from certain anyway. Two-thirds of the Red Army's officers had been liquidated in the recent purges, with a concomitantly 'disastrous effect' on its fighting capability. The Soviets were 'not capable of carrying the war into the enemy's territory with any hope of ultimate success'.[55]

Britain, the chiefs of staff conceded, might win a long war against Germany by dint of its superior economic resources. But such a war would probably not be confined to western and central Europe for long:

> Italy and Japan would seize the opportunity to further their own ends and in consequence the problem we have to envisage is not that of a limited European war, but of a world war [...] without overlooking the assistance we should hope to obtain from France and possibly other allies, we cannot foresee the time when our defence forces will be strong enough to safeguard our territory, trade and vital interests against Germany, Italy, and Japan simultaneously.[56]

Meanwhile, once the Luftwaffe had been relieved of its duties supporting the German army in its conquest of Czechoslovakia, it would, the chiefs of staff said, be free to begin strategic air attacks against London. They estimated that German aircraft would be able to drop 500 to 600 tons of bombs a day on the British capital for two months, causing hundreds of thousands of casualties.[57]

These appreciations can, in hindsight, be criticised in several ways. British air intelligence in 1938 grossly overestimated the ability and intention of the Luftwaffe to begin a war with a strategic 'knock-out blow' against London.[58] The chiefs of staff did not, importantly, consider what Germany's absorption of the rich Czech lands (including the Škoda armament works) would do to the overall strategic situation in Europe. Oliver Stanley, the president of the Board of Trade, asked them about this on mid-September 1938, but no study was made until long after Munich.[59]

All the same, the advice that Chamberlain received throughout 1938 was that going to war would result in disaster. Perhaps this is what he wanted to hear. But it came with the imprimatur of the country's most senior military experts. Chamberlain, as prime minister, was responsible for making the ultimate political decision about war and peace. But it would have been grossly negligent of him if he had disregarded the professional advice that had been laid out in front of him. He would, in fact, have been behaving like Hitler. If Chamberlain had gone ahead with a war in 1938 and that war had turned out calamitously, historians today would excoriate him for ignoring his chiefs of staff.[60]

After the war, Churchill's *The Gathering Storm* made much of the 'Oster conspiracy', a scheme, led by the former chief of the general staff Ludwig Beck, to overthrow Hitler as soon as he invaded Czechoslovakia. The Oster group was in secret contact with the British Foreign Office, and in September 1938 promised to act if the western powers stood firm over the Bad Godesberg demands. Chamberlain was aware of their existence. But he was sceptical of their motives and their capabilities. Even a vehement anti-appeaser like Sir Robert Vansittart, the government's chief diplomatic adviser, distrusted the Oster conspirators, regarding them as traditional German nationalists who only really differed with Hitler on matters of tactics. In the end, neither Beck nor any other German general needed Neville Chamberlain's permission to try to overthrow Hitler if he really wanted to. The fact that none of the anti-Nazi conspirators acted with any conviction until July 1944, by which time it was far too late, is all the commentary anyone needs on their sincerity and competence. Chamberlain was quite right to discount their feeble procrastination.[61]

The fact is that in September 1938 Chamberlain was faced, as national leaders sometimes are, with a truly horrible situation in which he did not get to choose between a good option and a bad one, but between several options all of which were bad in their own different ways. Many of Chamberlain's critics, if they had been in his place, would probably have done a deal of some sort with Hitler in the end.[62] We cannot even assume that the great anti-appeaser himself, Winston Churchill, would have gone to war for the Sudetenland. Churchill's actions in an alternative timeline in which he was prime minister throughout the Czech crisis would not necessarily have been the same as those actions he demanded as a powerless Commons back-bencher in 1938. In his later wartime dealings with Stalin, Churchill showed that he was just as capable as Chamberlain had been of behaving cynically about the rights of small nations at the behest of a foreign dictator when he felt it was in Britain's interests to do so. The 'percentages agreement' Churchill did with Stalin in October 1944 over the fates of the Balkan states was at least as cold-blooded as the Munich agreement. To object that Churchill had no choice in 1944 but to behave 'realistically' is to side-step the obvious: Chamberlain, in 1938, felt he had to behave realistically too. As for whether doing deals with Stalin was morally different from doing them with Hitler: who was – or is – to decide this?

One of Chamberlain's basic presumptions was that Hitler was a fundamentally rational actor like himself, making decisions based on enlightened self-interest – a belligerent windbag, to be sure, but one whose public statements were not always to be taken literally. The British prime minister assumed that his German counterpart was, at heart, just as keen to avoid unnecessary conflict as he himself was. Had Chamberlain been dealing with a man like Göring, who, despite his repulsive personal character, responded more conventionally to diplomatic cues than Hitler, then appeasement might well have worked – at least in the sense that war would not have been inevitable.[63]

He was not, of course, and trying to make peace with a man like Hitler, so intoxicated with the virtues of war, was probably futile in the long run – just as it was probably also futile to try to deter him from war, a point that often gets lost in the vituperations against Chamberlain. Once Hitler had consolidated his hold on power by mid-1934, the only way that war between Nazi Germany and Britain could have been avoided was if the Germans themselves had removed him through assassination or deposition. Neither of these things ever happened. Chamberlain once remarked on how frustrating it was that the Jews 'obstinately' refused to shoot Hitler, which would have made his life a great deal simpler.[64] It was equally frustrating from the prime minister's perspective that the 'moderate' men of the Nazi Party and German security and armed forces did not act against their *Führer*.

Short of Hitler's death or incapacitation, then, the only alternative open to the British government was to make peace with him or war against him. Before 1938 Hitler had done nothing sufficiently outrageous to provoke anything like the *casus belli* that would have been necessary for a pre-emptive strike against Nazi Germany. A technical violation of the Treaty of Versailles was just not enough. Nobody was going to support a war over the creation of the Wehrmacht or the remilitarisation of the Rhineland. The Nazis' behaviour towards their own citizens, especially Germany's Jews, was despicable long before the Czech crisis. But the Holocaust was still far in the future. Even *Kristallnacht* was yet to come. In September 1938 it was not so easy to draw a clear distinction between the anti-Semitic ugliness of the German National Socialists and that, for example, of Poland's governing 'Camp of National Unity', which Britain eventually went to war to defend. The nature of statecraft meant sometimes having to deal with governments with ideologies that were disagreeable to you.[65] In any case, the idea of a right to humanitarian intervention in the domestic affairs of other sovereign states did not exist in 1938. It would have seemed as presumptuous for Chamberlain to tell the

Germans how to treat Germany's Jews as for Mussolini to tell Chamberlain how to treat Palestine's Arabs or Ulster's Catholics.[66]

Appeasement, when stripped of all the lazy pejorative connotations of the last seventy years, was – and remains – simply a traditional method, employed by every state in history at some time or another, of trying to deal with a dangerous and unpredictable rival in circumstances in which going to war appeared to be either impossible or at least highly undesirable. Chamberlain never disputed that Germany represented the greatest ultimate threat to British security in the 1930s. That was all the more reason, as he saw it, to try to negotiate a lasting settlement with its government. A comprehensive agreement with Hitler about *all* European affairs would have then allowed Britain to withdraw from central European politics and to focus on the more manageable threats represented by the Italians in the Mediterranean and the Japanese in East Asia. 'We cannot exaggerate,' the chiefs of staff warned the prime minister in December 1937, 'the importance from the point of view of Imperial Defence of any political or international action which could be taken to reduce the number of our potential enemies and to gain the support of potential allies.'[67] Chamberlain had no qualms about standing up to states like Italy or Japan if he could remove Hitler from the picture. 'If only we could get on terms with the Germans I would not care a rap for Musso,' he said in July 1937.[68]

Once the Second World War began, some Conservatives defended the Munich agreement in hindsight because, however distasteful it had been, it had at least 'bought time' for Britain to complete its rearmament against Germany. 'The Munich respite achieved the military salvation of the British Empire,' the Tory MP Quintin Hogg argued in his 1945 book *The Left Was Never Right*.[69] Chamberlain made some remarks in 1938 that could be interpreted in that sense. As he was returning from Munich, he told Halifax that 'while hoping for the best, it is also necessary to prepare for the worst'.[70] Some of his senior military advisers had also suggested before the conference that extending the peace would buy useful time. 'If war with Germany has to come,' wrote Colonel Hastings 'Pug' Ismay, secretary to the Committee of Imperial Defence, on 20 September 1938, 'it would be better to fight her in say six- to twelve-months' time, than to accept the present challenge.'[71]

But if Chamberlain did think he was buying time at Munich, it was less about putting Britain in a better condition to go to war with Germany in the future than about creating a space in which the *Führer* would finally come to his senses, or at least about giving someone more chances to assassinate him.[72] Chamberlain's aim was not to fight a war with Hitler on more favourable terms, but to avoid fighting one entirely. In an address to a Birmingham audience in April 1938, he had said:

> An ancient historian once wrote of the Greeks that they had made gentle the life of the world. I do not know whether in these modern days it is possible for any nation to emulate the example of the Greeks, but I can imagine no nobler ambition for an English statesman than to win the same tribute for his own country.[73]

Statements such as these are often wielded against Chamberlain as examples of his pitiable naivety. They shouldn't be. There is nothing contemptible about regarding peace as the greatest of all political achievements. Chamberlain, like millions of his contemporaries, had lived through the First World War, then regarded as the most dreadful catastrophe humankind had ever experienced. He was determined to spare his nation and the world another such calamity. His own son Frank was a Territorial artilleryman who would be sent to the front if Britain fought Germany again. War was an issue that involved him as a father as well as a statesman.[74]

Detesting war is not a failing. Even Churchill, a man far more comfortable with the practices of state violence than Chamberlain ever was, sometimes found himself overwhelmed by the moral consequences of his actions. 'Are we beasts?' he once asked out loud while watching an Air Ministry film of an immolated *Stadt* during the Second World War. 'Are we taking this too far?' Chamberlain's error was not to hate war, but to assume that everyone else hated it as much as he did.

War's moral cost was only part of the issue, however. Chamberlain was a proud and anxious patriot. He believed in the essential goodness of the British Empire. He also believed that the Empire was not strong enough to withstand the stresses of another conflict against a power like Germany. 'I must in any given situation,' he once said, 'be sure in my own mind that the cost of war is not greater than the price of peace.'[75] In 1938 Herbert von Dirksen, the German ambassador in London, wrote a memorandum to his superiors in Berlin arguing that Chamberlain would never declare war on the Third Reich, no matter what the provocation, because he knew that 'the social structures of Britain, even the conception of the British Empire, would not survive the chaos of *even a victorious war*'.[76] Dirksen was, as the events of September 1939 proved, wrong. But he had caught an essential truth about the prime minister all the same. Chamberlain believed that any repetition of the First World War would be calamitous for Britain. It could and probably would beat Germany in the end, but it would be bankrupted in the process, with its imperial authority sharply abridged and its ability to serve as one of the great benign stabilising forces across the globe permanently shrunken. It would never emerge from victory the same again. There would only be two real winners in such a war, the Soviet Union and the USA. Their victory would leave the world much worse off.[77]

Chamberlain's fears about the rise of the USSR probably do not need spelling out. 'I must confess to the most profound mistrust of Russia,' he once wrote: 'I distrust her motives which seem to me to have little connection to our idea of liberty.'[78] His feelings about the United States need, perhaps, a little more explanation. Chamberlain was not an instinctive Americophobe. He believed that 'Americans and the British want the same fundamental things in the world'.[79] But he distrusted the United States' willingness to act on its principles and its capability to perform global responsibilities. He remembered 1919, after all. 'The real trouble with Yanks,' he said, was that they could 'never deliver the goods'. Chamberlain found Roosevelt's high-minded waffling about the dangers of dictatorship in the 1930s irritating, since the American president never showed the slightest willingness to do anything about it. 'It is always best and safest to count on nothing from the Americans except words,' he sniped in October 1937.[80]

Chamberlain understood that America's interests and those of his own country, while overlapping to some extent, were far from identical. The United States had economic designs on Britain's traditional world market-places. Its leaders would have no compunction about leveraging the circumstances of another world war to achieve those designs. That was why American involvement in a war against Germany would be such a double-edged sword. 'Heaven knows I don't want the Americans to fight for us,' he told Ida in January 1940. 'We should have to pay too dearly for that if they had a right to be in on the peace terms.'[81]

This point is often lost on modern Americans, who are a little too fond of dragging Chamberlain from the grave to serve as a symbol of naivety and cowardice, flattering themselves and their own fortitude in comparison. The United States was going to have a very fortunate Second World War. Its two oceanic buffer zones were an enormous privilege, allowing it to delay its entry into the conflict until the worst years of Allied military inferiority were over. America enjoyed victory at a remarkably low cost in human life and material destruction compared with that of its allies. It emerged in 1945 with its wealth and power not only undiminished but greatly enhanced. It had the inestimable advantage, in other words, of fighting a just war from which it also profited. It does not take any great moral courage to look back from a vantage point like that and feel it was all worth the risk. The outcome of the Second World War is a matter of historical record, and, from the American point of view, a highly appealing one.

Imagine, however, if the cost of 'standing up to Hitler' in 1938 had been the United States ceding Alaska to the Russians and California to Mexico, emptying Fort Knox's vaults, breaking the Wall Street banks, bankrupting General Motors and permanently reducing the United States to the rank of a second-rate regional power. Would Americans still be so glibly enthusiastic about their grandparents and great-grandparents 'taking a firm stand'? Chamberlain knew that the British Empire would have to pay a terrible price to beat the Nazis. It may be that the price was worth paying. It may be that that Empire that was sacrificed as payment was doomed anyway or not worth saving. But neither Chamberlain nor Churchill believed that. Of the two men, it was, perhaps, the former who was the more realistic about what another war would necessitate.

But – and this was von Dirksen's great error – Chamberlain also seems to have understood Macaulay's warning that 'governments, like men, may buy existence too dear'.[82] Great Powers need more than just bullion and coaling stations to survive. They need self-respect too. They need to believe in themselves. Appeasing Hitler meant sacrificing a good deal of that self-respect. Up to a certain point, that may have been a prudent calculation. But eventually a line had to be drawn. By 3 September 1939 it was no longer rational to keep conciliating the Nazis just to try to eke out a few more twilight years of imperial power. It would have been base. It would have been unworthy of the traditions of a great nation.

Chamberlain had personally had to sacrifice much of his own self-respect in a desperate, doomed bid to convince Hitler that another war would be a futile, self-destructive madness for Germany as well as Britain. But perhaps it had been worth it. It's important to appreciate the moral legitimacy that Chamberlain's efforts in 1938 gave Britain's decision to fight a year later. The 'piece of paper' signed by Hitler which the prime minister brought back with him to London from Munich is dismissed today as an example of Chamberlain's pathetic credulity. But this misses its point. Chamberlain hoped that Hitler would keep his promise to pursue his future diplomatic goals peacefully. But if he broke it, 'he would demonstrate to all the world that he was totally cynical and untrustworthy, and this would have its value in mobilising public opinion against him, particularly in America.'[83]

By exposing Hitler as a liar, Chamberlain demonstrated once and for all that Britain had no choice but to fight. The Second World War began in September 1939 with a moral clarity that would have been absent if it had broken out a year earlier over the Sudetenland. A war over Czechoslovakia would have divided the British people, the British Empire and the international community. Its first act would have been an imperial crisis. Canadian public opinion was deeply divided on the issue, and even if Canada had ultimately joined in, its home front would have been riven with dissent. South Africa, in all probability, would have stayed out.[84] For millions of people in the United States, meanwhile, a war for the Czechs would have looked a lot like just another senseless European squabble that they were well advised to keep out of. It would have been even harder for President Roosevelt to revise the various restrictions of the Neutrality Acts to assist the Allies than it turned out to be in 1939 – and that was hard enough.

Chamberlain's appeasement efforts failed. But in failing they also demonstrated to the world that he and the British nation had gone to every reasonable length to try to prevent a conflict with Hitler. 'No man can say that the Government could have done more to try to keep open the way for an honourable and equitable settlement of the dispute between Germany and Poland,' Chamberlain told the Commons on the day Hitler's Panzers crossed the Danzig frontier:

> Nor have we neglected any means of making it crystal clear to the German Government that if they insisted on using force again in the manner in which they had used it in the past we were resolved to oppose them by force [...] we shall stand at the bar of history knowing that the responsibility for this terrible catastrophe lies on the shoulders of one man – the German Chancellor, who has not hesitated to plunge the world into misery in order to serve his own senseless ambitions.[85]

Whatever moral confusion was to come later, the essential justice of the war was not in doubt from its first day. That advantage, at least, Chamberlain had secured for his country.

9

THE SHARPENING OF THE CLAWS

There are two things that everyone thinks they know about Neville Chamberlain. One is that he appeased Hitler. The other is that he neglected Britain's military defences. Chamberlain, the argument goes, shamefully ignored his country's need for military preparations in the years immediately before the Second World War, thus precipitating the disasters of 1940. 'Cato', writing shortly after the Allied collapse in France, placed the blame for the defeat squarely at the former prime minister's feet. *Guilty Men* condemned the 'leisurely manner' in which Chamberlain's government had rearmed during the late 1930s while the Nazis had been 'spending prodigiously' on armaments.[1] 'The soldiers of Britain had insufficient tanks and airplanes to protect them' at Dunkirk, claimed 'Cato', 'for the simple reason that insufficient money had been spent to buy them.'[2]

Guilty Men's coruscating accusations became orthodoxy after the war. In 1948's *The Gathering Storm*, Churchill recalled the whole interwar epoch as 'one of the awful periods which recur in our history, when the noble British nation [...] appears to cower from the menace of foreign peril, frothing pious platitudes while foemen forge their arms'. Much, he insisted, 'could have been done to make us better prepared and thus lessen our hazards' in the years leading up to the war. Chamberlain's naive trust in Hitler's good intentions and his fusty Victorian obsession with sound finance had, it seemed, combined to almost catastrophic effect. Chamberlain himself, long dead by 1948, was in no position to protest.

Yet if you had taken a walk through, say, Birkenhead on the northern tip of the Wirral peninsula ten years before *The Gathering Storm* was published, you would have seen a riot of martial activity. By the summer of 1938 more than 10,000 men were working in Cammell Laird shipbuilders' vast North and Tranmere Bay yards, within sight of the great port of Liverpool on the other side of the Mersey estuary. They teemed across the scaffolds and steel derricks, the noisy, smoke-blackened machine shops, the engine and boiler works, the timber yards, the sawmills and the smithies that stretched for acres along the estuary shoreline. At that moment Cammell Laird's slipways were packed with vessels contracted by the Royal Navy. Greatest of these new weapons of war rising on the Mersey skyline was the 35,000-ton battleship HMS *Prince of Wales*, one of five vessels of the King George V class under construction across the UK. Close by *Prince of Wales*, in Cammell Laird's fifteen-acre fitting-out basin, was HMS *Ark Royal*, the first aircraft carrier commissioned by the Royal Navy since 1924, and, at that moment, the most expensive warship the British government had ever built.[3]

All this activity along the Mersey, impressive in itself, represented just a fraction of the work being done under contract to the Royal Navy elsewhere in the UK in the summer of 1938 – at yards like Armstrong Whitworth and Swan Hunter on Tyneside, John Brown and Fairfield on Clydeside, Harland and Wolff in Belfast and the royal dockyards in Plymouth and Chatham. In addition to the five King George V class battleships, six even larger capital ships of the new Lion class were in the planning stage, with two of them about to be laid down (the second of these, HMS *Temeraire*, at Cammell Laird).[4] Six more aircraft carriers were being built to join HMS *Ark Royal*. Construction had begun on twenty-three cruisers, fifty-two destroyers, nine submarines and nine escort and patrol vessels. Britain had the largest, most ambitious maritime building programme of any nation in the world on the eve of the Second World War.

New tonnage was not the only measure of this naval rearmament. Although most of the Royal Navy's fifteen existing battleships had been built a generation earlier, between 1936 and 1939 five of them were chosen for extensive refitting, which meant essentially reconstructing them from scratch with new engines and boilers, armour, superstructures, fire control systems and anti-aircraft batteries. ASDIC (sonar), the sound propagation device for detecting submerged objects, which in 1938 seemed, at least, to have rendered the oceans transparent and the submarine threat to merchant trade insignificant, had been installed in most British destroyers and escort vessels. By the outbreak of war two Royal Navy vessels had already been fitted with experimental aircraft detection RDF ('Radio Direction Finding', or radar) systems. Others were awaiting their RDF refits.[5]

And the Royal Navy was not even the greatest beneficiary of military spending. By 1939 the Royal Air Force (RAF), now the *primus inter pares* of the British armed services, had risen to first place in defence expenditure.

At the outbreak of the Second World War the RAF's metropolitan forces consisted of thirty-three operational bomber squadrons and thirty-seven fighter squadrons, twenty-nine of the latter equipped with the latest monoplane interceptors, the Hawker Hurricane and the Supermarine Spitfire. RAF Fighter Command already possessed 670 Hurricanes and Spitfires, with another seventy-six of these state-of-the-art single-engine aircraft arriving from the factories every month. Plans were already under way to completely re-equip the RAF's two-engine bomber squadrons with much heavier four-engine planes. The first of the new 'heavies', the Short Stirling, had already made its inaugural test flight, and the Handley Page Halifax was only a few weeks away from doing so. In preparation for the arrival of the heavies, thirty-seven new airfields had already been constructed in Yorkshire, Lincolnshire and East Anglia, their locations reflecting the need for short flying times across the North Sea to attack targets in Germany.

Defensively, the RAF could now rely on twenty-one 'Chain Home' stations along the southern and eastern coastline of England to provide early warning of enemy raiders by RDF technology. A parallel 'Chain Home Low' system, to detect low-flying aircraft, was also being prepared. This early warning data could be transmitted by landline to Fighter Command's headquarters at Bentley Priory, near Harrow in north-western London, the hub of a revolutionary command and control system which, it was hoped, would maximise the efficiency of the air defences of Great Britain should war break out.[6]

Even that perennial Cinderella service the British Army, traditionally an afterthought where the country's military spending was concerned, was expanding rapidly by September 1939. That March the secretary of state for war had announced the doubling in size of the part-time Territorial Army (TA) from thirteen to twenty-six divisions. Then, the following month, peacetime conscription had been introduced for the first time in modern British history, with 35,000 young 'militiamen' selected for an initial six-month training programme. The Cabinet had approved the construction of a thirty-two-division force to be available for deployment no later than twelve months after the outbreak of a major European war – a force that would require up to 3 million soldiers. It had created a new Ministry of Supply to organise the production of the vast quantities of weapons, ammunition, vehicles, radios, uniforms and other stores that this mass army would need.

Moreover, this was to be a modern army equipped for the age of petrol rather than horses. Its excellent new 25-pounder field guns would arrive on the battlefield on motorised gun tractors, its infantrymen in lorries and armoured personnel carriers. All but a few of the regular and part-time yeomanry cavalry regiments would be mechanised by the outbreak of war. The Royal Tank Regiment (RTR) was about to receive deliveries of a new medium tank, the Matilda II, which had heavier armour than anything possessed by the German Panzer divisions of 1939.

In summary: Britain on the eve of the Second World War was undergoing the greatest peacetime military expansion in its history. To the journalist Philip Gibbs, Britain was no longer a land of peaceful Shire Folk but a country embarked on a 'colossal programme' of rearmament.[7] Its costs were remarkable. Over £284 million in government-ordered defence works – munitions and aircraft factories, airfields and port facilities, repair depots, stores, training camps and barracks – were under construction. Total combined annual expenditures on the armed services had more than tripled from £107 million to £383 million between 1933 and 1938.[8] By the summer of 1939 the government estimated that it would spend £730 million on defence by the end of the year. That was almost as much as the entire central government budget had been back in 1933. Such figures were, as the *Times* put it, 'monumental'.[9] The MP and playwright Stephen King-Hall was astounded at the 'vast sums' being spent on rearmament.[10] The government had committed to borrowing £800 million for a total rearmament programme that was now approaching £2 billion. So frantic was the pace that the Treasury was warning that if the rate of military expenditure did not slow down soon, the country was nine months away from a major financial crisis. And the warlord presiding over this military-industrial complex? Neville Chamberlain.[11]

*

Indeed, throughout the 1930s Chamberlain was routinely accused of being a belligerent sabre-rattler. His critics charged that he was accruing weapons of mass destruction simply for their own malevolent sake. Herbert Morrison, leader of London County Council, protested in 1935 that the government would only 'spend on the means of death, not on the means of life'.[12] To Labour MP Philip Noel-Baker in July 1936, the National Government's military spending was 'a race to destruction which can only have one end unless we stop it very soon'.[13] Major James Milner, another

Labour parliamentarian, called Chamberlain's military budget 'aggressive in character and provocative to the last degree'.[14] In February 1937 Aneurin Bevan wrote in the socialist journal *Tribune* that the Labour Party should oppose the government's armament plans 'root and branch'. Following the *Anschluss*, Stafford Cripps called Britain's military spending 'mad'.[15] After Munich, Cripps added that the 'new-found dove of peace' Chamberlain was really more interested in 'a sharpening of the claws'.[16] 'Neville annoys me by mouthing the arguments of complete pacifism while piling up armaments,' Clement Attlee complained as late as February 1939.[17]

This was an odd situation for Chamberlain to find himself in, because, unlike Churchill, he genuinely lacked any instinctive appetite for military spending. The prospect of playing at soldiers gave Chamberlain no schoolboy thrill. He retained throughout his life a Victorian liberal businessman's conviction that public money spent on defence was money that ought to be better spent in other ways. It was 'a sad, mad world' in which the earnings of virtuous British taxpayers had to be lavished on useless munitions, simply to 'frighten the Germans into keeping the peace'.[18] The effect of heavier military spending, he wrote in the spring of 1938, would be 'to set back the date of recovery and to add to the burdens of our people'.[19] The very idea 'that the hard-won savings of our people [...] should have to be dissipated upon the construction of weapons of war is hateful and damnable'.[20]

But by the late 1930s Chamberlain had accepted that he had little choice, given the threat that a reviving Germany represented to British security. Indeed, when it came to the challenge of the Third Reich, he had been among the first of the National Government's politicians to call for extensive military rearmament. In November 1932, before Hitler even came to power, Chamberlain was already warning the rest of the Cabinet that pacifist calls for wide-scale European disarmament were 'a gamble [...] on German good faith' that seemed naive without some tangible evidence of Berlin's honest intentions.[21] By the autumn of 1933, with the Nazis having seized control in Germany and withdrawn their country from the League of Nations, any hopes of good faith no longer seemed realistic. It was, Chamberlain thought, mere 'common prudence' to strengthen Britain's defences.[22] 'We are giving too much attention to the details of disarmament and not enough to security,' he warned.[23]

In the spring of 1934 Chamberlain argued vigorously and successfully for the Cabinet Defence Requirements sub-Committee (DRC), which had been established to consider security priorities, to focus its spending proposals on the German air threat to the United Kingdom rather than the Japanese threat to the Far East. This did not go down well with some of his colleagues. Maurice Hankey, the DRC's chairman, grumbled that Chamberlain was 'over obsessed with the threat from Germany'. The First Sea Lord, Ernle Chatfield, believed that the chancellor had 'taken the *Daily Mail* propaganda very much to heart' and seemed 'convinced' that Britain and Germany would go to war within a few years.[24] Chamberlain was unmoved. 'Hitler's Germany is the bully of Europe', he wrote to his sister Hilda in March 1935.[25]

That summer, in the face of Germany's reintroduction of military conscription and the creation of the Luftwaffe, Chamberlain put it to his Cabinet colleagues that the National Government should take the 'bold course' of fighting the general election due the coming winter on a platform of greater defence spending. The British public needed to be educated to understand the danger the Nazis represented. Germany, he wrote in his diary, 'is said to be borrowing over 1,000 millions a year to get herself rearmed [...] therefore we must hurry our own rearmament'. Britain needed to be 'strong enough to make it impossible for her wishes to be flouted'.[26] Baldwin, worried that the electorate would react badly if a rearmament programme featured too visibly in the campaign, chose to soft-pedal the issue. On the hustings Chamberlain argued for it anyway, provoking Labour's deputy leader, Arthur Greenwood – the very man who would take it on himself to 'speak for England' in September 1939 – to accuse the chancellor of the exchequer of 'the merest scaremongering, disgraceful in a statesman'.[27]

By May 1938 Chamberlain was conscious that the government's early rearmament efforts against Hitler had not been ambitious enough. 'The Germans who are bullies by nature are too conscious of their strength and our weakness [...] until we are as strong as they are we shall be kept in this state of chronic anxiety.'[28] That October, following the Munich conference, he noted that Britain would have to spend yet more on rearmament if it was to improve its credibility in any future negotiations with the Germans. 'Weakness in armed strength,' he observed, 'means weakness in diplomacy.'[29] In a letter to Lord Ponsonby, one of the leaders of the pacifist Peace Pledge Union, in February 1939 he declared that 'The stakes are so big, the existence of the British Empire as we have known it, that I dare not gamble them on trust in the pacific intentions of the dictators.'[30]

All in all, if advocacy of early rearmament against the Nazis is taken as the benchmark of wisdom in a 1930s politician, then Neville Chamberlain comes out looking rather good – certainly much better than most of his peers.

*

What, specifically, did Chamberlain want to see in a British rearmament programme? In many respects his core assumptions did not change all that much throughout the 1930s.

It needed to be directed primarily against Germany. Chamberlain, as a good imperialist, was not unaware of the dangers posed by Italy in the Mediterranean and Japan in the Far East. But he believed that Germany was by far the most powerful of all the British Empire's potential enemies. If Hitler could be deterred, then neither the Italians nor the Japanese would ever dare strike against Britain alone. For that reason, as much rearmament spending as possible ought to be directed against the primary threat in central Europe. That was the argument he used to challenge the DRC's proposal in 1934 to spend money on a new battleship fleet to be based in Singapore.[31] 'If the Admiralty were to advise that capital ships would be needed in a war against Germany,' Chamberlain told the Cabinet, he 'would accept that advice with the expenditure it involved.'[32] But building ships specifically in response to a Japanese threat was, he argued, a waste of resources. The Japanese would only ever risk attacking Britain's colonies in the Far East if Germany attacked first. After Hitler began constructing the Kriegsmarine in March 1935, Chamberlain recognised this as a primary threat to control of the home waters around the British Isles and agreed to a large-scale Royal Navy rearmament programme.

It had to be palatable to the electorate. The 1930s was the decade in which the members of the Oxford Union voted that they would 'in no circumstances fight for King and Country', in which 10 million participants in the League of Nations 'Peace Ballot' voted in favour of a worldwide reduction in armaments, in which Canon Dick Sheppard's Peace Pledge Union persuaded 135,000 young men to make a public commitment that they would never fight in another war. Peace candidates critical of the National Government's rearmament efforts did well in several by-elections in 1933 and 1934 – at Clay Cross, Fulham East (the disastrous result of which was later used by Baldwin to justify his decision to back-pedal on rearmament at the 1935 general election), Skipton and Cambridge.

Too much should not be read into any of these things. Chamberlain said that he 'did not lose a minute's sleep' over the defeat at Fulham East.[33] Still, he understood a need for caution. The public, he recognised, had an 'almost instinctive aversion from large-scale military preparations' in the mid-1930s.[34] Thoughtful mass education on the issue was necessary. What worried Chamberlain was that if the rearmament question was botched by demanding more than the electorate was yet willing to accept, then the National Government's parliamentary majority might be placed in jeopardy – and Chamberlain had no trust at all that the Labour Party, with its simultaneous (and to his mind incoherent) embrace of disarmament and collective security, could manage the threat from Hitler responsibly.

It had to be as cheap as possible. We will come back to this later. It's important to note now, however, that Chamberlain's desire for economy was not just the small-minded penny-pinching of the 'simple-minded businessman' that some of his snobbier critics accused him of being.[35] His concerns about the long-term relationship between the nation's military and financial security went much deeper than that.

The purpose of rearmament was deterrence, not war-fighting. He expressed this to Ida in a letter in July 1939:

> The longer war is put off the less likely it is to come at all as we go on perfecting our defences [...] that is what Winston & Co. never seem to realise. You don't need offensive forces sufficient to win a smashing victory. What you want are defensive forces sufficiently strong to make it impossible for the other side to win except at such a cost as to make it not worthwhile.[36]

Chamberlain did not want to prepare Britain for another world war. He wanted to prevent another world war from taking place at all. That was because he was convinced that, even if Britain won such a war, its cost would be so shattering as to wreck the country's standing as the leading global power. The proper application of rearmament moneys, then, was to build up a visible deterrent force for diplomatic, rather than strictly military, purposes. It was to create a deterrent 'so powerful as to render success in attack too doubtful to be worthwhile', and by doing so persuade Hitler, or any other would-be aggressor, that a war against the British Empire could not possibly be won, and that mutual negotiation was the only policy that could ever get them what they wanted.[37] Chamberlain always accepted the possibility that Britain might have to go to war if an enemy power like

Germany simply refused to see sense. But he gambled on the assumption that even a seeming fanatic such as the *Führer* was still bound by the basic rules of rational self-interest. Hitler, mercurial though he might appear, was surely capable of seeing that war was too costly to be worth it.

Rearmament should be a process with a definite end-point, rather than a new national way of life. Chamberlain wanted to avoid a 'hot' fighting war. But he wanted almost as much to avoid an interminable Cold War stand-off with Germany too – one in which the two sides, while nominally at peace, spent ever-increasing amounts of their national wealth building up armaments against one another. Such preparations would, he believed, bankrupt Britain even if no war ever broke out. Certainly, they would transform the country's economy and society in ways that were hateful to him. That is why Chamberlain believed that appeasement was the natural parallel policy to rearmament. Each complemented and reinforced the other. Successful deterrence would convince Hitler that the only way to resolve his grievances was at the negotiating table. Successful appeasement would resolve those grievances, and so reduce the need for further costly deterrence. Chamberlain's hope was that this virtuous circle would produce an authentic peace rather than merely a ruinous balance of terror.

*

What all this meant in practice was a rearmament programme that, from 1934 until the spring of 1939 anyway, strongly emphasised naval and air power – especially air power – while treating land power as a third, and rather regrettable, adjunct to these two.

British naval rearmament did not get off to a quick start. Battleship construction in the first half of the 1930s was restricted by the proscriptions of the Washington and London naval treaties with the United States and Japan, which had imposed a 'holiday' forbidding new vessels to be built. Even after the holiday ended in 1936, the Admiralty did not get Treasury approval to build to the 'Two Power Standard' it really wanted, which would have authorised it to create a surface fleet equal to Germany's and Japan's combined. Still, by September 1939 the Royal Navy had fifteen battleships to the Kriegsmarine's two (five if the small German 'pocket battleships' are counted), and enjoyed an enormous overall advantage in cruisers, destroyers and lighter craft. There were deficiencies, some of which – in maritime trade escort vessels and naval aviation especially

– were to prove dangerous later on. Nonetheless, with its King George V class battleships and Illustrious class aircraft carriers all approaching completion at the moment war broke out, the Admiralty had reason to be fairly satisfied with the balance of European naval power. If Britannia and her allies did not entirely rule the world's waves any longer, the crucial North Atlantic and Mediterranean lanes of communication at least were under their control.

It was the RAF, though, which really enjoyed Chamberlain's favour throughout the 1930s. He was an adamant airpower enthusiast. Under his direction, initially from the Treasury and later from Downing Street, the RAF's share of British annual defence expenditure rose from £16.7 million in 1933 to £143 million by 1938, from third place in the Forces pecking order to first.[38] Writing to his sisters in May 1935, Chamberlain described how he had insisted to the rest of the Cabinet 'on the need for such a recasting of our air programme as would show its truly formidable character and thus act as a deterrent'.[39] He called airpower 'a factor of first-rate, if not decisive importance'.[40]

Chamberlain's belief that air power had become the dominant new medium of military force was a popular one. The image that haunted the minds of millions of people when they thought about a future war was not a repeat of the trench fighting of the previous conflict but rather a 'knock-out blow' – a massive aerial onslaught by bomber planes, not against armies on the battlefield but against defenceless towns and cities, 'sudden rapid, and overwhelming [...] as impossible to predict as it [would be] to resist'.[41] London had already experienced such a blow in nascent form during the First World War, and though its physical effects had been primitive, it had terrified the capital's population all the same. By the mid-1930s fast mono-plane bombers had replaced the crude Zeppelins and Gothas of twenty years earlier. The possibilities of aerial apocalypse seemed far more dreadful than ever. Newsreel audiences had seen the pitiless bombing of civilians in China and Spain. An attack on Britain might use poison gas and incendi-ary firebombs as well as high explosive. In *War on Great Cities*, published in 1938, Frank Morison imagined a million Londoners suffocating to death in the opening hours of a Second World War as enemy aircraft seeded toxic clouds across the capital. This, he warned his readers, was 'no fanciful picture' but a frightful possibility.[42]

Official strategic planning documents were scarcely less alarmist. In October 1936 the chiefs of staff's Joint Planning Committee (JPC) drew up a draft report for the Cabinet of what an air war might look like, given a few more years of Luftwaffe rearmament. Its message was grim:

> We are [...] convinced that Germany would plan to gain her victory rapidly. Her first attacks would be designed as knock-out blows [...] in a war against us the concentration, from the first day of war, of the whole German air offensive ruthlessly against Great Britain would be possible. It would be the most promising way of trying to knock this country out.

The JPC's report forecast casualties of up to 150,000 people by the end of the first week of such a campaign, with hundreds of thousands more after a month. Food supplies to the capital would cease as infrastructure failed. Public morale and civil order would collapse; 'angry and frightened mobs of civilians' demanding an immediate ceasefire would attack RAF bases. A sudden strike from the air 'might well succeed' in defeating Britain in just a few weeks without the need for any land or naval operations at all.[43] The government took it as axiomatic throughout the 1930s that the main German threat to Britain was from the skies. As Sir Thomas Inskip, minister for co-ordination of defence from 1936 to 1939, put it, it was 'generally recognised' that 'the greatest danger against which we have to provide is attack from the air on the United Kingdom, designed to inflict a knock-out blow at the initial stage of a war'.[44]

Professional opinion was divided as to how the RAF could best deter such a knock-out blow. Most senior airmen believed that defence preparations were futile, because the bomber, as Stanley Baldwin famously put it, 'would always get through'. The only option was deterrence rather than defence: to build a counter-offensive bombing force so powerful that it would be able to launch a retaliatory knock-out blow of its own against Germany's cities and people, one at least as devastating as the threat that faced Britain. This echoed the all-offensive ethos established by the founding Chief of the Air Staff, Sir Hugh Trenchard, that 'the aeroplane as a weapon of attack cannot be too highly estimated'. Trenchard's mantra continued to resound throughout the halls of RAF Cranwell (the new service's officer training college) and the Air Ministry in the 1930s.[45]

Not every airman – nor all politicians – subscribed to this view. They believed, *pace* Trenchard, that attacking bombers might be vulnerable to intercepting fighter aircraft and anti-aircraft defences. If the Air Defence of

Great Britain (ADGB) was visibly formidable, the Germans could be made to realise that any attempt at a knock-out blow would fail.

Arguments about the pros and cons of defence versus deterrence went on throughout the 1930s. The all-bomber advocates largely held sway until early 1938, after which supporters of greater ADGB spending gained some ground. But these were considerations of detail. From a budgetary point of view, the issue was not whether Britain should build fighters or bombers. The issue was that, either way, it was primarily the RAF that would be needed to put the strategy into practice. Air power – 'the most formidable deterrent to war that could be devised', in Chamberlain's words – ought properly to receive the lion's share of rearmament funds.[46]

Where did that leave the Army? So far as Chamberlain was concerned, nowhere very much at all. He argued consistently for Army spending to be given the lowest priority of all the armed services. In particular, he objected vociferously to any proposal to man and equip a 'field force' to cross the Channel and fight in continental Europe alongside the French. In the summer of 1934 Chamberlain successfully scotched the DRC's attempt to create a five-division-strong field force.[47]

He was unable to veto a similar proposal when it resurfaced in early 1936. But shortly after becoming prime minister the following year, Chamberlain asked Sir Thomas Inskip to conduct a comprehensive survey of defence needs. Inskip's report of December 1937 quashed the European field force notion completely. Absolute priority, Inskip decided, was to be given to spending on anti-aircraft guns instead. The Army's task, such as it was, was to man imperial garrisons overseas and to maintain a small contingency force for operations in Egypt to deter the Italians from any designs on the Suez Canal. The generals looked on askance. 'The Cabinet, in a muddled kind of way, are terrified of making an expeditionary force [for Europe]' wrote General Sir Edmund Ironside, then the king's aide-de-camp, in his diary in the last days of December 1937:

> They dread a continental commitment [... they] also think that the Air Force can finish a campaign. They are terrified now of a war being finished in a few weeks by the annihilation of Great Britain. They can see no other kind of danger than air attack.[48]

Chamberlain argued that a field force would be so unpopular with the electorate it would discredit the whole idea of rearmament. The public, he argued, was 'strongly opposed to Continental adventures'. Inskip agreed: there was a 'universal unwillingness' among the British people to prepare the Army for European operations as in the First World War.[49] There was much less public opposition to spending on the RAF or on ADGB measures. Framing rearmament as a way to prevent a knock-out blow made it much more palatable to the democratic masses terrified of war.

Chamberlain also believed that his opposition to a field force reflected cutting-edge military science. In this he relied on the writings of Basil Liddell Hart, the most influential public commentator on defence matters in inter-war Britain. Liddell Hart was a gifted author of popular history, a tireless writer of letters (the catalogue of his papers lists 780 major correspondents alone) and a shameless self-publicist who rarely missed an opportunity to hawk his own intellectual brand. If he were alive today, he would have an award-winning YouTube channel and a couple of million Twitter followers. As it was, his position as a journalist, first for the *Daily Telegraph* and later for *The Times*, not to mention his many publications, public talks and prestigious contacts, gave him a privileged opportunity to influence the elite debate on rearmament. Chamberlain was in correspondence with Liddell Hart by 1937, and that same year he recommended the author's newest book, *Europe in Arms*, to his new secretary of state for war, Leslie Hore-Belisha. The introduction led to Liddell Hart becoming an *éminence grise* at the War Office, albeit a short-lived one.[50]

After the Second World War, Liddell Hart would claim with considerable success (and with the insincere co-operation of several ex-Nazi generals) that he had invented the *Blitzkrieg* methods of fast, mobile breakthrough warfare that were used so spectacularly by the Germans in 1940. This was, to say the least, disingenuous. He had certainly argued strongly for the mechanisation of armies in the 1930s. But what he later chose to forget was that, at the time, he believed mechanisation strongly favoured *defence*, not offence. Books like *Europe in Arms* argued that in a future war 'the machine-gun obstacle, intensified by wire entanglements and land minefields, will still have to be overcome [...] is there any more chance of success than in the last war? The contrary, rather.' Liddell Hart suggested that the prospect of rapid victory for land armies in a future European war was 'a dull one'. Germany's new Panzer divisions might fare well enough against an army inadequately equipped with modern anti-tank weapons and armoured vehicles of its own, but 'There is cause for doubt whether the German Army has yet developed either the equipment or the tactics to solve the problems created by the strong and thoroughly modern defence.'[51]

None of this was going to look very prophetic a few years later. In 1937, though, it provided Chamberlain with another argument against a British field force. There was no need to send British troops to the continent to aid the French because, unlike in 1914, the French army, safe behind its border fortifications, would be more than capable of handling the German army by itself. Perhaps the Germans would realise that too, and would focus exclusively on air operations. Either way, as Liddell Hart had put it, 'the balance seems to be heavily against the hope that a British field force on the Continent might have a military effect commensurate with the expense and the risk.' On the other hand, Liddell Hart noted, strategic air bombing offered Britain a new way of projecting power in the third dimension. 'The air force could act from its own shores and could intervene in the first hours' of any future war. 'The promise of such help would be more comfort to a threatened neighbour, and more deterrent to a would-be aggressor, than any force of the 1914 pattern.'[52]

'I cannot believe,' Chamberlain wrote to his sisters, 'that the next war, if it ever comes, will be like the last one.' Finite British resources would be 'more profitably employed in the air and on the sea than in building up great armies'.[53] A field force would be unpopular, expensive and would neither deter German aggression nor prevent it from succeeding if it was carried out. It was a bad bet all round.

*

In the end, Chamberlain's rearmament effort failed in two ways. It failed to deter war, and it failed to prevent the Germans from striking a mortal blow to France in 1940. Were his critics from *Guilty Men* onwards right, then, to declare his military preparations in the 1930s a disaster?

It might be argued that the pace of Chamberlain's rearmament was too slow. In 1936 Germany spent almost three times as much of its Gross National Product (GNP) on armaments as Britain. In 1938, though the gap had started to close, it was still spending over twice as much. Britain had almost caught up by the time of the invasion of Poland, and within a few months of war breaking out it had overtaken Germany.[54] But by then, of course, it was too late to deter. Perhaps, if spending had begun in earnest in 1935 or 1936, the British would have already been well ahead of the

Germans by war's outbreak. Or perhaps there would never have been a war, because Hitler might have been sufficiently overawed by this earlier burst of military production to show greater restraint at the time of the *Anschluss*, or Munich, or Prague.

The fact that Chamberlain did not become prime minister until the spring of 1937 does not exonerate him of this charge. He himself had boasted while he was MacDonald's and then Baldwin's chancellor of the exchequer of his dominance in Cabinet decision-making. No other politician shaped British rearmament policy so fundamentally during the 1930s. If Chamberlain had wanted to spend more money between 1934 and 1937, he could have made it happen. The virtues and deficiencies of Britain's military preparations at the outbreak of the Second World War were his.

Two things need to be borne in mind about the pace of rearmament. One is that money was not the only factor, or even the most important factor, that governed it. Production capacity mattered too: the availability of capital plant and specialist machine tools and, most of all, skilled manpower. This last resource was in short supply in the 1930s. Craftsmen took years to train: they could not simply be pulled from the dole queues. In April 1937 the Ministry of Labour estimated that there would be a need for an additional 70,000 men in skilled engineering trades over the next eighteen months in order to accommodate the growth in armament production. In January 1938 Vickers-Armstrongs advertised positions for 800 skilled men at its torpedo and tank plants at Scotswood and Elswick on Depression-hit Tyneside. Despite the high local unemployment rate, they were only able to engage nineteen suitable applicants.[55] The building trade was badly short of experienced bricklayers and other skilled workmen for constructing airfields and factories.

The manpower bottleneck could be widened in two ways. One was to redirect existing industry away from civilian production towards rearmament. The other was to expand the engineering and building trades by adding lower-skilled men to – 'diluting' – the workforce. The first of these, however, risked disrupting the peacetime economy, reducing living standards and jeopardising the balance of trade, while the second could only work with the co-operation of the trade unions, which were suspicious that dilution was really a ploy to dump unqualified workers into the labour pool to depress wages. It didn't help that the Amalgamated Engineering Union (AEU), the most important of the unions in the engineering industry, had a particularly fractious relationship with its management. At the time of the *Anschluss*, Chamberlain appealed to Walter Citrine, general secretary of the Trades Union Congress (TUC), to intervene to try to craft a dilution agreement with the AEU. But though Citrine was personally sympathetic towards the government's problem, the final document was not signed until four days before Germany's invasion of Poland.

The government could have simply bypassed these problems by taking control of national manpower and resource supply, as it eventually did during wartime. But taking such a drastic peremptory step in peacetime would have set off a major political crisis. It would have seemed like the act of a dictator. Creating a command economy was precisely the kind of creeping totalitarianism that Chamberlain thought Britain was supposed to be against.[56]

The second thing we need to remember about the pace of rearmament is that Chamberlain believed that Britain's fundamental security lay not in weapons but in sound finance. 'If we were to follow Winston's advice and sacrifice our commerce to the manufacture of arms,' he wrote in October 1936, 'we would inflict a certain injury to our trade from which it would take generations to recover. We should destroy the confidence which now so happily exists, and we should cripple the revenue.'[57]

This was not simply Victorian tight-fistedness. It was a coherent theory of the economy as a 'fourth arm of defence', a phrase coined by Sir Thomas Inskip, but which reflected Chamberlain's own views equally well. In his December 1937 report on rearmament Inskip set out the logic of this 'fourth arm':

> Our real resources consist not of money [...] but of our manpower and productive capacity, our power to maintain our credit, and the general balance of our trade. Owing to its shortage of native raw materials and foodstuffs, this country is particularly dependent upon imports which have to be paid for and can only be paid for if the volume of our export trade is not impaired. This factor of the general balance of our trade is closely connected with our credit. The amount of money which we can borrow without inflation is mainly dependent upon two factors: the savings of the country as a whole which are available for investment, and the maintenance of confidence in our financial stability. But these savings would be reduced and confidence would at once be weakened by any substantial disturbance of the general balance of trade. While if we were to raise sums in excess

of the sums available in the market, the result would be inflation; i.e. a general rise in prices which would have an immediate effect upon our export trade.

The maintenance of credit facilities and our general balance of trade are of vital importance, not merely from the point of view of our strength in peace-time, but equally for purposes of war. This country cannot hope to win a war against a major Power by a sudden knock-out blow; on the contrary, for success we must contemplate a long war, in the course of which we should have to mobilise all our resources and those of the Dominions and other countries overseas.

The outcome of a short war would be determined by the military forces on hand at its outset. The outcome of a long war lasting three years or more, however, would be determined by which side could out-manufacture and out-spend the other. Long wars, as Chamberlain put it, were won 'with the reserves of resources and credit', not standing armies.[58]

It was vital, then, to make it clear to an unfriendly power like Germany that it could win neither a short *nor* a long war. British military rearmament would prevent the possibility of Nazi victory in a short war. The way to deter a long war, however, was not to build lots of armaments in peacetime but to possess a self-evidently robust and stable economy more resilient than the Germans' own. The trick was to maintain the proper balance between strength now and strength in the future. Not spending enough on defence in the short term might embolden the Germans to try for a quick knock-out blow. But spending too much would strain the economy by diverting the nation's manufacturing capacity away from exports, threatening the balance of payments and undermining confidence in sterling. This might encourage Hitler to think he could, after all, win a long war. It was dangerous to rearm too slowly *and* too quickly.

What was that right balance? It was a question that Chamberlain's government was never able to answer, because it lacked the information it would have needed to do so. Deterrence strategy is as much a matter of psychology as military force. Perception is all. To deter, you must understand how your opponent subjectively interprets the balance of power, and how it will respond to changing circumstances. To deter the Germans, Britain did not necessarily need an air force literally capable of devastating Germany or fending off a knock-out blow. It only needed to convince Hitler that it had an air force that could do these things.

Yet the British pre-war intelligence community was unable to provide Chamberlain any useful insight into the minds of the Nazi leadership. This is perhaps surprising, given the central place that cloak-and-dagger exploits have occupied in Britain's memory of the Second World War. But the country's intelligence capabilities were disorganised and ineffective in the 1930s. A Joint Intelligence Committee (JIC) was established in 1936 to provide advice at the highest political levels. But in its first years all it did was collate the independent reports of the individual service ministries – even if they contradicted one another – rather than doing what was really needed, which was to provide the politicians and chiefs of staff with a broad synthetic overview of enemy capabilities and intentions. Too much early effort was wasted counting German aircraft and tanks, instead of thinking about how they might be used in a future war. The Secret Intelligence Service's (SIS's) pre-war efforts in continental Europe were a joke. The assistant chief at its key station in The Hague worked for the German intelligence service, the Abwehr, and blew the cover of Britain's two best-placed spies operating in the Nazi government. The RAF considered SIS intelligence on German air power '80% inaccurate'.[59]

Absent any way of evaluating what effect British rearmament was having on the Germans, then, all Chamberlain's government could do was try to catch up with Hitler's own armament spending and hope – wrongly, as it turned out – that its own preoccupation with knock-out blows was shared in Berlin.[60]

Catching up meant spending more and more each year. By late 1937 the fourth arm of defence was having to provide greater and greater funds for the other three. This threatened the fragile economic recovery that the National Government had negotiated since 1931. 'All the elements of danger are here,' Chamberlain fretted to his sister:

> Prices are bounding up now [...] increasing cost of living, jealousy of others' profits, a genuine feeling that things are not fairly shared out and I can see that we might easily run in no time into a series of crippling strikes, ruining our programme, a sharp steepening of costs due to wages increases, leading to the loss of our export trade, a feverish and artificial boom followed by a disastrous slump.

These fears were not imaginary. In the second half of 1937 the cost of rearmament began to upset the balance of payments deficit, which reached

£55 million. The following year proved to be no better. The economy started to overheat as the government pumped unprecedented amounts of money into military manufacturing. Inflation reached 3.4 per cent, a rate that had not been seen since 1920. The pound depreciated from a high of $5.02 to $4.67. British gold reserves fell from £800 million to £500 million. By the time of the Munich conference, Chamberlain was 'oppressed with the sense that the burden of armaments might break our backs'.[61]

Rearmament forced Chamberlain to abandon many of the axioms of Victorian sound finance. In 1937 he announced the floating of a defence loan of £400 million which later doubled, a move that three years earlier he had described as 'the broad road which [leads] to destruction'.[62] He tried to introduce a graduated levy on rearmament profits called the 'National Defence Contribution' as an alternative way of raising funds, but this was too controversial, and he fell back on a 5 per cent fixed rate business tax instead. In the spring of 1938, following the *Anschluss*, Chamberlain asked industry to prioritise defence contracts over civilian export manufacturing, even though this would have a negative effect on the balance of payments. He also increased the basic rate of income tax to 5s. 6d. (27.5 per cent), the same amount it had been at the height of the First World War. The 1939 budget doubled motor taxes and raised tobacco and sugar duties. None of these measures was enough. Military spending kept rising. By 1939, Chamberlain lamented, it had become a 'mockery' to say that Britain still had a peacetime economy.[63]

Indeed, by that point it had become clear that if the country continued spending on defence at the same rate for another twelve months, there would be an economic crisis. Chamberlain's only consolation as he reflected on this grim prognosis was that Germany, presumably, had to be feeling the same kind of strain given its even greater rearmament spending. Hitler had to be approaching a similar moment of decision. What would the German leader decide when the moment came? Chamberlain believed he knew: the *Führer*, on the brink of economic collapse, would reduce his arms budget and scale back his aggressive diplomacy. So the crisis in 1939 was, paradoxically, welcome. This helps to explain Chamberlain's optimistic mood even as the Danzig affair was gathering momentum. 'I can't help thinking [Hitler] is not such a fool as some hysterical people make out,' he told Hilda at the beginning of July.[64] The German leader, he added in another letter three weeks later, had surely concluded by now 'that we mean business and the time is not ripe for the major war [...] I go further and say that the longer the war is put off the less likely it is to come at all [...] at present the German feeling is it is not worthwhile *yet*, [but] they will presently come to realise that it will *never* be worthwhile.'[65]

Six weeks after Chamberlain wrote this, the Wehrmacht invaded Poland. Yet his insight had, in a sense, been correct. The Third Reich *had* reached a crisis point. Where Chamberlain erred was in assuming that Hitler would respond to this crisis as a sensible bourgeois politician like himself would, and retreat into financial orthodoxy. It did not occur to him that there was another, very different means of escape. Earlier in the year Halifax had warned the Cabinet that Hitler might seek a solution to his upcoming dilemma by 'exploding' in some direction, 'to secure by physical force the vast supplies of raw materials which Nazi Germany could no longer procure by legitimate trade'.[66] For Hitler, Germany's economic predicament by 1939 had not made further belligerence impossible. It had made it essential.[67]

*

What if someone like Churchill had overseen rearmament in the 1930s? How much difference would it have made? Presumably he would have tried to spend more money, and sooner. As early as 1932 Churchill was demanding that Britain procure a larger strategic bombing force. In November 1934 he complained that government proposals for RAF expansion were inadequate in the face of Germany's own rearmament. In April 1936 Churchill called for 'state of emergency preparations' in which defence contracts would be prioritised over normal export trade.[68] That July he led a delegation to Downing Street to ask Baldwin to create a Ministry of Supply. In October 1938 his complaints about the 'gross neglect and deficiency in our defences' had become familiar to the Commons.[69]

But if Churchill had tried to move Britain onto a wartime military production schedule in, say, 1936 or 1937, it would have had major political and economic ramifications. The national balance of payments would have been violently upended, domestic consumption curtailed, sterling sent into free fall and Labour and the trade unions provoked into revolt. As Sir Richard Hopkins at the Treasury put it at the time, Churchill was assuming 'a degree of forbearance on the part of the community which would only be forthcoming in the face of grave and imminent emergency' – a condition that did not yet seem to exist.[70]

Perhaps a politician with Churchill's energy, charisma and dynamism could have pulled it off anyway. But it's important to remember that the man attempting this would not have been the revered Churchill of modern-day memory. It would, rather, have been the Churchill who was seen by much of the nation as a reactionary Tory turncoat: the Churchill who had foolishly fought against reform of the Indian government and championed the Nazi-sympathising Edward VIII, the Churchill who had placed Britain disastrously back on the Gold Standard in 1925 and gleefully crushed the workers' General Strike a year later, the Churchill of Gallipoli and the Tonypandy riots, a Churchill, in short, who was widely unpopular and roundly distrusted. He certainly would have cut a more colourful figure as prime minister than the funereal Chamberlain in the 1930s. But there's not much reason to think that, in the absence of a clarifying national emergency, he would have been any more capable of negotiating a major economic and political crisis set off by faster rearmament.

Greater pre-war military spending might have deterred Hitler from war. Or it might have provoked him into war earlier, with consequences for Britain that are impossible to calculate. Or it might have made no difference at all, because in the end Hitler was not interested in being deterred. Victor Davis Hanson claims that the Second World War broke out because the British and French governments in the late 1930s 'lost a sense of the power of deterrence'.[71] But perhaps deterrence was never going to work against Hitler, no matter what they did.[72] The German leader seems to have viewed the prospect of an aerial knock-out blow against Germany with remarkable nonchalance.[73] 'There is no real rearmament in England,' he told his generals on 22 August 1939, 'only propaganda.'[74] That was an extraordinary conclusion to come to on the eve of the invasion of Poland. But then Hitler was simply not interested in seeing things that were inconvenient to him – a political failing in which he was hardly alone.

*

If Chamberlain could not have spent money on rearmament faster, could he have spent it better at least?

Rearmament money had been lavished on RAF Bomber Command, the nation's first line of offence when war broke out in September 1939. Yet on the day the Germans invaded Poland the RAF was incapable of performing the primary task for which all this money had been spent. As the official history of the strategic bombing war puts it, Bomber Command 'was not trained or equipped either to penetrate into enemy territory by day or to find its target areas, let alone its targets, by night'.[75] The only available bombsight available to it was little different from models used in the First World War. Navigation in enemy airspace remained a matter of looking out of the cockpit window. Early bombing trials suggested that perhaps three out of every hundred bombs dropped in daylight would hit their targets. At night, accuracy would presumably be far worse.[76] Britain's bombers in September 1939 were too small, underpowered and underarmed to present any kind of serious danger to German strategic targets. Its crewmen were unable to defend themselves properly against intercepting German day fighters.[77] Britain entered the war with a sketch of what a bombing force might look like some time in the future, nothing more.

Here was one of the worst consequences of treating rearmament as an exercise in avoiding war rather than preparation for warmaking. Chamberlain had been interested in a 'shop-window' air force designed to impress the Germans and the British electorate, rather than one capable of actually performing its mission. Large numbers of planes to boast of in the House of Commons were more important than a military force trained and equipped for viable operations against the enemy. A concomitant lack of seriousness had permeated the expansion efforts of Bomber Command until very late, despite the Trenchardian beat to which the RAF marched. Not until 1937 did it make any detailed study of the targets it might be possible to attack in Germany, what it would take to destroy such targets or what its own casualties were likely to be if it tried.[78]

But Britain did possess a genuinely effective strategic air defence system. It was this defence system which saved the country in 1940. RAF Fighter Command's Spitfires and Hurricanes, assisted by RDF, were able to prevent the Germans from acquiring daylight air superiority over southeastern England during the Battle of Britain. The new fighter aircraft and the Chain Home system were all established on Chamberlain's watch. 'Does it occur to you when you read of the "Men of Munich",' he wrote to Ida in July 1940, 'that the exploits of the Navy, RAF, and BEF must have been made possible by the "Men of Munich"? For no one can suppose that our equipment has all been turned out in the last six weeks.'[79]

Yet perhaps Chamberlain was demanding more credit than he deserved. While it was fortunate that the UK was well prepared to fight the Battle of Britain in 1940, it would have been better still if it had not had to fight it in the first place. The Germans only found themselves in a position to seriously threaten Britain in the summer of 1940 because they had successfully defeated France. And France's defeat might have been avoided if Britain had thought more seriously about its role in the land war in continental western Europe.

The single biggest failure of Chamberlain's rearmament programme was his unwillingness to prepare the British Army for a continental responsibility. By the late 1930s this had become the inevitable corollary of national grand strategy. If Britain was to be allied to France – and it had no choice but to be allied to France – it would have to send an army across the Channel when war broke out. As late as February 1939 Chamberlain was still convinced that 'when the French knew the details' they could be 'led to see' that British air and sea power were more valuable to it than land power. But then, as Norman Gibbs, the official historian of British rearmament, later put it, Chamberlain had 'an inward looking mind [...] he found it easy to ignore or to misunderstand the needs of others if those needs ran contrary to his own logic or predilections. Here was a case in point.'[80] The French were not interested in lectures from Chamberlain about strategy. They were interested in an *effort du sang*. The realities of democratic politics insisted on it. There was simply no way that France was ever going to go to war against Germany again without Britain showing some corresponding willingness to send its own young men in arm with their allies, *bras-dessus bras-dessous*.

Chamberlain accepted reality in the end, but he got there very, very late. By September 1939 the British Army had only had seven months to prepare for a continental commitment that was a complete volte-face from its previous strategic mission. It was only five months since the size of the Territorial Army had been doubled. It was only two months since the first 'militiamen' conscripts had arrived for their basic training. The British field force would, as a result, go to France in a state of considerable disorganisation, without a single armoured division accompanying the infantry and lacking any effective tactical close air support (CAS) from the RAF. Here were the seeds of disaster to come.

Yet, to be fair to Chamberlain, Churchill would have done no better if he had been in charge. He was just as uninterested in a continental land commitment in the 1930s.[81] After visiting Churchill in December 1937, General Ironside noted that 'I could get nothing out of him as to our need of sending an army to France.' Churchill regarded the French Army as 'unassailable' and capable of handling the German ground forces by itself.[82] He showed little enthusiasm about introducing compulsory military service before 1939. In May 1938 he wrote in a newspaper article that 'if our fleet and our air force are adequate, there is no need for conscription in time of peace.'[83] Even when the Conservative Party's back-bench 1922 Committee came out in favour of compulsory service after Prague in March 1939, Churchill remained silent on the issue.[84]

Ironically, building a larger land army was the one rearmament measure the British could have carried out that just possibly might have made Hitler pause for thought in the 1930s. 'How can the English picture a modern war when they can't even put two fully equipped divisions in the field!' he once observed to his aides mockingly.[85] But few people in Britain, whether supporters of Chamberlain or opponents of his, whether appeasers or anti-appeasers, were willing to seriously consider this option before 1939. Twenty-four years earlier, at the beginning of the First World War, Lord Kitchener had warned the British government of Herbert Asquith that it would have to 'make war as we must, and not as we should like to'.[86] During the first disastrous twelve months of the Second World War, Britain was to discover the grim consequences of its choice to ignore Kitchener's injunction.

PART THREE

COMPANIONS IN MISFORTUNE

10

THE OTHER DUNKIRK

'There is a sudden loud explosion close by. A dull thud; it has not hit us, but I'm not sure it was far away. I take a quick look; salvoes are landing beyond the jetty, there is also a lot of dust [...] the bastards will correct their aim and then it will be us.' Lieutenant Jean Boutron, commander of the forward gunnery control position on the French dreadnought *Bretagne*, found his first experience of combat to be a bewildering riot of noise. Imprisoned in a cramped turret in the sweltering heat of a North African summer, all he could do was listen and try to follow what was going on by the percussive slap of armour-piercing shells hitting water, concrete and steel just yards away.[1]

On the destroyer *Volta*, anchored near *Bretagne*, another French sailor, Sub-Lieutenant J. P. Bazard, was recording the action too. 'The huge splashes follow each other. After correction by the enemy, they start landing on the jetty.' Bazard watched as *Volta*'s sister ship *Mogador*, struggling to manoeuvre into a position to engage the opposing vessels, was struck by a shell directly on her quarterdeck. 'The whole ship vanishes in an immense cloud of black smoke and flames which rise rapidly [...] the shell has exploded her depth charges.' *Volta* herself now began attracting enemy fire. 'Everything hurtles by. Shell splinters and stones torn from the jetty give the effect on the water of a heavy rain storm.' *Mogador*, stationary and burning, presented a horrifying spectacle – 'flames, twisted blackened steel plates, and steam making a sinister sizzling noise [...] a man, broken in two, is held up by a life line.'[2]

The battle cruiser *Dunkerque*, one of the world's most modern warships and the vessel that had represented France at King George VI's coronation review in 1937, was struck by four shells. Two of them penetrated the ship's main belt armour and exploded within her interior. Almost 200 of *Dunkerque*'s officers and ratings were killed in the next few minutes, many of them scalded to death by escaping clouds of steam or incinerated by burning engine oil. Others were 'shredded to ribbons', in the words of the ship's damage report, 'their charred remains buried under an enormous heap of ironwork'.

Dunkerque endured its mutilation. *Bretagne* did not. A shell smashed into her side near one of her stern turrets, detonating a magazine and blowing open an enormous hole beneath the waterline that caused her to list at an alarming angle. Three further hits exploded deep within her belly, and within thirty seconds *Bretagne* was rolling over and disintegrating in an incandescent whirl of fire, steam and water. Boutron found himself swept off the ship's deck and sucked into a vortex of fuel oil. 'It didn't seem worthwhile to struggle,' he wrote afterwards: 'a quick thought of my mother and my son, that was all.' To his own astonishment he was pulled out of the water alive – one of just 180 of *Bretagne*'s 1,327 crewmen who survived the day.

The French fleet in the harbour of Mers-el-Kébir, just outside the city of Oran in north-western Algeria, had been mauled in the attack. *Bretagne* had sunk and *Dunkerque* been crippled, while a third battleship, *Provence*, had only escaped destruction thanks to the quick flooding of her main magazines. Though the French ships had attempted to exchange fire with their persecutors, they had been unable to score any hits on the enemy vessels. The engagement at Mers-el-Kébir on the evening of 3 July 1940 was the French Marine Nationale's first major battle of the Second World War. It had been a tragedy in two ways: first, because of the appalling human losses; second, because the enemy ships that had fired on Boutron and Bazard had not been German. They had been British.

*

The British national memory of the Second World War treats its first nine months as prologue. The period is largely dismissed as 'the Phoney War', an uneventful and slightly tiresome preamble that must be got through before the truly important parts of the story can begin – and by 'important' is meant the parts in which the British themselves play the role as sole saviours of the world. It's hardly surprising that they do not want to dwell too long on the war's first stage. It ends, after all, with an ignominious rout for the Allied coalition on the European continent, with the British Expeditionary Force (BEF) barely escaping from the beaches of Dunkirk and their French comrades defeated entirely. The British tend to look back on the whole episode from September 1939 to June 1940 as a mistake, and one that was not of their own making. After all, the British army survived to fight another day. The French army did not. France fell in 1940; Britain didn't. For the British, what followed the evacuation from Dunkirk was the heroic 'Finest Hour' of the Battle of Britain and the Blitz. For the French, what followed it were humiliation, occupation and collaboration.

In fact, even as the disaster was still unravelling in the summer of 1940, the British had already begun heaping recriminations on their former allies.[3] On 1 June, Neville Chamberlain wrote bitterly to Hilda that 'there seems to have been hardly any mistake that the French did not make [...] their generals were beneath contempt & with some notable exceptions the soldiers would not fight.'[4] The *Sunday Chronicle*'s war correspondent Jimmy Drysdale suggested to his editor that the French of 1940 were 'a different race from last war – all fighting spirit dead. Running away. German soldiers laughing.'[5] Once France had fallen to the Germans, some Britons even began arguing that it was actually better that their former allies had surrendered. Chamberlain rejoiced that 'we are at any rate free of our obligations', for the French had 'been nothing but a liability to us. It would have been far better if they had been neutral from the beginning.'[6] George VI delighted to his mother, Queen Mary, that 'we have no allies to be polite to and to pamper.'[7] The former Cabinet Secretary Maurice Hankey wrote to Lord Halifax that the French deserved everything they were getting, as they were 'more responsible for our present troubles than anyone else'.[8]

The dominant theme in the popular Anglophone narrative of 1940 ever since has been of blameless Shire Folk let down by their hopeless Gallic allies. The defeat in France and Belgium that year, according to this interpretation, was an inevitable result of French lethargy and corruption: certainly nothing for the British to feel guilty about. The Dunkirk evacuation, its one glorious chapter, was a deliverance from a hostile, foreign place back to a safe and familiar one – and, in a deeper sense, from a misbegotten partnership with an incompetent and untrustworthy pack of foreigners back to a noble self-sufficiency on home soil. In 1940, the story goes, the British took back control.

But there are other ways of thinking about what happened at the beginning of the Second World War. And some of them are a good deal less flattering to Anglo-Saxon sensibilities. The British think of their cross-Channel alliance ending with Dunkirk. The French think of it ending with the dying sailors of *Dunkerque* in Mers-el-Kébir harbour. The British version is all about escape and glorious self-discovery. The French version is all about wrecked hopes, false promises and cynical betrayal.

The British can argue that their attack on the French fleet in July 1940 was, however appalling, nonetheless a grim necessity. The circumstances at that moment were dire. France had just surrendered. The fate of the Marine Nationale, the fourth-largest navy in the world, was not clear under the terms of France's armistice with Hitler. The British worried that the Germans would seize the fleet and that France's government, prostrate in defeat, would be unable to do anything about it. Nazi control of the Marine Nationale would shift the naval balance of power in European waters in Germany's favour. It might make an invasion of the United Kingdom possible. The main French fleet in Mers-el-Kébir had to be neutralised one way or the other. Its commander had been offered compromises: to join the British, to hand over his ships, to seek internment in a neutral port. He had rebuffed all of them. Violence was the only option left. It was a decision the British hated to take. Vice-Admiral Sir James Somerville, whose ships opened fire on the French at Mers-el-Kébir, wrote afterwards to his wife that 'we all feel thoroughly dirty and ashamed'. He would refer to himself in later life as 'the unskilled butcher of Oran'.[9]

Perhaps this self-exculpation is fair; perhaps not. The wider point is that it would behove the British, and the rest of the English-speaking world with them, to consider both Dunkirks from the French point of view a little more often.[10] There was nothing inevitable about what happened in 1940 either in Flanders or in Algeria. Mistakes were made, not all of them by the French. Sins were committed, not all of them by the French. The fact that one people survived the year and another did not cannot be explained simply by appeals to national character or virtuous leadership. The catastrophe of 1940, perhaps the single most consequential event in the whole twentieth century, was a catastrophe of allies, and it can only be explained by looking at decisions made on both sides of the English Channel. The Second World War began not just as prologue to a Finest Hour but as an epilogue to years of star-crossed mistakes and fatal misconceptions.

11

CLASS WAR

'Dreamed last night. I was sorting rags swarming with maggots, to make shrouds for evacuated children,' East End schoolteacher Gladys Langford wrote in her diary on Tuesday, 29 August 1939:

> This morning, I dreamed I heard a bell ring and a voice said '*It is Colonel Death come to billet corpses on you. Don't keep him waiting. He can be very unpleasant.*' I thought I opened the door and a figure in black just like Conrad Veidt stood there. I wakened to find myself in my dressing gown on the doorstep.[1]

Bizarre and sinister apparitions had been disturbing Langford's sleep all week. On the previous Friday she had 'wept copiously and hysterically' in front of a London County Council doctor who had ordered her off work for a month suffering from 'psycho-asthenia', or what would now be called clinical depression. For Langford, none of this was new. She had suffered from bouts of crippling anxiety and suicidal impulses for years. But in the final week of August 1939 her fearful preoccupations seemed, if anything, perfectly reasonable. The end of civilisation appeared to be at hand. 'Notices about air-raid warnings garnish every blank wall,' she wrote. 'Children rehearse evacuation. Sandbags obscure windows of big buildings. Everyone talks to everyone else – and the heat is intense.'

War and rumours of war were all anyone could think about in the swelter of late-summer London. No one knew whether Britain and Germany would really fight over Poland or whether, after all the fear and fuss, it would turn out to be another false alarm, like the Sudeten crisis the previous year. 'I feel bordering on lunacy,' Langford confessed to her diary:

> Remembering newsreel pictures of bombardments. Cannot read or settle to anything [...] lots of people are carrying cats about in baskets,

evidently to be destroyed [...] ammunition on London fields camou-
flaged with green leaves.[2]

'Everyone leaving London who can,' she noted.[3] Langford herself could not
decide whether to flee the doomed city or not. On Saturday night, 2 September, with Hitler's bombers pounding Warsaw and war with Germany
apparently just hours away, she finally resolved to go. 'A nightmare journey
driving through the dark on an unknown road' into rural Essex followed,
with officious ARP wardens 'popping up from the darkness again and
again with exhortations and warnings'.[4] Langford heard the prime minister declare war on the radio at 11 a.m. the following morning as she sat
in a bucolic hamlet on the Cambridgeshire border. 'I am disgusted with
mankind,' she wrote. Aircraft kept passing over the house at high altitudes,
their nationality and destination unknown.[5]

*

'The mass of people and Mr. Chamberlain started this war expecting death
to rain from the air,' Tom Harrisson and Charles Madge wrote in *War
Begins at Home* in early 1940.[6] This last part was not quite right, though
they were not to know it. The prime minister had already concluded by the
end of August 1939 that the Germans would probably not, after all, begin a
war with a massive aerial knock-out blow against Britain.[7] But this was his
personal view; and in any case, neither central government nor the local
authorities could take any chances. The Ministry of Health was working on
the assumption that it might need up to 2.8 million hospital beds to cope
with the civilian wounded in the first two months of a bombing war. Tent
cities were ready to act as *ad hoc* casualty clearing stations. Furniture vans
had been requisitioned to remove corpses from the rubble. Warehouses
full of shrouds and papier mâché coffins had been stockpiled, though it
was anticipated that such niceties as individual burials might have to be
suspended in the emergency. Plans had been drawn up for the mass entomb-
ment of bodies in quicklime.[8]

Our mental image today is of British civilians facing the prospect of
German bombardment in 1939 with unruffled pertinacity, of Keeping
Calm and Carrying On with a tired grin and a cup of tea. No such Shire
Folk fortitude was assumed by the authorities. They expected mass panic.
The ubiquitous poster that has replicated itself across a million mugs and

tea towels was not created as a tribute to British resilience. It was created because the government feared the opposite – that in the wake of air raids by the Luftwaffe the public would be so distraught that there would need to be urgent reminders about self-control.[9]

Churchill himself had warned of this in 1934. Up to 4 million Londoners would flee the metropolis to escape an aerial knock-out blow, he warned:

> This vast mass of human beings, numerically far larger than any armies which have been fed and moved in war, without shelter and without food, without sanitation and without special provision for the maintenance of order, would confront the Government of the day with an administrative problem of the first magnitude, and would certainly absorb the energies of our small Army and of our Territorial Force.[10]

Robert Donington in *The Citizen Faces War* (1936) predicted 'a packed, stampeding crowd of city dwellers, flying without hope of getting clear [...] struggling and fighting again to get food, as food grows ever scarcer; dying now of hunger and exposure and wounds and disease.'[11] Respectable law-abiding behaviour, psychologists warned, would quickly give way to mass atavistic brutishness; civilisation was 'a very thin veneer over the primitive tendencies'.[12] Indeed, they argued that the security and creature comforts of twentieth-century living had made modern Britons more vulnerable than ever to panic. Spiritual defences had been 'impoverished' by the erosion of Victorian hierarchy and the decline of religious belief.[13] The 'utter helplessness' of the town dweller under aerial attack would be expressed in a bid for 'infantile security', either through flight into the countryside or a permanent retreat into the womb-like sanctuary of the underground air-raid shelter.[14] All that would matter would be the 'near bestial' scramble for self-preservation.[15] In 1938 the Home Office asked the Army to have on hand at least 17,000 troops to assist police and civil defence workers in controlling the exodus from London. The sight of armed men in uniform, it was hoped, would 'quieten the people'. Tens of thousands of special constables would form a cordon around the capital to corral the panicking mob.[16]

Aerial carnage was expected to cause millions to lose their sanity. Psychological casualties, it was predicted, would outnumber the physically wounded by three to one, meaning that the authorities would have to deal with perhaps 4 million cases of hysteria and derangement in the first six months of war. Roving teams of psychiatrists were expected to have to tour the refugee camps tending to the traumatised.[17]

The experience of the 1938 Sudetenland Crisis, when Britain had also been on the brink of war with Germany, was not encouraging. A stream of fleeing Londoners had clogged the road arteries leading from the capital in the final days before the Munich conference. Over 150,000 people had hurriedly decamped to Wales and the West Country.[18] 'Long faces, tearful women in streets,' Gladys Langford noted in her diary at the time. The noise of vehicles on the road to Great Yarmouth kept her awake all night.[19] 'Anyone who was in London in September and October, 1938, must have been aware of something new in the moral attitude of the people,' thought Wilfred Trotter, the social psychologist and author of the seminal work on group dynamics, *Instincts of the Herd in Peace and War*:

> Trenches were being feverishly scratched open, many of those who could afford it were openly running away, and people of whose nerves better might have been expected confessed to an uncontrollable alarm [...] in the blackest days of 1917 and 1918 no such moral landslide was seen. The stoical endurance of the Londoner had gone, and in its place was something to which the thoughtful mind could not refuse the ominous name of panic.[20]

Although in the end no Luftwaffe bomber appeared over the metropolis in September 1938, one of the consequences of the Munich scare was a rapid acceleration of the ARP and Civil Defence programmes. Already 38 million gas masks had been distributed free to the public and 1 million feet of trenchworks dug in parks and other public places to act as emergency shelters during air raids.[21] Now the national ARP workforce was increased to 1.6 million people, most of them part-time volunteers. Auxiliary fire, first aid and ambulance services were recruited. By the outbreak of war 1½ million corrugated steel 'Anderson' shelters had been distributed to householders in kit form which they could build in sunken garden plots.[22] Local authorities were encouraged to construct indoor and outdoor public shelters, the cost of which was subsidised by central government.

ARP measures were meant to accomplish a number of things: to protect civilians if the worst happened, of course, but also to offer a palliative to their morale before war's outbreak by suggesting that the people in power were 'doing something'. As a last resort, ARP workers would provide a reserve army to help control the population if panic broke out. There was an inherent tension in making such visible preparations for a knock-out blow – between, on the one hand, reassuring people that the state was protecting them, and, on the other, terrifying them about the seeming inevitability of war.

Disseminating official ARP advice was a hit-and-miss affair. During the Sudetenland crisis, a free pamphlet giving basic civil defence instructions was distributed to every address in Britain. But seven months later, four out of every five people polled by Gallup said they still had no idea what to do if an air raid took place.[23] When asked what the procedure was for disposing of an incendiary bomb, almost half the answers 'were so definitely wrong as to be a public danger'.[24] Four days before the war broke out, Edward Stebbing, a teenager living near Chelmsford, discovered that his twenty-five-year-old sister Betty didn't know there was an audible warning system.

> *'What should we have to do?'*
> 'Get under cover.'
> *'Where?'*
> 'Indoor, or in an air-raid shelter.'
> *'If there was a gas attack, how would we know when to come out?'*
> 'There's a signal for that too.'
> *'Oh, is there?'*[25]

At precisely 11.28 a.m. on Sunday, 3 September 1939, thirteen minutes after Chamberlain had broadcast to the nation announcing the declaration of war, the sirens went off across London and much of southern England for the first time. The official history of wartime civil defence recorded the moment like this:

> Civilians in the streets were shepherded without ceremony by police and steel-helmeted wardens into the nearest shelters. All traffic stopped. Casualty and rescue squads stood ready in depots to rush to the scenes of attack; and officials waited in town halls to hear where the first bombs had fallen.[26]

Other accounts of the morning belie such a stiff-upper-lip image. The authors of *War Begins at Home*, Tom Harrisson and Charles Madge, both amateur anthropologists, had founded the sociological survey organisation

Mass Observation in 1937. Its brief was to operate a national network of volunteers to record the patterns of ordinary British life. Today Mass Observation's publications, reports and diary collections offer historians a feast of information, albeit idiosyncratic, about wartime behaviour and attitudes. The air-raid warning of 3 September 1939 was their inaugural wartime subject. In a café in Fulham, a Mass Observation observer noted there was 'a second's silence' after the siren began wailing, then

> Panic [...] people in the street begin to run frantically. People in houses and shops rush to door. Remain crowded in doorway. People in streets diving for any open door they can see. Policeman on bike waves people at the café door back: '*Go in.*' People go in, and then, after a few seconds, return to door. Woman of 25 with pram rushes up and is helped into café by two men who push back other men in the way. She is rushed away downstairs through door at back. Then boy of about 15 runs up panting, looking terrified, and dives in.[27]

One of the commonest responses to that first air-raid warning seems to have been neither gibbering dread nor the stoic civic-mindedness recalled by the official historian but rather puzzlement. Was this a drill or the real thing? What was the difference between the sound of the warning and the all-clear? (One Civil Defence worker got the two mixed up and played the all-clear first.[28]) Had war even broken out? Many Londoners had still not worked out what was going on by the time it was all over, without event, twenty minutes later. Even the Chief of the Imperial General Staff had no idea whether it was a test or not.[29]

London on the morning of 3 September 1939 was a city much denuded of people. Two days earlier, Operation PIED PIPER had been put into effect. Over 650,000 children, mothers, pregnant women, disabled people and teaching staff were evacuated from the capital and its greater metropolitan area to what were assumed to be safer rural 'receiving areas' across south-eastern England. Parallel evacuations took place from all other major industrial cities across Britain. All told, almost 1.5 million people nationally participated in PIED PIPER.

So central has this experience become to Britain's memory of the outbreak of the war, particularly through literary memorials such as C. S. Lewis's *The Lion, The Witch and the Wardrobe* and Evelyn Waugh's more sardonic *Put Out More Flags*, we forget that the official evacuation of children represented only a fraction of the total population movement in September 1939. If 1.5 million PIED PIPER evacuees left the cities at the outbreak of war, then so did about 2 million 'private' evacuees – some of them young children with their mothers, but many others adult men and women travelling alone. In Devon private evacuees outnumbered official ones by seven to one.[30]

The truly archetypal evacuee at the beginning of the Second World War was not a red-eyed East End waif with a teddy bear and a string parcel but someone who looked a lot more like Gladys Langford – an adult, probably middle-class, fleeing to the countryside. Constantine FitzGibbon recalled such well-heeled exiles streaming in cars and taxis past his mother's Thames Valley home in the hours immediately following the invasion of Poland, a 'horde of satin-clad, pin-striped refugees [...] in various stages of hunger, exhaustion and fear, offering absurd sums' for accommodation and food, gorging themselves on everything for sale that could be eaten or drunk, before vanishing westwards.[31] On 28 August, George Orwell noted 'immense quantities' of expensive luggage building up at London railway stations.[32]

By the end of September 1939 Greater London had shrunk by 1.4 million people from its pre-crisis population of about 8.6 million. The Liverpool metropolitan area lost 86,500 residents in a matter of weeks, Manchester 123,000.[33] When we consider those additional Britons whose lives were disrupted by the hurried diaspora – those who stayed behind, and those whose responsibility it was to care for the people arriving in their towns and villages – it appears that up to a third of the national population was directly affected by the great *Völkerwanderung* of the autumn of 1939.[34]

To be fair, not all private evacuees were heading for the hills in panic. Some of them were workers whose employers had relocated (3,453 big firms had left the capital by the end of 1939).[35] Around 25,000 civil servants were swept up in Plan YELLOW, the compulsory dispersal of central government departments across the country. The old and the poor in public assistance facilities were turned out to fend for themselves. So were over 5,000 prisoners and borstal inmates. About 140,000 hospital patients, some seriously ill, were sent home to make way for the knock-out blow casualties that never, in the end, materialised.[36] But other evacuees from London had simply decided to make as much space between themselves and the German bombs as possible. A steady stream of Irish nationals headed home on the first weekend of the war. Around 5,000 people left for America from

Southampton within the first forty-eight hours of hostilities.[37] Some of the better-off retreated to private hotels and guest houses in Arcadian nooks not known on any Luftwaffe target map – 'funkholes', as they were disparagingly known to those left behind. There, in Lakeland valleys and seaside bays, they determined to see out the war discreetly playing backgammon, drinking sherry and knitting socks for the troops.[38]

It may be, then, that one of the reasons that there was no mass panic in the capital in September 1939 was that hundreds of thousands of those most likely to panic had already fled. Of course, the expected bombs did not suddenly fall from the sky that September. When the Blitz did begin, a year later, Londoners continued to defy the melancholy predictions of the pre-war social psychologists. But by then they had had plenty of time to mentally absorb and prepare for the ordeal ahead, while Britain's central and local governments had much improved their ARP provisions. In any case, the bombing never reached the apocalyptic proportions that the pre-war military prognosticators had feared. What would have happened at the beginning of the Second World War had the Luftwaffe actually been in a position to unleash, without warning, a knock-out blow against London on the scale that the experts dreaded – the contingency for which those 'Keep Calm and Carry On' posters were originally prepared – is, thankfully, a matter for the imagination only.

*

Gladys Langford stayed in Essex until 15 September. By that point, a fortnight into the war, there had not yet been a single air raid on London or, for that matter, anywhere else in the UK. It was becoming clear that the capital was not, after all, facing imminent destruction. Langford came back to a city that was not in fiery ruins or experiencing a mass psychological breakdown of its terrified survivors. The Stock Exchange and the banks had reopened; theatres, cinemas, sports grounds and dance halls were busy again. Londoners' struggles were with the prosaic inconveniences of wartime – most of all, the tedious nightly shrouding of doors and windows with heavy blackout material to accord with the ARP regulations enforced by overbearing neighbourhood wardens. 'Everyone loathes it and their nerves are on edge because of it,' she wrote of the blackout.[39] Friends and acquaintances had declared that they would not venture out at night any longer until the war was over. Langford was not ready to go quite that far:

but 'one *does* get depressed,' she admitted. 'Every wall is unsightly with plastered posters – indeed I am horrified at my beloved London's ugliness now. She's like an awfully ugly middle-aged woman who has lost all pride in her personal appearance.'[40]

Langford was not the only Londoner to slip quietly back to the city in the absence of Armageddon. By the end of September at least one in five PIED PIPER evacuees had been recalled home by their parents. If that rate of return was the same for private evacuees also, that means that about 400,000 people who had fled Britain's cities on the outbreak of war came back within four weeks. By the beginning of December over four in ten official evacuees had gone home. By January 1940 it was six in ten.[41] In February the government attempted to reboot the plan, distributing 9 million leaflets in a slightly desperate attempt to persuade parents to co-operate. But only one in five children in the evacuation zones registered.[42] The evacuees would leave the cities in the end, but only once bombing had actually begun.

This is another example of how the national myth of evacuation misremembers the experience. For most children swept up in PIED PIPER on 1 September 1939, evacuation was not an exile from home that lasted years without interruption but rather a short, confusing break from family routine that ended within a few weeks or months, the whole endeavour having turned out to be, on the face of it, rather a waste of time.

Indeed, by late autumn, a people who had grimly girded themselves for battle were starting to feel a more general sense of anticlimax, even a vague suspicion that they had been conned in some way. Nothing in this war had turned out the way they had been told to expect. 'It would be impossible to convey the sense of utter panic with which we heard the first air raid warning,' wrote George Beardmore, a clerk living in north London, in his diary. 'We pictured St Paul's in ruins and a hole in the ground where the Houses of Parliament stood. But nothing happened.'[43] May Smith, an elementary school teacher in Swadlincote, Derbyshire, was awoken at 3.30 a.m. on 4 September by the first air-raid warning in the East Midlands. 'Most terrifying,' she recorded afterwards:

Awoke with a start and a palpitating heart, flung on a dressing gown, shouted to Mother and Dad and dashed downstairs. Mother and I immediately fumbled with our gas masks and soon had them on and sat staring solemnly at each other.

The family ran outside and up the road to May's grandmother's house, which with its cellar seemed to offer greater protection. They hammered on the door to be let in and were eventually admitted. 'Fully expected to see enemy bombers bearing down on us any minute while we were still madly battering [...] after half an hour's awful suspense, the All Clear signal went. Mother thanked God in a devout tone.'[44] In Chelmsford the same night Edward Stebbing huddled in the dark awaiting the bombers, he in a self-confessed 'funk', his sister Betty 'trembling with fear'.[45]

Yet by mid-November, when the air-raid warning sounded during a dance at the parish hall, Stebbing noted in his diary that 'the dancing went on. Hardly anybody left [...] nobody seemed upset.'[46] Betty was already joking about how she had taken her gas mask with her to bed every night at the beginning of the war. How foolish it all seemed a dozen weeks later![47] In the first days of hostilities, sober middle-aged women had contemplated poisoning their husbands and children rather than see them torn apart by bombs.[48] Up to 400,000 family pets were euthanised, the corpses of cats and dogs piling up high at RSPCA clinics as staff worked night shifts to keep up.[49] In September, May Smith hadn't dared 'venture a yard' without her gas mask. After four uneventful months 'I seem lulled into such a false sense of normality that I never dream of yanking it out with me.'[50]

By Christmas 1939 there was, the home secretary, Sir John Anderson, warned the War Cabinet, a 'growing tendency' across Britain 'to decry as unnecessary and over-cautious many of the measures which have been taken to safeguard the national interest against air attack'. Much of this criticism was being directed at the PIED PIPER evacuation plan, which was now starting to look like a needless disruption of British family life and the school calendar. But this was merely

> symptomatic of a scepticism about the whole scale of Civil Defence preparations. Criticisms of the Black-Out, of the Civil Defence personnel, the emergency hospital scheme, all reflect the same tendency to call in question the need for the precautions which have been taken [...]
>
> For some time past the assumption had been that war with Germany would mean intensive air attack on this country from the first moment of hostilities. This assumption was fairly widely known, and when war came the people were braced to meet the shock of such an attack. Now that we have been at war for more than three

months and no such attack has been launched, it is only too easy for the average man to slip into a mood of complacency and to delude himself into supposing that, because this attack has not been delivered, the danger of it has now passed.[51]

For Gladys Langford, the sputtering out of the Apocalypse was suggestive of something fraudulent about the whole business of the war. What was really going on? Her host in rural Essex, 'whose faith in the National Government and the truth and purity of the English press was once so profound', had decided by 14 September that 'you can't believe anything or anybody NOW'.[52] Her friend Arthur Wellings, the owner of a chain of commercial libraries, believed that Chamberlain's government was secretly colluding with Germany and the USSR to destroy Poland. Nothing in the newspapers or on the BBC could be trusted, he insisted. When it was announced that the battleship HMS *Royal Oak* had been sunk by a German U-boat at Scapa Flow, in the Orkney Islands, in October, Wellings denounced the story as made up. He called what was going on a 'Phoney War' – not, though, in the sense that we use that term today, to describe the absence of major conflict, but rather to denote an experience that was counterfeit, sham, bogus.[53] The war was phoney, according to Wellings, because it was a manufactured pretence.

He may not have been the most rational of men. At the end of October he had some kind of mystical religious experience and announced to anyone who would listen that his landlady was really the Virgin Mary in disguise.[54] All the same, Wellings's conspiracy theory that the government was not being candid with the masses does seem have echoed a broader if more attenuated public scepticism about the war.

This was understandable enough under the circumstances. Think about how bewildering the whole seventeen-month period from August 1938 to December 1939 had been for the average Briton: the nauseating troughs of despair, followed soon afterwards by peaks of near-hysterical relief as war gave way to peace, only for the whole horrible process to begin again. The Sudetenland crisis had simmered away over the summer of 1938 until Chamberlain's dramatic flight to Obersalzberg had fashioned a diplomatic solution. But then within a few days there had been the Bad Godesberg ultimatum, and war, people were told, was just hours away. Barrage balloons had been hauled into the sky, gas masks distributed, trenches dug in the parks. The *Daily Mail* announced that only four days separated 'civilisation and catastrophe'.[55] Millions of lives were spared at the last moment by the Munich conference. Gloriously, a lasting European peace suddenly seemed to be within reach.

Soon enough, however, there was *Kristallnacht*, Prague, the Polish guarantee and, for the second time, the possibility of war with Germany. Many people refused to believe it any longer. In May 1939, two months after the fall of Czechoslovakia, 57 per cent of Britons polled still felt that the chance of war had decreased since the autumn.[56] On 7 August the *Daily Express* confidently asserted 'NO WAR THIS YEAR' on its front page.[57] But then there was the Danzig crisis: more barrage balloons, more gas masks, more trenches. This time the peace could not be saved. But the war, when it finally came, turned out to be a damp squib. 'My nerves have completely gone: we've been waiting a whole year not knowing if there'll be a war or not,' a Lancashire girl wrote in September 1939. 'I want a knock at Hitler.'[58]

Yet no knock came. The British had undergone months of psychological mobilisation for war, only to be left wondering whether the whole thing would sputter out with yet another inconclusive peace conference ('Is it the prelude to another Munich?' Londoners asked when Chamberlain travelled to Paris in the second week of September 1939).[59] Armageddon might be cancelled once more – but would it be for good this time, or just for another six months, perhaps a year? As one thirty-six-year-old commercial traveller put it:

> Things are not going a bit like we imagined they would, are they? I was led to expect that thousands of bombers would be over here the first day war was declared, and that we'd all be gassed and blown to pieces right away [...] doesn't seem as if we're doing much on land yet, does it? The papers say the boys are over there, but they haven't gone into action yet; still, you can't believe all you read, can you?[60]

Heavy-handed media management was eroding public trust in the press. Policemen descended on Fleet Street at midnight on 11 September 1939 to confiscate all the copies of the early morning newspapers when the War Office panicked about releasing information about the BEF – only to change its mind again a few hours later.[61] The Liberal Party leader, Archibald Sinclair, complained in Parliament that such fiascos were making people feel 'that things are being kept from them and that they cannot rely on the newspapers of this country'.[62] Clumsy censorship only sharpened suspicions that the government was covering things up. 'The public is longing to hear about sensational exploits by air, sea, and land, of batteries wiped out and woods occupied,' wrote George Beardmore on 28 September: 'what we get is one sentence to the effect that one German sortie has been repelled with loss.'[63]

The prestige of the Ministry of Information (MoI) fell so low in the first winter of the war that Chamberlain seriously considered winding it up.[64] In the end he stayed his hand, sacking its ineffectual head, Lord Macmillan, and replacing him with Sir John Reith, the founding director-general of the BBC. Reith held the office without enthusiasm for four months until he was sacked in his turn by Churchill, an old and bitter foe from the appeasement era. Reith brought some greater organisational coherence to the Ministry during his brief tenure, but he could do little to improve the MoI's battered reputation among journalists and the public. Its proclivity for pointless secrecy became a standing joke. According to one widely circulated story, a Ministry spokesman refused to give out the text of a propaganda leaflet dropped in its millions by the RAF the previous night over Germany because 'it would disclose information which might be of value to the enemy'.[65]

In the absence of reliable information, there was rumour. 'It is extraordinary that the responsible leaders could not have foreseen people's thirst for information,' wrote Harrisson and Madge in February 1940:

> People simply invented the news they were not given, in the image of the war that had so long been looming in their nightmares and daydreams [...] nearly every town was rumoured to have been bombed to ruins during the early days of the war. Planes had been *seen* by hundreds of eyewitnesses falling in flames.[66]

Fierce battles between German bombers and British anti-aircraft guns and fighter planes were solemnly reported in pubs and parlours across Britain. Witnesses swore to having seen damaged enemy machines crash-landed in fields and parks.[67] May Smith's Auntie Nell announced that Hitler was going to drop thousands of parachutists over England.[68] Edward Stebbing's father told him that the Germans had created a new powdered toxin that could penetrate gas masks.[69] 'Many people are now believing rumours in preference to official news,' warned Harrisson and Madge.[70] The MoI pushed back at this fevered military imaginary as best it could. 'Do not believe the tale the milkman tells,' counselled the author and MP A. P. Herbert:

> No troops have mutinied at Potters Bar.
> Nor are there submarines at Tunbridge Wells.
> The BBC will warn us when there are.[71]

But at this stage of the war few people were sure the BBC would do any such thing.

*

It's not that the British were against the war. Munich, however inglorious, had performed its necessary work. Hitler's abandonment of the peace vow that he had made to Chamberlain in the notorious 'piece of paper' had shown the world that the British leader had gone to all the reasonable lengths he could to try to prevent war. That war had come anyway was Hitler's choice.

Belief that the war was just in 1939 represented a significant consolidation of the fractured and uncertain national mood of a year earlier. One poll at the time of the Sudeten Crisis had suggested that only a minority of men under 30 would co-operate unconditionally with the authorities if war broke out with Germany. Fourteen per cent claimed they would actively resist the war effort, or at least refuse to take any part in it.[72] Probably such abstract declarations of defiance were never meant to be taken that seriously. But if even half of those young men had followed through on their threat, the wartime government would have faced a serious challenge to public order.

As it was, war resistance even of a passive kind barely flickered as a factor in the mobilisation of the autumn of 1939. Only twenty-two men out of every 1,000 who had to register for National Service in the first round of mass conscription in October 1939 requested a tribunal hearing on the grounds of conscientious objection (CO). Most of them ultimately accepted some conditional war work as an alternative to military enlistment. The country had accepted conscription with 'an apathetic equanimity impossible a year ago', thought Richard Crossman.[73] The number of registrants requesting CO tribunals slowly tapered off from the high point of October 1939 and fell dramatically once serious fighting began the following year.

The government took a relatively benign attitude towards conscientious objectors because they simply didn't matter very much.[74]

Pacifism, when put to the test in September 1939, proved to be a rather frail doctrine. This is not to say that it vanished entirely. The Women's International League of Peace and Freedom organised small anti-war demonstrations.[75] Two months after the war began, twenty-two Labour MPs signed a petition demanding an immediate armistice which was supported by over seventy of the Party's local constituency organisations.[76] But the large-scale organised political movement that pacifism had once boasted was no more. By the eve of the war, many of the local branches of the National Peace Council had ceased to function for lack of members, while after three years of strenuous campaigning the International Peace Campaign formally abandoned its opposition to the war in October 1939.[77] Prominent pacifists such as Bertrand Russell and C. M. Joad changed their minds. A handful of pacifist candidates stood in parliamentary by-elections during the Phoney War, but even the most successful of them, William Ross, a steelworker who identified himself as the 'Workers' and Pensioners' Anti-War' champion in Kettering in March 1940, was comfortably beaten by the Conservative nominee, John Profumo.

Abandoning pacifism was not an easy decision for many principled men and women who had taken the Peace Pledge Union's vow to renounce war in the 1930s. They wrestled for some time over the dilemma of whether violence could be condoned if it would serve to defeat Nazism. Most, in the end, chose violence. The writer Rose Macaulay summarised the situation in a May 1939 article for *Peace News*:

> Faced on one side with a regime more brutal than any we have had in Europe since [the sixteenth-century Spanish duke of] Alva and his Spanish torturers [... and] on the other with a horrible and inhuman war (which our Government would not wage to save the Czechs), what is the pacifist to feel or do? What attitude is possible that is neither callous, bellicose nor silly?
>
> It is no doubt because I am not a good pacifist that I cannot answer my own question.[78]

Perhaps there never were many really good pacifists. The majority of supporters of the Peace Pledge Union advocated what Martin Ceadel has called 'pacificism' rather than pacifism per se – a belief that the quest for peace was a vital moral duty, but that there might be occasions when it was justifiable, even imperative, to use armed force to secure it, just as a surgeon, while committed to doing no harm, might have to cut open a patient's belly to save a life.[79] This was a form of belief that could be reconciled with the government's foreign policy. Chamberlain himself could have been described as a pacificist. A few thousand unconditional anti-war supporters continued to protest against the conflict, some of them winding up imprisoned for their beliefs. The septuagenarian feminist Helena Swanwick killed herself with an overdose of sleeping pills, unable to face the 'lunatic days' ahead.[80] Most former peace campaigners, though, came to terms with the war. Hitler had clarified everyone's minds wonderfully.

It was the German dictator, personally, against whom many Britons considered they were fighting. Edward Stebbing noted how many people in his home village spoke of the enemy as 'he': 'I don't think he'll come; I don't think he'll bomb us.'[81] The war was 'all old Hitler's fault', according to Stebbing's sister: 'I'd like to be taken out there and shoot him myself.'[82] A friend's mother declared that 'I don't know what I should like to do to Hitler', the implication being that there was no imaginable punishment bad enough.[83] His villainous yet also faintly comic demeanour was a gift to propagandists. The day after war broke out, the *Daily Mirror* ran a *faux* Wanted poster for 'Adolf Schicklegruber', describing him as 'sallow complexion, stout build, suffering from acute monomania [...] harsh, guttural voice, and has a habit of raising right hand to shoulder level. DANGEROUS!'[84] A month later, the BBC broadcast *Adolf in Blunderland*, a parody of Lewis Carroll's fantasy in which the diminutive *Führer*, dressed in a Fauntleroy suit, meandered through encounters with the Deutsch-Hess and the Mock Gurbles (Goebbels).[85]

Focusing propaganda efforts on such a detestable man had obvious advantages in terms of rallying support for the war effort, but it also posed dangers. What if Hitler was assassinated or purged in an internal coup, and some faceless bureaucrat took his place as Nazi leader? Would popular enthusiasm for the war remain as strong? The British were emphatic, in a slightly self-regarding way in September 1939, that their enemy was Nazism rather than the German people – that they were not going to repeat the hysterical virulence against 'the Hun' of the previous war. There would be no banning Beethoven and kicking dachshunds this time.[86] That was all well and good, but it raised the question of whether the public's very particular hatred of Hitler could be redirected if the Third Reich found itself a new leader.

A belief that Hitler personally was the enemy made it easy to lose focus on the structural danger of the Nazi system in the absence of any new acts of outrage. Once Poland was defeated in early October 1939 and the long winter months of the Phoney War set in, there were fewer day-to-day opportunities to remind newspaper readers of the perfidy of the enemy regime (the horrors going on in occupied Poland were as yet largely unknown in Britain). Instead, by the end of 1939 it was the Soviet Union that had emerged as the most visible malefactor. Armed forces of the USSR had invaded eastern Poland on 17 September in obvious co-ordination with the Wehrmacht. On 28 September Germany and the Soviet Union issued a joint declaration that they might have to take 'necessary measures' against Britain and France should the Western Allies not make immediate peace with the Third Reich.[87] During the next two weeks the Baltic States of Estonia, Latvia and Lithuania were compelled to accept 'mutual assistance treaties' which allowed Soviet troops to enter their countries (annexation would follow the year after). When the Finns rejected a similar ultimatum in November, the Red Army invaded. Finland's plight and its heroic David-and-Goliath resistance against the might of the USSR in the 'Winter War' generated enormous sympathy in the West, and a sense that the USSR and Nazi Germany might really represent a single totalitarian enemy.

This sense transcended traditional political divides. The right-wing *Daily Sketch* suggested that 'Hitlerism [...] is still Hitlerism if the aggressor is called Stalin', while on the left Kingsley Martin asked in the *New Statesman* whether 'the ugly thing that now reigns from Vladivostok to Cologne is turning into the inevitable synthesis, National-Bolshevism'.[88] In March 1940 Clement Attlee and Arthur Greenwood issued a statement on 'the Red Czar' in the Kremlin which would not have sounded out of place in a Tory smoking room: 'Fascism and Bolshevism have identical political systems [... Stalin] has used a new social and political system to invent a new kind of slavery for the Russian people.'[89]

Too much should not, perhaps, be made of this. Even during the Winter War, only one in four people said that they thought the Soviet Union presented a more dangerous threat to Britain than Germany. All the same, in November 1939, 42 per cent of people polled by Gallup said that Britain ought to provide military assistance to any Scandinavian nation if it was invaded by the USSR, an act that would probably have led to war if the government had gone through with it. In January one in three people supported the idea of sending British troops to Finland.[90] By March, the month the Finns were forced to agree to an armistice, 47 per cent of Britons said that they did not want to establish friendly relations with the Soviets (against 41 per cent who did), and 41 per cent were sure that Britain would eventually go to war against the USSR (30 per cent felt otherwise).[91]

We now know that by the spring of 1940 the French government was seriously considering bombing the Soviet oil fields in the Caucasus as a way to break the war's deadlock, and the British government, though more sceptical about such a dangerous and unpredictable project, was starting to come around to the idea in the absence of anything better to suggest.[92] If fighting had not broken out in Norway in April 1940, the Second World War might have soon taken on a quite different character from the one it did historically. Many Britons, wearying of the drab and uneventful stand-off they were having with the Nazis, might just have found a greater moral purpose in a crusade against Bolshevism.

*

In the spring of 1940 the author Angela Thirkell completed her newest novel, *Cheerfulness Breaks In*, the ninth in her series of comedies of manners set in Anthony Trollope's fictional West Country 'Barsetshire'. Much of *Cheerfulness Breaks In* is devoted to Thirkell's arch observations about the lives of the rural upper-middle class. But by 1940 the war had intruded on Barsetshire. In the new instalment of her saga Thirkell included a number of scenes describing the arrival of urban working-class evacuee children to the community. It was not a sentimental portrayal. 'The London children, apart from their natural nostalgia for playing in dirty streets till midnight and living on fish and chips, settled down almost at once into the conditions of licence, dirt, overcrowding and margarine to which they were accustomed,' she wrote.[93] One of her characters, Mr Miller, admits to 'harboring un-Christian thoughts' about the refugee terror from the East End slums whom he has been landed with, a boy who has single-handedly murdered six of his hens. 'The old Adam rose in me and I beat him [...] not even after reflexion, I fear, but in anger,' he confesses to one of his neighbours:

> 'Then I am certain that you did him a great deal of good,' said Mrs Birkett firmly, 'and probably saved him from the gallows later' [...]
> 'Indeed, I hope that it may be so, though I fear the gallows are still

gaping for that boy. He has been trying to dig to Australia among the lettuces, thus causing considerable loss of good food.'[94]

Thirkell's American publisher, Knopf, was not sure about any of this. In a letter that August her US editor warned that readers on the other side of the Atlantic would find such comments about the evacuees 'a bit startling' and 'acid', and went on: 'Americans have become pretty sentimental about English children these days [... they] are going to gather from this book, I'm afraid, that you are a rather upstage and nasty sort of person.' Thirkell was unabashed. 'The evacuees must take their luck with the great sloppy-hearted USA public,' she retorted. 'They are far worse than anything I have said.'[95]

None of Thirkell's criticisms would have come as any surprise to her British middle-class readers. The First World War had begun with a spate of atrocity stories about brutish German soldiers bayoneting Belgian children. The Second World War started with atrocity stories too, only this time it was the children who were said to be committing the atrocities. 'I have a letter from a doctor who is a justice of the peace, and who writes on behalf of many people in his district,' complained Captain Colin Thornton-Kemsley MP when the House of Commons debated the evacuee issue on 14 September 1939:

> He says that the children and their mothers arrived in his district mostly in a very filthy and verminous condition and that many were very inadequately clad. Their habits were indescribable, and many cases had come to his notice where carpets, mattresses and bedding had had to be completely destroyed owing to the primitive habits of these evacuees.[96]

In the *Spectator* the Oxford historian R. C. K. Ensor described the new arrivals in his Home Counties village as 'the lowest grade of slum women – slatternly malodorous tatterdemalions trailing children to match', deposited in their squalor upon 'prosperous artisans with neat clean homes and habits of refinement'.[97] Why were these wretched refugees not being accommodated in tented camps and dormitories, where they could be safely monitored and controlled?

The government had been proud of itself in the immediate wake of PIED PIPER. One and a half million children, mothers and escorts had been swiftly and efficiently removed from the cities in under seventy-two hours without a single casualty. Perhaps too efficiently, as it turned out. The evacuees came disproportionately from the poorest districts of urban Britain. Their homes were in the densely packed Victorian tenements expected to be prime targets for the Luftwaffe. There was an unspoken belief in the official mind that such slum quarters were peculiarly vulnerable to mass panic.[98] According to L. E. O. Charlton in his 1935 book *War in the Air*, the 'labouring masses' would be 'the most difficult people to control' and likely to 'stampede when the air-raid warning goes'.[99] Official pre-war Civil Defence discussions had taken it for granted that 'the most unstable element [...] very susceptible to panic' would be found in London's East End.[100] There was, then, an urge to get poor women and children out of the cities as fast as possible without too much regard for where they ended up. At one London station on 1 September they were being dispatched at the rate of 8,000 an hour.[101]

Rather less care was taken about the conditions in which the evacuated were sent, or even where they ended up. Hundreds of thousands of children spent hours packed in stifling railway carriages in the late summer heat, with no opportunities to eat or use a toilet. They emerged at the other end exhausted, soiled and weepy. Frantic dispatchers caused chaos. One group of over 420 mothers and small children from Liverpool's Edge Hill district, who were supposed to go to Wrexham, were dumped instead in the small North Wales village of Aberdaron, which had no food or accommodation to offer them.[102] Local authority billeting officers, usually low-ranking civil servants unused to this level of responsibility, felt overwhelmed as complaints began to flood in from evacuees and hosts alike. By the end of September many of these complaints were ending up back in the original evacuation areas as the paperwork metastasised. At County Hall in London shorthand typists were drafted in to help process the gathering mountain of correspondence while queues formed in the corridors and the telephones rang incessantly.[103]

In Essex, Edward Stebbing recorded that 'many clean, decent country people have been shocked and hurt at the way in which some [evacuees] act in their new homes'. The local headmaster declared their behaviour 'disgusting'.[104] Nella Last, a middle-class housewife in Barrow-in-Furness, said that the locals had had 'the shock of their lives' at the wretched and verminous condition of evacuees from Manchester. 'There is a run on disinfectant and soap, while children who arrived with a crop of curls look like shorn lambs.'[105]

A national middle-class commentary began about the astonishing want and ignorance of many of the evacuees. Quite aside from the filth, the bed-wetting and the fear of contamination by lice, scabies and impetigo, thousands of them, it was said, had arrived bearing no change of clothing other than the miserable ensembles they were dressed in. They lacked underwear, pyjamas, washcloths, toothbrushes, combs and brushes. Their understanding of basic hygiene and toilet training was more appropriate to the cowshed than the modern home. They looked askance at knives and forks, were baffled by the mysteries of books and fresh vegetables, slept on the floor. Their negligent mothers decamped to the pub every evening, 'obviously meaning to enjoy a cheap country holiday of indefinite duration'.[106]

Many of these tales improved a good deal in the telling. It's true that pre-war school medical inspections had estimated that one London child in six and one Liverpool child in five were infested with lice. This was scarcely a discovery to make anyone comfortable, though it did mean, of course, that the great majority of such children were not lousy. Middle-class hosts could easily forget that their own expectations about proper dress, cleanliness and behaviour were not necessarily shared by the rest of the nation, nor did they amount to moral precepts. Adults who themselves had been sent to private boarding-schools in their youth were sometimes blind to the fact that long-term separation from their mothers and fathers was a new and frightening experience for working-class children. Any nightmares and bed-wetting that resulted from this were a natural reaction to trauma, not symptomatic of years of bad parenting.[107]

Evidence of widespread working-class poverty was abundant enough, however. It all added up, thought Harold Nicolson, to a most 'perplexing social event', the most dramatic encounter of rich and poor, city and country, in the nation's history. The effect, he hoped, would be 'to demonstrate to people how deplorable is the standard of life and civilisation among the urban proletariat'.[108] H. G. Wells reported, a little gloatingly, that 'parasites and skin diseases, vicious habits and insanitary practices have been spread, as if in a passion of equalitarian propaganda' from the nation's slums to its suburbs and villages.[109]

The official historian of evacuation, Richard Titmuss, concluded after the war that the evacuation 'aroused the conscience' of the British middle and upper classes to the plight of the nation's poor, stimulating calls for reform that were eventually articulated in the Labour Party's post-war health and social service policies.[110] To some extent this was true. One society hostess is said to have remarked in 1939 that 'I feel ashamed of having been so ignorant of my neighbours [...] for the rest of my life I mean to try & make amends by helping such people to live cleaner & healthier lives.'[111] Evacuation, seen from this point of view, was an important moment in class solidarity and the evolution of the idea of a People's War.

But not all of the evacuees' hosts drew a moral that greater state resources should be spent on improving life for the poor. On the contrary, a good many of them seem to have concluded that all the money that the central and local authorities had lavished on social reform before the war had been wasted. The thriftless and slovenly denizens of the slums were clearly in too degraded a state to be capable of improvement.[112] Harrisson and Madge thought that a few volunteers in support organisations such as the Women's Voluntary Services (WVS) had been moved to pity by the plight of evacuees, but most of the well-off had, rather, 'turned their horror into fear and even hatred, seeing in this level of humanity an animal threat, that vague and horrid revolution which lurks in the dreams of so many supertax payers'.[113]

Revulsion towards the labouring masses could lurk even in the most self-consciously left-wing mind. Gladys Langford thought of herself as progressive; she chided her fellow Londoners for not wanting to assist the depressed areas of the north. But a month into the war, she wrote in disgust that homes in Stoke Newington that had once housed 'Nonconformist ministers, upper grade civil servants and works managers' were now being leased to 'slatternly women and dirty children [who] crowd the streets'. It was, she thought, 'very frightening' to realise 'how powerful these mobs of uneducated, "unwashed", unthinking people could become! No wonder the government soddens them with radio and cheap cinemas so they've no time to become politically minded.'[114]

The years immediately before the war had been anxious ones for the British middle class, as rearmament spending and tax rises had seemed to shift the balance of economic and political power towards the working class. The first eight months of war only exacerbated those fears. Many middle-class Britons concluded that it was they, the thankless workhorses of the nation, who were the principal victims of this new war. The nation was demanding unique and inequitable sacrifices from their class and their class alone, while the forces of organised labour sat back and took advantage of their ordeal.

The plight of evacuee hosts was just one example of this. 'Apart from the disgraceful insistence of the billeting people in thrusting filthy women and children into the homes of decent, cleanly people, there is an economic hardship not yet mentioned,' complained 'A Victim' in the *Spectator*:

> Many of the evacuated children arrived with no change of various undergarments. This means that the struggling country worker's wife must buy new socks and vests for the slum children or allow them to become even more malodorous than they are already.[115]

The British state provided a host family 10s. 6d. for the first evacuee and 8s. 6d. for each additional child, a sum that was supposed to reimburse full board and lodging. Such an amount might have been adequate in a thrifty working-class household but was totally insufficient to match the needs of a middle-class housewife with more demanding standards.[116] Such hosts were expected to make up the difference themselves. The idea that the middle class were having to shoulder the burden of evacuation all by themselves was a myth. Most evacuees went to stay with working-class families not very different from their own, but it was a powerful myth for nurturing a sense of collective grievance. The historian W. L. Burn protested that the 'meretricious and sentimental appeal' of the evacuees was obscuring the 'heavy burden' that was being imposed on one section of the population alone.[117]

'Today, many persons who belong to the so-called middle classes are looking back a little wistfully at the past and facing the future with resignation,' wrote Rolfe Scott-James in the *Spectator* in November 1939:

> Circumstances and sentiment alike have conspired to increase the tendency towards economic levelling. The war has automatically robbed many people of their financial superiority, among them barristers, architects, Harley Street specialists, research-workers, well-known artists and actors [...] nor has the Chancellor of the Exchequer, supported by a House of Commons in its most sacrificial mood, failed to make the most of this spirit of equality and fraternity. He has, rightly or wrongly, heaped such taxes on the middle-classes as to leave them dubious of the right to be so-called [...]
>
> If the state seriously reduces the strength of this class it is cutting at the roots of progress, fineness, resilience – it is assisting the forces of decay and degeneracy.[118]

The first months of the war were not easy for salary earners and self-employed tradespeople. Its outbreak had brought the summer tourist season of 1939 to an abrupt early end, while the general cut-back in discretionary spending on non-essentials hit the tailoring and dressmaking trade, the motor industry and the sport and entertainment sectors hard. 'Unemployment,' thought George Beardmore as he awaited being laid off from his clerical firm, 'is today an even greater threat than Hitler.'[119] Urban retailers and professionals saw their clients vanish into the countryside. The government banned the import of many luxury goods, including clocks, watches, musical instruments, toys, perfume and cutlery. Non-manual workers earning more than £250 annually were not covered by the national unemployment insurance scheme, so while out-of-work labourers and craftsmen were returning to busy munitions and aircraft factories in the autumn of 1939, black-coated clerks and shopkeepers pummelled by the new economic realities of wartime had to rely on their savings to eke out what was looking like a precarious future.[120]

Some of them were now relying on meagre soldiers' pay. Middle-class young men were much less likely than their working-class peers to be included on the Schedule of Reserved Occupations excluding them from conscription. Either through coercion or patriotic impulse, they joined the armed forces at a disproportionately high rate during the Phoney War. But this came at a financial cost. A private soldier's basic rate of pay in 1939 was two shillings a day. Officers received more, of course, but they were also responsible for mess bills and the cost of much of their own kit. Some former civilian employers made up the difference in earnings. Others did not. The derisory rate of allowances to servicemen's families meant that the wives and children of middle-class soldiers could suddenly find themselves in a new category of genteel poverty.[121] This while engineering firms in the Midlands and north-west short of skilled labour were offering some manual workers the extraordinary sum of £8 a week.[122]

These shifts in income were taking place against a background of wartime tax increases, price rises and rationing. The first budget of the war was announced on 27 September 1939. The standard rate of income tax was raised by two shillings to 7s. 6d. in the pound (37.5 per cent) – 'a phenomenal figure', thought George Beardmore – and the threshold for eligibility lowered. Duties went up on beer, whisky, tobacco and sugar. Surtax and estate taxes were raised.[123] This was modest enough stuff in comparison with what was to come. But it seemed shocking to middle-income earners used to the Treasury's generosity during most of the 1930s. Gladys Langford expected to see her tax liability at least double: 'the income tax seems to bother people more than the war,' she thought.[124] 'None can say that this Budget favours the rich, is lenient to the middle classes, or peculiarly harsh to the poor,' grumbled the *Spectator*: 'It will mean for all middle-class families a drastic reduction in a standard of living already threatened by rising prices, and in the case of those who have fixed commitments it may mean extreme hardship.'[125] The *Times* warned that such a burden risked 'undermining that great professional and service middle class, which is commonly and rightly described as the backbone of this country'.[126]

Meanwhile, prices were rising. Much of Gladys Langford's diary for the first two months of the war is preoccupied with her search for scarce goods in the shops and her astonishment at their price when she found them. Slippers that had cost 2s. 11d. at the beginning of September 1939 were 4s. 11d. by mid-month.[127] By February 1940 the official Cost of Living Index, a highly conservative measure of price changes, recorded that food expenses had risen by one-seventh since the outbreak of war, and clothes costs by a quarter.[128] A Gallup survey in October 1939 suggested that, even leaving the Budget's tax rises aside, one in three people felt themselves to be worse off as a result of the war.[129] By the following March, 45 per cent of *Sunday Express* readers said they were poorer than they had been back in September.[130]

It was partly to offset price rises in staple goods, to maintain wage restraint and to head off embarrassing press accusations about profiteering that in the winter of 1939 the government implemented subsidies on essential foodstuffs such as bread, meat and milk. In January 1940 food rationing of key items was introduced for the first time: twelve ounces of sugar and four ounces of bacon, ham and butter per person per week.[131] Meat rationing followed in March, with tea and fats added during the summer.

These controls on price and quantity offset some of the earlier concerns about panic buying. The egalitarian message of 'fair shares for all' was broadly popular. But the burden fell particularly hard on the middle class. The poorest Britons were relatively unaffected by food rationing in its early stages, for they had never bought much meat and butter to begin with. Their diet continued to be dominated by unrationed bread and potatoes. Shortages of discretionary foodstuffs hit those higher up on the social ladder far harder. Middle-class culture was as much about performative consumption as about income. It was about behaving differently, purchasing differently, from the working class. Petrol rationing, introduced at the beginning of the war, took away one of the greatest pleasures of 1930s suburban life. Thousands of beloved Morris Minors and Austin 7s were locked away in garages, shrouded in tarpaulins for the duration. Clothes rationing, an even crueller blow to middle-class respectability, was still to come.

In the Phoney War the key site of contestation was not the battlefield but the dining table, and in particular the butter dish. In 1938 the average middle-class family of three had been purchasing about two-and-a-half pounds of butter a week, far in excess of the amount it could now claim by wartime rationing.[132] The thought of replacing this lost butter with margarine provoked an acute level of social anxiety in the middle-class housewife. According to a survey taken in 1938, nineteen out of twenty women before the war would have hesitated to offer such a *déclassé* item to their guests: 'no one has ever insulted me so [...] cheap food makes cheap people,' baulked one Tyneside housewife.[133] Angela Thirkell specifically singled out a liking for margarine as one of the tell-tale traits of the underclass. The usurpation of butter by margarine and the triumph of saccharine over sugar represented two of the most hateful utilitarian features of the new People's War.[134]

An almost total lack of military action to give these impositions some context and purpose meant that there was 'a sense of unreality [...] and a significant residue of puzzled indifference' towards the war among the mostly Conservative middle classes in the autumn of 1939. Many, perhaps, 'hoped they would wake up and find it was all a bad dream'.[135] Chamberlain himself noted this. 'This war twilight is trying people's nerves,' he wrote on 23 September: 'Without the strong centripetal forces of mortal danger all the injustices, inconveniences, hardships and uncertainties of wartime are resented more because they are felt to be unnecessary.'[136] By March 1940, two in five *Sunday Express* readers said that their foremost feeling about the war was that they were 'bewildered and not sure of what's happening'.[137]

To describe this as anti-war feeling would be to misunderstand it. The British middle class regarded itself as the moral bulwark of Nation and Empire. It was instinctively patriotic to the core. It had no difficulty imagining its sons sacrificing themselves in battle for King and Country. But an eight-month demi-war of social sacrifice without glory was a test of its loyalty that it had not expected.

Britain's social cohesion at the beginning of the Second World War was stronger than that of France. There is no reason to think that the antagonism between the wartime classes would have become so bad that a significant number of the wealthy would have preferred defeat in war to defeat by their own working class, as was the case across the Channel. All the same, by the late spring of 1940 it had clearly become rather galling for many middle-class Britons that the only thing this uneventful conflict seemed to be doing was undermining their own position in the social hierarchy.

This frustration manifested itself in different ways. For some it meant a need to prosecute the war more fiercely in order to make its sacrifices worthwhile. By March 1940 the newspapers were demanding action of some kind, any kind – even, if necessary, against the Soviet Union rather than Germany. 'We need more vigour and liveliness in the conduct of the war,' complained the *Times*: there was 'a slightly leisurely air about our methods' which was dispiriting. 'Are we hitting as often as we can and wherever we can?'[138] Press criticism such as this encouraged the government to move ahead with plans for an expedition to Norway the following month that, in the end, brought military disaster and Chamberlain's resignation.[139]

But the frustration may also have begun to stimulate a renewed willingness to consider the possibility of peace talks. By February 1940 the percentage of Britons who said that they approved of the idea of negotiations with the Germans had risen from 17 per cent the previous September to 29 per cent. A clear majority still disapproved of this idea.[140] It remained an unpopular view. But it was less unpopular than it had once been. An Easter survey showed that middle-class Britons were more likely than the working class to think that there 'was no harm in having a look' at what the Germans had to say.[141] 'We must not sheathe the sword until our wrongs are righted,' insisted the *Daily Express*. Nonetheless, 'we must not appear unwilling to make peace if we are offered security,' it went on:

> What do we claim from Germany? We claim the right to live our lives in quietness and confidence [...] we make no claim for the partition of Germany. We would ask for no territorial relinquishments on the part of that country whatsoever, so long as the German boundaries embraced ONLY German people. We desire peace as earnestly and fervently as any other nation in Europe.[142]

This was all a far cry from fighting on the beaches. Of course, much was to happen in the next few months. All the same, without the outbreak of major fighting it is curious to wonder how much longer the British middle class would have quietly acquiesced in its own impoverishment before it started to ask awkward questions about whether the war was really serving any proper purpose.

12

BRAS-DESSUS, BRAS-DESSOUS

In 1939 Hove, at the genteel west end of the Brighton seafront, was, much as it remains today, a charming residential town of wide boulevards and grand Regency mansions. It was the home of Sussex County Cricket Club and pensioned-off Indian Army colonels. It conjured up images of neatly mown lawns and faded repertory actors and respectable, boring holidays taken in the brisk sea air. It was not a place that would have come to anyone's mind if they had thought about the grand strategy of the great world powers. It may, then, have been with a sense of knowing bathos that the British War Cabinet arrived in Hove on the morning of 22 September 1939 for the first meeting on English soil of the Anglo-French Supreme War Council, the Allied decision-making body for the great crusade against Hitler's Third Reich.

Things began oddly that morning. The War Cabinet had been driven from the railway station and dropped off at the back door of the Town Hall, which was locked. They had to walk round to the front of the building, where they were eyed suspiciously by the municipal civil servants, who were unaware of what was going on. A clerk walked up to Lord Halifax and demanded to know if he was a government official ('*Yes*', the foreign secretary replied with laconic amusement). The ministerial party wandered the corridors looking at pictures of dead aldermen until the mayor ('the local butcher, I assume,' sniffed Cadogan) arrived out of breath. Someone recognised the prime minister and shouted 'Chamberlain! Cor blimey!' The French delegation arrived just after noon. Raoul Dautry, Daladier's minister of munitions, had had a bad flight across the Channel and could barely keep down his breakfast.[1]

Once the Supreme War Council was assembled, the meeting began. At its centre was a presentation by General Maurice Gamelin, the commander-in-chief of the French armed forces and (because it was subordinated to his control while on campaign) the British Expeditionary Force in France also. Gamelin explained to the British War Cabinet that the BEF had been assigned a twenty-five-mile sector of the front line between the River Lys and the River Scheldt on the border with Belgium. Overall, he thought that there were about ninety German divisions at that moment on the Western Front, against which the Allies could field somewhere between sixty-five and seventy of their own – more if Italy's neutrality could be assured and the troops guarding the Alpine front could be moved northwards. These numbers would rise on both sides. Gamelin left no doubt that the Western Front was the decisive theatre. 'If the bulk of the German forces were now turned against the Allied forces in France,' he argued, 'the issue of this battle might decide the war.'[2]

*

History has not been kind to Gamelin. The French commander-in-chief, aged sixty-six at the outbreak of war, is said to have epitomised the sclerotic obsolescence of his country's military leadership in the final years of the Third Republic. André Beaufre, one of Gamelin's own general staff officers, called him a 'placid and timorous man [...] who temporized over everything'.[3] Sir Arthur Barratt, the commander of the RAF's Advanced Air Striking Force (AASF), was rather less polite: 'a button-eyed, button-booted, pot-bellied little grocer' was his view.[4]

In the eyes of history, Gamelin committed the cardinal sin of the solider: he lost, and lost catastrophically. It was he, as commander-in-chief of the Allied forces, who made the military dispositions on the Western Front during the Phoney War. It was his plan that the Franco-British forces followed when the Germans attacked on 10 May 1940; and it was he, therefore, who took the blame when the plan collapsed and the Germans achieved a stunning victory in just six weeks.

Gamelin has been accused by generations of historians of lassitude and negligence, of trusting in the false assurances of the Maginot Line defences and the military maxims of 1918 rather than those of 1939. Of believing that the Second World War would play out much as the First had done, with sluggish mass infantry battles rather than the kind of rapid advances assisted by air and armour that the Germans were planning. Of complacently ignoring the possibility of an enemy offensive through the Ardennes forests of southern Belgium, allowing that sector to remain gravely ill-defended. Of stubbornness and vacillation in the hour of crisis, squandering the last opportunity to check the German *Blitzkrieg* and dooming his country to defeat. 'Even after the events of 1940, it was possible to discuss his military gifts,' wrote A. J. P. Taylor in a waspish review of Gamelin's post-war memoirs:

> After his book, controversy is ended. There are limits to absurdity even in a soldier [...] he followed the military principles of an earlier age, when men and not machines decided the lot of war [...] he was never guilty of an intrigue, of a harsh word, of an act of betrayal; alas, he was also never guilty of a victory.[5]

Yet in 1939 Gamelin was probably the most experienced and well-respected soldier in Europe. General Gerd von Rundstedt, who would command Hitler's Army Group A, the spearhead force that invaded France in 1940, had a healthy admiration for his talents. In the autumn of 1914 Gamelin had been responsible for the meticulous staff work that had saved France at the First Battle of the Marne. He was known for his keen mind and an intellectual curiosity unusual in a career soldier. He was an expert in Italian painting and Greek philosophy. Charles de Gaulle in his memoirs praised Gamelin's 'intelligence, subtlety, and self-control'. Another contemporary noted the 'impression of stolidity' offered by his 'measured but simple words, in a calm and resonant voice'. To his friends and enemies alike, Gamelin appeared to be a symbol of reliability and level-headedness, the ideal man to lead in a crisis.[6]

The idea that he was a senile Blimp unable to grasp the nature of modern war is quite wrong. On the contrary, for many years Gamelin had been one of the principal voices within the French Army arguing for faster mechanisation.[7] He was a passionate believer in the centrality of the tank in future conflicts. He had championed the creation of France's *Divisions Légères Mécaniques* (light mechanised divisions, or DLMs) and *Divisions Cuirassées de Reserve* (armoured reserve divisions, or DCRs), the equivalents of Germany's Panzer divisions. Gamelin wanted an army not just of rifles and bayonets but also of troop-carrying vehicles, anti-tank guns and anti-aircraft defences. Certainly, he was not a young man. But he was not much older than von Rundstedt or, for that matter, Winston Churchill. From its outbreak, Gamelin was under no illusions that the Second World War would simply be a replay of the previous conflict. 'The chief lesson to be learned from the Polish campaign,' he remarked in September 1939, 'is the penetrative power of the speedy and hard-hitting German armoured formations and the close co-operation of their Air Force.'[8]

Gamelin understood that his task for the first two or three years of a war against Germany would not be to defeat the enemy but to avoid being defeated. Neither France nor Britain would be in any immediate position to launch a large-scale ground offensive on the Western Front at the opening of hostilities. The Germans, however, might try such an attack themselves as they had done in 1914, in the hope of quickly knocking out France, or at least conquering its industrial north-eastern *départements* and the Low Countries as a base for further operations. Gamelin's job, then, was to hold the Germans along a line as far to the east as possible, ideally beyond French territory altogether. From within the security of such a position, the Allies could steadily mobilise their greatly superior but latent financial and man-power resources. If the Third Reich did not collapse internally from its own political and economic fragility, as many in the Allied camp hoped it might, the fully mobilised Franco-British forces would deliver a crushing *coup de main* some time in 1941 or 1942.

Gamelin's right flank along the Franco-German border from Luxembourg to Switzerland was secured by the famous 280-mile Maginot Line of fortifications. The Maginot Line is ridiculed today as exemplifying everything that was supposedly wrong with France's military preparations for the war. In fact, it was a perfectly sensible system of defence which in the event did exactly what it was supposed to do, which was to deter a direct German attack into Alsace-Lorraine. At a total cost of 5 billion francs, about 7.5 per cent of the French Army budget between 1928 and 1936, it was cheap at the price. It proved better value in 1940 than the Marine Nationale's luxurious battleship fleet, which, though far more expensive, did nothing whatsoever to save France and was ultimately smashed at Mers-el-Kébir.[9] The Maginot Line did not 'fail' in 1940 because France was defeated. It was never expected to stop a German invasion by itself. Its purpose was to channel such an invasion in a predictable direction which could then be countered by mobile ground forces.

Because of the Maginot Line, Gamelin knew that any German attack in the west would come elsewhere: either through Switzerland or, more probably, through the Low Countries. Gamelin was convinced that he had identified the most likely place the Germans would aim for: the Trouée de Gembloux (Gembloux Gap), a twenty-five-mile plateau in central Belgium between the towns of Wavre on the River Dyle and Namur on the Meuse.

With no natural obstacles impeding rapid movement in a south-westerly direction through this aperture, it offered the perfect route for Hitler's Panzers to advance from Maastricht and Liège towards Paris. This, believed Gamelin, was the most vulnerable point along the whole Western Front, because it afforded the maximum geographical advantages to a modern mechanised assault force.

The French had a keen respect for the Wehrmacht's quality, but they were not overawed by it, because they had been thinking about the problem of how to defend against a *Blitzkrieg*-style attack for many years. The idea that German tactics in 1940 were a total shock to them is a myth. As far back as 1932 the French Army had conducted field exercises which showed that even a powerful tank advance could be halted by a well-prepared defence-in-depth using minefields, anti-tank guns and mobile reserves for counter-attacks. These were the same tactics that would be used successfully against the Germans in North Africa in 1942 and Russia in 1943. Germany's Panzer I and Panzer II light tanks, the mainstay of the *Panzerdivisionen* in 1939, were fast but thinly armoured, and equipped only with machine guns and cannons. There was nothing invincible about them, and no reason to think that they could not be stopped by a sound, well-organised defence.[10]

Gamelin's dilemma, though, was a mismatch between the demands of doctrine and politics. He wanted dearly to avoid an encounter battle with the Germans – that is, the two sides advancing into one another in open country as they had done in 1914. The French army should, he believed, fight from a thoroughly prepared defensive position. But in 1936 the Belgians had withdrawn from their military alliance with France and declared neutrality.[11] A French army on the outbreak of war would have to wait on the border for permission to enter Belgium, which would probably only come the moment the Germans invaded. An encounter battle somewhere in the middle of Belgium seemed inevitable under these circumstances. The Belgians had constructed a fortified frontier line of their own along the Albert Canal from Antwerp to Liège, on the eastern border with Germany, but it was no Maginot Line, and it would not buy much time for the French to establish themselves within Belgium if the Germans attacked. Gamelin thought it would hold out for a week, the British CIGS General Ironside three days.[12]

The alternative was to abandon Belgium to its fate and remain on the French side of the border awaiting the Germans. This would eliminate the risk of an encounter battle and was Gamelin's own preference at the outbreak of war. But there were all kinds of problems with this. It would mean forgoing the assistance of Belgium's twenty-two divisions, which might not even put up a fight if it was obvious the French were not going to intervene. It would make it impossible to link up with the Dutch if they too were invaded. Gamelin was under pressure from his own government to keep the fighting as far away from French territory as possible: France's north-eastern *départements* were its industrial heartland, and their devastation during the First World War had enfeebled the national war economy. Moreover, the British were adamant that Belgium must not be ceded to the enemy because of its importance as a base of aerial operations against England, and perhaps Germany too. The Chief of the Air Staff, Sir Cyril Newall, was already eying up Belgian airfields for his squadrons should the RAF get its long-sought approval to begin bombing the Ruhr.[13]

Gamelin's dilemma would, of course, have been resolved if the Belgians had given up their neutrality and allowed Franco-British forces to enter their country. There was a perfect opportunity to do this in September 1939, when the German Army was occupied in Poland, but it was not taken up. In mid-January 1940, and again in April, it seemed to Gamelin that the Belgians might be about to change their mind. But in the end nothing happened. This refusal to co-operate caused no small amount of frustration in Paris and London, where it seemed that the Belgians were going out of their way to make the Allies' defence preparations unnecessarily difficult while still expecting help should the Germans invade. From the Belgians' point of view, abandoning neutrality would guarantee a Nazi invasion, and even if this was probably going to happen anyway, there was no point in exchanging the possibility of catastrophe for the certainty of it. It was, in any case, a bit rich for the British to be complaining about a refusal to co-operate with the French when as recently as February 1939 they had been just as obstinate about the same thing. At a meeting of the Supreme War Council on 23 April 1940 the Allies agreed that if the Germans invaded either Belgium or the Netherlands, they would immediately cross into Belgian territory no matter whether Brussels formally agreed to it or not.[14]

Gamelin's plan, completed in November 1939, was a compromise. Since in the event of a German invasion of Belgium it would likely be impossible to reach the Albert Canal in time before its fortifications capitulated, the French and British would aim to secure a defensive line instead from Antwerp southwards to Dinant, much of it running along the River Dyle (hence the name Dyle or D-Plan). This would involve a dash of up to seventy-five miles from the French frontier in the opening hours of the German attack. But most of the Allied troops would have less far to go than that, and it was reasonable to assume they would reach their assigned positions before the Germans beat them to it. Holding at the Dyle would mean abandoning about half of Belgium. But Brussels would be saved, the Gembloux Gap secured and much of the Belgian Army would be able to fall back to link up with the French and British. If it looked as though the Germans would reach the Dyle first, then there was a more cautious option to stop at the River Scheldt instead. This would sacrifice most of Belgium, but the Germans would at least be denied Ostend and Antwerp.

The Dyle Plan envisaged rushing twenty-five of the best Franco-British divisions into Belgium to hold the line from Antwerp to Namur. On the right shoulder of this force would be just sixteen mostly second-class divisions, which would be dug in on the south bank of the Meuse from Namur to the westernmost end of the Maginot Line, near Sedan. What if the Germans did not try to seize the Gembloux Gap, but instead directed the bulk of their forces towards this much weaker flank position? That, of course, is exactly what happened in May 1940, and ever since Gamelin has been excoriated for ignoring the possibility. He and the other French generals, it is said, clung to the obstinate belief that the Ardennes forest of southern Belgium was 'impenetrable' – a singular expression of their obsolete military thinking in 1940.

But the French were well aware of the fact that the Ardennes was 'penetrable'. How could they not have been? The Germans had sent three armies through it in 1914.[15] A French staff exercise in 1938 suggested that it would take about sixty hours for a German tank force to negotiate passage of it, which as it turned out was almost exactly right.[16] Gamelin had toured the area himself in May 1939 and wrote afterwards of his concern about the weakness of French defences along the Meuse. In conversation with Ironside in September, he speculated that the Wehrmacht might sweep through the Ardennes and try to force a river crossing south of Namur, which is not far off what they actually did the following year.[17]

What made him ultimately conclude that this was not very likely was not some geriatric hankering for the tactics of past wars, but rather a keen understanding of what was happening in the present one. Gamelin made a close study of the Polish campaign in October 1939, and recognised how critical the use of tanks, mobile infantry and close air support had been to the Germans' rapid victory. He knew that Hitler, conscious of Germany's fragile economy, would want to achieve an equally swift knock-out blow on the Western Front. The Ardennes seemed a poor avenue for such a project. To begin with, traversing its narrow forest roads with thousands of vehicles would be a logistical nightmare that would produce traffic jams stretching back tens, if not hundreds, of miles – easy targets for Allied bombers. But even once the Germans made it through and got to the Meuse, they would encounter the most formidable anti-tank obstacle in western Europe. 'How immensely strong by nature [are] the series of positions – the gorge of the Semois, the heights north of Sedan, and the Meuse – upon which the French might stand,' Liddell Hart wrote in 1939, speculating about such a German move:

> The Ardennes country east of the Meuse can be yielded to an invader without serious industrial or military risk. Indeed, because of its relative barrenness and difficulties of communication it might prove a strategic trap for an invader if he fails to cross the Meuse. Having pushed his head into the sack he might find it hard to break loose, and might be severely pummelled [...] an invader of the Ardennes who could push no further might find difficulty in maintaining the supply of his forces under concentrated air bombardment of the winding roads and narrow defiles in the Ardennes.[18]

In other words, if the Germans did attempt such a foolish venture in preference to the natural tank country of the central Belgium plain, so much the better. At the very worst, they would be held up for at least a week trying to cross the Meuse, allowing plenty of time for a counter-attack.

Liddell Hart's concerns in 1939 were focused on the other end of the Allied line. 'It has to be recognised,' he wrote,

> that [the] northern flank of Belgium's defences is relatively more vulnerable than the southern flank [...] an invading force which pounced on and occupied the part of Holland which lies south of the Rhine could dominate the Scheldt and Antwerp, threaten Belgium on her least fortified side, and establish air bases within a hundred miles of the English coast.[19]

It was concerns such as these that encouraged Gamelin to revise his plan in late 1939, removing the French Seventh Army from the strategic reserve and placing it on the leftmost flank of the Allied line. In the event of a German attack, it was now to dash along the Channel coast as far as Breda, allowing a link-up with the Dutch army and protecting the approaches to the Scheldt.

The removal of the Seventh Army's seven excellent divisions from the strategic reserve, including the only one of the three DLMs not already committed to defending the Gembloux Gap, worried General Georges, the commander of the north-eastern front, who would be responsible for putting the Dyle Plan into effect. What if a German assault on northern Belgium was just a feint? 'In the event of an attack [...] in the centre or on our front between the Meuse and the Moselle,' he wrote to Gamelin, 'we could find ourselves lacking the necessary means for a counter-attack.'[20] The commander-in-chief was unmoved by such fears. After all, he still held three DCRs in reserve. They ought to be more than adequate to stop a German breakthrough in any emergency – so long as they were used in a swift and co-ordinated way.

If his country had not been defeated in 1940, Gamelin's qualities as a scrupulous planner and affable committee man might have led to him becoming the French Eisenhower of the Second World War, the ideal commander to lead the Allied coalition to victory. His basic military judgement was not at fault. The Dyle Plan was a sound idea, given everything that could be reasonably assumed in November 1939. Gamelin was quite right that a German attack through the Ardennes was a doubtful venture because it was so imprudent. Most of Hitler's own generals thought so too. They called it 'crazy and foolhardy', and embarked on it not so much from any confidence that it would work but simply because the only alternative – charging into central Belgium – seemed too obvious to offer any prospect of success.[21] Franz Halder, chief of the German general staff, thought it would take nine days for armoured forces to cross the Ardennes. He wondered if the plan might have only a one-in-ten chance of succeeding.[22] General von Bock, who would command the German forces invading northern Belgium and the Netherlands, said it was 'transcending the frontiers of reason' to think that the Panzers could struggle through the Ardennes forest roads without first being smashed by Allied air power.[23]

Where Gamelin erred fatally was in ignoring the mounting intelligence evidence in the spring of 1940 that the Germans *were* going to attack through the Ardennes anyway, no matter how risky it was.[24] It was unfortunate that, for all his qualities, he was, as Julian Jackson puts it, 'temperamentally unwilling to confront unpleasant realities' that did not accord with his own assumptions. This was a mental stubbornness he shared with Neville Chamberlain. The two men were undone by the same flaw in May 1940.[25]

*

On 3 September 1939 the British Army could call on an official strength of 892,697 officers and men. Only about 224,000 of these were regular full-time soldiers, however. Around 131,100 were ex-regular reservists who were statutorily obligated to return to the colours in an emergency; 458,000 were the 'Saturday night soldiers' of the part-time Territorial Army; 42,600 were members of the Supplementary Reserve, a group of doctors, engineers, mechanics and other specialists who had agreed to perform service in the technical and medical branches of the Army in wartime; and 34,500 comprised the first cohort of twenty-year-old 'Militiamen' conscripts who had been called up for six months of service back in July. Only one in four of the soldiers in this nominal return could, therefore, really be said to be fully trained and prepared for war. France, by contrast, already had 900,000 men under arms when Germany invaded Poland, and 5 million reservists available for immediate call-up.[26]

The difference in size between these two mobilisations did not go unnoticed on either side of the Channel. Daladier commented to one of his generals in October that the British, protected by their moat defensive, had the advantage of being able to conserve their energies 'so as to last out, to wait for the Americans, perhaps the Russians'. His own nation, directly bordering Germany, enjoyed no such luxury: 'we risk becoming, after the Czechs, after the Poles, the prey of the Reich.'[27] France's ambassador in London, Charles Corbin, wrote that the British had 'such confidence in the French army that they are tempted to consider their military support as a gesture of solidarity rather than a vital friendship'. Churchill, now recalled to Chamberlain's War Cabinet as First Lord of the Admiralty, noted the barbed resentment underlying such remarks. 'I doubt,' he told his colleagues, 'whether the French would acquiesce in a division of effort which gives us the sea and the air and left them to pay almost the whole blood-tax on land.'[28]

Chamberlain, having resisted every attempt to enlarge the Army since he had entered the Cabinet in 1931, had been forced in February 1939 to assume a continental commitment. Now, as wartime prime minister, he had no choice but to accept that the Army must grow, and grow dramatically. In April he had agreed to double the size of the Territorial Army to 340,000 men, and to begin selective short-service conscription. The Cabinet agreed a target of a thirty-two-division army, including troops from the Dominions and India, within two years. In October the secretary of state for war, supported by Churchill and Lord Halifax, proposed that this all-imperial target be expanded still further to fifty-five divisions by 1941, thirty-two of them to be provided exclusively by troops from the UK. This, though a smaller army than the one that had been raised to fight in the previous world war, would still be a ground force of continental proportions.

The prime minister had many reasonable objections to this. It was not clear, for one thing, whether Britain was even capable of mustering enough men to deploy a thirty-two-division army (including all of the support and service personnel such a vast force would require behind the lines) while still keeping its war economy running properly. Nor was it clear whether Britain's factories would be able to produce the arms, vehicles and equipment such an army would need on a two-year deadline while at the same time keeping up the wartime expansion of the RAF and Royal Navy. But a start had to be made somewhere. The Cabinet agreed to the 32/55-division figure as a final mobilisation target, though an air of fantasy hung around it from the beginning. It was a number plucked from the rarefied atmosphere of a War Cabinet committee room and scribbled onto a memorandum, rather than the product of any serious investigation about needs and capabilities.[29]

All thoughts of dozens of divisions were, in September 1939, for the distant future anyway. An expeditionary force of the existing Army had to be sent to France immediately, if for no other reason than to give moral succour to Britain's ally. By early October a four-division-strong BEF, mostly made up of regular Army infantry battalions, had taken its place on the Franco-Belgian border. A fifth regular infantry division arrived in December. During the early months of 1940 five additional Territorial infantry divisions joined the regulars, and by late spring three 'labour' divisions of Territorials had also been sent to France. The troops of these last divisions had had almost no training and were equipped with little more than rifles and bayonets. The idea was to use them for construction duties behind the lines until they were fit for combat.

The BEF of 1940 has been talked up quite a bit recently by historians.

David Edgerton has called it 'a small but uniquely mechanised army', the 'mechanical Moloch on the Western Front'.[30] 'The best equipped and most modern [Army] in the world' is another sanguine judgement.[31] It's true that the BEF was unusually mobile for a force of its size, and it had some excellent weapons. Its artillery was towed entirely by lorries and gun tractors rather than horses, and the infantry could be moved about by road thanks to the Royal Army Service Corps's troop-carrying companies. Some units by 1940 were equipped with the Universal Carrier, an ingenious caterpillar-tracked tankette that could ferry a mortar or radio crew around the battlefield. The new section-level light machine gun, the Bren, was accurate and reliable, the QF 3.7-inch heavy anti-aircraft gun the most advanced of its type in the world. The QF 25-pounder was probably the best field gun of the Second World War.

But listing these vehicles and weapons on an official table of organisation and equipment was one thing, getting them into the hands of the troops in 1939 quite another. Furnishing even a ten-division army within a matter of months was too much for Britain's overstretched armaments and motor industry. Of the 240 heavy anti-aircraft guns the BEF was supposed to possess on its arrival in France in late September 1939, it had only seventy-two, many of them having been held back in the UK for fear of a Luftwaffe knock-out blow against London. Four in ten anti-tank guns had yet to be issued. None of the BEF's field artillery regiments had received any 25-pounder guns. Some units had not received their army lorries and had to rely on requisitioned civilian vehicles which quickly broke down.[32] Territorial units were even worse off than the regulars. TA divisions arrived in France in the spring of 1940 with, on average, only a quarter of the amount of equipment they were supposed to possess.[33]

Some of these deficiencies were made up in the months of inaction during the Phoney War. Many were not. In April 1940 the BEF's commander-in-chief, Viscount Gort, was still complaining to the War Office about critical shortages of material, particularly ammunition, vehicles and spare parts.[34] After one inspection visit he noted with disbelief that the troops did not even possess cutlery and mugs.[35]

A far bigger issue than equipment, though, was that the Army was having to prepare suddenly for a kind of military operation it had not thought much about for twenty years. It's true that the main Army doctrinal manual, *Field Service Regulations*, had continued between the wars to lay out tactics for full-scale, combined-arms battle against a modern

European enemy.[36] But if the Army had never entirely forgotten its continental role, it was certainly well out of practice of it by 1939. 'The purpose of the British Army is to maintain order in the British Empire only,' declared the secretary of state for war, Alfred Duff Cooper, in 1934.

Its organisational structure, equipment and training throughout the 1920s and 1930s had reflected this imperial reality. In January 1938 seventy-four out of its 138 infantry battalions were overseas, either fighting to suppress the Arab Revolt in Palestine or else on some other security or policing task east of Suez. The scattered nature of this littoral garrison army meant that there were few opportunities between the wars to conduct realistic training on a large scale. Only a single corps-size exercise took place in the whole period from 1925 to 1939. A counter-insurgency gendarmerie operating in built-up areas among civilians needed bolt-action rifles and bayonets, not automatic weapons wasteful of ammunition and indiscriminate in lethality. At a section and platoon level, the British Army would fight the Second World War at a significant firepower disadvantage to the Germans because of this pre-war preference for lighter, less profligate weaponry.[37]

Gort commanded ten divisions of infantry in France. But Gamelin had plenty of infantry of his own. What he really wanted from the British were tanks. A strong British armoured component, complementing France's own DLMs and DLCs, would provide a vital counter-balance to the German Panzer forces massing to the east. And yet not a single British armoured division arrived in France during the first eight months of the war. Britain had pioneered the tank in 1916 and maintained its lead in armoured technology and tactics up to the late 1920s. The 16-ton Vickers Mark III Medium was arguably the best tank in the world in 1930. But it was never developed beyond the prototype stage, owing to its high cost. The government's abandonment of the project and reluctance to pursue any further work on medium tanks caused a concomitant loss of commercial orders, a drying up of R&D budgets, and a drifting away of talented designers from the industry which set back Britain's armoured warfare development by at least a decade.[38]

Liddell Hart would later blame the Army's neglect of the tank on narrow-minded Blimps still obsessed with the cavalry glories of the past. But, if anything, British generals between the wars were unusually open to the idea of mechanisation.[39] The problem was not the Army's stubborn allegiance to Victorian ideas. It was that the government could see no point in spending money on the kind of heavier tanks that would be suitable for European warfare if the Army's mission was going to remain imperial security overseas and anti-aircraft defence at home. When, in February 1938, the Treasury asked the War Office to cut the Army's rearmament budget by 14 per cent to help pay for the RAF instead, over half the savings were taken from armoured vehicle spending.[40]

What money there was for mechanisation between the wars was spent mostly on light tanks such as the Vickers Mark VI, a fast vehicle suitable for desert and scrub conditions, but thinly armoured and equipped only with two machine guns. By May 1940 the BEF had 208 Mark VIs organised in seven Royal Armoured Corps (RAC) regiments. The only heavier British tanks in France were the 100 Matilda Infantry ('I') tanks of the independent 1st Army Tank Brigade. But of these just twenty-three were the Mark II type, equipped with an armour-piercing gun.[41] Except for the Mark IIs, the French regarded the tanks the British sent as 'quite useless'.[42]

In theory, the Army was committed at the outbreak of war to creating three 'mobile' armoured divisions similar to France's DLMs and the German *Panzerdivisionen*. But not one of these was ready for deployment in France by the following May.[43] The 1st Armoured Division was mostly equipped with light tanks. It had too few of the motorised infantry, artillery and engineer units it would need to perform as a proper combined-arms force, and those it did possess were picked off for use elsewhere anyway during the Phoney War. Most of its vehicles were still sitting idle in the UK when the Germans opened the campaign in the west on 10 May.[44]

Perhaps a commander-in-chief of energy and vision could have compensated for some of the deficiencies in his inchoate army by sheer force of will. Lord Gort, though an officer and gentleman with many sterling personal qualities, was not up to such a task. An Old Harrovian and Grenadier Guardsman, Gort was a sixth viscount of impeccable Anglo-Irish stock, a bona fide hero of the First World War, a recipient of the Victoria Cross and the DSO with two bars, and a man of great courage, integrity and industriousness. He could be a little stiff and shy in company, but despite his high rank and aristocratic pedigree he had no airs or graces. Gort relished the ascetic life of the soldier on campaign. His HQ during the Phoney War, Château d'Habarcq, west of Arras, had no hot running water, no electric lighting and no indoor lavatories. He regularly worked fourteen-hour days, sometimes driving over a hundred miles on difficult roads to visit scattered units of the BEF, nourished en route only by sandwiches and a Thermos flask.

It is not difficult to see how such an unassuming, hard-working and deeply honourable man – nicknamed affectionately 'Fat Boy' – could earn the passionate loyalty of his subordinates. Gort 'dazzled no one', conceded Sir Edward Spears, Churchill's liaison officer with the French, 'but [he] inspired confidence because he was completely trustworthy'.[45] But he never really got to grips with his role as the BEF's commander-in-chief. Mentally, he was still too much the regimental colonel. His mind was still too focused on the kind of ephemera best handled by battalion adjutants: what kind of igniting paper to use on signal rockets, the right mixture of anti-freeze for engines, the training of night-flying pigeons. One of the first things he set his mind to after arriving in France was deciding whether tin hats should be carried on the left or right shoulder.[46]

Perhaps his biggest handicap was his unwillingness to make a nuisance of himself. Gort had considerable private reservations about the wisdom of advancing into Belgium to take up defensive positions that had not been adequately reconnoitred beforehand. He worried about the ability of his untried army to fight a first-class enemy like the Wehrmacht, well equipped with armour and airpower. But he was conscious of the small size of the BEF, and this, plus his poor knowledge of French (sometimes he could not follow Gamelin's rapid speeches and just nodded along, smiling and muttering '*d'accord*'), his sense of loyalty to his superiors and his natural diffidence meant that he did not raise his concerns either in Paris or London. A more strident, even obnoxious, British commander-in-chief might have been better for everyone.[47]

*

One thing that Gort was emphatic about was the BEF's need for air support. 'The whole weight of our Metropolitan Air Forces will be needed to help in the formidable task of repelling the German onslaught when it begins,' he warned the secretary of state for war in April 1940.[48] From the beginning of the Phoney War, Daladier and Gamelin also pressed for a firm commitment from the RAF to be ready to take part in the battle for France if the Germans attacked.[49] Their own Armée de l'Air (AdA) was growing fast: Daladier's government had given priority to air rearmament back in 1938, and by the eve of the German offensive in the west the AdA had around 1,280 modern combat and reconnaissance aircraft, including some very advanced types such as the Dewoitine D520 fighter and the Breguet 693 ground-attack bomber. But multiple reorganisations had badly disrupted the efficiency of the French air arm, and it was plagued by manufacturing and maintenance problems and a very poor pilot training programme. The only way it could hope to balance out the Luftwaffe's advantage in numbers over French airspace would be through the active assistance of the RAF.[50]

The Royal Air Force had played a crucial tactical role in the victory of the Allied ground armies in 1918. By the final months of the First World War it had had eighty-four squadrons on the Western Front in direct co-operation with Field Marshal Haig's armies.[51] RAF aircrew were pioneers in the arts of Close Air Support (CAS) on the battlefield – acting as 'flying artillery' against enemy troops in the opposing trenches – as well as in the interdiction of German soldiers, supplies and communications further behind the front lines. But this powerful and highly experienced tactical air force was dissolved in the great post-war demobilisation of 1919, and as the British Army returned in the 1920s to its traditional role as a small imperial constabulary, it seemed unlikely that such a ground-support force would ever be needed again.

The RAF had other plans for its future. To guard its hard-won status as an independent service, it sought to craft a mission that went beyond simply acting as a tactical adjunct to the Army and Navy. The mission it embraced was strategic bombing, both in an offensive and a defensive form: the ability to threaten a knock-out blow against Britain's enemies and to defend against one at home. A CAS role had no place in this schema. The primacy of strategic bombing to the RAF was reflected in its division into three operational commands in 1936: Fighter, Bomber and Coastal. Fighter Command was to be responsible for the air defence of Great Britain, Bomber Command the knock-out blow deterrent and Coastal Command the protection of the maritime sea lanes. No Army Co-operation Command was created. The RAF did not contemplate 'any organised close support by aircraft at all', its Deputy Director of Operations, Robert Saundby, noted: 'no units are really trained in such work.'[52] The RAF inter-war *Manual of Combined Operations* devoted a grand total of three-and-a-half pages out of 272 to ground support.[53]

In 1936, to be fair, army co-operation did not seem all that urgent a consideration, given that the government was still solidly opposed to a continental commitment. But by the winter of 1939 that commitment had been re-embraced, the BEF was in France and plans were already coalescing for a fifty-five-division army. Such a mass force would surely need extensive tactical support from the RAF.

The Air Ministry's view, though, was that nothing had fundamentally changed. Diverting the RAF's mission to tactical ground support would be, as Sir Cyril Newall put it, 'a gross misuse' of its resources.[54] 'The aeroplane,' decreed John Slessor, Director of Plans at the Air Ministry, 'is not a battlefield weapon.'[55] Any objections by the Army that it had certainly seemed like a battlefield weapon back in 1918 were brushed aside. CAS missions had been useful in the First World War 'in an emergency', Slessor conceded, but were too costly in lives and machines. More recent experience in the Spanish Civil War and the Polish campaign was also deemed irrelevant. Spanish militiamen who had fled in terror from ground attacks by German dive-bombers had had poor training and morale.[56] As for Poland: 'I am aware that there were instances in which close support on the battlefield was effective,' wrote the secretary of state for air, Kingsley Wood, in November 1939. 'But by far the greatest effect was achieved by long-range bombers [...] operating against the enemy reserves, communications and headquarters, miles to the rear of his forward troops.'[57] The best way to support the BEF, the RAF insisted, would be for Bomber Command to begin raids on the Ruhr industrial basin as soon as any German offensive in the west began. A knock-out blow against German industry would assist the British Army far more than wasteful and ineffective attacks on battlefield targets.

Given the Air Ministry's undisguised lack of enthusiasm for the mission, the RAF complement that accompanied the BEF to France in the winter of 1939 was unsurprisingly meagre.[58] The 'Air Component' of the Expeditionary Force, as it was known, consisted of five squadrons of Westland Lysander reconnaissance aircraft, four of Bristol Blenheim light bombers and four of Hawker Hurricane fighters. There was also the 'Advanced Air Striking Force' (AASF), based near Rheims, which had eight squadrons of Fairey Battle light bombers, two of Blenheims and two of Hurricanes. From January 1940 onwards all the Air Component and AASF squadrons were under the command of Air Marshal Arthur Barratt, under the mantle of the British Air Forces in France (BAFF). Barratt's views on tactical ground support can be gleaned from a visit he made to French air bases in April 1939. He criticised the AdA for being 'entirely bound up with the use of land forces', and hoped the RAF would be able to guide it 'to more enlightened views on the subject of the use of air forces in war'.[59]

The AASF's Fairey Battles were going to play an especially poignant role in the disaster to come. It is worth looking at their story in some detail because of what it reveals about the RAF in the first year of the Second World War.[60] The Battle is one of the most undistinguished British combat aircraft in history. It is almost always described as a plane that was 'obsolete' at the outbreak of the war, a characterisation that tidily explains away its tragic performance in combat. But the Battle was not an ageing machine in 1939. It had entered service in June 1937, only a few months before the Hurricane. It used the same Rolls-Royce Merlin engine as the Hurricane and the Spitfire. It had many of the same innovative characteristics as other advanced monoplanes of the time – a light alloy and stressed-skin construction, an enclosed cockpit, a retractable undercarriage. It was easy to fly, reliable and tough. Many of its crews loved it. 'We all thought the world of the Battle,' said Flying Officer R. D. Max of the AASF's 103 Squadron. 'It was really a solid rugged aircraft [...] we all thought very highly of it and in fact we were not in a hurry to go rushing off to re-equip.'[61]

The Battle's main vulnerability was its speed. It could only manage 257 m.p.h. in level flight at high altitude, making it an easy target for much faster German interceptors such as the Messerschmitt Bf 109. But the reason it was slow was that the Air Ministry viewed it as a strategic day bomber, which ought to be able to fly a thousand miles to an industrial target like the Ruhr and back. Such a bomber needed a dedicated third crew member to serve as a navigator, in addition to the pilot and air-gunner. It also needed a bulky autopilot system and an auxiliary fuselage fuel tank. The Merlin was a powerful engine, but all that weight was too much for it.

The Air Ministry knew all about the Battle's deficiencies. Indeed, even before the first Battle had arrived at an operational squadron in 1937, the whole concept of the single-engine strategic bomber had been quietly written off. But Chamberlain's desire for a cheap, shop-window deterrent air force, as well as the need to keep the Fairey Aviation Company's establishment busy while better designs were still on the drawing board, kept the Battle project going.[62]

Within a month of the outbreak of war it was obvious that the sluggish, overladen Battle would be totally unable to perform strategic bombing in daylight. On 30 September 1939 five Battles flying a reconnaissance mission over Saarbrücken were ambushed by German fighters and every one of them quickly shot down. Further Battle flights over enemy airspace were banned for the time being.

What, then, to do with the over 100 Battles still remaining in France?

Air Chief Marshal Sir Robert Brooke-Popham, who was sent to inspect RAF squadrons in France in late 1939, had one suggestion. If the Battle could not be flown into Germany, then it really did not need its navigator, its autopilot or its auxiliary fuel tank. Getting rid of these would drastically cut its range but would also allow ground crews to fit several hundred pounds of additional armour protection to the engine and cockpit, plus a ventral rear-firing machine gun, all without compromising the plane's existing performance. It would no longer be capable of long-distance strategic bombing, but evidently it could not do that anyway. What it *would* be much more capable of doing, however, would be short-range, low-level CAS and interdiction bombing against German positions, with a far greater chance of surviving anti-aircraft fire on the run-in to the target.

Perhaps, if this new role was embraced, its paltry wing armament of one machine gun could be quadrupled, giving it a more effective ground strafing capability. Perhaps its four 250-lb high-explosive bombs, which could not be safely dropped from low level without a long fuse delay, making CAS targeting difficult, could be replaced with 40-lb anti-personnel bombs instead. None of these changes would suddenly turn the Battle into a superlative weapon of war. It would still be slow. But they would allow a useless strategic bomber to serve as a decent tactical bomber – just the kind of aircraft the Army was crying out for.

The Air Ministry would have none of it. It could not bring itself to strip away the Battle's long-range strategic bombing capability. Tactical air support remained a contemptible deviation from the true purpose of an air force. If necessary, when the day came, the Battles might be used for CAS and interdiction as a sop to Gort and Gamelin. But in the meantime there would be no attempt to prepare the planes or their crews to carry out such missions effectively. So no changes were made to equipment, armour or payload. Instead of practising 'hedge-hopping' flying and low-level attacks on enemy targets, the Battle squadrons in France during the Phoney War were given high-altitude night-flying exercises, since that might be a way for them still to bomb the Ruhr. The RAF did not even refit the Battles with self-sealing fuel tanks, despite the mounting evidence by the spring of 1940 that these were vital to protecting aircraft from catastrophic fires. The tragedy that was about to befall the brave young crew members of the AASF was one that the RAF chose, however unwittingly.

If any Allied bombing aircraft was to operate successfully over French or Belgian airspace when the Germans attacked, it would need the protection of friendly fighters. The six Hurricane squadrons attached to the BAFF were clearly not going to be enough, even in combination with the AdA, to wrest air superiority over the battlefield from the Luftwaffe's hundreds of Bf 109s and Bf 110s. But all attempts to increase the fighter commitment to France during the Phoney War ran into the implacable resistance of Air Marshal Sir Hugh Dowding, Air Officer Commanding-in-Chief (AOC-in-C) of RAF Fighter Command. Dowding regarded his own claim on fighters as superseding those of any other theatre commander. He complained to the Air Ministry in September 1939 that he had been asked to hand over the six BAFF Hurricane squadrons and to set aside another six squadrons for possible transfer to France if the Germans invaded. Dowding pointed out that he still did not have the fifty-three metropolitan squadrons which he regarded as a bare minimum for the Air Defence of Great Britain.[63] 'The Home Defence Organisation must not be regarded as co-equal with other Commands,' he insisted, 'but should receive priority to all other claims until it is firmly secured, since the continued existence of the nation, and all its services, depends upon the Royal Navy and Fighter Command.'[64]

Dowding's later role as leader of Fighter Command in the Battle of Britain in 1940 would raise him into the pantheon of British heroes of the Second World War. His reputation today stands almost as high as Churchill's. There is much to admire about this shy, self-effacing man with a 'soft voice and quiet manner'. The tragic circumstances of his personal life – his wife, to whom he was devoted, died two years into their marriage – add an undeniable pathos to his story. Even his taste for Theosophy and his belief that garden fairies helped plants grow are endearing quirks.[65] Dowding's standing as the providential saviour of his country has been polished by hundreds of adulatory pen portraits since 1940, and in particular by Laurence Olivier's portrayal of him in Harry Saltzman's 1969 film *Battle of Britain*. To question Dowding's judgement today seems almost impious. Yet his stubborn insistence during the Phoney War that the BEF should be given as little fighter support as possible helped to doom the British forces in France when the German attack came. His refusal to co-operate with Lord Gort placed Britain in jeopardy in a way it otherwise might not have been.

To be fair to Dowding, there were some sound practical reasons not to send Spitfires across the Channel in 1939. The plane's narrow undercarriage made it unsuitable for use on rougher French airfields.[66] As Fighter Command's AOC-in-C, Dowding's primary responsibility was the defence of the airspace over the United Kingdom, and so he can hardly be blamed for wanting to keep the maximum possible resources for that mission. He was certainly not the only senior commander to think that a Luftwaffe knock-out blow might be the main threat to the Allies. RAF Air Intelligence remained fixated on the idea.[67] On 4 May 1940, less than a week before the Germans invaded the Netherlands and Belgium, the chiefs of staff reported to the War Cabinet that an air attack on Britain was more likely than a ground offensive in the west.[68]

But Dowding was unwilling to consider how interrelated the needs of the BEF and the Air Defence of Great Britain were. A German aerial knock-out blow against the UK would be much more dangerous if the Luftwaffe could use air bases in the Low Countries and northern France. Defending that territory was precisely what the BEF had been sent to the continent to do. Dowding was reluctant to support Gort in France in anything more than the most grudging way because he was obsessed with the strategic bombing threat to the homeland. But his refusal to assist the BEF made that threat greater, not less.

Once the German assault in the West began on 10 May 1940, Dowding was on stronger ground in refusing to throw unprepared UK-based Fighter Command squadrons into the air war in piecemeal dribs and drabs. But he could have avoided this problem in the first place by a greater willingness to send some of them during the Phoney War, when their pilots would have had an opportunity to conduct proper training in army co-operation and close escort duties.[69] In the event, the political realities of the Allied coalition meant that he had to rush some of his precious squadrons across the Channel anyway. That was inevitable. Their poor preparation, and eventual defeat, were not.

13

IN THE NAME OF GOD

'My policy continues to be the same,' Chamberlain wrote to his sister Ida on 8 October 1939, just over a month after the outbreak of war:

> Hold on tight. Keep up the economic pressure, push on with munitions production and military preparations with the utmost energy, take no offensive unless Hitler begins it. I reckon that if we are allowed to carry on this policy we shall have won the war by the spring.[1]

Assurances such as this were going to look comically Panglossian after the dramatic events of the spring and summer of 1940. Indeed, within a year of his making this confident prediction, Chamberlain's leadership during the Phoney War was going to be condemned on all sides as complacent and pernicious. He had, his critics said, dawdled and delayed, refusing to take seriously the threat of Hitler's Wehrmacht. He had wasted precious months that could have been employed building up Allied strength by trusting instead to facile assumptions about the Third Reich's fragility. 'The British Government did not exert itself to any great extent in the arming of our country, even after we had clashed into war with the most tremendous military power of all times,' 'Cato' of *Guilty Men* wrote in the most famous and damning valediction to Chamberlain in July 1940:

> On the morning of May 10 [1940], with a roar which drowned the futile boasts and foolish brags of Britain's Prime Minister [...] the Nazi hordes streamed over the frontiers of Holland, Belgium and Luxemburg, with tanks, planes, guns and motorised infantry in endless columns. Within three weeks the tragedy of the Dunkirk beaches was enacted before the staring eyes of a trembling world.[2]

Historians since have been little kinder to Chamberlain. British policy during the Phoney War 'reflected a bureaucratic inertia bordering on pusil-lanimity', according to Williamson Murray.[3]

It's important, though, not to confuse contingent defeat with funda-mentally flawed strategy. No one would deny that events in 1940 turned out very differently (to put it mildly) from the way the British prime min-ister hoped. That does not mean that they were fated to turn out that way. Or that his approach to the war was inherently irrational or unrealistic.

It's important to remember that Chamberlain's war aim was not simply to defeat Hitler. He wanted to defeat Hitler while preserving the United Kingdom as the solvent centre of an undiminished world empire. He wanted to maintain a country with much the same social, economic and political systems at the end of the war as it had had at the beginning. To see Nazi Germany destroyed but Britain's wealth and authority swept away in the process, or its liberal-democratic-capitalist traditions perma-nently abandoned, would, for him, only be victory of a gravely Pyrrhic kind. Chamberlain was not the only Briton to be worrying about such an outcome in 1939. Geoffrey Crowther, the editor of *The Economist*, won-dered if his country was 'being driven, in an effort to defeat totalitarianism, to adapt all forms of totalitarianism itself [...] is democracy in Europe com-mitting suicide in self-defence?'[4] As Basil Liddell Hart had recently warned in *The Defence of Britain*, 'if you concentrate exclusively on victory, with no thought for the after-effect, you may be too exhausted to profit by the peace.'[5]

Chamberlain's cautious approach to the war has to be seen in that light. He understood that certain liberal-capitalist verities would have to be set aside for the duration. Indeed, suspending *laissez-faire* business-as-usual in September 1939 and introducing controls on manpower, production and financial transactions had been something of a relief, as it had brought the growing economic crisis of the final months of peace to an end. Chamber-lain accepted that even a short conflict would be very expensive; there was no avoiding that. And as a patriot who by the war's outbreak had come to personally loathe Hitler with a passionate and vindictive intensity, he also believed that, if it came to it, national bankruptcy was preferable to defeat by the Nazis.

But Chamberlain would certainly try to avoid either fate if possible. For the first six months or so of the war he felt satisfied that this was a realistic, indeed likely, goal. 'I have a hunch that the war will be over by the spring,' he wrote in November 1939. 'It won't be by defeat in the field but by

German realisation that they can't win and that it isn't worth their while to go on getting thinner & poorer when they might have instant relief [...] my belief is that a great many Germans are near that position now.'[6]

Britain and France had, as Liddell Hart put it, one important strategic advantage over Hitler. 'For him to succeed, he has to conquer. For them to succeed, they have only to convince him that he cannot conquer, and that continued effort will bring more loss than gain. They are thus able to wage a far less exhausting kind of war.' Faced with the underlying fragility of the German economy and the limited popular support of his regime, the Nazi dictator would, Chamberlain believed, have no choice but to try for a quick knock-out blow, either by land or by air, against the Allies, rather than hunker down for a long war of attrition that he could not win.

But since, to quote Liddell Hart again, 'the dominant lesson from the experience of land warfare, for more than a generation past, has been the superiority of the defence over attack', any assault against the Franco-British armies in the west would probably end in bloody failure; and the Luftwaffe's threat was now looking more manageable in the face of a vastly strengthened air defence system in Britain.[7] 'I cannot see how he can get a smashing military victory and the attempt whether successful or unsuccessful would entail such frightful losses as to endanger the whole Nazi system,' Chamberlain concluded in October 1939.[8]

The best course for the British and French, then, was steadily to tighten the grip on Germany's war industry by the application of blockade, to build up just enough defensive military force to absorb any knock-out blow and to wait for the Third Reich to collapse from within – by economic implosion, revolution or some combination of the two. No repeat of the gruesome mass battles of the First World War would be necessary; 'holocausts are [not] required to gain the victory, though they are certainly liable to lose us the peace,' Chamberlain thought.[9]

Victory would mean, at a non-negotiable minimum, Hitler's death or Napoleonesque departure to some distant prison. The apparatus of dictatorship in the Third Reich would have to be dismantled. That might not necessarily mean the removal of every leading Nazi, however. Chamberlain could still contemplate in November 1939 a man like Göring having 'some ornamental position in a transitional government'.[10] Most probably, he imagined the war ending somewhat as it had in 1918, with the German head of state and his principal cronies ousted and a coalition of 'moderate' Nazis and traditional conservatives replacing them and offering concessions (but not total capitulation) to the Allies. Poland and Czechoslovakia would have their sovereignty restored, but not necessarily with their old pre-war borders. Chamberlain was even willing to consider restoring some of Germany's old colonies if it would make the treaty more palatable.[11] The idea that peace would only come if the victorious Allied powers occupied every square inch of Reich territory and took it upon themselves to reconstruct German society from top to bottom would have seemed bizarrely excessive in 1939.

The Allies' Fabian strategy had disadvantages. It meant abandoning the Poles to their fate in the short term, a cynical desertion given the promises of military assistance they had made in the summer of 1939 – though defending Polish sovereignty had never been a cause particularly dear to British or French hearts. It meant, too, the Allies passing up the chance to try for a quick knock-out blow of their own while the German army was distracted in Poland in the first month of the war. This looks more like a lost opportunity now than it did at the time. It's true that the Wehrmacht had only a few divisions defending the western border in September 1939. It's equally true that rushing an Allied army with little training in offensive action into an improvised assault, for which no prior staff work had been done, would have risked a costly and humiliating defeat.

In any case, during the first few months of war it seemed that economic blockade through the Allies' massive naval superiority might quickly bring Germany down by itself. That, at least, was the optimistic prognosis supplied to the War Cabinet by the new Ministry of Economic Warfare (MEW). Germany lacked stockpiles of many key raw materials necessary for advanced war industry, including iron, chrome, nickel, copper and tin. Its agricultural labour force was inadequate; its railway system was strained; its gold and foreign currency reserves were minimal.[12] According to an interdepartmental committee in October, the Third Reich was liable to exhaust all its stockpiled petroleum within the first six months of the war, and by the spring of 1940 'Germany's oil position is likely to be critical'.[13] By Christmas 1939 the MEW was growing more confidant that 'in each principal section of [Germany's] war economy there is a weak link [...] which has introduced a type of vulnerability different in kind from that which existed in 1914–1918'.[14]

It turned out later that such expectations of German economic collapse were highly premature, but they were not totally fantastical. Germany really did go through a profound crisis in the winter of 1939, as imports were slashed to one-fifth of their peacetime level. Nazi collaboration with the USSR ameliorated some of the worst shortages of key raw materials, but it could not make up for the blockade's fundamental disruption of the economy at a time when Hitler was demanding rapid expansion of munitions and aircraft manufacturing. During the first seven months of 1940 total armaments production in Germany doubled. But this could be achieved only by a drastic contraction of civilian consumption. Clothing, housewares and furniture became scarcities. Coal disappeared from sale. Food rationing was introduced even before the invasion of Poland and was much more austere than its equivalent in Britain. In the first months of 1940 millions of Germans were already living on a monotonous regimen of bread, potatoes and artificial sausage. Resentment at the ostentatious diets of fat Nazi *Gauleiters* grew. Absentee rates in factories soared in protest at draconian new labour laws, which froze wages and made Sundays compulsory workdays. Nervous Gestapo officials wondered whether the Reich would make it through a full year of war.[15]

Hitler was aware of this crisis and its implications. 'Time is an ally of the western powers and not of ours,' he told his generals after the conquest of Poland. To the German dictator, this meant that either peace must be brokered with the Allies immediately or else an all-or-nothing strike launched against the West. His risk-taking mentality made that decision inevitable; as in the summer of 1939, he chose a violent plunge into the unknown rather than submission. 'I am staking my life's work on a gamble,' Hitler privately admitted: 'I have to choose between victory or destruction. I choose victory.' Within days of Poland's surrender he was already demanding that the invasion of France and the Low Countries, *Fall Gelb* (Plan Yellow), begin no later than 12 November. In the end, this date had to be cancelled because of bad weather, the first of eleven postponements between November 1939 and April 1940. Hitler's generals were aghast. As one put it: 'paying due credit to our Panzer successes in Poland, we must nevertheless note that our armour has little chance of success' against the British and French. Senior officers began plotting to overthrow the *Führer*, though only in the same hesitant and desultory way they had done at the time of the Sudeten Crisis. Halder, the army chief of staff, started carrying around a loaded pistol so he could shoot Hitler if he felt it was necessary. None of this amounted to anything, as usual. Still, in early 1940 the sense of gathering gloom in Berlin was palpable.[16]

*

Unfortunately for Chamberlain, however, it was beginning to look as though time might not be on the Allies' side either. Britain was not facing an imminent economic crisis in the same way as Germany, but the financial implications of the war stretching on for another two or three years were looming ominously all the same. Back in September the chancellor, Sir John Simon, had warned the Cabinet that the war was already costing the British state £210 million a month. And mobilisation, especially of the Army, had barely begun.[17] In January the railway chairman, Lord Stamp, delivered a sobering report on the state of national resources. By the end of the first year of war, he estimated, Britain would have a balance of payments deficit of £400 million. This was likely to be higher still in a second year. But it only possessed about £450 million in gold assets, with another £250 million realisable from sales of foreign securities.

Britain could, for the time being, defer debts to countries and colonies that used the pound as their principal currency, or else anchored their own currency to its value – the so-called 'Sterling Area'. This included most of the British Empire (though not Canada or Hong Kong), Iceland, Egypt and Iraq. Instead of paying directly for imports from Sterling Area members, the UK was able to run up a series of accumulating paper liabilities to be settled after the war – essentially an inexhaustible series of IOUs held by the Bank of England.

But Britain's most important source of imports was the United States, outside the Sterling Area. Because of the Neutrality Acts passed by Congress in the 1930s, American citizens were not allowed to extend lines of credit to belligerent powers. All US imports had to be paid for in gold or dollars and collected directly by British-flagged vessels ('cash and carry'). Stamp's conclusions were ominous. There was no hope of fighting a three-year war based on the existing level of expenditure. Britain was simply going to run out of money within two years.[18] 'Unless, when the time comes, the United States are prepared either to lend or to give us the money as required,' the Treasury warned, 'the prospects for a long war are exceedingly grim.'[19]

The French, alarmed by disappointing shortfalls in their own munitions production, shortages of food and petroleum and fears about possible communist-led war resistance, were also coming to pessimistic conclusions around this time. On 21 March 1940, Édouard Daladier's administration fell. He was replaced as premier by Paul Reynaud, his former finance minister. Reynaud had played a role somewhat akin to Churchill's in French politics in the 1930s. He had been one of the most prominent opponents of appeasing Hitler at Munich. His promotion brought a renewed energy and combativeness to the government in Paris, but he had been elected to the premiership by just one parliamentary vote and was aware of the fragility of his position. 'To believe that time is working for us is today a mistake,' he told the British on 25 March. 'We will only again assume control of the war if we are able to forestall the initiatives of the enemy by imposing our own.'[20] Chamberlain continued to maintain that the advantage in a long war of attrition lay with the Allies. But, perhaps frustrated that his predictions back in autumn that Germany would collapse within six months had not come true, he was now more open to the idea of widening the war. Even if Germany's economy was fated to collapse by itself, it might be necessary to give it a bit of a nudge.

This strategic uneasiness was the origin of the Norwegian campaign, which began on 8 April 1940. The idea of intervening in Norway had been floating about in Franco-British conversations since the beginning of the war and became entangled with the issue of the USSR's invasion of Finland in November 1939, but at its heart it was a project to tighten the economic screws on Germany. The Third Reich relied for much of its iron ore supply on imports from Sweden, which throughout the warmer months of the year were transportable across the Baltic Sea. But between October and April the Baltic route was unavailable because of ice, and so the ore was trans-shipped by rail across to the northern Norwegian port of Narvik instead, and from there ferried down the Skjaergaard coastal corridor in Norwegian territorial waters to Denmark's Jutland peninsula before being delivered to Hamburg and Bremen.[21] The MEW claimed that this iron ore source was so critical to Germany's economy that blockading the Norwegian route during the winter could 'end the war in a few months'.[22]

Churchill, who as First Lord of the Admiralty would take the leading role in a naval expedition across the North Sea, argued forcefully for landing troops at Narvik and perhaps other western Norwegian ports. Knowing his audience, he pitched the idea to the War Cabinet as a way of bringing the war swiftly, cheaply and bloodlessly to an end: 'no other measure is open to us,' he wrote in December, 'which gives so good a chance of abridging the waste and destruction of the conflict, or of perhaps preventing the vast slaughters which will attend the grapple of the main armies.' But blockading the Skjaergaard and occupying Narvik would be a blatant violation of Norwegian sovereignty. Britain was, after all, supposed to be fighting the war to defend the very principles of international law that it was now proposing to break. What would other neutrals like the United States think? Churchill was unmoved by what he saw as this pedantic objection. 'Small nations must not tie our hands when we are fighting for their rights and freedom,' he insisted.[23]

Arguments about the pros and cons of the idea dragged on throughout the winter. It was not until the meeting of the Anglo-French Supreme War Council on 28 March 1940 that the go-ahead was finally given. By this date the Swedish Baltic ports were on the verge of reopening again for the year, which meant that an expedition to Norway could not possibly have any short-term economic consequences for Germany even if everything went exactly to plan. Quite why it was still considered to be a good idea is unclear. Reynaud pushed hard for the project: perhaps he just needed some evidence of Allied belligerence to prop up his shaky parliamentary position back in Paris.

But Hitler had decided to pre-empt action against the Narvik iron ore route by invading Norway and Denmark himself. On the morning of 8 April, as Royal Navy destroyers began laying mines off the approaches to Narvik, German troops were already embarked on troopships in the Skagerrak. The following day they seized Oslo and Copenhagen. What had begun for the Allies as something perilously close to an act of unprovoked aggression against a peaceful neutral state had become, by accident, an emergency intervention to save Norway from German occupation.

The nine-week Norwegian campaign was Britain's first major combined-arms engagement of the Second World War. It did not go well. British troops landed in three locations in western Norway, including Narvik, but all but the last of these expeditions were evacuated in disarray at the beginning of May, and the Narvik force finally withdrew by sea on 8 June. British ground forces suffered over 1,860 casualties killed, wounded and captured. The Royal Navy lost the aircraft carrier HMS *Glorious* – sunk by the German battlecruisers *Scharnhorst* and *Gneisenau* under grotesquely needless circumstances – plus two cruisers, seven destroyers and three submarines, for a total loss of life of about 2,500.[24] The RAF had 163 aircraft lost, albeit many of them ageing biplanes.

The campaign had moments of unqualified heroism, the most famous of which was the fate of the destroyer HMS *Glowworm*, which, though hopelessly outgunned, attacked and rammed the much larger German cruiser *Admiral Hipper* off the coast of Trondheim on 8 April. *Glowworm's* captain, Lieutenant-Commander Gerard Roope, became the Second World War's first (posthumous) recipient of the Victoria Cross, an award he was granted largely thanks to testimony offered afterwards by *Admiral Hipper's* captain via the Red Cross. But Norway mainly demonstrated, as the official history of British grand strategy put it later, a 'total lack of realistic planning' by the chiefs of staff, owing to 'blunders [...] sheer miscalculation and failure of imagination'.[25] It was 'a fiasco', according to the historian and retired British Army general John Kiszely – 'a textbook example of how not to plan and conduct a military campaign'.[26]

Neither the Army nor the RAF emerged with much credit. Squadron Leader Jack Donaldson of 263 Squadron returned to Britain on 28 April with a litany of complaints about logistics: 'wrong aviation spirit, wrong oil, no serviceable starter batteries, unsuitable equipment, no maps, lack of ammunition.' He was told his squadron of 18 Gloster Gladiator biplanes, all of which had been destroyed or left unserviceable after just two days in Norway, had been sent out 'as a token sacrifice' only.[27] The Army did what it could, but the campaign revealed just how grievous the years of inadequate training and equipment had been, especially for the Territorial forces. They were sent into combat totally unprepared to engage a first-class enemy and were swiftly routed. The Norwegian campaign had serious consequences for the BEF in France. It diverted four badly needed infantry brigades from the Western Front, one of which, the 15th, had to be extracted from the front line and sent northwards directly into battle.[28]

There were just two points of satisfaction that the Allies could extract from this miserable debacle. One was that the Kriegsmarine suffered the destruction of three cruisers and ten destroyers, losses it could ill afford. The other was that conquering Norway turned out, in the end, to be a pointless, burdensome exercise for the Germans. When they occupied France later in 1940 they gained access to the extensive iron ore deposits in Lorraine, rendering the Swedish supply superfluous. Garrisoning the long Norwegian coastline against the threat of Allied invasion throughout the rest of the war tied down four times as many troops as it had taken to occupy Norway in the first place. The Allies, ultimately, never went back there until the war was won anyway.[29]

*

The fall of Neville Chamberlain is generally depicted as a very British affair lasting a few days, from the start of the Commons debate on the war on Tuesday, 7 May 1940, to Winston Churchill's appointment as prime minister on the evening of Friday, 10 May. But it's perhaps better to think of it as just one manifestation of a crisis that was affecting all the combatant powers in the early spring of 1940, a crisis brought on by a fear that time was running out, and that the upcoming campaigning season might represent the best chance – perhaps the only chance – of still winning the war.

In France, Daladier had already been forced out as prime minister at the end of March, and his replacement, Reynaud, had fought in vain to quell the feuding of his unstable coalition Cabinet in the two months since. On 9 May, Reynaud, still struggling to establish his authority, had decided to resign the premiership as a way of reforming his Cabinet. He planned to sack Daladier (who had stayed on as defence minister) and Gamelin the following day and would have done so had the German invasion of Belgium and the Netherlands not imposed itself on events. In Germany there was no way for such a crisis of confidence to express itself politically except through violence. That did not happen. The plotters against Hitler had long lost their nerve. But the *Führer's* decision to accept no more postponements and to launch *Fall Gelb* on 10 May, despite the grave misgivings of his generals about its likelihood of success, was Hitler's way of trying to escape the strategic trap the Third Reich appeared to have fallen into.

In Britain, Chamberlain had already had to respond to parliamentary and press criticism of his government's inaction with a Cabinet reshuffle at the beginning of April which had made Churchill a *de facto* minister of defence in charge of the general direction of the war effort. When the fighting began in Norway, Chamberlain's critics were briefly silenced. Here, at last, was evidence of some belligerent resolution on the part of the government. (The House was 'extremely calm' on the day the Germans took Oslo, thought Harold Nicolson. Everyone seemed to believe that 'Hitler has made a terrible mistake'.[30]) Optimistic press headlines fed to editors by the Ministry of Information suggested that the Allies were on the verge of a major victory in Norway.[31]

But the expedition's collapse at the beginning of May offered the prime minister's enemies an opportunity to slam his administration's vacillation and feebleness. To make matters worse, just before the German attack Chamberlain had claimed in a much-publicised speech in Westminster Hall that Hitler had 'missed the bus' by not immediately attacking Britain and France back in September 1939, when their military preparations were less advanced and his advantage much greater.[32] Hitler would have privately agreed with Chamberlain about this; he too felt that he had missed a great opportunity the previous year. But that was by the by. The 'missed the bus' comment looked grotesquely maladroit as Franco-British troops reeled from defeat in Norway. It was 'peace for our time' all over again.

The Allies evacuated central Norway on 2 May. On 7 May the Commons was due to consider a motion for adjournment for its two-week Whitsun recess, usually a formality. The opposition parties, in liaison with discontented National Government MPs, decided to use the motion to savage the prime minister about his government's conduct of the war.

The events of this 'Norway Debate' have become deeply embedded in the Churchillian mythology of 1940. For that reason, then, it's important to remember that no one knew on 7 May what the result of the upcoming debate would be. Nor, when it ended the following evening, was anyone immediately much the wiser what, if anything, had been accomplished. The Conservative chief whip, David Margesson, suspected beforehand it would be the most serious challenge to the government since 1931. But Chamberlain's Commons majority was so huge that there was virtually no chance of a censure vote succeeding, even if it came to that.

The speeches that subsequently became most famous were all fierce attacks on the prime minister: Sir Roger Keyes, dressed in his admiral's uniform, condemning the Norwegian campaign as 'a shocking story of ineptitude'; Leo Amery giving Chamberlain the Cromwellian exhortation 'In the name of God, go!' – all the more shocking as Amery was a fellow Birmingham Tory and a protégé of the prime minister's father, Joseph.

But the two speeches that perhaps made the most difference were in defence of the government. One was by Chamberlain himself at the beginning of the second day. Labour's Herbert Morrison started proceedings on 8 May by announcing that his party was going to call for a division at the end of the debate, a vote that would effectively be a motion of no confidence in the government. Chamberlain, his vanity stung by this but aware of the commanding Conservative majority of MPs, reminded Morrison, with what Harold Nicolson called 'a leer of triumph', that 'I have friends in the House'.[33] It was a disastrous miscalculation. Forcing a parliamentary division might well have rebounded badly on Labour by provoking the partisan instincts of even disaffected Conservative back-benchers. But Chamberlain's boasting about his 'friends' made it look as though he was turning a vital debate about the country's war effort into a referendum on his own popularity. It was trivialising and vulgar. It irritated otherwise reliable Tories who felt their loyalty was being taken for granted.

The other decisive speech was by Churchill, at the end of the second day. The First Lord of the Admiralty faced a daunting rhetorical challenge: to defend the conduct of the Navy and the government of which he was a prominent member, without at the same time damaging his own prestige by association with it. Churchill realised this might be a critical moment in his career. He had not always dazzled the House with his debating panache in previous weeks. On 11 April, Nicolson had noted how a weary First Lord, 'giving an imitation of himself', had alarmed the Commons by offering 'vague oratory coupled with tired gibes', hesitating, fumbling his notes and mis-speaking. But on 8 May Churchill's 'extraordinary force of personality' shone through. He demonstrated, thought Nicolson, 'by his brilliance that he really has nothing to do with this confused and timid gang'.

When the result of the division was announced, it was 281 for the government and 200 against. This is usually described as a 'crushing moral defeat' for Chamberlain and the virtual end of his premiership.[34] At the time, neither of these things was so clear. It's true that in theory the prime minister could have been able to draw on a parliamentary majority of just over 200 MPs. But in May 1940 many Members, including at least forty government supporters, were absent from Westminster on active service or other official duties. The last time Chamberlain had faced a no-confidence motion, in September 1939, his majority had been only 116. Before the 8 May division the Conservative whips had calculated that a majority of more than 100 would be a comfortable victory and one fewer than sixty would be a disaster that would probably require the Cabinet's immediate resignation. In other words, the eighty-one majority was ambiguous, neither putting the government wholly in the clear nor irrevocably compromising it. Thirty-eight Members on the government benches had voted with the opposition – but they represented fewer than one in ten National Government MPs. Derbyshire back-bencher Charles Waterhouse, a typical representative of the Tory shires, dismissed the rebels as 'the usual crowd of Anglo-American[s] [...] disgruntled [...] with a few well-meaning sentimentalists and amateur strategists thrown in'.[35] Cadogan thought it had gone 'badly' for Chamberlain, but, he added, 'I don't think it's fatal'.[36] Jock Colville thought the whips were 'fairly satisfied' with the outcome.[37]

Everyone sensed afterwards that the 8 May vote would cause *something* to happen. But what kind of something? Not all the rebels wanted the same thing. A few were inveterate anti-appeasers who had been after Chamberlain's scalp since Munich. Most, though, were normally loyal supporters who had become disillusioned with the government's performance – whether during the eight idle months of the Phoney War, the four disastrous weeks of the Norway campaign or the two days of the debate. They did not necessarily want to see Chamberlain go; indeed, many of them would have been horrified by the prospect. They did, however, want to see change. They wanted the government to adopt a much more vigorous approach to the war effort. This would mean a War Cabinet reshuffle. It would also probably mean bringing Opposition members into the coalition, so that a new deal could be struck with organised labour over more radical manpower and production measures.

On 9 May, then, it seemed to many well-informed observers that the most likely result of the debate would be the sacking of some of Baldwin's old gang, like Samuel Hoare and Sir John Simon, and places in government found for opposition men such as Clement Attlee and the Liberal leader, Archibald Sinclair. Chamberlain had been given a bruising, but he would probably stay on as prime minister, at least for now.

His survival, though, rested on Labour's willingness to serve under him. Chamberlain had invited Attlee to join him in coalition at the outbreak of war and had been rebuffed. Now he approached the Labour leader and his deputy, Arthur Greenwood, again on the evening of 9 May. The two Labour men were in a difficult position. Their party was haunted by the memory of 1931, when Labour's last prime minister, Ramsay MacDonald, had accepted the king's appeal to form a coalition with Baldwin's Conservatives against his own party's wishes. Labour had been torn apart by the decision in an internecine struggle from which it was still recovering almost a decade later. If Attlee and Greenwood simply agreed to Chamberlain's offer of War Cabinet places without the definite support of the rest of their party, they risked another split.

On the other hand, if they rejected it outright, it was possible that Chamberlain would seek out another prominent and ambitious Labour figure like Herbert Morrison, who had little loyalty to Attlee personally and who might well take the prime minister up on his offer. So the two Labour leaders gave no response other than to claim (on murky procedural grounds) that they had no power to answer until they first put the matter to the National Executive Committee, which was meeting at the party's annual conference in Bournemouth at that moment.[38]

At five o'clock in the afternoon the following day, 10 May, Attlee and Greenwood's answer arrived at Downing Street: Labour was willing to join a coalition, but not one led by Chamberlain. That qualification was, to no small degree, personal. It was their revenge for years of the prime minister's savage, sarcastic contempt for the opposition. The arch-appeaser had been brought down, in the end, by his record of belligerence towards his enemies.

The news was deeply disappointing but not really a shock. Chamberlain was mostly resigned to this fate by this point. He had spent much of the previous day considering who ought to replace him as prime minister if Labour refused to join his government. His first preference was the foreign secretary. On the surface, it seemed an obvious enough choice. Halifax would have certainly been the most popular nominee among Tory MPs on 10 May 1940, and probably most Labour MPs too. But he declined, offering all kinds of self-effacing doubts about his suitability for the premiership. That left Churchill as the only other plausible choice.

Halifax's demurrals need to be understood, at least in part, as a tactical calculation rather than a fundamental rejection of the premiership. He was just as ambitious as any politician. His problem in May 1940 was not lack of self-confidence. His problem was Churchill. The First Lord of the Admiralty was clearly the most dynamic member of the current War Cabinet and would remain the key figure in any Halifax administration. The foreign secretary had no desire to play the part of a merely 'honorary prime minister' in the First Lord's shadow, 'living in a kind of twilight just outside the things that really mattered'. Churchill must get a chance of his own first. He might well mess it up. If he did, the way would be cleared for Halifax to make his own move.[39]

Chamberlain drove to Buckingham Palace to tender his resignation and to advise George VI to offer Churchill the premiership. He announced his decision on the BBC at nine o'clock that night. Churchill went to bed 'conscious of a profound sense of relief', as he wrote later in *The Gathering Storm*:

> At last I had the authority to give directions over the whole scene.
> I felt as if I were walking with Destiny, and that all my past life had
> been but a preparation for this hour and for this trial [...] although

impatient for the morning, I slept soundly and had no need for cheering dreams. Facts are better than dreams.[40]

*

The British people learned that their prime minister had resigned on the BBC Home Service that Friday evening. 'Winston Churchill has been appointed in his place,' May Smith wrote in her diary. 'Felt frightfully sorry for the PM when he was speaking, although I have long felt that it would be best for him to go, and for us to have a change,' she added:

> His tones were really emotional as he said that we must rally round our new leader 'and with unshakeable courage fight and work until this wild beast that has sprung out of his lair upon us is finally disarmed and overthrown'.[41]

Given Chamberlain's fall from grace in the years since his resignation, it's surprising how popular he remained in Britain until very late. His national favourability, according to Gallup, had been 64 per cent in December 1939. When asked which of the two men they would, if given the choice, prefer as prime minister, 52 per cent of people polled went with Chamberlain. Only 30 per cent preferred Churchill.[42] Even as late as March 1940, when his government was coming under increasing criticism for its inaction, Chamberlain's favourability rating was still 57 per cent.[43] It only really collapsed in the first few days of May 1940.

It could be, as Mass Observation argued later, that this popularity had always been a lot more fragile than it seemed. Many Britons may have been nursing private doubts about the prime minister ever since the war began. But they very much *wanted* him to succeed: and perhaps because it seemed unpatriotic to criticise a national leader in time of war, and perhaps because of a sense of lingering obligation for his attempts to keep peace, they set aside their doubts. Only the humiliation of military defeat and evacuation in Norway finally offered a socially sanctioned way to express unhappiness with Chamberlain, tipping private doubts into public scorn. As one man put it:

> He was all right until a little while ago. Now I don't know. I'm sort of half-way. A little while ago I was a staunch Chamberlain supporter – I

agreed with him about Munich, and I felt he was the one man who could steer our course straight […] but I don't know. Now I'm half and half. I really can't decide one way or the other.[44]

Chamberlain's fall seems to have been a moment for people to start working through their complicated feelings about the events of the previous five years – a national coming to terms that would go on for some time, mixed up with pity, regret and a sense of guilt-ridden complicity in appeasement and the coming of war. 'This is what I have desired almost more than anything since Munich, but now that it has come there seems something rather pathetic about it,' one Mass Observation diarist wrote.[45] Another described how listening to the resignation 'made me feel conscience-stricken – almost personally responsible for his deposition'.[46] Edward Stebbing called Chamberlain 'a brave man, a good man, even a great man', but said the ex-prime minister was also 'unimaginative, weak, and inefficient'. Churchill, he added, 'is the best choice as successor'. Two days after the handover, Stebbing felt that the general mood in the country had become more optimistic – not so much, though, from the change of government, 'but because we can now get to grips with the enemy'.[47]

The point here is not that Churchill's subsequent popularity in 1940 was imaginary, but that it was highly situational. He was popular because he happened to fill a role that very badly needed filling at that moment. The period from 10 May to 31 October 1940 was going to be one of unremitting anxiety for the British people. Someone needed to be there to reassure them that everything was going to be all right. Churchill was sufficiently independent of the Chamberlain administration to distance himself from its failures. His anti-appeasement efforts before the war had given him a unique moral standing. He was perfectly placed to assume the mantle of national interpreter and consoler. 'Churchill should be OK,' a Mass Observation diarist wrote on the evening he came to power. 'We thought he was too fierce at the beginning of the war. But that is needed now.'[48]

How long he would be needed was less clear. No one in May 1940 could have predicted that he would be Britain's leader for the next five years. Indeed, there were good reasons for thinking that he would not be around for too long. One of the chief complaints that had settled on Chamberlain's War Cabinet in its twilight weeks was the age of its ministers. The government resembled 'an assembly of austere, upright, strict maiden aunts', thought George Beardmore.[49] Chamberlain himself was seventy-one. His chancellor, Sir John Simon, as well as Lord Chatfield, the minister for co-ordination of defence, were sixty-seven. Sam Hoare was sixty, Halifax fifty-nine. 'Talked with lots of people, and they all say [Chamberlain] is too old,' one Mass Observer wrote on 6 May: 'he is trying his best, but he is an old man.'[50] A Mass Observation report the following day noted that 'it would be useless in terms of mass enthusiasm, if a get-rid-of [Chamberlain] movement had as its end result the appointment of further *old* people to key positions.'[51] After Churchill was appointed prime minister, the *Daily Express* made a point of calculating that the average age of his ministers was only fifty-six.[52]

The great exception to this anti-ageing process was the new prime minister himself – sixty-five years old in May 1940, stout and of uncertain health. Churchill's energy for a man of his age was impressive. But how long, realistically, could he be expected to endure the stresses of wartime leadership? Perhaps, after a decent interval, he would give way to one of the rising new men in the Cabinet, such as the forty-two-year-old Anthony Eden. A poll back in March had indicated that Eden would be the most popular choice to replace Chamberlain if there were to be a new prime minister.[53] 'Eden is fundamentally the most mass-popular politician today,' Mass Observation noted on 7 May.[54] His reputation as an anti-appeaser was as solid as Churchill's, while he had retained far more sympathy on the Tory back benches during the Chamberlain years. Eden had good looks, patrician charm, apparent vigour, military experience. He had already been foreign secretary. Perhaps the Churchillian interregnum, necessary but brief, would be a transitional moment before the Eden wartime premiership.[55]

*

Before closing the story of Chamberlain's fall and Churchill's rise, it is worth thinking about one curious but rarely considered counter-factual possibility. On the morning of 10 May, as the political drama in London was reaching its climactic stage, German forces invaded Belgium and the Netherlands. It was the long-awaited Wehrmacht offensive in the west. When he heard the news, Chamberlain wondered if Hitler's attack offered him a last chance to hold on to power. He wrote to Lord Beaverbrook that 'we cannot consider changes in the government while we are in the throes of battle.'[56] Churchill wondered the same thing. He told his son Randolph that morning that he thought the whole matter of the premiership would probably be dropped, given that the fighting had started in the Low Coun-tries.[57] As it turned out, Chamberlain's hopes were in vain. Too much had already taken place since 7 May to save his career now. Labour's National Executive Committee, meeting away from London, were only vaguely aware of what was going on across the Channel that morning. The moment had passed.

Hitler, as we now know, postponed the opening date of his offensive half a dozen times in the first week of May 1940 for weather and other tech-nical reasons.[58] So what if, as was perfectly possible, *Fall Gelb* had begun forty-eight, or even just twenty-four hours earlier – that is to say, on 8 or 9 rather than 10 May? This minor change in the schedule would not have had any great military significance, but it would have had enormous rami-fications for the political drama going on in London. The outbreak of the long-awaited campaign in the west would have dramatically transformed the circumstances of the Norway debate.

If word of the German attack had reached the Commons on the day of the Norway division, many Conservative MPs would surely have thought twice before abstaining or voting against their leader on a confidence motion. Or, alternatively: what if the BEF had already been heading into battle in Belgium when Chamberlain appealed to Attlee and Greenwood to join his Cabinet? To refuse the prime minister's request at a moment of national emergency, simply on the grounds of personal enmity, would have risked seeming unpatriotically petty. Perhaps the Labour men would have swallowed their pride and accepted the offer. If they had, Chamberlain would, at the very least, have continued as prime minister through the rest of the fateful month of May 1940. The cause of this alternative historical path would have been almost trivial. Its consequences would have been vast and unforeseeable.

14

A CERTAIN EVENTUALITY

Flight Lieutenant William Simpson's war lasted only a couple of seconds. It was at about five o'clock in the afternoon of Friday, 10 May 1940, that his Fairey Battle, *V for Victor*, swept across a moon-shaped clearing on the Luxembourg–Junglinster road in southern Belgium. About thirty feet below him, he saw a cluster of German vehicles. His bomb aimer dropped the plane's four 250-lb bombs and they watched four large clouds of smoke erupt on the ground. That moment the Battle was raked with anti-aircraft cannon shells. Sticky glycol coolant sprayed into the pilot's compartment. The cockpit was filled with petrol fumes. Remnants of two molten cylinders burst out of the plane's Merlin engine, flames gushing from the serrated holes they left in the front cowling. Simpson turned the failing Battle westwards to try to make a crash-landing. He spotted a grass-covered glade in the woodland and ploughed *V for Victor* straight into it.

As the Battle staggered to a halt, the slipstream that had been suppressing the engine fire ebbed, and flames rushed back into the cockpit. It was saturated with petrol vapour. Simpson was still struggling with the release clip fixing him to his seat when the fumes ignited. 'Great sheets of searing flames rushed between my legs,' he wrote later:

> My hands were burned and they seized up solid. They were completely useless. I was trapped by my straps and could not move. The awful realisation that I was about to be burned to death took possession of my mind [...] I let my hands drop to my knees and curled myself up, waiting for the release of death.[1]

As he was being broiled alive, Simpson could hear the shrill of an electric klaxon behind his head, warning him that the Battle's landing gear had not been deployed in the proper wheels-down position.

One, two, three, four, five, six, seven, eight seconds. Get out of the burning cockpit of a Second World War aircraft in that time and you'd live, though you'd probably never fly again. Nine seconds, and you'd perhaps still make it out, though you'd leave your face or your hands behind. Ten seconds, and you wouldn't be getting out. This was the mordant arithmetic of combustion. Fire was the pilot's most terrible adversary, far more frightening than any human opponent. A combat aircraft, as Spitfire pilot Gordon Olive noted,

> was a structure full of petrol, oil, inflammable engine coolant, and explosive bullets or bombs [...] a single tracer bullet was more than enough to explode the lot. Once the petrol tank was set on fire, a vast sheen of brilliant orange flame trailed back from the tank, rapidly melting and consuming what was left of the frail aluminium structure.[2]

Ignited fuel would reach a temperature of several thousand degrees in a few seconds. Hot enough to melt steel, burn through thick leather and fabric flying clothes instantaneously, sear flesh like a blowtorch, dissolve fat and muscle into liquid.[3]

Airmen had already learned to their cost about the danger of engine fires during the First World War. During the 1930s the French and German air forces took steps to protect their crews from the risk by putting self-sealing rubber-lined fuel tanks in all their combat aircraft. The Royal Air Force was altogether tardier about this. By the spring of 1940 only certain RAF planes had received fuel tank refits. The Fairey Battles of the Advanced Air Striking Force (AASF) were not considered high priority. Their three-man crews continued to sit in what were essentially giant flying cigarette lighters.

Not that they thought to complain. 'Most of the officers behaved like the overgrown schoolboys they were,' remembered Simpson. He was twenty-six, which if anything was on the older side. Some of the other men were barely out of school. One hundred and sixty AASF Fairey Battles, organised into ten squadrons of about fifty aircrew and 300 ground crew each, had arrived in the Rheims area in September 1939.[4] Simpson's 12 Squadron was sent to Berry-au-Bac on the River Aisne. The men spent the first days of autumn in pioneer work, digging trenches and felling trees. Officers were installed in a small château at Guignicourt a few miles from the airfield, an ugly but comfortable red-brick building with central heating and hot water. As the bitter Phoney War winter took hold, they spent their duty time huddled over oil stoves in log-roofed dugouts, guarding the wooded clearings in which their Battles had been dispersed to hide them from enemy reconnaissance planes. 'After four months we were still playing at war,' Simpson recalled:

> Don, tall, fair, and proud of his Irish blood, lashing with his witty tongue all the bureaucratic institutions he hated so much. Blackie, short, red-headed Canadian, with a cheery, India-rubber face, cracking jokes at me or at his fellow Canadians. And all the others, each one so different in temperament – English, Scots, Canadian, Australian, and Irish – yet with so much in common. None of us was over 27. We knew nothing of war.[5]

Paul Richey, a Hurricane pilot with 1 Squadron, visited Simpson and his comrades at Berry-au-Bac that spring, and was struck with how 'pathetically confident' the Battle crew men were: 'We admired their flying and guts, but [...] we privately didn't give much for their chances.'[6] A lot of the confidence was for show. Simpson was aware of the Battle's dangerous weaknesses: its slow speed, its inadequate armour protection, its vulnerability to fire. In private discussions with 12 Squadron's other flight commanders, he guessed that, come the day they were thrown into combat, they would lose four out of every five of their aircraft and three out of five aircrew.[7] When *V for Victor* and three other 12 Squadron Battles were dispatched over southern Belgium to try to slow the German advance through the Ardennes on the afternoon of 10 May, William Simpson understood completely that the mathematics of the thing were badly against him.

He did not die in his burning cockpit. In an act of extraordinary courage his two crew mates, who had managed to scramble clear before *V for Victor* exploded, risked their lives again to come back and get him out. They hauled his charred, smouldering body away from the fuselage and over to the cool grass of the glade. The flames had done their work; Simpson was a hideous sight. Much of his face had melted away. His fingers had curled up into shrivelled talons. Delirious, and in gathering agony, he was carried off to a nearby convent. Eventually, after being moved around Belgium and France for several months, he would be taken prisoner by the Germans. An altogether different kind of battle lay ahead of him as he faced years of painful surgery for his disfiguring burns.

The Battle for France was less than a day old and already William Simpson and *V for Victor* were gone. But the melancholy ordeal of the rest of 12 Squadron's aircrew, and that of the other men of the Advanced Air Striking Force, was only beginning. RAF Battles flew thirty-two sorties on 10 May 1940. Fourteen of them were shot down. Eight more Battles were sent out the following day to attack the German columns advancing through Luxembourg. One eventually limped back to base, riddled with bullet holes. The rest were never seen again. On Sunday, 12 May, Allied air strength was directed northwards to the bridges over the Albert Canal near Maastricht. Twenty-four Blenheim medium bombers based in England launched the first attack on the bridges at nine o'clock that morning. Basil Embry, commanding officer of 107 Squadron, approached his target at 4,000 feet. 'A tornado of fire met us from the ground,' he recalled:

> Every few seconds my aircraft shook as it was struck by flying splinters [...] I turned my head to see how the others in my formation were faring and as I did so two aircraft burst into flames and went crashing down like meteors. Three more were to follow almost immediately.[8]

Ten of the Blenheims failed to return to base. They dropped ninety-six bombs, all of which missed.

As this was going on, five of 12 Squadron's Battles, led by twenty-one-year-old Flying Officer Donald Garland (the 'tall, fair, and proud' Irishman who had enlivened those winter months at Guignicourt), were making a simultaneous attack on the nearby bridges at Vroenhoven and Veldwezelt. None of the aircraft survived. Six of their crewmen were killed, including Garland and his navigator, twenty-five-year-old Sergeant Thomas 'Dolly' Grey, who both received posthumous Victoria Crosses.[9]

These operations, as the historian Greg Baughen has put it, 'had all the heroic and hopeless qualities associated with the Charge of the Light Brigade'.[10] But worse was to come. On the morning of 14 May the BAFF received an urgent request from the French high command to send as many bombers as it could to Sedan, on the River Meuse. The previous day the German mobile columns which William Simpson had first observed on the Luxembourg–Junglinster road had finally struggled their way through the narrow Ardennes forest and, after a furious supporting bombardment by Ju 87 Stuka dive-bombers, had made an opposed crossing of the Meuse. Gamelin's headquarters was belatedly starting to understand the significance of this move and, with a sense of growing panic, the awful consequences of a German armoured breakthrough at this weak point in the Allied line.

Barratt ordered an armada of seventy-one Battles and Bristol Blenheims, every bomber the British still had available in France, to join the Armée de l'Air to attack the Meuse bridges. The result was different from the disasters of the previous four days only in its murderous scale. The astonished Germans on the bridges watched the Allied planes slowly lining up to attack, each as it lumbered forward presenting a perfect target for their flak guns. A staff officer of the 1st Panzer Division, observing the carnage, wrote afterwards:

> Again and again, an enemy aircraft crashes out of the sky, dragging a long black plume of smoke behind it, which after the crash of the succeeding explosion remains for some time in the perpendicular air.[11]

Forty RAF aircraft, thirty-five of them Battles, did not return, including four out of five of 12 Squadron's remaining Battles. A few of the bridges were damaged, but the Germans were not seriously inconvenienced. Their tanks and infantry continued to cross the river. In all, the RAF flew 109 bombing sorties over Sedan on 14 May 1940. By the day's end, sixty-four British aircraft had either been destroyed or so badly damaged as to be irreparable. It was the single worst day in the history of the Royal Air Force.[12]

'An unimaginable hell, a real Valley of Death from which few emerged', was the way historian Alistair Horne described the attack on the Meuse bridges.[13] During the opening three weeks of the French campaign, more than 100 of the RAF's Fairey Battles were destroyed and 119 of its aircrew killed.[14] Such a figure bears comparison with the number of deaths in an infantry battalion on the first day of the Battle of the Somme in 1916. Indeed, if we thought about the Second World War in the same way that we do the First, then the doomed Battle crews of May 1940 might be as well known as the fallen of the Somme. Their fates might be invested with the same tragic solemnity. And we might ask the same questions about what happened to them – whether their sacrifice was worth it; whether they really had to die; whether someone, perhaps, had blundered.

The problem was not the aircraft. If the Fairey Battle was 'obsolete' in 1940, then so too was the German Ju 87 Stuka dive-bomber, which had entered service at exactly the same time, had more or less the same kind of armament and was even slower than the British plane. Yet no one says that the Stuka was obsolete at the time of the Battle of France. On the contrary, it's still seen today as an acme of modernity, a machine of terrifying, precision mass destruction, as representative of the ruthless cutting-edge efficiency of the Nazi *Blitzkrieg* as the Panzer. Plunging almost vertically from up to 12,000 feet onto their targets, with banshee sirens in their under-carriages wailing to terrify the infantry below, Stukas were able to reduce French defensive positions at Sedan into stunned submission. 'The gunners stopped firing and went to ground,' said a French report afterwards: 'dazed by the crash of bombs and the shriek of the dive bombers [...] five hours of this nightmare was enough to shatter their nerves.'[15]

But then the Germans understood that for their bombers like the Stuka to be able to do this, they needed to be able to fly in a secure air-space with plenty of protection from enemy interceptors. When Stukas were occasionally caught in less favourable circumstances, their limitations became as obvious as those of the Fairey Battle. On 12 May five French fighters bounced – ambushed – a dozen unescorted Stukas and promptly shot down the lot.[16]

It's impossible to say for certain how events would have unfolded in May 1940 if the RAF had protected its bombers over the battlefield as well as the Germans protected their Stukas. Probably the men of 12 Squadron would still have suffered grievously over Belgium and France. Still, equipped with appropriately armed and armoured Fairey Battles, given time to prac-tise low-level tactical manoeuvres and protected by a sufficient number of well-trained escort pilots, it's possible that they might have been able to slow down the German crossing of the Meuse just long enough to allow the French to bring forward reinforcements to plug the gap in the front line. That would have changed history. The Fairey Battle, not the Spitfire, would be the quintessential symbol of RAF history today. No one would talk of the Battle of Britain, because the Battle of Britain would never have had to happen.[17]

*

The RAF had always claimed that close air support was a misuse of its resources. The disasters of 10–14 May seemed to prove it – no matter that the Luftwaffe was making a rather good job of co-operating with *its* army. Sir Cyril Newall pressed for the RAF to be allowed to make its true stra-tegic contribution to the battle in France, rather than waste further planes and men on brave but futile sacrifices. In other words, he asked Churchill's Cabinet to be allowed to bomb the Ruhr. 'We [have] now reached a vital stage in the war,' Newall argued to the new prime minister:

and it had always been accepted that when that stage was reached we should be prepared to take decisive action [...] throughout the course of the war the enemy had so far seized the initiative every time, and we had been forced to follow his lead. From the psychological point of view alone it [is] now important that we should wrest the initiative from him.[18]

A strategic assault on the Ruhr had been an *idée fixe* of the RAF's leadership for a long time. 'The Ruhr is the most outstanding economic objective in Germany,' a chiefs of staff memorandum on air policy asserted in November 1939: 'its successful dislocation and even partial destruction would have a most important effect on Germany's capacity to continue the war.'[19] A force of 240 twin-engine bombers, the Air Ministry believed, would be able to drop 28 tons of bombs nightly on oil refineries, marshalling yards and factories in the Ruhr basin. All major targets would, with luck, be destroyed within eighteen days.[20] Even leaving aside the physical destruction that would be caused by bombing, the local population 'might be expected to crack under intensive air attack' within a short time.[21] 'The psychological effect of an immediate blow at the enemy's most vulnerable spot would be very great throughout the world,' Newall argued.[22] It might even end the war.

Churchill hesitated to give his approval throughout the first week of his premiership. Then, on 15 May, as the crisis developed on the Meuse, he finally agreed to the RAF plan. Bombing the Ruhr, he declared,

> would cut Germany at its tap root, and [...] might even provide an immediate contribution to the land battle. [It] should dispel French doubts about our willingness to suffer and also have a salutary effect on Italy. Finally, he considered that this was the psychological moment to strike Germany in her own country and convince the German people that we had both the will and the power to hit them hard.[23]

'I never saw anything so light up the faces of the RAF when they heard,' Ironside noted acerbically. 'They have built up their big bombers for this work [...] now they have got the chance.'[24] 'Now the "Total War" begins!' exulted Alexander Cadogan.[25]

That night, ninety-nine Wellington, Whitley and Hampden two-engine bombers attacked sixteen targets, most of them oil installations, in the Ruhr area.[26] Though no one in the British War Cabinet could have realised it at the time, their decision to allow the RAF to start bombing the Ruhr on 15 May 1940 was a watershed moment in the history of the Second World War. That first raid was merely the preliminary event in a campaign that was to go on virtually unabated for the next five years, and which would, for better or worse, absorb much of the war-making potential of the British Empire. No one could have had any inkling of what they had just set in motion.

Reports the morning afterwards were highly encouraging. The oil works at Duisburg, Ramen and Sterkrade Holten were said to be burning; the plant at Homberg had 'blown up violently'; there had been a 'tremendous explosion' at the Dortmund synthetic oil factory which had shaken one of the RAF bombers 10,000 feet above.[27] Follow-up raids over subsequent nights appeared to have been equally spectacular. Indeed, as the situation on the ground in France and Belgium deteriorated over the next several weeks, the War Cabinet's members continued to hope, though with diminishing optimism, that the good news from the Ruhr might produce the miraculous change in fortunes they needed so badly. On 30 May the Foreign Office reported that the destruction in the Ruhr was having 'terrible effects' and causing a crisis of political confidence in the Reich.[28] Surely the Germans would soon sue for peace as the RAF continued to sow chaos and destruction in the Ruhr.

But it was all fantasy. RAF damage appraisal was still in its infancy. No photographic evidence was as yet available to check whether the anecdotal tales told by returning aircrew were reliable or not. All information about target damage had to be derived second-hand from reports by British representatives in neutral countries or from neutral businessmen and diplomats in Germany. It was, as the official history of bombing readily admits, 'highly unreliable'.[29] In reality, most RAF bombs in the spring of 1940 were landing harmlessly across the German countryside miles away from their supposed targets. Even those bombs which came close to their targets were scattered so widely that it was impossible for the Germans to see any coherent pattern in them. Puzzled, they assumed that the RAF were conducting night training missions and dropping a little ordnance as an afterthought. The idea that they might be part of an all-out British offensive never even occurred to them. Not a single German fighter or anti-aircraft gun was transferred from the battlefield in France or Belgium back to the Ruhr as a result of the RAF's efforts in the spring of 1940. Not a single German bomber was redirected from close air support of the Wehrmacht to retaliatory strikes on Allied cities. The decision to start strategic bombing would have profound consequences for the future of the war. For now, though, it was a total waste of time, even if no one in Britain knew it.[30]

*

The RAF in May 1940 found it difficult to think of war in any other terms than strategic bombing. To its senior airmen, obsessed with the idea of the aerial knock-out blow, any fighting on the ground was merely an opening prelude to the real event. Soldiers, of course, thought differently. General Gamelin greeted the start of the German attack on 10 May in a mood of quiet confidence. He strode up and down the corridors at his headquarters at Vincennes 'humming, with a pleased and martial air'.[31] There was no reason for panic. All contingency plans had been laid down long before in binders inches thick. Now it was simply a case of carrying them out to their logical conclusion.

Alexander Geddes, a subaltern with the 92nd Royal Artillery Field Regiment, was one of the millions of soldiers set into motion by Gamelin's orders. On 11 May he arrived in Hersin-Coupigny, a little mining village between Arras and Béthune about twenty-five miles from the Belgian border. There he and the rest of the British Expeditionary Force's general reserve had been told to wait while the infantry divisions advanced into Belgium to take up their assigned positions along the River Dyle. At that moment, the war still seemed very far away from rural Artois. When Geddes asked a local farmer about whether it would be possible to construct a slit trench in one of his hayfields, the man kicked up a fuss about the damage to his property. Geddes asked him if he would prefer to wait and have the Germans do it instead. The farmer's face went white; this was not a possibility he had considered. 'The Germans won't come here,' he insisted. The Army of France would stop them; *la ligne Maginot* would stop them. The Germans couldn't reach Hersin-Coupigny. Could they? 'I assured him we would do our best to stop them,' replied Geddes. 'But I could not make any promises.'[32]

Over the next several days such qualms began to seem uncomfortably prescient. The Netherlands surrendered on the morning of 15 May. With the Dutch army gone, the Germans could begin pressing on Antwerp from the north. If the city fell, it would expose the whole left flank of the Allied

THE BATTLEFIELD OF MAY-JUNE 1940

▲▲▲▲	Belgian and Dutch forward defences
⌐¬	Fortress Holland
◄──	Movement of Allied forces, 10-13 May
──	The Dyle line
◄─ ■ ■	German offensives, 10-13 May
◄──	German offensives, 13-26 May
☂	German airborne landings, 10 May

North Sea

Groningen

NETHERLANDS

ENGLAND

Amsterdam

Deventer

The Hague

Utrecht

Rotterdam   Waal

Maas

Army
Group
B

GERMANY

Ostend   Bruges   Antwerp   Albert Canal

Gravelines   Dunkirk   Belgian
Calais   Army
          French   BELGIUM   Brussels ■
          Seventh
Boulogne   Army   Fort Eben Emael

BEF   Meuse   Liège

**21 May, counter offensive
by British armour**   Namur

          Mons   Army
French   Group
Novelles   First   Sambre   A
3pm, 20 May   Army
          Arras   Dinant

Abbeville   Cambrai
7pm, 20 May Somme

Amiens 18 May   St Quentin French
                        Ninth   ARDENNES   Army
N   Army   Montcornet   Group
                               15 May Donchery   C
          Laon   Doncournet Sedan
FRANCE   French   Meuse   LUXEMBOURG   WEST WALL
          counter-attacks
          17 May   French
                          Second Army   MAGINOT LINE

Rhine

20	40	60	80	100 mls	
40	80	120	160 kms		

line on the Dyle. That alone was a serious enough threat. But it was not even the worst of it, because the previous Monday the mobile infantry of the Wehrmacht's Army Group A had emerged from the Ardennes to assault the French defences along the Meuse near Sedan. Gamelin had been warned several times since the start of the offensive about Allied photo reconnaissance which showed that the Germans might, after all, be attempting this most audacious of moves. He ignored the warnings. By the evening of 13 May, thanks in part to the Luftwaffe's devastating close air support, the Germans had crossed the river in three places and were establishing bridgeheads on the south bank, in readiness to start bringing their tanks over the following day. As we have already seen, the British and French air force's attempts to destroy the Meuse bridges on 14 May were a gruesome failure.

General Georges, Gamelin's commander on the north-eastern front, had something close to a nervous breakdown when he heard the news. Sunk in a chair, head bowed, all could say was: 'our front has caved in … a rout!' Three DCR armoured divisions were ordered to retake the Meuse bridgeheads. The individual French tank units fought fiercely, but overall the counter-attack was dilatory and incoherent. It failed to regain any of the lost ground. By the evening of 15 May the French 9th Army defending the Meuse was in a state of near-disintegration, and the leading Panzers were almost forty miles from their bridgeheads, advancing westwards across Champagne into open country. No one on the Allied side knew whether they would turn for Paris or make for the Channel. Either way, their advance threatened to cut the lines of supply and communication to the Allied forces fighting in Belgium, including the BEF.

Rumours of the French collapse to the south had begun reaching the British troops on the Dyle on 14 May. They were holding their own reasonably enough against the German forces in front of them. But this Panzer advance from Sedan menaced their unprotected southern flank. 'I hope to God the French have some means of stopping them and closing the gap,' wrote Gort's chief of staff, Sir Henry Pownall, 'or we are *bust*.'[33] The lack of information was what was so frustrating for Gort and Pownall, though the British commander had not helped the situation by deciding to leave the main BEF headquarters behind at Arras on 10 May to establish a personal forward command post up with the fighting troops. Gort's decision to remain close to the front was entirely characteristic of his pugnacious desire to be in the thick of the action. But in doing so he severed communications with his own staff. Even his sympathetic biographer Jock Colville admits this was an 'administrative disaster'.[34] He made it almost impossible for his main HQ to keep him abreast of new information on enemy movements. As a result, throughout the campaign the BEF would have to rely on intelligence that was 'scanty, vague, and often inaccurate'.[35]

Gort finally got some orders in the early hours of 16 May. The entire Allied line was to start pulling out of Belgium. There would be a staged withdrawal back to the River Scheldt to the west. Back in London, Churchill was 'infuriated' when he heard of the decision. It was, he said, an absurd overreaction to the German crossing of the Meuse. 'It was ridiculous to think that France could be conquered by 120 tanks.'[36] This says much about how the significance of the breakthrough at Sedan was not yet understood back in Britain. Only after visiting Paris in person and receiving a sobering account of what had happened to the French 9th Army on the Meuse did Churchill begin to appreciate the danger. Even then, however, he insisted that 'we ought not to yield an inch of ground without fighting.'[37] When the prime minister gave his famous 'Fight on the Beaches' speech in the Commons a month later, he suggested that the 'colossal military disaster' that had destroyed the Allied armies had been caused by the French High Command failing to withdraw the northern armies as soon as they knew of the German breakthrough at Sedan.[38] This was disingenuous, to say the least. At the time, Churchill's voice had been one of the loudest opposing such a withdrawal.

By the evening of 19 May most of the BEF was back behind the Scheldt. It had not been an easy few days for the British troops. Barely a week had gone by since they had crossed the Belgian frontier. Dug in on the Dyle, they had appeared to be fully in control of the situation. Then, without explanation, they had been ordered to abandon the position they had defended so successfully and retreat almost back to where they had started. There was 'puzzlement and disappointment' in the ranks to compound the fatigue and frustration and hunger of days of forced marching, digging in and meagre suppers of cold rations.[39] They had advanced through Belgian towns and villages as heroes, to be greeted with cheers, kisses and bottles of lager. Now there were only sullen glances from behind closed windows as they struggled back through columns of civilians fleeing westwards too. South-west of Brussels, Alexander Geddes saw 'a variegated and multi-coloured flood of refugees' going ceaselessly by, at a rate of several thousand an hour:

Tired horses and grossly overloaded motors, buses, lorries, and tractors [...] bicycles loaded like pack mules [...] trams and wheelbarrows
have been impressed [...] two old women go trudging by, supporting
between them one even older; little children crying in their prams or
asleep from exhaustion in grotesque attitudes; a long file of impeccably dressed nuns carrying far less than anyone else; a streamlined
limousine with a mattress and a Persian rug on top, a bicycle in front
and two soldiers on the rear bumper! It is quite the most pathetic
scene I have ever seen.[40]

Though the BEF had now reached the Scheldt, it was far from safe. There
was a 'complete void' on the BEF's southern flank, Pownall noted, into
which a couple of German armoured divisions could enter without opposition.[41] Three options presented themselves. The BEF could sit tight where
it was and hope that the French armies to the south, on the Somme, could
link up with it again. It could make a fighting retreat south-west to try to
rejoin the French. Or it could withdraw towards one of the Channel ports
– Ostend, say, or Dunkirk – and hope for evacuation.

The first option seemed futile, given the lack of remaining French
reserves. The second would mean disengaging from the enemy forces on the
far bank of the Scheldt and marching across the axis of the German advance
– a manoeuvre that would require extraordinary good luck to work. The
third option might be the best remaining chance to save the BEF, or at least
a portion of it. But it had its own perils. And evacuation would have profound political consequences even if it worked, because it would represent
a British abandonment of the land battle – perhaps of the whole Anglo-
French alliance. Gort knew this. He was hesitant about even discussing the
idea with his superiors in London. But he felt he had no choice. On 19 May,
Pownall made two telephone calls to the War Office in which he suggested,
in oblique language, that it might be a good idea for the government to
start preparing evacuation plans.[42]

The response in London was swift and hostile. Churchill insisted that
Gort was exaggerating the BEF's predicament; if he could not hold on the
Scheldt, he must break out south-westwards towards the Somme instead.
The prime minister considered travelling to France to deliver the message to
Gort personally and was only talked out of the idea with difficulty. Ironside,
as CIGS, went instead, arriving at the BEF's headquarters at Wahagnies,
at dawn on 20 May. The visit was loaded with historical symbolism. In

September 1914, during the German march on Paris, Lord Kitchener, wearing his blue field marshal's uniform, had crossed the Channel under almost identical circumstances. Kitchener had told the BEF's then commander, Sir John French, in no uncertain terms that he was to abandon any thoughts of evacuation. Perhaps Churchill hoped Gort would recognise the precedent.

If he did, it made no difference. Gort immediately made it clear to Ironside that any plan to move south-westwards was a fantasy – 'a scandalous (i.e. Winstonian)' proposal, as Pownall put it.[43] The BEF's divisions were already heavily engaged with the Germans. His men were tired from nine days of marching and running low on ammunition and food. There was no way they could conduct a fighting advance across open country. Ironside quickly realised Gort was right.

The issue was soon moot anyway, because on the evening of 20 May the Germans captured Abbeville, at the mouth of the Somme, closing off the escape route to the south. Two of the BEF's Territorial 'labour' divisions had been hurriedly withdrawn from construction work behind the lines and ordered to defend Abbeville. They were pathetically unready for battle. One quarter of their men had not even finished basic rifle training. Some of them fought with astonishing bravery anyway. One private of the 5th Buffs stayed at his Bren gun post, surrounded, refusing repeated German appeals for surrender, until he was killed. A provost sergeant of the Tyneside Scottish (Black Watch) was last seen by his comrades standing on top of an enemy tank turret, trying to pry open the hatch with his bayonet like a tin of corned beef. But the Germans were advancing with seven armoured divisions towards Abbeville. No amount of gallantry could overcome such desperate odds. When the town fell, Gort's three corps to the north-east were all cut off.[44]

Gort had little optimism that he could break through this encirclement. But he agreed to make one limited counter-attack southwards on 21 May, around Arras, with an *ad hoc* force of tanks, infantry and artillery – the only British offensive of the whole campaign, as it turned out. Arras was a confused encounter battle. For a short time the British tanks ran amok. Enemy anti-tank shells simply bounced off the armour of the advancing Matilda IIs. The German artillerymen fled. But the British radio network broke down, the attack lost cohesion and in any case the attackers had only had sixteen of the Matildas to start with; by nightfall just two were still serviceable. The British force withdrew from the battlefield.

The counter-attack at Arras did not alter the overall situation one bit, but it inspired a brief alarm among the Germans out of all proportion to its real threat – a reminder that it was not just the Allies who were susceptible to panic in May 1940. The German commander at Arras was a then obscure Wehrmacht major-general called Erwin Rommel. The battle was his first encounter with the British – indeed, the first significant opposition of any sort he and his troops had met since crossing the Meuse the previous week. Rommel wildly overreacted to it, reporting to his superiors that he was being attacked by five British divisions.

That was enough to persuade General von Rundstedt on 22 May to halt any further progress towards Boulogne and Calais until the threat had been contained. For twenty-four hours five German Panzer divisions sat waiting to resist a British counter-attack that existed only in the heads of their commanding officers. Much attention would be given later to Hitler's forty-eight-hour 'halt order' to his tank crews on 24 May. But the halt two days earlier was far more significant. Had the German tanks continued to advance on 22 May at the same pace they had been doing for the last several days – and there is no obvious reason why they could not have done so – then Boulogne and Calais, still totally undefended, would have probably fallen without opposition within a few hours, and Dunkirk shortly afterwards. All the British troops further inland would have been trapped. Rommel's panic attack unintentionally saved the BEF.[45]

By 25 May a small garrison was in place in Calais which would hold the Germans up on the Channel coast for a couple of precious days. But the BEF's position remained extremely precarious. Gort's divisions were stretched out along a convoluted 97-mile front line. His troops were on half rations. Ammunition and fuel were running out. General Maxime Weygand, who had replaced the disgraced Gamelin as overall Allied commander-in-chief six days earlier, ordered Gort to use his last two reserve divisions (the 5th and 50th infantry) to make a breakout attempt to the south-west. The War Cabinet confirmed the order. Gort had dismissed such a plan as fantasy back on 20 May. It had even less chance of success now. He was also alarmed by reports that the Belgian army, on his left flank, was collapsing. If this was true, it would open a gap between Menin and the Channel coast that the Germans to the north could advance straight into. By chance, a British patrol that morning had captured a set of orders belonging to a Wehrmacht staff officer that showed the Germans were planning to do exactly this.[46]

At six o'clock on the evening of 25 May, then, Gort decided, in defiance of Weygand and his own government, to ignore the order to attack south-westwards and instead to move the two reserve divisions to close the gap to his north at Menin. In doing so, he knew he was abandoning any last chance of linking back up with the French on the Somme. Withdrawal to the coast and evacuation would now be the BEF's only remaining hope. 'Whether we ever get to the sea, how we get off the beach, how many of us survive is on the knees of the Gods,' wrote Pownall in his diary: 'But it's the only thing to be done. We cannot stay here without being surrounded and there is no other direction in which to go.'[47]

Gort's decision was insubordinate. It was filled with risks. But it was absolutely the correct thing to do, as was demonstrated the following morning, when the War Cabinet changed its mind and approved it. Had Gort sent his last two spare divisions south-westwards on 25 May, it's highly unlikely they could have accomplished anything. The BEF, meanwhile, would have been swiftly enveloped from the north and destroyed. If he had dithered for lack of instructions, the result would have been much the same. Gort was not a great general. His shortcomings had contributed to the disaster that had unfolded in France and Belgium, but his clear-minded courage on 25 May 1940 saved his army from capitulation and his country from losing the Second World War. Which is no bad epitaph to have.[48]

*

Alexander Geddes finally made it onto the Dunkirk beaches on the night of 1–2 June. During his retreat from Belgium he had been strafed by Bf 109s, dive-bombed by Stukas, shot at by snipers and seen his comrades blown up in front of him by enemy shellfire. He had stumbled into an abandoned convent school to find the corpses of sixty schoolgirls, killed in a Luftwaffe raid, neatly laid out in rows and columns, 'rigid and motionless, staring up at the sky'. At one stage during the retreat he had got only ten hours' sleep in a period of 110 hours and had to force himself to stay awake by eating chocolate bars and lumps of cold bully beef. When Geddes finally reached Dunkirk, he lost the rest of his battery in the darkness and wandered from the beaches to the outer harbour's East Mole (breakwater) and back, looking for a spare place on a ship. For the first and only time in the campaign, he fired his revolver – not at the Germans but at a group of British stretcher-bearers who were planning to abandon the wounded under their care on the quayside. Finally, back on the beach, Geddes heard the skipper of a small motor boat about 100 yards offshore call out for one or two more men:

> He looked on that shelving shore rather a frighteningly long way out and none of the [other] soldiers were prepared to take the plunge, nor was the boat risking coming in any further. Being very tall, I decided this was my chance, and using my spade as a walking stick, waded out till the water reached my neck [...] grasping the gunwale and at last dropping my spade, I tried to lever myself aboard, but the water in my clothes, added to the weight of my weariness, completely defeated me in my exhausted state. I was as if anchored to the sand. The long strong arm of the Navy at this moment grasped my webbing belt at the back, and without any misplaced tenderness, deposited me head first into the bottom of the boat. I have never been so grateful to be hurt.[49]

Geddes was among the last men of the BEF to be evacuated. The Admiralty had begun embarking 28,000 'useless mouths' – non-combatant soldiers from the rear area lines of communication – from Dunkirk as early as 20 May, long before the decision was taken to withdraw the whole of the British force. This was the most chaotic period of the whole operation; many of these 'useless mouths' lacked the good leadership and discipline of front-line troops, and there were examples of officers abandoning their men and mobs of panicking soldiers swamping boats.[50] Gort's deputy chief of staff, Oliver Leese, wrote of this period that 'it was nothing to see the whole beach strewn with rifles and Bren guns, and hundreds, if not thousands of men walking about, having thrown away their arms.'[51] Fortunately, the fighting soldiers generally behaved much better when they arrived at Dunkirk in the following days, and by then the Navy had landed shore parties to maintain military discipline.

Operation DYNAMO officially began on Churchill's instruction at 7 p.m. on 26 May. The operation was originally expected to last about two days and to save, at most, 45,000 troops.[52] In the end, it lasted until 4 June and rescued just over 338,000 men, 198,000 of them soldiers of the BEF. About 40,000 British troops were captured by the Germans during the campaign in France and Belgium, but the men who escaped at Dunkirk included almost all the country's trained officers and NCOs, 'the root and core and brain' needed to reconstitute a new British Army, as well as the senior officers (Brooke, Adam, Alexander, Montgomery) to lead it.[53]

One of the reasons why DYNAMO's success far exceeded the Admiralty's original predictions was that it took the Germans at least a week longer than expected to capture Dunkirk. Much of the credit for that belongs to one of Gort's corps commanders, Lieutenant-General Sir Ronald Adam, later the Army's adjutant-general, who established a very effective defensive perimeter.[54] Independent French forces still fighting in the interior of Flanders bought invaluable time too. Any British memory of Dunkirk that fails to include the stubborn stand of the 35,000 French troops besieged at Lille from 28 to 31 May is unjust. Their heroic, doomed resistance delayed seven German divisions and probably allowed 100,000 additional Allied troops to escape to the coast.

On the evening of 23 May, von Rundstedt ordered his *Panzerdivisionen* to halt their advance on Dunkirk to allow time for the German infantry to catch up. His order was confirmed by Hitler around noon the following day, and not rescinded until the evening of 26 May. Rumours circulated afterwards about the rationale for this famous 'halt order', the most sensational of which was that the *Führer* wished to spare the BEF from humiliating destruction as a goodwill gesture to the British government. There is no substance at all to this. Hitler probably saw the order simply as a way of imposing his will on his own commanding officers after days of confusion.[55] After the war, surviving veterans of the 1940 campaign such as Panzer general Heinz Guderian blamed the halt order for allowing the BEF to escape and throwing away the chance of a total strategic victory. But it's by no means obvious that the German tanks could have quickly seized Dunkirk even if they had been allowed to keep advancing on 23–4 May. Guderian's men were exhausted, his vehicles were badly in need of maintenance and the Allied defensive line was much stronger than it had been a couple of days earlier. If there was a lost opportunity, it was probably the earlier halt order on 21 May caused by Rommel's panicky overreaction to the Arras counter-offensive.[56]

The role of the RAF in the evacuation was contentious. Vice-Admiral Bertram Ramsay, DYNAMO's overall commander-in-chief, complained in his subsequent report to the Admiralty that 'full air protection was expected, but instead, for hours on end the ships off-shore were subjected to a murderous hail of bombs and machine-gun bullets.'[57] Many BEF veterans complained bitterly afterwards that the RAF ('Royal Absent Force') seemed entirely missing at Dunkirk. Throughout the summer of 1940, it was hazardous for men clad in Air Force blue to venture into English pubs filled with sullen men in khaki.

Dowding, in defence of Fighter Command's reputation, insisted that his squadrons had made an all-out effort for DYNAMO. Thirty-four of them were involved at one time or another over Dunkirk, including the first Spitfire squadrons to be seen in French airspace since the war's start. But this was questionable. Only 250 to 300 sorties were flown over the beaches each day, too few to provide continuous patrols in strength. The task of defending Dunkirk was left largely to Fighter Command's south-eastern 11 Group, equipped with only about 200 serviceable aircraft at the time. Dowding, despite being ordered by Newall to throw everything into the battle, deliberately held back many available squadrons in the Midlands and northern England, worried that the Germans might use the opportunity provided by the Dunkirk distraction to launch a knock-out blow against Britain's aircraft factories and ports. He had never been convinced of the importance of the land campaign. Indeed, he had been quietly worried that the Allied armies trapped in France would *not* be defeated, for that would mean that he would be pressured to send his priceless fighter squadrons back across the Channel again.[58]

Dowding's calculus, though well intentioned, was highly dubious in its strategic logic. If Britain was unable to extract enough of the BEF's troops from France, then the Luftwaffe bombing threat would be purely academic, because it was unlikely that Churchill's government would be able to carry on the war anyway. In the event, Fighter Command did just enough. But the RAF's obsession with knock-out blows was continuing to distort the war effort.[59]

The calm weather in the last week of May 1940 and the lack of heavy surf, which would have made lifting men off the beaches almost impossible, were hugely important to DYNAMO's success. Had the Channel experienced the sort of early summer squalls that made D-Day so challenging four years later, the evacuation would never have got properly started. Above all, there was the professional excellence of the Royal Navy. J. B. Priestley's famous BBC *Postscript* in June 1940, celebrating the 'little ships', helped to create a narrative of Dunkirk as an essentially civilian triumph, an example of the native British genius for muddling through.[60] This was a clever way of spinning the defeat as a kind of improvisational Shire Folk victory. But it misrepresented what had actually happened. The 203 requisitioned private motor boats and 230 trawlers and drifters did useful work ferrying men from the beaches to vessels standing offshore with larger draughts. But most of these little ships were manned by naval ratings throughout the operation, and the actual transportation of soldiers back to Britain was carried out overwhelmingly by RN destroyers and big passenger vessels.[61] The little ships were helpful, but they did not decide Dunkirk's outcome.

The key breakthrough was not their arrival but the realisation on 28 May by Captain William Tenant, senior naval officer onshore, that the East Mole of Dunkirk's outer harbour could be used as an *ad hoc* embarkation point in place of the inner harbour, which had been smashed up by a Luftwaffe attack the previous day. Ultimately, 239,000 soldiers, or seven out of every ten men evacuated, were taken off the Mole rather than the beaches. It was the competent professionalism of sailors like Tennant, Rear-Admiral Frederic Wake-Walker, who supervised the evacuation fleet, DYNAMO's overall commander Ramsay and his deputy, Vice-Admiral Sir James Somerville (soon to be, tragically, 'the unskilled butcher of Oran'), that made Dunkirk a success. Every time during the Second World War that the British attempted to muddle through with inspired amateurism, the result was a disaster. Every time they accomplished something, it was because of careful planning and professional expertise.

Dunkirk, though a successful military operation, marked the beginning of the disintegration of the Anglo-French alliance. The British accused the French (with fairness) of not acting with sufficient haste. The French accused the British (with fairness) of ignoring previous commitments they had made. On 26 May Churchill told Reynaud, who was visiting London, that the BEF was withdrawing back to the coast. The French premier immediately telegraphed Weygand, asking him to give similar orders to General Blanchard, the commander of the French units also trapped in the northern pocket. But whether out of mischief or confusion, Weygand failed to pass along the information clearly. Blanchard was shocked when Gort informed him that the BEF was leaving on 28 May. He had been under the impression that the Allies were going to try to hold the pocket as an embattled fortress, and that supplies and reinforcements would be coming *into* Dunkirk, not out of it. Weygand did not clarify the situation until the following day.[62]

In DYNAMO's final days there was an unfortunate disconnect between Churchill's promises to the French government and the orders given to the BEF's commanders on the scene. By the end of 30 May, only 6,000 of the 120,000 troops evacuated had been French. This was largely Weygand's fault, but Churchill recognised that 'it might do irreparable harm to the relations' between Britain and France if the inequity were not addressed.[63] Tempers were already flaring at Dunkirk as *poilus* (French troops) began pouring into the town, only to be told that the beaches and Mole were off-limits to them. Harsh words were accompanied by stand-offs with fixed bayonets and shots in the air.[64] At a Supreme War Council meeting in Paris on 31 May, Churchill, pressed on the point by Reynaud, agreed that the evacuation would henceforth take place on a 50:50 basis. Three remaining British divisions would help form the rearguard to allow more French troops to depart, and as a sacrificial gesture to their allies, British troops would make the final stand before the port's capitulation.[65]

But Gort, who held firmly to the view that 'every Frenchman embarked is at the cost of one Englishman', believed that his orders from the War Office had been clear: to prioritise British lives above all else.[66] Major-General Harold Alexander, one of the BEF corps commanders who took over when Gort was recalled home on 31 May, felt similarly that, while he was happy to 'assist' the French, he had been instructed to put the safety of his own 40,000 remaining troops first. After he assumed command, he told Admiral Jean-Marie Abrial, the senior French officer still remaining at Dunkirk, that he intended to withdraw the last of the BEF's soldiers as soon as possible. The 100,000 or so French troops still in the pocket would have to manage for themselves as best they could. Abrial showed him the memorandum from the Supreme War Council. Alexander replied that he was not bound by any such instructions. 'Your decision [...] dishonours England,' Abrial shouted at him angrily.[67]

The final British troops were embarked from Dunkirk around 9 p.m. on the night of 2 June. The French rearguard held on until the morning of 4 June. As it turned out, because the Germans took longer to capture the port than expected, the British were able to keep their 50:50 promise: between 30 May and the final surrender, 139,000 of the last 278,000 troops withdrawn were French.[68] But about 40,000 *poilus* were left behind. The Germans discovered disconsolate hordes of them sitting at Dunkirk's har-bourside and on the sand dunes, waiting forlornly for ships that never arrived.

*

Churchill's speech to the Commons on the day Dunkirk surrendered was remembered afterwards for its rousing peroration to 'fight on the beaches' of England if the Germans now tried to invade. But on 4 June 1940 it was still not clear if the battle for France was over and the Third Republic doomed. The prime minister hedged his bets in his speech. 'The British Empire and the French Republic, linked together in their cause and in their need, will defend to the death their native soil, aiding each other like good comrades to the utmost of their strength,' he insisted. Churchill was still proclaiming his commitment to the Anglo-French alliance and the continuation of the war on the other side of the Channel, even as he roared lone islander defiance at the Germans.[69]

The BEF might have departed, but large numbers of British military personnel remained in France after Dunkirk. The 51st (Highland) Infantry Division, which had been doing a tour of duty on the Maginot Line when the Germans attacked, and the incomplete 1st Armoured Division were still fighting. The AASF had six bomber and three fighter squadrons in the Orléans–Le Mans area. There were about 150,000 soldiers and RAF airmen serving at supply bases and depots throughout north-western France. Churchill promised Reynaud that these forces would be the kernel of a second British Expeditionary Force, which would now be reassembled south of the Somme. Orders were given for the 52nd (Lowland) and 1st Canadian Infantry Divisions to start embarking for France. He began sketching out plans for a new seven-division BEF once soldiers evacuated from Dunkirk had been reorganised and re-equipped.[70] The prime minister insisted that there should be no talk of the alliance collapsing. 'No tolerance should be given to the idea that France will make a separate peace,' Churchill warned his War Cabinet colleagues.[71]

Privately, he was aware that France might try to do just that. The point of a second BEF was to offer Reynaud's flagging government enough material assistance and moral support to keep it in power, and the French nation in the war, once the Germans turned south from Dunkirk. The second stage of the Wehrmacht offensive, against the new French defensive line on the Somme, began on 5 June. Despite being heavily outnumbered now, the defending forces fought much better than they had done in the earlier battles to the north. This belies the accusation that there was anything fundamentally wrong with French military morale or doctrine in 1940.

But the outcome on the Somme was never really in doubt, and Weygand had prepared no reserve line to fall back on. The French commander-in-chief's attitude towards the campaign had been sulkily defeatist ever since his appointment on 19 May. Weygand was far more worried about a Communard-style leftist insurrection than about military defeat by the Germans. His primary concern was no longer to win the war but to preserve enough army units to defend the existing social order from revolutionaries.

Reynaud wished to continue fighting no matter what. But he had little control over the French armed forces any longer – Weygand would only obey the orders that suited him – and his authority in his own Cabinet was undermined by the presence of the eighty-four-year-old First World War hero Philippe Pétain, who had been made deputy prime minister on 18 May. Pétain made no secret of his desire for an immediate armistice.

On 10 June the government left Paris for Tours. The capital was declared an open city, the Germans occupying it four days later. With the Third Republic beginning to disintegrate, Churchill made two final cross-Channel trips to try to persuade Reynaud's Cabinet to keep fighting, suggesting that, if necessary, it should raise an army of irregular *francs-tireurs* to conduct a guerrilla insurgency against the Germans. What the social conservatives Weygand and Pétain thought of that idea is not hard to imagine. Reynaud, under pressure from his own ministers, asked Churchill to release France from the commitment it had made in March 1940 never to negotiate a separate peace with the Germans. The War Cabinet in London reluctantly agreed to this to offer Reynaud some help, insisting as a condition, however, that all capital ships must sail to British ports during any armistice negotiations – the beginning of a wrangle over the French fleet's fate that would end in tragedy at Mers-el-Kébir. On 16 June, Churchill made a quixotic last-ditch proposal of full Anglo-French political union as a 'dramatic announcement [...] to [try to] keep the French going'.[72] But Reynaud's Cabinet barely discussed the idea before dismissing it as a cynical British ploy to steal France's colonies. Reynaud resigned in despair that night, and President Lebrun asked Pétain to form a new government. At noon the following day the new octogenarian premier broadcast to the French people that he was requesting peace terms from Hitler.

Throughout this political drama the so-called second BEF had been assembling in north-western France. Churchill enthused about the idea of building a 'Breton redoubt' to encourage further French resistance. But the War Office advised that such a fortified bridgehead would require a minimum of ten full-strength divisions to have any chance at succeeding, far more troops than were now available.[73] Lieutenant-General Alan Brooke,

Gort's former corps commander now appointed to lead the motley force, took a long time reaching his new HQ in Le Mans. By the time he did, it appears that he had already decided that the whole project was futile. On 14 June he cancelled the dispatch of any further reinforcements from England and issued orders for his units in France to retire to the coast to await evacuation. This provoked a peppery phone call from Churchill, who pointed out, quite correctly, that Brooke was exceeding his authority. But by the end of the conversation the prime minister had reluctantly conceded that the idea of the Breton redoubt was folly. He agreed to Brooke's withdrawal.

Operation AERIAL, the evacuation of all remaining British military personnel (and many civilians also), began the following day. It officially ended on 25 June, the day that France's armistice with Germany went into effect. AERIAL accomplished the rescue of almost 200,000 men, women and children. Aside from the sinking of the liner RMS *Lancastria* off St Nazaire on 17 June, with the loss of over 3,500 lives (more than twice as many passengers and crew as died on the *Titanic*), the operation proceeded without major enemy interruption. It was another feat of Royal Navy professionalism. Indeed, with only a single exception – the 51st (Highland) Infantry Division, trapped at St Valéry on 10 June – the Navy was able successfully to evacuate every large body of British troops that made it to the French coast during the campaign.

*

A few weeks earlier, when the Dunkirk evacuation had just been getting under way, the British chiefs of staff had delivered a report to the War Cabinet on what the strategic outlook would be if France fell. The report, though, spoke only of 'a Certain Eventuality' taking place. Why the euphemism was used is unclear. Perhaps, in late May 1940, it was still considered too dreadful a thing to spell out the possibility of French surrender.[74]

Within months of the signing of the armistice with Germany, however, people on both sides of the Channel were already musing about whether France's fall had been 'a certain eventuality' in a different sense – as something that was bound to take place, a doomed and inescapable result. Profound events seem to demand profound explanations. French writers began constructing a whole genre of polemical literature that sought to explain their country's defeat in terms of deep systemic causes – pre-war political atrophy, social dissension, cultural decadence, spiritual malaise.[75]

That sense of inevitability remained a dominant theme in writing about the collapse after the war. André Beaufre, one of Gamelin's former staff officers, wrote in his memoir that 'by 1940 there was nothing to be done: fate had stacked the cards too heavily against us'.[76]

British observers, too, switched from stunned incomprehension to claims that France's fall had been a foregone conclusion. On 25 May 1940, the day Gort decided that the BEF must withdraw from Dunkirk, Lord Halifax wrote: 'the mystery of what looks like the French failure is as great as ever. The one firm rock on which everybody had been willing to build for the last two years was the French Army, and the Germans [have] walked through it like they did through the Poles'.[77] Ordinary Britons were just as astonished. It was 'a complete and bewildering surprise', wrote teenager Edward Stebbing in his diary in July: 'Up to the time of the actual surrender, nobody thought it possible. "France will never give in" was the general opinion [...] even when the papers printed it in black and white it was hard to believe'.[78] By January 1941, however, deterministic conclusions were in vogue. 'The military defeat of France,' wrote the Scottish historian Denis Brogan, 'was only one aspect of a deeper defeat, of a loss of faith in herself, of a resignation to a passive role'.[79]

But there is no need to resort to deep theories about civilisational decline to explain what happened to France in 1940. The proximate reason the Third Republic fell was that its army failed to mount an effective counter-attack against the German bridgeheads over the Meuse between 14 and 16 May. That failure was the watershed. Before it, anything might have happened. After it, the most the Allies could probably have hoped for was a ceasefire leaving Hitler in control of the Low Countries and northern France. But events moved swiftly. By 20 May even that outcome was highly unlikely. By 25 May it was out of the question. All the rest from that point onwards was, as Churchill said later, though in a very different context, 'merely the proper application of overwhelming force'.

The idea that France's army in 1940 was incompetent, and uniquely so, is simply wrong. Like all the armies on both sides, the Armée Française in May 1940 was still struggling to organise and equip itself for a major European war during a period of rapid expansion. Many of the vehicles and weapons it had been promised had not yet been delivered. Many of its soldiers had not yet received enough training. Like all the armies, it had some excellent units, a lot that were average quality and some that were very poor. It was France's particular misfortune that the critical battle on the Meuse took place between some of the most elite Wehrmacht combat forces and some of its own worst. The brilliance of the German Army's overall victory in 1940 has obscured the fact that its individual units did not always put on such an impressive performance. Troops of the 3rd SS Panzer Division panicked and ran from British tanks at Arras. French heavy tanks rampaged through the German lines at Huppy, near Abbeville, on 28 May.

When the balance of quality on the battlefield was even, the result could be very different from that at Sedan. The great tank battle in the Gembloux Gap on 14–15 May is forgotten today because events further south rendered its outcome strategically irrelevant, but it was the only occasion in the campaign in which German *Panzerdivisionen* were met by their French equivalents on the battlefield on roughly equal terms, and General René Prioux's mechanised cavalry corps gave an excellent account of itself, destroying more enemy tanks than it lost.[80] During the campaign France may have lost as many as 92,000 men, including twelve generals. Over 13,000 of these troops were killed during the last ten days of the fighting, suggesting that there was no lack of willingness to continue dying for *la patrie* even when the odds had become hopeless.[81] The last French troops holding out in the Maginot Line did not surrender until ordered to do so on 4 July, nine days after the armistice came into effect.

Some of the French generals were simply not up to the job. But the French were hardly alone in this. Two of the BEF's generals, Michael Barker and Sir Charles 'Budget' Loyd, cracked up under the stress of battle and had to be relieved.[82] Many German generals in the Wehrmacht high command did not understood clearly what was going on at the beginning of the campaign either and tried to interfere in their own army's advance from Sedan, to the point where a furious and insubordinate Guderian had to threaten to resign in the midst of the battle to prevent further meddling from his superiors.

The French understood *Blitzkrieg* principles as well as any other army of the time. They knew in principle how to respond to them. One of the lessons of 1940 is that it is one thing to know in theory what to do in an emergency, quite another to be able to put it into practice when the emergency arrives.

But it is not difficult to imagine a very different outcome to the drama of May 1940. Had the French responded even a little more coherently and vigorously to the threat at the Meuse from 14 to 16 May, then von Rundstedt's daring breach of the line through the Ardennes might have turned into precisely the kind of fatal strategic trap that Liddell Hart had predicted a year earlier, with the Panzers stuck in the narrow, congested Belgian forest roads, unable to advance or escape.[83] Had that happened, the fighting on the Western Front would probably have become bogged down by the end of the summer into an inconclusive stalemate. Hitler's great gamble would have failed. His armoured units thrown into the Sedan battle were the Wehrmacht's greatest, irreplaceable military asset in 1940. Had they been smashed on the Meuse, the German Army's offensive capability would have been shot. There would have been no second chance to conquer France.[84] How the war would have proceeded from that point onward is anyone's guess, but Germany's parlous economic circumstances do not suggest that its chances in a long conflict were promising. Perhaps Hitler's generals, seeing their *Führer* fail spectacularly for the first time, would have finally summoned up the courage to do something about him. Perhaps Halder would finally have removed that pistol from his pocket. Certainly, the war – and the world – would have been very different afterwards.

The story of the Battle of France in 1940 is not one of militarism triumphing over meekness. Nor is it one about innovation overcoming stagnant thinking. For all the glamour attached to *Blitzkrieg*, it was the Germans, not the Allies, who planned to fight the campaign in the spring of 1940 on strictly traditional, even old-fashioned, lines. They had no time for novel theories like strategic bombing. Their conception of what they must do to win was one that Bismarck and Napoleon, and Alexander the Great for that matter, would have understood without difficulty: to use ground forces to smash a way through the enemy's defences, defeat its armies and compel its surrender by the physical occupation of its territory. It was a timeworn, hackneyed idea of how to fight a war, which happened to work brilliantly on this occasion.

*

'There is probably no more terrible trial for a people than the defeat of its armies: in the scale of crises, this is the supreme catastrophe,' the French historian René Rémond wrote of 1940: 'Defeat creates a deep and lasting traumatism in everyone. It wounds something essential in each of us: a certain confidence in life, a pride in oneself, an indispensable self-respect.'[85]

The British, though defeated in the spring of 1940, were spared this kind of trauma. The demise of the Western alliance was not met by much sense of guilt about what had happened. After all, it was a French army that had collapsed at Sedan, not a British one. It was the Belgians and the French who had surrendered, not the British. It was Reynaud's government that had broken the terms of the alliance by making a separate peace, not Churchill's. 'As usual, the brunt of all the hard fighting and the hard work fell upon the British,' wrote Chamberlain in his diary. Millions of his fellow countrymen and -women agreed with him.[86] For the British, 1940 would be a year of domestic recriminations aimed at Cato's Guilty Men. But this would not develop into any wider sense of responsibility for the Allied defeat, still less any sense of shame or remorse. The British spiritual revival of that year was about rediscovering a peculiar national genius, of looking inwards, not outwards. The British concluded that the alliance with France had been part of the problem, not something to apologise about.

Or at least most of them did. There were a few dissenting voices. At a War Cabinet meeting on 17 May, General Ironside turned angrily on Labour's Arthur Greenwood when he scoffed at 'these bloody gallant allies'. 'I told him that we had depended on the French Army,' wrote Ironside later: 'that we had made no army and that therefore it was not right to say, "these bloody allies." It was for them to say that of us.'[87] Churchill made a similar admission to Anthony Eden about the 'lamentable failure to support the French by an adequate BEF during the first year of the war'.[88]

The BEF's position on the Allied front line meant that by the time it was involved in any heavy fighting in May 1940 the crucial battles to the south had already been fought and lost. The British Army in France was simply too small to play any decisive role in the outcome of the campaign. But did it have to be that way?

What Gamelin had always really wanted from the British was not a huge infantry army – he had one of those already – but two or three fully equipped armoured divisions which, combined with one or two motorised infantry divisions, could have served as a high-quality mobile reserve. Had it existed, such a force would have been available to intervene against the German bridgeheads on the Meuse on 14 May, with incalculable but possibly decisive results.[89] There was no technical obstacle to its creation. It would not even have required the politically difficult introduction of peacetime conscription. Its absence in 1940 was a choice.

A larger and more powerful BEF would have required the War Office to think more carefully about higher command structures. The decision to appoint Gort as commander-in-chief in France in September 1939 was made at the last minute, and for reasons that had far more to do with Whitehall politics than any real suitability for the role. France's leadership structure in 1940 was handicapped by too many generals; Britain's, on the other hand, had too few. Gort was expected to lead three active corps in the field as well as to serve as the overall commander-in-chief of all British personnel in France, with the many important administrative and liaison duties that entailed. That was asking too much of any single man. He chose to concentrate on the first of his roles, the one he was best at, to the detriment of the second. Had the two responsibilities been formally divided up, as they surely would have had to be in a larger BEF, and someone like Ironside made overall commander-in-chief (with Sir John Dill, perhaps, in his place back in London as CIGS), then the British forces in France would have enjoyed far more attentive leadership.

If the British had had more troops in France, it might also have encouraged them to be less reticent in their early discussions about strategy with Gamelin. 'All through our dealings with the French,' Ironside wrote in 1943, 'we were beset with the trouble of not upsetting their Command. Our military contribution to the war was so small that we had to be careful.'[90] Gort had significant doubts about the wisdom of the Dyle Plan. But he kept them to himself, partly because he was burdened with a sense of how modest his own country's contribution to the defence of the Western Front was. A larger BEF might have given the British commanders more confidence to ask the awkward questions that so badly needed to be asked about Allied strategy.[91]

All this is speculation. But it's something Sir Thomas Inskip had speculated on back in December 1937, when the Cabinet agreed to continue focusing rearmament on the RAF rather than the Army:

> I must warn my colleagues of the possible consequences of this proposal [...] if France were again to be in danger of being overrun by land armies, a situation might arise when, as in the last war, we had to improvise an army to assist her. Should this happen, the Government of the day would most certainly be criticised for having neglected to provide against so obvious a contingency.[92]

But for Britain to have been adequately prepared in 1939 to fight the European land war it found itself in, not the war it wanted to fight, would have taken more than just a few last-minute changes to the defence budget. It would have required a fundamental early reconsideration of its place in the European security system. Throughout the 1930s there was no significant lobby pressing for such a rethink. Chamberlain believed Britain should remain aloof from a continental commitment. So, until very late, did Churchill. The Conservatives, the Liberals and the Labour Party were all united on the matter. Appeasers and anti-appeasers, militarists and pacifists: with very few exceptions, all wanted to keep out of Europe. There was no shortage of Guilty Men and Women on that score.

Britain maintained a semi-detached attitude towards the alliance throughout its existence. France had to sacrifice a lot to try to make it work. It set aside other diplomatic relationships – with Italy in 1935, Czechoslovakia in 1938, the USSR in 1939 – for Britain's sake. It scraped the bottom of its own manpower pool to build an army three-quarters as large as Germany's from a population base only half the size, while Britain, though more populous than France, mobilised only a fraction as many soldiers. The British argument was always that its key contribution to the alliance should be airpower rather than manpower. But after war broke out, the RAF persistently refused to send fighter squadrons across the Channel. When, in the critical weeks after 10 May, the French begged for air assistance, the answer was invariably no.

The British decided to withdraw the BEF from Dunkirk without asking the French first. They promised to maintain the final rearguard at the port, then changed their minds, leaving tens of thousands of French troops behind. Three weeks after Dunkirk they withdrew a second BEF from France, again without asking first. In a sentimental moment during the crisis, Churchill called the two countries 'companions in misfortune'.[93] Yet for his country it was a companionship that was highly conditional. Britain claimed that France had no right to negotiate a separate peace with Germany under the terms of their March 1940 agreement. So far as the French were concerned, the unilateral withdrawal of British forces from the continent released them from any moral obligation to that agreement. They suspected that the British might be about to make a separate peace deal with the Germans themselves. It was not a bizarre suspicion. Britain had, after all, done plenty of things without informing the French first.

After 1940 the British looked back at Dunkirk as the place in which they had rediscovered their true nature. The French could only agree, though for very different reasons. Dunkirk had, as they saw it, revealed what the British were truly like. 'They cannot resist the call of the ports,' said

Weygand.[94] The soldier-historian Marc Bloch felt that the French soldiers left behind in the wreckage of Dunkirk 'would have needed a superhuman dose of charity not to feel bitter as they saw ship after ship drawing away from the shore, carrying their foreign companions in arms to safety. Heroes they may have been, but they were not saints.'[95]

Churchill – who had stuck by the French longer than most of his countrymen – ultimately decided that British survival in 1940 mattered more than loyalty to the alliance. The French attitude was: *we entered this war together, so we should fight to the end together. If we can no longer win, let us at least battle the Germans to a standstill to get the best possible peace terms for us both.* Churchill's attitude was: *the only thing that matters in the end is that one of us fights on.* Whatever the rights and wrongs of 1940, he was ultimately correct. French defeat was not decisive for Britain. The war went on. Eventually, France was liberated by an expeditionary force dispatched from southern England. The British decision to abandon France after Dunkirk may not have been very noble. It may have been the result of years of its own complacent, solipsistic behaviour. All the same, perhaps it was the right choice to make under the circumstances.

The war that Britain was left with after France's fall was very different from the one Chamberlain had wanted to fight back in September 1939, however. All hope of restricting it to north-western Europe was gone. So too was any possibility of Britain and the British Empire emerging from it the same as they had been when it started. No matter who won, there was no going back any longer.

PART FOUR

AND ONLY ENGLAND STANDS

15

LUNATIC RELIEF

On Tuesday, 28 May 1940, a crowd of Fleet Street reporters clustered into a suite at the Berkeley Hotel in London's Knightsbridge. They were there to hear Major-General Noel Mason-MacFarlane, the Director of Military Intelligence for the British Expeditionary Force, give them an account of what was happening on the other side of the English Channel. There was much to explain. The reporters knew that the BEF had been fighting a desperate struggle against the German forces ever since the Panzers had broken through the Allied line at Sedan two weeks earlier. On Sunday, 26 May, the king had spoken at a prayer service at Westminster Abbey, broadcast nationally by BBC radio, for 'our soldiers in dire peril in France'.[1] But otherwise, news on the British side of the Channel remained very vague. The situation, while serious, did not yet appear to be catastrophic. 'BEF CHECK ENEMY IN BIG BATTLE', the headline in the *Daily Mirror* read that Tuesday morning. 'The British front is intact,' the *Daily Express* consoled its readers.

'Mason-Mac' was at the Berkeley to disabuse Fleet Street of any misplaced optimism. 'I am afraid there is going to be a considerable shock for the British public. It is your duty to act as shock absorbers,' he began. Gort's army, he revealed, was on the brink of total capitulation. Surrounded, squeezed against the Channel coastline, cut off from the main body of the French armies to the south, it was now just hours away from likely collapse and surrender. 'The leadership, the staff work and the stubborn defence manifested by our force will go down to history as one of the bravest and most efficient struggles against heavy odds in the annals of the British Army.'[2] But the outcome now looked inevitable. To the *Daily Mirror*'s correspondent Bernard Grey, it seemed that Mason-MacFarlane's job at the Berkeley was to give a 'funeral oration' for the British Army. The evacuation of the BEF from Dunkirk's beaches did not even get a mention in the briefing. Nor did Mason-Mac offer any hope for such a rescue. The BEF's fate seemed to be mass surrender.

In his memoirs, years later, Churchill wrote of that final week of May 1940 that 'the supreme question of whether we should fight on alone never found a place upon the War Cabinet agenda. It was taken for granted and as a matter of course.'[3] That was untrue. Indeed, David Reynolds has called it 'the most significant cover-up' in Churchill's post-war history of 'His Finest Hour'.[4] In fact, as Mason-MacFarlane's briefing shows, the overwhelming mood of the British establishment in the last week of May 1940 was one of doom. During the nine meetings of the War Cabinet held between 26 and 28 May, the question of peace was therefore debated at length and with considerable passion.

Lord Halifax was the principal advocate for seeking to hear German peace terms through the intermediary efforts of the still neutral Italians. Halifax had warned his War Cabinet colleagues back in December 1939 that 'if the French Government wanted to make peace, we should not be able to carry on the war by ourselves'. It was a bland assertion that had seemed commonsensical enough at the time.[5] Five months later, with the Allied front on the point of collapse and Reynaud likely to come under pressure from his colleagues in Paris to consider an armistice, its implications were acquiring a new and disquieting relevance.

The Foreign Secretary argued to his colleagues that an approach to Hitler via Rome offered a good chance of success. The Italians would surely be keen to persuade the Germans to take 'a more reasonable attitude' towards peace terms, given that 'the last thing that Signor Mussolini wanted was to see Herr Hitler dominating Europe'. Churchill was dubiously non-committal about the idea, warning that 'we must take care not to be forced into a weak position in which we went to Signor Mussolini and invited him to go to Herr Hitler and ask him to treat us nicely'. He wanted to wait at least until the results of Operation DYNAMO were established before considering any approach.[6]

The debate continued all the following day and into 28 May, at which point Halifax, accepting that the other three members of the War Cabinet had now aligned themselves with Churchill's view that it was better to fight on for the time being, conceded defeat. The prime minister brought the matter to a close with a rousing address to the outer Cabinet in the House of Commons on the evening of 28 May. According to the Labour MP Hugh Dalton, the new coalition minister of economic warfare, Churchill closed his remarks with the graphic peroration that 'if this long island story of ours is to end at last, let it end when each of us lies choking in his own blood upon the ground'.[7]

How close did Britain really come to making peace with Hitler in May 1940? And to what extent was Churchill's personal intervention in the matter critical? It's arguable that far too much is made of these secret talks-about-talks. Halifax's proposal never stood any real chance of gaining acceptance. The two Labour members of the War Cabinet, Attlee and Greenwood, said little throughout the three days of debate. But they were clearly unimpressed with what the foreign secretary was advocating. They never showed much likelihood of agreeing to his plan.

Chamberlain was equally unenthusiastic, suggesting at first only that it might be worth stringing out negotiations with the Italians for a while to buy some time. By 26 May he was in full agreement with Churchill, writing in his diary that 'it would be better for us to fight on in the hope of maintaining sufficient air strength to keep the Germans at bay until other forces can be mobilised, perhaps in USA'.[8] Chamberlain's support for the man who had just usurped him as prime minister may seem surprising, but it is one of the most under-appreciated factors in the story of 1940.[9] Churchill, Chamberlain conceded in a letter to Ida the day after he resigned the premiership, was 'surrounded by a different crowd from the one I am accustomed to'. But 'Winston has been most handsome in his appreciation of my willingness to help and my ability to do so.'[10] Vain, spiteful and narrow-minded he certainly was, but Neville Chamberlain was not the sort of man to stab a close colleague in the back, especially at a moment of national emergency. It was his 'unswerving allegiance' to the new prime minister during the first few months of the Churchill government that persuaded many Tory back-benchers suspicious of Churchill to stay loyal too.[11]

Halifax, in any case, always insisted that he was not advocating peace at any price. The idea of an armistice with the Germans was 'was probably academic', he conceded, 'since we were unlikely to receive any offer which would not come up against the fundamental conditions which were essential to us' – namely, a settlement that would guarantee the British Empire's continued independence and sovereignty.[12] Halifax simply felt that it would be foolish not to find out what the German terms were, at least, however unlikely it was that they would turn out to be acceptable.

What Halifax would have considered 'essential' to British independence and sovereignty was something he never laid out. He might have taken a more flexible attitude towards the 'essentialness' of certain things than Churchill. Halifax also never considered how even tentatively broaching the issue of peace with Hitler might have been interpreted in Berlin as a sign of weakness to be exploited. The effect on British public willingness to continue fighting if word of such an approach had got out could have been disastrous. But the foreign secretary was a conscientious patriot who had been responsible for taking a firmer stand against Hitler before Munich and again in 1939. To suggest (as films such as 2017's *Darkest Hour* have done) that he was a weakling defeatist plotting to turn over his country to Hitler is an outrageous calumny.[13]

The military background to what took place during these War Cabinet meetings is important. When discussions began on 26 May, Operation DYNAMO had only just been put into effect. About 25,000 British troops were extracted from the harbour and beaches of Dunkirk over the next forty-eight hours. Whether the Royal Navy could rescue many more soldiers than this was still not clear. If Dunkirk fell to the Germans quickly, as it seemed it might, only a small fraction of the total British force trapped in the Flanders pocket would get away. 'Of course, whatever happens at Dunkirk, we shall fight on,' Churchill said 'quite casually' at his meeting with the outer Cabinet on 28 May.[14] At the time, though, he had no way of knowing whether that was a pledge he could hold to. His statement to the Commons that evening was terse and gloomy. The House, he warned, 'should prepare itself for hard and heavy tidings'.[15] As Mason-MacFarlane's apocalyptic briefing in the Berkeley Hotel illustrates, the Army itself had no confidence in success.

What would have happened if DYNAMO had failed and most of the British troops in France and Flanders had been forced to surrender? Presumably, Churchill would have wanted to fight on regardless. There would have been voices in the Cabinet and the service ministries demanding the same. The RAF and RN might have insisted that the homeland was still safe from invasion by air and sea, for the time being anyway. But consider the context. The Germans would have just captured almost all the British Army. Hitler would be holding several hundred thousand soldiers, most of the country's trained military personnel, as hostages. If, on 4 June 1940, Churchill had had to return to the House of Commons to announce not 'a miracle of deliverance' at Dunkirk but a dreadful mass capitulation, lacking any redeeming counter-narrative to soften the blow of defeat, it's hard to imagine him being able then to go on to summon up much enthusiasm to fight on Britain's beaches. At the very least, Halifax would surely have seized the opportunity to reopen the discussion of peace talks that he had been forced to abandon on 28 May.

Churchillian hagiography today would have it that it was the prime minister's iron will alone which kept Britain in the war in 1940. 'Take away Churchill,' according to Charles Krauthammer, 'and Britain would have settled with Hitler – or worse. Nazism would have prevailed.'[16] Boris Johnson echoed the same view in 2014, when he wrote: 'without Churchill, Hitler would almost certainly have won [...] only he could have done it.'[17]

But it was the success of DYNAMO, not Churchill imposing his resolve, however formidable, on his foreign secretary, that clinched the matter of whether Britain fought on in May 1940. Prime ministerial will was important, to be sure. But it was never enough by itself.

*

When he heard the news of France's surrender, Sir Hugh Dowding thanked God.[18] Such avowals of deliverance were understandable as an attempt to buck up spirits. But if they were meant in any way seriously, then they were, as the historian John Terraine later called them, a 'lunatic relief' only.[19] It ought to have been obvious to anyone in Britain in June 1940 that the country's strategic situation was gravely compromised by France's surrender. Britain may, in a sense, have been released by the French armistice to fight the kind of non-continental sea and air war it had hoped and planned for until the spring of 1939. But it would now have to do so under circumstances very different from, and much more treacherous than, anything its leaders had ever envisaged in the 1930s.

Britain was now fighting a Germany that effectively controlled all the European mainland. Certainly, it was not fighting Hitler 'alone', thanks to the rest of the British Empire and the émigré forces of the conquered nations. But it was no longer fighting in alliance with any formidable Great Power. Its ability to project military force against the Third Reich had been limited to what were, as yet anyway, ineffectual bombing raids and pinprick commando sorties. Britain had lost access to vital supplies of raw materials from the continent. Before the war, 34 per cent of British imports by value had come from Europe.[20] The loss of continental and French colonial sources for food and raw materials meant the immediate loss of 94 per cent of the UK's iron ore supply, 90 per cent of its paper-making soft timber, 72 per cent of its bacon, 71 per cent of its eggs, 46 per cent of its butter. Supplies of linen and Scandinavian hardwoods for pit props and railway sleepers were decimated.[21] Some of these imports could be made good with substitutions; some of them could be produced at home instead. But many of them, or their equivalents, would now have to found elsewhere.

Germany's seizure of the Atlantic coastline from Norway to the Spanish border had greatly increased Hitler's ability to attack Britain's maritime lines of communication. All the coastal waters of the British Isles, including the crucial west coast ports, were now within the Luftwaffe's bombing range. German capital ships and U-boats could operate from French bases along the Bay of Biscay, allowing them much faster transit times to the Atlantic shipping lanes to harry eastbound convoys and the southern corridor to Gibraltar. At the same time, the Royal Navy would now be required to mount elaborate anti-invasion watches along the southern and eastern coastlines of Great Britain, tying up many of the destroyers, sloops and armed trawlers that would otherwise have been available to escort merchantmen across the Atlantic.

Worst of all, Britain would now be fighting not simply a limited war against Germany but the expanded world war the chiefs of staff had been dreading since 1937. Italy declared war on Britain on 10 June 1940. Mussolini's vulturine assault meant that the British position in Egypt, Sudan and the Middle East was now threatened by invasions from Libya and Ethiopia. Previously, the Royal Navy had been able to leave the defence of the Western Mediterranean to the French. Now it had to face the considerable fighting power of the Regia Marina alone. The closing of the Mediterranean to merchant traffic meant that convoys travelling from the UK to the Nile Delta would now take 13,000, not 3,000 miles. Bombay had become 11,000 miles away rather than 6,000.[22]

Japan would soon take advantage of Britain and France's discomfiture. In July, Tokyo demanded that Britain close the Burma Road, the circuitous 700-mile trail linking Burma to south-west China which was the principal supply route for the Kuomintang forces fighting the Japanese. When the demand came, the War Cabinet had to decide what to do. Lord Halifax was placed in the position of hawk for a change, warning his colleagues that to give in to this 'blackmail' would be to 'relinquish our principles'. It was Churchill, not one of the Chamberlain Guilty Men, who insisted on submission to the aggressor this time.[23] The Burma Road was closed for three months, albeit during the monsoon season, when it was least useful anyway. British strategy in the event of a Japanese threat to its colonies east of Suez had, since the 1920s, always been to hold out under siege until the

Mediterranean fleet could be dispatched to the naval base at Singapore. But conflict with Italy now made that relief expedition impossible.

David Reynolds has rightly called 1940 the 'fulcrum of the twentieth century'.[24] Had France survived the German attack that year, the Second World War would probably not have expanded into the Mediterranean and the Far East. Britain would not have found its imperial resources stretched almost to breaking point during the next twenty-four months as it faced a three-power assault on its Empire. Chamberlain's hope in September 1939 that the conflict would remain limited, and that Britain could emerge from it not just victorious but also much the same independent, unreduced and solvent state it had been when the war had begun, might possibly have come true. With France gone, that possibility was gone for ever too.

*

In their report on 'A Certain Eventuality' on 25 May, the chiefs of staff tried to put the most optimistic spin possible on the chances of British survival in the event of France's fall. Nonetheless, they admitted that 'it is impossible to say whether or not the United Kingdom could hold out in all circumstances' if France surrendered. Moreover, 'Our ability to bring the war to a successful conclusion [would depend] entirely upon full Pan-American economic and financial co-operation.'[25]

Britain was committed to enormous new army, navy and air force expansion programmes, including 6,600 front-line aircraft and enough equipment for fifty-five infantry and armoured divisions, all to be ready by the second half of 1942.[26] The country's own industrial plant was insufficient to produce such a vast arsenal by itself. Much of it, and the raw materials besides, would have to be obtained overseas. That could only mean in North America. Most of all, it could only mean the United States.

The US Neutrality Acts' 'cash-and-carry' restrictions meant, however, that Britain could only continue importing American goods while it still had dollars and bullion to pay for them. The UK could draw on the dollar earnings of Sterling Area members (especially Malaya's tin and rubber exports) and the gold production of South Africa and Australia. British citizens had large overseas investments which the government was empowered to compulsorily liquidate to raise more dollars. But by the summer of 1940 the sheer scale of British purchasing plans in America far exceeded the ability of even these imaginative devices to generate enough funds. The government expected to purchase £100 million worth of iron and steel imports alone from America by the end of the year.[27] All told, Britain was committed to $10 billion in orders and capital development in the United States. This was a spending spree that it could not possibly pay for under the cash-and-carry rules.[28]

This financial imprudence had been a deliberate choice. On 16 May, three days after the German tanks reached the Meuse, the War Cabinet had agreed that it had no choice but to abandon the last vestiges of Chamberlain's cautious spending policy of the 'the Fourth Arm of Defence'. Churchill had already written to President Roosevelt outlining Britain's most urgent *matériel* requirements and stating frankly that 'we shall go on paying dollars for as long as we can, but I should like to feel reasonably sure that when we can pay no more you will give us the stuff just the same.' On 3 July, Lord Lothian, the British ambassador in Washington, presented the Americans with an aide-mémoire laying out the same request in more formal terms. Britain, 'almost the last free country in Europe', would abide by cash-and-carry rules for as long as possible, but 'it will be utterly impossible for them to do this for any indefinite period in view of the scale on which they will need to obtain resources from the United States'. The implication was that the Americans must accept this and yet keep supplying Britain anyway.[29]

In recent years the question of whether Britain was really 'alone' after Dunkirk has come up for a good deal of public examination. The issue tends to be framed in terms of the contributions that the British Empire and Commonwealth and the various émigré nations of occupied Europe made to British survival in 1940. These contributions were very important indeed. But the most important factor that problematises Britain's 'aloneness' in its Finest Hour is overlooked. Without the active collaboration of the United States it simply would not have been possible for Britain to continue fighting for much longer. As the chiefs of staff put it in a report in September,

> Our reserves of gold and saleable foreign securities are limited, and at the present rate of expenditure are unlikely to last for more than another year. It is impossible for us to export on a scale nearly sufficient to defray our necessary purchases, and before very long it will be essential for us to obtain credits on a substantial scale from the United States. *This represents in the long run an indispensable condition to the successful conduct of the war.*[30]

1. The wreckage in Broadgate, Coventry's main shopping promenade, on 25 August 1939 after an Irish Republican Army (IRA) bomb left in a bicycle front basket exploded. Five people were killed and another sixty wounded. On the eve of the Second World War, Britain was experiencing its deadliest terrorist campaign since the Victorian era.

2. A British Army armoured car patrols the streets of Belfast in July 1935 following attacks by Protestant marchers on Catholics in the city. The violence that month left nine people dead and forced thousands of Belfast's Catholics to flee their homes. Northern Ireland's sectarian viciousness offered a striking contrast to the supposed liberal values of the interwar United Kingdom.

3. A factory worker at the Singer Motors works in Coventry applies an electric sander to a new car on the production line. While our memory of the 'Hungry Thirties' today is dominated by images of unemployment and poverty, towns and cities in the prosperous Midlands and south of England were booming at the time with new consumer manufacturing industries.

4. British troops blow up houses in the village of Miar, near Haifa, during the 'Arab Revolt' in British Mandate Palestine. This often-brutal counterinsurgency campaign from 1936 to 1939 exposed the violence which underlay much of British imperial rule across the globe. It also demonstrated Britain's vulnerability as an overstretched colonial power trying to respond to simultaneous crises in Europe and the Middle East.

5. Neville Chamberlain, British chancellor of the exchequer 1931–37 and prime minister 1937–40. At his death a few months after leaving 10 Downing Street for the last time, Chamberlain wrote that he would 'not fear the historians' verdict' about his career. But the man who led Britain into the Second World War has been excoriated ever since for his supposed cowardice, credulity and incompetence in dealing with Hitler.

6. British foreign secretary Austen Chamberlain (*right*), the older half-brother of Neville, signs the Locarno Treaty on 16 October, 1925 on behalf of his country. To his far left sits the Italian dictator Benito Mussolini. Locarno ostensibly pledged Britain to the defence of France against future aggression from Germany. But its terms were so vague that the nature of Britain's 'continental commitment' remained unclear.

7. Chamberlain shakes hands with Adolf Hitler at the conclusion of the Munich Conference in September 1938. Although Munich led the annexation of the Czech Sudetenland by Germany, both Chamberlain and Hitler believed that it was the British prime minister who had triumphed at the conference, and the German dictator who had been defeated. Hitler was furious with himself afterwards for not going to war.

8. Chamberlain in 1939 with the man who was to soon replace him as prime minister, Winston Churchill. Despite their disagreements over the appeasement of Germany, both politicians respected one another's talents and worked together well. 'I can't help liking Winston, even though I think him nearly always wrong,' Chamberlain once admitted.

9. The battleship HMS *Prince of Wales* is launched down the slipway at the Cammell Laird shipyard in Birkenhead, Merseyside, on 3 May 1939. Britain engaged in a massive rearmament programme in the six years before the outbreak of the Second World War, spending so much on imports for defence that the economy was suffering a serious balance of payments problem by 1939.

10. A French battleship in the harbour of Mers-el-Kébir, outside the city of Oran in north-western Algeria, burns on 3 July 1940 after being attacked by British warships. Almost 1,300 Frenchmen were killed by the Royal Navy. The British believed that they had no choice but to sink the French fleet after France's surrender to Germany. The attack was a tragic coda to the ill-fated alliance between the two Channel powers.

11. Evacuee children from London arrive in the coastal town of Eastbourne at the outbreak of war in September 1939. The evacuation scheme brought Britons of different classes and races into close – and often fraught – proximity with one another for the first time. Few British people in 1939 would have ever met Afro-Caribbean children such as those seen in this photograph.

12. Five of the key men who decided France's fate in 1940. From the left: Chief of the British Imperial General Staff Sir Edmund Ironside; General Alphonse Georges, commander of the critical French northeastern front; Winston Churchill, soon to be British prime minister; General Maurice Gamelin, commander-in-chief of the French armed forces; and Lord Gort, commander of the British Expeditionary Force in France.

13. British troops wait uncertainly outside a Norwegian coastal town in May 1940 watching a fuel dump burn after a Luftwaffe air raid. The British had mulled over intervening militarily in Norway for months at the beginning of the war. When finally forced to do so to try to thwart a German invasion, they experienced a humiliating defeat which spelled doom for Neville Chamberlain's government back in Britain.

14. One of the more than 100 RAF Fairey Battle light bombers shot down during the first three weeks of the German invasion of France and the Low Countries in May 1940. The slow, poorly armoured Battles were thrown into action by RAF commanders who disdained the idea of using aircraft for tactical air support of the Allied ground armies. Inadequately escorted by friendly fighters, hundreds of Battle aircrew were killed.

15. Desperate British troops on the Dunkirk beaches, awaiting evacuation in the final week of May 1940, fire their rifles at attacking Luftwaffe aircraft. For the British, the successful withdrawal by sea of almost 200,000 of their troops at Dunkirk was a glorious achievement in the midst of defeat. For their French allies left behind, it was a moment of bitterness about an alliance unravelling.

16. The foreign secretary Lord Halifax (*left*) leaves 10 Downing Street alongside the secretary of state for war Anthony Eden on 28 May 1940. This was the day on which Halifax's attempts to convince Churchill's War Cabinet to seek out possible peace terms with the Germans were finally rejected. Churchill sent Halifax to Washington, DC, as British ambassador in December, with Eden taking his place at the Foreign Office.

17. British troops watch for enemy invaders on a barbed-wire-laden beach on the south coast of England in early September 1940. After France's surrender, a possible German amphibious assault against Britain seemed a frightening possibility, though how seriously Hitler ever considered attempting invasion in the face of considerable British air and naval resistance is debatable.

18. Interned 'enemy aliens' arrive in a holding camp somewhere in Britain in 1940. Over 26,000 persons of German and Italian citizenship, most of them known to be harmless by the British authorities and many of them Jewish refugees from Hitler's persecutions, were arrested between May and July 1940. The government was motived less by genuine security fears than by the need to appease a xenophobic press-led scare campaign.

19. Air Chief Marshal Sir Hugh Dowding, commander-in-chief of RAF Fighter Command from 1936 to 1940. Unlike most senior RAF officers at the time, Dowding believed that fighter aircraft could successfully protect against a strategic bombing campaign. His 'Dowding System' of strategic air defence was one of the critical advantages the British possessed against the German Luftwaffe in 1940.

20. Aircrew of the RAF's 264 (Madras Presidency) Squadron cluster near one of their turret-armed Boulton Paul Defiant fighters to listen to their commanding officer, Squadron Leader Phil Hunter (*far left*) on 31 May 1940. Great things were expected of the Defiant by the Air Ministry, but it proved to be a disaster in daylight combat against German fighters. Hunter was killed in action on 24 August.

21. Hawker Hurricane fighters fly in formation during the Battle of Britain in summer 1940. Unlike the ill-fated Boulton Paul Defiant, the Hurricane, with its fixed wing machine-guns, proved to be a formidable daylight fighter against the Luftwaffe. But the Air Ministry initially insisted that its pilots fly in the rigid three-aircraft 'vic' formation seen here, which placed them at a disadvantage in combat against German Bf 109s.

22. Liverpool city centre after seven continuous nights of heavy bombing by the German air force in May 1941. The 'Blitz' against British civilians from 1940–41 was not experienced equally across the nation. Most bombs fell on London. Only Birmingham and Merseyside suffered anything like the same ordeal of sustained bombing night after night. In the end, the bombing failed to seriously interfere with British war production.

23. Air Raid Precautions (ARP) rescue workers extract dazed survivors from the rubble of a bombed house during the Blitz. British propaganda preferred to dwell on images of smiling civilians cheerfully Keeping Calm and Carrying On throughout the German bombing campaign. In reality, though there was no mass psychiatric crisis as some prewar experts had predicted, there was plenty of fear in the Blitz.

24. Supporters of the anti-war 'Mother's Crusade' protest near the US Capitol in Washington, DC, in February 1941 in a bid to prevent the passage of the Lend-Lease bill to assist Britain in its war effort against Nazi Germany. There was nothing inevitable about continued American aid to Britain after the fall of France. Plenty of US voices, some at the highest levels of power, argued that their country should remain strictly neutral.

25. Survivors of a merchant vessel torpedoed by a German U-boat in the north Atlantic await rescue by the Royal Navy in May 1940. Almost 14,000 Allied merchant seamen, most of them British, died in the first two-and-a-half years of the Second World War. The German attempt to defeat Britain by closing off its lines of maritime communication was the most serious threat to the nation's survival during the war.

26. General Sir John Dill (*left*), Chief of the Imperial General Staff from May 1940 to December 1941, and General Sir Archibald Wavell (*centre*), British Middle East commander-in-chief, confer with Lady Wavell in Cairo in 1941. Both men had a difficult relationship with Churchill, who regarded them as insufficiently aggressive. After defeats in Greece, Crete and Libya, the prime minister succeeded in shifting both to new jobs.

27. British Matilda II infantry tanks in action near Tobruk, Libya, in 1941. After easy initial victories against the Italians in the Western Desert, the British troops defending the Nile base had a nasty shock when German General Erwin Rommel's Afrika Korps arrived in North Africa in spring 1941. But Rommel could not advance into Egypt without taking the vital port of Tobruk, which held out successfully under siege.

28. Ivan Maisky, the Soviet ambassador to Britain, is presented with the first fighting vehicle built during 'Tanks for Russia Week' in September 1941. Hitler's decision to attack the USSR in June had transformed Britain's strategic position in the war, and Churchill was eager to offer Stalin as much material aid as possible. But allying with the Soviets after their ruthless actions in Poland and Finland morally disquieted many Britons.

29. A view of nighttime Berlin from the bomb-bay of a RAF bomber in September 1941. Bombs can be seen exploding at the bottom of the pictu the broad wavy lines are German searchlights. Bombi Germany seemed to offer the only viable route to victory in t West after France's defeat. But precisio raids on economic targets were failures leading to more indiscriminate attac on civilians.

With the end of the cross-Channel alliance, Britain had been relieved of its obligations to one power. But it had also, in consequence, had to take on more one-sided obligations to a further distant and altogether less reliable power than France.

For in the summer of 1940 it was highly uncertain whether the United States would accede to Britain's requests, however urgently framed. President Roosevelt had already had to apply a 'necessary douche of cold water' to British hopes that the US might be on the brink of entering the war itself.[31] On 11 June, FDR stated publicly that he had no intention of trying to repeal the cash-and-carry laws.[32] For six weeks following the fall of France he offered little encouragement to the British at all on the issue. Roosevelt seems at that moment to have been genuinely uncertain what to do next. There was an influential school of thought in Washington in the summer of 1940 that the British were probably finished, and that any arms or *matériel* sent across the Atlantic would either be destroyed or else fall into the hands of the Germans. Scepticism about Britain's chances was widespread. Only one in three Americans polled in late June expected the UK to win the war (82 per cent had expected this back in 1939).[33]

Even if the UK was not finished, the United States' own armed forces were desperately in need of weapons and equipment themselves. It made eminent sense to some policymakers to consider the defence of the western hemisphere first and to make British needs very much a secondary matter. Adolf Berle, one of FDR's closest advisers, argued on 15 May that 'our job is to collect the strongest and solidest defence forces we can, and not fritter away small detachments to the other side of the Atlantic.' War Department planners advised the President on 22 May to concentrate on defending the American continent and US Pacific territories only.[34]

The following month General George Marshall and Admiral Harold Stark, the army and navy chiefs of staff respectively, asked Roosevelt to ban any further arms sales to Britain. FDR would not go that far. But he did agree to sign a Congressional law that forbade the export of any more military equipment unless it was deemed 'not essential' to US interests – this at a time when the American military was so short of equipment itself that there was scarcely a single rifle in the country that could not be deemed 'essential'.[35] In London, Churchill, while maintaining nothing but confidence in American aid in his public statements, had been privately seething at the country's inaction for some time. 'The United States [has] given us practically no help in the war,' he complained to his War Cabinet colleagues at the end of May.[36]

The 'special relationship' between Churchill and Roosevelt has furnished a good deal of saccharine-coated nonsense over the years. It is important to remember that there was nothing inevitable about the Anglo-American alliance in the summer of 1940. The two countries' interests may have corresponded in many important respects, but they were far from overlapping. Nor were the British and Americans two peoples who understood and sympathised with one another well, for all their superficial similarities in language and culture. To the British elite, 'America' in 1940 still represented a land of brash hucksterism, po-faced evangelicals, tawdry Hollywood gossip and Chicago gangsters. Many Americans were repulsed – for good reasons – by British snobbery, condescension and imperial brutality. The two wartime leaders were initially cooler towards each other than the mythology suggests. 'I have always disliked [Churchill],' FDR is supposed to have told the US ambassador in London, Joseph Kennedy, in December 1939: 'He acted like a stinker at a dinner I attended, lording it all over us.'[37] Churchill's private feelings about the United States in 1940 were frequently dominated by 'disillusion and suspicion'.[38] His government resented the sense, unfamiliar to it, of being exploited by another power with greater security but less understanding. The American government resented the sense of being railroaded into a war that was not of its making for interests that were far different from its own.

*

If Roosevelt was to be persuaded that Britain was, all the same, worth backing, it would be necessary first to survive the German assault that would surely follow France's surrender. On 18 June, two weeks after DYNAMO's end, and four days before Pétain's armistice with Hitler, Churchill told the Commons, in one of his most famous perorations, that 'the Battle of France is over. I expect that the Battle of Britain is about to begin.'

> Upon this battle depends the survival of Christian civilisation. Upon it depends our own British life, and the long continuity of our institutions and our Empire. The whole fury and might of the enemy must very soon be turned on us. Hitler knows that he will have to break us in this island or lose the war.[39]

Theories of victory would have to wait for the time being. What would be required for the next three months was a plausible theory of survival. Britain was going to have to start winning, or at least not losing, a few battles for a change.

16

ALL OUR PAST PROCLAIMS OUR FUTURE

'An island fortress, England is fighting a war of redemption not only for Europe but for her own soul. Facing dangers greater than any in her history she has fallen back on the rock of her national character.'[1] So ends Arthur Bryant's *English Saga*, first published in November 1940. *English Saga* is a millenarian ode to a people in peril. It went through twelve printings during the war and launched its author on a profitable career writing sentimental historical potboilers for a mass audience.[2]

English Saga, needless to say, is Shire Folkery from start to finish. Bryant's Englishmen and women are shy, modest, gentle souls, with 'a sense of justice and an invincible love of decent and legalised dealing' and a 'temperamental inability to nurse a grudge'. Collectively, their only defect is their parochial lack of interest in events beyond their limited island horizons, and their tendency to overlook dangers from overseas for too long.[3] 'Wanting nothing but peace' in the inter-war years, Bryant argued, 'the British people assumed, in their insular, hopeful way that everyone else felt the same.' They ignored the distant rise of fascism as something which was no concern of their own. 'Easy-going, preoccupied' with 'pacific hopes,' they stumbled unhappily from appeasement to war in 1939, and then wasted the eight months of the Phoney War's false calm through the same 'fatal indecision' that had marked the 1930s more generally.[4] He went on:

> It was not till the Germans had struck with their full force at the Netherlands and sent France reeling that Britain awoke to the magnitude of her task [...] only to the enduring character of her people, made manifest on the Dunkirk beaches and the skies above the Channel and the Kentish weald, could Britain look for deliverance.[5]

This emphasis on national vulnerability – an enthusiastic embrace of it, even – was in stark contrast to the propaganda that had been published before May 1940. Writers then had sought to emphasise Britain's material strength: above all, its place at the hub of a mighty commercial empire commanding the world's greatest concentration of people, resources and wealth. The Ministry of Information's November 1939 pamphlet *Assurance of Victory* touted the British Empire's advantages in population, territory and industrial production over the Third Reich, guaranteeing its readers that 'this war will expose the fatal weakness of the Nazi structure [...] the immense staying power of democracy is the final guarantee of Allied triumph'.[6]

Before the disasters of May 1940 the possibility of invasion seemed far too fantastical to worry about. The decisive military conflict would surely take place in France and Flanders, just as it had done in the previous great war against Germany. England 'is more secure than ever before against invasion', Basil Liddell Hart reassured his readers in 1939's *The Defence of Britain*.[7] The danger to British people at home was from a Luftwaffe aerial knock-out blow, not paratroopers or landing craft. The public information film *If War Should Come*, prepared just before Hitler's attack on Poland, instructed citizens in the use of gas masks and air-raid shelters. The government regarded the risk of invasion as so marginal that references to it were deleted from the official Whitehall war plans.[8]

By the early summer of 1940, however, with France vanquished, German troops gazing on the White Cliffs of Dover from Cap Gris-Nez just twenty-one miles away, and only a narrow body of water preventing the Panzers from steamrolling through Kent and East Sussex as they had done through Champagne and Picardy, invasion seemed all too real and frightening a possibility. 'Every step one takes brings home the fact that we are not only at war, but in a corner. The fear of invasion hangs over every minute of the day,' George Beardmore wrote in his diary on 16 July:

The preparations for meeting an army among the fields around us, at home, fill us with dread [...] Winston talks in a grim and powerful speech of fighting if need be through the streets of London and in the colonies. Letters from the north contain only hints of what is happening there because information must not be given away. The names on post offices, sign-posts, on railway stations and AA call boxes have been obliterated. Steel helmets are carried by every other man. All the talk is of '*he's scratching his head how to get here*' and '*he'll make use of the first fog.*' That Channel, and what we owe to it![9]

Assurances of British material superiority which might have been appropriate for the Phoney War now looked absurd in the aftermath of the *Blitzkrieg*. So as far as propaganda was concerned, then, it was time for Powerhouse Britannia to be replaced by Plucky Little England: the island fortress, tiny but lion-hearted, alone but undaunted, defiant even in defeat. Where physical strength had failed on the continent, now history, landscape and national character would be mobilised in defence of the homeland. Rifles and bullets might be in short supply, but there were plenty of cultural munitions in reserve to draw on. As the *Daily Mirror* cartoonist Zec reminded his readers on 19 June, quoting Swinburne beside an illustration of Britannia staring down the aggressor:

All our past proclaims our future;
Shakespeare's voice and Nelson's hand,
Milton's faith and Wordsworth's trust
In this our chosen and chainless land,
Bear us witness: come the world against her,
England shall yet stand.[10]

The Ministry of Information film *Britain at Bay*, written by J. B. Priestley and released in the immediate aftermath of Dunkirk, took up this theme of reassuring historical continuity: 'For nearly a thousand years, these hills and fields and farmsteads of Britain have been free from foreign invasion,' it began. Arcadian rhythms and images of the pastoral Home Counties countryside accompanied Priestley's soothing Shire Folk narrative of doughty innocents. The British were 'as easy-going and good-natured as any folk in the world', asking 'for nothing belonging to others'; all they wanted was 'to be left alone to do what we like with our own'. France's surrender, the narration conceded, had left 'Britain alone, at bay'. But Priestley reminded his audience that 'it's not the first time she has been at bay against a conquering tyrant, for we were equally alone against the full might of Napoleon'.[11]

Comparisons between the present situation and invasion threats of the past – from Philip II, Louis XIV, Bonaparte – were dusted off from mothballed storage in 1940 to console and encourage once again. 'Europe is again despairing and England stands once more in the shadow of the invader,' declared *Picture Post* that July: 'in the spirit of the race, whose nonchalance in the face of impending danger has exasperated and baffled its enemies since Drake broke the might of Spain with a fleet of cockle boats and a handful of civilians, burns an unquenchable flame.'[12] Noël Coward, on a propaganda tour of Australia, reminded his audiences that the threat of a German landing was only a shocking thought 'for those of us who forget that England has thriven on invasion, not once but dozens of times'.[13] Indeed, to hear Coward tell it, it was almost as though Hitler had fallen into a cunning trap by conquering France as swiftly and effortlessly as he had. For now the British, 'with a sigh of relief', according to the *News Chronicle*'s Philip Jordan, had been unshackled from their useless continental partners, and were free to fight the kind of battle they had fought so often and so well in the past. They could now engage the Nazis on historical ground of their own choosing. As Dorothy L. Sayers put it:

> This is the war that England knows [...]
> When no allies are left, no help
> To count upon from alien hands,
> No waverers remain to woo,
> No more advice to listen to,
> And only England stands.[14]

David Edgerton has pointed out that this notion of 'aloneness' was complicated by the existence of the Empire.[15] To be sure, propagandists acknowledged it, but mostly as an afterthought. *Britain at Bay*, after its unhurried reflections on the 'island fortress of a thousand years of peace', mentions in passing that 'alongside us are men from the ends of the Earth – from our great Dominions'. But while the Empire certainly mattered a great deal to Britain's material ability to keep fighting in 1940, it was far too weak an ingredient in the national imagination to play anything more than a subordinate role in that year's emotional drama.[16] Stark geographical facts militated against its relevance. When the Luftwaffe's bombers were just a few minutes' flying time from Dover, how much consolation was there to be gained by a reminder that New Zealand, 11,500 miles away, was standing by the motherland? The existence of the Empire also raised embarrassing questions about why this easy-going people, who just wanted to be left alone, had somehow managed to conquer one fifth of the world's land surface. The historical myth-making of 1940 necessarily marginalised Britannia overseas. This was a story of a stocky, inward-looking island race.

It was also a story that marginalised the Scots, Welsh and Irish. The defeat of France in 1940 turned the Second World War into far more of a specifically English drama than the First World War had ever been. The Battle of Britain was fought in the skies above Kent and Sussex, Essex and Surrey. St Paul's Cathedral, the ecclesiastical heart of England's capital city, emerged, wreathed in smoke and flame, as the symbol of the Blitz. It was the farms and woodlands of the Weald and the Downs that were immediately threatened by invasion in the Spitfire summer of 1940. Writers like Priestley sometimes insisted that 'when I say "English" I really mean British'. More often, the opposite was the case.[17] To presume a seamless historical continuity linking the stories of the Spanish Armada, the Dutch Wars, Trafalgar and Dunkirk made little sense outside of a strictly English context.

At the time, this Anglocentricity did not seem to matter too much. It was dangerous, though, for British identity to become so heavily invested in events with less emotional purchase along the Celtic periphery than within the English heartland. Recently, as Britishness has begun to buckle and yield under the strain of reviving Caledonian nationhood, English appeals to memories of the Second World War have turned out to be a weak response. Symbolically it was never Scotland's war in quite the same way as it was England's. And Scotland will never care about it in quite the same way.

*

When would the invasion come? Would it come at all? Churchill seemed uncertain in his radio address to the nation on 14 July:

> Girt about by the seas and oceans where the Navy reigns; shielded from above by the prowess and devotion of our airmen, we await undismayed the impending assault [...] perhaps it will come tonight. Perhaps it will come next week. Perhaps it will never come. We must show ourselves equally capable of meeting a sudden violent shock or – what is perhaps a harder test – a prolonged vigil.[18]

It's been argued that Churchill never really believed there would be an invasion. He knew of the Royal Navy's ability to dominate Channel waters if the emergency ever came.[19] 'I see great reason for intense vigilance and exertion, but none whatever for panic or despair,' he had assured the Commons on 18 June.[20] According to Jock Colville, his confidence when speaking privately verged on the cynical. Invasion was a chimerical threat, quite impossible for the Germans to carry out. But it was, he said, useful to harp on 'the great invasion scare' now and again, in that it was 'keeping every man and woman tuned to a high state of readiness'.[21]

This is to overstate Churchill's real certainty in 1940. He was more sceptical about the possibility of invasion than some of his colleagues. But he could never dismiss it completely. The advice he received from the chiefs of staff, informed by top-secret deciphering of German signals (later known as ULTRA), gave every reason for concern. On 5 July the Joint Intelligence Committee warned that a 'full-scale invasion' attempt might be expected by mid-month.[22] Churchill remained uncertain. Five days later he told the chiefs of staff that he found it 'very difficult to visualise the kind of invasion all along the coast by troops carried in small craft' that the Admiralty was preparing for. Nonetheless, he agreed that it was still essential to allow for a worst-case scenario.[23]

Invasion fears lessened somewhat throughout August. But in early September photographic reconnaissance and ULTRA decrypts revealed a rapid build-up of barges and dive-bombers in forward bases in France. The JIC warned again that a full-scale invasion might be attempted at any moment.[24] Lieutenant-General Alan Brooke, commander of the UK Home Forces, wrote on the evening of 13 September that he expected a German landing the following morning somewhere between Portsmouth and Dover.[25] The morning came and went without incident. But senior figures remained anxious throughout the month. 'The PM seems rather more apprehensive than I had realised about the possibility of invasion in the immediate future,' wrote Colville on 21 September: 'he keeps on ringing up the Admiralty and asking about the weather in the Channel.'[26] The threat did not disappear even after the Luftwaffe gave up its daylight attacks on RAF bases. In October, the prime minister refused an Admiralty request to release twelve destroyers and thirty anti-submarine trawlers stationed on the Channel coast for Atlantic convoy escort duties instead.[27] Only on the last day of that month, with the weather now rapidly deteriorating, did it seem at last safe to regard invasion before the spring as a 'relatively remote' possibility.[28] Whether the Germans ever seriously considered mounting an invasion of Britain in 1940 is a question for another chapter. On the other side of the Straits of Dover, however, the threat seemed real enough.

Ordinary people were left to come to terms with the shock of defeat in France. Overly optimistic press coverage of the initial fighting back in May had not adequately prepared them for catastrophe. 'Not one person in a thousand could visualise the Germans breaking through into France,' noted the first report of the Ministry of Information's new Home Intelligence (HI) division, tasked with monitoring domestic morale.[29] With France gone, people had to come to terms with an awful new reality. By 30 May, HI was reporting that 'more people are facing up to the possibility of invasion and many people speak of it as certain.'[30] According to a schoolmaster in Bolton, his staff were 'going around looking as though they want to put their heads in a gas oven [...] morbid as hell'.[31] Mass Observation surveyed people in Aberdeen and Glasgow in early July about the likelihood of invasion; 87 per cent expected one imminently.[32] There were 'many reports of parachute landings and invading troops' on 2 July, and 'still much talk of the imminence of invasion, often supported by references to "official" statements that the invasion is only a matter of hours away'.[33] Certain dates that were considered to be particularly suitable for an invasion took hold in the popular imagination, encouraged by press speculation. HI reported on Wednesday, 17 July, that it was widely gossiped the Germans would attack that Friday, and that 'many people are seriously alarmed'.[34]

'We are given up to gloom – almost,' wrote George Beardmore in his diary three days after the Germans took Paris:

> Each tells the other about the Navy and the Army in the East, American aid, the nearness of Canada, the loyalty of Australia, Rhodesia, South Africa, the new government under Churchill. We remember that all Europe has been against us before and still we have come through. Underneath all these reassurances, a nameless dread.[35]

*

How would ordinary Britons respond if the invader came? Churchill, of course, offered little doubt in his public statements:

> I can easily understand how sympathetic onlookers across the Atlantic [...] may have feared for our survival when they saw so many States and kingdoms torn to pieces in a few weeks or even days by the monstrous force of the Nazi war machine. But Hitler has not yet been withstood by a great nation with a will power the equal of his own. Many of these countries had been poisoned by intrigue before they

were struck down by violence. They had been rotted from within before they were smitten from without [...]

But here, in our Island, we are in good health and in good heart [...]

Should the invader come to Britain, there will be no placid lying down of the people in submission before him, as we have seen, alas, in other countries. We shall defend every village, every town, and every city. The vast mass of London itself, fought street by street, could easily devour an entire hostile army; and we would rather see London laid in ruins and ashes than that it should be tamely and abjectly enslaved.

In private, the political elite were not so sure. Despite all those propaganda invocations about British steadfastness, the crisis of May–June 1940 was a moment of anxiety in high government circles about whether the people really would stand fast if the Germans landed. We tend to think of the Nazi conquest of the west as a military disaster, which of course it was, but at the time it also seemed to be a disaster for democracy. A whole way of organising political life had been tested and failed. The Netherlands had collapsed in less than a week, Belgium in less than three, France after barely a month. The German advance had been preceded by panic as millions of refugees had taken to the roads, hampering the Allied armies' efforts to confront the enemy. Hitlerian totalitarianism had triumphed.

There was no clear evidence that the British would behave any differently from the Dutch, Belgians or French if their turn came. Large-scale air raids had not yet taken place in June 1940. The pre-war assumption that civilians would flee the cities in terror if and when they did still seemed to have been borne out by similar events on the continent. The people would need close monitoring. The Ministry of Information established a Home Morale Emergency Committee to counter 'the danger of a break in morale', though it chose an odd assortment of men to take a democratic nation's pulse: the committee included Sir Kenneth Clark, director of the National Gallery, and Harold Nicolson, who despite being a National Labour MP seemed to regard the working class (according to one colleague) 'as barbarians to be feared'.[36]

Panic was the least of it, however. Churchill on 14 July spoke of 'traitors that may be found in our midst' – agents of a so-called 'Fifth Column' who might take the opportunity of invasion to aid enemy forces and act as saboteurs behind the lines. Within days of the start of the German offensive in the west, newspapers in London and Paris had been full of stories of enemy paratroopers dressed in fake uniforms and costumes (especially nuns' habits) and pro-Nazi French, Dutch and Belgian civilians sniping at Allied troops and assisting the invaders.[37] 'Cato's *Guilty Men* later proposed that 'Fifth Column treachery' was one of the key reasons for the German victory.[38]

There is not the slightest evidence any of this was true. But Fifth Column panic swiftly crossed the Channel anyway. General Ironside insisted that 'people are quite definitely preparing aerodromes in this country' for use by the Luftwaffe.[39] Admiral Ramsay, the hero of Dunkirk, claimed that Fifth Columnists in Dover were buying used cars at fantastic prices and leaving them parked around the town to impede military traffic.[40] MI5 spent many hours investigating mysterious marks on telegraph poles said to be secret code left by spies (actually the work of Boy Scouts and Girl Guides) and the possibility that sentries might be poisoned by enemy ice cream.[41] An innocent farmer was detained for seventeen hours after being named the kingpin of a spy and sabotage network in rural Oxfordshire – the fantasy, it turned out, of a disgruntled army deserter.[42] The fact that no Fifth Column activity could be discovered anywhere in the UK perversely became one more piece of evidence of how dangerous it was. 'The absence of sabotage up to date reinforces the view that such activities will only take place as part of a prearranged military plan,' suggested the JIC.[43]

All of this seemed to suggest that the democracy itself could not be trusted in a crisis.[44] Only by abandoning the 'present rather easy-going methods' of national life and adopting a set of restrictions 'which would approach the totalitarian' could Britain survive a Nazi onslaught, the Cabinet was warned by Chamberlain on 18 May.[45] The legal apparatus for such a siege dictatorship was established four days later, when a new Emergency Powers (Defence) Act was passed by the Commons in its entirety in just two hours. This was an extension of the existing emergency legislation passed at the outbreak of war which now gave the government almost unlimited authority to regulate people, property and capital without the need for parliamentary scrutiny. As the new minister for labour later observed, it made him 'a kind of *Führer* with powers to order anybody anywhere'.[46] A Treachery Act passed the same day made it a capital offence to assist the enemy's military operations or to hamper Britain's own.

As the *Times* put it, the Emergency Powers Act 'comes near to suspending the very essence of the Constitution as it has been built up in a thousand years. Our ancient liberties are placed in pawn for victory.'[47] A slew of regulations soon circumscribed even the most quotidian features of the British citizen's life. It was unlawful to 'endeavour to influence [...] public opinion in a manner likely to be prejudicial' to the war effort, to take part in a strike, to withhold information about an invention or patent if the state demanded it, to hold an unauthorised procession, to put out flags, to operate a car radio or to put icing on a cake (wickedly wasteful of sugar). Chamberlain hoped that public opinion would back these restrictions; but if not, recalcitrant non-cooperators could be drafted into a compulsory labour corps under prison discipline.[48]

The creation in mid-May 1940 of the Local Defence Volunteers (LDV), later renamed the Home Guard, ought to be seen in this context of government nervousness. Private citizens had responded to news of the German parachute landings in the Netherlands and Belgium by announcing the formation of *ad hoc* militia companies to defend their homeland. Whitehall felt it had to act quickly to control the process.[49] One quarter of a million men aged between seventeen and sixty-five registered to join the new auxiliary force within the first week of its announcement, and by July 1940 its nominal strength stood at 1.5 million.

Decades after the war, the gentle BBC sitcom *Dad's Army* would absorb the Home Guard into cosy Shire Folk memory. But the prospect of 1½ million armed men roaming the country, barely trained and operating under only the loosest military discipline, was a source of official anxiety at the time. 'The creation of private armies [...] has often proved fatal to the stability of the state,' the War Office's permanent under-secretary, Sir Edward Grigg, warned. Left-wing intellectuals like George Orwell hoped the LDV might become the kernel of a democratic people's militia, especially given the primitive democracy of its early days, when some of its officers and NCOs were elected by the ranks. A fellow Spanish Civil War veteran, Tom Wintringham, tried to put this idea into practice by creating a guerrilla warfare training programme at Osterley Park, near Hounslow, outside the control of the War Office. By the end of 1940, however, such dangerous innovations had been quietly stifled. The Home Guard was safely absorbed into the professional military apparatus as an auxiliary to the regular forces. The communist *Daily Worker* thought it a sinister Tory 'instrument of the class struggle' to suppress striking workers.[50]

In Northern Ireland, where Fifth Column paranoia was part of the warp and weft of life even in peacetime, the Home Guard was especially politicised. Rather than being placed under British Army jurisdiction, as elsewhere, Ulster's Home Guard was formed as an adjunct of the police reserve. Its officers, then, were not Pooterish Captain Mainwarings but the men of the B-Specials, despised in the province's Catholic community for their bigotry and quick resort to violence. Questions were raised in Westminster about the desirability (and constitutionality) of this, but the British government ultimately backed down in the face of Stormont's determination not to see weapons 'get into the hands of undesirable elements'. A few Catholics enlisted in the Ulster Home Guard but quickly dropped out as it was made clear that their presence in its Orange-dominated ranks was unwelcome.[51] They were to have no place in the 1940 story.

*

The government's fear of mass panic turned out to be unwarranted. Certainly, Home Intelligence detected what it called 'pockets of defeatism' here and there. Comments like 'if we're going to lose the war, why go on?' and 'I suppose we can only wait for Hitler now' were overheard by Ministry officials in mid-June.[52] In Bristol there were reports of 'cases of defeatism among isolated businessmen and some of the poor people'. In Reading there was 'some defeatist talk on the lines of "we couldn't be worse off under Hitler."'[53] 'It won't be long now,' a Bolton man was heard to say:

> We are in a bad way [...] what are we going to do now? That's the burning question. We are left absolutely on our own now. You heard what Winston Churchill said – we would fight on even if it came to street fighting and if the country was swimming in blood. That will be nice, won't it?[54]

People continued to expect invasion well into the autumn. Rumours of a seaborne landing were reported to be 'rife' in Bristol on 9 September. Across the country the following week, most people were said to 'anticipate invasion within a few days'.[55] Only in October did the danger definitely appear to recede.

But if the British expected an invasion, they also expected it to fail. 'In spite of this atmosphere of tension people are not depressed,' Home Intelligence insisted on 2 July. 'Many people say they think our defence preparations are inadequate but at the same time they say "we shall beat them off'", "we'll teach them a lesson", "let them come."'[56] Even in mid-June, when France surrendered and the outlook seemed bleakest, three-quarters of Britons polled expected the war to continue. Half were confident about fighting on alone.[57] In the weeks that followed, the stream of fresh disasters that the BBC and the press had been delivering almost daily since the end of May finally dried up. The lull in news gave people the opportunity to recover from the shock of defeat in France and take mental stock. If Britain's military situation was not improving, at least it was no longer getting any worse. Reports of the French fleet's destruction in early July were sensational, but also demonstrated a grim resolve to keep fighting using any ruthless means necessary. As the possibility of invasion lost its distressing novelty, so HI observers found that it was 'ceasing to be the terrifying idea that it once was'.[58] Mass Observation suggested on 17 July that public remarks by 'optimists' now outnumbered those by 'pessimists' by four to one.[59] Even the beginning of daylight air raids in August did not cause a new wave of distress. On the contrary: 'confidence is increased [...] there is a feeling of growing exhilaration.'[60]

If anything, the government was criticised for not giving the public enough of a martial role. In July, 15 million copies of an invasion advice leaflet, *Stay Where You Are*, were distributed to every home in Britain. As the title suggests, its main message was to warn people not to clog up militarily vital roads by fleeing from German forces. But it also cautioned those stouter hearts who might be thinking of taking a pot shot at the enemy themselves: '[set] a good example to others. Civilians who try to join in the fight are more likely to get in the way than to help.'[61] Mass Observation thought that such an instruction 'tended to be against the grain' for sending far too 'passive' and 'helpless' a message at a moment when the public wanted 'active and aggressive' directives. 'Reads as if it were written for a child' complained one man – 'why don't they say *kill the fascist* outright, good and strong?'[62]

Ordinary Britons were in much greater physical danger by July 1940 than they had been during the Phoney War. Their morale seemed paradoxically all the better for it. The *New Yorker*'s London correspondent Mollie Panter-Downes wrote that 'this country appears to be asking for and getting the self-sacrificing gestures of everyday life which the totalitarian governments have enforced on their people for years.'[63] The drama of air attack and possible invasion had at last given the war a revivifying psychological intensity absent throughout the dreariness of its first eight months: every man his own Achilles now, every woman her own Hippolyta. Wartime sacrifices and restrictions ceased to irritate as they had previously done with the sense people now had of being characters in a great national epic – something that might be frightening in the immediate moment, but which they would be able to look back on with pride.

Reading about the Dunkirk evacuation from her Barrow-in-Furness home, housewife Nella Last felt that 'I forgot I was a middle-aged woman who often got tired and had backache. The story made me feel part of something that was undying and never old [...] somehow I felt everything to be worthwhile, and I felt glad I was of the same race as the rescuers and rescued.'[64] According to the author Verily Anderson, then a twenty-five-year-old First Aid Nursing Yeomanry volunteer, 'even the very colours of the summer seemed heightened, the sky bluer, the clouds whiter, and the darkness darker'.[65] Panter-Downes suggested that the manufactured contrivances of the West End theatre were struggling to compete with this new melodramatic reality:

> What is happening on the stage of history is so tremendous that most thinking people find it difficult to take their eyes off the real thing [...] the footlights are already up and the orchestra is swinging into the somber and terrible overture.[66]

*

With soldiers patrolling high streets and with barbed wire and concrete fortifications appearing at country crossroads, Britain by the summer of 1940 had become 'a very unfamiliar place' compared with the country it had been just a year earlier.[67] 'I never thought,' wrote Vita Sackville-West, 'to spend an afternoon filling old wine bottles with petrol, paraffin and tar and finishing them off with two of Messrs Brock's gay blue Guy Fawkes squibs bound tightly to the sides.'[68] Policemen were walking their beats with pistols. Armed guards protected bus garages by night. The Army busied itself mining bridges and beaches, felling crops and woodlands to create firing arcs, placing machine-gun nests at the end of piers and strewing tank traps (at first old cars and tree trunks, later concrete blocks) at road junctions. Over 28,000 pillboxes and gun emplacements were hurriedly constructed, though often by inexperienced civilian contractors who in their haste erected them facing the wrong way.[69] Signposts, milestones and name boards were removed or painted over on roads and railway stations to confound the enemy – allowing people 'the exhilarating feeling of being explorers', the *Times* suggested hopefully. The military authorities were less delighted at this prospect after their baffled drivers began getting lost on unfamiliar roads, and they asked for the measure to be partially rescinded.[70]

The invasion threat altered the geography of risk. At the outbreak of war many thousands of children had been evacuated from the big cities to towns and villages along the south-eastern coastal belt from Great Yarmouth to Littlehampton. They now found themselves in the likely pathway of an invading German army. They were hurriedly re-dispatched to Wales and the Midlands, while plans were drawn up for the compulsory removal of up to 900,000 people from the invasion zone if necessary. These orders never had to be carried out, but tens of thousands of residents were encouraged to leave, so that by mid-July two-fifths of the population of coastal Kent and half of East Anglia had retreated inland.[71] In their wake, Army officers requisitioned seafront hotels (including many of the 'funk holes' that had sheltered comfortably-off city dwellers during the Phoney War) as command posts, laid out their sandbagged Bren gun positions on the promenades and trained their binoculars on the grey horizon.

The enthusiastic but raw recruits of the Home Guard brought a good deal of disruption to the country in their overzealous attempts to weed out disguised German parachutists and saboteurs. Most of this was amusingly harmless, at least to those not caught directly up in it. Lord Gort's staff car was commandeered one evening; hapless clergymen were accused of being Nazi spies; countless courting couples and night-time ramblers found themselves frog-marched to their local police stations at bayonet point. But even the most bumbling LDV militiaman was walking around with live ammunition, and with guest lecturers like General Ironside encouraging recruits to shoot first and ask questions later, it's not surprising that tragedies mounted up.[72] Two Home Guard sentries fired on a car in Romford, Essex, when the driver failed to hear their demands to halt because of a noisy exhaust: one of those inside was killed and another four wounded. The coroner dismissed the shooting as 'perfectly justified'. On one single night (4 June) four motorists in different locations across the country were killed.[73] A trigger-happy sentry wounded and almost shot dead Flight Lieutenant James Nicolson, RAF Fighter Command's only Victoria Cross winner during the Battle of Britain, when the badly burned pilot landed in a field after bailing out of his Hurricane.[74] Well-meaning its members may have been, but the Home Guard proved far more of a threat to life and limb in the United Kingdom than Göring's *Fallschirmjäger* division ever did.

Sir John Simon's 1938 prophecy that rearmament and war would turn Britain into 'a different kind of nation' seemed to have come true. Moreover, it had happened with a remarkable lack of discussion or opposition. 'A united nation feels no hesitation or misgiving' about the abandonment of its personal freedoms, insisted the *Times* when the Emergency Powers Act was rushed through Parliament: 'the temporary surrender [of liberties] is made with a glad heart and a confident spirit.'[75] That was not altogether true. There would be resistance to some of the more controversial powers the government had acquired for itself. That said, the assault on other values, particularly the presumption of innocence in law and the protection of minorities, inspired rather less sympathy.

The very British right to grumble out loud produced an early skirmish in this conflict over liberties. Regulation 39BA, introduced in June 1940, made it a criminal offence, punishable by up to a month in prison, to circulate 'any report or statement relating to matters connected with the war which is likely to cause alarm and despondency'. It was announced at the same moment the Ministry of Information launched a 'Silent Column' campaign that condemned spreading rumours and gossiping about the war effort.[76] The government was not shy about using its new power. By late July there had been over seventy prosecutions. A tradesman in Yeovil was jailed for thirty days for saying 'Hitler will be here in a month'. A Bristol septuagenarian earned himself a week in prison for claiming that the Swastika would soon fly over Parliament.[77]

As the summer wore on, however, a press backlash caused the government to retreat. Churchill admitted to the Commons on 23 July that, however 'well-meant' it had been, Regulation 39BA had had the unfortunate effect of criminalising 'silly vapourings which are best dealt with on the spur of the moment by verbal responses'.[78] The Silent Column was put into what he called 'innocuous desuetude', and the Home Secretary was asked to review all 'alarm and despondency' convictions. To what extent the Order's continued existence had a chilling effect on free expression is unknowable. ('Best to pass no opinion these days,' as one Briton was reported saying by Home Intelligence. 'You might get hung.'[79]) Could anyone be certain that that innocuous pollster or Mass Observer asking them questions about the war was not a government *provocateur*?

A more ominous issue came up in August, when the government sought to create special regulations to deal with a crisis in which heavy bombing or invasion had halted normal legal procedures in some parts of the country. It proposed the creation of regional 'War Zone courts', presided over by experienced judges and appointed by the lord chancellor. Although these would not be military tribunals or courts-martial, they would nonetheless have the power to impose death sentences without appeal.[80] 'If we are not shot by the Germans we are evidently going to be shot by our own people,' one Briton commented on hearing the news.[81] The proposal was attacked in the Commons as far too vague, considering its life-and-death stakes. The Home Secretary's reassurance that such courts would only operate with the greatest restraint was condemned as feeble by the barrister and Liberal MP Frank Kingsley Griffith: 'it is all very well for anybody to come before this House and say, "I have a Bill which entitles me to cut off your head, but I can assure you that I am only going to cut your toe nails."'[82] In the end, the government retreated and promised that all War Court sentences would be subject to appeal. They were, in the end, never used anyway.[83]

The Home Office received enough popular pushback against both Regulation 39BA and the War Zone courts for it to moderate its plans on the grounds of civil liberty. There was much less public concern provoked by the mass incarceration without trial of British citizens, which began on the morning of 23 May with the arrest of Sir Oswald Mosley, leader of the British Union of Fascists (BUF).[84] Under Defence Regulation 18B, the Home Secretary could detain indefinitely anyone of 'hostile origin or associations' or who had recently committed 'acts prejudicial to the public safety'. Anyone so interned had a right of appeal to an advisory committee, but they were not allowed to know who had recommended their arrest, or why.

Regulation 18B had existed since the outbreak of war but was only now applied with any seriousness. By July 1940 over 700 BUF members and fellow-travellers of the far right had been swept up, most to Brixton Prison (only a single Communist Party member, a Yorkshire shop steward accused of sabotaging workplace production, joined them).[85] Along with Mosley, some of the more notable detainees were: Admiral Barry Domvile, a former Director of Naval Intelligence; Harry St John Philby, father of *Times* correspondent and KGB spy Kim; and the Conservative MP Archibald Ramsay, one of the leaders of the anti-war group the Right Club, who just two weeks earlier had complained in the Commons to the Home Secretary about the 'Jew-ridden Press'.[86]

Ramsay had been implicated by association with another Right Club member, Tyler Kent, an American cipher clerk at the US Embassy who the Security Service (MI5) had discovered was stealing top-secret documents embarrassing to the Roosevelt administration and passing them along to the Italians. As for most of the other detainees, including Mosley, MI5 had little definite knowledge of any illegal acts. Its requests to infiltrate the BUF in the 1930s had been opposed by successive home secretaries who were far more concerned about the communist threat than that of the far right.[87] By February 1940 the Security Service was arguing that the BUF was effectively 'the English branch of the Nazi Party' with 'a core of fanatics' who should be apprehended immediately.[88] But while Mosley had been railing for an end to the 'Jewish war' since its outbreak, he had been careful not to say anything that would put him in explicit breach of the existing emergency regulations (he was 'too clever to put himself in the wrong by giving treasonable orders', as the home secretary, Sir John Anderson, told the Cabinet).[89]

This was justice of a rather blunt sort, then. But it was popular. 'Precautions that should have been taken years ago are now being applied to the Judas Association (British Branch),' the *Daily Mirror* exulted the day after Mosley's arrest.[90] The BUF had always existed on the margins of respectable politics only, and the outbreak of war had turned its leader into a hate figure: he had been almost lynched when he had tried to campaign in the Middleton and Prestwich by-election a few weeks earlier.[91] Mass Observation found the public's approval to be almost universal. 'Some people thought of it as a real achievement or victory – at least we have conquered one enemy in our midst.' A few commented on the troubling precedent of arresting someone for having unpopular views rather than for any definite crime: 'He's a pretty miserable fellow, but on the other hand it does mean the end of all political liberty,' one critic said.[92] The disquieted generally kept their thoughts to themselves, however. Ex-BUF member Anthony Heap, a clerk at Peter Robinson's department store in Oxford Street, wrote in his diary on the night of 24 May that

> the great democratic sham [is] exposed for what it's worth [...] our pro-Jewish, pro-Communist government knows the game is up and [this is] their last mean, vicious, desperate act of revenge before the Germans come here and kick the skunks out, assuming they haven't scuttled to America before that happens [...] poor Mosley has to pay

the price of real patriotism. I'm downright ashamed to be an English-man today.[93]

*

Mosley was soon moved from Brixton to a house in the grounds of Holloway Prison, along with his wife, Diana, herself a fervent fascist. He continued to work for the BUF until the party was proscribed on 10 July. After that he spent his time reading, listening to gramophone records and lounging in the sun. Other prisoners acted as domestic servants; the Mosleys were free to do their own cooking, use their own furniture and have free run of the house in daylight hours.[94] It was not, then, the most dreadful of incarcera-tions. Whatever the rights and wrongs of Regulation 18B, the unrepentant pair were never very compelling objects of sympathy.

The experience of the roughly 26,000 'enemy aliens' of German and Italian citizenship arrested between May and July 1940 offers a rather dif-ferent kind of story, one in which the government's instincts, for once, were more liberal than those of the public.[95] At the outbreak of war, about 75,000 holders of German passports were resident in Great Britain. The majority were refugees or exiles from the Third Reich, many of them, of course, Jewish. The wartime government's attitude towards them showed restraint at first. By the end of 1939 only just over 550 who were regarded as definite security risks had been detained. The remainder had been individually assessed by tribunals made up of local worthies and catego-rised according to likely political risk. About 8,300 were given 'Class B' status (allowed to remain free, but with some travel limitations), with the remainder, including almost all the refugees, unrestricted 'Class C' status.[96] Admittedly, the tribunals sometimes adjudicated according to the quirks and prejudices of their members. Aliens who had taken part in left-wing politics in pre-war Germany or Austria were viewed with extra suspicion.[97] At the same time, those with prosperous middle-class backgrounds who spoke excellent English were given disproportionately sympathetic treat-ment – even though these were precisely the people who would, on the face of it, have made the best Nazi spies.[98]

That liberal environment ended on 12 May 1940, when about 2,000 men of military enlistment age living in coastal areas were immediately interned. Three days later the Home Office ordered this round-up to be extended to all Class B males. When Italy declared war on 10 June, the decision was made, as Churchill put it, to 'collar the lot': 4,000 adult Italian men were immediately arrested, with no attempt made to distinguish between supporters and enemies of Mussolini. After the French surrender two weeks later, the process of detaining all the remaining Class C German males began. Some were given a few moments to pack, without being able to contact family or friends to say what was happening to them. Others were simply whisked off the street.[99] 'Thousands of Jewish refugees from Hitler heard an early morning knock on the door, in a land where such things were supposed to be unthinkable,' E. S. Turner reminds us:

> Sometimes the police arrived with truckloads of armed troops in attendance and the internees were swept variously into Black Marias, buses, taxis and Army transport [...] a police party walked into Hampstead Public Library and called for all Germans and Austrians to step outside. It was a harsh operation, disfigured by needless suicides.[100]

A handful of those taken into custody really were Nazi and fascist sympathisers. The vast majority were either opponents of the enemy regimes or indifferent to politics. Some had no sensible business being there at all. They included two bemused Scottish brothers, both miners, whose only link to Germany was that their father had happened to be working on contract in a Ruhr coalfield when they were born.[101]

In his memoirs Churchill later called mass internment a 'grave affront to the rights and liberties of the individual', but he argued that it had been regrettably necessary because 'our plight had seemed so grievous that no limits could be put upon the action of the State'.[102] Much of the Fifth Column hysteria of May–June 1940 was directed towards foreigners generally, and enemy aliens specifically. When Sir Nevile Bland, the former British minister to The Hague, returned home after the surrender of the Netherlands, he told a lurid story, subsequently given an airing on the BBC, of German- and Austrian-born traitors betraying the Dutch – the infidelity of domestic servants, a long-standing middle-class obsession, being given special emphasis. Even 'the paltriest kitchen maid' of German origins, Bland warned, 'not only can be, but generally is, a menace'. They might be 'superficially charming and devoted', but such people represented a 'real and grave menace', for 'when the signal is given, there will be satellites of the monster all over [Britain] who will at once embark on widespread sabotage and attacks on civilians and the military indiscriminately'.[103]

The *Sunday Express* warned its readers on 19 May about a Fifth Column plan to 'paralyse Britain' upon receiving word from Hitler – to 'seize power stations and broadcasting stations, sabotage railways, telephone exchanges [...] spread false information and create panic'. Some of the plans for this plot, which the paper alleged had been just discovered by the Security Service, were 'in the possession of Germans living here'.[104]

Spy fever brought on by *Blitzkrieg* nerves can, then, explain much of what happened in May and June 1940. But it would be overly generous to say that that was all there was to it. The fact is that the British press had been agitating that the government 'get tough' with enemy aliens long before the spring crisis. The experience of the Irish in Britain during the IRA's S-Plan campaign had already illustrated how prevailing public anxieties could easily find an expression in crude xenophobia. Within a month of the war breaking out, the *Daily Mail* was already warning of 'aliens in our midst' plotting treachery.[105] Frustration with the lack of progress in the war in early 1940 had provoked bouts of stories about grasping, disloyal foreigners with mysterious sources of overseas money. The *Sunday Express* told of 30,000 German émigrés – 'the nucleus of a Fifth Column' – snatching up vital government war contracts.[106] By April 1940 agitation for mass internment was growing. The *Sunday Dispatch* blamed 'namby pamby humanists' in Whitehall for stalling.[107]

Sir John Anderson had noted the increasing press agitation with disquiet. 'The newspapers are working up a feeling about aliens,' he had written back in March. 'I shall have to do something about it, or we may be stampeded into an unnecessarily oppressive policy.'[108] The Home Office quietly reserved accommodation for up to 18,000 potential detainees, even though it regarded such a plan as illiberal and militarily pointless.[109] With the start of the German offensive on 10 May, even the 'respectable' press joined in the clamour for internment. The Cabinet reviewed the issue the following week. A paper drafted by Anderson, Attlee and Greenwood argued that there were 'strong objections to wholesale internment' on grounds of practicality and justice. But the War Office continued to press for its imposition.[110] Churchill formed a Security Executive led by the former secretary of state for air, Lord Swinton, to root out the truth behind the Fifth Column threat. Unlike Anderson, who suspected that stories such as Sir Nevile Bland's were gossipy embroideries, Swinton was convinced that a powerful Fifth Column existed in Britain as it had on the continent, and that only wholesale internment would suppress it.[111] Reluctantly, Anderson gave in.

The onset of mass internment was, in part, the culmination of a general feeling of mistrust and resentment that the public had been directing against German refugees ever since Hitler had come to power. The British memory of refugee aid in the 1930s has, of late, become rather self-congratulatory. This is thanks to the rediscovery in popular culture of the *Kindertransport* evacuations of about 10,000 children, mostly from Germany and Czecho-slovakia, in 1938 and 1939.[112] The *Kindertransport* undoubtedly saved many young lives. Sir Nicholas Winton, the stockbroker who helped organise the programme, was rightly hailed as a hero when he reluctantly emerged into the public eye in the 1980s.

What the 'triumphalist narrative' of the *Kindertransport* tends to obscure, however, is that it took place in the face of a thoroughly hostile environment for refugees.[113] Throughout the 1930s the 1919 Aliens Act had been used to limit the number of German citizens given refuge in the United Kingdom. The government, under no legal obligation to assist refugees from the Third Reich, was particularly insistent that none of them should be a drain on state funds. Private charitable organisations that wished to sponsor refugees had to agree to strict terms, including a £50 deposit for each child (well beyond the means of most families) and a pledge that it would financially maintain anyone over the age of sixty for life.[114] Many Jewish Germans had been impoverished by confiscatory Nazi laws and no longer had any means to support themselves. A private fund set up by the former prime minister Stanley Baldwin and a Czech refugee fund organised by the lord mayor of London each raised half a million pounds, and the Council for German Jewry about the same amount. But that money was rapidly exhausted.[115] The *Kindertransport* children travelled unaccompanied by their parents because the government would not let the parents in.

British refugee policy in the 1930s evolved amid widespread parliamentary and press hostility. Refugees were said to be interlopers, stealers of jobs, benefit scroungers. The British Medical Association refused to recognise the credentials of German doctors for fear of professional competition. The *Daily Mail* warned that 'misguided sentimentalism' about the plight of refugees in the Third Reich would lead to 'the floodgates [being] opened [...] we should be inundated'. The trade unions were opposed.[116] The true loyalties of aliens in Britain were said to be to their home nations. Winston Churchill warned in Parliament in July 1937 that 'there may be 35,000 or 40,000 Germans or Italians in this country at any given moment', all of whom were receiving political instructions from their overseas govern-ments: 'nothing like this has ever been seen before.'[117]

In fact, by the end of 1937 government obstacles compounded by public indifference and distrust meant that only 5,500 Jewish refugees had been able to come to Britain. With the *Anschluss* in March 1938 and the *Kristallnacht* pogrom that November, that number increased rapidly.[118] The extraordinary violence meted out across Germany during *Kristallnacht* shifted popular sympathy in Britain somewhat.[119] The government began to encourage Jewish refugees of international distinction in the arts and sciences to come to Britain; such generosity, it was hoped, would create a good impression in the United States and elsewhere.[120] It also agreed to be more flexible about entry visas for children and domestic servants.[121]

But plenty of popular resentment survived even *Kristallnacht*. A month after the Nazi pogroms the home secretary received a delegation of back-bench Tory MPs unhappy about the volume of Jewish refugees entering Britain.[122] In February 1939 the king, disturbed by reports that German émigrés were illegally entering Palestine, wrote to Lord Halifax expressing the hope that 'steps are being taken to prevent these people leaving their country of origin'. The foreign secretary promptly asked the British ambassador in Berlin to urge Hitler's government to prevent the 'unauthorised emigration' of Jews.[123] Halifax himself later admitted that he had 'always been rather anti-Semitic'.[124] An attempt to start an imperial set-tlement scheme for German Jews outside of Palestine got nowhere thanks to problems with cost and objections from colonial administrators (Kenya's governor was willing to accept the 'right type' of Jew, but thought their presence on a large scale would be an 'undesirable feature' in his colony).[125]

In June 1939 the scurrilous anti-Semitic magazine *Truth*, surreptitiously run by Chamberlain's party fixer Sir Joseph Ball, was still complaining that London was 'crawling with foreign undesirables' and that 'one of the mys-teries of this present time is how the refugees who are pouring into Great Britain manage to present such a well-fed, well-dressed, and cheerful – not to say arrogant – appearance'.[126] By July, with the Danzig crisis deepening and charity organisations running out of money, Chamberlain reluctantly announced that the government was willing to re-examine the question of whether it should defray costs of emigration and settlement (though 'I don't care about [Jews] myself', he reminded his sister.)[127] On the brink of war, according to a Gallup survey, seven out of ten Britons thought that refugees ought to be allowed to enter the UK. But almost all of those who agreed added the proviso that there ought to be 'restrictions designed to safeguard British workers and taxpayers', making the commitment a rather shallow one.[128]

The invasion of Poland might have been expected to increase sympathy for Hitler's victims. If anything, the opposite was true. All Germans, no matter their religion or political views, were now the enemy. 'You cannot trust any Boche at any time', suggested the Tory MP Gilbert Acland-Troyte.[129] By April 1940, according to a Foreign Office minute, 'the hatred of Jews among the middle and lower strata of London's population' had 'increased greatly'.[130] Mass Observation agreed: popular anti-Semitism, always widespread but hitherto too impolite to be expressed too loudly in public, had been given a new respectability by the press's obsession with the Fifth Column. It had become 'quite the done thing' to speak your dislike of Jews out loud.[131] On the day the Germans invaded Belgium, a London County Council alderman complained that

> the idea of Germans taking charge of Britons in an air raid is grotesque, particularly as it is ten chances to one that the man dropping bombs is his cousin or some relative [...] these people are nationals of an enemy country, however much they may dislike the government now in power, and deep down they must have a love for their native land.[132]

Almost two-thirds of people polled by Gallup felt that the government had been too lenient with aliens up to this point in the war. Only 2 per cent thought it had been too strict.[133]

Italy's declaration of war on 10 June 1940 generated a wave of popular anger previously unseen even against the Germans. Mussolini's craven opportunism in turning against the Allies at their moment of vulnerability seemed especially contemptible. This anger in its most visceral form was directed against the Italian émigré community in Britain. Italian-owned restaurants, fish-and-chip cafés and ice-cream parlours in Liverpool, Cardiff, Swansea, Newport and London's Soho district had their windows smashed. Some were looted. The worst violence was in Scotland. Mobs rampaged through Italian districts in Glasgow, Clydebank and Edinburgh. Much of this was economic envy masquerading as patriotism, the work of 'hooligans' rather than concerned citizens, according to Home Intelligence.[134] The *Hotel Review* had already complained of 'the excessive Italianisation' of the British hotel industry. The war, it said, ought to see such foreign encroachment 'checked and eliminated'. Now the Italian *Duce* had done disgruntled fish-and-chip merchants a great favour by allowing them to smash up the competition's premises and see their rivals interned, all while wrapped up in a Union Jack.[135]

*

After their arrest, German and Italian internees were sent to military transit camps across the country. The original plan was to pass them along to long-term secure accommodation on the Isle of Man before final deportation to Canada. Little had been organised beforehand to make the transit camps tolerable. Warth Mill (known by its unlucky inmates as 'Wrath Mill'), near Bury, an abandoned rat-infested cotton factory with a broken glass roof, was notorious as the worst of the lot. Eighteen water taps had to provide for 2,000 internees. The lavatory facilities consisted of sixty buckets in the yard. At Sutton Coldfield men slept on ground sheets without even straw sacks as blankets.[136] Even at the better camps internees lacked furniture, medicines and nutritious food. The conditions might have been spartan but tolerable if all the interned had been healthy adults, but many were aged or sickly, despite the Home Office originally advising the police to leave such people unmolested. At Huyton camp, near Liverpool, one third of inmates were judged physically incapable of surviving the conditions for long. Some were crippled or suffering from serious mental disorders.[137]

Those in command were generally well intentioned, if not necessarily sympathetic towards their charges. Petty injustices were more the result of a lack of imagination than deliberate cruelty. In one camp the *Oxford Book of English Verse* was banned as subversive literature. In Kent a commandant was found guilty of stealing from the internees.[138] Newspapers were generally prohibited, leaving refugees and anti-Nazi activists fearful about the progress of the war. If Hitler's forces had invaded, their own chances were, after all, bleak. Should the Germans ever take over the UK, a letter writer noted to the *Times*, they would now 'be full of sardonic gratitude to us for so conveniently assembling the favourite victims of their sadism'.[139] Perhaps the cruellest consequence of the rush to intern was the failure of the authorities to keep track of whom they had in their custody. Communications with the outside world were limited, so interned aliens had no way of contacting their families to tell them where they were. The War Office simply lost people. Archibald Sinclair, the secretary of state for air, tried to intercede on behalf of one refugee family he knew personally, whose young son had been taken away and interned. 'We can't find the boy,' officials finally admitted.[140]

On 2 July the *Arandora Star*, a Blue Star Line transport carrying over 1,200 German and Italian internees to Newfoundland, was torpedoed off the north-west coast of Ireland and sank with the loss of 865 passengers. The deportation programme was suspended as a result. Even before this tragedy the panic that had provoked the original round-up had been ebbing away. As a result, the purpose and propriety of it all started to come under attack. On 24 July the internment of all the remaining enemy aliens in the country was stopped because of a lack of any more camp accommodation. It was never resumed.[141] By early August popular approval of the policy had fallen to 33 per cent.[142] When it was debated in the Commons on the 22nd, Sir John Anderson was savaged. 'We have, unwittingly I know, added to the sum total of misery caused by this war, and by doing so we have not in any way added to the efficiency of our war effort,' said the Tory MP Victor Cazalet.[143] 'Most regrettable and deplorable things' had happened in executing the policy, conceded Anderson. 'Great improvements are now being made rapidly.'[144]

What this meant in practice was the incremental release of all the Class C and many of the Class B internees. Churchill, who told the Commons in August that he had always thought the Fifth Column threat exaggerated (this was certainly not what he had said in private a few months earlier), now accused MI5 of 'witch-finding' and wanted the hunt for spies brought to an end.[145] But the process took time. By mid-October only one in five internees had been let free. In February 1941 three in five were still locked up. By November that year 3,695 enemy aliens remained interned in Britain, most of them by this time on the Isle of Man. Five thousand were also being held in captivity in the Dominions because they had been deported early in the process – these included many Class C Germans and Austrians who would have been released had they remained in Britain.[146]

Britain's experiment with the mass indiscriminate suspension of habeas corpus was largely over by late 1941. It is hard to know exactly what to say about it. On the one hand, it compares quite well with the US government's treatment of Japanese-Americans, which would begin after Pearl Harbor. The United States interned five times as many people for far longer – most were not released until the end of the war – and was much less discriminating about whom it interned. Tens of thousands of US citizens of Japanese ancestry were interned, without any tribunal process, an injustice that had no analogy in Britain.[147]

On the other hand, the mass internment of enemy aliens in 1940 was a policy that the Home Office embarked on not because it felt it was necessary or fair – it knew it was probably neither – but because it had been pressed into it by a confederacy of outraged special interests (MI5, the press, the trade unions) that were pandering to fashionable prejudice and an obsession with spies and traitors.[148] The best one can say about the whole unhappy episode is that its noblest feature was its brevity.

It was certainly freighted with irony. Henry Prais, who eventually had a distinguished career as a professor of modern languages, had come to Britain from Germany in February 1939 as a teenager. When war broke out, he tried to enlist in the British Army but was turned down. The following July he was interned and sent first to Prees Heath camp in Shropshire, and later to Onchan on the Isle of Man. He was eventually released in December 1940. He looked back on his involuntary sojourn with fatalism. 'From 1936 onwards you had become so accustomed to an insecure existence that you did not find injustice surprising,' he remembered afterwards. 'You were conditioned to the fact that life was going to be insecure from then on.' When he was released, the police gave him a form to fill out which, among other things, asked him if he had ever been in prison. 'November–December 1938: Buchenwald, on the charge of being a Jew. July–December 1940: Onchan, on the charge of being a German.'[149]

17

MARGINS

'We crossed the Thames and the Medway, leaving the towns with their moorings of toy balloons far beneath.' It was the morning on 28 August 1940, and Jim Bailey was a twenty-year-old Pilot Officer in RAF Fighter Command's 264 (Madras Presidency) Squadron, taking part in his first combat action. Twelve of 264's aircraft had been scrambled from the RAF base at Hornchurch in Essex to intercept a group of German bombers – several dozen Heinkel He 111s – detected heading northwards across the Channel from Calais. It was fifteen days since the Luftwaffe had begun its full-scale, systematic daylight raiding of south-eastern England, attacking RAF airfields in a bid to wear down Fighter Command's defences and so achieve local air superiority over Kent and Sussex – perhaps as a prelude to a ground invasion. Two days earlier, twenty-seven of the RAF's fighters had been destroyed and six pilots killed in massive aerial battles over the Home Counties. German losses were greater still, but they had had larger numbers to begin with. The strain on Fighter Command's young airmen was beginning to tell. The outcome of this battle – the 'Battle of Britain', as Churchill had already named it back in July – seemed very much in the balance.

In the distance, Bailey could see a drove of Heinkels approaching from the south-east, accompanied by dusty splatters of anti-aircraft fire. Far above them, 'small black motes in the empyrean', were the German Bf 109 escort fighters, buzzing about sinisterly. Bailey's orders were to ignore them and to stay rigidly in formation to attack the bombers, trusting that other nearby British fighters would deal with the Luftwaffe escorts. 'Then it happened', he said:

> They were about twenty or thirty large Heinkels flying in sections of three, line astern. My gunner began to fire. I concentrated on keeping formation, confident that the whole of 'B' Flight was behind,

protecting my tail. The four Brownings stuttered above my head. I became excited [...] the Heinkels looked as big as elephants.

I had felt jolts or rattles on my own aircraft, and a voice seemed to be saying down the intercom, '*I'm wounded.*' I flicked over, pulled back on the stick, and spiralled for the ground in a controlled blackout. At ground level I straightened out.

'*Are you all right?*' I shouted to the air-gunner down our faulty radio. '*Quite all right.*' '*I thought you said you were wounded?*' '*No!*' he said. '*Turn to starboard.*' Then the engine died.

With the throttle not responding and only a couple of hundred feet of altitude left between his aircraft and the soil of Kent, Bailey had no choice but to look for an emergency landing site. All the fields below were studded with wooden poles, planted earlier in the summer to thwart German invasion gliders. With all other options exhausted, Bailey brought his aircraft down hard into a hedgerow, just missing some overhanging high-tension cables as he plummeted to a halt. He bloodied his nose on the instrument panel at the moment of collision, but he was otherwise unhurt. He and his air-gunner, also luckily uninjured, climbed out to examine the fuselage of their crashed fighter. It was peppered with puncture wounds from machine-gun bullets and cannon shells. A kindly vicar appeared to offer them a drink of whisky, Bailey's second ever glass of it.[1]

Despite having been shot down, he and his crew mate John Hardie nonetheless felt 'jubilant'. They had damaged or destroyed a Heinkel and had survived their first combat encounter with only cuts and bruises to show for it. Only after returning to Hornchurch did their mood change as they found out what had happened to the rest of 264 Squadron. As the British planes had approached the enemy bombers, they had been 'bounced' – ambushed – by Bf 109s, led, though they did not know it, by two of the Luftwaffe's top fighter aces, Adolf Galland and Werner Mölders. Four of 264's dozen aircraft had been shot down, including the commanding officer's. Another five had been badly damaged. Five aircrew were dead. 'We were hushed all the next day', he remembered, 'quietly subdued in the mess.'[2]

Bailey's first daylight sortie in the Battle of Britain had turned out to be his last. The squadron's survivors were immediately transferred to an air base in Lincolnshire, far from the action over Kent. His squadron had been in the main battle area for five days. In that time it had lost eleven of its aircraft. It had, in effect, been wiped out as a fighting unit in less than a week. Such a rate of loss was not unprecedented, but it was unsustainable. Had it been experienced across all Fighter Command's squadrons that summer, the entire force would soon have been destroyed.[3]

The fate of 264 Squadron was particularly shocking because it was equipped with the most modern fighter aircraft the RAF possessed in the summer of 1940 – not the Supermarine Spitfire, nor the Hawker Hurricane, but the Boulton Paul Defiant. The Defiant, like the Fairey Battle, is not an aircraft that the modern RAF prefers to dwell on much. Its place in the story of the Second World War is relegated to the footnotes. No Defiant proudly occupies a place in the Battle of Britain Memorial Flight. No adulatory coffee table books have been written in its honour. No one invokes images of Defiants roaring above the Weald to epitomise Britain's pluck in its Finest Hour.

But before the war it had been regarded as the aircraft of the future. Great things were expected of it. The press gushed about its high speed, 'exceptionally powerful armament' and 'streamline shape'.[4] Part of its appeal was its novelty. The Defiant was a two-seat fighter armed not with forward-firing machine guns, like the Spitfire and Hurricane, but with four Browning .303s mounted in a manned, electrically powered turret, making it capable of engaging the enemy from the side and rear. Compared with this revolutionary design, the Spitfire and Hurricane could seem old-fashioned, 'obsolescent type[s] of fighter', as Sir Ernest Lemon, the Air Ministry's Director-General for Production, called them – useful as temporary stopgaps, perhaps, but no basis for a rapidly expanding air force.[5] Churchill wrote to Chamberlain bemoaning the money that was being spent on out-of-date fixed-gun fighters like the Spitfire and Hurricane. It was 'paramount', he wrote, that planes like the Defiant be given priority.[6] The Air Ministry's plan was to equip one third of all Fighter Command squadrons with Defiants by the summer of 1940.[7]

Enthusiasm for the Defiant appeared to be justified during the battle over the Dunkirk beaches. On 28 May, 264 Squadron claimed to shoot down thirty-seven German aircraft in a single day ('it was like knocking apples off a tree', one of the pilots told a reporter afterwards). Churchill, in his 'Fight them on the Beaches' speech on 4 June, said that the Defiant had been 'vindicated as superior' to all existing German fighter planes.[8] The Air Ministry was equally impressed. In July it ordered another 280 to add to its existing purchase of 650.[9]

In the event, production difficulties at Boulton Paul made it impossible to deliver more than a fraction of this total. Fighter Command had only two operational Defiant squadrons at the beginning of the Battle of Britain. That was fortunate, because the Defiant's success on 28 May turned out to be a fluke, never to be repeated. On 19 July nine Defiants of 141 Squadron tried to intercept a group of German Bf 110 twin-engine fighter-bombers attacking ships off Folkestone. They were bounced by Bf 109s. The single-seat Luftwaffe fighter was faster, more manoeuvrable and better armed than the Defiant. Moreover, movable turret-mounted rather than fixed forward-firing machine-guns turned out to be a huge liability rather than an advantage in a fighter duel. The Defiant's slow-moving turret simply could not keep up with the rapidly changing relative position of the twisting and diving aircraft; the gunner could not get an accurate shot against German fighters. Six out of 141's nine Defiants were shot down in the encounter, and ten of their aircrew killed. The squadron was immediately withdrawn to Scotland, its surviving pilots and air-gunners traumatised by the speed of their unit's destruction.[10] When 264 Squadron was similarly massacred at the end of August, the Defiant's career as a day fighter was brought to a hasty and ignominious end.

These twin tragedies made no difference to the outcome of the Battle of Britain because the number of planes involved was small. They represent, though, an alternative, might-have-been battle – the battle the Air Ministry was initially *hoping* to fight – which would have had a very different outcome from the historical one if chance had not haphazardly intervened. If the RAF had got the aircraft it originally wanted, it probably would have been beaten by the Luftwaffe in the summer of 1940. This is not because its leaders were stupid. There were rational reasons to plan for a different kind of Battle of Britain in the late 1930s, one for which an aircraft like the Defiant seemed a more appropriate choice of weapon system than the Spitfire or Hurricane. No one had any idea what modern air combat between two advanced industrial nations would be like. Nor could anyone have predicted the collapse of France in June 1940, which changed the strategic context of the battle entirely and rendered so many pre-existing assumptions moot.

The Battle of Britain tends to be interpreted at the extremes. The traditional, heroic view is that it was the unlikeliest of David and Goliath victories, the plucky 'Few' of Fighter Command somehow transcending the appalling odds stacked against them to avert Britain's almost inevitable defeat in the summer of 1940 – and the defeat, by extension, of all western democracy. This was the version of events that the Air Ministry sponsored in its authorised history in March 1941, written by Hilary Saunders, author of the 1927 psychological thriller that Alfred Hitchcock later adapted into the movie *Spellbound*. 'Men like these saved England,' Saunders wrote of the RAF Spitfire and Hurricane pilots of the previous year:

> What the Luftwaffe failed to do was to destroy the fighter squadrons of the Royal Air Force. This failure meant defeat – defeat of the German Air Force itself, defeat of a carefully designed strategical plan, defeat of that which Hitler most longed for – the invasion of this Island [...]
>
> Such was the Battle of Britain in 1940. Future historians may compare it with Marathon, Trafalgar and the Marne.[11]

'At the summit the stamina and valour of our fighter pilots remained unconquerable and supreme. Thus Britain was saved,' as Churchill put it in his own post-war variation on this narrative.[12]

In recent years, a more prosaic way of thinking about the summer of 1940 has emerged which challenges this victory-snatched-from-defeat interpretation of the battle. Historians have pointed out that the odds were never really so stacked against the RAF. The Luftwaffe was not the vast, unstoppable force it appeared. Moreover, even in the unlikely event that Fighter Command had been destroyed in the summer of 1940, there would still have been the matter of the Royal Navy to contend with. Hitler's invasion plan Operation *SEELÖWE* (SEA LION) took no proper account of how an armada of fragile German troop barges crossing the Channel could be protected from British surface vessels, which would have mounted a desperate, all-or-nothing attack. Some historians have concluded that the Battle of Britain air war, for all its fury and heroism, made little difference to the outcome of 1940 because a successful invasion was impossible anyway.[13] As Derek Robinson has concluded:

> Hitler knew the truth about a Channel crossing [...] he was no sailor; nonetheless, he knew the difference between a battleship and a barge; he knew the Royal Navy was massive and that it could, and would, sink his unprotected invasion fleets in a night [...] if the Royal Navy was supreme, then SEA LION was bound to fail.[14]

Perhaps, though, the Battle of Britain was neither a miracle of deliverance nor a strategic irrelevance. Popular memory exaggerates the degree to which the British were fighting against overwhelming odds in 1940. Germany's military victory in a campaign it had never expected to wage would have been a formidable challenge even if its leaders had made the best tactical decisions, which they did not. That does not mean that British survival in 1940 was an inevitability, however. Contingency played its part. Plenty of things could have gone wrong that summer, as the story of 264 Squadron demonstrates. The margins of permissible error were small. Britain survived partly through imaginative pre-war planning, partly through the mistakes of its enemy, partly through the astonishing youthful courage of men like Jim Bailey and partly through sheer bloody good luck.

*

France's surrender on 22 June left Hitler without any obvious military strategy to pursue. So far as he could see, continued fighting between Germany and Britain would weaken both nations and would work only in the interests of the United States and the USSR. The obvious answer, then, was a compromise Anglo-German peace which left Britain, for the time being anyway, in control of the world's oceans and its overseas empire while the Third Reich enjoyed hegemony over the European continent. Hitler had such high expectations that his enemy would recognise this logic that once the Armistice was signed with Pétain he forbade his planes from flying over British airspace for several weeks so as not to antagonise public feeling in the UK and jeopardise possible talks.[15]

Hitler's offer did not come until 19 July, in the coda to a long, rambling speech at Berlin's Kroll Opera House. The *Führer* declared himself 'compelled, standing before my conscience, to direct yet another appeal to reason in England'.[16] He offered no details of what Germany might demand for peace, only that it was Britain's last remaining option if it wished to avoid total destruction. He was far too late: the War Cabinet had already decided on 28 May to fight on for the time being, and Churchill had pledged the same to the Commons the following week. It was decided that Hitler's proposal, such as it was, did not merit the dignity of a further prime-ministerial rejection. Instead, it was left to Halifax to give the official reply in a BBC broadcast three nights later. 'There was in [Hitler's] speech no suggestion that peace must be based on justice, no word of recognition that the other nations of Europe had any right to self-determination,' the foreign secretary told his listeners: 'We never wanted the war; certainly no one here wants the war to go on for a day longer than is necessary. But we shall not stop fighting till freedom, for ourselves and others, is secure.'[17]

The public was underwhelmed by Halifax's desiccated radio performance – 'too much like a bishop', as one listener put it – but government policy was at least unequivocal. Peace, for now, was not a matter for discussion.[18] Hitler was left disappointed. A further demonstration of violence would, it seemed, be necessary to compel the British to the negotiating table. With a distinct lack of enthusiasm, the *Führer* ordered his general staff to prepare plans for a campaign against the island of 'England' (always the geographic enemy so far as the Germans were concerned).[19]

There were two ways this could be done: blockade and invasion. The first would require a campaign of attrition, comprehensively wearing down the British war economy and the country's ability to continue fighting. The focus would be not so much on military units as on the means of importing, manufacturing and supplying them: ports, warehouses, food storage centres and aircraft and munitions factories. In a blockade campaign the Luftwaffe would need to work in close co-ordination with the Kriegsmarine to attack merchant ships entering and exiting British home waters. It would be a national campaign, focusing not just on London and southern England but also on the western Atlantic ports and the Midlands and northern industrial centres. No swift result could be expected. It would be a campaign that would have to be sustained for at least several months, perhaps into 1941, until Britain, broken, isolated and starving, was reduced to such a parlous state that Churchill was overthrown or his government compelled to sue for peace.

The alternative to blockade was for the Luftwaffe to establish rapid air superiority over the Channel and south-eastern England and threaten or actually undertake an amphibious invasion. The principal target in that case would be the Royal Air Force: its fighter and bomber aerodromes, early warning stations, anti-aircraft units and, of course, its operational squadrons, either caught on the ground or shot down in aerial combat. Royal Navy warships would also be attacked where possible to reduce Britain's anti-invasion fleet. Ideally, the campaign would begin as soon as possible to take greatest advantage of the good weather and the British Army's disorientation in the wake of Dunkirk. Rather than a steadily attritional slog extending over many months, the attack would be one of terrifying ferocity lasting just a few weeks, or even days; after all, it would only be necessary to maintain a window of air supremacy over the sea approaches and beaches for a short time. Perhaps, in the final hours, the Luftwaffe could unleash indiscriminate terror bombing against London, terrifying the city's people into flight and so jamming the roads of southern England with refugees to delay British ground forces. Once the conditions for successful invasion were established, ideally the government in Westminster would see sense. If not, then, as a last resort, the operation could be carried out.

There were advantages and problems to both strategies. The essential point was that they were *different* strategies: they could not be executed coherently at the same time. A choice had to be made between the two. Yet Hitler, in effect, ignored that choice. His Directive No. 16, ordering the German armed forces 'to prepare a landing operation against England, and, if necessary, to carry it out', was distributed to his military commanders on 16 July. It envisaged 'a surprise crossing on a wide front from about Ramsgate to the area west of the Isle of Wight', and tasked the Luftwaffe with the sort of interdiction and CAS missions that might be expected in support of such an operation: engaging the RAF over the beachheads, destroying coastal fortresses, dropping airborne troops and attacking enemy ground and naval forces.[20] But on 1 August, Göring's air force received a supplementary directive ordering it 'to establish the necessary conditions for the final conquest of England'. This second directive talked of attacks 'against flying units, their ground installations, and their supply organisations' and the need to be ready at any moment to support SEA LION. But it also ordered attacks 'against the aircraft industry [...] ports [...] stores of food, and also against stores of provisions in the interior of the country'.[21] The Luftwaffe was being ordered to begin simultaneous campaigns of blockade *and* invasion preparation.

The confusion of effort was multiplied in Göring's tactical plan for the daylight offensive against the RAF, code-named *Adlerangriff* (Eagle Attack) and initially scheduled to begin on 10 August, though this was eventually pushed back due to poor weather until the 13th. Göring's two principal *Luftflotten* (air fleets) based along the French Channel coast – No. 2, commanded by Albert Kesselring, and No. 3, led by Hugo Sperrle – were ordered to attack a long and heterogeneous list of targets: RAF air bases, RDF (radar) stations, aircraft and motor factories, harbours, warships and, if Hitler allowed it, civilian residential areas. There was no priority given to any particular type of target. No logical effort was made to establish how attacking one target might affect a subsequent attack on another. There was not even any analysis of which specific RAF aerodromes in southern England might be most important to knock out. The German Army was not consulted, nor the German Navy. There was no proper discussion with Luftwaffe intelligence. The plan offered no cogent argument as to why it would destroy British resistance or create the appropriate conditions for SEA LION. It just declared that it would, and it would do it in a matter of days. As Stephen Bungay summed it up, 'Eagle Attack' 'barely merits the name of "plan" at all'. What it amounted to was

> little more than flying over England, dropping some bombs on various things to annoy people, and shooting down any fighters which came up as a result. Given that the German General Staff had just planned and executed one of the most innovative, brilliant and decisive conceptions in military history, [*Adlerangriff*] was astonishingly amateur.[22]

Throughout the summer of 1940 the contrast between the professional skill and courage of the Luftwaffe's aircrew and the complacent dilettantism of the men who led them would grow starker and starker.

*

The RAF had always expected to have to fight a Battle of Britain. It had been central to its strategic thinking in the 1930s that the main German effort against the UK if war broke out would be a large-scale aerial offensive, the much-feared 'knock-out blow'. What exactly that blow would consist of was, of course, unknown. But its broad parameters could be guessed from what the air force knew about its own plans for strategic bombing. There would be a short, sharp series of massive air raids against urban and industrial targets to try to smash the country's war economy and terrify its citizenry. They would take place in daylight. The raiders would fly from bases in north-western Germany across the North Sea, making landfall somewhere along the English east coast. The Luftwaffe's He 111 bombers had the range to attack targets anywhere east of a line stretching from Hull to Bognor, while its longer-legged Dornier Do 17s could range as far as Newcastle or Southampton. The bombers would fly mostly unescorted. The Luftwaffe's principal single-engine fighter, the Bf 109, lacked the fuel tanks to get to England and back from Germany.[23]

There was no expectation that the Germans would be trying to gain air superiority over British airspace to prepare the way for a land invasion. Such a scenario would have seemed absurdly pessimistic in 1939, given the strength of the French army. The RAF never imagined a scenario in which the Germans would control the entire seaboard from Brittany to northern Norway, leaving the southern English coastline just a few minutes' flying time from enemy air bases.

RAF plans to defend against a German knock-out blow had been shaped by its own assumptions about the power of strategic bombing. The most committed bomber advocates believed that nothing could stop a well-disciplined attacking formation from reaching its target: trying to mount a defence with fighter aircraft was a waste of resources. 'The bomb,' the 1935 RAF War Manual spelled out plainly, 'is the chief weapon of an air force.'[24] The only way to thwart an aerial attack was to mount an even bigger one of your own. Sir Edward Ellington, Chief of the Air Staff from 1933 to 1937, argued that 'every fighter is a loss to the striking force – the true defence against air attack'.[25] His successor, Sir Cyril Newall, grumbled in 1938 that he was being forced by the government to 'accept a vast output of obsolescent, if not obsolete, fighters [...] deferring the reequipment of the service with really powerful bombing aircraft'.[26] Fighter defence was 'amateur strategy' and, as one RAF officer put it, 'putting all your players in goal'.[27] This attitude died hard. Even as the Battle of Britain was being fought, the Air Ministry was still complaining about the priority that the Ministry of Aircraft Production was giving to fighters.[28] The 'Few,' it thought, ought to be even fewer.

Most RAF leaders were sceptical about the value of fighter escorts. Modern fast bombers, flying in tightly co-ordinated formations so that their front, side and rear machine-guns cocooned them in an overlapping defensive web, would have more than adequate protection. 'The whole conception of fighter escorts is essentially defective,' the Deputy Chief of the Air Staff, Sir Richard Peirse, wrote in February 1937.[29] The RAF assumed the Germans would feel the same way. It was a view that proved stubbornly resilient even in the face of appalling losses experienced by its own bomber crews. The Allies would not have an effective long-range daylight escort fighter until 1943.[30]

Bomber purism heavily influenced pre-war policy. But it could never set its terms entirely. The Air Ministry accepted that at least some fighter defence of Great Britain was necessary, if only to appease politicians and the public. For his part, Sir Hugh Dowding, the first AOC-in-C of RAF Fighter Command appointed in 1936, had no doubts about the wisdom of a defensive fighter force. 'The best defence of the country is the fear of the fighter,' he argued. 'If we are weak in fighter strength, [German] attacks will not be brought to a standstill and the productive capacity of the country will be virtually destroyed.'[31]

Dowding understood, however, that his fighters would have to meet the enemy in battle in inferior numbers. In 1936 it was assumed that the Germans were assembling a massive bomber fleet, and that its size would only increase with time. Intelligence estimates thereafter became more and more inflated, partly because of an assumption, not borne out in practice, that the Luftwaffe maintained more aircraft in reserve than it put in the front line. At the outbreak of war the British believed the Germans had 4,320 military aircraft when the real figure was only 3,647.[32] On the eve of the Battle of Britain in June 1940, when Fighter Command had about 760 operational aircraft, the Luftwaffe was estimated to possess 5,000 front-line machines, including 2,500 bombers, with 7,000 in reserve. Its actual strength at that moment was 2,000 front-line planes and just 1,000 in reserve.[33]

Numerical inferiority would mean that it would be vital for Dowding's aircraft to fight as efficiently as possible. Early warning and tracking of German bombers would be critical if he was to be able to assemble a concentration of force at the crisis point. Acoustic mirrors and gigantic horn-like listening devices had been used as detection systems during the First World War, but these had very limited utility. Electronics provided the breakthrough. The creation of the first 'Chain Home' (CH) RDF – Radio Direction Finding, or 'radar' – stations on the east coast of England in 1938 made pre-warning of German attacks a realistic proposition for the first time. By the eve of the Battle of Britain there were twenty-one fixed-mast CH stations in operation from Cornwall to the Shetlands, supplemented by thirty rotating aerial 'Chain Home Low' stations which could monitor shipping and low-flying aircraft.

Buried in the popular mythology of the Battle of Britain is the belief that radar was a purely British invention, that it was a mystery to the Germans in 1940 and that it played the signature role in the RAF's victory. None of these things is true. By the time the first CH stations went into service in 1938, the Germans were already working on an early warning radar system of their own that was even more advanced. One of their radar sets, known as 'Freya', performed the world's first successful electronic air defence interception in December 1939.[34] The French had a radar set of their own too, known as DEM, which, like Freya, was technologically superior to Chain Home in some respects.[35] By the late 1930s all the Great Powers understood the basic principles behind radar and were working on detection systems if they did not already possess them.[36]

The Germans knew about Chain Home, at least in outline. In the summer of 1939 the airship *Graf Zeppelin II* sortied across the North Sea packed with radiometric equipment to investigate mysterious steel towers that had begun to appear along the English coastline. Their suspicions that these were artefacts of a radar system were confirmed the following year. It seems odd, then, that the Germans attached so little importance to what they had found out. A detailed Luftwaffe intelligence report on the state of British defences in July 1940 did not even mention RDF.[37]

The problem was not ignorance of radar. If anything, it was precisely because the Germans already understood so much about it – and its weaknesses – that they deprecated its value. First-generation radar sets were highly temperamental. They were unreliable at estimating the height and number of incoming enemy planes. Most importantly, the information any single one of them provided was of limited usefulness because it gave only a narrow snapshot of what was happening within a three-dimensional battle space that could be hundreds of miles across. The data it produced could be more confusing than clarifying if there was no way to put it into context or to react to it efficiently in a very tight response window – after all, it only took six minutes for an aircraft to cross the Channel. The Germans had not found Freya to be all that useful because of poor communications between their own navy and air force staffs.[38]

It was information synthesis and co-ordinated response, rather than radar per se, that were the peculiar genius of the British air defence system in 1940. Dowding had developed an integrated early warning network that was fast, flexible and accurate enough to respond to a German air attack with great efficiency. At the heart of the system was the 'filter room' created at his headquarters at Bentley Priory in Harrow. All reports of air activity in or near UK airspace – not just from coastal CH stations but also from the 1,500 or so Royal Observer Corps's inland lookout posts scattered across the country, as well as the 'Y' interception station at Cheadle in Staffordshire, which could pick up Luftwaffe pilots' wireless traffic – was sent to this filter room. There plotters could synthesise that raw information minute by

THE BATTLE OF BRITAIN

RAF FIGHTER COMMAND

- ◎ Command headquarters
- ● Group headquarters
- □ Sector station
- ---- Sector station boundary (11 Group only)
- ✈ Fighter station
- 📡 Low-level radar station
- 📡 High-level radar station
- ▬ ▬ Command boundary

LUFTWAFFE BASES

- ✈ Bomber
- ✈ Fighter
- ▬ ▬ Command boundary

FIGHTER COMMAND
13 GROUP

Hull

Manchester

Sheffield

Nottingham

FIGHTER COMMAND
12 GROUP

Birmingham

Coventry

FIGHTER COMMAND
10 GROUP

Bristol

Ball

Bath

Andover

Middle Wallop

Southampton

Portsmouth

Tangmere

Ventnor

North
Sea

Norwich

Duxford

Debden

Martlesham
Ipswich

North Weald

Bentley Priory
Northolt
Uxbridge

London

Croydon

Kenley

Redhill

Rochford
Eastchurch

Hornchurch

Biggin
Hill

West
Malling

Detling

FIGHTER COMMAND
11 GROUP

Manston
Canterbury

Hawkinge
Lympne   Calais

Rotterc

Antwer

Ghent

Lille

English Channel

Cover of low-level
radar (500ft)

Amiens

LUFTTFLOTTE 2
(Kesselring)

Cherbourg

Le Havre

Cover of high-level
radar (15,000ft)

LUFTTFLOTTE 3
(Sperrle)

N

0	20	40	60	80	100 mls
0	40	80	120	160 kms	

minute, discarding dubious or duplicate reports and building up a holistic real-time picture of the situation across the aerial battlefield.

That processed information was then relayed by a secure telephone network to Fighter Command's four Group headquarters, each of which was responsible for one geographic section of the UK. The most important of these was 11 Group, responsible for defending airspace across south-eastern England in a roughly quadrilateral area from the Isle of Wight to Suffolk, including London. It was at the Group level that operational decisions were made about which German raiders should be intercepted, and with how many squadrons. Orders were sent to each of the Groups' principal airfields, known as 'sector stations'. From the sector stations individual aircraft were given instructions about the direction and height they should fly to bring them into contact with the enemy.[39]

Dowding's system was by no means perfect. It required a high degree of skill from the plotters to prevent the filter room becoming an information bottleneck. The operations rooms at sector stations were in unprotected buildings, vulnerable targets had the Luftwaffe ever chosen to attack them, which it never did in any methodical way. But the system was extraordinarily robust and flexible. It had enough built-in redundancy to allow for short-term breakdowns of any of its constituent parts. It was possible for information to pass up as well as down the chain, giving everyone within it the fullest possible picture of what was going on at any particular moment. Crucially, Dowding's system permitted Fighter Command to choose when and where to engage the Germans throughout their air offensive, neutralising much of the Luftwaffe's advantage in numbers. The Germans had nothing like it. As a result, they did not understand it. This would cost them dearly.

During the 1930s the British had gone to great lengths to prepare a strategic aerial defence-in-depth. In some ways this had been a bad choice, poorly aligned with the country's military needs by the outbreak of war. It had meant sending an expeditionary force to the continent that lacked proper tactical air support. The choice was partly to blame for the Allies' defeat in the Battle of France in May 1940. It might easily have lost Britain the war that month. But it did mean that when the Germans attempted a strategic air assault later in the summer of 1940, Britain was better prepared for it than any other country in the world would have been. That turned out to be decisive.

*

In July 1936, when Fighter Command was created, its fastest interceptor had been the Gloster Gauntlet, an open-cockpit biplane which could reach a maximum speed of 230 miles per hour, and which was armed with two Vickers machine-guns mounted in the fuselage within easy reach of the pilot. In appearance, the Gauntlet would not have looked out of place flying over the Western Front in the First World War. Four years later, it had been replaced by the Supermarine Spitfire Mark IA monoplane fighter. The Spitfire had a closed cockpit, stressed metal skin, low-drag elliptical wings and retractable undercarriage. It could reach 367 miles per hour and was armed with eight Browning .303 machine-guns each capable of firing twenty rounds a second. This was far more than an incremental improvement. The Spitfire was a plane of a new age entirely. In less than half a decade, military aviation had been technologically transformed.

No one in the spring of 1940 knew for sure what that would mean for aerial combat. No two first-rate air forces had yet gone into battle against one another equipped with the new machines. Could fighters still engage bombers when the aircraft would be approaching one another with a combined velocity close to the speed of sound? Would pilots pass out owing to the excruciating G-forces of high-speed manoeuvring?[40] The fate of empires would rest on such technical questions. The RAF spent much time in the late 1930s thinking about them.

It was clear that intercepting fighters, even if they could break through bombers' defensive screens, would have a very short time to fire at the enemy planes in a single pass because of their high relative speeds: perhaps two seconds only. Several conclusions emerged from this. One was that the two machine-guns per fighter which had sufficed in the First World War and which were still standard on planes like the Gloster Gauntlet would no longer provide a dense enough concentration of fire to do any damage in the brief window of opportunity. At least eight machine guns firing 480 rounds every three seconds would be the minimal necessity, though twelve would be better – and replacing machine-guns with cannons firing exploding shells would be best of all.

A second conclusion was that intercepting fighters would have to attack bombers in rigid formations to produce a cone of overlapping fire sufficiently wide to hit something. The days of lone fighter pilots stalking individual enemy bombers seemed to be over. A corollary of this was that

the one-man fighter armed with forward-firing fixed guns, like the Spitfire, might be heading for obsolescence. Anyone flying a fighter plane in
formation at over 300 miles per hour would have to focus simply on not
crashing into his comrades. He would have little mental energy left over to
aim his guns. In the First World War pilots had practised 'deflection shooting', approaching an enemy plane from the beam rather than from the front
or rear and firing at it slightly ahead to anticipate its forward movement.
Such rapid mental calculations might be impossible for a pilot with fixed
guns flying at modern speeds.[41]

Dowding had spelled out his own thoughts on the matter in a lecture
at RAF Uxbridge in May 1937. 'The increasing performance of the modern
bomber is rendering [deflection shooting] tactics obsolete,' he proposed:

> Single seat fighters, apart from the fact that their endurance is gener-
> ally inadequate or extremely ill-adapted to act as escort for bombers,
> can only shoot straight ahead [...] if a [bomber] armada were to fly in
> great depth on a narrow front it would be very difficult to bring large
> numbers of single seat fighters into action against it by attacks from
> astern, since only the rearmost formations would be vulnerable.[42]

This raised the question of whether, in the new fast fighters, it might be
better to decouple the tasks of flying and firing. A second crew member
operating a mobile turret could focus exclusively on the business of shooting down the opposition. Moreover, turret-mounted guns could be brought
to bear on an enemy bomber regardless of the relative angle of the two
planes, reviving the art of deflection shooting.[43] Peirse had already argued
back in July 1933 that 'the movable multi-gun multi-seat fighter is beyond
doubt the right answer [...] it is so far in advance of the single-seater that
the latter must be considered obsolescent now.'[44]

With all this in mind, it is understandable why many senior RAF figures
had their doubts about the Spitfire when it first flew in March 1936. Indeed,
given the prominent position the Spitfire now holds in the RAF's identity,
it is a little shocking to be reminded of how little faith key members of the
Air Ministry had in it right up to the eve of the Battle of Britain.

The initial RAF order for 310 Spitfires was placed with Supermarine (a
subsidiary of Vickers-Armstrong) in June 1936 for delivery within fifteen
months. Even then, it was unclear whether this new plane could expect a
long service life. Leaving aside its perceived shortcomings as a single-seat

fixed-gun fighter of the old-fashioned type, the Spitfire did not seem a good platform for future weapons upgrades. Its slender wings did not seem capable of absorbing the brutal recoil of cannon fire. Heavier aircraft in development such as the Westland Whirlwind, the Bristol Beaufighter and the Hawker Tornado (a planned successor to the Hurricane) looked to be much more promising as the RAF imagined the Fighter Command of 1940.

Supermarine's inability to deliver even the first order of Spitfires on time seemed likely to doom the plane anyway. Its novel elliptical wing required an unusually high degree of skill to manufacture – too demanding, it had turned out, for the Supermarine engineers at their Woolston, Southampton, factory to handle alone. But the company's reluctance to liaise properly with subcontractors meant that by the time of the Munich Crisis the RAF did not possess a single fully equipped Spitfire squadron. Only thirteen of the aircraft a month were being delivered (compared with twenty-six Hurricanes).[45]

The government had tried to boost this delivery process by asking Lord Nuffield, director of Morris Motors, to build and run a new factory at Castle Bromwich in Birmingham to produce 1,000 of the Mark II version of the Spitfire. Nuffield claimed that he would soon be building sixty machines a month. But managerial complacency and a shortage of skilled local labour meant that not a single Spitfire had been manufactured at Castle Bromwich by the outbreak of war.[46] Even Woolston had only completed 270 of its original order of 310.[47] The Air Ministry was by now running out of patience. The Spitfire had been an exciting, cutting-edge machine on its first flight over three years earlier, but it looked as though it would be obsolete before it ever arrived in squadron service in large enough numbers to make a difference. It was, perhaps, time to move on to more promising designs such as the Defiant, Tornado, Whirlwind and Beaufighter. The Spitfire and Hurricane would serve as useful stopgaps until then, but there was no point in ordering any more.[48] They could be quickly phased out of European service, though they might find a place in secondary theatres such as the Middle East.[49] The Spitfire survived 'almost by accident' – less because of any of its inherent virtues than because its competitors proved even more troublesome to build.[50]

On the eve of the Luftwaffe's assault in the summer of 1940, Fighter Command had almost fifty Spitfire and Hurricane squadrons. If the Air Ministry had had its way, it would have had fewer than twenty.[51] The consequences of this would probably have been disastrous. Turreted and twin-engine fighters proved perfectly capable of intercepting unescorted bombers. The Beaufighter had a very successful career as a night-fighter. But German bombers in the summer of 1940 were not unescorted in daylight, because they were flying from France. Victory on the continent had transformed the Luftwaffe's operational circumstances. It could now operate its Bf 109s from Channel bases as far as London and back. The RAF had never expected this. Heavy fighters like the Defiant and Beaufighter were far less manoeuvrable than one-man single-engine types, which had, as it turned out, defied all the pessimistic 1930s predictions that they would be helpless in modern combat. Without enough Hurricanes and Spitfires, the Battle of Britain could have been over in a couple of weeks.

*

Adlertag – the opening day of Eagle Attack – caught the British by surprise. ULTRA signals intelligence had earlier picked up talk of a planned 'Eagle Day', but no one knew what the code name meant.[52] Unfortunately for the Germans, 13 August was something of a damp squib. Unexpectedly thick cloud forced the cancellation of most of the morning's planned raids on RAF airfields. *Erprobungsgruppe* 210, an experimental fighter-bomber wing the Luftwaffe had set up to practise low-level precision attacks, had accomplished what could have been a vital coup the previous day by knocking out the RDF stations at Dover, Pevensey and Rye, and so disabling the early-warning system across Kent and Sussex. Ventnor RDF station on the Isle of Wight was also badly damaged. But because the Germans continued to underrate the importance of RDF, there were no rapid follow-up attacks on these or other stations to exploit this feat.[53] All but Ventnor were back in operation by the end of the day, and Ventnor was working again within three days.

Several RAF aerodromes were successfully attacked on *Adlertag*, but the targets chosen bore no relationship to their importance in the Fighter Command defence network. RAF Eastchurch on the Isle of Sheppey was heavily bombed on 13 August and on seven subsequent occasions over the next four weeks. But it was a Coastal Command air base irrelevant to the battle. Of the vital 11 Group sector stations, only one, RAF Middle Wallop in Hampshire, had any bombs dropped near it at all on 13 August, and those were by accident. The Luftwaffe lost forty-seven aircraft for its trouble, but believed it had destroyed eighty-four RAF fighters, many of them on the ground. In fact, only thirteen British fighters were lost in combat and three pilots killed, and while about fifty planes were indeed destroyed on the ground, only one of them was a fighter.[54] Fighter Command did not fully appreciate that the Luftwaffe had even begun its main offensive for another five days.

For the next three-and-a-half weeks, Kesselring and Sperrle's *Luftflotten* launched almost daily attacks on British targets, mainly 11 Group airfields, from the West Country to the Thames Estuary. Göring had originally hoped that after four days of *Adlerangriff* the RAF would be wiped out.[55] By the beginning of September that had clearly not happened. Even so, the Luftwaffe's progress reports, composed by its intelligence head, Joseph 'Beppo' Schmid, offered room for optimism. The Germans believed that since the start of the campaign eight British airfields had been made totally unusable and many others badly damaged, and 791 RAF aircraft had been destroyed – half the British starting fighter force – compared with just 169 German fighters. The British, they thought, probably only had 100 service-able Hurricanes and Spitfires left.[56]

Kesselring and Sperrle disagreed as to what this meant. Kesselring was convinced that Fighter Command was on the verge of disintegration, and that if enough of its remaining Hurricanes and Spitfires could be lured into the air, they could be destroyed. Sperrle was less sure. He was sceptical about the figures and believed attacks on airfields should continue. Göring sided with Kesselring. The Luftwaffe could not continue flying daylight sorties over England at such a frenetic pace for much longer. Losses were mounting. Nerves were strained. Reports of *Kanalkrank* ('Channel Sick-ness'), somewhat like the nervous condition known by the RAF later in the war as 'Lack of Moral Fibre', were rising – stomach cramps, irritabil-ity, drunkenness, missions aborted for dubious mechanical reasons. Crews had started to hold attack briefings near the toilets.[57] Presumably the RAF pilots must be in as bad a way too.

This was the context for the decision on 3 September to switch attacks from RAF airfields to London – the beginning of 'the Blitz'. If Fighter Command really was on the brink of collapse, then forcing its surviving pilots into the air to defend their capital would be a way of quickly finish-ing them off. The *Luftwaffe* would be able to roam freely above London thereafter, bombing at will. On the other hand, if the RAF was not really beaten at all, then it was time to transition to a more sustainable strategy of blockade anyway. The great sprawling morass of London had plenty of valuable economic targets, and with the unmistakable signature shape of the Thames to guide them in, the Luftwaffe's bomber pilots would find it impossible to miss and big enough to hit even in pitch darkness – and bombing at night would be much safer for the German aircrews.[58]

*

Who were the handful of callow-faced young men who stood in the way of Göring's dark ambitions? 'All over the country' in 1940, remarked Lord David Cecil,

> in lanes, in streets, saying goodbye at railway stations, leaning, glass in hand, over the bars of inns, we see the figures of the pilots, their faces for the most part so incongruously boyish above the misty blue of their uniform collars.[59]

In some respects, the Battle of Britain did not fit easily into the Shire Folk myth of 1940. The heroes at Dunkirk had been overwhelmingly civilians: weekend yacht-club sailors and calloused trawlermen delivering the BEF home to safety. In the Blitz, they would be portly ARP wardens and harried WVS volunteers dispensing hot tea and sympathy to the bombed-out. But the air campaign over Britain was a warrior's war, far removed physically and mentally from the rest of the population: a battle fought between tiny elite vanguards of highly trained, technologically adept myrmidons, duelling against one another thousands of feet above the masses.[60]

Perhaps it was for that reason that the 'Few' of the RAF Fighter Command adopted a rather mannered insouciance, a determination *not* to seem exceptional. 'The most striking thing about the fighter pilots,' insisted war artist Cuthbert Orde, who spent months embedded at an RAF station, 'is their ordinariness. Just you, I, us and co.; ordinary sons of ordinary parents from ordinary homes.'[61] The RAF discouraged the cult of celebrity that surrounded the Luftwaffe fighter aces, with their Knights Crosses and champagne and customised aircraft paint schemes. Bragging and grandstanding were considered poor form. Proper self-effacing British heroes, understated to the point of scruffiness in their dress, manners and discipline, did not seek individual glory or medals, but were content with the rewards of a quiet pipe and a pint at the local pub.[62]

They were barely men at all. Of the 2,937 RAF airmen who flew in the Battle of Britain, most were under twenty-six. To be 'young' meant under twenty-two.[63] Almost 600 were non-British, the majority of these from the Dominions and Empire, although there were also 145 émigré Poles and eighty-eight Czechs, who were allowed to serve operationally after much Air Ministry hesitation over language difficulties. About one-third of pilots had entered service through the Royal Air Force Volunteer Reserve (RAFVR) as sergeants, and so messed separately from their officer comrades.[64] This differential treatment does cast some doubt on George Orwell's claim that the RAF was 'hardly at all within the ruling-class orbit'. The moneyed antics of 601 (County of London) Squadron, 'the million-aires' squadron', with its polo and silk tailoring and fast cars, hardly fitted that mould. Still, only about 200 Battle of Britain pilots had attended elite institutions like Harrow and Winchester.[65] The campaign was one of grammar school boys rather than the scions of the aristocracy, won not on the fields of Eton but 'in the draughtsman's workrooms of Coventry'.[66]

They had little preparation for what was to come. The exigencies of wartime meant that the leisurely 1930s flight training programme of forty-four weeks had been cut in half by 1940.[67] Tom Neil, a nineteen-year-old bank clerk from Bootle, did not fly solo in a single-engine fighter until late May 1940. By August he was on combat ops in a Hurricane.[68] Fewer train-ing hours gave pilots less time to familiarise themselves with the handling characteristics of dangerous high-performance monoplanes. Accidents at operational squadrons were frequent. During July 1940, forty-seven out of 162 British fighters destroyed were written off through misadventure. Of the 107 pilots who died that month, eighteen did so in accidents.[69]

The small technical differences in the Spitfire, Hurricane and Bf 109 were far less important to the outcome of any individual engagement than the experience and skill of the pilots who were flying them and the combat environment they found themselves pitched into. This was why the tactical training that new RAF pilots had received had to be unlearned once they got to their squadrons, because so much of it was at best useless, at worst liable to get them killed. The 1938 Manual of Air Tactics, still the basic Fighter Command textbook in the Battle of Britain, held firmly to the pre-war views that RAF aircraft would only have to intercept unescorted enemy bombers, and that both sides would stay rigidly in close formation throughout any engagement.[70] It laid down several 'fighting area attacks' of increasingly rococo complexity, the basic unit of combat being the 'vic' of three aircraft in line astern, one central fighter slightly ahead of the others. Squadron commanders were warned 'not to practise forms of attack other than those laid down' unless given explicit permission by Fighter Command HQ.[71]

The limitations of the vic and the total irrelevance of the fighting area attacks to any realistic combat situation soon came to light. The Luftwaffe fighter crews had learned in the Spanish Civil War to fly in loose pairs (*Rotten*), with a leader engaging the enemy and his wingman scanning the skies and watching his tail; two *Rotten* made a *Schwarm* ('swarm').[72] They contemptuously dubbed the rigid British vics as *Idiotenreihen* ('rows of idiots').[73] The *Schwarm* – anglicised as the 'Finger-Four' – was so manifestly superior a formation to the vic that some Fighter Command squadrons began to adopt it in defiance of the Manual of Air Tactics. But the training units continued to adhere to that 'criminal document', as one pilot called it. And Dowding oddly refused to take a clear position on the matter, leaving it up to individual squadrons to decide which formation to adopt, and making no attempt to offer advice to new units or to disseminate tactical lessons learned by seasoned pilots.[74] At the end of the battle, some unfortunate squadrons were still flying vics. Newly trained pilots were still arriving at their units in 1941 knowing little else.[75]

In practice, most fledgling pilots lost any sense of situational awareness within seconds of entering the battle space, no matter what they tried to do. The tremendous speed of their aircraft made it almost impossible to follow what was going on. A fighter moving at 300 m.p.h. would travel a mile in twelve seconds. A speck on the horizon would be at point-blank range within half a minute, then would vanish with the blink of an eye. After entering a mad mêlée of perhaps 100 twisting and diving aircraft, all most pilots could do was to try to avoid colliding with anyone and take a few frantic shots at whichever enemy machine filled their sights for an instant.[76] Usually, it was a waste of time. It was estimated that ninety-seven out of every 100 bullets fired at other aircraft during the battle missed.[77] During his first few combat flights Tom Neil did not even have the chance to shoot as things were happening around him too quickly: 'If only they'd keep still for a moment!' he despaired afterwards in anger and shame.[78] One moment the sky would be full of planes, the next it was completely empty. 'You turn around [...] and you wonder where everyone's gone,' another pilot remembered.[79]

Air battles are imagined as lengthy balletic performances, with dog-fighting planes locked in single combat, each desperately pirouetting and wheeling to get on its opponent's tail. Such protracted duels were uncommon and rarely had a decisive result. The typical kill was an ambush or 'bounce', one aircraft descending out of the sun, closing to within a few hundred yards of its victim from astern, firing for a few seconds, then climbing or diving rapidly away. Most prey had no time to respond. Four out of five pilots shot down never even saw their attacker.[80] For most victims, the Battle of Britain ended with a sudden burst of point-blank machine-gun or cannon fire ripping into metal, fabric and flesh. The aerial battle zone was an arena of stark inequality, divided between a tiny number of expert hunters who did most of the killing and the rest who spent their time trying not to get killed. Only 15 per cent of fighter pilots ever shot down another aircraft during the battle.[81]

The least experienced aircrew were the likeliest to die. Sometimes they froze up in mid-flight terror, overcome with shock and confusion. 'I knew he was shooting at me,' recalled Spitfire pilot George Unwin during his first encounter with a Bf 109: 'and I did nothing, absolutely nothing. I was just, not petrified, but, I don't know, frozen, for ten or fifteen seconds [...] I just sat there and watched him shoot at me.'[82] Unwin was lucky; his would-be assassin missed, and he lived to become a fighter ace in his own right. Others were less fortunate. There were cases of men being killed on their first day after arriving from training school in the morning.[83] The rotating of untried rear-area squadrons into the front line of 11 Group could result in speedy massacres, causing Dowding to stop the practice in early September.

For those who were able to overcome their terror and shoot back, the feeling of battle was exhilarating. Tom Neil's first successful combat was on 7 September, over Maidstone. He lined up a 'big fat Heinkel' in his gunsight and pressed the fire button:

> The Hurricane's eight Brownings did not chatter, the noise was of a thick coarse fabric being ripped, a concentrated tearing noise which shook the aircraft with a vibration that was indescribably pleasant. Ahead, smoking tentacles reached out in clutching traces and felt about the leading vic of Heinkels with blind, exploring fingers. The briefest ripple of twinkling lights. Like a child's sparkler. I was hitting them! I couldn't miss!

Moments later, he shot at a Bf 109 which had strayed into his field of view:

I fired again. And again. A few bright strikes. A brief puff of dark smoke. A thin plume of white, then a slightly thicker tail of darkening grey. The 109 suddenly looked tired. It leaned slowly to its right and slid downwards gently. I fired again. And again. It sat there, tilting. In a way, pathetic. Then momentarily, a small puff of debris exploded into the air. It was dying. The aircraft was dying. Like an animal, mortally wounded. Not the pilot or a man, but an aircraft. It fell away. Sadly. The angle steepening, the trail thickening. I let it go.[84]

There was little room for pity or chivalry in air combat. Fighters descended on crippled enemy planes in a killing frenzy. At the final moment of victory there was a sharp impulse to hover and watch a doomed opponent slowly burn and disintegrate, an urge that long-lived pilots learned to suppress, for it left them vulnerable to ambush by another adversary.[85] From a distance, the destruction of a fighter or bomber might seem like the smashing up of a machine only. But at point-blank range the enemy aircrew could be seen moving about within their Perspex canopy prisons, the fear and pain on their faces a mirror-image of the pilot's own – provoking a mixture of recognition, detached curiosity, morbid excitement and revulsion. Geoffrey Page, twenty years old in the summer of 1940 and already an excellent fighter pilot, wrote in confession to a friend that 'I enjoy killing. It fascinates me beyond belief to see my bullets striking home and then to see the Hun blow up before me.' But his discovery of this ghoulish streak within himself made him nauseous. 'I feel I am selling my soul to the devil.'[86]

For those RAF pilots who might fantasise about a decorous, heroic death in battle, the air war provided plenty of disabusing reality. Pilot Officer Howard Perry Hill was a twenty-year-old New Zealander who had joined the air force in 1938. On 15 September 1940, flying with 92 Squadron from Biggin Hill, he was credited with the destruction of three German bombers. He shot down a fourth on the 18th. Two days after that, his Spitfire was bounced by Werner Mölders while at 27,000 feet over Dungeness. Hill's plane was seen to slowly descend, but no one witnessed him crash or bale out. Search parties could initially find nothing, and he was posted missing. Several days passed before his wrecked Spitfire was found lodged in a canopy of trees. Hill's partly decapitated corpse, still clutching the flight controls, was inside. He was buried in Hawkinge cemetery, near

Folkestone, along with nine other Allied and fifteen German airmen who died during the battle.[87]

*

Fighter Command assumed that the German raiders they detected on 7 September would be heading for 11 Group's airfields as usual. The turn towards London caught them by surprise and left the capital unguarded. In hindsight, the attack that day marks the start of the Blitz. At the time it seemed more like evidence of an invasion. The sheer unprecedented scale of the assault – 348 bombers and 617 fighters – and previous photographic evidence of a build-up of barges in Channel ports all suggested an amphibious attack might be imminent. The warning 'CROMWELL', indicating the likelihood of a German landing, was flashed to all Home Forces troops. The Royal Navy's battle fleet put to sea.[88]

No invasion came, though the threat continued to loom. The raiders returned to London on the night of 8 September, and in daylight again on the 9th. This time, though, Fighter Command was ready, and intercepted them in large numbers over Croydon. Twenty-four Luftwaffe aircraft were destroyed for the loss of seventeen RAF fighters. The German bombing of the capital was scattered and ineffective. On 11 September the Luftwaffe did rather better, breaking through to the London docklands and shooting down more British planes than they themselves lost. Churchill broadcast to the nation that night that 'if this invasion is going to be tried at all, it does not seem that it can be long delayed [...] we must regard the next week or so as a very important period in our history.'[89]

On Sunday morning, 15 September, the prime minister and his entourage left Chequers to visit 11 Group's Operations Room at Uxbridge. Keith Park warned his visitor that not much might happen that day, and reminded Churchill as tactfully as he could that there was no smoking in the underground bunker. By 11.15 a.m., however, the RDF stations had reported enough contacts to make it clear that something big was developing over the Channel. These were the first indications of a massive Luftwaffe effort that day that would involve around 500 bombers and 620 fighters. All of 11 Group's squadrons went up to meet them. Churchill, sitting in the 'dress circle' above the Ops Room map table, watching the plotters track the movement of friendly and enemy formations,

became conscious of the anxiety of [Park ...] hitherto I had watched
in silence. I now asked, '*What other reserves have we?*' '*There are none*',
said Air Vice-Marshal Park. In an account which he wrote about it
afterwards, he said that at this I '*looked grave*'. Well I might.[90]

In the event, 15 September was a remarkable success for Park's men.
Fifty-six German planes were destroyed, and 144 of their aircrew killed or
taken prisoner. The RAF lost twenty-nine aircraft of its own, with sixteen
pilots killed. Churchill later acclaimed it the 'crux' of the battle, the 'date
of the demise' of Hitler's hopes to invade in 1940. It entered national
mythology as Battle of Britain Day, the climactic moment of the campaign
– maybe of the war.[91]

It's doubtful that it really was that decisive a turning point. It's true
that Hitler postponed SEA LION two days later and cancelled it more
or less indefinitely on 2 October, but there's little evidence that the air
action on the 15th specifically had much to do with that decision, which
had been long in the making. At a conference on the 14th, Hitler had
conceded that the preconditions for an invasion did not yet exist. SEA
LION, in his view, was more valuable as a psychological weapon against
the 'nerves' of the British public than a viable military operation. Enough
'outbreaks of mass hysteria [might] yet occur' among bombed Londoners
to force Whitehall to seek terms.[92] As for Göring, he was undismayed by
the results of 15 September.[93] So far as he was concerned, the British effort
had represented a last gasp of Fighter Command, which probably only had
170 to 300 fighters left. He had never taken much interest in SEA LION
anyway and remained convinced that his Luftwaffe alone would defeat
Britain.[94] Further large-scale daylight raids were mounted on London on
27 and 30 September.

So, in the end, there was no dramatic conclusion to the daylight battle
in 1940, just a slow sputtering out through October as the weather deteriorated and German efforts switched over almost exclusively to night
bombing. The Air Ministry's 1941 history chose to formally conclude the
Battle of Britain on 31 October. This date subsequently became canonical,
defining, for instance, whether a pilot had a right to wear a Battle of Britain
campaign clasp on his 1939–45 War Medal. The decision, inherently arbi-
trary, introduced a certain unfairness to the subsequent commemoration
of the battle's dead. Archibald McKellar, the first RAF pilot of the war to
shoot down a German aircraft over the UK, was excluded from the Battle

of Britain Roll of Honour in Westminster Abbey because he was killed in combat on 1 November, a few hours too late. From the Luftwaffe's point of view, 31 October had no special significance at all. The 'bombing war against England' would continue in darkness throughout the winter and into the spring of 1941.

*

SEA LION was abandoned. Did it ever stand a hope? It's not difficult to put together an argument that it didn't. Göring's optimism throughout the Battle of Britain was based on a fundamental misunderstanding of how the two sides were doing. RAF Fighter Command's men – rising before dawn, flying up to four sorties a day – were certainly exhausted by early September, but the Luftwaffe's belief that British air defences were almost destroyed by that stage of the battle was nonsense. On 1 September the RAF had 648 serviceable fighters immediately on hand at squadrons – slightly more than it had had on 1 July – and hundreds more in reserve, plus 1,142 pilots at squadron readiness.[95] Beppo Schmid's intelligence reports were deeply flawed. His misconception was a dual failure – the result of greatly overestimating the German success rate and greatly underestimating the production capacity of the British aviation industry.

The latter had gone through a remarkable expansion in recent months. In June, July and August a total of 1,418 fighter aircraft were delivered from British factories, more than in the whole of 1939, and far exceeding the 444 machines that Fighter Command had lost in the battle since *Adlertag*.[96] This expansion was later mythologised (not least by himself) as the work of Lord Beaverbrook, the Mephistophelean crony Churchill had made minister of aircraft production in May 1940. It really had much more to do with the final bearing fruit of the expansion scheme that had begun under Chamberlain's rearmament programme in the late 1930s. In April 1940, before Beaverbrook was even appointed, fighter production was already two-and-a-half times higher than it had been six months earlier.

To be fair to Schmid, if he failed to gauge his enemy's combat losses accurately, then so too did his Air Ministry counterparts across the Channel. Neither side solved this problem in 1940. Estimated losses were compiled from pilots' after-action debriefings, which in turn relied on their memories of a few seconds of adrenaline-filled terror. In a confused dog-fight, multiple aircraft often fired at the same enemy machine, each pilot claiming to have shot it down afterwards. Pilots eager to see their personal 'score' increase erred on the side of confidence when assessing how successful they had been. One Dornier bomber that crashed on the forecourt of Victoria Station was afterwards claimed by nine Fighter Command pilots from four different squadrons.[97]

Intelligence officers approached pilots' assertions with a degree of scepticism. But ultimately they had little else to go on. The British at least could count the number of enemy wrecks that landed on their soil. Also, while the RAF exaggerated its successes, it had an exaggerated belief in the Luftwaffe's size, which meant that the two errors to some extent cancelled one another out. The Germans overestimated their victories *and* thought the RAF much smaller than it really was: their delusion was the greater. It did not help that Schmid was a careerist sycophant who knew his chief's proclivities well and tailored his intelligence reports to what Göring wanted to hear rather than what was really going on.[98]

Even if the Luftwaffe really had destroyed Fighter Command by early September, however, the Royal Navy would have still presented a formidable – maybe an insurmountable – challenge to any amphibious landing force. The RN had 5 capital ships, 2 aircraft carriers, 16 cruisers, 96 destroyers, 26 submarines and many smaller vessels, such as motor torpedo boats (MTBs), minesweepers, anti-submarine corvettes and armed trawlers, in British home waters. The Kriegsmarine had taken a battering in the Norway campaign. The most it could have assembled to defend its invasion barges would have been a paltry 2 cruisers, 7 destroyers, 16 U-boats and some MTBs and smaller craft.[99] The Luftwaffe would have tried to bomb any British warships that ventured into the Channel, but its anti-ship record in 1940 was not very good. Its pilots had no training in it. It possessed no air-launched torpedo.[100] The Germans had an ingenious new maritime weapon, the magnetic mine, with which they had been able to badly damage several Royal Navy warships in the first winter of the war. But by using these mines too profligately from the outset of the fighting rather than reserving them for a moment of opportunity like SEA LION, they squandered their surprise value. By the autumn of 1940 the British had already introduced effective counter-measures to them.[101]

The British Army was in much better shape by September 1940 than it had been three months earlier.[102] It's reasonable to assume that British troops would have fought as tenaciously in a life-or-death struggle for their homeland as the German defenders of the Reich did in 1945. Churchill's government intended to use its large stocks of chemical weapons for a last-ditch stand against Hitler. The vast natural fortress of London would have been a nightmare for the invader to take in brutal house-by-house street fighting, a Stalingrad on the Thames.

Looking at these obstacles, then, Peter Fleming's conclusion seems compelling: 'Operation SEA LION, as planned and mounted, was doomed to failure and, had it been launched, could only have ended in disaster.'[103] And yet ... on the face of it, Germany's attack against France in May 1940 was also doomed to failure. The obstacles to its success were also enormous, but looking back, we forget all that because we know that attack ultimately succeeded. A military campaign, as Clausewitz put it, is a product of the unpredictable forces of 'friction'. The fluke descent of a blanket of fog can obscure a fleet of invasion barges. A lucky hit can disable a battleship at a critical moment. Perhaps SEA LION had only a one-in-ten chance of succeeding. One-in-ten chances happen all the time. Even one-in-a-hundred chances come up occasionally. But to win such a gamble, Hitler would have had to be willing to take it.

This, for once, he would not do. Hitler had gambled everything on a desperate plunge into the unknown against France back in May 1940. He would do the same thing against the USSR the following year. But in the summer of 1940 he was seized with uncharacteristic doubt. Having achieved such a remarkable sequence of victories since April, Hitler seems to have feared that any interruption to his series of triumphs would be disastrous for the German public's confidence in him and his regime. At that moment, he was not willing to chance anything.

The only condition in which he would have conceived of going ahead with an invasion of the British Isles would have been if its success was guaranteed. He conceived it as a *Todesstoss* ('death blow') to follow some cataclysmic domestic event in the UK – a mass outbreak of civilian panic or a political or economic collapse – which would make any organised resistance to the Wehrmacht virtually impossible.[104] The Luftwaffe was not involved in invasion planning because there was not expected to be any serious fighting if it ever took place. In a sense, then, arguments about whether it was the Royal Navy or the RAF that prevented SEA LION are beside the point. It was never going to happen anyway unless both forces had already been neutralised.[105]

The real question, then, is whether *Adlerangriff* could ever have produced the conditions necessary for such a collapse. It is hard to see how it could have done in the dozen or so weeks the Luftwaffe had before winter weather set in in the autumn of 1940. Churchill's government was more stable and confident by September than it had been in May. Bombing did not produce the rapid breakdown of the public's nerve that airpower advocates on both sides had expected (Hitler, more than most wartime leaders, had always been sceptical about this anyway).[106]

This is not to say that the Luftwaffe could not have done a better job in 1940. Göring is often given the blame for its failure because, it is said, he meddled in his pilots' tactics, forcing the German fighter escort squadrons to fly too close to their bombers and so preventing them from engaging the British defenders to their best advantage. This allegation was given popular circulation in the 1969 film *Battle of Britain*. But it is unfair to Göring, whose tactical advice to his pilots was mostly sensible. Throughout the battle he always stressed that the German fighters should be given operational freedom to hunt enemy planes however they saw fit.[107]

If anything, Göring's mistake was that he did not meddle enough. Lazy and complacent, he whiled away the summer in his elaborate hunting lodge near Berlin, leaving the planning and execution of *Adlerangriff* to Kesselring and Sperrle. He did not impose any central focus or direction on his two *Luftflotten* commanders. His air force was trying to destroy RAF Fighter Command, but its leader never established any coherent theory about how to do this other than to try to destroy a lot of enemy planes on the ground (which the Luftwaffe hardly ever did) and a lot of enemy planes in the air (which it was better at, but not nearly better enough).

Too little thought was given to what the RAF's weaknesses might be. There were several vulnerable choke points in the aircraft manufacture process. In the summer of 1940 the Vickers works in Sheffield possessed the only drop hammer in Britain capable of forging the crankshaft casings for Merlin engines. Its loss would have been catastrophic, but it was not attacked.[108] Supermarine's Southampton factory was critical to the RAF's survival, though the Germans do not seem to have appreciated this. On 26 September it was gutted beyond repair in a devastating raid. Spitfire production fell by 70 per cent for several months. Fortunately for the British, the battle was largely over by this time anyway.[109]

The Dowding system was very robust, but it was not invulnerable. The coastal RDF stations were potential chinks in the armour. So too were the sector stations. Kesselring and Sperrle seem to have got an inkling of this in the final week of August and the first of September, when for the first time their bombers attacked and damaged six out of the seven 11 Group sector airfields.[110]

Even then, though, most of this bombing was directed at runways, buildings and hangars. The results looked spectacular from the air but accomplished less than they seemed. A runway pitted with craters could be filled in quickly enough, especially once Dowding attached permanent work parties, equipped with bulldozers, to the most vulnerable aerodromes. Aircraft were dispersed on the perimeters of their airfields in blast-proof shelters which could only be destroyed with a direct hit. The really vital targets at the sector stations were the Operations Rooms, from which squadrons were vectored to their targets using Bentley Priory's data. If the sector stations' communications and utilities lines could be cut, it could put them out of action for hours. If such attacks were mounted consistently, day after day, the defenders could find it impossible to restore normal service.

The experience of RAF Biggin Hill on the North Downs, sector station for 11 Group's Sector 'C' covering much of west Kent, gives a hint of how the Battle of Britain might have played out had the Luftwaffe been more consistent, imaginative and ruthless in its targeting. Biggin Hill was hardly touched by the Germans throughout the first two-and-a-half weeks of *Adlerangriff*. But on 30 August a precision strike ruptured the station's water and gas pipes and its telecommunications and electricity lines. The Germans returned the next day, breaking the telephone and power lines again. They also hit the station's Operations Room, the concrete roof of which collapsed, smashing the plotting table below into pieces. On 1 September raiders brought the power down once more, and most of the station's remaining surface structures were gutted. A temporary Ops Room was set up in a local chemist's shop a few miles from the airfield. By 4 September, Biggin Hill was so smashed up that it could only operate a single squadron. The raiders came back on 5 September and broke the telephone lines a further time. But this was the end of the airfield's ordeal: on 7 September the Luftwaffe went to London instead.

Because Biggin Hill's pummelling was exceptional, other less harassed sector stations were available to take over its duties while it was temporarily out of action. If, in addition to attacking Biggin Hill, the Germans had mounted simultaneous repeat attacks of equal ferocity and consistency against the neighbouring sector stations RAF Kenley and RAF Hornchurch, the Dowding defence system across Kent might well have started to collapse under the strain. But this would have required an attention to detail and a level of concentration that the Luftwaffe simply did not possess in the summer of 1940. Just half of all the air raids on fighter bases during the battle were against sector stations at all, even though they were the only targets that really mattered.[111] Göring actually discouraged Kesselring and Sperrle from attacking airfields on consecutive days – the one tactic that had a chance of working – because he thought it was a waste of effort.[112]

More, then, is made of the importance of the 'turn to London' on 7 September than is really warranted. Traditional accounts of the Battle of Britain suggest that Göring threw away victory just when the RAF was beginning to buckle. 'By the end of August [...] Fighter Command was coming under a strain which, if prolonged, might have proved fatal.'[113] But this overstates the crisis. The assault on 11 Group's sector stations had been an unpleasant development in late August, but it was conducted in far too desultory a way to have any decisive consequences. If the Germans had ignored London and kept on with their same tactics throughout the whole of September, then it would have made the battle costlier for the British, but the outcome probably would not have been any different.[114]

It was the German air force, not the RAF, that was under the greater strain even before the turn to London. On 1 September it had only 735 single-engine fighter pilots ready for duty, 134 fewer than on 1 August.[115] Not only was it losing more planes than its adversary, but it was not replenishing them at anything like the same rate. Germany's monthly fighter production in the second half of 1940 was 30 per cent of Britain's.[116] The Blitz did not save the RAF from destruction. It saved the Luftwaffe.

18

THE SCOURING OF THE SHIRE FOLK

The London Fire Brigade incident log records the effects of a high-explosive bomb landing at Old Tram Yard, Lakedale Road, Plumstead, at three minutes to five o'clock in the afternoon on 7 September 1940. '120 × 100 feet of garage, stables, and stores and contents, including two cars damaged. Two horses killed. Range of buildings and one floor 350 × 70 feet contents and stores damaged.' A surface air-raid shelter near by was damaged too; two people were killed.[1] The moment the bombs started to fall was impressed into the memory of Jack Garnham-Wright, an architecture student living with his parents a few streets away from Old Tram Yard, because, like countless other Londoners, he and his family were settling down for a cup of tea at the moment when the air-raid siren began its banshee wail. 'We all became conscious of a growing crescendo of noise [...] and then a series of enormous thuds growing near by.' The Wrights retreated to a cupboard under the stairs:

> The biggest crunch of all came with the hugest noise. The air of the parlour condensed and became opaque as if turned instantaneously to a red-brown fog, the floor heaved unbelievably, the wall leaned and rocked as if it had become flexible [...] the slates from the roof came pouring down, crashing through the roof of the glass conservatory with huge clatter, smashing all the glass and piling brokenly into the room. I could hear doors and windows crashing all over the place [...]
> The little china milk jug was lying on its side, and the spilt milk lay in a rivulet dripping over the edge of the table to a white pool in a thick layer of dust below. My mother made an instinctive movement to pick up the jug.[2]

Using the Fire Brigade's meticulous chronicle of what happened over the next two hours, we can follow the melancholy path of destruction traced by 348 Luftwaffe aircraft as they released their bombs over Plumstead and then droned westwards towards 'Target G', the bight in the Thames that was London's great dockland heart. The first fires were reported in Deptford at three minutes past five, North Woolwich at 5.24 p.m., the Royal Arsenal ten minutes later and Greenwich a minute after that. By 5.52 p.m. the bombers were over Millwall. Within seven minutes the 336-acre Surrey Commercial Docks were reported to be alight. The holocaust reached Rotherhithe and Wapping less than a minute afterwards. 'The whole bloody world's on fire,' a Fire Brigade station officer yelled to his telephonists as they called frantically across the city for reinforcements.

The dockland warehouses stretching from Woolwich to Tower Bridge were the great storage houses of Empire, full of precious (and highly flammable) commodities from across the world: Baltic and North American timber, pitch, spirits, sugar. Barrels of scalding rum exploded. Molten tar flooded the streets. Sheds of paint, varnish and rubber released noxious clouds of fumes, causing a panic among ARP personnel as it seemed the Germans might be dropping poison gas bombs. Storehouses of scorching pepper scalded firemen's breath. Other rescue workers struggled through floods of melting grain which attached itself like hot treacle to their boots. Rope moorings on the river quaysides burned through, allowing barges to drift lazily down the Thames, their paintwork blistered by the heat. Telegraph poles smoked and sizzled and burst into flame. In Finsbury, four miles away from the docks, Barbara Nixon watched the largest white cloud she had ever seen billow up into the sky. Every fire engine in London appeared to be racing towards the East End. The vast cloud turned an angry black-bordered red as the evening drew on: 'From our vantage point it was remote, and from a spectacular point of view, beautiful. One had to force oneself to picture the misery and havoc down below.'[3]

At 6.10 p.m. the all-clear sounded. But the respite was brief. At 8.30 p.m. the siren wailed again as 250 more German bombers appeared, guided easily to Target G now by the glow of the great conflagration below them and the satin plumes rising tens of thousands of feet into the air. This time the raiders kept coming until dawn. Battersea, Chelsea, Victoria, Hammersmith and Paddington were among the new sites of destruction, but the focus of the bombing remained the dockland tidal basin around the Isle of Dogs. In Silvertown and Rotherhithe thousands of people trapped between the water and the combusting warehouses had to be ferried to safety by riverboat. By morning 436 Londoners were dead, including seven firemen; 1,600 were seriously injured. Major fires continued out of control in many boroughs.

On Sunday night, 200 German bombers returned, reigniting smouldering pyres across the East End and killing another 412 men, women and children. Monday night's raid lasted for ten hours and killed 370 more people. By this point much of central London was at a standstill, with factories and businesses closed and streets blocked off by yawning craters and unexploded bombs. Dazed citizens stumbled out of their basements and shelters to encounter an uncanny new world of rubble, smashed timber, broken glass, smoke, grime and dust that would assume an ashen familiarity over the months to follow.

'This is perhaps the strangest and greatest period in the world's history,' the journalist James Lansdale Hodson wrote from London a week after Black Saturday.[4] The Blitz had begun – an assault on Britain's towns and cities that would continue on and off for the next four-and-a-half years. Black Saturday was not the first day on which British civilians had been victims of the Luftwaffe. The proximity of residential to industrial areas meant that attacks on ostensibly military targets during the Battle of Britain had already caused plenty of collateral civilian casualties. Cambridge had suffered the first serious air raid of the war on 19 June, with nine people killed. That same night the first bombs of the war fell on Greater London. Thereafter, Luftwaffe raids took place against British urban areas almost uninterruptedly. In July German bombers attacked Norwich, Cardiff, Portland, Portsmouth, Aberdeen, Swansea, Falmouth and Hartlepool. During August the first bombs fell on Birmingham, Coventry, Bristol, Liverpool (for four continuous nights), Port Talbot, Boston and Rotherham.

By mid-August 1940 German raiders were creeping closer and closer to central London. Over sixty civilians were killed in Croydon on 15 August. Wimbledon was hit four days later, Harrow and Wealdstone three days after that. During the early hours of 25 August there was an exceptionally widespread Luftwaffe attack across the capital, with bombs landing in Lewisham, Uxbridge, Hayes and, for the first time, in the City itself, in Fore Street, near the Barbican. The German crews on this occasion had probably mistaken the Thames for the Medway. But the pattern remained the same. By the end of August, Finchley, St Pancras, Wembley and Wood Green had all suffered raids as well. 'LONGEST BLITZ NIGHT' was the *Daily Express* headline on 29 August: 'the air Blitzkrieg mounted this morning to a fierce crescendo [...] fire bombs, screaming bombs, high-explosive bombs, London had them all.'[5] Even before Black Saturday, 1,698 British civilians had already died as a result of aerial bombardment – 257 of them in London – and 2,289 had been seriously injured.

Nonetheless, Black Saturday marked a new chapter in Britain's war. For one thing, the Germans' decision to switch to full-scale air attacks on civilian targets meant that they were tacitly abandoning their invasion strategy of the summer and committing themselves to blockade instead – a campaign of economic strangulation against Britain's stocks of food and raw materials and its concomitant industrial capacity. Black Saturday was the moment in which the Second World War turned, for the British, into a fully fledged war of peoples. There had been a taste of this already at Dunkirk. During the Blitz, Britain's civilians, not the army or navy or air force, became the definite main target of enemy violence.

This would make the Blitz the central mythic experience of Britain's war. It was the Shire Folk story in its most perfect form: a battle of soulless, technologically sophisticated weaponry against the stout hearts of unarmed Little Men, and women, and children. It was an epic about

> the moral authority of a people, virtually defenceless against an indiscriminate and brutal attack, responding stoically to the challenge of the community, their families, their civic buildings, their sense of the past and therefore, their identity in the present. The heroes were not only members of the same communities but also heroes of passive defence, and therefore morally unchallengeable – firemen, air-raid wardens, heavy rescue squads, bomb disposal squads.[6]

Black Saturday marked the point at which, for the British, the Second World War became a different kind of national experience from the First, one defined in the popular consciousness far more by civilian than by military suffering. Just over 11,000 soldiers of the BEF had been killed in the campaign in France and Flanders from May to June 1940.[7] Yet during the 115 days from Black Saturday to New Year's Eve 1940, over twice as many British civilians died as a result of enemy bombing. The usual moral economy of wartime sacrifice had, it seemed, been profoundly disrupted. Britain's cities had become the front line, and its citizens the new fighting ranks. 'We're not really civilians any longer but a mixed lot of soldiers,' J. B. Priestley suggested in his radio *Postscript* the evening after Black Saturday – 'machine-minding soldiers, milkmen and postmen soldiers, housewife and mother soldiers.'[8] This, as it turned out, was a temporary phenomenon. The traditional casualty pattern of war reasserted itself from the summer of 1941 onwards as the Blitz ebbed in intensity and British forces became more heavily engaged in overseas combat. But British collective memory after 1945 privileged the Blitz experience above all others. Sacrifice out of military uniform would be remembered in the years following the war as at least as important as sacrifice in it – perhaps more so.[9]

In recent years the Blitz has become the go-to myth of the Anglophone world in crisis. After the 9/11 suicide attacks in New York City it was the memory of London's resilience in the Blitz, rather than, say, Pearl Harbor, that mayor Rudy Giuliani invoked as a model of courage in the face of terror.[10] The connection was made even more forcefully when London endured its own suicide bombing ordeal on 7 July 2005.[11] But such evocations of the Blitz experience misunderstand it because they interpret it entirely through the reductive lens of national character.[12] That was a habit acquired during the war itself. 'British morale springs from within,' Stephen Spender, writing in 1945, argued: '[Britons'] will to resist [...] is the resistance of their whole nature, their whole history, the whole pattern of their culture, against any attempt to impose on them the behaviour of another nation.'[13]

The British, according to this interpretation, survived the Blitz because of their essential Shire Folk qualities of cheerfulness, quiet patience and inconspicuous toughness – their spiritual core of 'nonchalance, bloody-mindedness and defiance'.[14] Churchill claimed they possessed the innate confidence 'of an unconquered people in their bones'.[15]

Such a belief in the endurance of national character is what continues to make the Blitz myth so compelling and useful. For, as Ian McLaine has argued, the myth 'encapsulates for its believers all the qualities they see themselves as possessing in circumstances of extreme adversity'.[16] Hence its relevance to more recent tests of popular will. If it was 'British phlegm', inheritable and unchanging, that made the Blitz endurable in 1940, then twenty-first-century terrorism can presumably be endured too.[17] Tony Blair, speaking immediately after the 7/7 suicide bombings in 2005, invoked the traditional 'stoicism and resilience', 'spirit and dignity' and 'quiet and true strength' of the British as expressed in the Second World War. The Metropolitan Police Commissioner declared that 'if London could survive the Blitz, it can survive this'.[18] Alan Massie, writing in the *Independent* that same week, consoled his readers that

London's response to yesterday's evil acts shows that any doubts or fears we may have had were groundless. We are the same people we were sixty years ago, capable of the same stoicism. London can take it.[19]

But the Blitz experience was far more complicated than that. There were reasons why the British people endured in 1940 that had nothing to do with any innate qualities of character. The Blitz has lessons to offer today, but they are not necessarily the lessons we would like them to be.

*

The bombing of Britain's towns and cities continued in a desultory way all the way from the summer of 1940 until March 1945, by which time 60,595 civilians had been killed and 86,182 seriously injured. But the greatest continual period of threat was from 7 September 1940 to 16 May 1941, an eight-month Calvary during which about two-thirds of all the war's British civilian deaths and injuries occurred.[20] In this, the 'Big Blitz', London experienced seventy-one major air raids (in each of which at least 100 tons of bombs were dropped) and the rest of the country another fifty-six. In addition to the major raids, the Luftwaffe also mounted several thousand smaller *Störangriffe* (dislocation or nuisance raids) to whittle away at the nation's defences, damage its war economy and sap the energy and morale of its people.[21]

The Big Blitz can be roughly divided into two periods. Between 7 September and early November 1940 London was the Germans' almost exclusive target. September and October 1940 were the capital's two worst months of the war. It suffered forty-nine major raids, almost six a week, with an average of 160 German bombers coming over each night and, in all, about 20,000 bombs landing somewhere in the metropolitan Civil Defence Region.[22] Over 10,400 people were killed – over one-third of all London's wartime fatalities – and another 37,700 seriously injured. The Thames docklands and the East End remained the focus of the Luftwaffe's attention throughout. But bombs also landed across Westminster and the City and as far afield as Enfield, Kensington, Chiswick, Stoke Newington, Willesden, Balham, Twickenham and Sidcup. During the first six weeks of the bombing about 16,000 houses were destroyed or wrecked beyond repair across London, and another 60,000 were seriously damaged.[23]

London's tourist sites shared in the destruction. Buckingham Palace was hit, wrecking its chapel. So were St Paul's Cathedral, the Royal Courts of Justice, BBC Broadcasting House and the National Gallery. The equestrian statue of Richard the Lionheart outside the Palace of Westminster had its sword bent and its horse's mane shrapnel-peppered. A bomb hit the Conservative Party's Carlton Club at dinnertime, almost killing half the members of the War Cabinet at a stroke. The prime minister and his wife, Clementine, had a close escape on 14 October when a bomb landed in Treasury Gardens, just a few yards from 10 Downing Street. The Churchills were unharmed, but three civil servants sheltering near them were killed, and the premier's private kitchen and pantry were wrecked. John Lewis's department store in Oxford Street was burned out by incendiaries, its 'wrecked and gutted' interior afterwards showing 'gaunt girders already rusting, enclosed here and there by unwilling masonry'.[24] In all, between Black Saturday and 3 November 1940 there was not a single twenty-four-hour period when the air-raid sirens did not go off across London at some point.

Most Londoners survived these two months without injury to person or property. The capital was simply too big, its population too large, for any German destruction to be more than sporadic. But they had to endure week after week of torments during that miserable autumn all the same – the fatigue of sleeplessness, the time-wasting drudgery of navigating the city's mangled public transport system every morning and evening, the constant anxiety that they, or one of their loved ones, might be the raiders' next victim. 'Many recollections of that hectic time return,' Londoner Max Cohen wrote in 1953:

> of nights when all Hell seemed to have broken loose, when a mad cacophony of guns and bombs assailed the black empty streets with crashing and shattering explosions, when the house was shaken with a violent bout of *delirium tremens*, when into the turmoil of conflicting noises came the dry scratching rattle of shrapnel on the roof. Nights when through the uncurtained bedroom window came a bewildering display of pyrotechnics, flashes and flickerings and explosions of red, yellow, green, white, chasing and tumbling over one another and mingling with one another in a fantastic series of cosmic fireworks.[25]

German bombs smashed up the fragile linkages of transport,

communication, power and hygiene necessary to maintain a normal urban existence. Over 4,000 water mains were broken in London in the first three months of the Blitz.[26] Telephone exchanges were knocked out, letters and parcels destroyed in the flames, postal services delayed. Roads were blocked by craters and unexploded bombs. The metropolitan railway system was particularly badly affected. More than 100 railway bridges were disabled by November 1940, some of them for up to a month.[27] In a Gallup poll a few weeks after Black Saturday, only 3 per cent of people said they had personally suffered injury in an air raid, but 19 per cent complained that the raids were causing difficulty getting to work.[28] It was 'endless inconveniences' of the Blitz such as these that George Orwell found more trying than its physical danger. 'One seems to spend half one's time trying to buy a sack of coal because the electricity has failed,' he wrote to American readers of *Partisan Review*, 'or trying to put through telephone calls on a wire that has gone dead, or wandering about looking for a bus.'[29]

Night-time air defence was difficult. The RAF had always expected the Germans to turn to city bombing. As an organisation itself obsessed by the power of the strategic bomber, it had never thought of invasion as anything other than a secondary threat.[30] Yet its pre-war planners had taken it for granted that the Luftwaffe would fly to London by day; daylight attacks would, after all, be so destructive that there would be little point in doing anything else. So the start of full-scale night bombing represented an unanticipated challenge. Scant attention had been given before the war to the problem of interdicting enemy raiders in darkness.[31] CHAIN HOME could detect incoming flights of night bombers approaching the coast, but once inland it was impossible to track them manually by visual means as it was by day. A typical Luftwaffe night raid involved one incoming aircraft, travelling at 180 m.p.h., entering British airspace every five minutes at a height ranging from 10,000 to 20,000 feet. Each enemy bomber had an average of 345 pitch-black cubic miles to itself. This made finding them without specialised equipment a matter of pure luck.[32]

Night interception of bombers would become a realistic proposition only when two new paired technologies had become widely available. The first was a ground radar set that an operator could use to direct a night fighter to within a few miles of an enemy bomber. The second was a multiseat interceptor aircraft with its own radar set that could complete the kill. A suitable flying machine, the Bristol Beaufighter Mark 1F equipped with a Mark IV Airborne Interception radar, had its first operational flight in

October 1940. A month later an aircraft of this type detected and shot down a Junkers Ju 88 over Chichester, the first kill of its kind. But Beaufighters did not arrive from the production lines in large numbers until the spring of 1941. In the meantime, Fighter Command had to manage as best it could with repurposed day-fighters like the Defiant and the Blenheim. Results were correspondingly disappointing. On the night of 14 November 1940 the RAF put up 125 sorties. The weather was good, ideal for interception. Seven enemy aircraft were reported spotted. Two British planes claimed to open fire at a target that night. No German bombers were destroyed.[33] After the great daylight tallies of September, it was meagre stuff.

The artillery problem on the ground was just as bad. Customised radar equipment was again the only real answer to the night bomber menace, and until it arrived in large quantities, there was little chance of Anti-Aircraft Command's gunners being able to hit anything. All they could do for the time being was to fire as many shells as they could into the coal-black void in the hope that the cacophony would at least cheer citizens hunkered below in their shelters. Such bombardments posed little risk to the Germans. On the night of 15 October, Anti-Aircraft (AA) Command fired 8,300 rounds at almost 400 Luftwaffe raiders over London. But it only shot down two.[34] The falling shrapnel from the shells caused far more injuries to British civilians than they did to German airmen, but the guns probably did help to bolster morale.

A variety of other anti-raider technologies were tried out during the Blitz, some more hare-brained than others. Frederick Lindemann, Churchill's personal scientific adviser, was an advocate of creating 'aerial minefields' of small explosives attached to parachutes by piano wire and either dropped from aircraft or fired from the ground by rockets. Large amounts of time and money were devoted to this chimerical project, which came to nothing. On the other hand, paraffin-soaked straw fires on the outskirts of cities were a simple but effective way to fool German raiders into thinking that they were over a burning target and releasing their bomb loads prematurely. Known as 'Starfish' sites, it's been estimated that these rural decoys successfully lured in one in twenty German bombs dropped during the Blitz.[35]

The blackness of the night was just as much a challenge to navigation and targeting for the Germans as it was for the British. But during the first few weeks of the Blitz the RAF was surprised to discover that the Luftwaffe could fly accurate night raids even during bad weather conditions that would have stymied Britain's own Bomber Command. Herein lay an irony. The RAF, which had planned for strategic bombing for years, started the war with no reliable method for night navigation. But the Luftwaffe, even though it had made no such plans, did have one. It had created a set of electronic direction-finding systems using radio signals beamed from transmission stations on the continent.

The simplest of these signals, called *Knickebein* ('Crooked Leg'), could be picked up by any standard German bomber. *Knickebein* could place an aircraft over its target with an accuracy of about one mile – not precision bombing, but far better than anything the RAF was capable of at that moment. The *X-Gerät* and *Y-Gerät* beam systems, refinements on the same principle, were more accurate: they could direct a bomber to within a few hundred yards of its target. These, though, required specialist equipment to be fitted to detecting aircraft. Pathfinder bombers capable of following the beams therefore flew ahead of the main force, dropping incendiaries to mark the target.

Fortunately for the British, they had heard whispers of the Luftwaffe beam technologies in October 1939, when a disaffected German physicist had leaked information about several top-secret Nazi weapons projects. *Knickebein* beams were detected in UK airspace for the first time early in 1940. Further evidence acquired from salvaged German aircraft and prisoner interrogations gave a brilliant young research scientist working for the Air Ministry, called R. V. Jones, an insight into how to jam the signals – first *Knickebein,* and then eventually *X-* and *Y-Gerät.* By the spring of 1941 his disruption campaign had mostly succeeded, and the Luftwaffe had lost the 'Battle of the Beams'. But they had brought catastrophe to the Midlands and Liverpool in the meantime.

*

At the beginning of November 1940 deciphered German radio traffic suggested that the Luftwaffe would make an especially heavy raid during the upcoming mid-month full moon period. But what the target of this offensive, code-named 'MOONLIGHT SONATA', would be was unclear. London? Or a provincial city? Up till late afternoon on 14 November the former seemed the likeliest. But then *X-Gerät* beams were detected intersecting over Coventry. Jamming counter-measures proved unsuccessful and Coventry's Civil Defence services received no warning until the bombers were already in the air – though whether a few hours' difference could have done anything to mitigate the city's agony is doubtful anyway. (A myth persists, based on an incomplete understanding of this story, that Churchill deliberately 'sacrificed' Coventry to keep the breaking of German codes a secret.)

The Luftwaffe pathfinders dropped their 10,000 incendiaries exactly as planned that night. Coventry was already crowned with a 'halo of red flames' visible for tens of miles when the 430 bombers of the main force arrived. Over 560 Coventrians were killed in a crucible of fire that gutted the medieval town centre (including Broadgate, the scene of the IRA's bombing attack a year earlier) and left one in twelve houses destroyed or uninhabitable and the remaining two-thirds damaged. Within a few hours the cathedral church of St Michael was 'a seething mass of flame and piled-up blazing beams and timbers', according to one eyewitness.[36] In the morning all that was left of the 600-year-old building was a blackened ruin, the molten lead from its vanished roof coating the broken masonry. Goebbels's propaganda machine was exultant at the bombers' success. Crowing a little too loudly for its own good, it created the unhappy neologism 'to Coventrate' to describe what had happened to the Midlands city.

The Luftwaffe returned to London the night after MOONLIGHT SONATA, but the attack on Coventry had marked a turning point in the campaign. The Germans' focus now shifted from the British capital to industrial cities in the north and Midlands, crucial to aircraft and munitions production, as well as to the Atlantic ports, which were the conduits for essential goods arriving from North America. Southampton, Bristol, Manchester, Portsmouth, Plymouth, Sheffield, Cardiff, Swansea, Clydeside, Newcastle, Belfast, Hull – all experienced their own bespoke horrors in the six months following MOONLIGHT SONATA. The Blitz had become a provincial as much as a metropolitan experience. During 1941 two Britons outside the capital would die for every Londoner killed in an air raid.

The provincial raids, while ferocious, generally each lasted only a night or two before the Luftwaffe moved on to find a new target. Coventry was not attacked in force a second time until April 1941. Only Birmingham and Merseyside experienced anything like the same weight and intensity of bombing as London's East End during the Blitz. Both cities suffered eight major individual raids and had over 1,800 cumulative tons of high explosive dropped on them in 1940–41. They were the only two places outside the British capital to experience the distinctively unpleasant phenomenon of unbroken heavy raids night after night for a week or more.

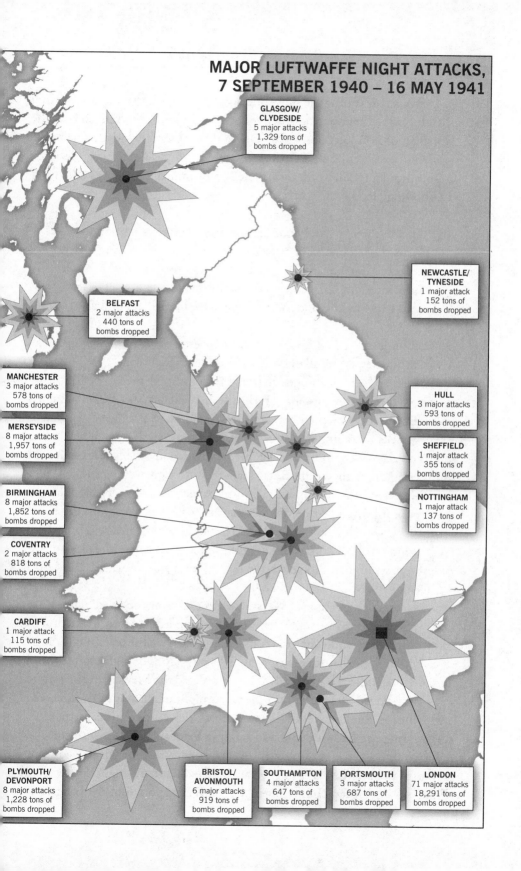

MAJOR LUFTWAFFE NIGHT ATTACKS, 7 SEPTEMBER 1940 – 16 MAY 1941

GLASGOW/ CLYDESIDE
5 major attacks
1,329 tons of
bombs dropped

NEWCASTLE/ TYNESIDE
1 major attack
152 tons of
bombs dropped

BELFAST
2 major attacks
440 tons of
bombs dropped

MANCHESTER
3 major attacks
578 tons of
bombs dropped

HULL
3 major attacks
593 tons of
bombs dropped

MERSEYSIDE
8 major attacks
1,957 tons of
bombs dropped

SHEFFIELD
1 major attack
355 tons of
bombs dropped

BIRMINGHAM
8 major attacks
1,852 tons of
bombs dropped

NOTTINGHAM
1 major attack
137 tons of
bombs dropped

COVENTRY
2 major attacks
818 tons of
bombs dropped

CARDIFF
1 major attack
115 tons of
bombs dropped

PLYMOUTH/ DEVONPORT
8 major attacks
1,228 tons of
bombs dropped

BRISTOL/ AVONMOUTH
6 major attacks
919 tons of
bombs dropped

SOUTHAMPTON
4 major attacks
647 tons of
bombs dropped

PORTSMOUTH
3 major attacks
687 tons of
bombs dropped

LONDON
71 major attacks
18,291 tons of
bombs dropped

On average during the Blitz, one bomb fell on every ten acres of central Birmingham. That was a destructive concentration that compared with the worst-hit of London's boroughs. 'Oh God, what a night,' wrote one of the city's housewives in her diary after the raid of 19–20 November 1940, the beginning of a ten-day ordeal that left 800 Brummagem citizens killed and 20,000 homeless:

> Ten-and-three-quarter hours of anguish, misery, hunger, and sleeplessness [...] as one wave of planes came over and was dying away so the next came into hearing every three minutes. That went on for hours intermingled with violent earth-shakings, the click-clack of incendiaries falling, and shrapnel which fell like hail around us.

A local undertaker had forty-six sacks delivered to him by Birmingham's civic authorities, each full of body parts to be reassembled.[37]

The first German bombs fell on Liverpool and the other industrial towns of the Mersey estuary – Birkenhead, Wallasey, Bootle – in August 1940. By the end of September, 327 Merseysiders had already been killed in small attacks averaging one every other night. Then, during eight horrific hours on 28–9 November, 300 people were killed in the biggest single raid on the region of the entire Blitz. Half these victims were entombed in a basement beneath a collapsed technical college. Three more big raids on Liverpool followed just before Christmas. St George's Hall, in the heart of the city, was almost gutted. The Liverpool–Leeds canal was breached. Warehouses, rubber storage tanks and timber yards across the city's docksides were set on fire. Birkenhead town hall was badly damaged, and 8,000 of Bootle's 17,000 houses wrecked.

Merseyside's greatest test was still to come. During the seven nights from 1 to 7 May 1941 the Luftwaffe threw every resource it had into an attempt to destroy the eleven miles of wharfs and quays that were the terminus for Britain's key North Atlantic convoy route. Over 860 tons of high explosive and 106,000 incendiary bombs fell on Liverpool and the Mersey littoral during this 'May Week' offensive.[38] On the worst night of all, 3–4 May, a moored ammunition ship in Liverpool's Huskisson Dock caught fire and exploded, devastating the harbour area and sending flames 1,600 feet into the sky. 'We would sometimes turn off the lights, go into the bay-windowed front room, draw back the black-out curtains and peer into the night sky,' recalled Francis Oakley, then a boy living in the south Liverpool suburb of Garston:

The sight was a mesmerising one. The whole arc of the sky took on the appearance of a darkened lunar landscape, pitted, pocked, and cratered by the constant succession of exploding anti-aircraft shells and lanced by moving fingers of light as searchlights, trying to pin-point enemy aircraft, probed relentlessly into the nooks and crannies of the night.[39]

When May Week was over, 1,900 Merseysiders were dead, 70,000 were homeless, half of Liverpool's shipping berths had been rendered unusable and all road, rail, postal and telephone connections into the region were severed. Wild rumours circulated across the Lancashire hinterland that Liverpool was under martial law and its half-crazed survivors were marching in the streets, demanding the government make immediate peace with Hitler. This was not true. But May Week showed that even the citizens of a gritty working-class port like Liverpool, already inured to hardship by years of poverty, unemployment and the austere seagoing life, could be traumatised by 'perhaps the worst continuous battering any people yet have had in this country in this war'.[40]

Belfast was only 230 miles further from the Luftwaffe's French air bases than Liverpool, placing it well within the bombers' operating range. The December 1940 raids on Merseyside should have alerted Stormont to Belfast's vulnerability, especially given the obvious strategic value of the city's Harland and Wolff shipyard, the largest in Europe. But geography fostered complacency. ARP precautions in Northern Ireland were rudimentary and uninspired. Barely a quarter of Belfast's 425,000 residents had a public shelter to go to in the event of attack. Few children had been evacuated. The black-out was only half-heartedly enforced. There were no searchlights and only seven anti-aircraft batteries. The Auxiliary Fire Service (AFS) had no modern appliances and had not been properly trained in the use of the few pumps and hoses it did possess. By the spring of 1941 there was probably no major city anywhere in the United Kingdom so grotesquely ill prepared to withstand aerial bombardment.[41]

Almost 200 German bombers began dropping flares over Belfast a little before 11 p.m. on the night of 15 April, shortly after the air-raid sirens had sounded. The greatest concentration of explosives fell on the cluttered, dingy working-class tenements of the New Lodge and Antrim Road area just to the west of the dockyards. Entire streets were levelled as paper-thin, crumbling house walls toppled domino-like onto one another. Dozens of people were trapped in public shelters which imploded under the percussive impact of explosives. Around 1.45 a.m. a bomb destroyed the city's central telephone exchange, cutting off all phone contact with the rest of the United Kingdom and disrupting communications to the nearby RAF station at Aldergrove. The Luftwaffe had the skies to itself over Belfast for five and a half hours.

The all-clear was sounded just before 5 a.m. Belfast 'looked like photographs of Spain or China,' reported one witness who trekked into the city centre by bicycle: 'houses roofless, windowless, burnt out or burning, familiar landmarks gone and in their place vast craters and mounds of rubble.' A treacly yellow fog of smoke, ash and dust enveloped an area up to ten miles from the city centre. The official record was of 745 people killed and 430 seriously injured, making it the second worst attack of the Blitz anywhere in Britain so far. The victims were warehoused in the city's mortuaries and municipal baths, heaped in irreverent disarray – arms outstretched, legs twisted and interlaced, mouths gaping and astonished, fingers pointing judgementally. 'It was grotesque, repulsive, horrible,' wrote one volunteer worker assigned to identify and catalogue the dead. 'No attendant had soothed the last moment of these victims [...] with tangled hair, staring eyes, clutching hands, their grey faces covered in dust, they lay', most still in their soiled and stinking clothing, men's corpses heaved onto women's, children's onto adults', from floor to ceiling.[42]

London never experienced another long unbroken period of heavy bombing after November 1940. But the Luftwaffe kept returning to the capital all the same, if only to keep the defenders guessing and to prevent the withdrawal of anti-aircraft guns and searchlights to the provinces. Some of these later raids were individually much worse than anything that had happened on Black Saturday. The period immediately leading up to and following Christmas 1940 was quiet, which made the massive attack on the night of 29–30 December all the more shocking. *X-Gerät* pathfinders scattered their incendiaries perfectly onto the narrow winding alleyways immediately around St Paul's Cathedral at the heart of the historic square mile of the City. Nature worked against London that night. There was a full moon, an especially low tide and a strong south-westerly wind acting as a treacherous, highly efficient bellows. Thousands of small offices, workshops, warehouses and churches, most of them ancient timber- and brick-built, were locked up, empty, for the holidays. Within three hours over 22,000 incendiaries had fallen, and half a square mile of the City circumscribed by

Moorgate, Aldersgate, Cannon Street and Old Street was on fire. The raid that night was the closest Britain ever came to a firestorm of the kind that would obliterate Hamburg, Dresden and Tokyo later in the war. Redcross Street Fire Station in Cripplegate caught fire, and the chief fire officer for London Region, the splendidly named Aylmer Firebrace, had to rush to safety along with the rest of his staff. 'The air is filled with a fierce driving rain of red-hot sparks and burning brands,' he wrote in his diary: 'The clouds overhead are a rose-pink from the reflected glow of the fires [...] burnt-out and abandoned fire appliances lie smouldering in the roadway, their rubber tyres completely melted.'[43]

Thankfully, bad weather in France that night forced the Germans to cancel a potentially devastating second strike. Only 163 people were killed in the raid, a reflection of the City's tiny residential population, but the physical geography of central London was changed permanently; centuries of architectural heritage had been consumed in a few hours of inferno, including many of the civic buildings that had been constructed after the great fire of 1666. The Guildhall, eight Wren churches and numerous livery company halls were lost. Seventeen publishing houses and over 20 million volumes went up in ash and smoke as Paternoster Row, the centre of the book trade, was razed to the ground. St Paul's itself was hit by twenty-eight bombs, and only through good fortune and the heroic efforts of its fire-watching volunteers armed with stirrup pumps and buckets was the wooden interior of the dome prevented from collapse. But 'the bulk of the City is destroyed complete and utterly', wrote Anthony Heap the following week. 'Every street has its huge gaping voids, gutted buildings and choked roadways. The odour of charred wood still lingers in the air.'[44]

There were four more major raids on London in mid-January 1941 before an eight-week respite brought on by heavy cloud and fog. But late spring saw three raids of a terrifying new intensity.[45] The German raid on 16–17 April ('The Wednesday', as it became known) lasted over eight hours, during which the Germans dropped 150,000 incendiaries and 890 tons of high explosive. Over 1,180 Londoners died. St Paul's probably came closer to destruction that night than on any other during the Blitz when an enormous bomb crashed through its North Transept and exploded in the crypt. Three nights later ('The Saturday'), there was an even more punishing raid – in fact, the heaviest mounted against Britain in the whole war – when over 1,000 tons of high-explosive (HE) and 153,000 incendiaries were dropped, and more than 1,200 people killed. A parachute mine hit a school being used as a fire sub-station in Bromley-by-Bow, killing thirty-six firefighters in what was the greatest disaster in the history of the service.[46]

The five-hour raid of the weekend of 10–11 May saw slightly fewer bombs dropped than on 19 April. But the number of casualties was even greater – 1,436 killed and 1,800 seriously wounded, the deadliest single night of the Blitz. Over 2,100 individual fires were soon blazing across London. The worst of the destruction was, as usual, concentrated on the riverfront between Waterloo Bridge and Woolwich. But the night is most famous for the partial destruction of the Houses of Parliament. One MP on ARP duty personally wielded an axe to stave in one of the ancient oak doors of Westminster Hall to allow firemen access to save its 500-year-old hammer-beam roof from the flames. Choices had to be made, however, and the decision to protect Westminster Hall meant that the nearby House of Commons Chamber was left to burn. Harold Nicolson, inspecting what remained a few days later, discovered 'a sort of Tintern Abbey gaping before me [...] there was absolutely nothing'.[47] Winston Churchill, who also visited the ruins, in silent reflection, had presided over the Commons as prime minister for exactly one year.

'We are slowly, painfully, fighting our way to that command of the air which *must* be a part of this new and intensified Battle of Britain,' the *Daily Mirror* insisted on the Monday after the destruction of the Commons Chamber.[48] This was not merely defiant wishful thinking. Britain's night defences, so feeble at the beginning of the Blitz, really were becoming much more formidable by the spring of 1941. Anti-aircraft fire was more intense and accurate. Total 'rounds per bird', the number of shells necessary to destroy one bomber on average, had fallen from 20,000 at the start of the Blitz to 4,000.[49] Radar-equipped night-fighters had come to represent a real threat to the enemy bomber stream. During the 10–11 May raid, RAF interceptors shot down seven German attackers. Overall Luftwaffe losses that month were eighty-one planes destroyed, compared with just forty-two in March.

The Luftwaffe was also struggling to keep up in the technology war. Its radio beam systems were now routinely being jammed over UK airspace. By May 1941 only one pathfinder bomber in four was successfully receiving a signal from *X*- and *Y-Gerät*. In the absence of such navigational assistance, crews were having to rely (like RAF Bomber Command) on old-fashioned plotting methods, which made targeting at night much more difficult. Losses of experienced aircrew meant that pilots with fewer flying hours were having to make the long and difficult journey over the UK, often in poor weather. Casualties from accidents rose sharply.[50]

In fact, the 'new Battle of Britain' was at an end, even if the British did not realise it. After the great raid of 10–11 May the Luftwaffe made one more major attack on Birmingham. Further raids took place against Merseyside, Manchester and Hull later in 1941. But otherwise, the Germans returned to a *Störangriffe* air strategy. Most of the Luftwaffe bomber fleet transferred to the Eastern Front in mid-May in preparation for the invasion of the USSR the following month. No really big raids on British cities would take place again until 1942. Even then, they would not compare to the unbroken ferocity of the Big Blitz. Hitler's attempt at a knock-out blow was over.

*

The British state had sought to prepare the civilian population for the threat of the bomber in the 1930s. The responsibilities of the Home Office's Air-Raid Precautions Department grew until in 1939 it became a government department, the Ministry of Home Security, headed by the Home Secretary. By the outbreak of war, the central government was spending £56 million a year in various kinds of ARP-related measures. Over 400,000 people were in full-time paid employment as Civil Defence workers.[51]

The purpose of ARP was to protect people and property from the enemy's destruction to the greatest extent possible, and to repair the fractured networks of civil society once raiders had gone. No one knew for certain how difficult that would be. No major European city in the 1930s had ever experienced a knock-out blow on the scale anticipated in a major modern conflict. All the planners could do was extrapolate from data drawn from the First World War and events in war-torn Spain.

Their calculations produced grim data. It was anticipated that for every ton of bombs dropped on a densely crowded urban area, twenty-four people would be killed and forty-eight injured, half of them seriously. The Air Ministry anticipated that the Luftwaffe would be able to begin any major attack against London by dropping 3,500 tons of bombs in the first twenty-four hours, and 700 tons a day for the two weeks following. This meant that the first fortnight of war would see roughly 300,000 Britons killed. Within sixty days twice as many might be dead. Perhaps one quarter of the Luftwaffe's bombs would be filled with poison gas, which would kill even more people.[52] In the face of such apocalyptic predictions, any civil defence preparation could seem futile. Indeed, some left-wing councils refused to have anything to do with them, insisting that ARP's claim to mitigate the effects of bombing merely licensed politicians to imagine war as an acceptable form of state policy.

The Big Blitz tested the reality of what bombing could really do against pre-war assumptions, and in many respects the results were not nearly as bad as had been feared. Between Black Saturday and MOONLIGHT SONATA the *Luftwaffe* dropped 13,651 tons of high explosive on London. During approximately that same period – the worst and most intense of the whole Blitz – 10,820 Londoners were killed and 16,271 injured.[53] Awful though those figures were, they meant that each ton of German bombs had killed only 0.8 civilians and injured 1.2. This was a far cry from the macabre prophecies of the 1930s. At such a rate of attrition, it would take not two weeks but four and a half years to kill 300,000 Londoners.

From an actuarial point of view the Blitz's effect would turn out to be surprisingly modest. A British citizen only stood a 1-in-272 chance of being killed or injured in an air raid during the Second World War.[54] In 1940 the death rate across the London County Council region only rose to 18.6 per thousand people from 12.0 per thousand the year before. More London-ers died from cancer and TB in 1940 than were killed in air raids.[55] The corporeal consequences of attack turned out to be only a fraction of what had been feared.

Why? Addressing the House of Commons on 8 October 1940, the prime minister argued that there could be only one explanation: 'namely, the vastly improved methods of shelter which have been adopted'.[56] In the 1939 Civil Defence Act the government had agreed to provide a free or subsidised six-person domestic garden shelter (the corrugated-steel type known as the 'Anderson', named after Sir John Anderson, head of the ARP Department) to any householder in a vulnerable urban area. More than 2 million Andersons had been distributed by the summer of 1940.[57] The Anderson had many virtues. It was relatively cheap to produce at around £7 10s. per occupant; it was easily manufactured; and it appeared to provide at least some protection against the shrapnel and blast effects of high-explosive bombs.[58] Its close proximity to the home offered the psychological reassurance of the familiar.[59]

The humble garden shelter named after Sir John performed rather well under fire. A properly entrenched Anderson proved capable of protecting its occupants from the blast and splinters of a 50 kg bomb landing as close as six feet away, or twenty feet away in the case of a 250 kg bomb. A direct hit on an Anderson's thin metal shell was a different matter, of course. Stanley Rothwell, an ARP warden in Lambeth, attended an incident where an Anderson had been blasted clear of the ground by a German bomb. 'I could see what looked like treacle sliding down the wall,' he wrote later: 'I realised what it was.' He and his colleagues had to clear up the human remains with brooms, rakes and shovels:

> The only tangible things were a man's hand with a bent ring on a finger, a woman's foot in a shoe [...] in one corner of the garden was a bundle of something held together with a leather strap. As I disturbed it, it fell to pieces steaming. It was part of a torso.[60]

For all the Anderson shelter's virtues, millions of working-class people in flats and tenements lacked the garden space necessary to erect one. In Gateshead, for instance, only 7,000 out of 31,000 households were found to be suitable for the use of an Anderson.[61] For such residents, as well as passers-by caught in the street at the outbreak of an air raid, local authorities had been directed before the war to provide public shelters, in the form of either park trenches, custom-built brick surface structures or existing basements reinforced with steel and timber.

Reinforced basement shelters, though they might look secure enough, were as vulnerable to direct hits as an Anderson. Planning for them had assumed that the debris load from an explosion would fall straight down onto the support strutting. But sometimes a bomb would land at the side of a building, exposing the shelter beneath to a horizontal strain it was never designed to take. The result could be total collapse. One of the worst individual disasters of the Blitz occurred in Stoke Newington on the night of 13 October 1940, when a large high-explosive bomb stove in the side-wall of a basement shelter beneath a five-storey tenement building, fracturing a water main in the process.[62] Over 250 people were in the shelter at the time. 'There was a dull thud, a sound of falling masonry, and total darkness,' an eleven-year-old boy remembered later:

> Somebody lit a torch [...] suddenly I felt my feet getting very cold, and I realised that water was covering my shoes. We were at the end of the room farthest from the exit. I noticed my father trying to wake the

man in the bunk above him, but without success – a reinforcing steel beam in the ceiling had fallen down and was lying on him.

The water was rising, and I started to make my way to the far end, where the emergency exit was situated [...] it was very cold and dark, and I was shivering. The air was thick with brick dust, which got into my mouth, the water was squelching in my shoes. I still dream of, and recall, the smell of that night, and the water creeping up my body.[63]

It took three weeks to dig through the rubble, by which time 157 bodies had been recovered. Many of them were never successfully identified.

Thousands of brick surface shelters had been hastily erected by local authorities in the year before the Blitz. Many of them had been poorly constructed using the cheapest materials to hand, such as sand lime mortar, which gave their walls no tensile strength. Some of them, the government privately admitted in November 1940, had been 'practically disintegrated' by bomb blasts in the first weeks of the bombing, crushing their occupants when their reinforced concrete roofs collapsed on everyone inside. One such shelter had been demolished from a sideways blast 195 feet away.[64] Londoners grew to distrust them once the Blitz began ('they're about as much use as a sick headache') and rumours spread that 'a breath of wind would knock them down'.[65] Eighteen-year-old Margaret Turpin was trapped in a surface shelter along with the rest of her family when it collapsed on them during a raid:

I felt somebody's blood was dripping on me from above [...] I tried to move my head, but of course it was a narrow space and I couldn't get my head away from the blood. And I heard a long time afterwards that the man was already dead. But it couldn't have been my father because he was taken out of the shelter and he didn't die till two days later [...] he died, my mother died, my baby sister died, my younger sister died. I had two aunts and they died, and my uncle died [...]

When I got to the house [after hospital], there were milk bottles outside, and I just knew then that nobody had come home.[66]

Still, catastrophes like these were rare. The biggest drawback of all the pre-war shelters was not so much their structural integrity as their lack of amenities. This reflected a fundamental misunderstanding about what strategic bombing would be like. It had always been assumed that bombing raids would take place in daylight and a raid would be brief – perhaps an hour or two at most. Few people had ever anticipated that millions of Britons might have to take refuge in a shelter for eight hours or more, night after night, in all seasons and all weathers. None of the government's pre-war-designed shelters was equipped with lighting, heating or ventilation. There was nowhere to cook food, nowhere to sleep, nowhere to wash, nowhere to use the toilet other than a bucket. The Anderson, in particular, suffered from flooding in wet weather. 'There'll be more deaths from pleurisy than bombs,' a London wit predicted.[67] A few enterprising householders rigged up lighting and gas cooking in their Andersons, but this was both a fire hazard and beyond the means or ingenuity of most people.

In despair at these inadequacies, some Londoners in the autumn of 1940 took to the same sanctuaries that their parents had used in the First World War: church crypts, warehouses, factory cellars and railway arches. In Tilbury, in the borough of Stepney, a complex of vaults was commandeered by up to 16,000 people. Other cockneys headed westwards to safer boroughs such as Westminster, Kensington and Chelsea. Home Intelligence observers noted convoys of taxis depositing East Enders and their belongings at Euston and Paddington stations as night fell. Some Londoners made for Epping Forest, others the Kent countryside.[68]

The phenomenon of 'trekking' out of other vulnerable cities like Coventry, Southampton, Plymouth and Clydebank to safer rural areas subsequently became one of the most characteristic features of the provincial Blitz. By the summer of 1941 up to 9,000 dock workers and their families were leaving Hull each night to sleep in improvised dormitories – or barns and pigsties if necessary – in the rural East Yorkshire hinterland. The government was initially alarmed at these 'night vagrant populations', worried that they were symptomatic of mass panic. But as it became evident that the dawn and dusk processions were being conducted in an orderly way, were not affecting daytime war production and were unstoppable anyway, the authorities came to tolerate them grudgingly as a necessary safety valve for morale. The government eventually co-operated in the setting up of temporary rest centres, billets and canteens.[69]

Frightened Londoners fled most of all to the Underground. Some of them had already begun taking shelter on Tube platforms in late August. Two weeks before Black Saturday, George Beardmore saw people camping out for the night on the platforms of the Central Underground Line – 'transform the tiled walls and advertisements into rock', he thought, 'and one already had a fair idea of what life must have been like in Neolithic times.'[70] But on the nights following 7 September that initial trickle became a flood. The government's first instinct, as with trekking, was to resist this act of mass trespass. But within a week the sheer numbers involved had forced it to concede the point, and it had started drawing up ways to regulate rather than forbid Underground sheltering. As many as 177,000 people may have descended into Tube tunnels every night in late September, although their numbers declined afterwards to around 65,000 a night.[71]

The adoption of improvised deep sheltering like this revived a pre-war question: should the government build permanent underground ARP facilities for the citizenry, rather than just relying on above-ground shelters like the Anderson and *ad hoc* converted basements? The London University geneticist J. B. S. Haldane's influential book *ARP*, published during the Munich Crisis in 1938, had demanded a scheme of deep underground public shelters which Haldane believed had been 'conclusively demonstrated' in Spain to be the best means of protecting civilians from bombing.[72] He envisioned 1,400 miles of gas-proof, brick-lined tunnel bored sixty feet underneath London's streets, capable of sheltering up to 5½ million people. Similar schemes could be created for other vulnerable British cities.[73]

Sir John Anderson had opposed the idea. He had argued that the excessive amount of time and resources that would be required to complete a civil engineering project of the kind imagined by Haldane made deep shelters unrealistic. Building such shelters for all the urban population of Britain would, it was estimated, require an expenditure of up to £400 million, which was greater than the annual peacetime defence budget.[74] 'We believe that most British citizens would prefer to count upon a less effective protection at their homes, even though this may make no pretence of warding off direct or near hits of bombs,' was Anderson's verdict.[75] The government also worried that 'shelter mentality' might take hold among the terrified populace if they were hidden deep underground. Perhaps they would refuse to emerge from their subterranean sanctuaries even after air raids ended.

As the Blitz showed, even a Tube tunnel deep beneath London's streets was no guarantee of safety from the Luftwaffe. On 14 October an armour-piercing bomb penetrated forty feet down to the platform of Balham Station, breaking water and sewage pipes along the way, and killed almost seventy people by asphyxiation and drowning. The following January, another 111 died when the booking hall at Bank Station received a direct hit which carved out a hole in the roadway above so large that the Royal Engineers had to build a bridge over it. Nonetheless, according to a Gallup survey in October 1940, over six in every ten Britons wanted deep shelters built.[76]

The problem had by then passed from Anderson to Herbert Morrison, who had been appointed home secretary and minister for home security in the new government coalition on 4 October. Before the war Morrison had been one of the loudest of the government's critics demanding deep shelters. Now, however, as poacher-turned-gamekeeper, he demurred. 'Anything like a universal policy of deep shelter, for the whole population or the greater part of it, is beyond the bounds of practical possibility,' he explained in a BBC broadcast on 3 November 1940. Still, he added, a limited number of extensions to the existing London Underground system would be bored out for use as public shelters in the capital.[77] Work began on this new scheme – at Clapham, Stockwell, Goodge Street, Chancery Lane, Camden Town and Belsize Park – in late 1941. This was months after the Big Blitz had ended. The new deep shelters, capable of holding 8,000 people each, were finished in time to shield some Londoners from the pilotless V-1 and V-2 attacks at the end of the war. Otherwise they played no part in events. They are still there to this day, used for everything from hydroponic farming to archival storage to occasional sets for episodes of *Doctor Who*.

Few images are as redolent of the Blitz as those of weary men, women and children camping down for the night on Underground platforms. Yet only a minority of Londoners ever sheltered in the Tube. Surprisingly few used formal shelters of any kind. A survey of air-raid habits in early November 1940 found that 27 per cent of Londoners were using Andersons, 9 per cent small public surface shelters and 4 per cent the Tube and other big basement shelters. The rest were either at work during raids (possibly taking cover, possibly not) or stayed in their own homes.[78] In January 1941, 45 per cent of people polled by Gallup said they used no special shelter during air raids.[79] By spring, only 16 per cent of people in the London Civil Defence region were believed to be regularly sheltering in places other than their own homes.[80] This was despite Morrison's elaborate reforms over the winter to address the problems of sleeping arrangements, heating, lighting and sanitation in public shelters, including the Tube.

In the end, then, Sir John Anderson's intuition was correct. Most Britons, whatever they thought about deep sheltering in principle, preferred to stay in their homes in time of danger. The subterranean impulse certainly compelled some people to find refuge deep below the ground, and not just in London. Bombed Bristolians took refuge in the abandoned Clifton Rocks underground railway, Liverpudlians in the road tunnel under the River Mersey. Public shelters offered companionship and mutual assistance, which could have an appeal at moments of high stress. Residents of working-class tenements in which community life had always been tribal, and sleeping in closely packed confines the norm, may have been drawn to them especially. But most people had a powerful urge to stay at home during air raids – whether from a desire for privacy, a fear of looters, the demands of bourgeois respectability, the need to look after bedridden relatives, the expectation that it might make for longer and better sleep or simply from the psychological comfort of the familiar. 'You're not safe anywhere,' one Londoner argued. 'But I'd prefer to stop at home than run out all over the place every time that the warning goes.'[81]

*

The physical destruction wrought by German bombs must have seemed at times overwhelming during the Blitz. 'There is a smell of death and destruction everywhere – blasted windows – clocks without hands – great mounds of yellow rubble,' Londoner M. Morris wrote in the spring of 1941. 'There is a poisonous tang of damp plaster and coal gas, a reminder that 18,000 have died here.'[82]

Yet for all its sound and fury and bloodshed, the Luftwaffe's attempt to knock out Britain's war industry by air attack was totally unsuccessful. It was sometimes hard to appreciate this in the chaotic wake of a large raid. Coventry, for instance, appeared to have been devastated by the MOON-LIGHT SONATA bombing of 14 November 1940. The city's electric, gas and water network was shattered. Twenty-one factories producing war-related materials, including twelve involved in aircraft production, were destroyed or severely damaged by fire and explosives. Some famous industrial buildings in the heart of the city, such as the Triumph plant and the GEC cable works, both near the cathedral, were burned to the ground.

But the newer, larger factories dispersed on the city's outskirts survived mostly intact. Many workshops suffered damage to roofs and windows, but this was easily repairable. The machinery within was far more robust than glass and timber. Within four days of MOONLIGHT SONATA half the municipal electric supply in Coventry had been restored and all of the city's water pumping stations were back in operation. The War Cabinet in London noted that 'damage to munitions production was less extensive than feared'. Output was back to pre-raid levels within six weeks. And Coventry represented an unusually severe case of disruption. Most British cities in 1940–41 resumed full industrial operation within three to eight days of a big raid. Overall, the government estimated after the Blitz that the bombing had caused a loss of national production of just 5 per cent.[83] Such a meagre rate of attrition was never going to win the war for Hitler.

Why did the Luftwaffe fail to win the Blitz? For much the same reasons it failed to win the Battle of Britain. Partly, it was a consequence of the German air force's modest size. Bombing an industrial economy turned out to be far harder than anyone before the war had appreciated. Subsequent British and American strategic bombing efforts against Germany would be on a vastly larger scale than anything the Luftwaffe was capable of in the Big Blitz. But even then, grinding down the German war economy would prove to be an excruciatingly slow and difficult task.

The Luftwaffe's failure in 1940–41 also reflected the same planning incoherence it had demonstrated during the Battle of Britain. There was, for instance, no attempt to follow up MOONLIGHT SONATA with two or three similar-sized raids against Coventry in quick succession, before the city had time to recover. Weather conditions for an equally devastating attack existed on 19 November. But the Luftwaffe switched to Birmingham that night instead.[84] No big raid was mounted on Coventry again until April 1941, by which time the city had recuperated from its ordeal five months before.

German air intelligence in 1940 had in its possession an extremely detailed and accurate picture of the geographical distribution of key British industries, accumulated through meticulous pre-war reconnaissance.[85] What it lacked, however, was any sense of how these industries operated as a network, what the vulnerabilities of that network might be and what would be the most efficient way of breaking it down. It lacked, in other words, a plan for the Blitz. A plan would not necessarily have produced victory. As we'll see, RAF Bomber Command had plenty of plans for its own campaign against the Ruhr in the winter of 1940–41, though none of them did it any good. But a plan was at least a start. The absence of one guaranteed a desultory bombing campaign that had to be improvised from day to day, targets chosen almost at random. 'This erratic pattern,' Tom Harrisson wrote after the war, seems in retrospect to be nearly senseless. The sequences show no logic, no discernible theory of what such attacks were supposed to achieve; nor any reason why one place was left alone for weeks or months, while another was given serial assault, though still never with any consistency.[86]

Apparently satisfied that it had done its job with a single raid, or two or three at most, the Luftwaffe rarely bothered to press home any of its attacks on provincial targets. This gave the bombed cities a critical opportunity to repair their damaged factories and utilities before the next onslaught, which might take months to arrive or might never arrive at all. This was no way to destroy a war economy. The Blitz did not fail just because of British pluck. It failed because the Germans had no idea what they were doing. From the point of view of winning the war, it was an enormous, amateurish, bloody waste of effort.

*

Just as the Blitz failed to destroy the British war economy, so it also failed to destroy the British will to fight. By the end of the Blitz, in the summer of 1941, it had become clear that, despite all the pre-war predictions about mass civilian psychosis beneath the bombs, people had held up to the ordeal well. British air intelligence concluded in an August 1941 report that 'no town in England has suffered a breakdown in morale'.[87] Psychiatrists such as Edward Glover, who had been deeply pessimistic about civilian responses to air attack, confessed that, after all, 'there has been no outbreak of war neuroses in the civilian population. Such signs of panic [...] never assumed a serious form.'[88] The London clinic that Glover had established at the outbreak of war to deal with traumatised air-raid victims closed for lack of patients.[89] His colleague P. E. Vernon contrasted the 'imperturbability of the majority of the population' to the shell shock of the First World War trenches.[90] Despite all the pre-war fear about 'deep shelter mentality', there was only one recorded case, in Ramsgate, of a group of Blitzed civilians refusing to emerge from their underground tunnel sanctuary for days on end.[91]

This relief soon acquired a self-congratulatory tone as commentators compared British stoicism with the panic they had seen or expected from the French and Germans. The American journalist Virginia Cowles wrote:

'there was no break in the dam here as there was in France [...] even the weakest link in the chain was reliable. From the highest to the humblest, each person played his part.'[92] Government officials planning the strategic bombing war against Germany assured their leaders that the enemy masses would not hold up to the strain as the British had done. 'The Germans, for all their present confidence and cockiness, will not stand a quarter of the bombing that the British have shown they can take', a Ministry of Information report reassured Churchill in January 1941.[93]

Here was the beginning of the myth of the Blitz as a triumph of national character, which continues to enjoy such purchase in popular memory. 'A people who can remain steadfast under bombardment from dusk to dawn for weeks on end deserve to win,' surmised one survivor of the bombing in 1942.[94] The same reassuring message is delivered today in the face of the terrorism threat, which, like the Luftwaffe's bombing, is violence directed by the armed against the unarmed. The Blitz is valuable as a reassuring precedent that urban life can go on even under the most terrible of ordeals.

It is important to remember, however, that while memories of the Blitz evoke the idea of a national community enduring a common ordeal, bombing was highly inegalitarian. Its risks were never evenly divided out. Half the British people were never bombed at all during the Second World War. They experienced the Blitz the same way we do today, by reading about it. The countryside was scarcely affected at all, aside from the odd stray bomb jettisoned by a Luftwaffe plane heading elsewhere. The only wartime fatalities in north Devon were caused by crashed RAF aircraft.[95] Small towns might be at the receiving end of one or two *Störangriffe* raids that left a few craters. London's experience of persistent bombing night after night was unique, with only Birmingham and Liverpool coming close. Even in London the distribution of risk was highly uneven. Essentially, the closer you lived to London Bridge during the Blitz, the likelier it was that the Germans were going to kill you. Four miles from the bridge, the bomb density per acre was half that at the epicentre. At ten miles, it was one-eighth.[96] There were twenty-three casualties per thousand residents in the borough of Poplar, six per thousand in Fulham.[97] Greater London was so vast that even a heavy raid would leave most areas of the city untouched; the sirens and the anti-aircraft guns in the distance disrupted sleep, but no bombs fell.

Moreover, many of the most vulnerable or frightened quickly left the cities. From September 1940 a great exodus of people departed London and other urban areas as the unrealised threats of a year before now became horribly real. By February 1941 the number of people billeted away from home in the official evacuation scheme had leaped from a pre-Blitz total of 550,000 to over 1.3 million.[98] Over 142,000 people from Glasgow and Clydebank alone were officially living in reception districts across rural Scotland by the summer of 1941.[99]

It's not known how many people left the cities through their own devices, either briefly or for the rest of the war. Within a few weeks of Black Saturday it was evidently impossible to book a hotel room within seventy miles of London.[100] The city's population was estimated by December 1940 to have fallen to 6.4 million residents from 8.6 million before the war (a decline that persisted into the post-war period for economic reasons and would not be fully reversed until 2015). The population fall in some of London's inner boroughs was particularly dramatic. By December 1940 there were just 92,000 people still resident in the East End borough of Stepney, compared with 197,000 before the war; by the end of 1941 there were just 69,000.[101] When we think about the Blitz spirit, we need to remember that there was an element of self-selection to this process. Not everyone who was frightened had the means or opportunity to get out of the cities. But tens of thousands did. Those who stayed behind were the stoic volunteer rearguard – or those who had nowhere else to go.

This inequality of experience produced the much-resented phenomenon of Blitz tourism.[102] At night, curious groups of voyeuristic onlookers would find high vantage points to gaze on the destruction from a distance. Margaret Turpin, who had lost seven family members to a bomb, was sent from the East End to the village of Harefield, near Watford, which was perched on a hill about seventeen miles from Charing Cross. She bitterly resented the fact that the locals would go out to watch the fires in the evening: 'to view it like a spectacle – I couldn't stand that.'[103] After big raids, sightseers from elsewhere in London would descend on Blitzed boroughs. The *Daily Express* condemned the 'gawkers' who enjoyed a day out in central London after the 10 May 1941 raid:

> They came in droves to look at the seared ruins, to block the streets, to trample on hoses, to hold up fire engines, to gawk at the weary, blistered firemen, to fill the roads with their cars, to hamper the police, to stare at the grimy half-clad homeless. It was a day out.[104]

Similar 'gawking' had followed MOONLIGHT SONATA, as rural Warwickshire residents had travelled into Coventry to see the destruction. Police had had to erect roadblocks on the city's outskirts to keep them out. Whitley Bay, north of Tynemouth, was attacked several times in April 1941 as the Luftwaffe tried to bomb the newly completed aircraft carrier HMS *Victorious* before it could leave the nearby Vickers-Armstrongs works. So many sightseers came into town, hampering rescue work, that Civil Defence workers had to be delegated to crowd control.[105]

*

ARP warden Barbara Nixon was cycling up a grubby, derelict street in East London ten days after Black Saturday when she experienced her first Blitz 'incident'. 'Suddenly, before I heard a sound, the shabby, ill-lit, five-storey building ahead of me swelled out like a child's balloon, or like a Walt Disney house having hiccups', she remembered.

> I looked at it in astonishment that bricks and mortar could stretch like rubber. At the point when it must burst, the glass fell out. It did not hurtle, it simply cracked and dropped out [...] almost instantaneously there was a crash and a double explosion in the street to my right. As the blast of air reached me I left my saddle and sailed through the air, heading for the area railings. The tin hat on my shoulder took the impact.

Standing up, finding herself unhurt, she approached the remains of the wrecked tenement building thirty yards away. 'In the middle of the street lay the remains of a baby. It had been blown clean through the window, and burst on striking the roadway.' Nixon found a torn piece of curtain to wrap the cadaver in. Five or six other mutilated bodies lay scattered about, and she covered them in blankets. Eleven people in all had been killed and a larger number still badly injured. One teenage boy had had his leg torn off.

Nixon had not been sure what her reaction would be to the first sight of casualties. 'I had never seen a dead body, and I was terrified that I might be sick when I saw my first entrails.' But it turned out that, to her 'intense relief, pitiful and horrible though it was', she was not nauseated. Self-consciousness had afforded her a detachment from the grotesque situation she found herself in. Later, in other bloody incidents, she was simply too busy to reflect on the horror.[106]

Most Britons did not receive so stark an introduction to the human cost of the Blitz as Barbara Nixon's, but few people exposed to the bombing in 1940 and 1941 had ever undergone anything like it before. They wondered, as Nixon did, how they would cope with the possible sight of mutilation and death, and wondered too whether they would be able to adjust to the trauma of air raids. The author C. P. Snow discovered to his shame that he was 'less brave than the average man [...] I could just put some sort of face on it, but I dreaded the evening coming.'[107] George Beardmore, in Weald-stone in north-west London, was first sent leaping out of bed by the 'dull but resounding whhooomph!' of bombs landing on the local cinema and a branch of Barclay's Bank in the early hours of 23 August 1940. Listening for the siren thereafter became a part of his and his wife's nightly routine for many months. Lying beneath the sheets in the darkness like millions of other Londoners, listening to the distant crashing of explosives, Beardmore admitted to feeling 'hopelessly exposed and afraid'.[108]

For the unlucky minority who were persistently exposed to bombs, there was plenty of fear in the Blitz. Housewives surveyed in Hull said that the worst moments were when the raiders were directly overhead – with the noise of the droning aircraft engines, the shrieking of the plummeting bombs and the explosions especially frightening.[109] Bombs were ear-split-tingly loud, as were the anti-aircraft shells fired to stop them. Only one in four people surveyed in five London boroughs in mid-September 1940 said that they were getting more than four hours' sleep a night.[110] 'There is something especially vicious about this swishing and whistling of a bomb, because one sits underneath and waits where it is going to drop,' Austrian refugee Klara Modern wrote to her family in the USA: 'One goes to sleep with great effort, hoping that bombs will not drop on the house [...] closing one's ears to the noise of the guns and the nasty throbbing sound of the planes.'[111]

People tried to cope with their fear in different ways. Shelterers took books, cards, games, knitting and other distractions with them to pass the time and take their minds off what was going on above.[112] Some wrapped shawls round their heads, put in earplugs or doped themselves up with hot milk and aspirin to try to dull the noise. For the religious, there were the consolations of prayer. ('I heard German planes high up and found myself reciting the 23rd Psalm almost like a charm,' said one Fulham resident.[113])

The Ministry of Information tried to remind citizens of the low probability of being killed or injured in any given air raid.[114] In his booklet *Nerves versus Nazis*, war correspondent John Langdon-Davies suggested that anxious readers should stand over a map of their town and drop grains of salt on it to see how unlikely it was that a bomb would ever hit their house in particular.[115]

This attempt at reassurance, though, vied in people's minds with the less rational but entirely human instinct that the Germans were aiming at them specifically. One Liverpool mother insisted that her family unplug the radio each night in case the Luftwaffe was homing in on it.[116] There was an apparently common belief that surface shelters were visible to German air-crews looking down – perhaps a by-product of the exaggerated tales of RAF accuracy in raids on the Ruhr. 'We've put leaves and things over the top of ours to camouflage it, so they can't see us,' one London shelterer reported.[117] The perverse whimsies of fate played on people's nerves. Those who had been missed by previous air raids worried if it was 'their turn' next because their luck couldn't hold for ever (some who had actually been bombed, meanwhile, assumed they'd had their turn and were hereafter immune).[118]

Overt displays of fear were inhibited by diffidence and shame. Britons were fully aware of the cultural expectations of quiet sang-froid they were supposed to live by. Shelterers who showed signs of hysteria or emotional breakdown during raids were removed into ignominious quarantine in a corner.[119] No one wanted to be seen to be letting the side down. 'Few people will admit they are themselves afraid,' noted Mass Observation of East Enders in September 1940. To get around this, they would justify their anxious behaviour by ascribing it to concern for other members of their family, especially if they could point to women and children, who had greater leeway to be seen as fearful: 'I think I shall make the bedroom downstairs. It's the wife that worries me – a bundle of nerves', or 'I think I ought to go to the shelter – because of the children.'[120]

When in private, more people were willing to confess to their own fears. 'I've not heard a warning for weeks, but today I heard almost every one and each time it gave me a horrible heave inside,' Viola Bawtree of Sutton, south London, wrote in her diary in November 1940. 'I don't know how to describe it, like you might get if you heard a sudden wail of someone in distress, or a shriek of pain.'[121] Earlier that year Marie Lawrence admitted to getting 'in a terrific state' when she heard the bombers overhead. 'It was just like having a bad stomach ache. Slowly the pain would come on, get worse, and then lie down [...] then a nasty feeling and another would come over.'[122] Tom Harrisson noted in an article in the *British Medical Journal* in the spring of 1941 that after heavy bombing people could 'cave in': 'they have simply taken to bed and stayed in bed for weeks at a time.'[123] Confidential interviews in Hull showed many residents developing worrying behavioural problems after air raids. One housewife had begun wetting herself; another shook uncontrollably throughout raids; a dock worker had started drinking to excess every night to calm his nerves.[124]

Anxiety was expressed psychosomatically in an epidemic of peptic ulcers, gastrointestinal pain, lack of bladder control and menstrual problems. But the traumatised were often reluctant to talk to their doctors or other authority figures about what they assumed was a personal and shameful failure of character. Instead, they bought patent cures from the chemists, stayed off work sick or slumped into apathy.[125] Such silent suffering went unrecorded in sanguine tales of Britain cheerfully 'taking it'.

In the end, however, people were willing to endure. In some respects, the Blitz had turned out to be less horrible than they had expected. The Germans had not, for instance, used the kind of poison-gas bombs that had dominated so many of the nightmarish fantasies about bombing before the war. A great deal of civil defence spending in the 1930s had been devoted to the poison gas threat. More than 44 million gas masks had been distributed across Britain by September 1939 (cluttering the nation's lost-property offices for the next six years). The country began the war with the most elaborately trained and best-equipped gas decontamination service in the world.

In the event, it all proved unnecessary. The Germans, whether from want of ability or desire, did not employ gas as a strategic weapon against British cities.[126] This is not to say that fears about its use vanished immediately. In February 1941 Birmingham housewife Evelyn Saunders had it on good authority from the local rumour mill that the Germans would soon start dropping gas-filled incendiary bombs as 'the full force of Hitler's hate' was unleashed on Warwickshire.[127] Churchill too continued to worry that the Germans, frustrated by their lack of progress during the bombing campaign, might resort to chemical warfare to try to finish off the war quickly.[128] But such anxieties were happily unfounded. Shrapnel, masonry, glass, smoke and fire were the more prosaic threats to British bodies during the Blitz.

Bombing, it turned out, was something you could get used to. The

Blitz was preceded by two years of mental habituation in which the British adjusted their peacetime habits to the state-directed conduct of total war – by carrying gas masks, submitting to rationing and the black-out, practising air-raid and first-aid drills, building Anderson shelters and so on.[129] Even before Black Saturday, Londoners had been schooled in the customs and risks of aerial warfare. The most intense period of the bombing of the capital offered a certain predictable routine. Londoners may have been frightened, but at least they knew what to expect night by night. 'Hardening' helped to calm the nerves.

The most traumatic experiences of bombing during the Blitz, the ones in which it really did seem as though public confidence might collapse for a time, took place in cities in which the citizens had not experienced the same hardening before their first major raid. Coventry was one example. Mass Observation reporters spoke of 'an unprecedented dislocation and depression' after MOONLIGHT SONATA: there were 'more open signs of hysteria, terror, neurosis observed in one evening [in Coventry] than during the whole past two months together' in the capital. 'Women were seen to cry, scream, to tremble all over, to faint in the street, to attack firemen.'[130] An unnerving bolt from the blue – smashing up normal lives in a matter of minutes, rather like a modern terrorist attack – was more terrifying than a predictable nightly visitation from the Luftwaffe.

Ultimately, people were willing to endure the Blitz because they believed that the underlying political struggle in which they were taking part was a just one. Phoney War hesitations about whether the war was a worthwhile cause had vanished with Dunkirk. By the time the first German bombs fell in the autumn of 1940, the British had a clear sense who they were fighting against and why. The cause was popular, and the goal – the destruction of Hitler and the Nazi regime – clear as well.

Also – and perhaps more controversially – people endured because they believed the RAF was 'giving it back' to the Germans each night at least as hard. The desire for reprisal raids in 1940–41 was played down after the war by some Blitz historians like Tom Harrisson. Such a streak of vindictiveness did not fit into the Shire Folk myth, but it certainly existed as an important motivator at the time. In late September 1940 four out of five readers' letters sent to the *Daily Mail* were demands for reprisal raids on German cities to avenge the Blitz on London.[131] Harrisson's own Mass Observation recorded a typical conversation in Hull the following August:

E's getting it now. RAF's giving it to 'im worse than what we 'ad it.

    Yes, it's every night now they go over there. 'E won't be able to stand it like we did.[132]

This fillip that the RAF strategic bombing campaign gave to British morale in 1940–41 is probably the best justification for it (it was achieving little else). It was hugely important to British civilians to believe that they were not simply passive victims of violence, but rather participants in a struggle in which they were able to give as good as they were getting.

    Moreover, the intensity of the bombing duel in 1940–41 gave civilians hope that their ordeal would not last long because the conflict itself could not last long. Bombing was so unendurable that it could surely not be sustained for more than a few months more. As one person put it: 'If the bombing gets bad in both Britain and Germany this winter, I don't think the war will last long.'[133] Londoners in September 1940 had no idea that they would still be getting bombed from the air four years later. If they had known, it's interesting to wonder what the effect would have been on their willingness to continue indefinitely 'taking it'. Ignorance, perhaps, was bliss in the Blitz.

Part Five

'A NEW AND MOST BITTER PHASE OF THE WAR'

19

AMERICAN *LEBENSRAUM*

At 4 p.m. on Tuesday, 17 December 1940, Franklin D. Roosevelt, newly re-elected for an unprecedented third term as US President, held a press conference in the White House to announce a programme of aid for Great Britain. 'There is absolutely no doubt in the mind of a very overwhelming number of Americans that the best immediate defense of the United States is the success of Great Britain in defending itself,' he began:

> and that, therefore, quite aside from our historic and current interest in the survival of democracy [...] it is equally important from a selfish point of view of American defense, that we should do everything to help the British Empire to defend itself.

What he had in mind, Roosevelt explained, was neither a conventional extension of credit nor a simple gift. Rather, what he was proposing was that the American government should take over future British orders of war materials in US factories – after all, he pointed out, 'they are essentially the same kind of munitions that we use ourselves' – and then afterwards divvy them out 'as the military events of the future determine', keeping some of them for the use of the US armed forces and leasing or selling others to the British on terms to be negotiated after the war. The point, Roosevelt insisted, was to 'eliminate the dollar sign [...] the silly, foolish old dollar sign' from the whole question of aid to Britain. After all, he added in one of his folksy analogies,

> suppose my neighbor's home catches fire, and I have a length of garden hose ... if he can take my garden hose and connect it up with his hydrant, I may help him to put out his fire. Now, what do I do? I don't say to him before that operation, 'Neighbor, my garden hose

cost me \$15; you have to pay me \$15 for it' [...] I don't want \$15 – I want my garden hose back after the fire is over.[1]

In this way, as Churchill put it in his war memoirs, 'the glorious conception of Lend-Lease was proclaimed' to the world. In 1949 the former prime minister was keen to place his own fingerprints all over FDR's decision nine years earlier. As he pointed out in *Their Finest Hour*, a week before the White House press conference Churchill had sent a long letter to Roosevelt – 'one of the most important I ever wrote' – laying out the precarity of Britain's financial position. 'The danger of Great Britain being destroyed by a swift, overwhelming blow has for the time being very greatly receded' thanks to victory in the Battle of Britain, he noted. But any programme for victory would have to rely on enormous material assistance from the United States. And

> the more rapid and abundant the flow of munitions and ships which you are able to send us, the sooner will our dollar credits be exhausted [...] the moment approaches when we shall no longer be able to pay cash for shipping and other supplies.

From this letter 'there sprang a wonderful decision', Churchill concluded in 1949.[2] In fact, although the missive from London may have helped to crystallise Roosevelt's thoughts on the matter, the American president had already been musing about ways to resolve Britain's dollar problem for some weeks. In early November he had told his Cabinet that 'the time would surely come when Great Britain would need loans or credits', and that some leasing arrangement for war *matériel* might be a way to work around the restrictions of Congress's Neutrality Acts.[3]

More fundamentally, Roosevelt had already decided to make Britain's survival a paramount objective of US foreign policy. As we saw earlier, it was not at all inevitable that he would do that after the fall of France in the summer of 1940. Making a heavy investment in the UK war effort was a risk, given the possibility that the British would collapse as the French had done. But the RAF's victory against the Luftwaffe's daylight attacks and the stoicism of British civilians under night bombing had persuaded FDR that the transatlantic partnership was worth investing in. On 11 November, Roosevelt received a planning memorandum on future US grand strategy drafted by Admiral Stark, Chief of Naval Operations. Stark posited that 'if

Britain wins decisively against Germany we could win everywhere; but that if she loses the problem confronting us would be very great; and, while we might not lose everywhere, we might, possibly, not win anywhere.' Consequent to this, Stark argued that 'the continued existence of the British Empire, combined with building up a strong protection in our home areas, will do most to [...] promote our principal national interests.'[4]

Roosevelt never formally responded to this 'Plan Dog' memorandum. But then, as David Reynolds points out, 'presidential silence often signified tacit consent' in the FDR administration.[5] The assumptions about the primacy of the Anglo-American relationship expressed in 'Plan Dog' represented the kernel of US strategic planning from November 1940 onwards. Lend-Lease was simply a practical expression of that commitment.

The details of the Lend-Lease bill ('An Act to Promote the Defense of the United States') were published on 10 January 1941. It became law on 11 March, having been approved by Congress by a comfortable, though largely partisan, majority. Churchill called it 'the most unsordid act in the whole of recorded history' in a Mansion House speech that November.[6] 'It transformed immediately [our] whole position,' he added in his memoirs: 'it made us free to shape by agreement long-term plans of vast extent for all our needs.'[7] Back in May 1940, when deliberating on Britain's chances in the 'Certain Eventuality' of a French surrender, the chiefs of staff had been emphatic that obtaining substantial credits from the United States would be an 'indispensable condition to the successful conduct of the war' in the long term.[8] Lend-Lease confirmed Washington's commitment to that condition.

But in the short term Lend-Lease offered little practical assistance to the British war effort. Indeed its detailed terms, once it had emerged from the legislative process, were deeply disquieting to the War Cabinet. No Lend-Lease appropriations would be used to pay for British orders for war materials placed in the United States prior to 11 March 1941, orders that already represented a staggering burden on HM Treasury. Roosevelt, like many members of Congress, was under the impression that Britain's financial resources were adequate to cover its standing liabilities. 'They have plenty of exchange, you know,' he had reassured reporters at his 17 December press conference. The problem as he saw it was not in paying for existing orders, but in additions to those orders.[9]

Throughout the winter of 1940–41 the Americans continued to demand payment firmly from Britain's dwindling gold and dollar reserves. Six days after the unveiling of his Lend-Lease proposals FDR casually informed the British that a US Navy destroyer was on its way to South Africa to collect £50 million from the fast-shrinking imperial bullion reserve. Shortly before the final vote on Lend-Lease, FDR's Treasury Secretary, Henry Morgenthau, gave London a blunt ultimatum: to sweeten the bill's passage, the massive British-owned American Viscose Corporation would have to be sold off to a US banking consortium at a fire-sale price as a gesture of goodwill. On 13 March the British learned that another US destroyer was on its way to Cape Town to pick up gold. An exasperated Churchill drafted a complaint to Roosevelt, never sent, that the American actions were akin to 'a sheriff collecting the last assets of a helpless debtor'.[10]

Of course, for the leader of the largest empire in the world to fume about inequitable treatment at the hands of another country might have been regarded as a bit rich. An Indian or Malayan taxpayer could have pointed out to Churchill that the limitless IOUs being run up in London at that moment by Sterling Area nations – IOUs that were allowing the British to finance much of their war effort on terms convenient to themselves – were a much heavier-handed form of economic appropriation than anything represented by Lend-Lease. Still, it was a novel experience for the British to be on the receiving end of such humiliating treatment. And the final terms by which Lend-Lease would be settled after the war remained unnegotiated, opening up the ominous possibility that, even if Hitler were defeated, Britain might find its wealth dissipated, its empire dismantled and its supplicant status to the emerging American superpower made permanent. The United States, protected by the Royal Navy from German aggression, was, it seemed, sanctimoniously extending the hand of charity while quietly ensuring it profited from the British Empire's discomfiture.

Already, in order to secure the delivery of fifty ageing US Navy destroyers of dubious military value, the British had been required to offer to the United States ninety-nine-year rent-free leases on several Atlantic territories extending from Newfoundland to Guyana, including Bermuda, Jamaica and the Bahamas. 'This rather smacks of Russia's demands on Finland,' Jock Colville noted sourly in his diary.[11] Beaverbrook complained that 'they have taken our bases without valuable consideration. They have taken our gold [...] and offered us a thoroughly inadequate service in return.'[12] The Americans, complained Lord Chatfield, would 'fight the battle for freedom to the last Briton, but save their own skins!'[13] That proud imperialist Leo Amery hinted darkly of Roosevelt's bid for 'American *Lebensraum*'.[14]

*

A few weeks before Roosevelt's Lend-Lease press conference, Neville Chamberlain, staying at a country home in Hampshire, had died, quietly and without fuss, from the terminal bowel cancer he had been diagnosed with earlier in the year. 'People ask me how we are ever going to win this war,' he wrote in one of his last letters to his sister Hilda:

> I suppose it's a very natural question, but I don't think the time has come to answer it. We must just go on fighting as hard as we can in the belief that some time – perhaps sooner than we think – the other side will crack.[15]

Churchill would not have disagreed. There was, yet, no obvious theory of victory in the final months of 1940, given the catastrophes of the spring, only a hope that something would come along sooner or later: that the German economy would collapse, the peoples of conquered Europe rise in revolt or perhaps RAF bombing drive the maddened Nazi citizenry to depose their leader – 'more an article of faith than the product of a coherent plan', as one historian has called it.[16] Chamberlain's hopes that war could be avoided entirely or, failing that, at least be fought on a strict basis of limited liability had both perished. Now a protracted, total war, with all its portentous implications for long-term British power, was unavoidable. Somehow it would have to be won anyway: the cost of failure was too great and terrible to imagine.

Increased American assistance would, of course, be an enormous asset going ahead. But, as Chamberlain recognised even before the announcement of Lend-Lease, there could be no great military help from across the Atlantic in the immediate term. 'It will be a long time before they can give us any material aid to speak of. Their neglect of their defences has been even greater than ours and they haven't even the potential capacity to produce what is needed to fill the gaps.'[17] Vast amounts of British money had been spent in the USA so far in the war, but little as yet had actually been delivered.

Much could be expected from American factories, armouries and shipyards in the future, but in 1941 there was still precious little of a military-industrial complex available in the United States to provide, as FDR evocatively put it, 'the arsenal of democracy'. Over the nine months following Lend-Lease's passage in Congress, $14 billion in aid would be promised – but only $1 billion of munitions actually delivered to Britain. Only 1 per cent of the armaments used by forces of the British Empire in 1941 would be supplied under Lend-Lease terms. Britain received just 2,400 aircraft from American manufacturers that year – the equivalent of about six weeks' worth of UK output – with all but 100 of them paid for in cash. Food supplies were a more significant immediate by-product of the Lend-Lease deal, and far from unimportant. But you could not bring down the Third Reich with Spam alone.

For the time being, then, the British Empire would need to continue to confront the Axis powers largely alone: on the steep Atlantic stream, in the olive groves of the Aegean and the febrile wastes of the North African desert, in the black, brumal skies over the Ruhr. There were many painful defeats still to come. The rout was not over yet. 'We are entering on a new and most bitter phase of the war,' James Lansdale Hodson wrote the same month that Lend-Lease passed into US law. 'The next six months will be crucial and terrific. On them our fate depends.'[18]

20

SHAPELESS, MEASURELESS PERIL

The RMS *Empress of Britain* was about seventy miles north-west of the Atlantic coast of Ireland on the morning of 26 October 1940 when her lookouts sighted a Focke-Wulf Fw 200 Condor bomber heading straight for the ship. A 550-lb bomb struck the vessel amidships and penetrated the deck, enveloping her in yellow-black smoke. 'Christ! That was a bloody bomb!' one of the passengers, Colonel Stevenson of the Seaforth Highlanders, shouted as he emerged from below, blood flowing from lacerations on his face caused by flying wood splinters. The Condor made a second pass, machine-guns strafing the ship, but missed with its bomb this time. On the third pass it was luckier. The explosion set off a fire which greedily began to consume the liner's innards. The lights and communications systems failed as the electrical system sputtered out. All water pressure ceased, meaning that the ship's firefighting equipment was inoperable too. Dust, smoke and flames obscured vision within the cabins and passageways of the dying vessel.

Empress of Britain had no business being at war at all. She was intended for an altogether more serene existence. The 42,348-ton liner had been built on the Clyde by the Canadian Pacific Steamship Company and had gone into service in 1931 to compete in the lucrative transatlantic passenger trade. Slightly smaller than the *Titanic*, she was not the largest liner afloat in the 1930s. But what she lacked in size she made up for in luxurious features: swimming-pools, Turkish baths, cinemas, concert halls, gymnasiums, squash and tennis courts, hairdressing and beauty salons. In her brief happy life before the war she had carried millionaires, Hollywood celebrities and members of the royal family from Southampton to Quebec and back, as well as on eight world cruises. At the outbreak of hostilities she was requisitioned as a troopship and her gaudy peacetime colours gave way to a sombre grey. On 23 September 1940, at the start of what turned out to be her last voyage, she departed Suez, rounding the coast of Africa en route to

Liverpool with over 200 military personnel and civilians on board in addition to her 419 crew. *Empress of Britain* travelled alone and unescorted on this final trip. Her high speed (an average of 20 knots) would, it was hoped, protect her from German U-boats.

As the Condor departed the scene, it left behind it shrieks and crying and the smell of burning varnish. Mr Howell, the *Empress of Britain*'s fourth officer, discovered an injured woman in the lounge, bloodied and dishevelled, screaming for help by the side of a dead or unconscious soldier. He half-carried, half-led her out to the stairway, tripping over bodies and wreckage along the way. 'He's there – there ... don't you understand? He'll die ... go and help him,' she wailed at Howell. The ship's officer put on a gas mask and tried to return to the lounge to find the prostrate soldier. But the smoke and heat made it impossible: he could feel his face burning beneath the mask's rubber. Pitch bubbled and steamed in *Empress of Britain*'s planking.[1]

After thirty minutes the captain gave the order to abandon ship. On deck, smashed and burning lifeboats hung uselessly from their davits. One winchman yelled at the passengers mobbing the boats: 'for Christ's sake, get a move on! Me backside's burning off.' Jimmy England, an old crew hand, middle-aged and plump, no hero to look at, tied a water-soaked handkerchief around his mouth and journeyed up and down inside the ship five times to rescue comrades, navigating his way around its flooded and burning passageways with great ingenuity. Other crewmen prevailed upon him to stop before his luck ran out, but he ignored them. He did not return from his sixth trip below.[2]

Twenty-five crew members, including Jimmy England, and twenty passengers were killed, the youngest of them sixteen years old. The survivors were picked up by two Royal Navy destroyers and an armed trawler. *Empress of Britain* was assumed to be lost, but to everyone's surprise she did not sink. She could no longer move under her own power, but a salvage party which re-boarded her the morning after the Condor's attack was able to attach tow ropes to two tugs. They began hauling her towards land, though at a fraction of her former speed, exposing her to new dangers.

The U-boat *U-32*, alerted to the opportunity, moved into position to intercept the crippled giant on the morning of 28 October, while she was still far out to sea north-west of Co. Donegal. Wounded, sluggish, she offered an easy target. *U-32* fired three torpedoes at the liner, two of which hit and detonated. The ship's boilers exploded, and she began to flood.

Soon she was listing heavily to port. The tugs slipped their lines, and the RMS *Empress of Britain* went down in nine minutes. She would be, as it turned out, the largest British ship sunk by a U-boat in the Second World War. The German press gloried at the destruction of what it called 'the plutocrats' liner'. The Condor captain received a Knight's Cross for his efforts. The skipper of *U-32* got rather less. His submarine was captured two days after the *Empress of Britain* sank, and he spent the rest of the war in a POW camp.[3]

The *Empress of Britain* was just one of fifty-six British and Allied merchant ships sunk in the North Atlantic in October 1940, one of 349 sunk that year and one of 2,223 sunk throughout the whole of the Second World War.[4] The Battle of the Atlantic, as it became known, had begun on the day war broke out with the torpedoing of the passenger liner SS *Athenia*. It continued until 7 May 1945, when the little Norwegian steamer *Sneland I*, carrying a cargo of coal in the Firth of Forth, achieved melancholy fame by being the last merchant vessel sunk by a U-boat. In between, the Kriegsmarine's submarine service had mounted the longest and most existentially threatening challenge to British survival in the whole war. Pre-war strategists had feared the aerial knock-out blow. The silhouette of a submarine periscope turned out to be a far greater danger to British survival.

And this, really, made eminent sense. Britain was either a maritime nation or it was nothing. Seaborne lines of communication were essential to its day-to-day economy and society. In peacetime, the United Kingdom relied on thirty to thirty-five ships of 1,600 tons or more arriving at its ports every twenty-four hours, disembarking 68 million tons of imports a year – food, lumber, oil, iron ore and other vital raw materials.[5] Two-thirds of the calories consumed by Britons in the 1930s came from overseas.[6] Were the Germans to choke off this supply, the UK would be incapable of continuing to fight. Churchill claimed afterwards that the U-boat threat was 'the only thing that ever really frightened me'. It demanded great heroism on both sides, but there was nothing romantic about it. It was not a war

> of flaring battles and glittering achievements. It manifested itself through statistics, diagrams, and curves unknown to the nation, incomprehensible to the public. How much would the U-boat warfare reduce our imports and shipping? Would it ever reach the point where our life would be destroyed? Here was no field for gestures or sensations; only the slow, cold drawing of lines on charts,

which showed potential strangulation [...] either the food, supplies, and arms from the New World and from the British Empire arrived across the oceans, or they failed.[7]

'How willingly,' Churchill admitted, 'would I have exchanged a full-scale attempt at invasion for this shapeless, measureless peril, expressed in charts, curves, and statistics!'[8]

*

The foundational terms of the Battle of the Atlantic were set on 19 June 1935, with the signing of the Anglo-German Naval Agreement. This bilateral treaty gave the Third Reich the right to build a new navy with a maximum tonnage up to 35 per cent of that of the British fleet. Hitler eventually denounced the agreement in April 1939. But it formed the basis for the Kriegsmarine's expansion in the years immediately preceding the Second World War and shaped the enemy fleet that faced the Royal Navy when that conflict broke out.

The agreement has not gone down well among most historians. It has been characterised as 'a triumph for brisk Nazi bargaining tactics' and 'a conspicuous symptom of Britain's great power decline'.[9] Churchill described it in his memoirs as a 'marked gain to Hitler at an important and critical moment in his policy'.[10] The Treaty did have several undesirable consequences. Germany's possession of large warships had been forbidden by the Treaty of Versailles. By signing the agreement, Britain became the first Great Power to sanction German defiance of one of Versailles's arms limitation clauses. Having already conceded the principle, it was difficult to mount a persuasive complaint when Hitler abrogated the rest of those restrictions later. The British did not consult the French before signing the agreement, though France's security was certainly affected by it, damaging the two countries' subsequent relationship. Any treaty that legitimised German military rearmament might appear, on the face of it, to have been nothing more than a short-sighted concession to a belligerent, expansionist Third Reich, a hallmark of the naivety and self-destructiveness of the whole appeasement era.

But the Royal Navy, which strongly supported the agreement, knew what it was doing. The greatest threat that Germany might pose to British maritime power in a future war, it believed, would be to attack the UK's trade lines of communication with relatively small, fast vessels suitable for commerce raiding (*Kreuzerkrieg*). By 1935 the British feared that Hitler would begin building lots of U-boats, light cruisers and *Panzerschiffe* ('pocket battleships') perfect for such piratical tactics. The point of the Anglo-German Naval Agreement was to channel Nazi Germany's taste for warship construction into what were, so far as the British were concerned, less menacing avenues. If the Germans were determined to build a new fleet, then no one could stop them. But Hitler could, perhaps, be lulled into building as ineffective a fleet as possible. The agreement specifically condoned the construction of full-size battleships and aircraft carriers; it therefore encouraged the Germans to build them. For the Royal Navy, this was all to the good.[11]

By the beginning of 1939, thanks to the Treaty, Hitler's Kriegsmarine had a little bit of everything and nothing much of any one thing – two giant 42,000-ton battleships (*Bismarck* and *Tirpitz*) and two aircraft carriers under construction; two smaller 32,000-ton battleships (*Gneisenau* and *Scharnhorst*) already completed; three *Panzerschiffe*; three modern cruisers; twenty destroyers; and about fifty U-boats, half of which were suitable for Atlantic operations. It was an ostensibly impressive fleet. But it was too 'balanced' to be capable of any single mission effectively. There were not enough battleships to mount a serious challenge to the Royal Navy's command of the sea. At the same time, there were not enough commerce raiders to perform a really threatening *Kreuzerkrieg* campaign. The biggest vessels proved, in the event, to be a huge waste of resources. *Bismarck* performed one theatrical sortie into the Atlantic in the spring of 1941 before being sunk. *Tirpitz* spent most of the war skulking from one Norwegian fjord to another, never firing its main guns in anger. The two aircraft carriers were scrapped before completion.

This was deeply frustrating for Admiral Karl Dönitz, the commander-in-chief of the Nazi U-boat fleet. Dönitz was a veteran of Germany's submarine service in the First World War, which had mounted a ferocious campaign of blockade against Britain in the first half of 1917 that had come close to choking off the Atlantic line of communication to North America. Dönitz believed that with larger numbers – at least 300 submarines – and more sophisticated tactics his U-boats could succeed a second time. But he faced the indifference of many of his Kriegsmarine colleagues who preferred the glamour of big capital ships to tiny, drab submersibles. He was also at the mercy of Hitler's mercurial approach to rearmament. In January

1939 it seemed briefly as though the German Navy's expansion plans would be prioritised over those of the Army and Luftwaffe. Almost 250 U-boats were to be built, along with a plethora of other surface vessels. Enormous dry dock facilities were begun at Wilhelmshaven and Hamburg.[12]

But by the invasion of Poland that autumn Hitler's attention had already shifted back again to Germany's land and air forces. Between September 1939 and June 1940, despite having originally been promised twenty-nine new U-boats a month, Dönitz received an average of two. That, plus the fact that even after delivery from the shipyard a new submarine required three to four months of trials and training before it could become operational, meant that during the first ten months of the war Dönitz had to rely largely on the meagre forces he had possessed at its outbreak.[13] He was given permission to start commerce raiding against Britain from the first day of the war, but the initial results were disappointing. Not only did Dönitz lack numbers and reliable torpedoes (serious malfunctions in their detonators and depth-keeping equipment were not identified and fixed for many months), but the war's geography initially worked against him. Having to operate from Germany's North Sea ports, his U-boats could only enter the North Atlantic hunting grounds by first making the lengthy journey around Scotland, greatly cutting down their patrol endurance.

Two of the more intrepid of Dönitz's commanders pulled off spectacular coups in the first weeks of the war when they sank the aircraft carrier HMS *Courageous* off the coast of Ireland and the battleship HMS *Royal Oak* at anchor in Scapa Flow. But the tally of merchantmen was disappointing. Between the start of the war and June 1940 British and neutral merchant shipping losses from all causes (including aircraft, mines and surface vessels as well as submarines) averaged only 233,000 tons a month, 74,000 of these tons in the North Atlantic.[14] This was far below Dönitz's goal of sinking 750,000 tons a month, which he estimated would be enough to force Britain out of the war within a year.[15]

*

The Royal Navy, then, could look back on the first ten months of the war in the Atlantic with a certain amount of satisfaction. The losses of *Courageous* and *Royal Oak* were embarrassing (and tragic – 1,353 men died) but did not gravely disturb the naval balance of power. One of Hitler's pocket battleships, *Admiral Graf Spee*, which had represented Germany in the 1937

Coronation naval review in Portsmouth, made a brief sortie into the South Atlantic in the autumn of 1939, sinking 50,000 tons of merchant shipping. But it was then intercepted by three British cruisers off the coast of Uruguay and forced to take shelter in Montevideo. *Graf Spee*'s captain, believing himself (wrongly) to be trapped by the bulk of the RN fleet lurking just beyond the River Plate estuary, scuttled his ship and committed suicide. This was the only serious German attempt to perform surface *Kreuzerkrieg* before the fall of France.

As for the defence of merchant shipping from the U-boat, two pre-war innovations – one administrative, one technological – appeared to have, if not neutralised, then at least significantly diminished the submarine threat. The first was the organisation of merchant vessels into convoys which could be shepherded to their destination by specialist anti-submarine escort vessels. The introduction of convoys had been deeply contested in 1917. But its value in reducing the danger of U-boat attacks was so obvious in hindsight that it was introduced on key coastal and oceanic routes immediately on the outbreak of war in September 1939. The first outward-bound transatlantic convoy sailed on 7 September; the first homeward-bound one left Halifax, Nova Scotia, twelve days later. Similar convoy systems were arranged from Sierra Leone and Gibraltar to the UK and back.

The technological innovation was ASDIC, better known today as 'sonar', a detection system that could locate submarines by listening for the echoed reflections of underwater sound pulses. ASDIC had been fitted on RN destroyers starting in 1923, and by the outbreak of war there were 180 vessels equipped with it.[16] Although the details of the system remained top secret, the Admiralty deliberately leaked hints about ASDIC's amazing anti-submarine efficacy in the 1930s to discourage the Germans from bothering to build U-boats.[17] There was an element of disinformation to this, but the Navy's basic confidence in ASDIC was not feigned. In exercises in 1936, six out of ten ASDIC-guided destroyer attacks on submarines were judged to have been 'decisive'.[18] The Admiralty remarked the following year that 'the submarine menace will never be what is was before [...] we have taken effective steps to prevent that.'[19] Churchill wrote a memorandum to Chamberlain in March 1939 claiming that 'the submarine has been mastered'.[20]

This self-assurance encouraged complacency. If the U-boat had been mastered and the Germans knew it, the argument went, then there would be no Battle of the Atlantic in a future war: what, then, was the point of spending lots of money on convoy protection? Anti-submarine vessels were given low priority in rearmament budgeting. In March 1938, under pressure to reduce the naval estimates, the government deferred the building of two new flotillas of destroyers, two escort vessels, three patrol vessels and four minesweepers.[21] It was only a few days before the outbreak of war that the Admiralty finally placed orders for fifty-six new anti-submarine escort sloops equipped with ASDIC, depth charges and four-inch guns. These were the first of the so-called 'Flower' class corvettes which would be vital to the defence of the North Atlantic trade route over the next six years. But most of the Flower class corvettes would not be ready for commissioning until 1941. Only about 100 vessels suitable for anti-submarine escort were available to the Royal Navy in September 1939, a very modest force to defend up to 3,000 ocean-going merchant ships.[22] As a result, only an average of two escorts could be provided for each transatlantic convoy at the start of the war. And these could only operate as far as twelve degrees longitude west – barely beyond the west coast of Ireland – or occasionally fifteen degrees west. Beyond that, the merchantmen were on their own.[23]

Nor was this escort force particularly well trained or organised. Perhaps lulled into torpor by its confidence in ASDIC, the Admiralty had paid little attention to escort tactics and procedures before the war. No practical exercises in how best to protect a merchant convoy using the new technology were carried out during the 1920s or 1930s.[24] Scant energy was devoted to thinking about the role of airpower in a future Battle of the Atlantic either, though it had been key in 1917. The RAF's Coastal Command had been directed in 1937 to concentrate its role on reconnaissance for the main battle fleet and attacks on enemy capital ships, not the defence of merchant vessels.[25] Coastal Command in September 1939 possessed only three squadrons of aircraft with range and armament suitable for anti-submarine ship protection. These squadrons could mount a few patrols up to eight degrees west.[26]

All the same, by the end of May 1940, Dönitz's men had not been able to take much advantage of any of these weaknesses. Their U-boats had so far only succeeded in sinking 215 merchant ships and two escorts for the loss of twenty-three of their own vessels. Almost all these sinkings had taken place in home waters around the north-east of Scotland, the Straits of Dover and off southern Ireland and south-west of Cornwall. Almost all of them – 200 – had been ships sailing independently or stragglers which had broken off from a convoy. While any vessel sunk was an individual defeat for the

British, this was not the sort of tally that was going to win Germany the war. Such relatively affordable losses could justify a certain confidence in the robustness of the lines of maritime communication.[27]

What transformed the situation calamitously was the fall of France. The loss of continental markets meant a great westward reconfiguration of Britain's maritime trading network, forcing its mariners to travel much further distances through far rougher waters in more dangerous circumstances. During the Phoney War, 36 per cent of Britain's dry cargo imports had come from North America. By the end of 1940, that share had risen to 51 per cent.[28] The average round-time length of voyages for ships bringing imports into Great Britain increased from ninety days to 122.[29]

Moreover, the whole military geography of the Atlantic war was altered with Paris's surrender. The U-boats were now released from their captivity in the south-eastern nook of the North Sea. The first of Dönitz's submarines arrived in the port of Lorient in north-western France on 7 July 1940. By August a string of U-boat bases were under construction there and elsewhere along the French Atlantic coast – in Brest, La Pallice, St Nazaire, Bordeaux – each with elaborate reinforced concrete pens that proved virtually invulnerable to RAF Bomber Command's attacks.[30] At a stroke, 450 miles had been eliminated from a submarine's journey to the hunting areas, adding up to a week to the length of time it could remain on patrol. From western France, U-boats could now operate as far as twenty-five degrees longitude west, far beyond the range of British surface escorts in the summer of 1940.[31] And the elaborate dockyard facilities in ports like Lorient, captured from the French intact, allowed Dönitz to put 22 per cent more of his boats to sea at any one time.[32]

Faced with this sudden outflanking manoeuvre, the British had no choice but to re-route their Atlantic maritime traffic as far away from the Bay of Biscay as possible. Ships from Halifax, which had previously made their way south of Ireland to reach the UK's west coast ports via St George's Channel, now had to steer the far northern route around Ulster and enter the Irish Sea through the North Channel. Those bound for London and the southern ports (while they still could) had to go around the north of Scotland. This meant, for one thing, that Dönitz's small coastal U-boats operating from Norway could now prey on traffic travelling down the Scottish east coast.[33] For British merchantmen it also meant a longer and much more hazardous journey through rougher northern Atlantic waters. Ships that were never designed to take the battering of Force-8 gales south

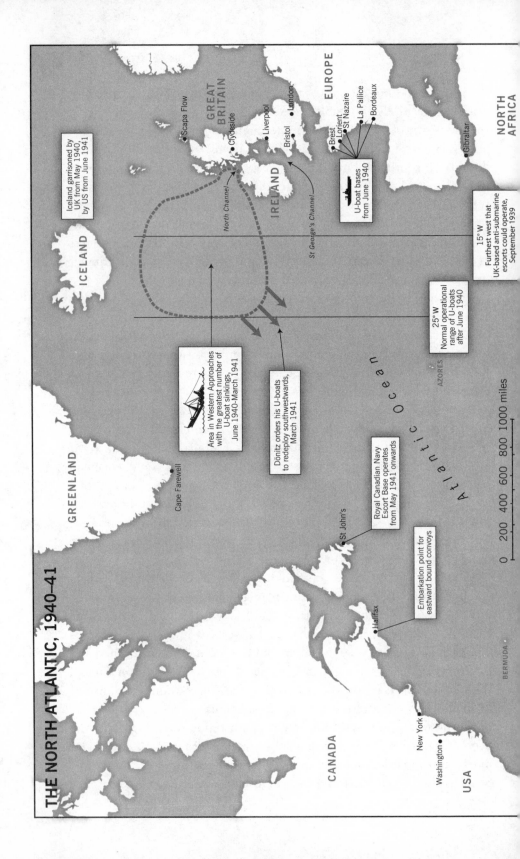

THE NORTH ATLANTIC, 1940–41

ICELAND

Iceland garrisoned by UK from May 1940, by US from June 1941

GREENLAND

Cape Farewell

GREAT BRITAIN

Scapa Flow
Clydeside
Liverpool
Bristol
London

IRELAND

North Channel
St George's Channel

EUROPE

Brest
Lorient
St Nazaire
La Pallice
Bordeaux

U-boat bases from June 1940

NORTH AFRICA

Gibraltar

15° W
Furthest west that UK-based anti-submarine escorts could operate, September 1939

25° W
Normal operational range of U-boats after June 1940

Area in Western Approaches with the greatest number of U-boat sinkings, June 1940–March 1941

Dönitz orders his U-boats to redeploy southwestwards, March 1941

Royal Canadian Navy Escort Base operates from May 1941 onwards

St John's

Halifax

Embarkation point for eastward bound convoys

AZORES

Atlantic Ocean

0 200 400 600 800 1000 miles

CANADA

New York

Washington

USA

BERMUDA

of Iceland now had to risk foundering under waves that could be seventy metres high. Crews unused to thick summer fogs and drift ice had to navigate these lethal natural hazards as well as scanning the horizon for periscopes.

The threat of invasion meant that the already stretched escort fleet was stretched yet further. Destroyers, corvettes and other anti-submarine patrol boats had to be redeployed away from the Western Approaches shipping lanes to southern England to be ready to sally against SEA LION transports. This meant that the average number of escorts per convoy fell from an already paltry two in January 1940 to half an escort in July.[34]

This collection of fortuitous circumstances would produce what U-boat crews would later look back on, in grimmer days, as their first 'happy time' of the war. Merchant tonnage losses in the North Atlantic rose from fewer than 50,000 tons in May 1940 to 296,000 tons in June. They averaged 227,000 tons a month for the next half a year. Total British losses in all waters in the second half of 1940 averaged over 400,000 tons. And only eight U-boats were lost between July and December, compared with fifteen in the first half of 1940.[35] Dönitz's tally included the savage mauling in October of two convoys, SC 7 and HX 79, which had thirty-two out of eighty-four ships sunk between them, in an early demonstration of what co-ordinated U-boat attacks could achieve against weakly escorted prey. But most of the destruction during the 'happy time' was wreaked by submarines operating alone in the North-Western Approaches against independently sailing ships such as RMS *Empress of Britain*.

This was the era of the 'U-boat ace' captains who rose to fame back in Germany – Joachim Schepke, Günther Prien (who sank HMS *Royal Oak*) and, most celebrated of all, 'Silent Otto' Kretschmer, who sent forty-five ships of 258,900 cumulative tons to the ocean bed during his brief career, a figure not surpassed by any other German submarine commander of the war. Kretschmer's patrol of 25 July–5 August 1940 illustrates something of the misery of the British Merchant Navy at this time. Operating from Lorient, Kretschmer's U-boat *U-99* sank three independently sailing merchantmen off the north-west coast of Ireland which were carrying a total of 21,000 tons of metals, hides, grain and fruit. Then he turned on the outward-bound convoy OB-191, sinking another merchant vessel and damaging three more.[36] OB-191's escorts had abandoned their charges before Kretschmer's attack, searching fruitlessly for another suspected U-boat. This indiscipline, typical of the period – escorts in 1940 would sometimes chase off as much as fifty miles in search of enemy submarines, inevitably without result – allowed Kretschmer to slip right into the ranks of the convoy itself at night and fire torpedoes from the surface at just a few hundred metres' range, unseen and unopposed.[37]

Even when escorts stayed on station, they now discovered a disconcerting flaw in their defensive tactics that wily U-boat commanders like Kretschmer were quick to exploit. ASDIC, so effective at detecting submerged submarines, was useless if the enemy attacked on the surface instead. It was virtually impossible to spot the sleek night-time silhouette of a U-boat lurking among columns of much larger merchantmen. Even if it was spotted, a Type VII German submarine with a surface speed of seventeen knots was faster than a Flower class corvette and could make its getaway without difficulty. The result so often in that bleak second half of 1940 was, as John Terraine puts it, 'dire confusion in the ghostly moonlight; ubiquitous explosions; the cries of abandoned sailors in the water; the helplessness of the weak and distracted escort'.[38] The British remember that year for its glorious Spitfire victories. But in the darkness, many hundreds of miles from the wheat fields of Kent and Sussex, the Royal Navy's 'Few' was losing its battles against ghostly persecutors far more unremitting than Göring's Luftwaffe.

*

The Merchant Navy that endured the 'happy time' of Kretschmer and his comrades occupied a curious place in British mid-century mythology. Central to national self-identity yet underpaid and neglected, its men were valorised in principle even as they were quietly disdained in practice.[39] The idea of the British as a maritime people was a commonplace – 'we are a seafaring race and we understand the call of the sea', as Churchill put it in 1941.[40] The vital role of maritime trade to the UK's wealth and influence was noted in every schoolchild's geography book. Yet though the British merchant fleet remained the largest in the world in 1939, the economic weakness of the inter-war years had withered it. On the eve of the war it comprised about 17.4 million total gross tons, ranging from the 81,000-ton passenger liner RMS *Queen Mary*, pride of the Cunard White Star Line, to little coastal colliers of a few hundred tons which shuttled coal from the Northumbrian and Welsh pits to London's ravenous power stations.[41] Of the 2,400 vessels of the ocean-going fleet, about 500 were oil tankers. Another 739 were 'tramp steamers', owned mostly by small companies, which wandered back and forth across the world's sea lanes picking up cargoes as they could.[42]

Around one third of the world's deep-water tonnage in 1939 was British-registered. But the British fleet had declined in size by 7.7 per cent since 1914, while those of the United States and Japan had risen by 361 per cent and 162 per cent respectively.[43] British ships were ageing. Over 6 million new tons had been launched in the three years before the First World War, compared with just 3.9 million tons completed between 1932 and 1938.[44] The decline of the coal trade between the wars had discouraged new investment. Only a quarter of British vessels in 1939 used modern diesel engines (compared with 62 per cent of Scandinavian ships), making them relatively slow and inefficient. Most British tramp steamers were dirty, rat- and cockroach-infested, coal-puffing relics, barely capable of 8 or 9 knots under full steam, while equivalent Norwegian ships could manage up to 13 knots.[45] Accommodation and victualling on British-flagged vessels were notoriously sub-standard.

During the early 1930s, when the economic malaise was at its worst, up to 3.5 million tons of British shipping had been laid up unused for want of cargoes.[46] Unemployment among British merchant sailors in the 1930s had rarely fallen below 20 per cent, hardly encouraging young men of initiative and talent to consider a career at sea. The fleet's manpower represented Britain's global reach. Of the roughly 193,000 men regularly engaged on vessels before the war, 132,000 were UK residents (one in twenty non-white), with 51,000 of them 'lascars' – Indian, Chinese, African and Arab sailors who had signed on overseas under special articles of service.[47] Most British-born merchant sailors came from the working-class slums of Liverpool, London, Glasgow and Tyneside. Many were well into middle age, though the youngest cabin and deck boys were children – Kretschmer's *U-99* drowned a fourteen- and a fifteen-year-old in October 1940.

Even before the hazards of war intruded, life at sea had been austere and precarious. Men on tramp steamers were expected to provide their own bedding, usually a straw palliasse or coarse sack. Living conditions 'compared unfavourably with a dirty farmyard'.[48] Food was unrefrigerated and consisted largely of salted meat and tinned butter. There was little ventilation and not much fresh water, perilous in the baking conditions of the Red Sea or Persian Gulf in summer. Seamen were three times more likely than other men of their age to die of TB, three times more likely than coal miners to die in an industrial accident.[49]

Pay was not good: in September 1939 the typical British able seaman received a little over £2 a week, when an unskilled Coventry car worker might be making twice that. There was no security of employment. Under the casual labour system, crewmen signed articles at the beginning of a voyage and were paid off at its end, their subsequent re-hire entirely at the whim of the individual shipowner. While this meant men could move from vessel to vessel as they chose, it could also mean months on the dole queue. In practice, because of the vagaries of the maritime life (a couple of weeks ashore followed by a six-month voyage, perhaps), few sailors had the chance to settle down to respectable marriage and family. 'Home' for men of this nomadic, bibulous, liminal civilisation was largely aboard ship. But there was little camaraderie on vessels, with a constantly changing roster of crewmen, in which sailors of different ranks and occupations worked and messed separately. Life in shore towns was divided between flophouses, bars and brothels, with local residents looking on in distaste. A Mass Observer described Cardiff's Tiger Bay as 'like being in some foreign and faraway town' when the ships were in:

> When the pubs are open, out of them comes an exceptional clatter [...] we never before saw so much steady, solid drinking. The overwhelming impression made upon us was of utter dullness, of meaningless spending, of men glad to be alive and ashore who had nothing better to do than soak and get soaked.[50]

Hostilities brought any improvement in pay in the form of a War Risk premium (an additional £10 a month for over-eighteens). More importantly, for the first time in decades merchant seamen found themselves with some leverage over the shipowners. A shortage of manpower meant the labour market was suddenly less coercive. Seamen could be pickier about which ships to sail on and which to avoid, according to conditions and discipline, subjects that were widely circulated in gossip networks in pubs and hotels worldwide. In theory, men who refused new articles could be conscripted into the armed forces instead. But in practice it was hard for the authorities to catch them. Even legally enforceable contracts were of little use when sailors could easily slip away while in port to sign up on other ships or on better-paid industrial war work. 'Untraced absenteeism' was by far one of the commonest charges handled at the 505 Naval Courts held between 1939 and 1944 (there had been just five such courts held from 1930 to 1939).[51]

Lascars, previously seen as an especially pliable and docile labour pool before the war, became more aggressive about demanding their rights as they became conscious of their heightened market value. Strikes and mass desertions began from late 1939 onwards to protest against the inequity in wages and premiums between white and non-white mariners (a Chinese able seaman at the outbreak of war received less than one-fifth the pay of one of his European comrades). In February 1941 eighty-seven Indians were packed into a Liverpool courtroom because they had refused to put to sea unless they were paid the same War Risk bonus as fellow white crew members. The men were found guilty and sentenced to one day's imprisonment each – but probably paid the higher rate afterwards too.[52]

The Royal Navy had always harboured the prejudice that its Merchant Navy cousins were a fractious rabble. One Admiralty proposal to quell any occupational militancy was to enlist all merchant seamen for the duration of the war as RN auxiliaries – ostensibly to increase their prestige but, more cynically, to put them under the full authority of naval law. In the end, though, the government preferred a more benign form of regulation. An Essential Work Order (EWO) covering the Merchant Navy was introduced in May 1941. Men paid off at the end of their voyages now entered a reserve pool from which they could, if necessary, be compulsorily allocated to a new ship of the government's choosing. Typically, though, they could reject the first two ship offerings if they wished. Also, the EWO introduced paid leave for the first time and eliminated the cruel loophole which had previously meant that a sailor whose vessel was sunk had his pay stopped from the day of the attack, even if he had spent many subsequent days in a lifeboat awaiting rescue.

Most voyages passed uneventfully even at the worst moments of the Battle of the Atlantic. The loss rate of ships sailing independently in the north-east Atlantic in the final four months of 1940 – an exceptionally dangerous period – was 5.3 per cent, and 1.7 per cent for those in convoy.[53] Such statistics cannot, of course, account for the emotional stress caused by fear of attack, whether ultimately realised or not.

If an attack did happen, it was usually terrifying and frequently deadly. Most U-boats hunted their prey at night. This added to the confusion among men who had not always been competently drilled in emergency procedures. Poorly maintained lifeboats could turn out to have rusted winches or be nailed to their chocks. Sometimes they were lowered too quickly, fouling their ropes or capsizing or swamping them. Torpedoed

ships typically sank within fifteen minutes, giving frightened and disori-
ented sailors, many of whom might have been asleep at the moment of
attack, little time to gather their most vital belongings and head for deck.
Stokers and engine-room men working below the waterline had to negotiate flooded passageways, super-heated steam gushing from broken pipes,
and choking coal dust before they could make their way to safety. Most
deaths happened in the first few minutes of an attack as sailors failed to
reach the lifeboats. The average number of merchant mariners killed per
month grew from 125 to 470 between 1939 and 1940.[54]

For those men who did get to the lifeboats, subsequent survival chances
varied greatly depending on weather, sea state, proximity to land and other
ships, and whether their radio operator had had a chance to signal a distress call before the ship foundered. In the well-trafficked North Atlantic,
half of crews were rescued within an hour of their vessel being sunk, two-
thirds within one day. But one in five was adrift for more than a week.
Survival chances were excellent in the first forty-eight hours but then grad-
ually declined, and fell precipitously after fifteen days. There were some
extraordinary exceptions to this. Two of the original seven survivors of the
SS *Anglo Saxon* lived through a seventy-day, 2,800-mile lifeboat voyage in
the summer of 1940. Weather conditions mattered a great deal to survival
chances. If the sea temperature was below 5° C, there was a one-in-four
chance of dying of hypothermia and exposure before you could be rescued.

For men on well-organised ships whose vessels sank slowly in good
weather, with rescue boats near by to pick up the survivors, U-boat attack
was a dramatic but relatively low-risk event.[55] For others it was a nightmare
they would never be able to forget. The 12,000-ton steam tanker *Cadillac* was 300 miles north-west of the Outer Hebrides at four minutes to
midnight on 1 March 1941 when she was torpedoed twice. Her highly
flammable cargo immediately caught fire. A tremendous explosion almost
ripped the ship apart, sending her settling fast by the bow. Only one of the
lifeboats could be launched in time, with twenty-six men packed on board.
R. A. Smith, second mate and one of the survivors, recalled later that

> the sea was already a mass of flames from the burning oil running out
> of the ship, so I gave orders to cast off. We got out the oars and tried
> to pull away from the flames, but it was hopeless. There was a wall of
> flame around us, we could hardly breathe and could see nothing. Then
> [...] most of the men in the boat jumped into the water with the oars.

They were nearly mad with the heat and pain and some were calling
out and others were praying, they did not know what they were doing.

Smith and four other men lay down in a foot of water at the bottom of
the lifeboat, where it was slightly easier to breathe. They were picked up
by a destroyer after about ninety minutes. They were, they discovered, the
sole survivors of a ship's company of thirty-four and three passengers. All
five men had to be taken to hospital on landing for treatment for their
burns. One of them, who had had no heavy clothing to protect him from
the flames, died of his injuries the following night.[56]

*

To turn from such a desperate ordeal to the dry minutiae of import statistics might seem bathetic, even distasteful. Yet the single biggest crisis facing
the British in the winter of 1940–41 was a crisis of logistics. It had been
caused by the peculiar new military geography of the war. In peacetime,
London and the south and east coast ports normally accounted for about
60 per cent of the handling of Britain's dry cargo imports. But by the final
months of 1940 this proportion had fallen to just 18 per cent.[57] Germany's
occupation of the French, Belgian, Dutch and Norwegian coasts meant
that it was no longer safe for most merchant traffic to use south-eastern
ports for fear of air and naval attack. As a result, almost all of Britain's trade
had to be redirected to the west coast ports on the Clyde, Mersey and Avon.

In the case of some of these western ports, especially Glasgow and
Greenock, the result was a massive increase in the volume of traffic being
handled: in the case of the Clyde ports, from 321,000 tons a month in
April–June 1940 to 421,000 tons in October–December. Storage sheds
designed to handle up to 2,000 tons of goods were suddenly being required
to house four times as much material. In other ports, such as Liverpool, the
absolute growth in volume was not so great.[58] But the type of cargoes that
were now arriving were different from in peacetime, and that mattered a lot
because each port was equipped with specialised kinds of fixed infrastructure – cranes, warehouses, rolling stock – that were suited to its pre-war
needs alone.

The loss, for instance, of iron ore supplies from continental Europe and
North Africa meant that Britain had to switch to the importation of huge
amounts of steel from North America. This made sense, in that importing

a compact finished product rather than a bulky raw material saved overall shipping space. But unloading steel required heavy-lift cranes and specialised wagons, which ports like Liverpool had never needed before and so did not possess. The result was that cargoes began to pile up on the quaysides uncollected for days or weeks, while ships – arriving in convoy simultaneously rather than in the usual looser movement patterns of peacetime – waited in harbour to be unloaded.[59] These congestion delays added, on average, about five days to the round-voyage time of each vessel in the winter of 1940–41. That may not sound like much, but collectively it amounted to perhaps 3 million tons of lost import capacity.[60]

Moreover, carrying heavy cargoes like finished steel in vessels that were never designed for them was causing severe marine damage. Over 350 British vessels were lost for reasons other than enemy action in 1940, largely as the result of accidents and bad weather.[61] Even for vessels that did not founder, marine damage still meant many weeks laid up in repair yards. Normally, in peacetime, about 7 per cent of the nation's ocean-going dry-cargo fleet would be immobilised under repair at any given moment. By January 1941, however, this proportion had almost doubled. Some of the damage that needed to be repaired had been inflicted by German submarines, mines and aircraft. But most of it was simply a product of the hazardous new circumstances in which the Merchant Navy was having to operate – with unsuitable cargoes carried along rougher northern routes.[62]

Here, then, was a consequence of the fall of France that tends to be overlooked in the literature on the Battle of the Atlantic. Yet it was even more threatening to Britain's capacity to continue fighting than the enemy submarine fleet.[63] After all, the point of the U-boat war from the German point of view was to choke off Britain's ability to import food and raw materials. Sinking merchant ships was a means to that end, but it was only one means and not the only possible means. It did not matter in what way precisely each thousand tons of lost import capacity was inflicted on the British economy, only that it was inflicted. By January 1941 the British had lost more than twice as much cumulative import tonnage because of the need for wartime ship repairs than through sinking by U-boats.[64] In other words, if Britain did not resolve its logistical problems, the Germans just might win the Battle of the Atlantic.

The crisis in the ports had already attracted the prime minister's attention by the end of 1940. On 27 December he wrote to the minister of shipping, Ronald Cross, demanding action. Within three days the decision was made to appoint 'Regional Port Directors' to the key west coast ports to sort out the muddle. These Port Directors brought in new railway wagons and road transport, requisitioned storage facilities and, crucially, decasualised the dock labour system at the quaysides. British dockers, like the nation's merchant seamen, had enjoyed no security of employment before the war. Industrial relations at the ports between workers and owners had been characterised by mutual suspicion and 'a more or less constant state of friction'.[65] As a result, even after war broke out, the dockers had insisted on continuing traditional peacetime restrictive practices to choose and refuse which cargoes to unload. It was a system that created artificial labour shortages. By introducing guaranteed minimum wages and a more rational system of productivity wage bonuses, the Port Directors were able to convince the dockers to set aside such restrictive practices.[66]

The backlog in ship repairs and alterations also dramatically improved in the first half of 1941. Tonnage laid up fell from a high of 2.6 million to 1.6 million tons. This was thanks in part to the passage of the Lend-Lease Act, which meant that British merchant vessels could be repaired in US yards without depleting the Treasury's dollar holdings.[67]

By the late spring of 1941, thanks to such innovations, the western port crisis was largely over. It's telling that, by comparison, the May Blitz on Merseyside, the most furious of all military offensives against Britain's port system, had hardly any effect on import capacity. The Luftwaffe bombing only inflicted the equivalent of three working days' loss of activity on the Liverpool dock area.[68]

*

While conditions may have been improving on land in the first months of 1941, at sea they brought, at first, new misery. Sinkings per month averaged 485,000 tons, 289,000 of them in the North Atlantic. In April, the worst month of the whole war so far, total losses peaked at 687,000 tons. Prospects for the year looked grim. Then, however, the numbers began to fall. At first, this was a slow improvement, but then, from July onwards, the fall was precipitous. Average sinkings from July to November 1941 were just 172,000 in all maritime theatres and 114,000 on the North Atlantic routes.[69] The U-boat 'happy time' was over.

This improvement had happened even though Dönitz had more U-boats than ever before. His total fleet size increased from seventy-three vessels in December 1940 to 138 by the end of June 1941 and would reach 256 by December. This meant that from the summer of 1941 onwards he was able to maintain thirty or more submarines on patrol in the Atlantic at any one time, up from just eight at the beginning of the year.[70] Dönitz now had enough U-boats on station to mount large-scale combined assaults on convoys for the first time – his famous 'Wolf Pack' (*Rudeltaktik*) methods. In May nine German submarines descended on convoy HX 126 south of Greenland. Over three nights in September no fewer than fourteen U-boats mauled convoy SC 42 in the most ferocious Wolf Pack attack mounted since the beginning of the war. In November a Wolf Pack achieved an unprecedented strategic victory, the only one of its type, in fact, in the whole conflict: it succeeded in terrorising an eastbound convoy (SC 52) so badly that it was forced to turn back to Canada.

But for all this, the overall productivity of Dönitz's boats by the end of the year was only a fraction of what it had been at the beginning. Gross tons sunk per U-boat at sea fell from 484 in the first six months of 1941 to just 119 from July to December.[71] There were now plenty of U-boats, but individually they were not achieving nearly as much as they had done the previous year. Something from the German point of view had started to go very badly awry in the Battle of the Atlantic.

Today, it's commonly assumed that that 'thing' was cipher security. If any image of the Battle of the Atlantic has impressed in the public imagination in recent years, it's one of eccentric professors sitting in damp huts in an English country house garden, fighting the German submariners with tables of incomprehensible mathematical formulae and primitive mechanical computers. The image in question is, of course, Bletchley Park, the Buckinghamshire mansion that was the home to the wartime Government Code and Cypher School (GC&CS). GC&CS was the top-secret organisation that broke the German ENIGMA wireless cipher in 1940, and thus provided throughout the rest of the war a unique window into Nazi strategy. Known as ULTRA, the Bletchley Park intelligence programme included, among other things, key information on U-boat movements, allowing the Admiralty to re-route Atlantic convoys safely out of danger.

Since the ULTRA secret was first revealed in the early 1970s it has steadily grown to greater and greater prominence in the popular consciousness. Its fame had been accompanied by the parallel rise to celebrity of GC&CS's most famous employee, Alan Turing. Turing – gay, diffident, donnish, possibly autistic, certainly unconventional, the theorist and founding father of computer science and artificial intelligence, a man whose sexual ambivalence was persecuted by a bigoted and ungrateful post-war state – is a highly sympathetic figure to modern eyes. The spectacle of a lone genius such as him defeating the Nazi war machine using only the power of his brilliant nonconformist mind is irresistible. The 2014 film *The Imitation Game* portrayed Turing, played by Benedict Cumberbatch, standing in front of a gigantic map of the North Atlantic with God-like omniscience, making decisions about the life and death of millions. 'There are five people in the world who know the position of every ship in the Atlantic. They are all in this room,' one of his awed colleagues says to Turing at one point in the film.

Was it Bletchley Park, then, that turned things around in the Atlantic in 1941? On the face of it, it might appear so. On 9 May 1941, east of Greenland's Cape Farewell, *U-110* (commanded by Fritz-Julius Lemp, the captain who had sunk the liner SS *Athenia* on the day war broke out) was detected on ASDIC by a British destroyer and depth-charged to the surface. A Royal Navy boarding party retrieved the submarine's ENIGMA machine and codebooks before she sank. These documents, in conjunction with materials taken from German meteorological ships around the same time, provided Bletchley Park with a vital insight into 'Dolphin', the particular form of ENIGMA cipher used for U-boat signals traffic between Dönitz's headquarters and boats at sea.

Dolphin had previously been almost unreadable by the British. For eight months from June 1941 onwards, the ULTRA code-breakers could read the Kriegsmarine's messages to its U-boats almost as quickly as the German submariners could decode them themselves. The information accrued about U-boat positions was used by the Admiralty's Operational Intelligence Centre (OIC), housed in the brutalist 'Citadel' building adjoining Horse Guards Parade, to re-route North Atlantic convoys safely away from the Wolf Packs. The results for the Germans were stark. For six weeks in June and July, Dönitz's boats intercepted no transatlantic convoys at all. September saw a brief re-escalation in *Rudeltaktik* attacks, but then there was a further drought until the end of the year. The correlation between Bletchley Park's success and Dönitz's failure in 1941 seems clear.

But what was going on was rather more complicated than just a cryptanalytical miracle. Ship re-routings prompted by ULTRA warnings certainly helped to reduce loss rates in 1941. But monthly losses of merchantmen in the North Atlantic started to fall in April, a month before

U-110's codebooks were delivered into the hands of Turing's men. Gross tons sunk per U-boat at sea had already started to decline in March. Bletchley Park's breakthrough with Dolphin had only accelerated a shift in fortunes that had begun already.[72]

What brought the 'happy time' in the Atlantic to an end was not code-breaking genius but a ruder assembly of military *matériel*: more (and better) escorts; more (and better) aircraft; and, eventually, more (and better-protected) convoys.

The escort situation began to improve in October 1940 as the immediate threat of SEA LION receded and ships could be released from the south and east coast of England back to anti-submarine duties. Many of the Flower class Corvettes ordered in 1939 were now finishing their sea trials and had become available for convoy operations. More important still, the new year brought the opening of new transatlantic bases, which greatly increased the endurance of escorts. In April 1941, anti-submarine vessels and RAF Coastal Command aircraft began operating from Iceland, extending the defensible area of the Atlantic to thirty-five degrees west. At the end of May, the Royal Canadian Navy (RCN) Newfoundland Escort Force base was inaugurated with thirteen destroyers and twenty-one corvettes. This lengthened the range of the escorts in the western Atlantic by 900 miles and made it possible for the first time to escort convoys all the way from Canada to the UK west coast ports.

Anti-submarine technology had also started to improve at this time. The first seaborne surface radar sets were installed in escorts starting in March 1941. These could detect surfaced U-boats at a distance of up to 8,000 yards. In July, experiments began with seaborne high-frequency direction-finding, known as HF/DF or 'Huff-Duff'. Huff-Duff could detect the origin point of radio signals from U-boats via a process of triangulation. Trials of 'snowflake' illuminating rocket flares commenced in the autumn of 1941, which robbed the Germans of the benefits of night-time invisibility.[73] Perhaps most crucial of all was a tactical innovation: escorts were now being formed into permanently operating groups which could train and practise anti-submarine drills together, rather than having to rely on hasty improvisation in the battle area itself.

Air power also played a vital role in changing the tide. By June 1941 the total number of operational aircraft available to RAF Coastal Command at any given time was 305. This was still an inadequate air fleet for the task at hand across a vast geographical area.[74] Nonetheless, the quality of the aircraft was improving as well as the number of them. In addition to British-built Sunderlands, Beaufighters and Wellingtons, Coastal Command now possessed a small number of American-built long-range Catalina flying boats and B-24 Liberator heavy bombers. Many planes were now equipped with airborne radar.

None of these Coastal Command aircraft was, as yet, very good at sinking U-boats. By the end of 1941 land-based aviators had only succeeded in destroying three enemy submarines (one of them Italian) by their own unaided efforts, and had co-operated with the Royal Navy in sinking another four.[75] They still lacked a decent air-dropped depth charge and a way to see U-boats at close range on the night-time surface of the water. But to look only at these particular results is to miss the point. The real success of the RAF in 1941 was to disrupt German submarine activity by forcing the U-boats to dive for safety whenever an aircraft appeared. By doing this, they frustrated the efforts of Dönitz's men to reconnoitre targets and to place themselves in a good attack position ahead of a convoy's path. It is telling that by October 1941 no ships were being lost within 400 miles of Coastal Command's bomber bases.[76]

This touches on a larger point that was often lost on the more aggressively minded members of the armed services and the Cabinet – including the prime minister. The purpose of trade protection was to prevent the loss of ships. It was not to sink enemy submarines. Any time a U-boat was sunk that was all to the good, obviously, in that it helped to reduce the sinking of more merchantmen. But that was not the aim of the campaign. Frustrating U-boat attacks by denying them targets was just as good a way of defeating them as sinking them. It was, in fact, a much more efficient way as it turned out.

The key to understanding what went wrong for Dönitz in 1941 can be found in an order he gave in March to his U-boat commanders in the North Atlantic to shift their patrol areas 200 miles to the south-west.[77] Ever since the summer of 1940 his submarines had been concentrated close to the British Isles, in the approaches to the North Channel immediately to the north-west of the Irish coast, where inbound or outbound vessels on transatlantic voyages were funnelled into a relatively narrow body of water that was easy to reconnoitre. It was the ideal killing ground. Dönitz was sorely reluctant to abandon it, but he had no choice. The influx of British aircraft and escorts in the area had begun to take a toll on his U-boat aces. On 7 March, Günther Prien's *U-47* was reported missing, believed destroyed by depth charges. Ten days later Dönitz suffered a terrible double blow: during an attack on convoy HX 112, Joachim Schepke was killed when his vessel was rammed by a RN destroyer, while Kretschmer's *U-99* was disabled and 'Silent Otto' taken prisoner.

Transferring operations further south-west into the Atlantic would, Dönitz hoped, take his U-boats out of range of Coastal Command patrols and so reduce their unacceptable loss rates. So it did – for the time being anyway. But the move also reduced the number of Allied ships the U-boats could sink. Dönitz's men, scattered now over a much wider area with a far thinner density of merchant vessels crossing it, simply could not make contact with targets in the way they had been able to do a year before in the congested North Channel. Convoy re-routings thanks to ULTRA intelligence made the situation more difficult still for the Germans. But even if Bletchley Park had not been able to read a word of Dönitz's signals, his submariners would have still had to struggle with the same basic dilemma.

Dispersing beyond the range of RAF Coastal Command's patrols meant dispersing beyond the range of German air cover. Ever since the fall of France, a Focke-Wulf Condor unit had been flying daily reconnaissance missions above the U-boats' rich hunting zone in the North Channel. There were never very many Condors – only two a day on average – and with the exception of the jackpot success of the RMS *Empress of Britain* they did not sink many British merchant ships in their own right.[78] But they had been invaluable to Dönitz's men in identifying potential targets. Now those roving aerial eyes were lost to the U-boats. Required to rely on their own reconnoitring abilities, the submariners' victories declined fast.

The significance of this shift in the battleground would have been even clearer if it had not coincided with a British initiative which was so unfortunate that, for a few months in early 1941, it virtually cancelled out all the benefits of pushing the U-boats away from the North Channel. This was the decision to allow merchant ships capable of making between 13 and 15 knots to travel independently rather than in a convoy. Churchill had been pushing for such a move since November 1940, despite the Admiralty's considerable doubts about its wisdom. The idea was logical enough on the face of it. Since convoys tended to slow down the rate of loading and unloading time in ports because all the ships arrived together, having more vessels travel independently would spread the workload out more and reduce the import congestion problem.

The problem was that any advantage gained from this in the ports was more than outweighed by the loss of the ships themselves while at sea. A speed of 15 knots was simply not fast enough to save a vessel from submarine attack. This was reflected in loss statistics. In March 1941 U-boats sank sixteen merchantmen. In April they sank thirty-two. In May they sank forty-three.[79] Almost all these new losses were among ships travelling independently under the new regulations.[80] Merchantmen were being sent unnecessarily to their doom. The Admiralty approached Churchill with the figures, but the prime minister stubbornly insisted that 'no definite conclusions could [yet] be drawn from the percentages'. The ill-fated experiment continued. Finally, at the end of June, in the face of even more losses, he relented. The rule again became that only vessels that could travel faster than 15 knots would be allowed to travel independently. Ship sinkings fell back immediately to eleven a month.[81] Now the importance of Dönitz's retreat from the North Channel could be fully appreciated.

Understanding what happened in the North Atlantic in 1941 allows us to see Dönitz's Wolf Pack tactics in a new light. They were not a bold new intensification of the German campaign. They were an act of desperation by an enemy who knew he was losing ground. The U-boats switched to *Rudeltaktik* not because it was a better method of sinking merchant ships but because they had no choice. The easy victories against ships in the North Channel, especially ships travelling alone, were over. The great tallies of the U-boat aces during 'the happy time' would not be repeated, at least not on the eastern side of the Atlantic. U-boats under the new conditions of war in 1941 would have to focus on convoys rather than lone victims. Those convoys were far better protected than they had been a year earlier. A well-coordinated Wolf Pack attack *might*, if the Germans were skilful and lucky, be capable of doing great damage to an individual convoy, but the investment of total effort did not justify the results.

In 1941 there were 13,183 convoyed ship crossings of the Atlantic in 378 convoys. One hundred and eighty-three of those convoyed ships were sunk. That was a loss rate of 1.4 per cent.[82] Its human toll was tragic. Almost 14,000 Allied merchant seamen died in the first two and a half years of the Second World War, a figure worth bearing in mind when we consider that only 1,542 RAF aircrew were killed in the Battle of Britain.[83] But this was not the kind of loss rate that was going to force Britain into surrender. During the spring of 1941 stockpiles of imported food and raw materials in Britain reached a low of 15.7 million tons. But the government had already calculated that it could manage if the figure remained above 11.5 million tons.[84]

None of this means that the Battle of the Atlantic was over. There were many great convoy battles still to come. There would even be another 'happy time' on the other side of the Atlantic. But Dönitz's best chance to win the war with his U-boats had already passed, even if he did not know it.

And Dönitz now had another problem on his hands: strategic dispersion of his efforts. In June 1941 Germany invaded the USSR, and he was forced to redeploy eight of his precious submarines to the Baltic to support operations against the Soviet Red Navy. Another six boats had to be detached to the Arctic. Worse still, from his point of view, was Hitler's decision on 26 August to send ten U-boats from the Atlantic through the Strait of Gibraltar to operate against British vessels in the Mediterranean. The Kriegsmarine High Command informed Dönitz that the Mediterranean, not the Atlantic, was to be regarded as 'the main theatre of operations' for the time being, whether he liked it or not.[85] The war was widening geographically in the summer of 1941. Dönitz was not the first military commander to be vexed by a Mediterranean diversion. Nor would he be the last.

21

THE CAROTID ARTERY OF EMPIRE

'Jesus Christ.'

'Fuckin' Hell.'

I didn't say a word, because I wanted to throw up.

Before war broke out, Douglas Arthur, a nineteen-year-old junior sales-man in the bathroom and fittings showroom of a Liverpool plumbers' and builders' merchants, had never been further from home than a day trip to Llandudno in north Wales. Yet at dawn on 6 February 1941 he and his fellow squaddies of Number 1 Battery, 106th (Lancashire Hussars) regiment, Royal Horse Artillery, were lying in wait at the deserted village of Beda Fomm on the Gulf of Sirte, sixty miles or so south of Libya's lush Jebel Akhdar highlands. In front of them they could hear the 'low, menacing, rumbling noise' of hundreds of vehicles approaching from the north. As the light improved, a motorised armada began to emerge from the gloom:

> Dozens of huge Italian five-ton troop carriers with their billowing canvas covers; motorbikes and sidecars, each carrying three men, their rifles plainly visible, slung over their shoulders; heavy field artillery with ammunition limbers trailing behind them [...] private cars, looking as if they had been freshly polished that morning; open-topped staff cars, all carrying four or five people; water bowsers, and, unbelievably, two long, single-decker, fifty-seater civilian coaches, their glossy white enamelled paint contrasting sharply with the drab military vehicles. All slowly crawling along the dim light of the dawn, without any semblance of order except for the squadron of black lumbering tanks at their head.
>
> They were heading directly towards us.[1]

Beda Fomm was an inconsequential desert hamlet. Its only feature of importance was strategic: it straddled the coastal road (the *Via Balbia*) that led from Benghazi to Agedabia and then onwards, hundreds of miles to the west, to Tripoli, the Italian colony's capital. An army that held Beda Fomm, in other words, could prevent any enemy force from withdrawing from Libya's eastern province, Cyrenaica, west into Tripolitania. This was why Arthur's regiment and the other tanks, armoured cars, artillery and infantry of the British 4th Armoured Brigade had seized the village after a punishing 150-mile cross-desert dash across largely unmapped country strewn with rocks and boulders. Now, the entire Italian 10th Army was bearing down from the north against their scrappy, hopelessly outnumbered force.

Cyril Joly, a subaltern in the 2nd Royal Tank Regiment (RTR), was also lying in wait on the flank of the main blocking force occupying Beda Fomm. 'I was staggered by the amazing scene in front of me,' he remembered later:

> South, to my left, I could see the puffs of the shell bursts on the brilliant white dunes which marked the positions of the blocking force. From there, and directly in front of me and to my right, stretching as far as the eye could see, the main road and the flat ground on each side of it were packed tight with every conceivable type of enemy vehicle and equipment. At this point, where the Italians were still unaware that they were menaced, groups of men were wandering about between the equipment as if they were out for a Sunday stroll in the park. With black clouds low in the east, directly behind us [...] we moved into the attack.[2]

The battle was touch-and-go for the British; 4th Armoured Brigade was outnumbered, its men exhausted, its vehicles badly in need of maintenance. All fuel, ammunition and food were in short supply. No reserves were available to fall back on if anything went wrong. The dash to Beda Fomm had been an audacious gamble, as much a bluff as a considered military manoeuvre. 'It was remarkable,' thought Arthur, 'now that it had come to the crunch, how, with a sort of unspoken resolve, we all seemed to realise that there was nothing much we could do about the advancing horde of trucks, except stop them if we could.'[3]

Fighting at Beda Fomm went on throughout the day and into the night. On the morning of 7 February, Joly and his comrades watched with 'ominous foreboding' the 'huge and menacing' Italian column still in front of them. 'Each of us knew by what slim margin we still held dominance over the battlefield. Our threat was but a façade.' But then he became aware 'of a startling change' in the Italian ranks, as

> first one and then another white flag appeared in the host of vehicles. More and more became visible, until the whole column was a forest of waving white banners [...] Italians of all shapes and sizes, all ranks, all regiments and all services swarmed out to be taken prisoner.[4]

'We stood either side of the now-moving line of despondent Italians,' recalled Douglas Arthur. 'It was not long before I saw that they were being relieved of their wristwatches and cameras. I saw some of my crew with watches adorning their arms from the wrist to elbow. I had never seen so many wristwatches since the last time I walked past Boodle & Dunthorpe's in Lord Street.'[5]

The remnants of the entire Italian 10th Army, 25,000 men in all, had capitulated to the tiny, battered British force. Barely a single Italian soldier had escaped past Beda Fomm to Tripolitania. All eastern Libya, including the port of Tobruk, the only natural harbour in the whole region, was now in British hands. The road to Tripoli itself appeared wide open and undefended.

*

The Battle of Beda Fomm was a stunning reverse in a campaign that had begun the previous June under very different circumstances when Italian dictator Benito Mussolini, flushed with hubris and eager to partake in the spoils of victory, had declared war on Britain and France. Italy's entry into the conflict in alliance with Nazi Germany had had little effect on the outcome of the Battle of France in 1940, which the Allies had already as good as lost before Mussolini got involved. But it made a huge difference to the future direction of the Second World War. What had up to that point been a conflict largely confined to land fighting in north-west Europe now expanded to the whole of Africa and the Middle East, the Balkans and the Mediterranean islands. Italian belligerence transformed the character of the war's fighting armies as well. The conflict assumed a much more cosmopolitan, polyglot character than it had had in its first

nine months. Thanks to Mussolini's decision to fight, Cypriots and Nige-
rians, Afrikaners and Palestinians, Punjabi Sikhs and New Zealand Maoris
would find themselves killing and dying from Egypt to Ethiopia, the Peloponnese to Iraq.

The opening of a Mediterranean front in the summer of 1940 was a
crisis for the British. Churchill called the inland sea 'the carotid artery
of Empire'.[6] It was the United Kingdom's direct line of communication to India and Singapore, via Gibraltar and the Suez Canal. A hostile
Italy made that line of communication untenable. All shipping to South
and South-East Asia now had to be redirected round the Cape of Good
Hope. Defending British colonial territories in the Mediterranean and
East Africa tied up troops, aircraft and ships the country could ill afford to
divert from the defence of the home islands and the Atlantic supply routes,
not to mention the rest of the Empire. Middle Eastern oil was an important but vulnerable British military resource, and a tempting prize for the
petroleum-greedy Axis powers. The Arab revolt in Palestine in the 1930s
had already demonstrated how unpopular the British colonial presence in
the region was among millions of indigenous people. The spectre of a Pan-
Arab, Pan-Islamic insurrection across the British imperial world which had
haunted strategists between the wars was now revived, but in vastly more
dangerous circumstances than before – during a military assault from two
European Great Powers.

But a war in the Mediterranean was an opportunity for the British
too. After the fall of France, American economic support was essential
for continuing any conflict with Germany. That support was going to be
contingent on some hard evidence that Britain was an ally worth investing
in, however. With France gone, there was no realistic possibility of British
forces successfully fighting on the European mainland again for years to
come. Britain would have to demonstrate it was taking the war to the enemy
elsewhere. The Mediterranean would be a useful showcase for British military prowess – especially since the fighting there would be mostly against
Germany's less formidable Italian partner. Perhaps victory against the Italians would encourage a Balkan alliance against Hitler. Perhaps it would
even open a southern route to Berlin. The possibilities were intriguing.

The Mediterranean would also be a showcase for the military ingenui-
ties of the new British prime minister. Churchill had not had enough time
to imprint his strategic ideas on the Battle for France before it was over. A
war against the Italians, however, would be his to shape as he saw fit from

the start. He had a high opinion of his own talents as an amateur generalissimo. When he had first become prime minister, Churchill had claimed the additional title of 'minister of defence', a deliberately undefined personal office which afforded him the right to chair two defence committees of the War Cabinet, 'Operations' and 'Supply'. It was the former of these committees, usually attended by Churchill himself, the service secretaries-of-state and the chiefs of staff or their deputies, that became the prime minister's chief instrument for directing the high strategy of the war. The War Cabinet was kept informed of military events, but henceforth it restricted itself to matters diplomatic and domestic. Prosecuting the fighting war on a day-to-day basis would be Churchill's affair. He had created a unique relationship between himself and his military advisers, one that (as a staff officer at the time put it) made him 'as near to being a dictator as anyone in this country since Oliver Cromwell'.[7]

Audiences with the prime minister were a severe test of the chiefs of staff's constitutions. As his aide Jock Colville later noted, 'Churchill fascinated and impressed the Service Chiefs, but he often exasperated them with proposals they deemed unrealistic or, at their most extravagant, sheer fantasy.'[8] By the autumn of 1940 all of them were already exhausted by stress, ill-health or both. Churchill added considerably to their physical and mental burdens. Air Chief Marshal Sir Cyril Newall, Chief of the Air Staff, would soon retire, his departure prefigured by a whispering campaign, probably led by Churchill's crony Lord Beaverbrook, that he possessed 'inadequate mental ability [and] weakness of character'.[9] Admiral Sir Dudley Pound, First Sea Lord, had painful osteoarthritis, was visibly unwell – he often fell asleep in meetings – and finally succumbed to a brain tumour on Trafalgar Day, October 1943. Working for Churchill was not good for your health or actuarial prospects.

Two soldiers played a critical role in Churchill's early war in the Mediterranean. Neither is especially well known today, perhaps because they had the misfortune of leading British armies in the unglamorous locust years of the war, when mere survival was itself an achievement. General Sir John Dill, Chief of the Imperial General Staff, replaced Ironside as the Army's senior commander during the Battle of France. His first impressions of Churchill were not promising. 'I'm not sure that Winston isn't the greatest menace,' he wrote. 'No one seems to be able to control him. He is full of ideas, many brilliant, but most of them impracticable. He has such drive and personality that no one seems able to stand up to him.'[10] For his part,

Churchill soon nicknamed his new CIGS 'Dilly Dally' and complained that he represented 'the dead hand of inanition'.[11]

Anthony Eden described meetings of the Defence Committee in this period as 'disturbing – a monologue – any opposition [to the prime minister] treated as faction – policies and operations decided by impulse – no proper planning'.[12] Churchill was not incapable of having his mind changed. But he wanted to be bludgeoned into it in brilliant, aggressive verbal sparring, preferably conducted long into the early morning hours with brandy and cigars. Dill offered long, well-considered, dry-as-dust memos instead. Where the prime minister yearned for panache and ingenuity, Dill offered dull caution. He had little time for Churchillian truculence. 'The Prime Minister lost his temper with me,' he told a colleague after one altercation: 'I could see the blood come up in his great neck and his eyes began to flash.'[13] It was not a relationship fated to succeed.

Dill's job was to give Churchill direction at the highest level of strategy in Whitehall. The job of directly managing the war in the Mediterranean on the ground belonged to General Sir Archibald Wavell, the second of the two soldiers who shaped the early Mediterranean War. He was commander-in-chief of Middle East Command, a sprawling responsibility that included Egypt, Palestine, Transjordan, Cyprus, Sudan, British Somaliland, Aden and Iraq. Wavell was a remarkable soldier-scholar, 'a man of immense strength, simplicity, and dignity of character' according to one biographer, an expert horseman and passionate student of poetry who with little prompting could recite long passages of the Greek classics from memory.[14] It was Wavell, not Montgomery, who the 'Desert Fox' Erwin Rommel would later say 'showed a touch of genius' unique among the British wartime commanders in North Africa.[15]

His interactions with Churchill, perhaps the most self-assertive, disputatious and dogmatic prime minister in history, were to be as fractious as Dill's. The two men met for the first time in early August 1940, when Wavell briefly returned from Cairo to London to receive instructions from the new prime minister. 'I admired his fine qualities,' Churchill tactfully recorded in his war memoirs.[16] At the time, his opinion was less complimentary. 'I do not feel in him that sense of mental vigour and resolve to overcome obstacles, which is indispensable to successful war,' the prime minister wrote to Eden of Wavell: 'I find instead tame acceptance.' Wavell was 'a good average colonel and would make a good chairman of a Tory association'.[17]

Churchill's determination to control every aspect of Mediterranean strategy and Wavell's equal determination to remain his own man caused tension even before the commander-in-chief returned to Egypt. 'I could feel the temperature rising between him and the PM,' Wavell's intelligence chief Brigadier John Shearer recalled after a particularly quarrelsome chiefs of staff meeting that summer. 'Commander in chief, you said ...,' began Churchill at one point: 'I did not', Wavell spat out.[18] The prime minister prepared a 'General Directive' for operations in the Middle East which went into the most meticulous details about the deployment of individual battalions, the use of desert wells and the maintenance of the coastal road: basically, had Wavell accepted it, it would have reduced his office to that of Churchill's adjutant. 'It showed clearly that Winston did not trust me to run my own show,' he wrote later.[19] The chiefs of staff managed to persuade Churchill that such micro-management was in no one's interest and the directive was reduced to the status of advice rather than instruction. But the lack of confidence was manifest and the damaged relationship unhealed. Wavell never disputed his ultimate subordination to his political master. But he was not someone to be bullied or strong-armed. His was to be the first of a string of ill-starred relationships between Churchill and his generals.

*

Wavell returned to Cairo in late August 1940 facing what looked like a grim military prospect. Mussolini's 10th Army, then about 150,000 men strong, was amassing just across the border in Italian-controlled Libya. Egypt's only garrison was the 'Western Desert Force' (WDF), less than a quarter the size of the 10th Army, with fewer than half its tanks and aircraft and thirteen times fewer artillery pieces. Holding back the juggernaut Italian force as it drove towards the Suez Canal looked like a hopeless endeavour.

But the Italian army lacked a resolution befitting its size. The 10th Army crossed the frontier on 9 September after being pushed very hard to do so by Mussolini. After a week of very little fighting and only sixty-five miles from its starting-point, it halted and encamped at the Egyptian village of Sidi Barrani, its commander demanding that Rome provide more vehicles and supplies if his men were to proceed any further eastwards.

This gift of a breathing space allowed Wavell and the WDF's commander, Major-General Richard O'Connor, an opportunity to plan a riposte. The WDF, they decided, would cross Egypt's Western Desert, slip through the wide gaps separating the Italian fortified camps and attack them from the rear. With the onset of winter and the ending of the immediate invasion threat to the British Isles, almost 70,000 reinforcements were sent from the UK to the Middle East, including 100 tanks (half of which were the powerful Matilda II), plus 50,000 additional troops from the Empire and Dominions.[20] The WDF would still be outnumbered despite these additions, and Wavell was realistic about what any offensive could surely produce. 'I do not entertain extravagant hopes of this operation,' he wrote. He expected it to be a limited spoiling raid lasting perhaps five days.[21]

But Operation COMPASS, Wavell's offensive, resulted instead in a spectacular rout of Mussolini's troops that began within a matter of hours of its start on 9 December. The Italians were soon fleeing westwards towards the Libyan border in a state of panic. The WDF (now renamed 13 Corps) pursued the 10th Army along the coastal road, capturing Bardia on 1 January 1941, Tobruk on 22 January and Derna in the Jebel Akhdar six days after that. With the remnants of 10th Army in disorganised flight towards Tripolitania along the *Via Balbia*, O'Connor decided to try to collar the lot with a dash across the desert interior to Beda Fomm. As we have seen, it worked. By 7 February, when COMPASS finally came to an end, 13 Corps had advanced over 500 miles in all, capturing in the process 130,000 Italian prisoners, almost 400 tanks and 845 guns. It had lost just 500 of its own men killed.[22] In London, Eden quipped to Churchill that never had so much been surrendered by so few. The news of the catastrophe was greeted in Rome with furious diatribes about racial decline. Mussolini had already ranted after Sidi Barrani about the 'good-for-nothing... mediocre' men letting down the Italian nation.[23]

The detritus of the army wiped out at Beda Fomm, its vast piles of broken and abandoned weapons and equipment scattered across the desert surface – rifles, ammunition boxes, vehicles, tents, furniture – were epitaph enough for what had happened there. The sight, too, of a few wry, scruffy Tommies escorting tens of thousands of cheerful Italian prisoners eastwards into captivity said everything that could be said about Mussolini's grandiose dreams of Mediterranean empire.

For the British, Operation COMPASS was the first land victory of the war, the first real success in sixteen months of fighting – and, as it turned out, the last uncontestable one in North Africa for twenty-one months to come. But no one knew that in February 1941. What they knew, or felt they knew anyway, was that the stigma of Dunkirk had been wiped clean from the British Army's record at last. Britain's citizen-soldiers had proved themselves worthy after all. 'Considering that eighteen months before,' noted Douglas Arthur,

> the men taking part were clerks and shop assistants, labourers and bricklayers, jam-boilers and dustmen, and that we had only received three weeks' hurried training ... [we] acquitted [our]selves with distinction.[24]

Churchill had an opportunity, for once, to crow. 'The crafty, cold-blooded, black-hearted Italian, who had thought to gain an empire on the cheap, [has] got into trouble,' he told BBC radio listeners on 9 February. 'We have all been entertained, and I trust edified, by the exposure and humiliation of what Byron called Those Pagod things of sabre sway/ With fronts of brass and feet of clay.'[25]

Wavell's victory, however welcome, brought new strategic dilemmas. No one, including Churchill, had ever expected a rout in Cyrenaica so sudden and so absolute. The assumption before the launch of COMPASS had been that 13 Corps would remain afterwards on the defensive in Egypt. Now it was not so clear what to do next. O'Connor was all for continuing the offensive in Libya all the way to Tripoli and knocking the Italians out of North Africa entirely. Immediately following Beda Fomm one of his staff officers rushed back to Cairo to request permission to continue the operation. But at the end of a thirty-two-hour journey he was told by Wavell that the British forces in Cyrenaica would halt at El Agheila, at the southern-most base of the Gulf of Sirte, still 450 miles short of Tripoli. There would be no further advance along the *Via Balbia* that spring. All attention in Cairo was now directed northwards, towards Greece and the Balkans.[26]

Greece in 1940 was not, on the face of it, a very edifying potential ally. Its ruler, General Ioannis Metaxas, had seized power in a coup four years earlier. His attempts to create a fascist-like cult of personality around himself had mostly flopped, but his brutal persecution of his political opponents had not. No matter how distasteful the character of its government, however, Britain saw Greece as a potential bridgehead on the northern Mediterranean shoreline. Greece was also a victim of Axis aggression, albeit not very competent aggression. In October 1940 Mussolini – without informing Hitler, and much to the latter's subsequent irritation – had declared war and invaded. Italian hopes of quickly turning the Aegean into a private lake were frustrated by dogged Greek resistance. The heroic stand of the Hellenes against their more powerful persecutors inspired a good deal of international sympathy, rather as Finland had enjoyed during the Winter War against the USSR.

The British initially sent a few RAF squadrons to the Greek mainland and an infantry brigade to garrison Crete, but with the simultaneous Italian threat to Egypt there were no more forces in the Middle East theatre to spare. The success of COMPASS offered a chance to reappraise this. Metaxas, who had been hesitant about major British assistance, fearing that it would provoke the Germans into intervening too, died suddenly in January 1941, opening the possibility of building a new, closer Anglo-Greek relationship with his successor, Alexandros Koryzis.

Anthony Eden had replaced Lord Halifax as foreign secretary when the latter was dispatched to be the new British ambassador in Washington DC in December 1940. Eden saw the eastern Mediterranean as a place to stamp his personal mark on British diplomacy. Accompanied by Dill, he set off on a joint military-diplomatic mission to Athens and Ankara in mid-February 1941. Eden's hope was that, if Britain sent a full expeditionary force to Greece, it might inspire an anti-German 'Balkan Front' that Turkey, Yugoslavia and Bulgaria could be persuaded to join. The chances of this were always rather forlorn, and when Eden and Dill arrived in the Turkish capital their hosts made it clear that they had no desire to antagonise Hitler by defending a neighbouring state, Greece, that they did not much care for anyway. To make things worse, Bulgaria formally joined the Axis military coalition on 2 March. Yet despite all this, Eden formally promised the Greeks an expeditionary force two days later. The troops for this would have to come from the Middle East. Wavell concurred. Indeed, having initially been sceptical about a Balkan intervention, he was now one of its most enthusiastic advocates.

No one in London seriously opposed Eden's promise. Nor, truth be told, did they greet it with much optimism. As March drew on, its prospects looked more and more dubious. The Greeks refused to withdraw their forces on their northern border, which were liable to be outmanoeuvred if the Germans decided to invade, to a more defensible southern position. War correspondents assigned to the British expedition drank a gloomy toast before their departure to 'the new Dunkirk'.[27] Sir Alexander Cadogan thought that 'on all moral and sentimental (and consequently

American) grounds' intervention in Greece was a necessity. In Washington, Congress was about to begin debating Roosevelt's Lend-Lease bill. It would look impressive to American eyes if Britain was heroically intervening to support another small neutral power against Axis invasion. It might even tip the balance of the vote.[28] Nonetheless, 'it must, in the end, be a failure. However, perhaps better to have failed in a decent project than never to have tried at all.'[29]

Two infantry divisions and an armoured brigade, supported by eight RAF squadrons, were detached from Middle East forces and sent to Piraeus during the last weeks of March. It was not much of an expedition to hold back the Wehrmacht. The Greeks had hoped for at least nine divisions.[30] But even this small 'W Force', named after its commander, Lieutenant-General Henry 'Jumbo' Wilson, had to bring all its own food, fuel and stores with it from Egypt, and these were unloaded literally before the eyes of the still neutral German military attaché, who solemnly counted off the crates one by one.[31] On 6 April, German neutrality ended when Hitler suddenly attacked Greece and Yugoslavia.

After the heady triumph of Beda Fomm two months earlier, what followed for the British was a relapse back to the miseries of 1940. In principle, W Force's chances were not so bad. Wilson was well afforded with ULTRA signals intelligence about German movements. The mountainous Greek interior was ideally suited to defensive warfare. But the Greek army, which had stood so resolutely against the Italians, was exhausted from its long struggle, and could not stand against this much more formidable enemy. To add to that, Yugoslavia's rapid fall meant that the main British lines on the River Aliákmon north of Mount Olympus were quickly outflanked. Almost from the campaign's first day, W Force was in retreat.

The withdrawal revealed the fragility of British-built armoured vehicles, a fact that was to be such a depressing feature of the Mediterranean war's early years. The Greek passes were soon littered with tanks abandoned by their crews because of broken tracks and failed transmissions. The labyrinthine supply chain from Piraeus collapsed under constant harassment from the Luftwaffe, which had wrested control of Greek airspace from the RAF without difficulty. 'There was never a period of more than half an hour when there was not an enemy plane overhead,' remembered a lieutenant with the Royal Tank Regiment:

It was the unrelenting pressure of noise and the threat of destruction in every hour which accentuated the psychological consequences of continuous retreat [...] I had never seen so many men so unashamedly afraid.[32]

By 20 April, W Force had retired behind Thermopylae. This had a spirited classical ring to it. However, Wilson's job, as he now realised, was not to mount a suicidal last stand but to get as many of his troops safely evacuated as possible. The retreat to the Peloponnese beaches over the next ten days was mostly successful, and the Royal Navy was able to take off about 50,000 of the original 58,000 British and Allied forces in Greece. It was, after all, getting well practised at this sort of thing. As wags at home suggested, 'BEF' had come to stand for 'Back Every Fortnight'.

Greece was bad. The worst was still to come. About half the evacuees were taken to nearby Crete. The island's military commander, the New Zealander Major-General Bernard Freyberg, had orders to hold it at all costs. Whether this was still a good idea following Greece's fall was questionable. With the Luftwaffe now able to use air bases on the mainland, and Crete's only harbour lying on its vulnerable northern coast, keeping any viable maritime line of communication back to Egypt was going to be a daunting challenge.

But it would be a challenge for the Germans to take the island too. And Freyberg had one extraordinary secret advantage. A set of operational orders for the German attack, code-named MERKUR (MERCURY), had been transmitted by Luftwaffe ENIGMA and intercepted and deciphered by GC&CS at Bletchley Park. Freyberg thus knew in advance that his opponent was planning a combined parachute and amphibious assault, and he knew the details of when and where the enemy troops would arrive. Few military commanders in history have ever been the beneficiaries of such an intelligence scoop on the eve of battle. Freyberg telegraphed London that he was 'not in the least anxious' about the threat.[33] Churchill expected the German attack to be a catastrophic failure.

That Freyberg's advantage did not, in the end, turn the Battle for Crete into a British victory is instructive of the limitations even of the most excellent signals intelligence. It was one thing for him to know what was going to happen, another thing altogether for him to be able to do anything about it. ULTRA assistance had not saved Wilson in Greece, and it could do nothing to allay Freyberg's basic material difficulties either. Thanks to local levies and the evacuees from W Force, Crete's garrison in May 1941 was a nominally impressive 42,000 troops. But most of the new soldiers had arrived carrying, at most, their rifles and Bren guns. Armoured vehicles, artillery, lorries, radios and other supplies had all been left behind on the Greek mainland. While a few tanks were sent from Alexandria, Crete was therefore nevertheless packed with poorly equipped, demoralised soldiers, many of them stragglers or deserters from their original units, who were more of a logistical burden than an asset.

Airfields at Maleme, Retimo and Heraklion on the north coast of the island had been prepared over the winter. But the RAF had already withdrawn the few serviceable aircraft it possessed that had survived the Greek campaign. Attempts to build up Crete's anti-aircraft defences had been hampered by the need to support W Force. The cession of air superiority to the Luftwaffe meant that it was impossible to bring in new supplies by sea or to evacuate in advance any more than a few thousand of the most 'useless mouths'.

This is not to say that the attackers had it all their own way. On the morning of 20 May, after a week of intense air bombardment, thousands of German *Fallschirmjäger* began dropping from parachutes and gliders onto the three Cretan airfields. It was just as ULTRA had predicted. For many of the attacking German troops, the parachute drop was a short and final journey. They were shot while still dangling helplessly in their harnesses in the sky or bayoneted while hanging from the olive trees. Those German paratroopers who survived the initial drop established tiny bridgeheads, but by dusk they had captured none of their objectives. Lacking heavy weaponry, the situation appeared bleak for them.

During the night, however, a New Zealand infantry battalion commander at Maleme pulled back his troops from the heights overlooking the airfield – which, inexplicably, had not been rendered unusable with ditches and obstacles prior to the invasion. With the telephone lines cut, and worried that his initial withdrawal line was about to be outflanked, the officer had been unclear whether reinforcements he had been promised would ever arrive. Assuming, wrongly, that they would not, he took the decision to retreat before his men were overrun.[34] In this way, the absence of a few field radios on the British side at Crete undid all of Bletchley Park's work.

Thanks to the withdrawal, the Germans were able to take control of Maleme on 21 May. With such a vital conduit for air supply and reinforcement under enemy control, the British situation speedily unravelled. As in Greece, the Luftwaffe's total air superiority unnerved the defending troops to the point where they were paralysed into inactivity. On 26 May, Freyberg informed Wavell that the battle for Crete was lost. Two days later a new evacuation plan began. About 18,600 of the defending troops were brought off the island. But this time the Royal Navy, operating under constant Luftwaffe attack, suffered grievously for its courage. Three cruisers and six destroyers were sunk.

In London, Churchill was incandescent about a defeat that had been suffered despite the unique intelligence coup provided by ULTRA:

> I cannot feel that there was any real grip shown by Middle East HQ upon the operation of the defence of Crete [...] no one in high authority seems to have sat down for two or three mornings together and endeavoured to take a full forward view of what would happen in the light of our information [...] the slowness in acting upon the precise intelligence with which they were furnished, and the general evidence of lack of drive and precision fill me with disquiet.[35]

As the official history of the Bletchley Park story notes, however, in May 1941 'the Germans had the strength to offset bad intelligence', whereas the British, 'whether from weakness or for other reasons, were not in a position to make better use' of it.[36]

*

O'Connor had been frustrated by the decision to halt at El Agheila rather than proceed on to Tripoli after the victory at Beda Fomm. But it had not necessarily been the wrong decision. Back in London, the chiefs of staff argued that even the capture of all of Libya would not much alter the strategic situation in the Mediterranean. It would still be closed to British merchant traffic while the Italians held the north shore of the Sicilian Narrows. Seizing Tripoli would just add 450 miles onto an already overextended British supply line from the Suez Canal. Tripolitania, they concluded, could be left in Italian hands for now. So long as the flank was kept secure at Benghazi, then Tobruk, and Egypt beyond it, were safe. The problem was that by the mid-spring of 1941 the flank at Benghazi was no longer secure.[37]

For one thing, the Italians had responded to their calamity in Libya with surprising energy. The image of the hapless 'Eyetie' fleeing from the battlefield into happy captivity was affixed in Anglophone memory thanks to Beda Fomm. But Britain had come close to having a few Beda Fomms of its own since the war's outbreak. After all, the British troops in western France in June 1940 would have capitulated to the Germans just as quickly if evacuation had not saved them. In any case, the shock of the 10th Army's defeat had provoked a bout of serious reorganisation and rethinking in the Italian Army. Training in desert tactics was improved. Much better units, including a motorised division (the 102nd 'Trento') and an armoured division (the 132nd 'Ariete'), arrived in Tripolitania. These gave the Italian forces in North Africa a large-scale, modern, mobile strike force for the first time. Major deficiencies in the Italian order of battle remained, to be sure, because of the absence of powerful and reliable armoured cars and tanks. But the days of easy victories for the British were over. It's often forgotten that the bulk of the troops led by Erwin Rommel that inflicted numerous painful defeats on the British over the eighteen months that followed Beda Fomm were not German but Italian.[38]

The presence of any Germans at all in North Africa in 1941 was an unfortunate and unexpected consequence of COMPASS. Hitler had always been 'bored and exasperated' by the Mediterranean, and had no natural inclination to intervene there.[39] In the midsummer of 1940 he had formulated plans for an attack on Gibraltar (Operation FELIX) to try to put further pressure on the British to make peace. But to accomplish such a scheme would require Spanish co-operation, and at their personal meeting that October, Generalísimo Franco told Hitler that the price for his country's military intervention in the war would be elaborate economic assistance and French North African territory. Since Hitler could not spare the *matériel* and did not want to alienate the Vichy regime at a time when he was also trying to court Pétain, he demurred. FELIX was shelved indefinitely.

COMPASS, however, meant that Hitler was now forced to pay more attention to the Mediterranean. On 10 December 1940, the day following the start of O'Connor's offensive, he ordered the Luftwaffe's specialised coastal attack 10th Air Corps (*Fliegerkorps X*), of around 200 combat aircraft, to redeploy to Sicily to help defend Italian convoys crossing to Tripoli. The arrival of these well-equipped and experienced combat aviators was a nasty shock to the Royal Navy. It had just been tasked with escorting a special fast convoy carrying food and aircraft from Gibraltar to the British island colony of Malta before heading onwards to Greece. On 10 January

1941 one of the convoy's escorts, the aircraft carrier HMS *Illustrious*, was attacked by Heinkel He IIIs and Stuka dive-bombers of *Fliegerkorps X* just west of Malta. One of several bomb hits penetrated her armoured deck and exploded in the main aircraft hangar beneath, setting off a gruesome internal fire. *Illustrious* drifted into the Grand Harbour at Valletta, her steering system smashed. After a further aerial pummelling which left her listing to port and one of her turbines cracked, she was able to make it to safety in Alexandria. The merchant convoy she had escorted also survived. But as a result of the attacks by the German planes, *Illustrious* was out of action for the best part of a year. The British Mediterranean fleet was robbed of its only modern aircraft carrier for some weeks until a replacement could arrive. The appearance of *Fliegerkorps X* in the North African theatre 'may be the beginning of evil developments', Churchill commented to the chiefs of staff.[40]

He was more right than he knew. On 11 January 1941, as *Illustrious* burned and O'Connor's victorious Western Desert Force approached Tobruk, Hitler issued Führer Directive 22, which declared that 'for strategic, political and psychological reasons the Mediterranean situation [...] requires German assistance'. This was initially to be in the form of a single 13,000-strong light mechanised division acting as a *Sperrverband* ('blocking detachment'). But on 5 February, on the eve of Beda Fomm, Hitler decided the situation was too precarious for such a small commitment. He decided to dispatch in addition the full 18,000-strong 15th Panzer division to Libya as well.[41] This expeditionary force would be known as the 'German Africa Corps' (*Deutsches Afrikakorps*, or DAK). Its appointed commander, Erwin Rommel, was so far largely unknown to the British. He set foot in Africa for the first time on 12 February 1941.

Rommel's orders from the German general staff were to use the DAK to prevent the British from advancing any further towards Tripoli. The modest number of troops Rommel had initially been given and the time it would take to deploy them to Libya seemed to preclude any more ambitious use. Wavell learned of the new German force and its composition from deciphered ENIGMA messages passed along by Bletchley Park. He was not unduly alarmed. Given its small size, he felt reassured that the Italo-German army in Libya would be unable to mount any kind of major offensive until May 1941 at the earliest.

This was just as well from Wavell's point of view, because to find troops for the campaign in Greece, plus an operation to capture the Italian colonies in East Africa, he had had to disperse the veteran formations that had been victorious in Operation COMPASS. Two inexperienced and under-strength divisions were left holding the line in Cyrenaica. Even O'Connor was gone, recuperating from illness in Egypt. Lieutenant-General Philip Neame had assumed operational leadership at the front. Neame recognised the deficiencies of his command and requested reinforcements urgently. Nothing could be spared until late spring, he was told. But Wavell was sanguine. On 2 March he telegraphed the War Cabinet that, with the forces currently at their disposal, it seemed doubtful that the Axis army would try to retake Benghazi 'before the end of the summer', if at all.[42] ULTRA gave him no reason to doubt this. On 27 March he reassured Churchill that the Germans in Libya were a 'small stiffening' of the mostly Italian forces. Their numbers were 'probably much exaggerated'.[43]

Wavell's poise was not irrational. The Wehrmacht High Command had warned Rommel in a briefing in Berlin on 21 March not to attempt any advance further east than Agedabia, sixty miles from El Agheila.[44] But Rommel was a general of limitless ambition and self-confidence, with a less than punctilious attitude towards orders (unless he had given them himself). Immediately on his return to Libya from Germany, he began an advance. Agedabia fell to little resistance on 2 April. The following evening he and the Italian commander-in-chief in Libya, General Italo Gariboldi, got into a violent argument about what to do next. Gariboldi, nominally Rommel's superior, pointed out, accurately enough, that the Axis forces did not have enough supplies to embark on a major offensive. But Rommel's eyes were already fixed on distant Suez.

At that moment a message arrived from Hitler which reiterated the German General Staff's earlier caution. But it also said, crucially, that an advance of the DAK was permissible 'if it can be determined beyond any doubt that the enemy is withdrawing most of his mobile units from Cyrenaica'. On this rather flimsy pretext Rommel not only declared himself free to continue the advance but also argued that he was now empowered to act independently of Italian orders. Gariboldi submitted unhappily. The Italians never got back moral authority in North Africa again. From April 1941 what had been a parallel but equal war fought alongside the Germans (*guerra parallela*) became a conflict in which Italian forces served in sullen subordination to the wishes of their senior partners (*guerra subalterna*).[45]

Emboldened, Rommel ordered his Panzers to drive on past Agedabia. His tiny force – scattered into small columns, short of petrol, the air filters on its Maybach tank engines clogged with desert sand, its troops, still unaccustomed to the climate, fainting in the 120° F heat – had no business staying in one piece, let alone winning battles. But British resistance in Cyrenaica crumbled as fast as Italian resistance had three months earlier. Confusion was once again followed by panic. In Benghazi, Major John Devine watched as British soldiers streamed northwards in a desperate rush to escape the Panzers, a bitter reversal of Beda Fomm. 'Past us continually were troops moving, cars roaring along the road [...] there were rumours, the sound of guns, the sound of dumps being blown up, wounded arriving, tank people passing whose tanks had run out of petrol and had to be blown up.'[46] Some vehicles were driven off cliffs in their drivers' haste to escape.

Wavell fired Neame and reinstated O'Connor. But the latter, pleading unfamiliarity with the new units defending the front line, asked to be appointed as an 'adviser' to Neame instead – a clumsy division of command that was to become an unfortunate tenet of Britain's desert war. As it turned out, it did not matter which of the two men Wavell put in charge. On 6 April the pair of generals, inspecting the front line together in a staff car, got lost and stumbled into a DAK patrol, which took them prisoner. Benghazi had fallen two days earlier; Derna fell a day later. By 24 April, Rommel's reconnaissance troops had reached the Egyptian frontier, 400 miles from where they had started three weeks earlier.

The DAK did not, however, get to Tobruk fast enough to prevent the Australian 9th Infantry Division from withdrawing inside the town. Perhaps expecting a second Dunkirk, Rommel pressed an immediate assault. But his troops were bloodily rebuffed for the first time. This was positional warfare of a very different character from the frantic 'Benghazi Handicap' that had preceded it. With the Royal Navy controlling the sea lanes, albeit precariously, Tobruk could be supplied and reinforced indefinitely so long as its ramparts held. Rommel blasted his Italian allies (quite unfairly) for the failure to take the port and demanded additional forces from the Wehrmacht High Command.

So far as the exasperated General Halder, chief of staff back in Berlin, was concerned, this was precisely why he had told Rommel not to undertake any major offensive in the first place. The last thing the Wehrmacht needed at that moment was an expanding side-show on the fringes of Europe when the invasion of the Soviet Union was imminent. Rommel, he observed, had gone 'stark mad'.[47] The DAK could not advance into Egypt without taking Tobruk to its rear, a feat that was beyond it with the meagre forces at its disposal. Nor could it withdraw back to Tripolitania without incurring a major propaganda defeat. Not for the last time, the Desert Fox's audacity had collided with logistical reality.

That was little comfort to Wavell in Cairo, however. COMPASS's amazing gains had been almost wiped out in less than a month. And the defeat in Cyrenaica had other disturbing ramifications more than a thousand miles to the east.

Iraq had been independent of Britain since 1932, but it remained, by treaty, an important part of the imperial communications and energy network. The RAF maintained two important bases, at Habbaniya on the Euphrates west of Baghdad, and at Basra at the Persian Gulf delta. These provided refuelling sites for the air link between Egypt and India and protected the oil pipelines to Haifa. Iraq's Hashemite monarchy was traditionally pro-British. But the country's politics had been radicalised by the Arab Revolt in Palestine. Haj Amin al-Husseini, the 'Grand Mufti of Jerusalem', one of the instigators of that revolt, was now living openly in Baghdad. His seditious pronouncements and covert links with German diplomats alarmed the British.

The dramatic reversals of fortune in Cyrenaica in early 1941 reverberated in Baghdad. In the immediate wake of Beda Fomm the Hashemite regent for the infant King Faisal II felt confident enough about future British success to sack his pro-Axis prime minister, Rashid Ali al-Gaylani. But the start of Rommel's offensive in April inspired a quadrumvirate of Iraqi generals known as 'the Golden Square' to launch an anti-British coup. The Hashemites were deposed. The regent fled to British territory. Al-Gaylani was reinstated as Iraqi prime minister. His government promptly reached out to Berlin and secured an agreement to receive thirty Luftwaffe fighters and bombers with aircrews and maintenance staff. These would arrive via the Vichy French colonies of Lebanon and Syria. Admiral Darlan, who was now Marshal Pétain's prime minister, saw in this collaborative agreement his chance to avenge Mers-el-Kébir. On 30 April, Iraqi troops with tanks and artillery took the heights overlooking RAF Habbiniya and placed the air base under siege. Ten days later, the Grand Mufti broadcast by radio a *fatwa* prevailing on Muslims across the British imperial world to protect Iraq. War had come to Mesopotamia.

*

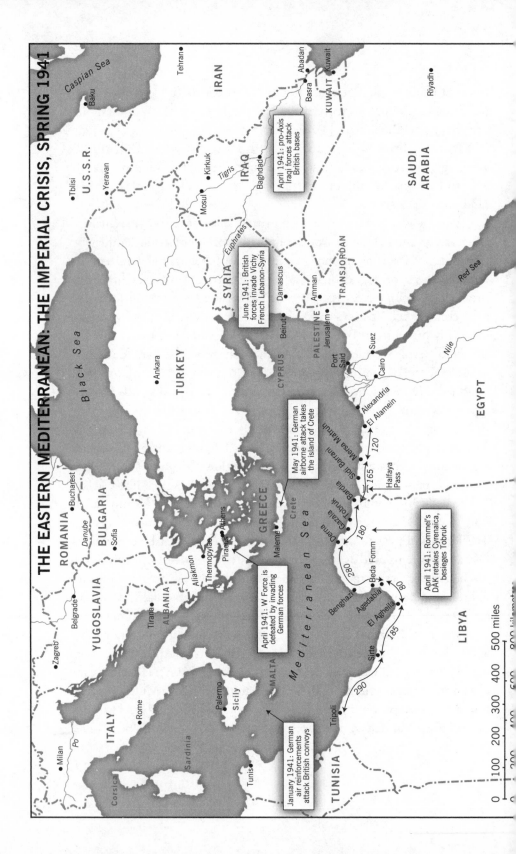

THE EASTERN MEDITERRANEAN: THE IMPERIAL CRISIS, SPRING 1941

April 1941: pro-Axis Iraqi forces attack British bases

June 1941: British forces invade Vichy French Lebanon-Syria

May 1941: German airborne attack takes the island of Crete

April 1941: W Force is defeated by invading German forces

April 1941: Rommel's DAK retakes Cyrenaica, besieges Tobruk

January 1941: German air reinforcements attack British convoys

Caspian Sea

Baku
Tehran•
•Tbilisi
Yeravan
Baghdad

U.S.S.R.
IRAN
Abadan
Basra
Kuwait

KUWAIT

Tigris
Mosul
Kirkuk
IRAQ

Euphrates
SYRIA
Damascus
Beirut
Amman

SAUDI ARABIA
Riyadh•

TRANSJORDAN
PALESTINE
Jerusalem

Red Sea

Ankara•

TURKEY

Suez
Port Said
Cairo
Nile
Alexandria
El Alamein
Mersa Matruh

EGYPT

Black Sea

ROMANIA
Bucharest•
Danube
BULGARIA
Sofia•

Belgrade•
Zagreb•
YUGOSLAVIA

120
165
Sidi Barrani
Bardia
Halfaya Pass
Tobruk
Gazala
Derna

GREECE
Crete
Maleme
Athens
Piraeus
Thermopylae
Aliakmon
ALBANIA
Tirana•

CYPRUS

180
280
Beda Fomm
Benghazi
Agedabia
El Agheila
80

MALTA

Mediterranean Sea

ITALY
Rome•
Milan•
Po
Sardinia
Corsica
Palermo
Sicily

185
Sirte
290
Tripoli

LIBYA
TUNISIA
Tunis

0   100   200   300   400   500 miles

It was at this critical juncture, as it seemed that the British Nile base might fall from attacks to the east and west, that a clash grew back in London between Churchill and Dill about what the priorities of British grand strategy ought to be. On 28 April the prime minister minuted the service chiefs that

> The loss of Egypt and the Middle East would be a disaster of the first magnitude to Great Britain, second only to successful invasion and final conquest. Every effort is to be made to reinforce General Wavell and military and air forces, and if Admiral Cunningham [Commander-in-Chief of the Mediterranean fleet, based in Alexandria] requires more ships, the Admiralty will make proposals for supplying them.[48]

Dill responded to Churchill on 6 May. He conceded that the loss of Egypt 'would be a calamity [...] and one which we would not accept without a most desperate fight'. But, he added, 'it would not end the war.' Only an invasion of the United Kingdom itself could do that. Furthermore,

> Egypt is not even second in order of priority, for it has been an accepted principle in our strategy that in the last resort the security of Singapore comes before that of Egypt. Yet the defences of Singapore are still considerably below standard.[49]

This touched on a basic question that had major political as well as military implications. Ever since the ending of the Anglo-Japanese alliance in 1922 and the souring of relations between the two states, British strategy for the defence of Australia, New Zealand and the South-East Asian colonies had been centred on Singapore. If the Japanese ever attacked British territory in the region, they would have to take Singapore before moving further south. As a result, an elaborate naval base with the largest dry dock in the world was constructed there during the inter-war years (albeit tardily, given Treasury hesitations over the budget) and completed in early 1938, at a total cost of £60 million.

But it was an empty shell of a base. There was no permanent Royal Navy battle fleet available to sally from it. Instead the idea developed of the 'Main Fleet to Singapore' strategy – that in the event of a crisis in the Far East, the British Mediterranean fleet, perhaps supplemented by warships from home waters, would sail for the Strait of Malacca. This would be a way of avoiding building two permanent fleets. But it also meant that at the start of any crisis with Japan there would be a delay before the Mediterranean fleet could get to Singapore.

This 'period before relief', during which the Singapore base would simply have to hold out as best it could, was originally calculated in the early 1930s as forty days. But it grew longer and longer as the European situation worsened. By September 1939 it was reckoned to be at least 180 days. Churchill, at that time Chamberlain's First Lord of the Admiralty, reassured the Australian government that the defence of Singapore nonetheless remained paramount to British grand strategy. 'If the choice were presented of defending Australia against a serious attack or sacrificing British interests in the Mediterranean, our duty to Australia would take precedence,' he told Canberra on 17 November 1939.[50] The following August he reiterated to the Antipodean Dominions that, if Japan ever threatened to invade Australia or New Zealand, 'we would cut our losses in the Mediterranean and sacrifice every interest' except the defence of the United Kingdom itself to defend them.'[51] It was based on these reassurances that the Australian War Cabinet agreed the following month to commit to sending two infantry divisions, almost the only trained and equipped troops the Dominion had, to the Middle East to assist Wavell rather than remaining in Asia.[52]

It was to these long-standing commitments to the Australians and New Zealanders that Dill was referring in his 6 May 1941 memorandum to the prime minister. After all, the threat from Japan was no longer an abstraction. The previous September the Tokyo government had agreed to the Tripartite Pact with Germany and Italy, formally creating the Axis alliance. In April 1941 the Japanese foreign minister had visited Moscow, signing a non-aggression treaty with the USSR which left Japan's northern flank secure should it choose to expand southwards. In July, Japanese troops completed the occupation of French Indo-China, placing Malaya within bombing range of land-based aircraft. Churchill was aware of the danger, though he downplayed it in his conversations with the Dominion prime ministers. 'The danger of Japan going to war with the British Empire [...] is definitely less,' he had assured the Australian leader, Robert Menzies, back in December. Just a few days earlier, however, Churchill had written to Roosevelt that 'it seems clear that the Japanese are thrusting southwards [...] thus bringing them within a comparatively short distance of Singapore.'[53]

The problem of defending the Singapore base from a Japanese threat was no longer just a matter of sending a fleet. Back in the 1920s, it had been assumed that any attack on the city would have to come by sea because the jungle of the Malayan peninsula was too impenetrable to provide a practical invasion route from the north. But by the mid-1930s Malaya's inland road system linking its rubber plantations to Singapore had become sophisticated enough to make that assumption insecure. The Japanese could now approach Singapore from Thailand or by amphibious invasion of Malaya. The whole peninsula, in other words, needed defending. The RAF had agreed to take over the defence of Malaya in 1936. It established a series of airfields across the colony. But there were no spare aircraft to send to them. In mid-1940 the chiefs of staff estimated that twenty-two squadrons with 336 first-line aircraft were the minimum requirement to secure British South-East Asia. The local commanders had only eighty-eight aircraft. By December the estimate of the smallest viable force had risen to 566 aircraft, but no reinforcements came.[54]

Resources, though, were pouring into Egypt at that moment. Between January and July 1941, 239,000 troops arrived, 144,000 of them from the UK. Over a million tons of military stores, vehicles and aircraft were delivered. An additional 770 tanks, 600 field guns and 200 anti-tank guns would arrive in the autumn.[55] The threat to Egypt was real, to be sure, but was it worth compromising British imperial security everywhere else to neutralise it – especially given the promises made to the Australians and New Zealanders? That was the basis of Dill's query.

'I was astonished to receive this document,' Churchill said in his memoirs about Dill's memorandum of 6 May. He responded to his CIGS a week later:

> I gather you would be prepared to face the loss of Egypt and the Nile Valley, together with the surrender or ruin of the army of half a million we have concentrated there, rather than lose Singapore. I do not take that view, nor do I think the alternative is likely to present itself. The defence of Singapore is an operation requiring only a very small fraction of the troops required to defend the Nile Valley against the Germans and Italians.
>
> I have already given you the political data upon which the military arrangements for the defence of Singapore should be based, namely, that should Japan enter the war the United States will in all probability come in on our side; and in any case Japan would not be

likely to besiege Singapore at the outset, as this would be an operation far more dangerous to her and less harmful to us than spreading her cruisers and battle-cruisers on the Eastern trade routes.[56]

Dill responded on 15 May, a fact omitted from Churchill's account in *The Grand Alliance*. He pointed out that his argument that the defence of Singapore had a greater strategic priority than the defence of Egypt was simply a repetition of Churchill's own statements on the matter. In addition,

> I agree with you that the defence of Singapore requires only a fraction of the troops required for the defence of Egypt. That is the very reason why I am so anxious not to starve Malaya at the expense of Egypt. Quite a small addition at Singapore will make all the difference between running a serious risk and achieving full security [...] if we wait till emergency arises in the Far East, we shall be too late.[57]

Churchill was unmoved. 'I had no difficulty in convincing my political colleagues, and I was of course supported by the Chiefs of the Navy and the Air,' he records with satisfaction in *The Grand Alliance*. 'My views therefore prevailed and the flow of reinforcements to the Middle East continued unabated.'[58] Privately, he was incensed by Dill's defiance. Ismay thought him 'shaken to the core' by what he considered the CIGS's defeatist attitude.[59] The prime minister described Dill as 'very tired, disheartened and over-impressed with the might of Germany'.[60] 'Dilly-Dally's' days in the War Office were numbered. In December 1941 Churchill took the opportunity to promote him to field marshal and send him to Washington DC as chief of the British joint staff mission. He made a highly favourable impression among the Americans and was given the honour of burial in Arlington Cemetery when he died from an autoimmune disease in November 1944.

Churchill won the argument in May 1941. Whether he was right and Dill wrong is, of course, a different matter. Prioritising the defence of the 'carotid artery of Empire' was part of Churchill's wider strategy to impress on the Americans that Britain was taking the fight to the enemy by land, sea and air. The Mediterranean had become a central battleground of the war in 1941 largely by accident. Had the Italian advance into Egypt simply become bogged down into a stalemate somewhere in the Western Desert, the Germans probably would have declined to get involved. It was the success of Operation COMPASS that alarmed them into intervention and began the saga of Rommel's Afrika Korps. Once the Germans were in the theatre, however, it was the one place that British land forces could fight them with some possibility of success. Churchill was not unaware of the price that would have to be paid for prioritising the Mediterranean. He understood how scarce the Empire's military resources were. But he argued that, no matter what promises had been made to the Australians and New Zealanders earlier in the war, it was better to deploy such forces as Britain had in a theatre where there definitely was a war going on than a theatre in which war was, as yet, merely a possibility. All Britain could do for Singapore for the time being was hope for the best – and for the Americans.

That last point is important. Churchill was placing a bet that, first, the Japanese would not dare attack Britain's colonies in the Far East, and that, second, if they *did* attack, the United States would feel compelled to intervene no matter whether its own territory had been violated or not. It is worth emphasising that right until the final week before Pearl Harbor, Churchill had no idea if this was true. In August he pressed the Americans to deliver a sharp message to the Tokyo government warning it that an attack on Malaya or the Dutch East Indies would mean war with the United States. Roosevelt agreed, but the subsequent statement was so watered down as to be meaningless. The British nightmare that they might find themselves simultaneously at war, alone, against Germany, Italy and Japan was not assuaged.[61]

The war in 1941 had transformed from a Battle of Britain into a Battle of the British Empire. But *which* British Empire was most at risk, which was most valuable and which of them ought to be defended to the hilt at the expense of others? That remained a matter for disagreement which would go on, sometimes furiously, for years to come.

*

The siege of RAF Habbiniya had a pleasing Shire Folk quality to it. Almost all the ninety-six aircraft stationed there were obsolete trainer types, totally unsuited to modern warfare, while the surrounding Iraqi troops were well trained with the latest British-supplied weapons and equipment. But the RAF ground crew at Habbiniya were able to jury-rig dozens of the trainers into *ad hoc* bombers, and this whimsical air fleet pounded the Iraqi positions in round-the-clock sorties for five days. At that point, as British reinforcements arrived from Basra and Palestine, the frustrated Iraqis abandoned the siege and withdrew back towards Baghdad. The coup began to collapse. On 29 May, with the capital's surrender imminent, al-Gaylani and the Grand Mufti fled to Iran. The Iraqi royal family was restored to power and a pro-British government reinstalled.

The Luftwaffe reinforcements destined for the Golden Square regime arrived too late to make any impression on the campaign in Iraq. But the logistical assistance given to them by the Vichy administration in Lebanon–Syria persuaded the British that a move against Damascus was necessary to secure Middle East Command's north-eastern flank. Having 'liquidated this tiresome Iraq business', as he put it, Wavell sent a force of 34,000 men into the Vichy colony on 8 June.[62] As at Mers-el-Kébir, the world was once again treated to the melancholy site of erstwhile allies killing one another. The Vichy troops had no intention of handing over the colony, and fierce fighting with about 10,000 casualties on all sides lasted until an armistice on 12 July. Lebanon–Syria was turned over to a Free French administration under the auspices of General Charles de Gaulle.

Any victories after the fiascos of Greece and Crete were welcome in the early summer of 1941. But defeating Iraqi and Vichy French troops was one thing: what the British Army had yet to accomplish – had yet to prove it could do – was to inflict a defeat on the Wehrmacht. 'Far more important than the loss of ground is the idea that we cannot face the Germans and that their appearance is enough to drive us back many scores of miles,' Churchill complained to Eden.[63] This was why, as soon as Rommel's troops reached the Egyptian border, the prime minister began pressing for a quick riposte to relieve the besieged Tobruk garrison. On 15 May a limited operation (BREVITY) was launched along the Egypt–Libya border. This briefly took Halfaya ('Hellfire') Pass, the only natural route up from the narrow coastal plain to a 180-metre escarpment a few miles inland which the British would have to climb if they wished to make further progress westwards into Cyrenaica. But Rommel, who could see the significance of Halfaya as clearly as anyone, fooled the British with a feint eleven days later, retaking the poorly garrisoned pass while most of its defenders were chasing phantom Panzers elsewhere.

Churchill, frustrated with his generals as usual, demanded an immediate further offensive with the troops now arriving daily in Egypt. Wavell preferred to wait. He was nervous about the distracting situation in Lebanon–Syria and wanted in any case to allow his newly arrived reinforcements to acclimate themselves properly to desert warfare conditions before committing them to action. He warned London that he had less than 'perfect confidence' about an attack so soon.[64] But the prime minister persisted. Operation BATTLEAXE, then, began at dawn on 15 June. A squadron of twelve Matilda II tanks, supported by a motorised infantry battalion, approached Halfaya. But the Germans had positioned powerful anti-tank defences in the pass after recapturing it, including five of their fearsome high-velocity 88-mm guns, which could punch through a British tank more than a mile away 'like a hot knife through butter'.[65] One by one, accompanied by the sinister whip-crack of an 88-mm shell, the Matildas were picked off far beyond the effective range of their own comparatively puny main guns. Many more victims of the 88s were to follow.

Cyril Joly commanded a tank in the BATTEAXE offensive. In his lightly fictionalised memoir *Take These Men* he recalled his vehicle being 'brewed up' by a German anti-tank round:

> All was chaos. There was a clang of steel on the turret front and a blast of flame and smoke from the same place, which seemed to spread into the turret, where it was followed by another dull explosion. The shock-wave which followed swept past me, still standing in the cupola, singed my hands and face and left me breathless and dazed. I looked down into the turret. It was a shambles. The shot had penetrated the front of the turret just in front of King, the loader. It had twisted the machine-gun out of its mounting. It, or a jagged piece of the torn turret, had then hit the round that King had been holding ready – had set it on fire. The explosion had wrecked the wireless, torn King's head and shoulders from the rest of his body and started a fire among the machine-gun boxes stowed on the floor. Smoke, and the acrid fumes of cordite filled the turret. On the floor, licking menacingly near the main ammunition storage bin, there were innumerable small tongues of flame. If these caught on, the charge in the rounds would explode, taking with it the turret and all it contained.
>
> I felt too dazed to move. My limbs seemed to be anchored, and I wondered vaguely how long I had been standing there and what I ought to do next.[66]

Joly escaped from the brewed-up tank with one other survivor from his crew.

I turned and looked past and to the left of our burning tank [...] beyond the left-hand tank of my troop, which was still exchanging shot for shot with the enemy, I could see all three tanks of Egerton's troop halted and in flames. A large column of black smoke and a long tongue of flame was shooting out of the cupola of Egerton's tank [...] a feeling of desolation settled on me.[67]

BATTLEAXE exposed some of the dangers of learning too many lessons from the victory at Beda Fomm – a battle fought in very different circumstances against a far more vulnerable opponent. The armoured dash to the coast to trap the Italian 10th Army had suggested to the British that tanks alone, if used with sufficiently aggressive speed and élan, could shock an enemy into defeat. The Western Desert Force had not thought sufficiently about the importance of co-ordinating armour with infantry and artillery support. O'Connor had dispersed his meagre forces during Operation COMPASS for lack of any realistic alternative. Inspired by his amazing achievement, O'Connor's successors, though commanding much larger numbers of troops, now continued this unfortunate habit of subdividing their forces in over-complicated plans of attack. This ignored the fact that Rommel's most powerful counter-strokes came when he amassed his troops and tanks to force a decision at one concentrated point. It would be more than a year before some of the misapplied lessons of COMPASS were effectively unlearned by the British desert army.[68]

BATTLEAXE was abandoned after two days. Of the 190 tanks that Wavell had committed to the battle, ninety-one had been destroyed or had had to be abandoned. The Germans had lost only half as many, with just twelve permanently knocked out in action. Halfaya Pass remained in Axis hands.[69]

Rommel, writing later in the war, was magnanimous towards his BATTLEAXE foe. Wavell's strategic planning had been 'excellent', he suggested. 'What distinguished him from other British army commanders was his great and well-balanced strategic courage, which permitted him to concentrate his forces regardless of the opponent's possible moves.' But the slow speed of his heavy tanks had let him down.[70] What Rommel did not mention was that he had known Wavell was coming the day before BATTLEAXE even began. The DAK had arrived in North Africa with an excellent signals intelligence unit, the 621st Short Range Reconnaissance Company, which was able to exploit the lax security on the British wireless network to listen in on communications traffic between units and commands.[71] The Germans had no equivalent to Bletchley Park, but when it came to low-grade battlefield SIGINT, they were miles ahead of the British in 1941.

In London, Churchill was not so generous as Rommel at the failure of BATTLEAXE. Apoplectic would be a more accurate description. 'Every single one of our plans has failed,' he railed at the chiefs of staff. 'The enemy has completely established himself in the central Mediterranean [...] have we really got to accept this?'[72] The lustre Wavell had enjoyed since COMPASS had finally worn thin. Calling the British Middle East commander 'a tired man', Churchill decided to have him swap jobs with General Sir Claude Auchinleck, the commander-in-chief in India. Dill, who had always been Wavell's staunchest defender, argued that perhaps he ought to be given a month's leave in England instead to reinvigorate him. 'Wavell is undoubtedly able and has the confidence of his troops [... and] is a considerable personage in the eyes of the public.' Churchill, though, was unmovable on the matter. Dill reluctantly gave in.[73]

Wavell received the news, which he had been expecting, in Cairo on the morning of Sunday, 22 June 1941. A few hours later he heard the astonishing announcement on the radio that Germany had invaded the USSR. The Mediterranean was now just one more front in an expanding war.

22

TAKING THE GLOVES OFF

Germany invaded the Soviet Union in the early hours of Sunday, 22 June 1941. The Communist writer Naomi Mitchison heard the announcement on the BBC morning news and 'began to sob and shake with hysterics [...] now at last we are on the same side; this ache I have had all the war because of the Soviet Union is now healed.'[1] In Co. Durham, schoolteacher Matthew Walton 'didn't know what to think'. He was 'astounded'. His family were 'unanimous in hoping that the Red Army would get its blow in first. If they can stand up against the German legions, they have a chance to become world heroes.'

> Why has Hitler done it? Is he hoping for compliance from us? Is there some underground agreement? [...] what <u>can</u> the attitude of our government be? At least, that section of it whose whole life is built up on anti-communism?[2]

Edith Oakley's colleagues discussed the attack in their Glasgow shipping company office on Monday morning. Miss Bousie, 'as a great admirer of Russia', applauded the new association with the USSR. 'Agnes is convinced that the Russians are going to murder "*every German*". Mr Mitchell wants, when we have won the war, for <u>all</u> the Germans, eighty million-odd, to be put in camps and gassed like vermin.' Oakley herself was not optimistic about victory in the east: 'I think Russia is against it.'[3] In Sheffield, though, Edward Stebbing and his army comrades were convinced that 'the Russians will slaughter the Jerries'.[4] The general verdict among George Beardmore's friends was that 'the more Russians kill the more Germans, and vice versa, the better'.[5]

Churchill had received news that Operation BARBAROSSA, the code name for Hitler's attack on the USSR, had begun while staying at his country residence, Chequers, on Sunday morning. General Dill briefed him on what was known so far. Hundreds of Axis divisions had attacked the Soviets on a vast front extending from the Baltic to the Black Sea, supported by intensive Luftwaffe attacks. Large numbers of Soviet aircraft had apparently been destroyed. How the Red Army was faring was unknown.

BARBAROSSA provoked 'amazement' and 'bewilderment' among most ordinary people, according to Mass Observation.[6] But not Churchill. ULTRA had been predicting the opening of an Eastern Front for months. The prime minister had repeatedly prevailed on Stalin, without success, to prepare for it. What Churchill had not yet decided on the morning of 22 June was how he should respond to the invasion in public. He spent much of the day in seclusion writing a radio address for delivery on BBC radio. 'The Nazi regime,' he told his audience that night, 'is indistinguishable from the worst features of Communism.'

> It is devoid of all theme and principle except appetite and racial domination. It excels in all forms of human wickedness, in the efficiency of its cruelty and ferocious aggression. No one has been a more consistent opponent of Communism than I have for the last twenty-five years. I will unsay no words that I've spoken about it.
>
> But all this fades away before the spectacle which is now unfolding. The past, with its crimes, its follies and its tragedies, flashes away.
>
> I see the Russian soldiers standing on the threshold of their native land, guarding the fields which their fathers have tilled from time immemorial. I see them guarding their homes; their mothers and wives pray – ah yes, for there are times when all pray for the safety of their loved ones – for the return of the breadwinner, of the champion, of their protectors [...]
>
> Any man or State who fights against Nazism will have our aid. Any man or State who marches with Hitler is our foe [...] that is our policy and that is our declaration.[7]

George Orwell thought the speech 'very good'. It would, he guessed, 'not please the Left. But they forget that he has to speak to the whole world e.g. to middle-western Americans, airmen and naval officers, disgruntled shopkeepers and farmers [...] his hostile references to Communism were entirely right and simply emphasised that this offer of help was sincere.'[8] It was not just sections of the left who were unhappy, however. So were some of Churchill's own colleagues. Eden and Lord Cranbourne, the

Dominions secretary, had wanted the prime minister to stick strictly to military matters. 'Politically,' they argued, 'Russia [is] as bad as Germany.' Half the country would surely object to any close association with the USSR.[9] The Foreign Office had argued in an internal meeting before the invasion that any attempt to 'treat Russia as an ally' after a German invasion should be 'resisted'.[10]

Churchill had carefully avoided describing the Soviets using those words in his broadcast. That remained the official British position in the immediate term. The BBC had not played the 'Internationale' along with the national anthems of the other allied nations after the nine o'clock news on the night of the invasion.[11] Diplomatic posts abroad were warned not to speak of the USSR as an ally of Britain.[12] Clearly, though, Hitler's attack meant that the UK and the USSR, previously quasi-belligerents, were now going to have a very different relationship with one another. While for admirers of the Soviet system, such as Naomi Mitchison, this was a source of profound relief, for others the association left a nasty taste in the mouth. To General Ismay, Churchill's military chief of staff, the prospect of an alliance with the Bolsheviks was 'repugnant'.[13]

In hindsight, we think of Hitler's invasion of the Soviet Union as a crucial turning point in the Second World War which helped to swing the balance of the outcome in the Allies' favour. Churchill could see clearly enough in June 1941 that it was a critical moment – the 'fourth climacteric' of the war, he called it, the first three having been the fall of France, the Battle of Britain and the announcement of Lend-Lease. But whether BARBAROSSA would serve Britain's interests was still unclear in the first few days after the invasion.[14] The Soviet Union's chances looked grim. Alexander Cadogan described Dill as 'very gloomy about Russian prospects' in a presentation before the War Cabinet on 30 June.[15] General Brooke thought the Soviets had four months at most.[16] The Joint Intelligence Committee believed that Nazi tanks might be in Moscow in a matter of weeks.

It was possible, then, that a rapid German victory in BARBAROSSA would be followed by an immediate German invasion of the British Isles, as Hitler, freed from any threat to his eastern border, found himself in a position to try to bring the war to a conclusion before winter. On 25 June, urged by the chiefs of staff, Churchill ordered anti-invasion forces to be put on high alert.[17] Defeat in Crete had revived old fears of airborne attack. 'We have to contemplate the descent from the air of perhaps one quarter of a million parachutists,' the prime minister informed Dill. He requested the rapid manufacture of pikes and maces to make sure every man in the armed forces had a weapon to hand.[18] On the south and east coast of England the summer of 1941 was an uneasy reprise of the year before.

The possibility of the Red Army's collapse made American entry into the war more vital than ever from the British point of view. This, rather than a protracted Eastern Front, was what Churchill pinned his hopes on most in the early summer of 1941. The prospects did seem encouraging. Lend-Lease, a vast and very un-neutral American commitment to the British war effort, had been agreed. The Battle of the Atlantic was raising US–German tensions. On 21 May the New York-registered steamship SS *Robin Moor* was torpedoed and sunk by a U-boat off the coast of West Africa. President Roosevelt, in response, closed German and Italian consulates in the United States and froze the two countries' financial assets. A week later FDR told American radio listeners that 'what started as a European war has developed, just as the Nazis always intended it should develop, into a war for world domination'.[19] The British public interpreted this as tantamount to a declaration of war. 'The entry of America into the war seems imminent,' Edward Stebbing wrote in his diary in Sheffield on 29 May.[20]

Churchill travelled to Placentia Bay, Newfoundland, on board the battleship HMS *Prince of Wales* for his first face-to-face summit with Roosevelt on 9 August, hopeful that the meeting might culminate in the president declaring war against Germany. He told Queen Elizabeth before departing: 'I do not think our friend would have asked me to go so far [...] unless he had in mind some further forward step.'[21] But although the meeting at Placentia Bay provided some valuable symbolic imagery of the two Anglophone leaders sitting next to one another at a joint prayer service, singing hymns familiar to both, it was frustratingly short on practical results. The 'Atlantic Charter' that the two leaders signed, a high-minded but abstract declaration of joint principles (some of which were to have unfortunate imperial consequences for the British later), was no substitute for an American commitment to fight. Leo Amery thought it 'fluffy flapdoodle'.[22]

For over a year Churchill had been assuring his colleagues in London that Roosevelt was itching to fight and was secretly looking for a *Lusitania*-like 'incident' to prod Congress into military action against Germany. After Placentia Bay, the British prime minister had to come to terms with the possibility that the President really meant it when he said he wanted to keep America out of the war. Churchill telegraphed FDR's adviser Harry

Hopkins reporting a 'wave of depression' in the British War Cabinet following his return from Placentia Bay.[23]

With the White House continuing to procrastinate, and the Red Army looking like it might have some fight in it after all, the British began to start taking the relationship with the Soviet Union more seriously.[24] The two countries settled a tentative treaty on 12 July, agreeing to provide mutual aid to one another and pledging that neither would sign a separate peace with Hitler. The latter was an especial fear of Stalin's given that it was known that Rudolf Hess, the Third Reich's Deputy Führer, had flown to Scotland in early May on some mysterious diplomatic initiative and was being held prisoner in the UK. Hess had, in fact, made the journey for his own quixotic reasons, not as an accredited agent of the Nazi state. After interrogation, he had been dismissed by the British as mentally unstable and would remain locked up for the remainder of the war. But given the Soviet Union's own recent collaboration with Nazi Germany, it is not surprising that Stalin could easily imagine Churchill cheerfully betraying him and leaving him to fight it out with Hitler alone in the east.

Within a week of the German invasion the USSR had made its first requests for material aid from Britain: ASDIC sets, anti-aircraft guns and 6,000 combat aircraft.[25] Many more appeals for weapons and equipment would follow. In time Russian attention would shift to the United States as a source of aid. In November 1941 FDR secured Congressional approval for the Soviet Union to be included in the US Lend-Lease programme. But during the first year of the German–Soviet war, it was Britain that provided the lion's share of Allied *matériel* assistance to the USSR. It was not on a huge scale, but it was important all the same, given the Soviet Union's fragility. By the end of 1941, 466 British tanks had been delivered to the USSR. They represented about a quarter of the Red Army's medium and heavy tank strength in the crucial months as the Wehrmacht approached Moscow and the USSR's own industrial production was still in disarray.[26] About 15 per cent of the aircraft that defended the airspace over the Soviet capital in December 1941 were Hawker Hurricanes and Curtis P-40 Tomahawks, the former built in Britain, the latter purchased by the UK from America and then trans-shipped to the USSR.[27] As Dan Todman has noted, if the United States was the arsenal of democracy in 1941, then Britain served very effectively as the arsenal of Bolshevik-style totalitarianism.[28]

The only way to deliver such materials from Britain to the USSR in mid-1941 was the Arctic passage to Archangel and Murmansk around the northern Scandinavian coastline. Convoys began making the treacherous journey twice monthly, starting in late August, to transport munitions to the Soviets. The sailors endured freezing temperatures and drift ice, as well as the threat of U-boats, land-based Luftwaffe bombers and German surface warships. It was far from an ideal route, and to begin with not much could be sent. The first convoy, which arrived in Murmansk on 31 August, consisted of just six merchant ships carrying tin, wood and fifteen crated Hurricane fighters.[29] Planners in both Britain and the USSR began to sound out better alternatives.

A much safer, if more circuital, possibility would be to send convoys from the UK around the Cape of Good Hope to the Persian Gulf, and from there transport goods by land across Iran to Soviet Azerbaijan. This, though, would require the co-operation of Iran's ruler, Reza Shah. On 5 July he declined a Soviet request to allow war materials through his country, arguing that to do so would compromise his country's neutrality.[30]

Iran played an important role in British imperial logistics. The Anglo-Iranian Oil Company's refinery at Abadan was the largest in the world, and critical to the supply of oil to British forces across the Middle East. But relations between the two countries had been deteriorating for some time. The British suspected Reza Shah of pro-Nazi sympathies, citing the presence of several thousand German residents in Iran. The Grand Mufti of Jerusalem and the deposed prime minister Rashid Ali al-Gaylani had been given shelter in Tehran after the failed anti-British uprising in Iraq. The possibility of Iran similarly throwing its support to Hitler and handing over the Abadan refinery to the Germans had haunted Whitehall for many months. But prior to June 1941 direct military intervention against Reza Shah had been ruled out because of fear of the Soviet response. BARBAROSSA now removed that constraint.

On 17 August an ultimatum was sent to Reza Shah's government demanding the expulsion of all German nationals from its territory. The Iranians, who could see that their strategic situation had worsened thanks to BARBAROSSA, had in fact already begun this process. But the demand was a pretext. On the morning of 25 August the Royal Navy sloop HMS *Shoreham* attacked the Iranian warship *Palang*, moored at the pier at Abadan. An explosion engulfed the *Palang* and she sank quickly. It was a Pearl Harbor-style attack, albeit on a modest scale: as *Shoreham*'s guns opened fire, the British and Soviet ambassadors were still driving up to the prime minister's residence in Tehran to announce that a state of hostilities had begun.[31] Later that morning British and Soviet troops crossed the Iranian border.

After some desultory and ineffectual resistance in the first few days, the Iranian government, seeing the hopelessness of the situation, ordered the Shah's troops to return to barracks. On 17 September the Anglo-Soviet forces reached Tehran. Reza Shah was forced to abdicate in favour of his son, and the country was effectively partitioned between the two occupiers for the duration of the war, the British taking the south, the Soviets the north. The Grand Mufti made yet another successful escape from British territory, pretending this time to be a diplomat's footman.[32] He eventually found his way to Berlin, where he became a well-remunerated broadcaster of Nazi propaganda to the Islamic world, and the organiser of Bosnian Muslim recruits for the Waffen-SS.

In his memoirs Churchill ascribed the Anglo-Soviet attack to 'the recalcitrance of the Persian Government' and its 'unsatisfactory reply' to the British ultimatum.[33] Privately, he had cabled to Stalin on 29 August that 'even more than safeguarding the oilfields, our object in entering Persia has been to get another through route to you which cannot be cut.'[34] In Whitehall there was some embarrassment at the brazenness of what the British and Soviets had done. Eden's principal private secretary in the Foreign Office, Oliver Harvey, admitted in his diary that it was 'our first act of "naked aggression"' in the war. Eden, he noted, was 'rather ashamed of himself, so too is PM'.[35] If Britain had dabbled in illegality in its actions towards Norway in the spring of 1940, this was a clear-cut case of brute power defying international law. Indeed, the carve-up of Iran, though conducted with much less violence, bore an uncomfortable resemblance to the division of Poland in September 1939. Here was another sovereign state with the misfortune to be standing in the way of the geopolitical ambitions of two great powers; and now it was Britain playing the part of Germany.

The attack on Iran was not going to be the last occasion on which the Anglo-Soviet *rapprochement* would require London to set aside its ethical qualms. Stalin soon demanded that the British declare war on Hungary, Romania and Finland, the armies of which were all participating in BARBAROSSA. There was an argument for this, if only on the grounds of military consistency. But in the case of the latter two states there were some uncomfortable ironies at work too. Both Romania and Finland had had territory seized from them by the Soviets in 1940. According to Chamberlain's 1939 guarantee to Romania, which had never been disavowed by the

British government, the UK should really have gone to war with the USSR over this blatant act of theft. It had declined to do so because of its parlous circumstances after the fall of France, not from any demonstrable principle.

As for Finland – 'heroic, nay, sublime' Finland, as Churchill had called it during the Winter War – the legitimacy of its grievances with the Soviets were hard to challenge. International sentiment still favoured the Finns, particularly in the USA. As Eden pointed out to the War Cabinet on 23 October 1941, 'a declaration of war on Finland would be likely to be distasteful to a large body of American public opinion, which still thinks of the Finns as a gallant little people'. But 'the importance at this juncture of not rebuffing or discouraging our Russian allies' was ultimately judged to override any other considerations. Britain duly went to war with Hungary, Romania and Finland at midnight on 6 December 1941, just hours before the Japanese raid on Pearl Harbor.[36] The coincidence introduced new ironies. Moscow had insisted that Britain wage war on its attackers. But the Soviets saw no corresponding obligation to declare war on the Japanese after the invasion of Hong Kong or Malaya.[37]

But there was hardly anything about the alliance with the USSR that was not pregnant with terrible irony. Even Churchill's poetic description of Red Army soldiers 'standing on the threshold of their native land, guarding the fields which their fathers have tilled from time immemorial' overlooked the fact that the Soviet border forces on 22 June 1941 were defending territory in eastern Poland, the Baltic States and Romania that they had illegally acquired a year earlier.[38] The seizure of that territory in 1939 and 1940 had been accompanied by arrests, deportations to labour camps, show trials, confessions extracted under torture, executions and state-organised mass murders.[39] In the Romanian province of Bessarabia alone, 8,000 people were shot or killed under interrogation by the Soviet secret police, the NKVD.[40] Around 22,000 Polish Army officers and NCOs, policemen and members of the Polish professional and intellectual classes were secretly murdered at Stalin's instigation in the spring of 1940, many of them in Katyn Forest near Minsk. A month after Katyn's corpse-stacked pits were covered with lime, the Soviet foreign minister Molotov extended his 'warmest congratulations' to the Germans on the 'splendid success' of their armed forces in France.[41]

The German attack on the USSR transformed the character of the Second World War. A rather pointless argument has gone on for years about whether it was the Soviet Union or the western Allies that were 'really' responsible for defeating Hitler. The question makes about as much sense as asking whether petrol or motor oil is more important to making an engine run. Certainly BARBAROSSA made it easier for Britain to fight the kind of war it wanted to fight, a machine-intensive, largely air and sea war in which it was not necessary to build land armies on the scale of 1916–18. Britain could devote much of its manpower to industrial mobilisation on the home front because the Red Army was there to fight the Wehrmacht on its behalf. That fact alone kept Britain's casualty figures during the six years of the war much lower than they otherwise would have been. Alliance with the Soviets was, in that sense, a blessing for the British people, and later the people of the United States. No sensible government would have abjured it.

The fact remains, though, that from 22 June 1941 onwards the moral clarity of the Second World War was never so sharp again. Before this, it had been possible to think of the war as a straightforward battle between parliamentary democracies (albeit imperial ones) and totalitarian states. The alignment of the Hammer and Sickle and the Swastika after the Molotov–Ribbentrop Pact of August 1939 had simplified the stakes greatly. In Evelyn Waugh's semi-autobiographical *Sword of Honour* trilogy the protagonist, Guy Crouchback, greets the news of the German–Soviet pact with a curious sense of liberation. 'A decade of shame seemed to be ending in light and reason,' he thinks: 'the Enemy was plain in view, huge and hateful, all disguise cast off.' But after BARBAROSSA two years later, Crouchback's 'hallucination is dissolved'. He finds himself unhappily watching his country 'led blundering into dishonour' even as its military fortunes improve.[42]

What followed BARBAROSSA was an extraordinary contortion in the attitude towards the USSR and its leadership, promoted from the highest institutions of the British state in order to obscure this moral problem. At the height of the Winter War, Churchill had said that 'Communism rots the soul of a nation [...] makes it hungry and abject in peace, and proves it base and abominable in war.'[43] Two years later, he described Stalin to the House of Commons after their first meeting in Moscow as a man

> of massive outstanding personality, suited to the sombre and stormy times in which his life has been cast; a man of inexhaustible courage and will-power [...] a man with that saving sense of humour which is of high importance to all men and all nations, but particularly to great men and great nations. Stalin also left upon me the impression of a deep, cool wisdom.[44]

Hitler's decision to invade the USSR greatly enhanced Britain's chances of winning the war. It also greatly compromised the legal and moral foundations on which the legitimacy of the war had been built.

*

Four weeks after the start of BARBAROSSA, Stalin wrote to Churchill asking for the British to start a second land front against the Germans in western Europe, perhaps by an invasion of Norway.[45] The prime minister responded two days later that 'anything sensible and effective that we can do to help will be done', but that the Soviet leader must 'realise [the] limitations imposed upon us by our resources and geographical position'.[46] His demurral did not impress the Soviet leader. Further requests for a second front would follow and become more strident. In September, Stalin demanded a major British raid against the French or Balkan coasts to tie up forty German divisions. When the idea was rejected, he upped the ante, asking for thirty British divisions to be immediately dispatched to Archangel or the Caucasus to fight on the Eastern Front. That the entire British Army only had twenty-eight divisions at that moment says a lot about Moscow's lack of understanding of British military capabilities. Churchill insisted that an attack on France was 'impossible' under present circumstances, and that any move against the Balkans would be 'unrealistic [... without] the forces, the aviation, or the tanks' necessary for success.[47]

In fact, Churchill had been pressing his own chiefs of staff for more aggressive action ever since the German invasion of the USSR. The day after the start of BARBAROSSA, Churchill wrote to Ismay proposing 'a large raid' of 25,000–30,000 men on the French coast. 'Now the enemy is busy in Russia is the time to "make Hell while the sun shines"', he argued.[48] In early September he directed the chiefs of staff to draw up a plan to land four British divisions in northern Norway to link up with the Red Army fighting in the Arctic Circle. The chiefs were unpersuaded. They pointed out that the grand strategy agreed in the autumn of 1940 was to stay off the European mainland until the German army had been so worn down by bombing, blockade or subversion that it could not offer significant resistance. 'The Russian war does not change this fundamental concept,' they explained to Churchill. 'Our time for entering the Continent [is] still distant.'[49] A rushed, opportunistic attack risked undoing all the work of rebuilding the army since Dunkirk.

The prime minister found this 'passive inactivity' typical of Dill's War Office, but he would not override his professional advisers on such a central matter of strategy. That still left him with the problem of persuading Stalin that the British were taking the war seriously, however. The Russian leader was unimpressed with the campaign in the Mediterranean, which in mid-1941 was still taking place far from Rome, let alone Berlin. There were some small-scale British attempts to intervene in the war on the Eastern Front, but the results could be embarrassing. On 30 July 1941 torpedo-bombers from the aircraft carriers HMS *Victorious* and *Furious* made a night attack on German merchant ships in the far northern Norwegian port of Kirkenes and the Finnish port of Petsamo. The planes sank one small enemy cargo ship. But flying in the midnight sun they had no hope of surprise, and one third were shot down. The whole operation was, as one historian observes, an 'unqualified disaster'.[50]

Churchill's best line of argument that the British were contributing to the war effort was through the strategic bombing campaign. On 7 July he wrote to Stalin explaining that the RAF was 'making very heavy attacks both day and night [...] upon all German-occupied territory and all Germany within our reach'.[51] Three weeks later the Soviet leader was promised that 'a terrible winter of bombing lies before Germany. No one has yet had what they are going to get'.[52] The prime minister told his Air Staff that the 'devastation of German cities' was needed 'urgently [...] to take the weight off the Russians'.[53] Strategic bombing had become as much an instrument of alliance diplomacy as a military policy. Just as retaliatory raids had helped to sustain British morale on the home front during the Blitz, now they were an expression of commitment to the USSR at a time when precious little else could be offered.[54]

*

After the Battle of Britain the RAF's senior leadership was reorganised. In October 1940 the exhausted Sir Cyril Newall stepped down as chief of the Air Staff, to be replaced by Sir Charles Portal, previously the commander-in-chief of Bomber Command. Aged forty-seven at the time, Portal was seven years younger than Newall, and the youngest member of the chiefs of staff by more than a decade. His physical robustness would be needed over the next five years, as he worked regular fifteen-hour days, including attendance at over 2,000 chiefs-of-staff meetings and regular visits to Chequers to listen to the prime minister's rambling nocturnal strategising.

Churchill's doctor, Charles Moran, said of Portal, 'his head is unduly small and shaped like a sugar loaf, with a bald circle at the summit; his great beaked nose is always in some book or paper [...] his aspect checks curiosity; it seems to say *"all trespassers will be prosecuted."*'[55] General Sir Leslie Hollis, a member of the War Cabinet Office secretariat, described him as a

calm character with a brain like a rapier [...] I never saw him ruffled, even under vicious and uninformed attacks on the Air Force. He would sit surveying the critic coldly from beneath his heavy-lidded eyes, never raising his voice or losing his temper, but replying to rhetoric with facts.[56]

Throughout the war Portal delegated the day-to-day management of the RAF largely to his vice-chief, Sir Wilfrid Freeman. This left him free to concentrate on matters of higher policy. His goals were twofold: to defend the independence of the RAF fiercely against the demands of the War Office and Admiralty, and to maintain the strategic bombing campaign's place at the fulcrum of British grand strategy. He largely succeeded in both. Unlike Dill, Portal was able to stand up to Churchill without infuriating him. His polite but unyielding firmness ultimately won the prime minister over: there was never any question of replacing him while the war was on. From the War Office's point of view, Portal 'was much too good', Major-General John Kennedy ruefully observed.[57]

Portal's arrival at the Air Ministry was followed by a reshuffle at Fighter Command. On 24 November, Sir Hugh Dowding was replaced at Bentley Priory by William Sholto Douglas. On 18 December, Keith Park, commander of 11 Group during the Battle of Britain, made way for the former 12 Group commander, Trafford Leigh-Mallory. Dowding was now fifty-eight and already overdue for retirement. But the brusque manner of his removal seemed a tactless coda to the career of a man who had arguably just saved his country from defeat. Dowding went unmentioned in the 1941 Air Ministry narrative of the Battle of Britain, causing Churchill to complain about the 'jealousies and cliquism' that had excised the chief protagonist from the story. 'What,' he asked the Air Ministry, 'would have been said [...] if the Admiralty had told the tale of Trafalgar and left Lord Nelson out of it?'[58]

Douglas and Leigh-Mallory faced a much-altered aerial battlefield at the beginning of 1941. The night Blitz was at its height, but the German bombers had mostly ceased to fly by day. This was an opportunity, then, to take the battle to the enemy on the other side of the Channel. Douglas and Leigh-Mallory were staunch advocates of the cult of the aerial offensive. Plans were drawn up for a campaign of raids over northern France. These would be of two types. The first, 'rhubarbs', would be small-scale all-fighter sweeps. The second, 'circuses', would be much larger operations, in which two or three Bomber Command squadrons would be escorted by formations of several hundred fighters. The object of both rhubarbs and circuses was less to damage any enemy ground targets than to lure Luftwaffe fighters into the air, where they could be engaged and, hopefully, overwhelmed. Douglas called the new approach 'leaning forward into France'.

Throughout 1941, under this new direction, Fighter Command waged what amounted to a second Battle of Britain, fought not over the wheat fields and orchards of Kent and Sussex this time, however, but in the skies above Picardy and Artois. The fact that this second battle has almost completely disappeared from British memory says much about its outcome. For Fighter Command was to discover in this second confrontation with the Luftwaffe that all the conditions that had worked to its advantage in 1940 now worked against it. Now it was British short-range fighters which had to operate at the extreme limits of their fuel supply over hostile territory, while the German 'Few', scrambling to intercept them with the assistance of their own radar defence screen, had the comparative luxury of being able to bail out or crash-land onto friendly soil.

The Germans were actually in a better position than the British had been in 1940, because while Luftwaffe raids over England had been so large the RAF had had no choice but to intercept them, the rather modest number of Blenheims and Hampdens that Douglas could muster over France (Bomber Command had no enthusiasm for circuses and provided only grudging assistance) were incapable of doing any serious damage. The Germans could pick and choose which attacks to engage and which to sit out, based on the amount of tactical advantage they were likely to enjoy. 'Our idea,' Douglas complained to Leigh-Mallory, 'was to go over the other side and leap on the enemy from a great height in superior numbers; instead of which it looks as though we ourselves are being leapt on.'[59]

Douglas later defended his aggressive policy of 1941 from internal complaints that it was a 'waste of effort'. It wrested the initiative away from the Germans in the west, he insisted. It prevented the Luftwaffe from transferring squadrons from France to support BARBAROSSA. It taught aircrew valuable tactical lessons. It inculcated a necessary fighting spirit. All these claims were dubious. Certainly the Germans ceded the initiative to the British in north-west Europe in 1941. But that was an inevitable corollary of their embarking on the invasion of the USSR; they had chosen to abandon it. The Luftwaffe would have been required to maintain a fairly large fighter force in France no matter what the British did. The decision to keep seventy-five day-fighter squadrons in the United Kingdom, however, was a voluntary one which had unfortunate opportunity costs elsewhere. It badly depleted the British air forces available in North Africa and the Far East, to catastrophic effect in the latter case.

As for experience and morale, Fighter Command claimed by the end of 1941 to have destroyed 800 enemy aircraft for the loss of just 462 of its own. In fact, only 183 German planes had been shot down. The RAF actually lost more fighter pilots in 1941 than it had done in the Battle of Britain. These included some of the most experienced veterans of the 1940 battle. In the last seven months of the year, when rhubarb and circus sorties were at their most intense, the RAF lost thirty flight lieutenants, twenty squadron leaders, six wing commanders (including famous legless ace Douglas Bader) and one group captain either killed or shot down and captured over France. The bemused Germans referred to Douglas's leaning forward as the 'nonsense offensive'. It is not hard to see why.[60]

*

Churchill was not very interested in fighter sweeps. The air war he wanted was a bombing war. Bombing offered a theory of victory that he could offer to sceptics at home and abroad: an argument that Britain could do more than just hang on against the Germans but could actually defeat them. 'There is one thing that will bring [Hitler] back and bring him down,' he told Beaverbrook, 'and that is an absolutely devastating, exterminating attack by very heavy bombers from this country upon the Nazi homeland.'[61] In his speech to the House of Commons on 20 August 1940 at the height of the Battle of Britain, he famously said of the air force's pilots: 'Never in the field of human conflict was so much owed by so many to so few.' But while he went on to make a perfunctory gesture of gratitude to Fighter Command, the focus of his attention that day was clearly elsewhere:

All hearts go out to the fighter pilots, whose brilliant actions we see with our own eyes day after day; but we must never forget that all the time, night after night, month after month, our bomber squadrons travel far into Germany, find their targets in the darkness by the highest navigational skill, aim their attacks, often under the heaviest fire, often with serious loss, with deliberate careful discrimination, and inflict shattering blows upon the whole of the technical and war-making structure of the Nazi power [...]

I have no hesitation in saying that this process of bombing the military industries and communications of Germany [...] affords one at least of the most certain, if not the shortest of all the roads to victory.[62]

Flying operations over Germany in the bombers available to the RAF at that moment – two-engine Whitleys, Hampdens and Wellingtons – was a precarious business. None of these planes was adequately weatherproofed to manage the sub-zero temperatures found at high altitude, especially as the cold winter nights drew in. The Whitley's engine pitch controls could freeze up above 10,000, feet, making it impossible to continue climbing. The fluid inside the lines had to be restored with an injection of coffee, or, failing that, the crew's urine. Ice jammed gun turrets and clumped onto propellers in alarming lumps.[63] Crews could find themselves so short of oxygen that they had to bang their heads on the fuselage to distract themselves from the pain.[64] The German night-fighter force was still not a major threat at this stage in the war. But anti-aircraft fire – flak – was terrifying and deadly. One Whitley pilot found himself caught in a three-sided 'box' barrage trap over Kiel for ten minutes one night: 'Fear broke its dams and swept over me in an almost irresistible flood,' he recalled later:

> Concentrating all my energies, I forced myself to sit motionless in my seat, fighting back an insane impulse to run [...] as the gunfire got heavier, light Flak joined in, and I gazed, fascinated, as if at a deadly snake, when a stream of incendiary shells came up in a lazy red arc which rapidly increased speed as it got nearer and at last flashed past a few inches above the wing on my side [...] by now the aircraft was becoming filled with the fumes of cordite from the bursting Flak shells. It seemed each second must be our last, and that we must surely disintegrate in a blinding flash at any moment.[65]

He survived to get home, but plenty of unluckier crews did not. Between the outbreak of war and September 1941, 875 Bomber Command aircrew were killed on operations. Training conditions were even more hazardous than enemy action: during the same time period 1,157 aircrew died in non-operational accidents.[66]

Flying in such conditions took guts. But by early 1941 it was not obvious that the valour of Bomber Command's crewmen was being expended to much use. Portal's first directive to his replacement at Bomber Command, Sir Richard Peirse, was to attack German oil refineries and storage depots. Oil, the Air Ministry had concluded, was 'the weakest link in Germany's war economy'.[67] An Air Staff report calculated that if the RAF could destroy the seventeen most important synthetic oil plants in the Third Reich within four months, then 1.5 million tons of production would be lost, a potentially fatal blow to Hitler's war economy.[68]

To destroy these oil plants, however, Bomber Command would have to hit them first. This, it discovered, was much easier said than done. In November 1940 the RAF formed a Spitfire-equipped photographic reconnaissance flight. This gave it a means for the first time of objectively evaluating bombing results rather than having to rely on anecdotal accounts by returning crews and vague reports from foreign diplomats. The result was disquieting. On Christmas Eve 1940, for instance, reconnaissance Spitfires took photographs of the Gelsenkirchen oil plant in North Rhine-Westphalia, which had just been attacked by 196 aircraft dropping 260 tons of bombs. The photographs revealed hardly any evidence of bomb craters or damage to the plant at all. Most of the crews had dropped their bombs somewhere else entirely.[69] This put the whole basis of the Oil Plan into question. Portal had assumed in his original calculations that one in every two bombers would find their target. Peirse had thought that the true figure would be more like one in three or one in five. Now even that more modest estimate seemed ludicrously overconfident.[70]

Sometimes the crews did not just get the wrong town: they got the wrong country. On one mission against Mannheim a Whitley bombed Épinal in France, 130 miles away, by mistake. Another Bomber Command crew dispatched to bomb a Luftwaffe airfield in the Netherlands had its compass thrown off by a magnetic storm and attacked RAF Bassingbourn in Cambridgeshire instead. Fortunately, its bombing accuracy was as bad as usual and no one on the ground was hurt. Two Spitfires flew from Bassingbourn to the bombers' home base in North Yorkshire and dropped Iron

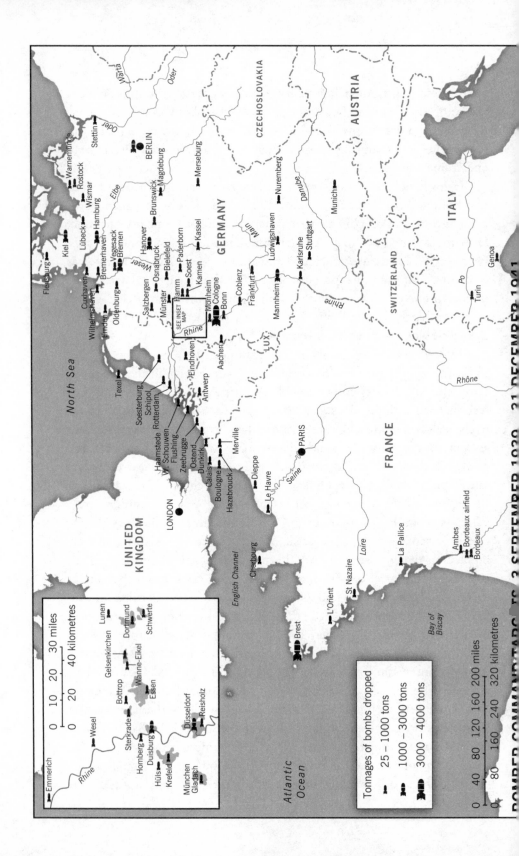

BOMBER COMMAND TARGETS, 3 SEPTEMBER 1939 – 31 DECEMBER 1941

Cross medals in tribute.[71] Humour could not disguise the uncomfortable corollary to these errors: 'precision' bombing was still a fiction.

Worse news was to come in a comprehensive survey of photographic reconnaissance conducted by the economist David Bensusan-Butt in the summer of 1941. The 'Butt Report' was damning. By its author's calculation only one in every five RAF aircraft sent on a bombing mission was dropping its payload anywhere within five miles of its target. Portal pushed back, criticising the methodology. But subsequent investigations by Bomber Command suggested that, if anything, Bensusan-Butt had been too optimistic. The true figure was more like three aircraft in twenty.[72] 'It is an awful thought that perhaps three-quarters of our bombs go astray,' Churchill complained to Portal.[73] Three-quarters was probably a rosy view.

*

In truth, the prime minister had never been very keen on the Oil Plan anyway. To attack oil refineries was a very desiccated response to the Blitz on Britain's own cities. 'We have seen what inconvenience the attack on the British civilian population has caused us, and there is no reason why the enemy should be freed from all such embarrassments,' Churchill urged the Air Ministry.[74] A feeling was growing in the War Cabinet too that, as the official historian of the campaign puts it,

> Bomber Command should become more ruthless in its reply to what was regarded as the German method of total war. Britain should give at least as good as she was getting. Bomber Command should turn the focus of its attack not on to specific targets, such as oil plants, but on to whole German towns.[75]

From a professional point of view, Bomber Command had been underwhelmed by the Blitz. Peirse thought that Göring's raids lacked the necessary 'planned and relentless' character and were much too 'sporadic and mainly harassing' to be effective.[76] But it was impressed with the Luft-waffe's use of incendiary bombs. The big raid on the City of London in December 1940 was afforded considerable admiring scrutiny afterwards because of the damage it had caused in the narrow streets around St Paul's Cathedral and the way the build-up of many simultaneous conflagrations had eventually overwhelmed the London Fire Brigade. 'Fire,' a Ministry of

Home Security report concluded later, 'will always be the optimum agent for the complete destruction of buildings, factories etc.'[77] Incendiary bombs were calculated to be five times as destructive per ton as high explosive.[78] Also large fires had the advantage of illuminating the target for many miles, making it much easier for aircraft lacking electronic navigation systems to find their way to the right place in the dark.

Evidence from the Blitz also suggested that it might be worth moving away from abstract economic systems as targets and more towards the German people themselves. 'British experience leads us to believe that loss of output [...] through absenteeism and other dislocation consequent upon the destruction of workers' dwellings and shopping centres is likely to be as great as, if not greater than, the production loss which we can expect to inflict by heavy damage,' the Ministry of Economic Warfare advised Bomber Command. Perhaps the best way to reduce the Third Reich's industrial output was to kill, maim and render homeless as many Germans as possible in the dense working-class tenement districts of their towns and cities. This would also be a much more psychologically satisfying way of paying them back for the misery they had inflicted on countless British (and Polish and Dutch and Belgian and French) civilians. And it would bring home to the Nazi *Burgher* and his family the cost of the war that their government had so recklessly embarked on. The Director of RAF Air Intelligence welcomed an attack on 'the livelihood, the homes, the cooking, heating, lighting and family life of that section of the population which, in any country, is least mobile and most vulnerable to a general air attack – the working class'.[79]

If the RAF wanted approval to attack German morale, however, it faced the awkward riposte that British morale had not collapsed under similar attack in the Blitz. The way around this was to assert that Germans were *different* – psychologically more fragile, more prone to hysteria and panic, constitutionally lacking in Shire Folk phlegm. 'The morale of the average German civilian will weaken quicker than that of a population such as our own as a consequence of direct attack,' an air bombardment report argued in January 1941. 'The Germans have been under-nourished and subjected to a permanent strain equivalent to that of war conditions during almost the whole period of Hitler's regime, and for this reason will be liable to crack before a nation of greater stamina.'[80] The RAF's founding father, Lord Trenchard, long retired to an exalted viscountcy but still an influential man on airpower matters behind the scenes, argued in a May 1941 memorandum that

The German nation is peculiarly susceptible to air bombing [...] their total disregard to the well-being of the population leads to a dislocation of ordinary life which has its inevitable reaction on civilian morale [...] virtually imprisoned in their shelters or within the bombed area, they remain passive and easy prey to hysteria and panic without anything to mitigate the inevitable confusion and chaos. There is no joking in the German shelters as there is in ours.[81]

How precisely Trenchard knew of the volume of laughter in German shelters he did not explain. But his view was shared. In a contest of wills, Portal believed, the British would surely 'prove themselves tougher than the Germans'.[82]

Deliberate attacks on German civilians might be effective, but would they be legal? This was hard to say because at the outbreak of the Second World War there was no single body of agreed law against which the RAF could measure its conduct. An attempt had been made by jurists in The Hague in 1923 to draw up rules of conduct for air warfare which would have made 'the bombardment of cities [...] not in the immediate neighbourhood of the operations of land forces' unlawful.[83] But these were never ratified by any Great Power.

Chamberlain had been questioned on the issue in the Commons in June 1938. He confirmed that there was no internationally agreed set of rules regulating strategic bombing. He insisted, however, that Britain would always respect certain underlying principles of just conduct in war. These included restricting bombing to 'legitimate military objectives' and keeping civilian casualties as low as possible.[84]

The Air Ministry took the view – practical or cynical – that, if war broke out, such restraint would only be exercised while it remained expedient to do so. For its part, it would initially concentrate on narrowly defined military targets, if only because this would impress neutral, particularly American, opinion. If – and more probably, when – the Germans began indiscriminate bombing, however, the RAF would feel itself released from any legal and moral limits. As Newall put it in September 1938, 'we obviously cannot be the first "to take gloves off".' Yet off they would surely come, sooner or later.[85]

Newall's palliative euphemism was revealing. To describe strategic bombing using a pugilistic metaphor reminiscent of the school gymnasium rather than the battlefield was to avoid spelling out what was being proposed, which was the deliberate killing of unarmed men, women and children. The British were deeply uncomfortable discussing something that seemed so inimical to their Shire Folk sensibilities. The bombing of towns was 'a method of warfare which is revolting and un-English', the Admiralty suggested in 1932.[86] That attitude extended into the war itself at first. In April 1940 Sir Samuel Hoare, then the secretary of state for air, disavowed the 'dastardly conduct' of the Germans, promising: 'we will not bomb open towns.'[87]

Yet there was a degree of hypocrisy to this. Unrestricted warfare which recognised no distinction between combatants and non-combatants was normal practice in the British imperial world. Colonial violence had always been directed as much against the societies of indigenous people as their armies. Anyone who wanted to know if the British always limited their use of force to 'legitimate military targets' only had to ask the Ashanti – or the Irish.[88] The RAF's early experiments with 'aerial policing' in the Middle East and South-West Asia in the 1920s had explicitly involved the punitive bombing of rebellious civilian villages, with no consideration for who might be killed.

In fact, just a week after war had broken out, the Air Ministry had already decided that it had been freed from any restrictions on its own choice of targets by the ruthless German bombing raids on Polish cities. Henceforth, Newall argued, 'our action is governed entirely by expediency.' Prohibitions would continue to be honoured only in so much as they were deemed to be in the British interest.[89]

Those prohibitions were steadily abandoned from the second half of 1940 on. In June, Portal, still at Bomber Command, was warned by the Air Ministry that 'in no circumstances should night bombing be allowed to degenerate into mere indiscriminate action'.[90] But it added that attacks on military targets 'in the widest sense' could be made, even though it was accepted these would cause civilian casualties. In July pilots who could not locate their primary target, or who found it obscured by cloud once they were over it, were given permission to choose any alternative target they could see – a choice they were free to exercise their own judgement about. In September, Bomber Command crews were told to bomb anything in Germany they deemed worth attacking rather than bring their bombs home, which had been the old practice.[91] In October, Portal told Peirse that 'if bombing is to have its full moral effect it must on occasions produce heavy material destruction'. Consequently, primary targets that were 'suitably placed in the centres of the towns or populated districts' would now be acceptable, and indeed preferable – because, though he did not quite spell it out, the bombs that missed the target would probably cause incidental civilian casualties.[92]

It's often suggested that the RAF switched from precision to 'area' bombing in the spring of 1942. In fact, Bomber Command's first explicitly area bombing attack of the Second World War was on the night of 16–17 December 1940. The target was Mannheim, in Baden-Württemberg, the occasion an experiment-cum-revenge raid provoked by the MOON-LIGHT SONATA destruction of Coventry. It was neither a very successful experiment nor much of a retaliation. The pathfinder aircraft equipped with incendiaries which tried to start a firestorm in Mannheim's city centre were inaccurate and the bombing pattern was scattered. Just thirty-four Germans were killed and 1,266 made homeless.[93] The death toll in Coventry had been sixteen times greater. All the same, Mannheim was an important intellectual and moral step. The RAF was already well on its way to normalising the idea of indiscriminate area bombing by fire.

Portal's revised directive to Peirse the following July reflected this new, more uncompromising attitude. The Oil Plan was out – even Portal was disillusioned with it after nine months of lack of results. Now, 'the weakest points in [Germany's] armour' were said to 'lie in the morale of the civil population and in [its] inland transportation system'. Peirse was told to aim at 'dislocating the German transportation system and destroying the morale of the civil population as a whole, and of industrial workers in particular'. A list of major railway, canal and road targets in the Rhine–Ruhr area followed – Hamm, Osnabrück, Cologne, Düsseldorf, Duisburg – with a note commenting that

> Most of the railway centres [...] lie in congested industrial areas and near concentrations of workers' dwellings. These objectives are therefore to be considered as suitably located for obtaining incidental effect on the morale of the industrial population. Moreover, the dislocation of the railway system will serve further to disturb the normal life of the community and will consequently have an indirect effect on the morale of the population, even when they are not subject to direct attack.[94]

'Incidental effect', 'dislocation', 'disturb normal life' – this was text as subtext. Area bombing did not quite dare to speak its own name yet. But it was getting bolder.

*

Portal's problem, though, was that he was just not getting results, no matter what his crews tried to hit. The strategic bombing offensive, far from getting into its stride in the autumn of 1941, was winding down. In September 1941 Bomber Command performed 2,621 night sorties over Germany. That was 520 fewer than it had been able to carry out the previous September.[95] The first of the four-engine 'heavies' ordered in the late 1930s, the Short Stirling and the Handley Page Halifax, were finally making their operational debut, but there were still very few of them. Only forty-one heavy bombers had been manufactured in Britain in 1940. Another 498 would be produced in 1941. During the same two years British factories had built 11,347 fighters.[96] Bomber Command was still having to rely on the same two-engine planes it had started the war with. No significant navigational or bomb aiming aids had been introduced yet.

On the night of 7–8 September 1941, in one of its biggest raids of the month, 197 RAF aircraft attacked Berlin. Only sixteen of the planes were four-engine heavies. Most of the bombs hit the eastern and northern suburbs of the city. Thirty-six Berliners were killed. Of the raiders, fifteen aircraft – with eighty-seven crew members aboard – were lost.[97] At this rate, Bomber Command would be wiped out long before Germany. Portal was frustrated. He told Churchill that he needed 4,000 heavies to make strategic bombing work.

By September 1941, however, the prime minister was no longer the enthusiastic believer in bombing he had been a year earlier. There had been too many false starts and over-optimistic predictions. 'It is very disputable whether bombing by itself will be a decisive factor in the present war,' he told Portal. On the contrary, he added,

> all that we have learnt since the war began shows that its effects, both physical and moral, are greatly exaggerated [...] the most we can say is that it will be a heavy and I trust a seriously increasing annoyance.[98]

Portal's stung response came on 2 October. 'If the most we can hope to achieve with our bomber force is a heavy and increasing annoyance,' he wrote to Churchill, 'then, as I see it, the strategic concept to which we have been working must dissolve, and we must find a new plan. We could, for example, return to the conception of defeating Germany with the Army as the primary weapon.' As the chief of the Air Staff knew perfectly well, Churchill had no interest in doing that. 'There is no intention of changing the policy,' he shot back five days later. 'It is the most potent method of impairing the enemy's morale at the present time.'[99] Churchill needed to be able to offer a sop to the Soviets in the absence of any major land fighting.

Path dependency alone required Britain to keep to its strategy. Production decisions had been made in the late 1930s that could not now be undone without massive economic dislocation. A few weeks after Churchill and Portal's exchange, the first production model of the Avro Lancaster, the most successful of the four-engine heavies, made its inaugural flight. Over 1,000 Lancasters were already on order. Portal was not going to get all his 4,000 heavies, not yet anyway. But until the Americans came along, or some other way of winning the war presented itself, he would get to carry on his campaign, if only for lack of any better ideas.

In doing so, he and Bomber Command would go even further down the road to fiery *Götterdämmerung* than they had already. A new bombing directive was approaching that would finally abandon the euphemisms of the past, and a new zealously dedicated commander-in-chief would come with it, prepared to carry it out to its ruthless conclusion. The gloves were truly coming off in this war. New powerful but unsavoury alliances had been negotiated, new compromises with laws and ethics drawn up, new terrifying feats of violence imagined. The British – the gentle, peaceable, civilised, *nice* Shire Folk – were about to start doing things to their enemies that they would have considered monstrous just a couple of years earlier.

23

MARCH ON TO BETTER DAYS

Wednesday, 3 September 1941, marked the second anniversary of the outbreak of the war. All in all, it passed quietly across the United Kingdom. No major enemy activity was reported in British airspace. A German raider dropped four high-explosive bombs on the Imperial Chemical Industries (ICI) factory at Billingham-on-Tees in Co. Durham, damaging a research workshop. On Monday night, twenty-eight German bombers had raided Newcastle, killing fifty-seven people, demolishing 100 houses and destroying the New Bridge Street railways goods depot, which burned for a week, taking 1,500 tons of flour, 160 tons of sugar, 20 tons of bacon and 85 million cigarettes along with it. Molten caramel ran in the city's gutters, sweetening the air across Tyneside with the scent of syrupy tobacco.[1] But this was, as it turned out, the last big air raid on Britain of the year. Most of the Luftwaffe's bombers were busy now over Russia and Ukraine.

One-hundred-and-twenty-six RAF aircraft attacked Frankfurt in the early hours of Wednesday morning. 'Many bursts were seen in and around the industrial and railway centres and near the inland docks', according to the chiefs of staff report for the War Cabinet afterwards. A smaller raid on Berlin the same night dropped fifty tons of bombs and 1,850 incendiaries: 'the objectives in the city were clearly identified, and bursts followed by fires were seen at various points within a radius of one mile of the Alexanderplatz.' In fact, German records show that no serious damage was done to either city. One in ten of the bombers in the Berlin raid was shot down, an unsustainable loss rate in the long run.[2] Reviewing the bombing strategy of the preceding three months, the chiefs conceded that 'no spectacular success has been recorded'. But they insisted that 'reliable reports are now coming in, in increasing numbers, to show that the effect of our attack is being felt.' They did not elaborate on what, precisely, the effect was.[3]

In the Atlantic there was little drama on 3 September. Convoy HX 145, with eighty-five merchant ships, one of the largest yet assembled, had arrived in Liverpool on 31 August without incident. Another, HX 146, with sixty-two vessels, was expected in the Mersey on Saturday. It too would make port with no losses. But a third convoy of sixty-four ships, SC 42, carrying half a million tons of supplies, which had left Nova Scotia on 30 August and was steaming that Wednesday eastwards in the direction of Cape Farewell, Greenland, would not be so lucky. It was heading straight towards the *Markgraf* Wolf Pack, of fourteen U-boats, which was assembling south-west of Iceland. Bletchley Park had detected the build-up of *Markgraf* thanks to deciphered ENIGMA traffic, but it could not identify the exact location of each submarine. Plus, rough seas and gale-force winds prevented the convoy from steering a wide detour around the danger area. SC 42's twelve columns of merchant ships, covering twenty-five square miles of ocean, staggering along at barely 5 knots, weakly protected by an inexperienced Canadian escort group of one destroyer and three corvettes, were a fat and easy target for Dönitz's men. Their first victim, the 5,591-ton steam merchant *Empire Springbuck*, carrying steel and phosphates, was sunk on the morning of 9 September with the deaths of her entire crew of thirty-nine. By the time SC 42 finally staggered into Liverpool Bay on 15 September it had lost sixteen ships and 278 men, the worst mauling of a convoy for a year. The only scant consolation was the destruction of *U-501*, the first Royal Canadian Navy victory of the Battle of the Atlantic.[4]

Thousands of miles from the frigid Denmark Strait, in the balmier waters of the central Mediterranean, it was British submarines that were attacking Axis merchantmen. On Wednesday afternoon, about 175 miles east of Malta, HMS *Otus*, an O class submarine, fired four torpedoes at an Italian merchant convoy steaming southwards to take supplies to Rommel's forces in North Africa. All four either missed or were duds. Fairey Swordfish torpedo bombers operating from Malta had more luck, hitting the 6,300-ton cargo ship *Andrea Gritti*, which was carrying ammunition. Her cargo detonated. There was 'an explosion accompanied by a very high and wide column of terrifying and vivid reddish smoke, with falling sparks and flashes', according to one eyewitness. All but two of the 349 men on board *Andrea Gritti* perished.[5]

In Libya and Egypt the day passed without much incident. The German-Italian forces surrounding Tobruk continued their ineffectual siege. With his supplies limited and a hostile Tobruk at his back, Rommel could not try to press further into Egypt, and his troops were still deployed more or less where they had been at the end of BATTLEAXE, holding the crucial

Halfaya Pass on the coastal road. Wavell's replacement as Middle East commander, General Sir Claude Auchinleck, was meanwhile drawing up plans for his desert force, about to be renamed the British Eighth Army, to go on the offensive to recapture Cyrenaica and relieve Tobruk. Hundreds of tanks, lorries and field guns and tens of thousands of reinforcement infantry were at that moment streaming into training depots at the vast and growing Nile Delta base. Auchinleck was aware that his political master in London expected him to use this cornucopia of arms as soon as possible, ideally by the end of September. But Auchinleck had no wish to repeat the mistakes of BATTLEAXE. He insisted that his fresh troops were not yet ready to take on Rommel. He would not be hurried. The offensive, code-named CRUSADER, would take place no earlier than November 1941. Until then, the Western Desert war would remain a stand-off.

In Iran, by contrast, British imperial forces were moving rapidly to wrap up the invasion of Reza Shah's inconveniently stubborn kingdom. On Monday, 1 September, the 10th Indian Infantry Division, advancing from Iraq, had marched into Kermanshah, about 325 miles south-west of Tehran. Soviet divisions were heading towards the Iranian capital from the north. 'The inhabitants are friendly everywhere and our forces are now engaged in minor operations against independent bands of armed soldiers and in restoring order generally,' the chiefs of staff noted with satisfaction.[6] Reza Shah's more pliable son would shortly assume the Peacock Throne. All fighting would cease, and the Persian Corridor supply route from Basra to Azerbaijan would begin funnelling Valentine tanks built in distant Smethwick and Hurricane fighters from far-off Surrey to the bloody battlefields of Russia.

Such aid was vital. The situation on the Eastern Front was bleak. On 3 September, German forces encircling Leningrad, the USSR's second city, began shelling the defenders within for the first time. Heinz Guderian's 2nd Panzer Army, having already captured Smolensk, was at that moment wheeling south to trap over 600,000 Red Army troops in a vast pocket around Kiev. That triumph accomplished, it and the rest of the Wehrmacht's Army Group Centre would be free to resume the drive on Moscow, barely 200 miles from the spearhead of the German advance. 'The Russians are hard pressed,' Jock Colville wrote in his diary on Friday. 'We look like being faced with a decision of the same kind as that in the closing stages of the Battle of France; throw in everything to save our allies or reserve our strength in case the worst happens.'[7]

*

For Churchill, 3 September 1941 was a typical day of exasperation. His memoranda expressed his dissatisfaction with his military commanders. He berated the First Sea Lord for the 'melancholy failure' of the Royal Navy to stop a German tanker, the *Ossag*, from reaching Benghazi with a cargo of valuable aviation fuel for the Luftwaffe.[8] He demanded that Sir Charles Portal respond to the 'very serious paper' he had just received on the inaccuracy of RAF Bomber Command's attacks on German targets.[9] Above all, he vented his spleen at the Army for its failure to act decisively enough in North Africa. At a Defence Operations committee meeting that evening, Colville recorded that Churchill 'expressed himself forcibly about the pusillanimity and negative attitude shown by our military advisers'. No one, not even his loyal chief staff officer 'Pug' Ismay, was spared. 'And you are one of the worst,' Churchill shouted at the 'indignant' Pug.[10]

It had been a remarkable, if testing, four years for Winston Churchill. In September 1938 he had not just been out of the Conservative-led government but on the verge of being thrown out of the Conservative Party altogether for his defiance of the front-bench line on appeasement. Members of Churchill's constituency association in Epping, infuriated at his disloyalty to Chamberlain, had talked of deselecting him. He had pondered resigning the Tory whip. In July 1939 four out of five Tory back-benchers said they would not tolerate him being given a Cabinet position.[11] Just two months after that, he was indeed back in the Conservative War Cabinet as First Lord of the Admiralty. Eight months after that, he was prime minister – though how long he would survive in office, or for that matter remain alive, was far from clear with the unfolding disaster in France and the possibility of Nazi invasion. 'You and I will be dead in three months' time,' he had told Ismay in a bleak moment in June 1940.[12] But the immediate danger passed that summer, and on 9 October, the terminally ill Chamberlain having resigned, Churchill had been elected leader of a political party that had been on the verge of expelling him eighteen months earlier.

Few Conservatives had greeted his rise with much enthusiasm at first. Some were stupefied by Churchill's appointment as prime minister, others apoplectic. 'W.C. is really the counterpart of Göring,' the socialite Nancy Dugdale wrote to her Tory MP husband, Tommy (a future party chairman): 'full of the desire for blood, "Blitzkrieg" and bloated with ego and over-feeding, the same treachery running through his veins, punctuated by heroics and hot air'.[13] Alec Douglas-Home, who would briefly become prime minister a quarter century later, said that 'since W. came in, the House of Commons [has] stunk in the nostrils of the decent people.'[14] R. A. Butler, Lord Halifax's under-secretary-of-state at the Foreign Office, grumbled that 'the good clean tradition of English politics' had been 'weakly surrendered to a half-breed American'.[15] Halifax himself lamented to Butler that 'the gangsters will shortly be in complete control'.[16]

But Churchill's success in rallying the nation in the Battle of Britain that summer won over most of the naysayers. There is a glimpse of how the Conservative rank-and-file adapted themselves to their unorthodox new leader in the diary of Sir Cuthbert Headlam, a provincial worthy and backbench MP for Newcastle North from 1940 to 1951. 'I don't want Winston', Headlam had written bluntly in February 1940, when the prospect of a possible replacement for Chamberlain had come up.[17] 'I have never believed in him,' he added when Churchill became prime minister three months later. 'I only hope that my judgement of the man will be proved wrong.'[18] As the summer of 1940 wore on, however, Headlam's assessment became friendlier. 'I have never been one of [Churchill's] admirers,' he wrote on 18 June, the day of the 'Finest Hour' speech,

> But this does not imply that I do not admire his courage, his abilities, his quickness of uptake and his fervid patriotism. In many ways he is the right man for the present situation.[19]

'It is certainly his hour', Headlam added a month later. 'And the confidence in him is growing on all sides.'[20]

Having seen off Hitler's invasion threat by autumn gave Churchill the security to move against the old gang in his own party and create a government more to his own liking. Chamberlain's death in November 1940 removed a powerful alternative focus of Tory loyalty. In December, thanks to another death, that of Lord Lothian, British ambassador in Washington, Churchill was able to lever Halifax out of the Foreign Office with a veneer of dignity. He also took the opportunity to remove David Margesson, an old foe, as Tory chief whip. In July 1941 the purge was completed when Halifax's former deputy, Butler, was replaced at the Foreign Office. Brendan Bracken, a Tipperary *arriviste* and long-time hanger-on, was made minister of information, and the prime minister's own son-in-law Duncan Sandys installed in a junior position at the War Office.[21]

By the autumn of 1941, Churchill's grip on Parliament was virtually complete. The only wobble had come that May after the defeats in Greece and Cyrenaica, when Leslie Hore-Belisha, a disaffected Chamberlain loyalist, and the septuagenarian former prime minister David Lloyd George, who had a quixotic fancy that he might replace Churchill as wartime leader, both criticised the government's direction of the war effort in the Commons. 'We must really have an end of the kind of blunders which have discredited and weakened us,' Lloyd George insisted.[22] The prime minister responded with a robust defence of his record:

> In some quarters of the House [...] there is a very acute realisation of the gravity of our problems and of our dangers. I have never underrated them. I feel we are fighting for life and survival from day to day and from hour to hour. But, believe me, Herr Hitler has his problems, too, and if we only remain united and strive our utmost to increase our exertions, and work like one great family, standing together and helping each other, as five million families in Britain are doing today under the fire of the enemy, I cannot conceive how anyone can doubt that victory will crown the good cause we serve.[23]

'He [held] the House from the very first moment,' Harold Nicolson wrote. 'Very amusing ... very frank.'[24] The subsequent vote of confidence was 447 in support of the prime minister, just three against. Churchill had more serious Parliamentary troubles ahead of him. But in September 1941 his role as Britain's frock-coated generalissimo was unchallenged – even if he had nothing but weary contempt at times for the senior soldiers, sailors and airmen to whom he issued his instructions.

*

What was the mood of the people after two years of war? Mass Observation was out on the streets as usual on 3 September 1941, taking the nation's pulse:

> I'd like to put paid to this war. It's gone on too long for my liking. I don't see the end of it in sight, not by a long way. It's depressing. I want to go back to my wife again. I don't want to go on leading this kind of life. [fifty-year-old man]

It seems like a hell of a stretch since it was peace [...] I suppose it's all for the best, but I'm fed up of wars. [forty-five-year-old man]

I'm just forgetting there was a peace. It's no use remembering things you can't have. I don't like the war, but you've got to put up with it, haven't you, same as everyone else. [forty-year-old man][25]

The Ministry of Information's weekly summary of the nation's morale suggested that 'on the second anniversary of the war, the consensus of opinion is that "we start the third year with immeasurably better chances of victory" [...] all reports agree that there is no lack of confidence in the outcome of the war.' But, it added, 'there is now little talk of it being over this year.' The absence of any major air raids or news from the Mediterranean front had introduced 'a mild satisfaction, and a mild boredom' in people. 'Individual problems' – rationing, shortages, the inconveniences of the black-out, queues, form-filling – preoccupied the national mind for the moment.[26]

It is salutary to be reminded that, while we think of the Second World primarily as a dramatic public experience, for millions of Britons the most important things that took place during it were personal and quotidian: falling in love, falling out of love, getting a new job, losing an old job, getting married, becoming a parent, watching a parent die, leaving school, moving home, falling ill, getting better ... the 'state of the nation' after two years was an aggregate of forty million individual lives, many of which were being shaped by people and events that had little or nothing to do with the conflict directly. Life, in lots of ways, went on as it had always done.

In a retrospective on New Year's Eve nine months earlier, thirty-year-old St Pancras clerk Anthony Heap had written in his diary that 'more happened to me in 1940 than in the whole previous ten years put together'. To have lived through that year, as Heap did, at the heart of the nation's capital, within sight of many of its great collective dramas, would, you might think, have been an extraordinary experience that would have powerfully impressed itself on his memory. It is easy to imagine him looking back at its world-shaking events: Chamberlain's fall and Churchill's rise to power, Dunkirk, the fall of France, the Battle of Britain, the Blitz. But his mind had been altogether elsewhere:

For the first time in my life, I fell really and truly in love. It was a 'grand passion' fated, alas, not to survive the year in which it started. It was an emotional upheaval such as I'd never experienced before and from which I have not even yet fully recovered – and may indeed never quite do so.

[...] the other thing which made 1940 a destiny year for me was the fact that after thirteen-and-a-half years at Peter Robinson's [the department store in Oxford Street], I at last lost my job and, even more remarkable, got another with St Pancras Borough Council.[27]

On the second anniversary of the war millions of other Britons were also focused on the commonplace. A Gallup poll asked people what were the chief changes that the conflict had made to their lives so far. The most popular choices were:

Break-up of family – 15 per cent
Change of job – 12 per cent
Working harder – 9 per cent
Removal to a new home through evacuation, bombing, new job –
    6 per cent
Loss of income – 6 per cent
General depression – 6 per cent[28]

Daily Express journalist Grace Herbert went out to the Victoria Embankment Gardens near Westminster Bridge at lunchtime on 2 September 1941 to ask Londoners their feelings about the milestone date the following day. Mrs Piggott, a part-time factory worker, had a husband serving in India. 'I wish somebody'd start a correspondence course on how to write letters,' she told Herbert:

I just can't explain myself when I write to my husband. How I envy the people who know how. This is how my life has changed: I wait on the doorstep for the post to arrive, instead of for my husband to come home.

A Mr Still told her: 'in six months' time I shall be in the Fleet Air Arm. Before the war I thought I'd be a clerk all my life. This is a break for me.' For W. R. Holden of Shoreditch, whose wife and children were evacuees outside Leicester, the biggest change the war had brought was that he had been forced to learn how to darn, scrub floors, cook, wash up, do the laundry and get in the weekly shopping. Mr Erich of Edgware, in his mid-sixties, had retired before the war. 'Now I've taken a small job. It helps to release a younger man,' he explained to Herbert. Other older people told her that the war had given them a new purpose in life. 'I no longer have the feeling I'm on the shelf,' one said.[29]

'Most people are still living in the present,' Mass Observation noted. 'But at the same time, they are beginning to form definite opinions about the nature of the post-war world.'[30] In Barrow-in-Furness on Tuesday, 2 September 1941, housewife Nella Last had been involved in 'a queer line of talk' with other women,

> a kind of 'turn the clock back, if but for an hour'. It started about peace again, and led on to whether we would like the world to step back to old days and ways. I said, 'speaking personally, I'd not live a year of my life over again, or go back to anything. I'd rather "march on" to better days than go back to any I've lived.'[31]

Already by September 1941 there were faint inklings that the post-war political scene might be quite different from the one Britain had left behind two years earlier. The discrediting of Chamberlain's foreign policy and military preparations had started to spill over into a more general complaint about the whole record of the pre-war National Government. As early as 1 July 1940 the *Times*, normally a bastion of the Establishment, had run a leader column (written by the historian E. H. Carr) which said that 'we must digest the hard lessons of the war as it goes on; and these lessons have not all been military.'

> The anarchic tendencies of *laissez-faire* are as obsolete internationally as they are in domestic politics [...] if we speak of democracy, we do not mean a democracy which maintains the right to vote but forgets the right to work and the right to live. If we speak of freedom, we do not mean a rugged individualism which excludes social organisation and economic planning.[32]

Even a landed Tory like Halifax had begun to accept that, when peace came, it would be 'necessary to have a greater regard to the human values and not allow them to be smothered by considerations of old-fashioned financial purity'. He noted 'the whirling pace' at which thought seemed to be moving on matters of social policy. In his cautious Christian progressive way, Halifax could not help but contrast the nation's willingness to spend £9 million a day on the war effort with the National Government's pre-war refusal to part with £10 million to provide relief for unemployed miners.[33] In the world after Hitler, things were going to have to be different.

The Conservative Party would need to shape and channel this inchoate but potentially powerful new mood if it was to maintain its dominance of the Commons after the war. Sir Cuthbert Headlam, who was elected chairman of the party's local associations union for a one-year term in March 1941, was more acutely conscious of this than most Tory MPs. But with the party's most energetic members serving in the coalition government or in military uniform, its network of regional agents unravelling, its coffers drying up and its leader uninterested in matters of post-war reconstruction ('Winston is quite incapable of the job'[34]), he could not see how it was to be done. 'There is nothing I can do to keep Conservatism alive without workers and without money,' Headlam complained: 'chaos is looming ahead: all the cranks and faddists are getting ready.'[35] Already he was lamenting that 'the Party is ceasing to exist'.[36] The war was not yet close to being won. But the battle for the post-war future of Britain was already getting under way.

*

In many respects September 1941 was the quietest September Britain had experienced for four years. In September 1938 there had been the drama of the Sudetenland Crisis and the terrifying prospect of death by a knock-out blow, only averted at the last moment. In September 1939 war had actually broken out. In September 1940 there had been the Battle of Britain, the Blitz and the prospect of invasion. Now the war had taken a curious turn with the German invasion of the USSR, something that might – or might not – turn out to Britain's advantage. The prospect of immediate defeat was probably ended, the dreadful series of military routs over, for the time being anyway. It was even possible to dimly glimpse a potential for victory. But it would be a long time coming. 'We are in for a long, dreary, exhausting war, with everyone growing poorer all the time,' George Orwell lamented in the final entry of a diary he had begun during the Dunkirk evacuation fifteen months earlier.[37] The war was entering a new stage, one as yet filled with doubt and uncertainty. All the British could do was march on, like Nella Last, to what were hopefully better days.

Three things happened in the opening week of September 1941 – one of them a world-redounding story, the other two secrets, known only to a select handful of men – that would profoundly shape this new, second stage of the Second World War, and the British Empire's future along with it.

The first of them happened off the south-west coast of Iceland on the morning of 4 September, when a US Navy destroyer, USS *Greer*, carrying mail and passengers to the American military garrison at Reykjavik, picked up a suspicious underwater contact on her sonar. The *Greer* had been forewarned that a U-boat might be operating in the area and reported the contact to a patrolling RAF aircraft, which dropped four depth charges. Shortly afterwards, the ship's crew spotted a torpedo track about 100 yards to her stern. The *Greer* immediately attacked the suspected location of her adversary, and over the next two hours dropped nineteen more depth charges, though without result (the German submarine responsible, *U-562*, slipped away, undamaged, to the west, and a few days later participated in the massacre of convoy SC 42).

Had the *Greer* been a Royal Navy ship, the encounter would have been too inconsequential for anyone much to care. But she was the first American warship to be fired on in the Battle of the Atlantic. Roosevelt had another 'incident' to exploit, like the sinking of the SS *Robin Moor* back in May. On 11 September the President made the *Greer*'s story the centrepiece of his radio 'Fireside Chat' to the American people. 'This was piracy – piracy legally and morally,' the President thundered (misleadingly omitting the fact that the US destroyer had been participating in a hunt for the German submarine when it was attacked). 'American naval vessels and American planes will no longer wait until Axis submarines lurking under the water, or Axis raiders on the surface of the sea, strike their deadly blow first.'[38] The US Navy would henceforth protect merchant vessels of all Allied and neutral nations, and attack on contact any U-boat its warships detected within the 'Western Hemisphere Zone', which FDR had defined in late spring – a zone extending over three-quarters of the North Atlantic, ending just 400 miles west of Scotland. On 17 September, American vessels began Atlantic convoy escort duty for the first time.

This was not a declaration of war against Germany. Roosevelt knew that was still impossible. The mood in the US Congress towards outright belligerency remained hostile. When FDR's administration moved to repeal certain sections of the Neutrality Act in response to the attack on the *Greer*, opposition, including on the Democratic Party side, was stiffer than it had been over Lend-Lease. All the same, 'from the date of the *Greer* incident, 4 September 1941', as the official US naval historian Samuel Eliot Morison later put it, 'The United States was engaged in a *de facto* naval war with Germany on the Atlantic Ocean.'[39]

Up to this point, American assistance to Britain's war effort had been economic or symbolic. Now US fighting men were being put directly in harm's way. The prospect of further 'incidents' rose dramatically. They were not long coming. On the night of 17 October the destroyer USS *Kearny* was struck by a torpedo, and eleven of its sailors killed. Two weeks after that, another destroyer, the USS *Reuben James*, on convoy duty near Iceland, had her bow blown off in a U-boat attack aimed at a merchant ship she was escorting. Her magazine exploded and she promptly sank, taking 100 of her 144 crew with her. No one could say for certain when the United States would go to war with Germany, but it was no longer a question of 'if'. Churchill's grand bet placed all the way back in May 1940 was going to pay off.

America's entry into the war would be complicated by another event of consequence to happen the same week the *Greer* was attacked, however. On Saturday, 6 September, an imperial conference (*Gozen Kaigi*) was held in Tokyo in the presence of Emperor Hirohito, with the main attendees being the prime minister, Prince Fumimaro Konoe, the minister of war, General Hideki Tōjō, and the chief of the Japanese naval staff, Admiral Osami Nagano. The Japanese faced a stark decision. On 26 July, responding to the Japanese occupation of southern Indo-China, the United States had embargoed all further exports of oil. This came in the wake of a ban on metal exports and the freezing of Japanese assets in the US. Japan's reliance on the United States for essential raw materials was almost total. The Imperial Navy could manage for eighteen months on its existing oil reserves, the Japanese Army perhaps a year. Cotton, rice, rubber and iron ore were also in desperately short supply. The choice was clear. Either Japan had to re-establish normal trade relations with the United States, which might mean a humiliating retreat from its conquests in China, or it had to seize these raw materials from somewhere else – the Dutch East Indies (modern-day Indonesia) and the British protectorate of Brunei, both major oil sources, being the chief targets – though this would almost certainly mean war with the US and Britain. Konoe favoured negotiations, Tōjō and Nagano (more ambivalently) war. The conference finally agreed on a compromise. Japan would continue to seek a diplomatic outcome until mid-October 1941, after which, if no progress had been made, it would immediately prepare for hostilities with Britain and the United States.[40]

The meeting on 6 September 1941 'was the turning point on the road to Pearl Harbor', as one historian has put it.[41] For the US, it would mean a much more complicated two-ocean war. For Britain, it would be the calling of a bluff that had kept the Far Eastern Empire precariously intact for more than two decades. Churchill had neglected the defences of Malaya and Singapore in favour of the Mediterranean in the hope that war with Japan could be avoided. Tokyo's decision to strike the American Pacific Fleet in Hawaii in the opening hours of the war at least guaranteed that Britain would not be facing the nightmare scenario of a strictly Anglo-Japanese conflict in which the American position might be uncertain. But inattention to imperial security east of the Chittagong was now going to have dreadful consequences. Britain was on the brink of military humiliations to make even Dunkirk, Crete and the Benghazi Handicap look like minor set-backs.

War with Japan – and a great many other things besides – would ultimately be settled by the third critical event of early September 1941, which took place not in the Hyperborean waters off Iceland, nor in an imperial conference chamber in Japan, but in an anonymous room in Whitehall. Seventeen months earlier, a working group of chemists and physicists at Oxford, Cambridge and the universities of Birmingham and Liverpool had been formed to explore the intriguing possibilities of creating a sustainable nuclear chain reaction in certain isotopes of uranium through bombardment by neutrons. It was an idea that had been originally developed by Rudolf Peierls and Otto Frisch, two émigré German-Jewish scientists who had been excluded from radar research in the Phoney War because, as enemy aliens, they were regarded as a security risk. By July 1941 the working group, known as the MAUD Committee, was ready to produce a report for the British government. James Chadwick, the Lyon Jones professor of physics at the University of Liverpool, was asked to author it. Chadwick wrote:

> We have now reached the conclusion that it will be possible to make an effective uranium bomb which, containing some 25 lb. of active material, would be equivalent as regards destructive effect to 1,800 tons of T.N.T. and would also release large quantities of radioactive

substance, which would make places near to where the bomb exploded dangerous to human life for a long period.

Such a programme was both 'practicable and likely to lead to decisive results in the war', he concluded. With appropriate funding a bomb could be ready by end of 1943.[42]

The MAUD Committee report reached Churchill's desk in late August via his scientific adviser Frederick Lindemann. 'Although personally I am quite content with the existing explosives,' Churchill wrote to the chiefs of staff, 'I feel we must not stand in the path of improvement.'[43] On 3 September the chiefs confirmed that, in their view, the MAUD scientists should be allowed to proceed and moreover that no time, labour, resources or expense ought to be spared in pursuit of such an important new device.[44]

In this pedestrian way, on the second anniversary of Neville Chamberlain's declaration of war on Germany, with the flick of a bureaucratic pen, without fuss or much reflection, the Shire Folk became the first people in the history of the world to commit to a nuclear weapons programme.

The war was going to be very different from this point onwards.

NOTES

1: Shire Folk

1. John Ellison, '"The Legendary War and the Real One": The Lord of the Rings and the Climate of Its Times', *Mallorn: The Journal of the Tolkien Society*, vol. 26, 1989, p. 17; 'Author Quotes: W. H. Lewis' First Impressions of Lord of the Rings', *M. Landers*, https://mlanders.com/2014/03/16/author-quotes-w-h-lewis-first-impressions-of-lord-of-the-rings/ [accessed 6 February 2020].

2. J. R. R. Tolkien, *The Fellowship of the Ring*, Boston, MA, Houghton Mifflin, 1994, pp. xiv–xv.

3. Humphrey Carpenter, ed., *The Letters of J. R. R. Tolkien: A Selection*, Boston, MA, Houghton Mifflin, 2000, p. 235.

4. Angus Calder, *The Myth of the Blitz*, London, Pimlico, 1991, pp. 180–208.

5. Tolkien, *The Fellowship of the Ring*, p. 48.

6. Peter Mandler, The *English National Character*, New Haven, CT, Yale University Press, 2006, pp. 164–5.

7. Arthur Bryant, *The National Character*, London, Longman, 1934, p. 18.

8. W. R. Inge, 'Religion', in Hugh Kingsmill, ed., *The English Genius: A Survey of the English Achievement and Character*, London, Right Book Club, 1938, pp. 4–5.

9. Tolkien, *The Fellowship of the Ring*, pp. 1–2.

10. Carpenter, ed., *The Letters of J. R. R. Tolkien*, p. 66.

11. Humphrey Carpenter, *J. R. R. Tolkien: A Biography*, Boston, MA, Houghton Mifflin, 2000, p. 193.

12. Carpenter, ed., *The Letters of J. R. R. Tolkien*, p. 65.

13. Carpenter, *J. R. R. Tolkien: A Biography*, p. 197.

14. Ellison, 'The Legendary War and the Real One', p. 18; T. A. Shippey, *J. R. R. Tolkien: Author of the Century*, Boston, MA, Houghton Mifflin, 2002, pp. 164–5.

15. Harold Nicolson, *Why Britain Is at War*, Harmondsworth, Penguin, 1939, pp. 128–9.

16. J. B. Priestley, *Postscripts*, London, Heinemann, 1940, pp. 8, 21.

17. Priestley, *Postscripts*, pp. 2–3.

18. W. S. Churchill, *The Second World War*, vol. 1: *The Gathering Storm*, New York, RosettaBooks, 2002, pp. ix, 228.

19. Tolkien, *The Fellowship of the Ring*, p. 6.

2: Ulster *Kristallnacht*

1. Details of the Broadgate bombing and the IRA's S-Plan come from Jane Cole Woods, '"To Blow and Burn England from Her Moorings": The Irish Republican Army and the English Bombing Campaign of 1939', PhD diss., University of Kentucky, 1995; David O'Donoghue, *The Devil's Deal: The IRA, Nazi Germany and the Double Life of Jim O'Donovan*, Dublin, New Island, 2010; M. Moulton, *Ireland and the Irish in Interwar England*, Cambridge, Cambridge University Press, 2014; S. Shaw, '"Not Forgotten", the 1939 IRA Bomb Attack', *Historic Coventry*, http://www.historiccoventry.co.uk/articles/s-shaw.php [accessed 15 June 2016].

2. Joshua Levine, *The Secret History of the Blitz*, New York, Simon & Schuster, 2016, p. 95.

3. The last IRA member executed in the United Kingdom was Tom Williams, who was hanged at Crumlin Road Gaol in Belfast in 1942 for the murder of a police officer.

4. National Archives UK (NA): CAB 24/287/30, IRA Outrages, 30 June 1939, p. 9.

5. O'Donoghue, *The Devil's Deal*, p. 254.

6. Woods, 'To Blow and Burn England from Her Moorings', p. 144.

7. O'Donoghue, *The Devil's Deal*, pp. 160–64.

8. Andrew Staniforth, *The Routledge Companion to UK Counter-Terrorism*, Oxford, Routledge, 2013, p. 50.

9. House of Commons Debates (HC Deb) 24 July 1939, vol. 350, cols. 1052, 1083–4.

10. K. D. Ewing and C. A. Gearty, *The Struggle for Civil Liberties: Political Freedom and the Rule of Law in Britain, 1914–1945*, Oxford, Oxford University Press, 2000, p. 413; NA: CAB 24/287/30, p. 1.

11. Woods, 'To Blow and Burn England from Her Moorings', p. 159.

12. O'Donoghue, *The Devil's Deal*.

13. Jon Lawrence, 'Forging a Peaceable Kingdom: War, Violence, and Fear of Brutalization in Post-First World War Britain', *The Journal of Modern History*, vol. 75, no. 3, 2003.

14. Mandler, *The English National Character*, p. 146.

15. Jon Lawrence, 'Fascist Violence and the Politics of Public Order in Inter-War Britain: The Olympia Debate Revisited', *Historical Research*, vol. 76, no. 192, 2003. Oswald Mosley, leader of the British Union of Fascists, tried repeatedly,

though without much success, to disassociate his party from violent tactics; he was all too aware that violence of any kind was regarded as deeply un-British. Adrian Gregory, 'Peculiarities of the English? War, Violence, and Politics: 1900–1939', *Journal of Modern European History*, vol. 1, no. 12, 2003.

16. Clive Emsley, *Hard Men: The English and Violence since 1750*, London, Hambledon and London, 2005, pp. 4, 128.

17. Peter Davison, ed. *The Complete Works of George Orwell: A Patriot After All, 1940–1941*, London, Secker & Warburg, 2000, p. 395.

18. Emsley, *Hard Men*, p. 110; Mandler, *English National Character*, p. 151.

19. Mandler, *English National Character*, p. 170.

20. Patricia and Robert Malcolmson, eds., *A Free-Spirited Woman: The London Diaries of Gladys Langford, 1936–1940*, London, London Record Society, 2014, p. 51 (18 April 1938).

21. Gregory, 'Peculiarities of the English?', p. 55; Emsley, *Hard Men*, p. 141; Stephen Kelly, *Idle Hands, Clenched Fists: The Depression in a Shipyard Town*, Nottingham, Spokesman, 1987, p. 68.

22. *The British Way and Purpose Consolidated Edition*, London, Directorate of Army Education, 1944.

23. Hugh Kearny, *The British Isles: A History of Four Nations*, Cambridge, Cambridge University Press, 2006, pp. 280–92.

24. Kearny, *The British Isles*, p. 283.

25. James Loughlin, *Ulster Unionism and British National Identity since 1885*, London, Pinter, 1995, p. 95; Brian Barton, *Northern Ireland in the Second World War*, Belfast, Ulster Historical Foundation, 1995, p. 3.

26. In a March 1938 Gallup survey, more Britons (28 per cent) said they wanted to see a united Ireland than were opposed to the idea (26 per cent). Robert Wybrow, *Britain Speaks Out, 1937–87: A Social History as Seen through the Gallup Data*, Basingstoke, Macmillan, 1989.

27. Robert F. Foster, *Modern Ireland, 1600–1972*, London, Penguin, 1989, p. 556; Ronaldo Munck and Bill Rolston, *Belfast in the 1930s: An Oral History*, New York, St. Martin's Press, 1987, pp. 18–19, 64–71; Barton, *Northern Ireland*, p. 2.

28. Munck and Rolston, *Belfast in the 1930s*, pp. 24–5, 90.

29. Chris Ryder, *The RUC: A Force Under Fire*, London, Mandarin, 1997, pp. 69, 73.

30. Foster, *Modern Ireland*, p. 529.

31. Kearny, *The British Isles*, p. 290.

32. Thomas Hennessey, *A History of Northern Ireland*, New York, St. Martin's Press, 1997, pp. 61–70.

33. Patrick Buckland, *The Factory of Grievances: Devolved Government in Northern Ireland, 1921–39*, Dublin, Gill and Macmillan, 1979, p. 22.

34. Munck and Rolston, *Belfast in the 1930s*, p. 44. Brooke was the nephew of General Sir Alan Brooke, later Churchill's chief of the Imperial General Staff.

35. Laura K. Donohue, 'Regulating Northern Ireland: The Special Powers Acts, 1922–1972', *The Historical Journal*, vol. 41, no. 4, 1998, pp. 1090–91.

36. National Council for Civil Liberties, *Report of a Commission of Inquiry Appointed to Examine the Purpose and Effect of the Civil Authorities (Special Powers) Acts (Northern Ireland) 1922 & 1933*, London, NCCL, 1936, p. 39.

37. Ian S. Wood, *Britain, Ireland and the Second World War*, Edinburgh, Edinburgh University Press, 2010, p. 188.

38. A. C. Hepburn, 'The Belfast Riots of 1935', *Social History*, vol. 15, no. 1, 1990.

39. Munck and Rolston, *Belfast in the 1930s*, p. 58.

40. Munck and Rolston, *Belfast in the 1930s*, p. 54.

41. Munck and Rolston, *Belfast in the 1930s*, p. 59.

42. Donald M. MacRaild, *The Irish Diaspora in Britain, 1750–1939*, London, Palgrave, 2011, p. 30.

43. *Times*, 5 August 1936, p. 7.

44. Richard Weight, *Patriots: National Identity in Britain, 1940–2000*, London, Macmillan, 2002, p. 59.

45. MacRaild, *The Irish Diaspora*, p. 187.

46. Kearny, *The British Isles*, p. 293.

47. Bryce Evans, 'Fear and Loathing in Liverpool: The IRA's 1939 Bombing Campaign on Merseyside', *Transactions of the Lancashire and Cheshire Historical Society*, vol. 162, 2013; M. Moulton, *Ireland and the Irish*, pp. 300–01.

48. Details in Woods, 'To Blow and Burn England from Her Moorings', and Moulton, *Ireland and the Irish*.

49. Guy Woodward, *Culture, Northern Ireland, & the Second World War*, Oxford, Oxford University Press, 2015, p. 191.

50. Loughlin, *Ulster Unionism and British National Identity*, p. 130.

51. HC Deb 24 July 1939, vol. 350, col. 1054.

52. HC Deb 24 July 1939, vol. 350, col. 1111.

53. HC Deb 26 July 1939, vol. 350, col. 1577.

54. NA: CAB 24/287/30, p. 7; J. McKenna, *The IRA Bombing Campaign against Britain, 1939–1940*, Jefferson, NC, McFarland, 2016, p. 77.

55. HC Deb 24 July 1939, vol. 350, col. 1054.

3: A Different Kind of Nation

1. Charles Saumarez Smith, *The Building of Castle Howard*, London, Pimlico, 1997, p. xviii.

2. David Cannadine, *The Decline and Fall of the British Aristocracy*, London, Penguin, 2005, p. 206.

3. B. Seebohm Rowntree, *Poverty and Progress: A Second Social Survey of York*, London, Longman, 1941, p. 476.

4. Tony Mason, "Hunger ... Is a Very Good Thing': Britain in the 1930s', in Nick Tiratsoo, ed., *From Blitz to Blair: A New History of Britain since 1939*, London, Phoenix, 1998, pp. 8–12.

5. Wybrow, *Britain Speaks Out*, p. 1.

6. J. B. Priestley, *English Journey*, London, Heinemann, 1934, p. 111–12.

7. Cannadine, *The Decline and Fall*, p. 127; Trevor Wilson, *The Myriad Faces of War: Britain and the Great War, 1914–1918*, Cambridge, Polity, 1986, pp. 771–2.

8. Cannadine, *The Decline and Fall*, p. 545.

9. Venetia Murray, *Castle Howard: The Life and Times of a Stately Home*, London, Viking, 1994, pp. 208–21.

10. Andrew Thorpe, *Britain in the 1930s: The Deceptive Decade*, Oxford, Blackwell, 1995, p. 91.

11. Rowntree, *Poverty and Progress*, pp. 476, 454.

12. Peter Dewey, *War and Progress: Britain 1914–1945*, London, Longman, 1997, p. 272.

13. Dewey, *War and Progress*, p. 166.

14. 'A View from the Motor Coach: J. B. Priestley's English Journey Scrapbook', *100 Objects from Special Collections at the University of Bradford*, https://1000objectsbradford.wordpress.com/2011/11/16/a-view-from-the-motor-coach-j-b-priestleys-english-journey-scrapbook/ [accessed 19 December 2019].

15. The damage done by the Germans in 1940 made the post-war plans of Coventry's developers far easier by removing much of the ancient city centre without the need for so much as a permit, though naturally they had to be discreet about appearing to be too pleased.

16. Both buildings were incinerated by the Luftwaffe a few years after opening, alas.

17. Lesley Whitworth, 'Men, Women, Shops, and "Little Shiny Homes": The Consuming of Coventry, 1930–1939', PhD diss., University of Warwick, 1997; D. McGrory, *A History of Coventry*, Chichester, Phillimore, 2003; P. Walters, *The Story of Coventry*, Stroud, The History Press, 2013. F. Taylor, *Coventry: Thursday, 14th November 1940*, London, Bloomsbury, 2015.

18. Priestley, *English Journey*, p. 375.

19. Davison, ed., *The Complete Works of George Orwell: A Patriot After All, 1940–1941*, p. 408.

20. R. C. Self, *Neville Chamberlain: A Biography*, Aldershot, Ashgate, 2006, p. 28.

21. Cannadine, *The Decline and Fall*, p. 229; David Cannadine, *The Rise and Fall of Class in Britain*, New York, Columbia University Press, 1999, p. 134.

22. Kevin Jefferys, *Politics and the People: A History of British Democracy since 1918*, London, Atlantic, 2007, pp. 38–9.

23. John Campbell, *The Iron Lady*, London, Vintage, 2008, pp. 1–4; Meredith Veldman, *Margaret Thatcher: Shaping the New Conservatism*, New York, Oxford University Press, 2015, pp. 16–24.

24. Margaret Thatcher, *The Path to Power*, London, HarperCollins, 1995, pp. 5, 6, 11.

25. Veldman, *Margaret Thatcher*, p. 22.

26. Thatcher, *The Path to Power*, p. 23.

27. Veldman, *Margaret Thatcher*, p. 21.

28. Ross McKibbin, *The Ideologies of Class: Social Relations in Britain, 1880–1950*, Oxford, Clarendon Press, 1990, pp. 269–70; Ross McKibbin, *Classes and Cultures: England, 1918–1951*. Oxford, Oxford University Press, 1998, p. 77; Alan Jackson, *The Middle Classes, 1900–1950*, Newton Abbott, Thomas, 1991, p. 94.

29. Tom Stannage, *Baldwin Thwarts the Opposition: The British General Election of 1935*, London, Croom Helm, 1980, pp. 248–9.

30. John Barnes, ed., *The Empire at Bay: The Leo Amery Diaries, 1929–1945*, London, Hutchinson, 1988, p. 403 (14–16 November 1935).

31. G. K. Fry, 'A Reconsideration of the British General Election of 1935 and the Electoral Revolution of 1945', *History*, vol. 76, no. 246, 1991.

32. Fry, 'A Reconsideration', p. 54.

33. Bernard Harris, *The Origins of the British Welfare State: Society, State, and Social Welfare in England and Wales, 1800–1945*, Basingstoke, Palgrave, 2004, p. 199.

34. McKibbin, *The Ideologies of Class*, pp. 283–4, 289–90.

35. Cannadine, *The Rise and Fall of Class*, p. 142.

36. G. K. Fry, *The Politics of Crisis: An Interpretation*, Basingstoke, Palgrave, 2001, p. 80.

37. J. B. Priestley, *Out of the People*, New York, Harper, 1941, pp. 45, 106.

38. Davison, ed., *The Complete Works of George Orwell: A Patriot After All, 1940–1941*, p. 400.

39. John Baxendale and Chris Pawling, *Narrating the Thirties: A Decade in the Making, 1930 to the Present*, Basingstoke, Macmillan, 1996, pp. 116–18.

40. Julian Jackson, *The Fall of France: The Nazi Invasion of 1940*, Oxford, Oxford University Press, 2003, pp. 108–11.

41. *Times*, 16 November 1935, p. 13.

42. *Daily Express*, 16 November 1935, p. 10.

43. Andrew Taylor, 'Speaking to Democracy: The Conservative Party and Mass Opinion from the 1920s to the 1950s', in Stuart Ball and Ian Holliday, eds., *Mass*

Conservatism: The Conservatives and the Public since the 1880s, London, Frank Cass, 2002, p. 79.

44. Richard Weight, *Patriots: National Identity in Britain, 1940–2000*, London, Macmillan, 2002, p. 23.

45. Ernest Barker, ed., *The Character of England*, Oxford, Clarendon Press, 1947.

46. Roland Quinalt, *British Prime Ministers and Democracy*, London, Continuum, 2011, p. 106.

47. Cannadine, *The Decline and Fall*, p. 277.

48. Norman Rose, *Harold Nicolson*, London, Jonathan Cape, 2005, p. 36.

49. Roland Quinault, 'Churchill and Democracy', in David Cannadine and Roland Quinault, eds., *Winston Churchill in the Twenty-First Century*, Cambridge, Cambridge University Press, 2005, pp. 36–7.

50. HC Deb 8 December 1944, vol. 406, cols. 925–6. Edith Summerskill interrupted Churchill to point out that women too were British subjects and voters, a point that the prime minister conceded.

51. Julie B. Gottlieb, *'Guilty Women', Foreign Policy, and Appeasement in Inter-war Britain*, Basingstoke, Palgrave, 2015, pp. 11, 164; John Charmley, *Chamberlain and the Lost Peace*, London, Macmillan, 1991, p. 147.

52. Raphael Samuel, 'Suburbs under Siege: The Middle Class between the Wars, Part III', *New Socialist*, no. 11, May–June 1983; Selina Todd, 'Class, Experience, and Britain's Twentieth Century', *Social History*, vol. 39, no. 4, 2014, p. 504.

53. McKibbin, *The Ideologies of Class*, pp. 271–2; Wilson, *The Myriad Faces of War*, p. 778.

54. Wilson, *The Myriad Faces of War*, pp. 773–80.

55. N. J. Crowson, *Facing Fascism: The Conservative Party and the European Dictators, 1935–1940*, London, Routledge, 1997, p. 128.

56. *The Economist*, 22 April 1939.

57. Scott Newton, *Profits of Peace: The Political Economy of Anglo-German Appeasement*, Oxford, Clarendon Press, 1996, p. 118.

58. McKibbin, *The Ideologies of Class*, p. 290.

59. HC Deb 22 April 1936, vol. 311, col. 201.

60. Cannadine, *The Rise and Fall of Class*, p. 120.

61. Newton, *Profits of Peace*, p. 72.

62. Oliver Harvey, *The Diplomatic Diaries of Oliver Harvey, 1937–1940*, New York, St. Martin's Press, 1971, p. 222.

63. Maurice Cowling, *The Impact of Hitler: British Politics and British Policy, 1933–1940*, Cambridge, Cambridge University Press, 1975, p. 387.

4: The School of Empire

1. Carel Willem M. van de Velde, *Narrative of a Journey through Syria and Palestine in 1851 and 1852*, Edinburgh and London, Blackwood, 1854, pp. 252–3.
2. Details of the events at al-Bassa below are taken from Matthew Hughes, *Britain's Pacification of Palestine: The British Army, the Colonial State, and the Arab Revolt, 1936–1939*, Cambridge, Cambridge University Press, 2019; Matthew Hughes, 'The Banality of Brutality: British Armed Forces and the Repression of the Arab Revolt in Palestine, 1936–39', *English Historical Review* vol. CXXIV, no. 507; Matthew Hughes, 'The Practice and Theory of British Counterinsurgency: The Histories of the Atrocities at the Palestinian Villages of al-Bassa and Halhul, 1938–1939', *Small Wars & Insurgencies*, vol. 20, no. 3–4, 2009; Jacob Norris, 'Repression and Rebellion: Britain's Response to the Arab Revolt in Palestine of 1936–39', *Journal of Imperial and Commonwealth History* vol. 36, no. 1, 2008; Harry Arrigonie, *British Colonialism: 30 Years Serving Democracy or Hypocrisy?* Bideford, Lazarus Press, 1998, pp. 35–6.
3. Imperial War Museum (IWM): SA 15255, C. Tinson.
4. IWM: SA 23846, D. Woods.
5. Arrigonie, *British Colonialism*, p. 36.
6. M. Hughes, *Britain's Pacification of Palestine*, p. 332.
7. IWM: D. Woods, SA 23846. No one lives in al-Bassa any more. It was destroyed, and its people scattered into exile, by the Haganah during the 1948 Arab–Israeli War.
8. M. Hughes, 'The Banality of Brutality'; Norris, 'Repression and Rebellion'.
9. M. Hughes, 'The Banality of Brutality', p. 346.
10. E. Keith-Roach to Richard O'Connor, 24 October 1938, Liddell Hart Centre for Military Archives, King's College London (LHCMA), General Sir Richard O'Connor papers, 3–1.
11. IWM: D 78/27/1, p. 103, B. A. Pond.
12. M. Hughes, 'The Banality of Brutality', p. 354.
13. Arthur Lane, *Empire Soldier*, Stockport, Nesa News Publishers, 2004, p. 16.
14. Douglas V. Duff, *Bailing with a Teaspoon*, London, John Long, 1953, p. 46.
15. Richard J. Overy, *The Road to War*, London, Macmillan, 1989, pp. 348–9.
16. Bernard Porter, *The Absent-Minded Imperialists: Empire, Society, and Culture in Britain*, Oxford, Oxford University Press, 2004, p. 266.
17. Porter, *The Absent-Minded Imperialists*, pp. 259–73.
18. For an alternative view, see David Edgerton, *Britain's War Machine: Weapons, Resources and Experts in the Second World War*, London, Penguin, 2011, pp. 47–51.
19. L. S. Amery, *The Forward View*, London, Unwin, 1935, p. 168.
20. Overy, *The Road to War*, p. 74.

21. Corelli Barnett, *The Collapse of British Power*, London, Eyre Methuen, 1972, p. 72.

22. Ian F. W. Beckett, *The Great War, 1914–1918*, London, Pearson, 2001, pp. 68–73.

23. Bernard Porter, *The Lion's Share: A Short History of British Imperialism, 1850–2004*, London, Pearson, 2004, pp. 252–3.

24. Amery, *The Forward View*, p. 110.

25. Brendan Simms, *Hitler: A Global Biography*, New York, Basic Books, 2019, p. 89.

26. John Darwin, *The Empire Project: The Rise and Fall of the British World-System, 1830–1970*, Cambridge, Cambridge University Press, 2011, p. 493.

27. G. C. Peden, 'The Burden of Imperial Defence and the Continental Commitment Reconsidered', *The Historical Journal*, vol. 27, no. 2, 1984, p. 416.

28. Graham Freudenberg, *Churchill and Australia*, Sydney, Macmillan, 2008, p. 3.

29. John Charmley, *Chamberlain and the Lost Peace*, London, Macmillan, 1991, p. 14.

30. Victor Rothwell, *Anthony Eden: A Political Biography, 1931–1957*, Manchester, Manchester University Press, 1992, p. 42.

31. Francis R. Nicosia, *Nazi Germany and the Arab World*, Cambridge, Cambridge University Press, 2014, p. 54.

32. Mark Mazower, *Hitler's Empire: Nazi Rule in Occupied Europe*, London, Penguin, 2009, p. 3.

33. Wilfred Campbell, *Sagas of Vaster Britain: Poems of the Race, the Empire and the Divinity of Man*, London, Hodder & Stoughton, 1914, p. 86.

34. *The British Way and Purpose Consolidated Edition*, p. 126.

35. Porter, *The Absent-Minded Imperialists*, pp. 274–9.

36. Jan Morris, *Sound the Trumpets: An Imperial Retreat*, Harmondsworth, Penguin, 1982, p. 311.

37. Mandler, *English National Character*, p. 166.

38. Darwin, *The Empire Project*, p. 449.

39. Gopal, 'Churchill and India', p. 458.

40. Tom Segev, *One Palestine, Complete: Jews and Arabs under the British Mandate*, New York, Metropolitan Books, 2000, p. 442.

41. Edward Keith-Roach, *Pasha of Jerusalem*, London, Palgrave Macmillan, 1994, p. 185.

42. Keith-Roach, *Pasha of Jerusalem*, p. 192.

43. John Connell, *Wavell: Scholar and Soldier*, London, Collins, 1964, p. 168.

44. It still commands a magnificent view of the Temple Mount as the headquarters of the UN peacekeeping force in Israel.

45. A. J. Sherman, *Mandate Days: British Lives in Palestine, 1918–1948*, London,

Thames and Hudson, 1997, pp. 14–52; Naomi Shepherd, *Ploughing Sand: British Rule in Palestine, 1917–1948*, London, John Murray, 1989, p. 183.

46. Shepherd, *Ploughing Sand*, p. 126.

47. William Roger Louis, *In the Name of God, Go! Leo Amery and the British Empire in the Age of Churchill*, New York, W. W. Norton, 1992, pp. 90–91.

48. Louis, *In the Name of God, Go!*, p. 22.

49. Michael Howard, *The Continental Commitment: The Dilemma of British Defence Policy in the Era of the Two World Wars*, London, Temple Smith, 1972, p. 71.

50. Anglo-American Committee of Inquiry, *A Survey of Palestine*, p. 185.

51. Bruce Hoffman, *Anonymous Soldiers: The Struggle for Israel, 1917–1947*, New York, Knopf, 2015, pp. 42–3.

52. For general accounts of the Revolt, see Anthony Clayton, *The British Empire as a Superpower, 1919–39*, Athens, GA, University of Georgia, 1986, pp. 487–507; Charles Townshend, 'The First Intifada: Rebellion in Palestine, 1936–39', *History Today*, vol. 39, July 1989; Segev, *One Palestine, Complete*; Hoffman, *Anonymous Soldiers*.

53. Clayton, *The British Empire as a Superpower*, pp. 494–7.

54. IWM: D 88/8/1, S. Burr, 1 June 1938.

55. Shepherd, *Ploughing Sand*, p. 206.

56. Joseph Nevo, 'Palestinian-Arab Violent Activity during the 1930s', in Michael J. Cohen and Martin Kolinsky, eds., *Britain and the Middle East in the 1930s: Security Problems, 1935–39*, New York, St. Martin's Press, 1992; Townshend, 'The First Intifada', p. 17; Segev, *One Palestine, Complete*, pp. 423–4.

57. Townshend, 'The First Intifada', p. 18.

58. Michael J. Cohen, *Britain's Moment in Palestine: Retrospect and Perspectives, 1917–1948*, London, Routledge, 2014, p. 275.

59. Francis Robinson, 'The British Empire and the Muslim World', in William Roger Louis, ed., *The Oxford History of the British Empire*, vol. 4: *The Twentieth Century*, Oxford, Oxford University Press, 1999, p. 398; Townshend, 'The First Intifada', p. 14.

60. Martin Kolinsky, *Britain's War in the Middle East: Strategy and Diplomacy, 1936–42*, Basingstoke, Macmillan, 1999, p. 233n.

61. Brian Bond, *British Military Policy between the Two World Wars*, Oxford, Oxford University Press, 1980, pp. 268–9.

62. Shepherd, *Ploughing Sand*, pp. 206–7.

63. Hoffman, *Anonymous Soldiers*, pp. 72–4; Hughes, 'The Banality of Brutality', p. 331; Keith-Roach, *Pasha of Jerusalem*, p. 191.

64. Hughes, 'The Banality of Brutality', pp. 316–17; Norris, 'Repression and Rebellion', pp. 28–9.

65. IWM: D 88/8/1, S. Burr, 29 December 1937.

66. Hughes, 'The Banality of Brutality', p. 321.

67. Shepherd, *Ploughing Sand*, p. 212.

68. C. E. V. Buxton to chief secretary, Government of Palestine, 16 March 1939, LHCMA, O'Connor, 3–1.

69. Keith-Roach, *Pasha of Jerusalem*, pp. 194–5.

70. Hoffman, *Anonymous Soldiers*, pp. 88–9.

71. *Dispatch on the Operations Carried Out by the British Forces in Palestine and Trans-Jordan, 1 November 1938–31 March 1939*, 6, LHCMA, O'Connor, 3–1.

72. Sir Miles Lampson to Lord Halifax, 6 December 1938, CAB 24 281.

73. Kolinsky, *Britain's War in the Middle East*, p. 80.

74. Segev, *One Palestine, Complete*, p. 436.

75. Segev, *One Palestine, Complete*, pp. 440–41.

76. Daniel Todman, *Britain's War: Into Battle, 1937–1941*, London, Penguin, 2016, p. 164.

5: Guilty Man

1. Sidney Aster, '"Guilty Men": The Case of Neville Chamberlain', in Robert Boyce and Esmonde M. Robertson, eds., *Paths to War: New Essays on the Origins of the Second World War*, London, Palgrave, 1989, p. 234; K. O. Morgan, *Michael Foot: A Life*, London, HarperPress, 2007, pp. 73–5, 79; David Dutton, *Neville Chamberlain*, London, Arnold, 2000.

2. 'Cato', *Guilty Men*, London, Victor Gollancz, 1940, pp. 70, 74.

3. 'Cato', *Guilty Men*, p. 16.

4. 'Cato', *Guilty Men*, pp. 124–5.

5. Dutton, *Neville Chamberlain*, p. 80.

6. Charmley, *Chamberlain and the Lost Peace*, p. 1.

7. Dutton, *Neville Chamberlain*, p. 71.

8. Churchill, *The Gathering Storm*, pp. 266–7.

9. Lewis Bernstein Namier, *Diplomatic Prelude, 1939–1939*, London, Macmillan, 1948, p. 41.

10. A. L. Rowse, *All Souls and Appeasement*, London, Macmillan, 1961, p. 13.

11. Dutton, *Neville Chamberlain*, p. 84. See also Robert J. Caputi, *Neville Chamberlain and Appeasement: Fifty Years of Conflict*, Selinsgrove, PA, Susquehanna University Press, 1999.

12. Patrick Benedict Finney, *Remembering the Road to World War Two: International History, National Identity, Collective Memory*, London, Routledge, 2011, pp. 188–225.

13. Victor Davis Hanson, *The Second World Wars: How the First Global Conflict was Fought and Won*, New York, Basic Books, 2017, pp. 31, 32, 393.

14. Roy Jenkins, *The Chancellors*, London, Macmillan, 1998, p. 364.

6: The Bones of a British Grenadier

1. Robert C. Self, ed., *The Neville Chamberlain Diary Letters*, vol. 4: *The Downing Street Years, 1934–1940*, Aldershot, Aldgate, 2005, pp. 362–3 (letter to Ida, 13 November 1938).

2. Self, ed., *The Neville Chamberlain Diary Letters*, vol. 4, p. 354 (letter to Ida, 9 October 1938).

3. Self, ed., *The Neville Chamberlain Diary Letters*, vol. 4, p. 358 (letter to Ida, 24 October 1938).

4. Self, ed., *The Neville Chamberlain Diary Letters*, vol. 4, p. 364 (letter to Hilda, 27 November 1938).

5. Self, ed., *The Neville Chamberlain Diary Letters*, vol. 4, p. 374 (letter to Hilda, 15 January 1939).

6. Self, ed., *The Neville Chamberlain Diary Letters*, vol. 4, p. 349 (letter to Ida, 19 September 1938).

7. Anthony Adamthwaite, 'The British Government and the Media, 1937–1938', *Journal of Contemporary History*, vol. 18, no. 2, 1983.

8. Nick Smart, *Neville Chamberlain*, London, Routledge, 2009, p. xiv.

9. Richard J. Aldridge and Rory Cormac, *The Black Door: Spies, Secret Intelligence and British Prime Ministers*, London, William Collins, 2016, p. 82.

10. Dutton, *Neville Chamberlain*, p. 31.

11. Barnes, ed., *The Empire at Bay: The Leo Amery Diaries, 1929–1945*, p. 442 (27 May 1937).

12. Dutton, *Neville Chamberlain*, p. 42.

13. Robert C. Self, *Neville Chamberlain: A Biography*, Aldershot, Ashgate, 2006, p. 8.

14. Charmley, *Chamberlain and the Lost Peace*, p. 154.

15. Self, ed., *The Neville Chamberlain Diary Letters*, vol. 4, p. 283 (letter to Hilda, 21 November 1937).

16. Aside from his height, Chamberlain was a dead ringer for Strube's 'Little Man'.

17. Arthur Salter, *Personality in Politics*, London, Faber & Faber, 1948, p. 85.

18. Self, *Neville Chamberlain*, p. 7.

19. John Ramsden, *The Age of Balfour and Baldwin, 1902–1940*, London, Longman, 1978, p. 359.

20. Self, *Neville Chamberlain*, p. 14.

21. Charmley, *Chamberlain and the Lost Peace*, p. 82.

22. HC Deb 28 February 1939, vol. 344, cols. 1099–1154; Dutton, *Neville Chamberlain*, p. 43; Ramsden, *The Age of Balfour and Baldwin*, p. 357.

23. John Ruggiero, *Hitler's Enabler: Neville Chamberlain and the Origins of the Second World War*, Santa Barbara, CA, Praeger, 2015, p. 50.

24. Andrew David Stedman, *Alternatives to Appeasement: Neville Chamberlain and Hitler's Germany*, London, I. B. Tauris, 2011, p. 11.

25. Charmley, *Chamberlain and the Lost Peace*, p. 13.

26. Ramsden, *The Age of Balfour and Baldwin*, p. 359.

27. Ramsden, *The Age of Balfour and Baldwin*, pp. 354–6.

28. Jenkins, *The Chancellors*, p. 339.

29. Jenkins, *The Chancellors*, p. 335.

30. Self, *Neville Chamberlain*, p. 364.

31. Charmley, *Chamberlain and the Lost Peace*, p. 27.

32. Aldridge and Cormac, *The Black Door*, pp. 74–6, 81.

33. Charmley, *Chamberlain and the Lost Peace*, pp. 22–3.

34. Dutton, *Neville Chamberlain*, pp. 111–12.

35. Charmley, *Chamberlain and the Lost Peace*, p. 13.

36. NA: CAB 23/95, Cabinet Conclusions, 17 September 1938.

37. Overy, *The Road to War*, p. 351.

38. Overy, *The Road to War*, pp. 75–6.

39. Overy, *The Road to War*, p. 95.

40. Stedman, *Alternatives to Appeasement*, p. 218.

41. Overy, *The Road to War*, p. 95; Stedman, *Alternatives to Appeasement*, p. 218; Charmley, *Chamberlain and the Lost Peace*, p. 73.

42. Self, *Neville Chamberlain*, p. 357.

43. Stedman, *Alternatives to Appeasement*, pp. 206–8.

44. Len Deighton, *Blood, Tears and Folly*, London, Cape, 1993, p. 156.

45. Alan Sharp, 'Anglo-French Relations from Versailles to Locarno', in Alan Sharp and Glyn Stone, eds., *Anglo-French Relations in the Twentieth Century*, London, Routledge, 2002, pp. 121–2.

46. John C. Cairns, 'A Nation of Shopkeepers in Search of a Suitable France: 1919–40', *The American Historical Review*, vol. 79, no. 3, 1974, p. 721; Anthony Lentin, 'Lloyd George, Clemenceau, and the Elusive Anglo-French Guarantee Treaty, 1919', in Sharp and Stone, eds., *Anglo-French Relations in the Twentieth Century*.

47. David Dutton, *Austen Chamberlain: Gentleman in Politics*, Bolton, Ross Anderson, 1985, p. 238.

48. Frank Magee, '"Limited Liability"? Britain and the Treaty of Locarno', *Twentieth Century British History*, vol. 6, no. 1, 1995, p. 16; N. H. Gibbs, *Grand Strategy*, vol. 1: *Rearmament Policy*, London, HMSO, 1976, p. 41.

49. Dutton, *Austen Chamberlain*, p. 239.

50. Dutton, *Austen Chamberlain*, p. 241; Cairns, 'A Nation of Shopkeepers', p. 726.

51. Paul W. Doerr, *British Foreign Policy, 1919–1939*, Manchester, Manchester University Press, 1998, p. 60; Philip M. H. Bell, *France and Britain, 1900–1940: Entente and Estrangement*, London, Longman, 1996, p. 161.

52. Brendan Simms, *Britain's Europe*, London, Allen Lane, 2016, p. 152.

53. Cairns, 'A Nation of Shopkeepers', p. 719.

54. Cairns, 'A Nation of Shopkeepers', pp. 725, 723.

55. Basil H. Liddell Hart, *The British Way in Warfare*, London, Faber & Faber, 1932, p. 15.

56. Dutton, *Austen Chamberlain*, pp. 249–50.

57. Dutton, *Austen Chamberlain*, p. 251.

58. Howard, *The Continental Commitment*, pp. 94–5.

59. Simms, *Britain's Europe*, p. 157.

60. Zara Steiner, *The Lights that Failed: European International History, 1919–1933*, Oxford, Oxford University Press, 2005, p. 402.

61. Dutton, *Austen Chamberlain*, p. 250.

62. Overy, *The Road to War*, p. 83.

63. Bell, *France and Britain*, p. 178.

64. Cairns, 'A Nation of Shopkeepers', p. 730.

65. Douglas Johnson, 'Churchill and France', in Robert Blake and William Roger Louis, eds., *Churchill*, Oxford, Clarendon Press, 1996, p. 52; Robert Alexander Clarke Parker, *Churchill and Appeasement*, London, Macmillan, 2000, p. 31.

66. Gibbs, *Grand Strategy*, vol. 1, p. 799.

67. Bell, *France and Britain*, pp. 176–7.

68. Bell, *France and Britain*, p. 179.

69. Talbot Imlay, *Facing the Second World War: Strategy, Politics, and Economics in Britain and France, 1938–1940*, Oxford, Oxford University Press, 2003, p. 28.

70. Donald S. Birn, 'The League of Nations and Collective Security', *Journal of Contemporary History*, vol. 9, no. 3, 1974, pp. 131–2.

71. Birn, 'The League of Nations and Collective Security', p. 135.

72. Azar Gat, *Fascist and Liberal Visions of War: Fuller, Liddell Hart, Douhet, and other Modernists*, Oxford, Clarendon, 1998, pp. 215–16.

73. Stedman, *Alternatives to Appeasement*, p. 108; Birn, 'The League of Nations and Collective Security', p. 133.

74. G. Bruce Strang, '"The Worst of All Worlds": Oil Sanctions and Italy's Invasion of Abyssinia, 1935–1936', *Diplomacy and Statecraft*, vol. 19, no. 2, 2008.

75. Strang, 'The Worst of All Worlds', p. 228.

76. N. J. Crowson, *Britain and Europe: A Political History since 1918*, London, Routledge, 2010, pp. 40–41.

77. Stedman, *Alternatives to Appeasement*, p. 109.

7: The Stupidest Thing That Has Ever Been Done

1. L. S. Amery, *My Political Life*, vol. 3: *The Unforgiving Years, 1929–1940*, London, Hutchinson, 1955, pp. 129–30.

2. Barnes, ed., *The Empire at Bay: The Leo Amery Diaries, 1929–1945*, p. 397 (13 August 1935).

3. Crowson, *Facing Fascism*, p. 40.

4. Somerset de Chair, *The Impending Storm*, New York, Richard R. Smith, 1930, p. 5. He predicted (pp. 126–7) that the Second World War would find Britain, Germany and Japan fighting in alliance against France, the USSR, Poland and, possibly, the United States.

5. Amery's eldest son John ('Jack') later became a passionate Nazi, decamped to Germany during the war and tried to establish a pro-Axis 'British Free Corps', an act for which he was subsequently hanged. Whether this was all part of some grotesque Oedipal drama arising from the Amery family's part-Jewishness will never be known for certain. See David Faber, *Speaking for England: Leo, Julian and John Amery, The Tragedy of a Political Family*, London, Free Press, 2005, p. 519.

6. Barnes, ed., *The Empire at Bay*, p. 459 (26 February 1938).

7. Stedman, *Alternatives to Appeasement*, pp. 232–3.

8. Neville Thompson, *The Anti-Appeasers: Conservative Opposition to Appeasement in the 1930s*, Oxford, Clarendon, 1971, p. 175.

9. Faber, *Speaking for England*, p. 340.

10. Charmley, *Chamberlain and the Lost Peace*, p. 53.

11. Richard S. Grayson, 'Imperialism in Conservative Defence and Foreign Policy: Leo Amery and the Chamberlains, 1903–39', *The Journal of Imperial and Commonwealth History*, vol. 34, no. 4, 2006, p. 511.

12. Stedman, *Alternatives to Appeasement*, p. 31.

13. Barnes, ed., *The Empire at Bay*, p. 424 (12 July 1936).

14. Barnes, ed., *The Empire at Bay*, p. 427 (30 August 1936).

15. Barnes, ed., *The Empire at Bay*, p. 503 (20 April 1938).

16. Barnes, ed., *The Empire at Bay*, p. 410 (7 March 1936).

17. Louis, *In the Name of God, Go!*, pp. 115–18.

18. Dutton, *Neville Chamberlain*, p. 111; David Reynolds, *In Command of History: Churchill Fighting and Writing the Second World War*, London, Penguin, 2005, p. 101; Churchill, *The Gathering Storm*, p. 202.

19. D. C. Watt, 'Churchill and Appeasement', in Blake and Louis, eds., *Churchill*, p. 211.

20. Reynolds, *In Command of History*, p. 102.

21. Philip M. H. Bell, '"Thank God for the French Army": Churchill, France, and an Alternative to Appeasement in the 1930s', in Christopher Baxter el al., eds.,

Britain in Global Politics, vol. 1: *From Gladstone to Churchill*, London, Palgrave Macmillan, 2013, p. 183; Parker, *Churchill and Appeasement*, p. 86.

22. Richard M. Langsworth, 'Did Churchill Ever Admire Hitler?' *Finest Hour*, vol. 156, 2012, p. 33.

23. Self, ed., *The Neville Chamberlain Diary Letters*, vol. 4, p. 81 (letter to Hilda, 28 July 1934).

24. Dutton, *Neville Chamberlain*, pp. 112–13.

25. Parker, *Churchill and Appeasement*, p. 165.

26. Watt, 'Churchill and Appeasement', p. 205; Stedman, *Alternatives to Appeasement*, p. 148; Bell, 'Thank God for the French Army', pp. 180–81.

27. Self, ed., *The Neville Chamberlain Diary Letters*, vol. 4, p. 311 (letter to Hilda, 27 March 1938).

28. Graham Stewart, *Burying Caesar: The Churchill-Chamberlain Rivalry*, London, Weidenfield, 1999, pp. 340–41.

29. Charmley, *Chamberlain and the Lost Peace*, p. 97.

30. Self, ed., *The Neville Chamberlain Diary Letters*, vol. 4, p. 265 (letter to Ida, 8 August 1937).

31. Self, ed., *The Neville Chamberlain Diary Letters*, vol. 4, p. 303 (letter to Hilda, 27 February 1938).

32. Churchill, *The Gathering Storm*, p. 307.

33. Ramsden, *The Age of Balfour and Baldwin*, p. 366.

34. Faber, *Speaking for England*, p. 345.

35. Andrew Roberts, *Eminent Churchillians*, London, Weidenfeld & Nicolson, 1994, p. 172.

36. Charmley, *Chamberlain and the Lost Peace*, p. 16.

37. Smart, *Neville Chamberlain*, p. 225.

38. Thomas Childers, *The Third Reich: A History of Nazi Germany*, New York, Simon & Schuster, 2017, p. 400.

39. Self, ed., *The Neville Chamberlain Diary Letters*, vol. 4, p. 304 (letter to Hilda, 13 March 1938).

40. Aster, 'Guilty Men', p. 249.

41. Barnes, ed., *The Empire at Bay*, p. 496 (12 March 1938).

42. Barnes, ed., *The Empire at Bay*, p. 498 (20 March 1938).

43. Parker, *Churchill and Appeasement*, pp. 163–4.

44. Zara Steiner, *The Triumph of the Dark: European International History 1933–1939*, Oxford, Oxford University Press, 2013, pp. 560–61.

45. Self, ed., *The Neville Chamberlain Diary Letters*, vol. 4, p. 325 (letter to Ida, 28 May 1938).

46. Barnes, ed., *The Empire at Bay*, p. 506 (30 May 1938).

47. Steiner, *The Triumph of the Dark*, p. 572.

48. Smart, *Neville Chamberlain*, p. 236.
49. Bell, *France and Britain, 1900–1940: Entente and Estrangement*, p. 211.
50. Steiner, *The Triumph of the Dark*, p. 581.
51. Barnes, ed., *The Empire at Bay*, p. 509 (16 September 1938).
52. Charmley, *Chamberlain and the Lost Peace*, p. 110.
53. Self, ed., *The Neville Chamberlain Diary Letters*, vol. 4, pp. 346–8 (letter to Ida, 19 September 1938).
54. NA: CAB 23/95, Cabinet Conclusions, 17 September 1938.
55. Self, ed., *The Neville Chamberlain Diary Letters*, vol. 4, p. 348 (letter to Ida, 19 September 1938).
56. Charmley, *Chamberlain and the Lost Peace*, p. 120.
57. Steiner, *The Triumph of the Dark*, p. 613.
58. Parker, *Churchill and Appeasement*, p. 167.
59. Steiner, *The Triumph of the Dark*, p. 617.
60. Charmley, *Chamberlain and the Lost Peace*, p. 125.
61. Faber, *Speaking for England*, p. 338.
62. Steiner, *The Triumph of the Dark*, p. 626.
63. Barnes, ed., *The Empire at Bay*, p. 518 (26 September 1938).
64. Steiner, *The Triumph of the Dark*, p. 639.
65. Self, ed., *The Neville Chamberlain Diary Letters*, vol. 4, pp. 350–51 (letter to Hilda, 2 October 1938).
66. Charmley, *Chamberlain and the Lost Peace*, p. 140.

8: To Make Gentle the Life of the World

1. I. Kershaw, *Hitler, 1936–1945: Nemesis*, London, Penguin, 2000, p. 403.
2. Steiner, *The Triumph of the Dark*, p. 672.
3. Self, ed., *The Neville Chamberlain Diary Letters*, vol. 4, p. 369 (letter to Hilda, 11 December 1938).
4. Deighton, *Blood, Tears and Folly*, pp. 175–6.
5. Charmley, *Chamberlain and the Lost Peace*, p. 142.
6. Self, ed., *The Neville Chamberlain Diary Letters*, vol. 4, p. 363 (letter to Ida, 13 November 1938); Steiner, *The Triumph of the Dark*, p. 679.
7. Bell, *France and Britain*, pp. 215–21.
8. Vincent Orange, *Dowding of Fighter Command*, London, Grub Street, 2011, p. 109.
9. N. H. Gibbs, *Grand Strategy*, vol. 1, p. 494.
10. N. H. Gibbs, *Grand Strategy*, vol. 1, p. 495.
11. N. H. Gibbs, *Grand Strategy*, vol. 1, p. 496.
12. Howard, *The Continental Commitment*, pp. 126–7; Bell, *France and Britain*, p. 222.

13. HC Deb 6 February 1939, vol. 343, col. 623; Steiner, *The Triumph of the Dark*, p. 724.
14. Deighton, *Blood, Tears and Folly*, p. 178.
15. Barnes, ed., *The Empire at Bay*, p. 529 (8 October 1938).
16. *Daily Express*, 15 March 1939, p. 12.
17. HC Deb 15 March 1939, vol. 345, cols. 440–41.
18. *Daily Telegraph*, 16 March 1939.
19. Wesley K. Wark, *The Ultimate Enemy: British Intelligence and Nazi Germany, 1933–1939*, Ithaca, NY, Cornell University Press, 2010, pp. 213–22.
20. NA: CAB 23/98, Cabinet Conclusions, 18 March 1939.
21. Charmley, *Chamberlain and the Lost Peace*, p. 172.
22. Parker, *Chamberlain and Appeasement*, pp. 189–90.
23. Harvey, *The Diplomatic Diaries of Oliver Harvey*, p. 265 (20 March 1939).
24. Daniel Hucker, *Public Opinion and the End of Appeasement in Britain and France*, Farnham, Ashgate, 2011, p. 134.
25. Overy, *The Road to War*, pp. 7–9.
26. Overy, *The Road to War*, p. 11.
27. Charmley, *Chamberlain and the Lost Peace*, p. 187.
28. S. Ball, ed., *Parliament and Politics in the Age of Churchill and Attlee: The Headlam Diaries, 1935–1951*, Cambridge, Cambridge University Press, 1999, p. 158 (3 June 1939).
29. Overy, *The Road to War*, pp. 6–10.
30. Self, ed., *The Neville Chamberlain Diary Letters*, vol. 4, p. 401 (letter to Hilda, 2 April 1939).
31. Charmley, *Chamberlain and the Lost Peace*, p. 187.
32. Howard, *The Continental Commitment*, p. 131.
33. Self, ed., *The Neville Chamberlain Diary Letters*, vol. 4, p. 435 (letter to Hilda, 30 July 1939).
34. Childers, *The Third Reich*, p. 416.
35. Overy, *The Road to War*, p. 65.
36. Childers, *The Third Reich*, p. 432.
37. Steiner, *The Triumph of the Dark*, p. 996.
38. NA: CAB 23/100, Cabinet Conclusions, 1 September 1939.
39. Faber, *Speaking for England*, p. 354; Amery, *My Political Life*, vol. 3, pp. 323–4.
40. Self, ed., *The Neville Chamberlain Diary Letters*, vol. 4, p. 444 (letter to Ida, 10 September 1939).
41. Julie V. Gottlieb, 'Neville Chamberlain's Umbrella: "Object" Lessons in the History of Appeasement', *Twentieth Century British History*, vol. 27, no. 3, 2016, p. 377; Dutton, *Neville Chamberlain*, p. xi.

42. Self, ed., *The Neville Chamberlain Diary Letters*, vol. 4, p. 348 (letter to Ida, 19 September 1938).

43. Smart, *Neville Chamberlain*, pp. 228–9.

44. Charmley, *Chamberlain and the Lost Peace*, p. 110.

45. Self, *Neville Chamberlain*, p. 13.

46. Charmley, *Chamberlain and the Lost Peace*, p. 106.

47. Barnes, ed., *The Empire at Bay*, p. 516 (25 September 1938).

48. NA: CAB 23/94, Cabinet Conclusions, 30 August 1938.

49. HC Deb 5 October 1938, vol. 339, col. 361.

50. Williamson Murray, *The Change in the European Balance of Power, 1938–1939: The Path to Ruin*, Princeton, NJ, Princeton University Press, 1984, p. 263.

51. Self, *Neville Chamberlain*, p. 413.

52. Steiner, *The Triumph of the Dark*, p. 672.

53. Hinsley, *British Intelligence in the Second World War*, vol. 1: *Its Influence on Strategy and Operations*, London, HMSO, 1979, p. 81.

54. Wark, *The Ultimate Enemy*, p. 207.

55. Charmley, *Chamberlain and the Lost Peace*, p. 73.

56. Murray, *The Change in the European Balance of Power*, p. 159.

57. Barnett, *The Collapse of British Power*, p. 526; Howard, *The Continental Commitment*, p. 111.

58. Wark, *The Ultimate Enemy*, pp. 65–8.

59. Murray, *The Change in the European Balance of Power*, p. 210; Wark, *The Ultimate Enemy*, p. 207; Bond, *British Military Policy between the Two World Wars*, p. 280–81.

60. Charmley, *Chamberlain and the Lost Peace*, p. 134.

61. Steiner, *The Triumph of the Dark*, pp. 590, 629; see also Gat, *Fascist and Liberal Visions of War*, p. 201n.; Kershaw, *Hitler, 1936–1945*, pp. 123, 262–78; Richard J. Evans, *The Third Reich in Power*, London, Penguin, 2006, pp. 670–71, 703.

62. Dutton, *Neville Chamberlain*, p. 56.

63. Stedman, *Alternatives to Appeasement*, p. 238; Kershaw, *Hitler, 1936–1945*, pp. 67–8.

64. Self, ed., *The Neville Chamberlain Diary Letters*, vol. 4, p. 419 (letter to Hilda, 28 May 1939).

65. Dutton, *Neville Chamberlain*, pp. 198–9; Stedman, *Alternatives to Appeasement*, p. 238.

66. In relation to this, it is worth considering the editorial comment of *The Times* as late as 28 January 1941: 'We do not make war for the subversion of the institutions of others [...] we are not now fighting Germany and Italy because they are governed by dictatorships; what form of government they choose for themselves, and for themselves alone, is their business and not ours.'

67. Paul M. Kennedy, *Strategy and Diplomacy, 1870–1945: Eight Studies*, London, Fontana, 1984, p. 28.

68. David Reynolds, *The Creation of the Anglo-American Alliance, 1937–41: A Study in Competitive Co-operation*, London, Europa, 1981, p. 8; Self, ed., *The Neville Chamberlain Diary Letters*, vol. 4, p. 259 (letter to Ida, 4 July 1937).

69. Quintin McGarel Hogg, *The Left Was Never Right*, London, Faber & Faber, 1945, p. 208.

70. Ramsden, *The Age of Balfour and Baldwin*, p. 366, Self, ed., *The Neville Chamberlain Diary Letters*, vol. 4, p. 6.

71. Wark, *The Ultimate Enemy*, p. 207; Howard, *The Continental Commitment*, p. 123; Murray, *The Change in the European Balance of Power*, p. 210.

72. Aster, 'Guilty Men', pp. 249–50.

73. Charmley, *Chamberlain and the Lost Peace*, p. 72.

74. Frank served in the Warwickshire Regiment from 1939 to 1945, surviving the war. In later life he became director of a manufacturing company. He died in 1965.

75. Self, *Neville Chamberlain*, p. 362.

76. Overy, *The Road to War*, p. 65 (my emphasis).

77. Gat, *Fascist and Liberal Visions of War*, p. 187.

78. Self, *Neville Chamberlain*, p. 366.

79. Stedman, *Alternatives to Appeasement*, p. 144.

80. Stedman, *Alternatives to Appeasement*, pp. 140–41.

81. Self, ed., *The Neville Chamberlain Diary Letters*, vol. 4, p. 492 (letter to Ida, 27 January 1940).

82. Thomas Babington Macaulay, *Speeches of Lord Macaulay*, London, Longman, 1877, p. 77.

83. Jeffrey L. Hughes, 'The Origins of World War II in Europe: British Deterrence Failure and German Expansionism', *The Journal of Interdisciplinary History*, vol. 18, no. 4, 1988, p. 868.

84. Barnett, *The Collapse of British Power*, p. 519.

85. HC Deb 1 September 1939, vol. 351, col. 127.

9: The Sharpening of the Claws

1. 'Cato', *Guilty Men*, p. 99.

2. 'Cato', *Guilty Men*, p. 113.

3. K. Warren, *Steel, Ships and Men: Cammell Laird, 1824–1993*, Liverpool, Liverpool University Press, 1998, p. 253; Ian Johnston and Ian Buxton, *The Battleship Builders: Constructing and Arming British Capital Ships*, Barnsley, Seaforth, 2013, p. 71; 'Ships Built by Cammell Laird', *Wirral Archives*, https://

www.wirral.gov.uk/sites/default/files/all/ Libraries%20and%20archives/
List%20of%20Cammell%20Laird%20Ships.pdf [accessed 1 January 2020].

4. All the Lion class battleships were ultimately cancelled before their
construction was completed.

5. Edgerton, *Britain's War Machine: Weapons, Resources and Experts in the Second
World War*.

6. Chaz Bowyer, *The Royal Air Force, 1939–1945*, Barnsley, Pen & Sword, 1996.

7. Philip Gibbs, *Ordeal in England*, London, Heinemann, 1937, p. 375.

8. N. H. Gibbs, *Grand Strategy*, vol. 1, p. 532.

9. *Times*, 20 February 1939, p. 13.

10. Stephen King-Hall, *Our Own Times, 1913–1938*, London, Nicholson & Watson,
1938, p. 753.

11. As it happens, as a former director of the Birmingham Small Arms Company,
Chamberlain was one of the few British politicians who had ever really been in
the weapons trade.

12. Stedman, *Alternatives to Appeasement*, pp. 181, 190.

13. HC Deb 20 July 1936, vol. 315, col. 123.

14. HC Deb 12 November 1936, vol. 317, col. 1118.

15. Hogg, *The Left Was Never Right*, pp. 78–9.

16. Stedman, *Alternatives to Appeasement*, pp. 181, 190.

17. Quoted in Cowling, *The Impact of Hitler*, p. 177; Stedman, *Alternatives to
Appeasement*, p. 191. See also Overy, *The Road to War*, p. 91.

18. Self, *Neville Chamberlain*, p. 252.

19. Self, ed., *The Neville Chamberlain Diary Letters*, vol. 4, p. 305 (letter to Hilda,
13 March 1938).

20. Dutton, *Neville Chamberlain*, p. 194.

21. Joseph Maiolo, *Cry Havoc: How the Arms Race Drove the World to War,
1931–1941*, New York, Basic Books, 2010, pp. 93–4.

22. Maiolo, *Cry Havoc*, p. 95.

23. Jeffrey L. Hughes, 'The Origins of World War II in Europe', p. 856.

24. Maiolo, *Cry Havoc*, p. 101, Keith Neilson, 'The Defence Requirements Sub-
Committee, British Strategic Foreign Policy, Neville Chamberlain and the Path
to Appeasement', *English Historical Review*, vol. CXVIII, no. 477, 2003, p. 675.

25. Self, ed., *The Neville Chamberlain Diary Letters*, vol. 4, p. 123 (letter to Hilda,
18 March 1935).

26. Dutton, *Neville Chamberlain*, pp. 172–3; Maiolo, *Cry Havoc*, pp. 159–60.

27. Stannage, *Baldwin Thwarts the Opposition*, pp. 135–6; Dutton, *Neville
Chamberlain*, p. 40.

28. Self, *Neville Chamberlain*, p. 304.

29. Self, *Neville Chamberlain*, p. 333.

30. Self, *Neville Chamberlain*, p. 332.

31. Neilson, 'The Defence Requirements Sub-Committee'.

32. Uri Bialer, *The Shadow of the Bomber: The Fear of Air Attack and British Politics, 1932–1939*, London, Royal Historical Society, 1980, p. 185.

33. C. T. Stannage, 'The Fulham By-Election, 25 October 1933', *The Historical Journal*, vol. 14, no. 1, 1971; Martin Ceadel, 'Interpreting East Fulham', in Chris Cook and John Ramsden, eds., *By-Elections in British Politics*, London, UCL Press, 1997.

34. N. H. Gibbs, *Grand Strategy*, vol. 1, p. 447.

35. Dutton, *Neville Chamberlain*, p. 91.

36. Self, ed., *The Neville Chamberlain Diary Letters*, vol. 4, p. 431 (letter to Ida, 23 July 1939).

37. Neilson, 'The Defence Requirements Sub-Committee', p. 675.

38. Robert Paul Shay, *British Rearmament in the Thirties*, Princeton, NJ, Princeton University Press, 1977, p. 297.

39. N. H. Gibbs, *Grand Strategy*, vol. 1, p. 175n.

40. N. H. Gibbs, *Grand Strategy*, vol. 1, p. 534.

41. Brett Holman, *The Next War in the Air: Britain's Fear of the Bomber, 1908–1941*, Farnham, Ashgate, 2014, p. 3.

42. Richard J. Overy, *The Bombing War: Europe 1939–1945*, London, Penguin, 2014, p. 26.

43. John Terraine, *The Right of the Line*, London, Hodder & Stoughton, 1985, p. 49; Wark, *The Ultimate Enemy*, p. 195. Group Captain Arthur Harris was the RAF representative on the JPC.

44. N. H. Gibbs, *Grand Strategy*, vol. 1, p. 533.

45. Terraine, *The Right of the Line*, p. 20.

46. Dutton, *Neville Chamberlain*, p. 171.

47. No one even dared using the term 'expeditionary force' at this stage, given what General Edmund Ironside called the 'unpleasant inferences in the public mind' that such an overt connection to the BEF of 1914 conjured up. Fry, *The Politics of Crisis*, p. 102.

48. Roderick MacLeod, ed., *Time Unguarded: The Ironside Diaries, 1937–1940*, New York, McKay, 1963, p. 42 (29 December 1937).

49. N. H. Gibbs, *Grand Strategy*, vol. 1, p. 535.

50. Gat, *Fascist and Liberal Visions of War*, pp. 207–9; Caputi, *Neville Chamberlain and Appeasement*, p. 118.

51. Basil H. Liddell Hart, *Europe in Arms*, London, Faber & Faber, 1937, pp. 272–3, 41.

52. Liddell Hart, *Europe in Arms*, pp. 143, 93–4.

53. Self, ed., *The Neville Chamberlain Diary Letters*, vol. 4, p. 175 (letter to Hilda, 9 February 1936).
54. G. C. Peden, 'A Matter of Timing: The Economic Background to British Foreign Policy, 1937–1939', *History*, vol. 69, no. 225, 1984, p. 25.
55. Robert Alexander Clarke Parker, 'British Rearmament 1936–9: Treasury, Trade Unions and Skilled Labour', *English Historical Review*, vol. 96, no. 379, 1981, p. 330.
56. Maiolo, *Cry Havoc*, pp. 175–6.
57. Stedman, *Alternatives to Appeasement*, p. 183.
58. Dutton, *Neville Chamberlain*, p. 135.
59. Hinsley, *British Intelligence in the Second World War*, vol. 1, p. 55.
60. Aldrich and Cormac, *The Black Door*, pp. 72–3; Richard J. Overy, 'Air Power and the Origins of Deterrence Theory before 1939', *Journal of Strategic Studies*, vol. 15, no. 1, 1992, p. 91.
61. Peden, 'A Matter of Timing', pp. 15–17.
62. N. H. Gibbs, *Grand Strategy*, vol. 1, p. 125.
63. Maiolo, *Cry Havoc*, p. 297.
64. Self, ed., *The Neville Chamberlain Diary Letters*, vol. 4, p. 426 (letter to Hilda, 2 July 1939).
65. Self, ed., *The Neville Chamberlain Diary Letters*, vol. 4, p. 431 (letter to Ida, 23 July 1939).
66. Peden, 'A Matter of Timing', p. 19.
67. Adam Tooze, *The Wages of Destruction: The Making and Breaking of the Nazi Economy*, New York, Penguin, 2008, pp. 321–5.
68. Parker, *Churchill and Appeasement*, pp. 307–8; Maiolo, *Cry Havoc*, p. 173.
69. Parker, *Churchill and Appeasement*, p. 95; Stedman, *Alternatives to Appeasement*, p. 173.
70. Parker, *Churchill and Appeasement*, p. 103.
71. Victor Davis Hanson, *The Second World Wars: How the First Global Conflict was Fought and Won*, New York, Basic Books, 2017, p. 529.
72. Evans, *The Third Reich in Power*, p. 705; Kershaw, *Hitler, 1936–1945*, pp. 500–01.
73. Hitler had great faith in Germany's anti-aircraft defences, especially its 88-mm AA gun. Richard J. Overy, 'Air Power and the Origins of Deterrence Theory', pp. 86, 88–9; Richard J. Overy, 'Hitler and Air Strategy', *Journal of Contemporary History*, vol. 15, no. 3, 1980, p. 409.
74. Evans, *The Third Reich in Power*, p. 698.
75. Charles Webster and Noble Frankland, *The Strategic Air Offensive against Germany, 1939–1945*, 4 vols, London, HMSO, 1961, vol. 1, p. 125.
76. Overy, *The Bombing War*, pp. 50–51.
77. Overy, 'Air Power and the Origins of Deterrence Theory', p. 89.

78. Webster and Frankland, *The Strategic Air Offensive against Germany*, vol. 1, p. 91.
79. Self, ed., *The Neville Chamberlain Diary Letters*, vol. 4, p. 553 (letter to Ida, 20 July 1940).
80. N. H. Gibbs, *Grand Strategy*, vol. 1, p. 510.
81. D. C. Watt, 'Churchill and Appeasement', in Robert Blake and Wiliam Roger Louis, eds., *Churchill*, Oxford, Clarendon Press, 1996, pp. 204–5; N. J. Crowson, 'The Conservative Party and the Call for National Service, 1937–1939: Compulsion versus Voluntarism', *Contemporary British History*, vol. 9, no. 3, 1995, p. 522.
82. MacLeod, ed., *Time Unguarded: The Ironside Diaries* , p. 41 (6 December 1937).
83. David Reynolds, 'Churchill and the Gathering Storm', in David Cannadine and Roland Quinault, eds., *Winston Churchill in the Twenty-First Century*, Cambridge, Cambridge University Press, 2005, p. 131.
84. Crowson, *Facing Fascism*, p. 161.
85. Childers, *The Third Reich*, p. 426.
86. Geoffrey Best, *Churchill and War*, London, Hambledon, 2005, p. 73.

10: The Other Dunkirk

1. For details of the attack on Mers-el-Kébir, including Boutron's account, see Colin Smith, *England's Last War against France: Fighting Vichy, 1940–1942*, London, Phoenix, 2010, pp. 57–88; John Jordan and Robert Dumas, *French Battleships, 1922–1956*, Barnsley, Seaforth Publishing, 2009, pp. 73–86.
2. IWM: D *Bombardment of the French Fleet at Oran*, Misc. 21 (381).
3. M. Alexander, 'Dunkirk in Military Operations, Myths, and Memories', in Robert Tombs and Emile Chabal, eds., *Britain and France in Two World Wars*, London, Bloomsbury, 2013, pp. 98–102; Malcolm Smith, *Britain and 1940: History, Myth, and Popular Memory*, London, Routledge, 2000, pp. 39–40.
4. Self, ed., *The Neville Chamberlain Diary Letters*, vol. 4, pp. 534–5 (letter to Hilda, 1 June 1940).
5. Alexander, 'Dunkirk in Military Operations', p. 100.
6. Self, ed., *The Neville Chamberlain Diary Letters*, vol. 4, p. 546 (letter to Hilda, 29 June 1940).
7. Michael Glover, *Invasion Scare 1940*, London, Leo Cooper, 1990, p. 51.
8. Cairns, 'A Nation of Shopkeepers', p. 742.
9. C. Smith, *England's Last War against France*, p. 86, 88.
10. Robert Frank, 'The Second World War through French and British Eyes', in Tombs and Chabal, eds., *Britain and France in Two World Wars*, p. 182.

11: Class War

1. Veidt was a German actor, a fierce opponent of the Nazis, who moved to Britain in 1933 and later emigrated to the United States. He tended to play sinister Teutonic villains on screen, most famously Major Heinrich Strasser in *Casablanca* (1942).

2. P. and R. Malcolmson, eds., *A Free-Spirited Woman*, pp. 116–19 (26– 30 August 1939).

3. P. and R. Malcolmson, eds., *A Free-Spirited Woman*, p. 120 (31 August 1939).

4. P. and R. Malcolmson, eds., *A Free-Spirited Woman*, p. 121 (2 September 1939).

5. P. and R. Malcolmson, eds., *A Free-Spirited Woman*, p. 122 (3, 4 September 1939).

6. Tom Harrisson and Charles Madge, *War Begins at Home*, London, Chatto & Windus, 1940, p. 49.

7. NA: CAB 23/100, Cabinet Conclusions, 30 August, 1 September 1939.

8. Richard M. Titmuss, *Problems of Social Policy*, London, HMSO, 1950, pp. 12, 93–4.

9. Bex Lewis, *Keep Calm and Carry On*, London, Imperial War Museum, 2017, p. 50.

10. HC Deb 28 November 1934, vol. 295, col. 859.

11. Quoted in I. Patterson, *Guernica and Total War*, London, Profile, 2008, p. 113.

12. J. Bourke, *Fear: A Cultural History*, Berkeley, CA, Shoemaker & Hoard, 2007, p. 69; Overy, *The Bombing War*, pp. 26–7.

13. *British Medical Journal*, 24 December 1938, pp. 1328–9.

14. Tom Harrisson, *Living through the Blitz*, London, Collins, 1976, p. 308.

15. Bourke, *Fear*, p. 228.

16. Titmuss, *Problems of Social Policy*, pp. 14–15, 19–21; MacLeod, ed., *Time Unguarded: The Ironside Diaries*, p. 61 (19 September 1938).

17. Titmuss, *Problems of Social Policy*, pp. 19–21.

18. Titmuss, *Problems of Social Policy*, p. 31; Terence O'Brien, *Civil Defence*, London, HMSO, 1955, p. 164.

19. P. and R. Malcolmson, eds., *A Free-Spirited Woman*, p. 72 (28 September 1938).

20. *British Medical Journal*, 17 February 1940, p. 270.

21. O'Brien, *Civil Defence*, p. 165.

22. Named after the lord privy seal (later home secretary) Sir John Anderson, who had been put in charge of ARP preparations after Munich.

23. G. H. Gallup, ed., *The Gallup International Public Opinion Polls: Great Britain 1937–1975*, vol. 1: *1937–1964*, New York, Random House, 1976, p. 16.

24. Mass Observation File Report 4, *ARP Instructions*, October 1939, p. 2.

25. E. Stebbing, *Diary of a Decade, 1939–50*, Lewes, Book Guild, 1998, p. 1 (30 August 1939).

26. O'Brien, *Civil Defence*, p. 281.
27. Harrisson and Madge, *War Begins at Home*, pp. 45–6.
28. Harrisson, *Living through the Blitz*, p. 43.
29. MacLeod, ed., *Time Unguarded: The Ironside Diaries*, pp. 92–3 (3 September 1939).
30. Titmuss, *Problems of Social Policy*, p. 547.
31. Constantine FitzGibbon, *The Blitz*, London, MacDonald, 1970, p. 26.
32. Peter Davison, ed. *The Complete Works of George Orwell: Facing Unpleasant Facts, 1937–1939*, London, Secker & Warburg, 2000, p. 400 (diary, 28 August 1939).
33. Titmuss, *Problems of Social Policy*, p. 543.
34. Titmuss, *Problems of Social Policy*, p. 137.
35. Harrisson and Madge, *War Begins at Home*, p. 337.
36. Turner, *The Phoney War on the Home Front*, London, M. Joseph, 1961, pp. 133–4; Titmuss, *Problems of Social Policy*, p. 101.
37. Titmuss, *Problems of Social Policy*, p. 90.
38. Angus Calder, *The People's War: Britain, 1939–1945*, London, Jonathan Cape, 1969, p. 36.
39. P. and R. Malcolmson, eds., *A Free-Spirited Woman*, p. 124 (14 September 1939).
40. P. and R. Malcolmson, eds., *A Free-Spirited Woman*, p. 126 (15 September 1939).
41. Titmuss, *Problems of Social Policy*, p. 544.
42. Titmuss, *Problems of Social Policy*, p. 175.
43. George Beardmore, *Civilians at War*, London, John Murray, 1984, p. 34 (3 September 1939).
44. May Smith, *These Wonderful Rumours! A Young Schoolteacher's Wartime Diaries, 1939–1945*, London, Virago, 2012, p. 35.
45. Stebbing, *Diary of a Decade*, pp. 3–4 (4 September 1939).
46. Stebbing, *Diary of a Decade*, p. 16 (22 November 1939).
47. Stebbing, *Diary of a Decade*, pp. 14–15 (12 November 1939).
48. Mass Observation, *Britain*, Harmondsworth, Penguin, 1939, pp. 49–50.
49. H. Kean, *The Great Cat and Dog Massacre*, Chicago, IL, University of Chicago Press, 2017, pp. 48–9.
50. May Smith, *These Wonderful Rumours!*, p. 75.
51. NA: CAB 67/3/159, Scale of Public Opinion As Regards Civil Defence Measures, 20 December 1939.
52. P. and R. Malcolmson, eds., *A Free-Spirited Woman*, p. 124 (14 September 1939).
53. P. and R. Malcolmson, eds., *A Free-Spirited Woman*, pp. 137–40 (27 September, 1 October 1939); p. 149 (17 October 1939).

54. P. and R. Malcolmson, eds., *A Free-Spirited Woman*, p. 158 (29 October 1939).

55. *Daily Mail*, 27 September 1938, p. 10.

56. Gallup, ed., *The Gallup International Public Opinion Polls*, p. 19.

57. M. Hicks, '"No War this Year': Selkirk Panton and the Editorial Policy of the Daily Express 1938–39', *Media History*, vol. 14, no. 2, 2008.

58. Harrisson, *Living through the Blitz*, p. 27.

59. P. & R. Malcolmson, eds., *A Free-Spirited Woman*, p. 124 (12 September 1939).

60. Harrisson and Madge, *War Begins at Home*, p. 152.

61. Ian McLaine, *Ministry of Morale*, London, Allen & Unwin, 1979, p. 38.

62. HC Deb 13 September 1939, vol. 351, col. 681.

63. Beardmore, *Civilians at War*, p. 40 (28 September 1939).

64. David Dilks, ed., *The Diaries of Sir Alexander Cadogan, O.M., 1938–1945*, London, Cassell, 1971, p. 225 (21 October 1939).

65. McLaine, *Ministry of Morale*, p. 40; N. Nicolson, ed., *The Diaries and Letters of Harold Nicolson: The War Years, 1939–1945*, New York, Atheneum, 1966, p. 32 (14 September 1939).

66. Harrisson and Madge, *War Begins at Home*, p. 57.

67. Harrisson and Madge, *War Begins at Home*, pp. 58–67.

68. May Smith, *These Wonderful Rumours!*, p. 49.

69. Stebbing, *Diary of a Decade*, p. 19 (19 December 1939).

70. Mass Observation File Report 4, p. 5.

71. Calder, *The People's War*, p. 134.

72. Mass Observation, *Britain*, p. 48.

73. R. H. S. Crossman, 'Labour and Compulsory Military Service', *The Political Quarterly*, vol. 10, no. 3, 1939, p. 309.

74. Martin Ceadel, *Pacifism in Britain, 1914–1945*, Oxford, Clarendon Press, 1980, p. 283.

75. Richard J. Overy, *The Morbid Age*, London, Penguin, 2010, p. 354.

76. Stephen Brooke, *Labour's War*, Oxford, Clarendon Press, 1992, pp. 34–5.

77. Overy, *The Morbid Age*, pp. 353, 358.

78. Ann Kramer, *Conscientious Objectors of the Second World War: Refusing to Fight*, Barnsley, Pen & Sword, 2013, p. 32.

79. Ceadel, *Pacifism in Britain*, pp. 4–5.

80. Overy, *The Morbid Age*, p. 359.

81. Stebbing, *Diary of a Decade*, pp. 10–11 (16 October 1939).

82. Stebbing, *Diary of a Decade*, p. 5 (7 September 1939).

83. Stebbing, *Diary of a Decade*, p. 12 (22 October 1939).

84. *Daily Mirror*, 4 September 1939, p. 10.

85. James Dyrenforth et al., *Adolf in Blunderland*, London, Muller, 1939.

86. See, for example, *The Spectator*, 22 September 1939, p. 9.

87. http://avalon.law.yale.edu/20th_century/dec939.asp
88. Roger Moorhouse, *The Devils' Alliance: Hitler's Pact with Stalin, 1939–1941*, New York, Basic Books, 2014, pp. 75, 109–10.
89. David Carlton, *Churchill and the Soviet Union*, Manchester, Manchester University Press, 2000, p. 75.
90. Gallup, ed., *The Gallup International Public Opinion Polls*, pp. 26–9.
91. Gallup, ed., *The Gallup International Public Opinion Polls*, p. 32.
92. Imlay, *Facing the Second World War*, p. 24.
93. Angela Thirkell, *Cheerfulness Breaks In*, New York, Knopf, 1941, p. 136.
94. Thirkell, *Cheerfulness Breaks In*, p. 318.
95. M. Strickland, *Angela Thirkell: Portrait of a Lady Novelist*, London, Duckworth, 1977, pp. 130–31.
96. HC Deb 14 September 1939, vol. 351, col. 818.
97. *Spectator*, 8 September 1939, p. 9.
98. Calder, *The People's War*, pp. 38–9.
99. Tami Davis Biddle, *Rhetoric and Reality in Air Warfare: The Evolution of British and American Ideas about Strategic Bombing, 1914–1945*, Princeton, NJ, Princeton University Press, 2002, pp. 108–9.
100. Geoffrey G. Field, *Blood, Sweat, and Toil: Remaking the British Working Class, 1939–1945*, Oxford, Oxford University Press, 2011, p. 41.
101. Field, *Blood, Sweat, and Toil*, p. 11.
102. Field, *Blood, Sweat, and Toil*, pp. 12–13.
103. Travis L. Crosby, *The Impact of Civilian Evacuation in the Second World War*, London, Croom Helm, 1986, pp. 31–3.
104. Stebbing, *Diary of a Decade*, p. 10 (13 October 1939).
105. Nella Last, *Nella Last's War*, London, Profile, 2006, p. 5 (6 September 1939).
106. *Spectator*, 22 September 1939, p. 11.
107. Calder, *The People's War*, p. 43; Field, *Blood, Sweat, and Toil*, p. 13.
108. Nicolson, ed., *The Diaries and Letters of Harold Nicolson*, p. 33 (14 September 1939).
109. Calder, *The People's War*, p. 43; Alan Jackson, *The Middle Classes, 1900–1950*, Newton Abbott, Thomas, 1991, p. 329; Derek Fraser, *The Evolution of the British Welfare State*, London, Macmillan, 1973, p. 20.
110. Titmuss, *Problems of Social Policy*, pp. 507–8.
111. D. Todman, *Britain's War: Into Battle, 1937–1941*, London, Penguin, 2016, p. 257.
112. Crosby, *The Impact of Civilian Evacuation*, p. 33.
113. Harrisson and Madge, *War Begins at Home*, pp. 336–7.
114. P. and R. Malcolmson, eds., *A Free-Spirited Woman*, p. 149 (17 October 1939).
115. *Spectator*, 15 September 1939, p. 18.

116. Calder, *The People's War*, pp. 45–6.

117. *Spectator*, 22 September 1939, p. 11.

118. *Spectator*, 24 November 1939, p. 10.

119. Beardmore, *Civilians at War*, p. 37 (7 September 1939).

120. *Times*, 26 September 1939, p. 9; *Times*, 3 February 1940, p. 4; Turner, *The Phoney War on the Home Front*, p. 128.

121. *Spectator*, 17 November 1939.

122. Calder, *The People's War*, p. 73.

123. Beardmore, *Civilians at War*, p. 39 (28 September 1939). There were further rises in duty on beer, whisky and tobacco in April 1940, and an increase in the postage rate.

124. P. and R. Malcolmson, eds., *A Free-Spirited Woman*, p. 139 (29 September 1939).

125. *Spectator*, 29 September 1939, p. 1.

126. *Times*, 2 October 1939, p. 9.

127. P. and R. Malcolmson, eds., *A Free-Spirited Woman*, pp. 126–7 (16 September 1939).

128. W. K. Hancock and M. M. Gowing, *The British War Economy*, London, HMSO, 1949, p. 166.

129. Gallup, ed., *The Gallup International Public Opinion Polls*, p. 24.

130. *Sunday Express*, 17 March 1940, p. 11.

131. The butter and bacon rations were doubled soon afterwards.

132. Mass Observation File Report A5, *Expenditure of 1,380 Middle Class Households in 1938–39*, January 1938, p. 24.

133. Mass Observation File Report A9, *Social Attitudes to Margarine*, December 1938, p. 2.

134. Ina Zweiniger-Bargielowska, *Austerity in Britain*, Oxford, Oxford University Press, 2002, p. 71.

135. Alan Jackson, *The Middle Classes*, p. 326.

136. Self, ed., *The Neville Chamberlain Diary Letters*, vol. 4, p. 451 (letter to Ida, 23 September 1939).

137. *Sunday Express*, 17 March 1940, p. 11.

138. *Times*, 18 March 1940, p. 9.

139. John Kiszely, *Anatomy of a Campaign: The British Fiasco in Norway, 1940*, Cambridge, Cambridge University Press, 2017, p. 283.

140. Gallup, ed., *The Gallup International Public Opinion Polls*, pp. 22, 30.

141. Mass Observation File Report 63, *Peace – Sylt*, March 1940, p. 5.

142. *Daily Express*, 18 March 1940, p. 6.

12: *Bras-Dessus, Bras-Dessous*

1.   Dilks, ed., *The Diaries of Sir Alexander Cadogan*, p. 218 (22 September 1939).

2. NA: CAB 66/1/47, Minutes of 2nd SWC Meeting, 22 September 1939.
3. André Beaufre, *1940: The Fall of France*, New York, Knopf, 1968, p. 163.
4. Alistair Horne, *To Lose a Battle*, London, Macmillan, 1969, p. 150.
5. A. J. P. Taylor, *Europe: Grandeur and Decline*, Harmondsworth, Penguin, 1961, pp. 289–94.
6. Ernest R. May, *Strange Victory: Hitler's Conquest of France*, New York, Hill and Wang, 2000, pp. 129–38; Julian Jackson, *The Fall of France*, p. 11.
7. Robert Forczyk, *Case Red*, London, Osprey, 2017, pp. 21–2.
8. Martin S. Alexander, *The Republic in Danger: General Maurice Gamelin and the Politics of French Defence, 1933–1940*, Cambridge, Cambridge University Press, 1992, p. 201; May, *Strange Victory*, pp. 289–95.
9. Forczyk, *Case Red*, pp. 19–20.
10. Forczyk, *Case Red*, pp. 49–50.
11. Jonathan A. Epstein, *Belgium's Dilemma: The Formation of the Belgian Defense Policy, 1932–1940*, Leiden, Brill, 2014, p. 266.
12. MacLeod, ed., *Time Unguarded: The Ironside Diaries*, pp. 150–51.
13. NA: CAB 66/3/118, Chiefs of Staff on Air Policy, 11 November 1939.
14. Julian Jackson, *The Fall of France*, p. 76.
15. Alexander, *The Republic in Danger*, p. 487.
16. Karl-Heinz Frieser, *The Blitzkrieg Legend: The 1940 Campaign in the West*, Annapolis, MD, Naval Institute Press, 2005, p. 140, Julian Jackson, *The Fall of France*, p. 32.
17. May, *Strange Victory*, p. 289, MacLeod, ed., *Time Unguarded: The Ironside Diaries*, p. 118.
18. Liddell Hart, *The Defence of Britain*, pp. 217–18.
19. Liddell Hart, *The Defence of Britain*, pp. 223–4.
20. Julian Jackson, *The Fall of France*, p. 28.
21. Frieser, *The Blitzkrieg Legend*, pp. 94–8.
22. Frieser, *The Blitzkrieg Legend*, p. 140; Julian Jackson, *The Fall of France*, p. 32.
23. Karl-Heinz Frieser, 'The War in the West, 1939–1940: An Unplanned Blitzkrieg', in John Ferris and Evan Mawdsley, eds., *The Cambridge History of the Second World War*, vol. 1: *Fighting the War*, Cambridge, Cambridge University Press, 2015, p. 297.
24. Forczyk, *Case Red*, p. 139; May, *Strange Victory*, pp. 357–61.
25. Julian Jackson, *The Fall of France*, pp. 219–20.
26. David French, *Raising Churchill's Army*, Oxford, Oxford University Press, 2000, p. 63.
27. Bell, *France and Britain, 1900–1940: Entente and Estrangement*, p. 230.
28. May, *Strange Victory*, p. 309.
29. Todman, *Britain's War: Into Battle, 1937–1941*, pp. 204–6.

30. Edgerton, *Britain's War Machine: Weapons, Resources and Experts in the Second World War*, pp. 2, 61.

31. James Holland, *The Rise of Germany 1939–1941*, New York, Grove Atlantic, 2015, p. 99.

32. Brian Bond, 'Preparing the Field Force, February 1939–May 1940', in Brian Bond and Michael Taylor, eds., *The Battle of France and Flanders, 1940: Sixty Years On*, London, Leo Cooper, 2001, p. 5.

33. Hew Strachan, 'The Territorial Army and National Defence', in Keith Neilson, ed., *The British Way in Warfare: Power and the International System, 1856–1956*, London, Routledge, 2016, p. 172.

34. NA: CAB 66/7/30, Letter from the Commander-in-Chief, British Expeditionary Force, 11 April 1940.

35. John Rupert Colville, *Man of Valour: The Life of Field-Marshal the Viscount Gort*, London, Collins, 1972, pp. 177–8.

36. Jonathan Fennell, *Fighting the People's War*, Cambridge, Cambridge University Press, 2018, pp. 45–6.

37. Edward Smalley, *The British Expeditionary Force, 1939–40*, New York, Palgrave, 2015, pp. 38–9; French, *Raising Churchill's Army*, pp. 84–7.

38. J. P. Harris, *Men, Ideas, and Tanks*, Manchester, Manchester University Press, 1995, p. 238.

39. D. French, 'The Mechanization of the British Cavalry between the World Wars', *War in History*, vol. 10, no. 3, 2003.

40. J. P. Harris, *Men, Ideas, and Tanks*, pp. 293–4.

41. Forczyk, *Case Red*, p. 144.

42. Forczyk, *Case Red*, pp. 112–13.

43. J. P. Harris, *Men, Ideas, and Tanks*, pp. 303–4. A mobile division was forming in Egypt and would become the 7th Armoured Division.

44. Forczyk, *Case Red*, p. 137.

45. Edward Louis Spears, *Assignment to Catastrophe*, vol. 1: *Prelude to Dunkirk, July 1939–May 1940*, London, Heinemann, 1954, p. 167.

46. Colville, *Man of Valour*, p. 156; Julian Jackson, *The Fall of France*, p. 78.

47. Colville, *Man of Valour*, p. 155; Julian Jackson, *The Fall of France*, p. 70.

48. NA: CAB 66/7/30.

49. NA: CAB 66/1/44, Conversation with M. Daladier and General Gamelin, 21 September 1939.

50. Bond, 'Preparing the Field Force'; Julian Jackson, *The Fall of France*, pp. 18–20.

51. Richard J. Overy, *The Birth of the RAF, 1918*, London, Allen Lane, 2018, p. 63.

52. Biddle, *Rhetoric and Reality in Air Warfare*, p. 116.

53. Overy, *The Birth of the RAF, 1918*, p. 136.

54. Terraine, *The Right of the Line*, p. 64; David Ian Hall, *Strategy for Victory: The*

Development of British Tactical Air Power, 1919–1943, Westport, CT, Praeger, 2008, p. xii.

55. Overy, *The Birth of the RAF, 1918*, p. 137.

56. Biddle, *Rhetoric and Reality in Air Warfare*, p. 116.

57. NA: CAB 66/3/12, Air Requirements for the Army, 3 November 1939, p. 3.

58. Matthew Lee Powell, 'Army Co-Operation Command and Tactical Air Power Development in Britain, 1940–1943', PhD diss., University of Birmingham, 2013, pp. 90–91.

59. M. L. Dockrill, *British Establishment Perspectives on France, 1936–40*, New York, St. Martin's Press, 1999, p. 137.

60. Greg Baughen, *The Fairey Battle*, Stroud, Fonthill, 2017; Greg Baughen, *The RAF in the Battle of France and the Battle of Britain*, Stroud, Fonthill, 2016, pp. 62–3.

61. Norman L. R. Franks, *Valiant Wings: The Battle and Blenheim Squadrons over France, 1940*, London, William Kimber, 1988, p. 108.

62. Malcolm Smith, *British Air Strategy between the Wars*, Oxford, Clarendon Press, 1984, pp. 253–7.

63. Basil Collier, *The Defence of the United Kingdom*, London, HMSO, 1957, p. 89.

64. Terraine, *The Right of the Line*, p. 76.

65. Stephen Bungay, *The Most Dangerous Enemy*, London, Aurum, 2010, p. 58; Orange, *Dowding of Fighter Command*, p. 263.

66. Francis K. Mason, *The British Fighter since 1912*, London, Putnam, 1992, p. 259.

67. Hinsley, *British Intelligence in the Second World War*, vol. 1, p. 110.

68. NA: CAB 66/7/25, Review of the Strategical Situation, 4 May 1940.

69. Baughen, *The RAF in the Battle of France*, p. 82.

13: In the Name of God

1. Self, ed., *The Neville Chamberlain Diary Letters*, vol. 4, p. 456 (letter to Ida, 8 October 1939).

2. 'Cato', *Guilty Men*, pp. 113–16.

3. Williamson Murray, 'British Grand Strategy 1933–1942', in Williamson Murray et al., eds., *The Shaping of Grand Strategy: Policy, Diplomacy, and War*, Cambridge, Cambridge University Press, 2011, p. 167.

4. Maiolo, *Cry Havoc*, p. 315.

5. Liddell Hart, *The Defence of Britain*, pp. 25–6.

6. Self, ed., *The Neville Chamberlain Diary Letters*, vol. 4, p. 467 (letter to Ida, 5 November 1939).

7. Liddell Hart, *The Defence of Britain*, pp. 25–6.

8. Self, ed., *The Neville Chamberlain Diary Letters*, vol. 4, p. 460 (letter to Ida, 22 October 1939).

9. Self, ed., *The Neville Chamberlain Diary Letters*, vol. 4, p. 451 (letter to Ida, 23 September 1939).

10. Self, ed., *The Neville Chamberlain Diary Letters*, vol. 4, p. 467 (letter to Ida, 5 November 1939).

11. Charmley, *Chamberlain and the Lost Peace*, p. 211.

12. CAB 68/1/9, Economic Warfare, 1st Monthly Report, 12 September 1939.

13. CAB 66/2/40, Germany: Stocks and Supplies of Petroleum, 13 October 1939, p. 7.

14. CAB 68/4/43, Economic Warfare, 5th Monthly Report, February 1940, pp. 12–13; James Ramsay Montagu Butler, *Grand Strategy*, vol. 2: *September 1939–June 1941*, London, HMSO, 1967, pp. 72–3.

15. Tooze, *The Wages of Destruction*, pp. 326–67; Nicholas Stargardt, *The German War: A Nation under Arms, 1939–45*, New York, Basic Books, 2015, pp. 56–9.

16. Childers, *The Third Reich*, p. 453; Maiolo, *Cry Havoc*, pp. 328–9.

17. CAB 66/1/42, note by the chancellor of the exchequer, 21 September 1939.

18. CAB 67/4/35, survey of the National Resources, 30 January 1940; CAB 65/5 War Cabinet Conclusions, 13 February 1940; Hancock and Gowing, *The British War Economy*, pp. 114–15.

19. David Reynolds, *From Munich to Pearl Harbor: Roosevelt's America and the Origins of the Second World War*, Chicago, IL, Ivan R. Dee, 2001, p. 72.

20. Julian Jackson, *The Fall of France*, p. 127; CAB 66/6/39, French Government's Views on the Future Conduct of the War, 26 March 1940.

21. Imlay, *Facing the Second World War*, p. 118.

22. Todman, *Britain's War: Into Battle, 1937–1941*, p. 294.

23. CAB 66/4/12 Norway – Iron Ore Traffic, 16 December 1939.

24. Anthony J. Cumming, *The Battle for Britain: Interservice Rivalry between the Royal Air Force and Royal Navy, 1909–1940*, Annapolis, MD, Naval Institute Press, 2015, p. 116.

25. Butler, *Grand Strategy*, vol. 2, p. 149.

26. Kiszely, *Anatomy of a Campaign*, p. 299.

27. Orange, *Dowding of Fighter Command*, p. 158.

28. Brian Bond, *Britain, France, and Belgium, 1939–1940*, London, Brassey's, 1990, p. 50.

29. Kiszely, *Anatomy of a Campaign*, p. 275.

30. Nicolson, ed., *The Diaries and Letters of Harold Nicolson*, p. 69 (9 April 1940).

31. Kiszely, *Anatomy of a Campaign*, p. 236.

32. *Times*, 5 April 1940, p. 8.

33. Nicolson, ed., *The Diaries and Letters of Harold Nicolson*, p. 78 (8 May 1940).

34. Paul Addison, *The Road to 1945: British Politics and the Second World War*, London, Pimlico, 1994, pp. 97–8.

35. Roberts, *Eminent Churchillians*, p. 145.
36. Dilks, ed., *The Diaries of Sir Alexander Cadogan*, p. 277 (8 May 1940).
37. John Rupert Colville, *The Fringes of Power*, London, Hodder & Stoughton, 1985, p. 119 (8 May 1940); N. Smart, 'Four Days in May: The Norway Debate and the Downfall of Neville Chamberlain', *Parliamentary History*, vol. 17, no. 2, 1998.
38. Todman, *Britain's War: Into Battle, 1937–1941*, p. 318.
39. Andrew Roberts, *The Holy Fox: A Biography of Lord Halifax*, London, Weidenfeld & Nicolson, 1991, p. 277.
40. Churchill, *The Gathering Storm*, p. 771.
41. May Smith, *These Wonderful Rumours!*, p. 110.
42. Gallup, ed., *The Gallup International Public Opinion Polls*, p. 26 (December 1939).
43. Gallup, ed., *The Gallup International Public Opinion Polls*, p. 32 (March 1940).
44. Mass Observation: File Report 99, *Political Crisis Report*, May 1940, p. 26.
45. Mass Observation Diarist 5382, 10 May 1940.
46. Mass Observation Diarist 5396 15 May 1940.
47. Stebbing, *Diary of a Decade, 1939–50*, p. 12 (10 May 1940).
48. Mass Observation Diarist 5175, 10 May 1940.
49. Beardmore, *Civilians at War*, p. 52 (12 May 1940).
50. Mass Observation Diarist 5341, 6 May 1940.
51. Mass Observation File Report 251, *Public Opinion about Mr. Chamberlain*, June 1940, p. 7 (emphasis in original).
52. *Daily Express*, 15 May 1940, p. 2.
53. Gallup, ed., *The Gallup International Public Opinion Polls*, p. 32 (March 1940).
54. Mass Observation File Report 251, p. 7.
55. Ramsden, *The Age of Balfour and Baldwin*, p. 375.
56. Addison, *The Road to 1945*, p. 99.
57. M. Gilbert, *Finest Hour: Winston S. Churchill 1939–1941*, London, Heinemann, 1983, p. 306.
58. 'Planned Dates for the Attack on the Western Front 1940', *Axis History Forum*, https://forum.axishistory.com/ viewtopic.php?t=159879 [accessed 9 January 2020].

14: A Certain Eventuality

1. William Simpson, *One of Our Pilots is Safe*, London, Hamish Hamilton, 1942; Franks, *Valiant Wings*, pp. 93–5.
2. Gordon Olive, *Spitfire Ace*, Stroud, Amberley, 2015, p. 150.
3. Bungay, *The Most Dangerous Enemy*, pp. 176–7.

4.   Two of the Battle squadrons were later converted to Blenheims during the Phoney War.

5.   W. Simpson, *One of Our Pilots is Safe*, p. 25.

6.   Terraine, *The Right of the Line*, p. 123.

7.   W. Simpson, *One of Our Pilots is Safe*, p. 47.

8.   Basil Embry, *Mission Completed*, London, Methuen, 1957, p. 146.

9.   Franks, *Valiant Wings*, pp. 118–22.

10. Baughen, *The Fairey Battle*, p. 73.

11. Horne, *To Lose a Battle*, p. 378.

12. Franks, *Valiant Wings*, pp. 146–66.

13. Horne, *To Lose a Battle*, p. 378.

14. Baughen, *The Fairey Battle*, p. 87.

15. Horne, *To Lose a Battle*, p. 331.

16. John Buckley, 'The Air War in France', in Bond and Taylor, eds., *The Battle of France and Flanders, 1940*.

17. For a plausible counterfactual describing this scenario in detail, see 'How the Fairey Battle Won the War', *Hush-Kit*, https://hushkit.net/2017/06/13/how-the-fairey-battle-won-the-war/ [accessed 11 January 2020].

18. NA: CAB 65/13, War Cabinet Conclusions, Confidential Annexes, 12 May 1940.

19. NA: CAB 66/3/18, Chiefs of Staff on Air Policy, 11 November 1939.

20. Butler, *Grand Strategy*, vol. 2, p. 171.

21. Webster and Frankland, *The Strategic Air Offensive against Germany*, vol. 1, p. 136.

22. NA: CAB 65 7, War Cabinet Conclusions, 10 May 1940.

23. NA: CAB 65/13, War Cabinet Conclusions, Confidential Annexes, 15 May 1940.

24. MacLeod, ed., *Time Unguarded: The Ironside Diaries*, p. 309 (15 May 1940).

25. Dilks, ed., *The Diaries of Sir Alexander Cadogan*, p. 283 (15 May 1940).

26. Martin Middlebrook and Chris Everitt, *The Bomber Command War Diaries*, London, Penguin, 1990, p. 43.

27. NA: CAB 65 7, War Cabinet Conclusions, 13 May 1940.

28. Overy, *The Bombing War*, p. 247.

29. Webster and Frankland, *The Strategic Air Offensive against Germany*, vol. 1, p. 267.

30. Baughen, *The RAF in the Battle of France*, p. 134; Denis Richards and Hilary Aldan St George Saunders, *The Royal Air Force, 1939–1945*, 3 vols, London, HMSO, 1953, vol. 1, pp. 123–4.

31. Beaufre, *1940: The Fall of France*, p. 180.

32. NA: CAB 106 253, 'Crowded Hour', Personal Account of Action in France, by A. C. Geddes, 1940.

33. Brian Bond, ed., *Chief of Staff: The Diaries of Lieutenant-General Sir Henry Pownall*, vol. 1, *1933–1940*, London, Archon Books, 1973, p. 317 (16 May 1940).

34. Colville, *Man of Valour*, p. 190.

35. Hinsley, *British Intelligence in the Second World War*, vol. 1, p. 147.

36. Dilks, ed., *The Diaries of Sir Alexander Cadogan*, p. 284 (16 May 1940).

37. Gilbert, ed., *The Churchill Documents*, vol. 15, p. 66 (17 May 1940).

38. Gilbert, ed., *The Churchill Documents*, vol. 15, p. 360 (18 June 1940).

39. Lionel Ellis, *The War in France and Flanders, 1939–40*, London, HMSO, 1954, p. 60.

40. NA: CAB 106 253, pp. 82–3.

41. Bond, ed., *Chief of Staff*, p. 322 (19 May 1940).

42. Bond, *Britain, France, and Belgium, 1939–1940*, p. 68.

43. Bond, ed., *Chief of Staff*, p. 323 (20 May 1940).

44. J. Thompson, *Dunkirk*, London, Sidgwick & Jackson, 2008, pp. 67–8.

45. Frieser, *The Blitzkrieg Legend*, pp. 286–8.

46. M. R. H. Piercy, 'The Manoeuvre that Saved the Field Force', in Bond and Taylor, eds., *The Battle of France and Flanders, 1940*.

47. Bond, ed., *Chief of Staff*, p. 342 (26 May 1940).

48. Gort was ordered home from France on 31 May 1940. He later served as governor of Gibraltar (1941–2) and Malta (1942–4) and high commissioner for Palestine and Transjordan (1945).

49. NA: CAB 106 253, p. 177.

50. Robin Prior, *When Britain Saved the West: The Story of 1940*, London, Yale University Press, 2015, p. 111.

51. NA: CAB 106/273, Correspondence on Draft Official History, 1947–52.

52. Ellis, *The War in France and Flanders*, p. 183.

53. The phrase is Churchill's from his 'Fight on the Beaches' speech.

54. Jeremy A. Crang, 'The Defence of the Dunkirk Perimeter', in Bond and Taylor, eds., *The Battle of France and Flanders, 1940*.

55. Frieser, *The Blitzkrieg Legend*, pp. 312–14.

56. Forczyk, *Case Red*, pp. 217–18.

57. Richards and Saunders, *The Royal Air Force*, vol. 1, p. 132.

58. Baughen, *The RAF in the Battle of France*, p. 133

59. Baughen, *The RAF in the Battle of France*, pp. 144–5; Prior, *When Britain Saved the West*, p. 113.

60. Alexander, 'Dunkirk in Military Operations, Myths, and Memories', p. 99.

61. Stephen Roskill, *The War at Sea*, vol. 1: *The Defensive*, London, HMSO, 1954, p. 228.

62. Colville, *Man of Valour*, pp. 221–3; Bond, *Britain, France, and Belgium*, p. 88.

63. Gilbert, ed., *The Churchill Documents*, vol. 15, p. 204 (30 May 1940).

64. J. C. Cairns, 'The French View of Dunkirk', in Bond and Taylor, eds., *The Battle of France and Flanders, 1940*, p. 89.

65. NA: CAB 66/8/18, Resolutions of the 10th Meeting of the Supreme War Council, 31 May 1940; Julian Jackson, *The Fall of France*, p. 95; Cairns, 'The French View of Dunkirk', p. 93.

66. Cairns, 'The French View of Dunkirk', p. 89.

67. Bond, *Britain, France, and Belgium*, pp. 110–14; Cairns, 'The French View of Dunkirk', p. 94; Prior, *When Britain Saved the West*, p. 131.

68. Prior, *When Britain Saved the West*, p. 133.

69. Gilbert, ed., *The Churchill Documents*, vol. 15, p. 247 (4 June 1940).

70. Gilbert, ed., *The Churchill Documents*, vol. 15, p. 268 (8 June 1940).

71. Gilbert, ed., *The Churchill Documents*, vol. 15, p. 187 (29 May 1940).

72. Gilbert, ed., *The Churchill Documents*, vol. 15, p. 348 (16 June 1940).

73. Forczyk, *Case Red*, p. 359.

74. NA: CAB 66/7/48, British Strategy in a Certain Eventuality, 25 May 1940.

75. Richard Carswell, *The Fall of France in the Second World War: History and Memory*, London, Palgrave, 2019.

76. Beaufre, *1940: The Fall of France*, p. 213.

77. Julian Jackson, *The Fall of France*, p. 3.

78. Stebbing, *Diary of a Decade*, p. 39 (8 July 1940).

79. D. W. Brogan, 'What Happened to France', *The Political Quarterly*, vol. 12, no. 1, 1941, p. 1.

80. Julian Jackson, *The Fall of France*, p. 38.

81. Forczyk, *Case Red*, p. 399. Other estimates (Julian Jackson, *The Fall of France*, p. 179) have suggested 50,000–90,000.

82. French, *Raising Churchill's Army*, p. 183.

83. Liddell Hart, *The Defence of Britain*, pp. 217–18.

84. Tooze, *The Wages of Destruction*, p. 380.

85. Julian Jackson, *The Fall of France*, p. 2.

86. Self, ed., *The Neville Chamberlain Diary Letters*, vol. 4, pp. 534–5 (letter to Hilda, 1 June 1940).

87. MacLeod, ed., *Time Unguarded: The Ironside Diaries*, p. 313 (17 May 1940).

88. Gilbert, ed., *The Churchill Documents*, vol. 15, p. 261 (6 June 1940).

89. Gibbs, *Grand Strategy*, vol. 1, p. 524.

90. NA: CAB 106/223, Letter by Field Marshal Lord Ironside on Relations with the French General Staff, 1940.

91. Colville, *Man of Valour*, p. 155.

92. Gibbs, *Grand Strategy*, vol. 1, p. 469.

93. Bond, *Britain, France, and Belgium*, p. 107.
94. Cairns, 'The French View of Dunkirk', p. 98.
95. Cairns, 'The French View of Dunkirk', p. 101.

15: Lunatic Relief

1. Nicholas Harman, *Dunkirk: The Necessary Myth*, London, Hodder & Stoughton, 1980, pp. 222–3.
2. The account of Mason-MacFarlane's briefing is from Bernard Grey, *War Reporter*, London, Robert Hale, 1942, pp. 119–24.
3. W. S. Churchill, *The Second World War*, vol. 2: *Their Finest Hour*, New York, RosettaBooks, 2002, p. 225.
4. David Reynolds, *In Command of History: Churchill Fighting and Writing the Second World War*, London, Penguin, 2005, p. 169.
5. NA: CAB 65/2, War Cabinet Conclusions, 7 December 1939.
6. NA: CAB 65/13, War Cabinet Conclusions, Confidential Annexes, 26 May 1940.
7. John Lukacs, *Five Days in London, May 1940*, London, Yale University Press, 1990, p. 5. Dalton had originally written 'only when we are rolling senseless on the ground'; the better-known phrase was a marginal annotation added later, possibly after consulting with Churchill.
8. Reynolds, *The Creation of the Anglo-American Alliance*, p. 104.
9. Graham Stewart, *Burying Caesar: The Churchill–Chamberlain Rivalry*, London, Weidenfield, 1999, p. 425.
10. Self, ed., *The Neville Chamberlain Diary Letters*, vol. 4, p. 530 (letter to Ida, 11 May 1940).
11. Roberts, *Eminent Churchillians*, p. 154.
12. NA: CAB 65/13, War Cabinet Conclusions, Confidential Annexes, 27 May 1940.
13. A. Roberts, *The Holy Fox: A Biography of Lord Halifax*, London, Weidenfeld & Nicolson, 1991, p. 214.
14. Churchill, *Their Finest Hour*, p. 130.
15. HC Deb 28 May 1940, vol. 361, col. 422.
16. 'The Indispensable Man', *The Churchill Society of New Orleans*, http://www.churchillsocietyneworleans.com/the-indispensable-man/ [accessed 15 January 2020].
17. B. Johnson, *The Churchill Factor*, London, Riverhead, 2015, p. 5.
18. Terraine, *The Right of the Line*, p. 170.
19. Terraine, *The Right of the Line*, p. 63.
20. Erin M. K. Weir, 'The Nazi Submarine Blockade: A Near Victory of Economic Warfare', MA diss., University of Calgary, 2007, p. 33.

21. Edgerton, *Britain's War Machine*, p. 52.

22. Tony Lane, *The Merchant Seamen's War*, Manchester, Manchester University Press, 1991, p. 13.

23. NA: CAB 65/8, War Cabinet Conclusions, 5 July 1940.

24. David Reynolds, '1940: Fulcrum of the Twentieth Century?' *International Affairs*, vol. 66, no. 2, 1990.

25. NA: CAB 66/7/48, British Strategy in a Certain Eventuality, 25 May 1940.

26. Hancock and Gowing, *The British War Economy*, p. 213.

27. M. Postan, *British War Production*, London, HMSO, 1952, p. 156.

28. Hancock and Gowing, *The British War Economy*, p. 232.

29. Hancock and Gowing, *The British War Economy*, p. 119.

30. CAB 66/11/42 Future Strategy, 4 September 1940 (my emphasis).

31. Philip M. H. Bell, *A Certain Eventuality: Britain and the Fall of France*, London, Saxon House, 1974, p. 66.

32. Reynolds, *The Creation of the Anglo-American Alliance*, p. 112.

33. Bungay, *The Most Dangerous Enemy*, p. 16.

34. Reynolds, *The Creation of the Anglo-American Alliance*, p. 110.

35. Reynolds, *From Munich to Pearl Harbor*, pp. 81–2.

36. NA: CAB 65/7, War Cabinet Conclusions, 27 May 1940.

37. Reynolds, *The Creation of the Anglo-American Alliance*, p. 320, n.134.

38. D. Reynolds, 'Churchill and the British "Decision" to Fight On in 1940', in R. Langhorne, ed., *Diplomacy and Intelligence during the Second World War*, Cambridge, Cambridge University Press, 1985.

39. Gilbert, ed., *The Churchill Documents*, vol. 15, p. 368 (18 June 1940).

16: All Our Past Proclaims Our Future

1. Arthur Bryant, *English Saga*, London, Collins, 1940, p. 378.

2. John Baxendale, '"You and I – All of Us Ordinary People": Renegotiating "Britishness" in Wartime', in Nick Hayes and Jeff Hill, eds., *Millions Like Us? British Culture in the Second World War*, Liverpool, Liverpool University Press, 1999, p. 312.

3. Bryant, *English Saga*, pp. 344, 351.

4. Bryant, *English Saga*, pp. 352–3, 355.

5. Bryant, *English Saga*, p. 356.

6. *Times*, 23 December 1939, p. 8.

7. Liddell Hart, *The Defence of Britain*.

8. B. Collier, *The Defence of the United Kingdom*, London, HMSO, 1957, p. 85.

9. Beardmore, *Civilians at War*, pp. 69–70 (16 July 1940).

10. *Daily Mirror*, 19 June 1940, p. 7.

11. BFI Film and Video Distribution, *Land of Promise: The British Documentary Movement, 1930–1950*, London, BFI Video, 2008.

12. Mark Connelly, *We Can Take It! Britain and the Memory of the Second World War*, New York, Pearson Longman, 2004, p. 109.

13. N. Coward, *Australia Visited*, London, Heinemann, 1940, p. 39.

14. *Times Literary Supplement*, 7 September 1940, p. 445.

15. David Edgerton, *The Rise and Fall of the British Nation*, London, Allen Lane, 2018, pp. 23, 26; Edgerton, *Britain's War Machine: Weapons, Resources and Experts in the Second World War*, pp. 47–51.

16. Baxendale, 'You and I – All of Us Ordinary People', p. 304.

17. Priestley, *Postscripts*, p. 2.

18. Gilbert, ed., *The Churchill Documents*, vol. 15, p. 518 (14 July 1940).

19. Cumming, *The Battle for Britain*, pp. 104–5.

20. HC Deb 18 June 1940, vol. 362, col. 59.

21. Colville, *The Fringes of Power*, p. 192 (12 July 1940).

22. Hinsley, *British Intelligence in the Second World War*, vol. 1, p. 174.

23. Hinsley, *British Intelligence in the Second World War*, vol. 1, p. 175.

24. Hinsley, *British Intelligence in the Second World War*, vol. 1, p. 185.

25. Alex Danchev and Daniel Todman, *War Diaries 1939–1945 Field Marshal Lord Alanbrooke*, Berkeley, CA, University of California Press, 2001, p. 107 (13 September 1940).

26. Colville, *The Fringes of Power*, p. 246 (21 September 1940).

27. Christopher M. Bell, 'The View from the Top: Winston Churchill, British Grand Strategy, and the Battle of the Atlantic', in Marcus Faulkner and Christopher M. Bell, eds., *Decision in the Atlantic*, Lexington, KY, Andarta Books, 2019, p. 22

28. Hinsley, *British Intelligence in the Second World War*, vol. 1, p. 190.

29. McLaine, *Ministry of Morale*, p. 62.

30. NA: INF 1/264, Home Intelligence Daily Report no. 12, 30 May 1940.

31. Mass Observation: File Report 181, *Capitulation Talk in Worktown*, June 1940, p. 1.

32. Mass Observation: File Report 284, *Survey of Public Opinion*, June 1940, p. 2.

33. NA: INF 1/264, Home Intelligence Daily Report no. 39, 2 July 1940.

34. NA: INF 1/264, Home Intelligence Daily Report no. 52, 17 July 1940.

35. Beardmore, *Civilians at War*, p. 64 (17 June 1940).

36. McLaine, *Ministry of Morale*, pp. 62–3.

37. Glyn Prysor, 'The "Fifth Column" and the British Experience of Retreat, 1940', *War in History*, vol. 12, no. 4, 2005.

38. 'Cato', *Guilty Men*, p. 118.

39. Christopher Andrew, *Defend the Realm: The Authorized History of MI5*, London, Allen Lane, 2009, p. 224.

40. P. Fleming, *Invasion 1940*, London, Rupert Hart-Davis, 1957, p. 62.

41. Andrew, *Defend the Realm*, p. 223.

42. Turner, *The Phoney War on the Home Front*, p. 224.

43. Angus Calder, 'The Myth of 1940', *London Review of Books*, vol. 2, no. 20, 16 October 1980, pp. 18–19.

44. McLaine, *Ministry of Morale*, p. 61; Gerry Rubin, 'In the Highest Degree Ominous: Hitler's Threatened Invasion and the British War Zone Courts', in Katherine O'Donovan and Gerry Rubin, eds., *Human Rights and Legal History*, Oxford, Oxford University Press, 2000, p. 90.

45. NA: CAB 65/13, War Cabinet Conclusions, Confidential Annexes, 18 May 1940.

46. Todman, *Britain's War: Into Battle, 1937–1941*, p. 372.

47. *Times*, 23 May 1940, p. 7.

48. NA: CAB 65/13, War Cabinet Conclusions, Confidential Annexes, 18 May 1940.

49. S. P. MacKenzie, *The Home Guard*, Oxford, Oxford University Press, 1995, pp. 25–8.

50. MacKenzie, *The Home Guard*, p. 68.

51. R. Fisk, *In Time of War: Ireland, Ulster and the Price of Neutrality, 1939–45*, London, Andre Deutsch, 1983, p. 269; MacKenzie, *The Home Guard*, pp. 84–5.

52. NA: INF 1/264, Home Intelligence Daily Report no. 29, 19 June 1940.

53. NA: INF 1/264, Home Intelligence Daily Report no. 44, 8 July 1940.

54. Mass Observation: File Report 181, *Capitulation Talk in Worktown*, June 1940, p. 3.

55. NA: INF 1/264, Home Intelligence Daily Report no. 95, 9 September 1940; no. 101, 16 September 1940; no. 102, 17 September 1940.

56. NA: INF 1/264, Home Intelligence Daily Report no. 39, 2 July 1940.

57. NA: INF 1/264, Home Intelligence Daily Report no. 28, 18 June 1940.

58. NA: INF 1/264, Home Intelligence Daily Report no. 45, 9 July 1940.

59. Mass Observation: File Report 282, *General Morale Report*, June [sic] 1940.

60. NA: INF 1/264, Home Intelligence Daily Report no. 78, 17 August 1940.

61. Turner, *The Phoney War on the Home Front*, p. 238.

62. Mass Observation: File Report 349, *'Stay Where You Are' Leaflet*, August 1940.

63. Mollie Panter-Downes, *London War Notes 1939–1945*, New York, Farrar, 1971, p. 75.

64. Last, *Nella Last's War*, p. 54.

65. V. Anderson, *Spam Tomorrow*, London, Rupert Hart-Davis, 1956, p. 74.

66. *New Yorker*, 6 July 1940, p. 36.

67. Malcolm Smith, *Britain and 1940: History, Myth, and Popular Memory*, pp. 60–61.

68. Turner, *The Phoney War on the Home Front*, p. 244.

69. Todman, *Britain's War*, p. 405; Collier, *The Defence of the United Kingdom*, p. 142.

70. Fleming, *Invasion 1940*, p. 60.

71. Collier, *The Defence of the United Kingdom*, p. 144; Titmuss, *Problems of Social Policy*, pp. 243–5.

72. MacKenzie, *The Home Guard*, pp. 56–7.

73. Fleming, *Invasion 1940*, p. 68.

74. Turner, *The Phoney War on the Home Front*, pp. 245–6.

75. *Times*, 23 May 1940, p. 7.

76. Turner, *The Phoney War on the Home Front*, p. 269.

77. Turner, *The Phoney War on the Home Front*, pp. 273–4.

78. HC Deb 23 July 1940, vol. 363, cols. 597–8.

79. NA: INF 1/264, Home Intelligence Daily Report no. 52, 17 July 1940.

80. Rubin, 'In the Highest Degree Ominous'.

81. NA: INF 1/264, Home Intelligence Daily Report no. 52, 17 July 1940.

82. HC Deb 6 August 1940, vol. 363, col. 80.

83. Turner, *The Phoney War on the Home Front*, p. 250.

84. A. W. Brian Simpson, *In the Highest Degree Odious: Detention without Trial in Wartime Britain*, Oxford, Clarendon Press, 1992.

85. Moorhouse, *The Devils' Alliance*, p. 152.

86. HC Deb 9 May 1940, vol. 360, col. 1380.

87. Andrew, *Defend the Realm*, p. 222.

88. A. W. B. Simpson, *In the Highest Degree Odious*, pp. 93–4.

89. R. Griffiths, 'A Note on Mosley, the "Jewish War" and Conscientious Objection', *Journal of Contemporary History*, vol. 40, no. 4 (2005), p. 677.

90. *Daily Mirror*, 24 May 1940, p. 7.

91. A. W. B. Simpson, *In the Highest Degree Odious*, p. 135.

92. Mass Observation: File Report 135, *Reactions to Internment of Mosley*, May 1940.

93. R. Woolven, ed., *The London Diary of Anthony Heap, 1931–1945*, Woodbridge, Boydell & Brewer, 2017, p. 290 (24 May 1940).

94. A. de Courcy, *Diana Mosley*, London, Chatto & Windus, 2003, pp. 254–63.

95. Andrew, *Defend the Realm*, p. 227.

96. B. Wasserstein, *Britain and the Jews of Europe, 1939–1945*, London, Clarendon Press, 1979, p. 85.

97. Neil Stammers, *Civil Liberties in Britain during the Second World War*, London, Croom Helm, 1983, p. 36.

98. Rachel Pistol, *Internment during the Second World War: A Comparative Study of Great Britain and the USA*, London, Bloomsbury, 2017, pp. 17–18.

99. Stammers, *Civil Liberties*, p. 42.

100. Turner, *The Phoney War on the Home Front*, p. 227.

101. Calder, 'The Myth of 1940', pp. 18–19.

102. Churchill, *Their Finest Hour*, p. 854.

103. Wasserstein, *Britain and the Jews of Europe*, p. 88.

104. *Sunday Express*, 19 May 1940, p. 7.

105. Tony Kushner, *The Persistence of Prejudice: Antisemitism in British Society during the Second World War*, Manchester, Manchester University Press, 1989, p. 143.

106. *Sunday Express*, 3 March 1940, p. 1.

107. Kushner, *The Persistence of Prejudice*, p. 144.

108. Wasserstein, *Britain and the Jews of Europe*, p. 86.

109. A. W. B. Simpson, *In the Highest Degree Odious*, pp. 52–3.

110. Stammers, *Civil Liberties*, p. 38.

111. Andrew, *Defend the Realm*, p. 227.

112. J. Craig-Norton, 'Contesting the Kindertransport as a "Model" Refugee Response', *European Judaism*, vol. 50, no. 24, 2017.

113. T. Kushner, 'Truly, Madly, Deeply ... Nostalgically? Britain's On–Off Love Affair with Refugees, Past and Present', *Patterns of Prejudice*, vol. 52, no. 2–3, 2018.

114. A. J. Sherman, *Island Refuge: Britain and Refugees from the Third Reich, 1933–1939*, London, Elek, 1973, p. 243.

115. H. Defries, *Conservative Party Attitudes to Jews, 1900–1950*, London, Frank Cass, 2001, p. 140.

116. Wasserstein, *Britain and the Jews of Europe*, p. 10.

117. Crowson, *Facing Fascism*, p. 33.

118. Pistol, *Internment during the Second World War*, p. 13.

119. Defries, *Conservative Party Attitudes to Jews*, p. 130.

120. Defries, *Conservative Party Attitudes to Jews*, p. 122.

121. Sherman, *Island Refuge*, p. 262.

122. Crowson, *Facing Fascism*, p. 31.

123. Roberts, *Eminent Churchillians*, p. 13.

124. Defries, *Conservative Party Attitudes to Jews*, p. 134.

125. Sherman, *Island Refuge*, p. 263; L. James, *The Rise and Fall of the British Empire*, London, Little, Brown, 1994, p. 410.

126. Defries, *Conservative Party Attitudes to Jews*, p. 134.

127. Crowson, *Facing Fascism*, p. 31.

128. Gallup, ed., *The Gallup International Public Opinion Polls*, p. 22 (July 1939).

129. Wasserstein, *Britain and the Jews of Europe*, p. 87.

130. Wasserstein, *Britain and the Jews of Europe*, p. 94.

131. Kushner, *The Persistence of Prejudice*, p. 147; Wasserstein, *Britain and the Jews of Europe*, p. 90.

132. Wasserstein, *Britain and the Jews of Europe*, p. 94.

133. Gallup, ed., *The Gallup International Public Opinion Polls*, p. 33 (May 1940).

134. NA: INF 1/264, Home Intelligence Daily Report no. 22, 11 June 1940.

135. Turner, *The Phoney War on the Home Front*, p. 233.

136. Pistol, *Internment during the Second World War*, p. 36; Stammers, *Civil Liberties*, p. 43.

137. Stammers, *Civil Liberties*, p. 42; NA: CAB 66/13/43, Huyton Camp, 25 November 1940.

138. Wasserstein, *Britain and the Jews of Europe*, p. 106.

139. *Times*, 20 May 1940, p. 4.

140. Stammers, *Civil Liberties*, p. 49.

141. Andrew, *Defend the Realm*, p. 230.

142. Kushner, *The Persistence of Prejudice*, p. 147.

143. HC Deb 22 August 1940, vol. 364, col. 1534.

144. HC Deb 22 August 1940, vol. 364, col. 1542.

145. Andrew, *Defend the Realm*, p. 230; Wasserstein, *Britain and the Jews of Europe*, p. 107.

146. Stammers, *Civil Liberties*, pp. 54–6.

147. Pistol, *Internment during the Second World War*, p. 135.

148. Kushner, *The Persistence of Prejudice*, p. 151.

149. Miriam Kochan, *Britain's Internees in the Second World War*, London, Macmillan, 1983, p. 176.

17: Margins

1. James Bailey, *The Sky Suspended*, London, Bloomsbury, 1964, pp. 40–42.

2. Bailey, *The Sky Suspended*, p. 43.

3. Alec Brew, *The Turret Fighters: Defiant and Roc*, Marlborough, Crowood Press, 2002, p. 72.

4. *Times*, 1 February 1939, p. 8.

5. Leo McKinstry, *Spitfire*, London, John Murray, 2007, pp. 131–2.

6. William Manchester, *The Last Lion: Winston Spencer Churchill: Alone, 1932–1940*, Boston, MA, Little, Brown, 1983, p. 123; Vincent Orange, *Churchill and His Airmen*, London, Grub Street, 2012, p. 96.

7. Baughen, *The RAF in the Battle of France and the Battle of Britain*, p. 186.

8. Gilbert, ed., *The Churchill Documents*, vol. 15, p. 244 (4 June 1940).

9. Brew, *The Turret Fighters*, pp. 36, 57, 67.

10. Brew, *The Turret Fighters*, p. 65–6.
11. Air Ministry [H. Saunders], *The Battle of Britain*, London, HMSO, 1941.
12. Churchill, *Their Finest Hour*, p. 411.
13. Cumming, *The Battle for Britain*.
14. Derek Robinson, *Invasion 1940*, London, Constable, 2005, pp. 265–6.
15. Bungay, *The Most Dangerous Enemy*, p. 109.
16. 'My Last Appeal to Great Britain: Adolf Hitler, Speech made to the Reichstag, July 19, 1940', *World War II Resources*, http://www.ibiblio.org/pha/policy/1940/1940–07–19b.html [accessed 22 January 2020].
17. 'Great Britain Shall Go Forward: Lord Halifax, Radio Address, 22 July, 1940', *World War II Resources*, http://www.ibiblio.org/pha/policy/1940/1940–07–22a.html [accessed 22 January 2020].
18. NA: INF 1/264, Home Intelligence Daily Report no. 56, 23 July 1940.
19. Militärgeschichtliches Forschungsamt (Potsdam), *Germany and the Second World War*, 13 vols, Oxford, Clarendon Press, 1990, vol. 2, p. 366.
20. Bob Carruthers, *Hitler's Wartime Orders*, Barnsley, Pen & Sword, 2018, pp. 47–8.
21. Carruthers, *Hitler's Wartime Orders*, p. 52.
22. Bungay, *The Most Dangerous Enemy*, p. 125.
23. Norman L. R. Franks, *RAF Fighter Command, 1936–1968*, Somerset, Patrick Stephens, 1992, p. 36.
24. Overy, *The Bombing War*, pp. 47–8.
25. Orange, *Dowding of Fighter Command*, p. 93.
26. McKinstry, *Spitfire*, p. 97.
27. Wark, *The Ultimate Enemy*, p. 62.
28. Baughen, *The RAF in the Battle of France*, p. 158.
29. Biddle, *Rhetoric and Reality in Air Warfare*, p. 119.
30. Franks, *Valiant Wings*, pp. 297–8; C. Sinnott, *The RAF and Aircraft Design, 1923–1939*, London, Frank Cass, 2001, p. 226.
31. Bungay, *The Most Dangerous Enemy*, p. 59.
32. Hinsley, *British Intelligence in the Second World War*, vol. 1, p. 75.
33. Richard J. Overy, *The Battle of Britain*, New York, W. W. Norton, 2002, p. 34; Sebastian Cox, 'A Comparative Analysis of RAF and Luftwaffe Intelligence in the Battle of Britain, 1940', in Michael Handel, ed., *Intelligence and Military Operations*, London, Cass, 1988, p. 430.
34. Terraine, *The Right of the Line*, p. 183.
35. Forczyk, *Case Red*, p. 263.
36. Overy, *The Bombing War*, p. 40.
37. Terraine, *The Right of the Line*, p. 176.

38. M. W. Kirby, *Operational Research in War and Peace*, London, Imperial College Press, 2003, p. 81.

39. Prior, *When Britain Saved the West*, pp. 181–4; Bungay, *The Most Dangerous Enemy*, pp. 63–7; S. Puri, 'The Role of Intelligence in Deciding the Battle of Britain', *Intelligence and National Security*, vol. 21, no. 3, 2006.

40. Sinnott, *The RAF and Aircraft Design*, pp. 221–2.

41. Liddell Hart, *The Defence of Britain*, p. 156; Mason, *The British Fighter since 1912*, p. 253; John Ferris, 'Achieving Air Ascendancy: Challenge and Response in British Strategic Air Defence, 1915–40', in Sebastian Cox, ed., *Air Power History: Turning Points from Kitty Hawk to Kosovo*, London, Frank Cass, 2002, p. 37.

42. Franks, *RAF Fighter Command 1936–1968*, pp. 22–5.

43. Sinnott, *The RAF and Aircraft Design*, p. 184; Brew, *The Turret Fighters*, p. 5.

44. McKinstry, *Spitfire*, p. 53.

45. McKinstry, *Spitfire*, p. 130; From Peace to War: Royal Air Force Rearmament Programme, 1934–1940', *The Spitfire Site*, http://spitfiresite.com/2010/04/from-peace-to-war-royal-air-force-rearmament-programme-1934–1940.html [accessed 22 January 2020].

46. McKinstry, *Spitfire*, pp. 144–5.

47. McKinstry, *Spitfire*, p. 135.

48. Baughen, *The RAF in the Battle of France*, pp. 73–4.

49. McKinstry, *Spitfire*, pp. 141–3.

50. Ferris, 'Achieving Air Ascendancy', p. 44; Baughen, *The RAF in the Battle of France*, pp. 80–81.

51. Baughen, *The RAF in the Battle of France*, p. 186.

52. Hinsley, *British Intelligence in the Second World War*, vol. 1, p. 178.

53. Cox, 'A Comparative Analysis', p. 437.

54. Bungay, *The Most Dangerous Enemy*, p. 211.

55. Overy, *The Bombing War*, p. 73.

56. Overy, *The Battle of Britain*, pp. 78, 80.

57. John P. Ray, *The Night Blitz, 1940–1941*, London, Cassell, 1996, p. 102; Bungay, *The Most Dangerous Enemy*, p. 303.

58. Bungay, *The Most Dangerous Enemy*, p. 312.

59. Martin Francis, *The Flyer: British Culture and the Royal Air Force, 1939–1945*, Oxford, Oxford University Press, 2008, p. 1.

60. Malcolm Smith, *Britain and 1940*, pp. 63–5.

61. Patrick Bishop, *Fighter Boys: The Battle of Britain, 1940*, New York, Viking, 2003, p. 6.

62. Francis, *The Flyer*, p. 33.

63. Bishop, *Fighter Boys*, pp. 241, 187.

64. Bungay, *The Most Dangerous Enemy*, p. 85.
65. Thomas E. Ricks, *Churchill and Orwell*, London, Penguin, 2017, p. 133.
66. Francis, *The Flyer*, p. 49.
67. Bishop, *Fighter Boys*, p. 218.
68. Tom Neil, *Gun Button to Fire*, London, William Kimber, 1987, p. 14.
69. Bungay, *The Most Dangerous Enemy*, p. 194.
70. Orange, *Dowding of Fighter Command*, p. 102.
71. Bungay, *The Most Dangerous Enemy*, p. 250; Franks, *RAF Fighter Command, 1936–1968*, p. 138.
72. Bishop, *Fighter Boys*, pp. 305–6.
73. Bungay, *The Most Dangerous Enemy*, p. 260.
74. McKinstry, *Spitfire*, p. 169; Baughen, *The RAF in the Battle of France*, p. 185.
75. Bishop, *Fighter Boys*, p. 305; Bungay, *The Most Dangerous Enemy*, p. 250.
76. Bungay, *The Most Dangerous Enemy*, p. 263.
77. Cumming, *The Battle for Britain*, p. 91.
78. Neil, *Gun Button to Fire*, p. 88.
79. Bishop, *Fighter Boys*, p. 365.
80. Bungay, *The Most Dangerous Enemy*, pp. 240–41.
81. Cumming, *The Battle for Britain*, p. 99.
82. Bishop, *Fighter Boys*, p. 205.
83. Bishop, *Fighter Boys*, p. 288.
84. Neil, *Gun Button to Fire*, pp. 94–5.
85. Olive, *Spitfire Ace*, p. 128.
86. Bishop, *Fighter Boys*, p. 248.
87. Bishop, *Fighter Boys*, p. 377.
88. Collier, *The Defence of the United Kingdom*, p. 225.
89. Gilbert, ed., *The Churchill Documents*, vol. 15, p. 802 (11 September 1940).
90. Churchill, *Their Finest Hour*, p. 406.
91. Churchill, *Their Finest Hour*, pp. 407–8.
92. Militärgeschichtliches Forschungsamt (Potsdam), *Germany and the Second World War*, vol. 2, p. 391.
93. Overy, *The Bombing War*, pp. 87–8.
94. Militärgeschichtliches Forschungsamt (Potsdam), *Germany and the Second World War*, vol. 2, pp. 396–7.
95. Bungay, *The Most Dangerous Enemy*, Appendix III.
96. M. Postan, *British War Production*, London, HMSO, 1952, p. 484; Overy, *The Battle of Britain*, p. 80.
97. Bungay, *The Most Dangerous Enemy*, pp. 190–91.
98. Cox, 'A Comparative Analysis', pp. 426–7.

99.   Robert Forczyk, *We March against England*, London, Osprey, 2016, pp. 208, 327–30.

100. Cumming, *The Battle for Britain*, p. 126.

101. Maiolo, *The Royal Navy and Nazi Germany, 1933–39*, p. 85.

102. Forczyk, *We March against England*, p. 218.

103. Peter Fleming, *Invasion 1940*, London, Rupert Hart-Davis, 1957, p. 298.

104. John Ferris and Evan Mawdsley, 'The War in the West, 1939–40: The Battle of Britain?', in John Ferris and Evan Mawdsley, eds., *The Cambridge History of the Second World War*, vol. 1: *Fighting the War*, Cambridge, Cambridge University Press, 2015, p. 317.

105. Militärgeschichtliches Forschungsamt (Potsdam), *Germany and the Second World War*, vol. 2, p. 374.

106. Overy, *The Bombing War*, pp. 89–90.

107. Bungay, *The Most Dangerous Enemy*, p. 158.

108. Richard Hough and Denis Richards, *The Battle of Britain*, New York, Norton, 2008, p. 248.

109. Baughen, *The RAF in the Battle of France*, pp. 205–6; Prior, *When Britain Saved the West*, p. 232.

110. Cox, 'A Comparative Analysis', p. 439; Baughen, *The RAF in the Battle of France*, pp. 197–8.

111. Prior, *When Britain Saved the West*, p. 216.

112. Bungay, *The Most Dangerous Enemy*, p. 219.

113. Hough and Richards, *The Battle of Britain*, pp. 307–8.

114. Bungay, *The Most Dangerous Enemy*, p. 369.

115. R. Overy, *The Battle of Britain*, p. 162.

116. Williamson Murray, *Strategy for Defeat: The Luftwaffe, 1933–1945*, Maxwell AFB, AL, Air University Press, 1982, p. 104.

18: The Scouring of the Shire Folk

1.   'London Blitz 1940: The First Day's Bomb Attacks Listed in Full', *The Guardian Datablog*, https://www.theguardian.com/news/datablog/2010/sep/06/london-blitz-bomb-map-september-7–1940 [accessed 24 January 2020].

2.   IWM: 97/19/1, D J. Garnham-Wright.

3.   Barbara Nixon, *Raiders Overhead: A Diary of the London Blitz*, Banbury, Gulliver, 1980, p. 13. For much of the incidental detail in this chapter see: Ray, *The Night Blitz, 1940–1941*; J. Gardiner, *The Blitz*, London, HarperPress, 2010; and Overy, *The Bombing War*.

4.   James Lansdale Hodson, *Through the Dark Night*, London, Gollancz, 1941, p. 319 (12 September 1940).

5.   *Daily Express*, 29 August 1940, p. 1.

6. Malcolm Smith, *Britain and 1940*, p. 89.
7. Alan Allport, *Browned Off and Bloody-Minded: The British Soldier Goes to War, 1939–1945*, London, Yale University Press, 2015, p. 56.
8. Priestley, *Postscripts*, p. 68.
9. Daniel Todman, 'Defining Deaths: Richard Titmuss's Problems of Social Policy and the Meaning of Britain's Second World War', in Nicholas Martin, et al., eds., *Aftermath: Legacies and Memories of War in Europe, 1918–1945–1989*, London, Ashgate, 1989.
10. G. Field, 'Nights Underground in Darkest London: The Blitz, 1940–1941', *International Labor and Working-Class History*, vol. 62, no. 3, 2002.
11. D. Kelsey, *Media, Myth, and Terrorism: A Discourse-Mythological Analysis of the 'Blitz Spirit' in British Newspaper Responses to the July 7th Bombings*, London, Palgrave, 2014.
12. Mandler, The *English National Character*, pp. 187, 213.
13. Amy Helen Bell, *London Was Ours*, London, I. B. Tauris, 2008, pp. 54–5.
14. D. Kelsey, *Media, Myth, and Terrorism*, p. 159.
15. Churchill, *Their Finest Hour*, p. 432.
16. McLaine, *Ministry of Morale*, p. 1.
17. Churchill, *Their Finest Hour*, p. 441.
18. P. Stansky, *The First Day of the Blitz*, London, Yale University Press, 2008, p. 6; J. Levine, *The Secret History of the Blitz*, New York, Simon & Schuster, 2016, p. 314.
19. Kelsey, *Media, Myth, and Terrorism*, p. 115.
20. O'Brien, *Civil Defence*, p. 677. The last major night raid of the 'Big Blitz' was on 16 May 1941, against Birmingham and Nuneaton.
21. Ray, *The Night Blitz*, Appendix B.
22. Collier, *The Defence of the United Kingdom*, p. 256.
23. Titmuss, *Problems of Social Policy*, p. 276.
24. Beardmore, *Civilians at War*, p. 92 (24 September 1940).
25. Max Cohen, *What Nobody Told the Foreman*, London, Spalding & Levy, 1953, p. 128.
26. NA: CAB 67/9/44, Air Raids on London, September–November 1940, 5 May 1941, p. 3.
27. Collier, *The Defence of the United Kingdom*, p. 257.
28. Gallup, ed., *The Gallup International Public Opinion Polls*, p. 35 (October 1940).
29. Davison, ed., *The Complete Works of George Orwell: A Patriot After All, 1940–1941*, p. 356 (3 January 1941).
30. Baughen, *The RAF in the Battle of France and the Battle of Britain*, p. 215.
31. Sinnott, *The RAF and Aircraft Design*, p. 225.

32. Ray, *The Night Blitz*, Appendix G.
33. Collier, *The Defence of the United Kingdom*, p. 264.
34. Ray, *The Night Blitz*, p. 131.
35. Edgerton, *Britain's War Machine*, p. 68.
36. F. Taylor, *Coventry: Thursday, 14th November 1940*, p. 156.
37. Mass Observation Diarist 5420, 19–20 November 1940.
38. O'Brien, *Civil Defence*, p. 418.
39. 'The Luftwaffe over Liverpool: Memories of a Wartime Childhood', *Commonweal*, https://www.commonwealmagazine.org/luftwaffe-over-liverpool [accessed 24 January 2020].
40. Mass Observation File Report 706, *Liverpool*, May 1941.
41. Fisk, *In Time of War*, pp. 476–81.
42. Ian S. Wood, *Britain, Ireland and the Second World War*, Edinburgh, Edinburgh University Press, 2010, pp. 175–6.
43. Margaret Gaskin, *Blitz: The Story of December 29, 1940*, Orlando, FL, Harcourt, 2006, p. 286.
44. Woolven, ed., *The London Diary of Anthony Heap, 1931–1945*, p. 341 (5 January 1941).
45. Overy, *The Bombing War*, p. 107.
46. Rosemary Taylor and Christopher Lloyd, *The East End at War*, Stroud, Sutton, 2012, p. 109.
47. Nicolson, ed., *The Diaries and Letters of Harold Nicolson*, p. 166 (16 May 1941).
48. *Daily Mirror*, 12 May 1941, p. 4.
49. Kirby, *Operational Research in War and Peace*, p. 94.
50. Overy, *The Bombing War*, pp. 96–7.
51. O'Brien, *Civil Defence*, p. 172; Titmuss, *Problems of Social Policy*, p. 140.
52. Titmuss, *Problems of Social Policy*, pp. 6–16; Sinnott, *The RAF and Aircraft Design*, p. 12.
53. Harrisson, *Living through the Blitz*, p. 128; Robin Woolven, 'Civil Defence in London 1935–1945', PhD diss., King's College London, 2001, p. 144. Figures for the number and tonnage of bombs dropped during the Blitz vary greatly, depending on whether they come from German or British sources.
54. Edgar Jones, 'Public Panic and Morale: Second World War Civilian Responses Re-Examined in the Light of the Current Anti-Terrorist Campaign', *Journal of Risk Research*, vol. 9, no. 1, 2006, p. 61.
55. Woolven, 'Civil Defence in London', p. 284.
56. HC Deb 8 October 1940, vol. 365, col. 291.
57. O'Brien, *Civil Defence*, p. 368.
58. Woolven, 'Civil Defence in London', p. 213.
59. Mass Observation File Report 436, *Shelter in London*, October 1940, p. 3.

60. Gardiner, *The Blitz*, p. 112.
61. Overy, *The Bombing War*, p. 138.
62. NA: CAB 67/9/44, pp. 13, 20.
63. 'Coronation Avenue, Stoke Newington, in the Blitz', *BBC WW2 People's War*, https://www.bbc.co.uk/history/ ww2peopleswar/stories/26/a2090026.shtml [accessed 24 January 2020].
64. NA: CAB 67/9/44, p. 12.
65. Mass Observation File Report 436, p. 5.
66. IWM: D, Thames TV Interviews for a Documentary on the Blitz, 67/262/1.
67. Mass Observation File Report 436, p. 4.
68. NA: INF 1/264, Home Intelligence Daily Report no. 96, 10 September 1940.
69. Overy, *The Bombing War*, pp. 143–4.
70. Beardmore, *Civilians at War*, p. 76 (27 August 1940).
71. Woolven, 'Civil Defence in London', p. 188.
72. J. B. S. Haldane, *ARP*, London, Gollancz, 1938, p. 228.
73. Haldane, *ARP*, pp. 212, 254.
74. Overy, *The Bombing War*, p. 36.
75. J. S. Meisel, 'Air Raid Shelter Policy and its Critics in Britain before the Second World War', *Twentieth Century British History*, vol. 5, no. 3, 1994, p. 314.
76. Gallup, ed., *The Gallup International Public Opinion Polls*, p. 35 (October 1940).
77. NA: CAB 67/8/80, Air Raid Shelter Policy, 31 October 1940.
78. Harrisson, *Living through the Blitz*, p. 112.
79. Gallup, ed., *The Gallup International Public Opinion Polls*, p. 39 (January 1941).
80. Woolven, 'Civil Defence in London', p. 187.
81. Mass Observation File Report 436, p. 9.
82. IWM: 80/38/1, D M. Morris, 9 May 1941.
83. Collier, *The Defence of the United Kingdom*, p. 265; Overy, *The Bombing War*, p. 114.
84. Collier, *The Defence of the United Kingdom*, p. 266.
85. Overy, *The Bombing War*, pp. 70–71.
86. Harrisson, *Living through the Blitz*, p. 144.
87. Overy, *The Bombing War*, p. 114.
88. Edward Glover, 'Notes on the Psychological Effects of War Conditions', *The International Journal of Psychoanalysis*, vol. 22, 1941, p. 133.
89. Edgar Jones et al., 'Civilian Morale during the Second World War: Responses to Air Raids Re-Examined', *Social History of Medicine*, vol. 17, no. 3, 2004, p. 474.
90. P. E. Vernon, 'Psychological Effects of Air Raids', *Journal of Abnormal and Social Psychology*, vol. 36, 1941, p. 457.
91. Jones, 'Public Panic and Morale', p. 62.

92. Overy, *The Bombing War*, p. 174.

93. R. J. Overy, '"The Weak Link"? The Perception of the German Working Class by RAF Bomber Command, 1940–1945', *Labour History Review*, vol. 77, 2012, p. 15.

94. Amy Bell, 'Landscapes of Fear: Wartime London, 1939–1945', *Journal of British Studies*, vol. 48, no. 1, 2009, p. 161.

95. Overy, *The Bombing War*, pp. 141–2.

96. NA: CAB 67/9/44.

97. Woolven, 'Civil Defence in London', p. 193.

98. Titmuss, *Problems of Social Policy*, p. 356.

99. Titmuss, *Problems of Social Policy*, p. 362.

100. Overy, *The Bombing War*, p. 143.

101. Woolven, 'Civil Defence in London', p. 191.

102. Field, 'Nights Underground in Darkest London', p. 16.

103. IWM: D, Thames TV Interviews for a Documentary on the Blitz, 67/262/1.

104. *Daily Express*, 12 May 1941, p. 1.

105. Overy, *The Bombing War*, p. 179.

106. Nixon, *Raiders Overhead*, pp. 25–7.

107. Levine, *The Secret History of the Blitz*, pp. 41–2.

108. Beardmore, *Civilians at War*, pp. 74–9 (23 August–3 September 1940).

109. Overy, *The Bombing War*, p. 178.

110. Harrisson, *Living through the Blitz*, p. 106.

111. R. Deveson, ed., *My Dearest Family: An Austrian Refugee's Letters to London from America, 1938–1945*, privately published, 2017, p. 101 (23 October 1940).

112. Mass Observation File Report 436, p. 12.

113. Mass Observation File Report 408, *Human Adjustments in Air Raids*, September 1940, p. 50.

114. Bourke, *Fear: A Cultural History*, p. 248.

115. Overy, *The Battle of Britain*, p. 100.

116. R. Mackay, *Half the Battle: Civilian Morale in Britain During the Second World War*, Manchester, Manchester University Press, 2002, p. 77.

117. Mass Observation File Report 436, p. 5.

118. Jones et al., 'Civilian Morale during the Second World War', p. 475.

119. Overy, *The Bombing War*, pp. 184–5.

120. Mass Observation File Report 408, pp. 46, 48–9.

121. IWM: 91/5/1, D V. Bawtree.

122. A. Bell, 'Landscapes of Fear', p. 160.

123. Hazel Croft, 'Rethinking Civilian Neuroses in the Second World War', in P. Leese et al., eds., *Traumatic Memories of the Second World War and After*, London, Palgrave, 2018, p. 106.

124. Overy, *The Bombing War*, pp. 170–71.

125. Jones et al., 'Civilian Morale during the Second World War', p. 476; Croft, 'Rethinking Civilian Neuroses', pp. 103–4.

126. By the end of the war the Luftwaffe had 500,000 poison gas bombs, and German factories were producing not just phosgene and mustard gases but also new nerve agents such as tabun and sarin, but it does not appear to have had any appreciable chemical warfare capability in 1940. K. Coleman, *A History of Chemical Warfare*, New York, Palgrave, 2005, pp. 61–8.

127. Mass Observation Diarist 5420, February 1941.

128. Overy, *The Bombing War*, p. 106.

129. Jones, 'Public Panic and Morale', p. 59.

130. Mass Observation File Report 495, *Coventry*, November 1940, p. 2.

131. Brett Holman, '"Bomb Back, and Bomb Hard": Debating Reprisals during the Blitz', *Australian Journal of Politics & History*, vol. 58, no. 3, 2012, p. 405.

132. Mass Observation File Report 844, *Hull*, August 1941.

133. Mass Observation FR 408.

19: American *Lebensraum*

1. 'Franklin Roosevelt's Press Conference, December 17, 1940', *Franklin D. Roosevelt Presidential Library and Museum*, http://docs.fdrlibrary.marist.edu/odllpc2.html [accessed 25 January 2020].

2. Churchill, *Their Finest Hour*, pp. 671–83.

3. Reynolds, *The Creation of the Anglo-American Alliance*, p. 153.

4. G. H. Bennett, ed., *Roosevelt's Peacetime Administrations, 1933–41: A Documentary History*, Manchester, Manchester University Press, 2004, pp. 183, 190–91.

5. Reynolds, *From Munich to Pearl Harbor*, p. 92.

6. Gaskin, *Blitz*, p. 415.

7. Churchill, *Their Finest Hour*, p. 684.

8. NA: CAB 66/7/48, British Strategy in a Certain Eventuality, 25 May 1940.

9. 'Franklin Roosevelt's Press Conference, December 17, 1940'.

10. Reynolds, *The Creation of the Anglo-American Alliance*, p. 159.

11. Colville, *The Fringes of Power*, p. 223 (15 August 1940).

12. B. J. C. McKercher, *Transition of Power: Britain's Loss of Global Preeminence to the United States, 1930–1945*, Cambridge, Cambridge University Press, 1998, p. 302.

13. Reynolds, *From Munich to Pearl Harbor*, p. 73.

14. W. R. Louis, *In the Name of God, Go! Leo Amery and the British Empire in the Age of Churchill*, New York, W. W. Norton, 1992, p. 26.

15. Self, ed., *The Neville Chamberlain Diary Letters*, vol. 4, p. 551 (letter to Hilda, 14 July 1940).

16. Abraham M. Roof, 'A Separate Peace? The Soviet Union and the Making of British Strategy in the Wake of "Barbarossa", June–September 1941', *The Journal of Slavic Military Studies*, vol. 22, no. 2, 2009, p. 237.

17. Self, ed., *The Neville Chamberlain Diary Letters*, vol. 4, p. 553 (letter to Ida, 20 July 1940).

18. James Lansdale Hodson, *Towards the Morning*, London, Gollancz, 1941, p. 214 (31 March 1941).

20: Shapeless, Measureless Peril

1. R. Seamer, *The Floating Inferno: The Story of the Loss of the Empress of Britain*, Wellingborough, Stephens, 1990, pp. 40–41.

2. Seamer, *The Floating Inferno*, pp. 73–4, 82–3.

3. J. Terraine, *Business in Great Waters: The U-Boat Wars, 1916–1945*, London, Leo Cooper, 1989, pp. 269–70.

4. Terraine, *Business in Great Waters*, Appendix D.

5. E. Grove, *The Defeat of the Enemy Attack upon Shipping, 1939–1945*, Aldershot, Ashgate [for the Navy Records Society], 1998, p. 53; L. Collingham, *The Taste of War*, London, Allen Lane, 2011, p. 67.

6. Erin M. K. Weir, 'The Nazi Submarine Blockade: A Near Victory of Economic Warfare?', MA diss., University of Calgary, 2007, p. 25.

7. Churchill, *Their Finest Hour*, pp. 718–19.

8. W. S. Churchill, *The Second World War*, vol. 3: *The Grand Alliance*, New York, RosettaBooks, 2002, p. 157.

9. J. A. Maiolo, 'The Admiralty and the Anglo–German Naval Agreement of 18 June 1935', *Diplomacy & Statecraft*, vol. 10, no. 1., 1999, p. 87.

10. Churchill, *The Gathering Storm*, p. 422.

11. Maiolo, *The Royal Navy and Nazi Germany*, pp. 190–91.

12. Tooze, *The Wages of Destruction*, pp. 288–9.

13. Tooze, *The Wages of Destruction*, p. 399.

14. Terraine, *Business in Great Waters*, Appendix D.

15. Overy, *The Bombing War*, p. 92.

16. Terraine, *Business in Great Waters*, p. 177; Grove, *The Defeat of the Enemy Attack upon Shipping*, p. 18.

17. J. A. Maiolo, 'Deception and Intelligence Failure: Anglo-German Preparations for U-Boat Warfare in the 1930s', *Journal of Strategic Studies*, vol. 22, no. 4, 1999, p. 56.

18. Maiolo, 'Deception and Intelligence Failure', p. 62.

19. Grove, *The Defeat of the Enemy Attack upon Shipping*, p. 63.

20. Terraine, *Business in Great Waters*, p. 177.
21. Grove, *The Defeat of the Enemy Attack upon Shipping*, p. 17.
22. Terraine, *Business in Great Waters*, p. 244.
23. Grove, *The Defeat of the Enemy Attack upon Shipping*, p. 30.
24. Terraine, *Business in Great Waters*, p. 177.
25. Grove, *The Defeat of the Enemy Attack upon Shipping*, p. 64.
26. Henry Probert, 'Allied Land-Based Anti-Submarine Warfare', in Stephen Howarth and Derek Law, eds., *The Battle of the Atlantic 1939–1945*, London, Greenhill Books, 1994, p. 371; Grove, *The Defeat of the Enemy Attack upon Shipping*, p. 30.
27. Grove, *The Defeat of the Enemy Attack upon Shipping*, p. 56.
28. Hancock and Gowing, *The British War Economy*, p. 251.
29. C. B. Behrens, *Merchant Shipping and the Demands of War*, London, HMSO, 1956, p. 109.
30. Grove, *The Defeat of the Enemy Attack upon Shipping*, p. 60. One U-boat (U-93) was slightly damaged by a raid on a U-boat pen during the war.
31. Terraine, *Business in Great Waters*, p. 262.
32. Terraine, *Business in Great Waters*, pp. 256–7.
33. Grove, *The Defeat of the Enemy Attack upon Shipping*, p. 59.
34. Grove, *The Defeat of the Enemy Attack upon Shipping*, p. Table 11.
35. Terraine, *Business in Great Waters*, Appendix D.
36. 'Patrol Information for U-99, 25 July–5 August, 1940', *U-boat.net*, https://uboat.net/boats/patrols/ patrol_4756.html [accessed 27 January 2020].
37. Gordon Williamson, *U-Boat Tactics in World War II*, Oxford, Osprey, 2010, pp. 8–9; Grove, *The Defeat of the Enemy Attack upon Shipping*, p. 61.
38. Terraine, *Business in Great Waters*, pp. 267–8.
39. Unless otherwise noted, all details from this section are from Lane, *The Merchant Seamen's War*.
40. P. Elphick, *Lifeline: The Merchant Navy at War, 1939–1945*, London, Chatham, 1999, p. 10.
41. Behrens, *Merchant Shipping*, p. 17.
42. R. Woodman, *The Real Cruel Sea: The Merchant Navy in the Battle of the Atlantic, 1939–1943*, London, John Murray, 2004, p. 45.
43. Behrens, *Merchant Shipping*, p. 17.
44. Behrens, *Merchant Shipping*, p. 22.
45. Woodman, *The Real Cruel Sea*, p. 39; Lane, *The Merchant Seamen's War*, pp. 13–14.
46. Behrens, *Merchant Shipping*, p. 21.
47. Woodman, *The Real Cruel Sea*, p. 26.
48. Lane, *The Merchant Seamen's War*, p. 30.

49. Woodman, *The Real Cruel Sea*, p. 44.
50. Lane, *The Merchant Seamen's War*, p. 85.
51. Lane, *The Merchant Seamen's War*, pp. 110–11.
52. Lane, *The Merchant Seamen's War*, p. 177.
53. Grove, *The Defeat of the Enemy Attack upon Shipping*, p. 303.
54. G. H. Bennett and R. Bennett, *Survivors: British Merchant Seamen in the Second World War*, London, Hambeldon, 1999, p. 33.
55. Specifically delegated rescue ships were introduced to convoys in January 1941. Grove, *The Defeat of the Enemy Attack upon Shipping*, p. 45.
56. Lane, *The Merchant Seamen's War*, p. 237; 'Cadillac: British Steam Tanker', *U-boat.net*, https://uboat.net/ allies/merchants/ship/796.html [accessed 27 January 2020].
57. Terraine, *Business in Great Waters*, p. 299.
58. Behrens, *Merchant Shipping*, pp. 134, 147.
59. Weir, *The Nazi Submarine Blockade*, pp. 35–6.
60. Behrens, *Merchant Shipping*, p. 146.
61. Grove, *The Defeat of the Enemy Attack upon Shipping*, Table 16.
62. Behrens, *Merchant Shipping*, p. 143.
63. M. Milner, 'The Battle of the Atlantic', *Journal of Strategic Studies*, vol. 13, no. 1, 1990, p. 46.
64. Kevin Smith, '"Immobilized by Reason of Repair" and by the Choice "Between Lithgow and Hitler"', in Marcus Faulkner and Christopher M. Bell, eds., *Decision in the Atlantic*, Lexington, KY, Andarta Books, 2019, p. 76.
65. Behrens, *Merchant Shipping*, p. 131.
66. Greg Kennedy, *The Merchant Marine in International Affairs, 1850–1950*, London, Cass, 2000, pp. 157–8.
67. M. Schoenfeld, 'Winston Churchill as War Manager: The Battle of the Atlantic Committee, 1941', in *Military Affairs*, vol. 52, no. 3, 1988, pp. 125–6.
68. Overy, *The Bombing War*, p. 161.
69. Terraine, *Business in Great Waters*, Appendix D.
70. W. J. R. Gardner, *Decoding History: The Battle of the Atlantic and Ultra*, Basingstoke, Macmillan, 1999, pp. 149–51.
71. Kirby, *Operational Research in War and Peace*, London, Imperial College Press, 2003, p. 96.
72. Gardner, *Decoding History*, pp. 175–7.
73. Grove, *The Defeat of the Enemy Attack upon Shipping*, p. 67.
74. Terraine, *The Right of the Line*, p. 407.
75. Grove, *The Defeat of the Enemy Attack upon Shipping*, Table 9.
76. Grove, *The Defeat of the Enemy Attack upon Shipping*, p. 73.

77. Militärgeschichtliches Forschungsamt (Potsdam), *Germany and the Second World War*, vol. 2, p. 346.
78. Militärgeschichtliches Forschungsamt (Potsdam), *Germany and the Second World War*, vol. 2, p. 347.
79. Grove, *The Defeat of the Enemy Attack upon Shipping*, Table 13.
80. Grove, *The Defeat of the Enemy Attack upon Shipping*, p. 303.
81. Schoenfeld, 'Winston Churchill as War Manager', p. 125.
82. Grove, *The Defeat of the Enemy Attack upon Shipping*, Table 12.
83. Grove, *The Defeat of the Enemy Attack upon Shipping*, Table 15.
84. Behrens, *Merchant Shipping*, p. 325.
85. Terraine, *Business in Great Waters*, p. 360.

21: The Carotid Artery of Empire

1. Douglas Arthur, *Desert Watch*, Bedale, Blaisdon, 2000, pp. 236–7.
2. Cyril Joly, *Take These Men*, London, Constable, 1953, p. 78.
3. Arthur, *Desert Watch*, p. 238.
4. Joly, *Take These Men*, pp. 86–7.
5. Arthur, *Desert Watch*, pp. 242–3.
6. Douglas Porch, *The Path to Victory*, New York, Farrar, Straus and Giroux, 2004, p. 7.
7. Alex Danchev, 'The Central Direction of War, 1940–41', in John Sweetman, ed., *Sword & Mace: Twentieth Century Civil–Military Relations*, London, Brassey's, 1986, p. 57.
8. John Rupert Colville, *Winston Churchill and His Inner Circle*, New York, Wyndham, 1981, p. 163.
9. Terraine, *The Right of the Line*, p. 252.
10. Alex Danchev, '"Dilly-Dally", or Having the Last Word: Field Marshal Sir John Dill and Prime Minister Winston Churchill', *Journal of Contemporary History*, vol. 22, no. 1, 1987, p. 24.
11. Danchev, 'Dilly-Dally', p. 21.
12. Danchev, 'The Central Direction of War', p. 66.
13. Danchev, 'Dilly-Dally', p. 21.
14. Harold E. Raugh, *Wavell in the Middle East, 1939–1941*, Norman, OK, University of Oklahoma, 2013, p. 266.
15. Raugh, *Wavell in the Middle East*, p. 270.
16. Churchill, *Their Finest Hour*, p. 511.
17. Raugh, *Wavell in the Middle East*, p. 80.
18. Raugh, *Wavell in the Middle East*, p. 78.
19. Connell, *Wavell: Scholar and Soldier*, p. 266.

20. Jonathan Fennell, *Fighting the People's War*, Cambridge, Cambridge University Press, 2018, p. 119.

21. I. S. O. Playfair, *The Mediterranean and Middle East*, vol. 1: *The Early Successes against Italy, to May 1941*, London, HMSO, 1954, p. 265.

22. Playfair, *The Mediterranean and Middle East*, vol. 1, p. 362.

23. Robert Lyman, *Tobruk: The Battle That Saved North Africa*, London, Macmillan, 2009, p. 56.

24. Arthur, *Desert Watch*, p. 254.

25. Martin Gilbert, ed., *The Churchill Documents*, vol. 16: *The Ever-Widening War, 1941*, Hillsdale, MI, Hillsdale College Press, 2011, pp. 192–3 (9 February 1941).

26. Lyman, *Tobruk*, p. 88.

27. Porch, *The Path to Victory*, p. 147.

28. Fennell, *Fighting the People's War*, pp. 127–8.

29. Dilks, ed., *The Diaries of Sir Alexander Cadogan*, p. 358 (24 February 1941).

30. Porch, *The Path to Victory*, p. 148.

31. I. S. O. Playfair, *The Mediterranean and Middle East*, vol. 2: *The Germans Come to the Help of Their Ally, 1941*, London, HMSO, 1956, p. 79.

32. Fennell, *Fighting the People's War*, p. 132.

33. Fennell, *Fighting the People's War*, p. 135.

34. Playfair, *The Mediterranean and Middle East*, vol. 2, pp. 132–3.

35. Gilbert, ed., *The Churchill Documents*, vol. 16, p. 804 (14 June 1941).

36. Hinsley, *British Intelligence in the Second World War*, vol. 1, p. 421.

37. Butler, *Grand Strategy*, vol. 2, pp. 384–5.

38. R. Carrier, 'Some Reflections on the Fighting Power of the Italian Army in North Africa, 1940–1943', *War in History*, vol. 22, no. 4, 2015; D. French, *Raising Churchill's Army*, Oxford, Oxford University Press, 2000, p. 219.

39. Porch, *The Path to Victory*, p. 69.

40. Gilbert, ed., *The Churchill Documents*, vol. 16, p. 82 (13 January 1941).

41. Playfair, *The Mediterranean and Middle East*, vol. 1, p. 315; Butler, *Grand Strategy*, vol. 2, p. 386.

42. NA: CAB 66/15/26, Telegram from Commander-in-Chief, Middle East, to the War Office, 7 March 1941.

43. Hinsley, *British Intelligence in the Second World War*, vol. 1, p. 392.

44. Militärgeschichtliches Forschungsamt (Potsdam), *Germany and the Second World War*, vol. 3, p. 674.

45. Carrier, 'Some Reflections', p. 506.

46. Lyman, *Tobruk*, p. 101.

47. Militärgeschichtliches Forschungsamt (Potsdam), *Germany and the Second World War*, vol. 3, p. 685.

48. Butler, *Grand Strategy*, vol. 2, Appendix IV.

49. Gilbert, ed., *The Churchill Documents*, vol. 16, p. 556 (28 April 1941).
50. Butler, *Grand Strategy*, vol. 2, Appendix IV; Freudenberg, *Churchill and Australia*, p. 210.
51. Freudenberg, *Churchill and Australia*, pp. 229–30.
52. Freudenberg, *Churchill and Australia*, p. 232.
53. Freudenberg, *Churchill and Australia*, pp. 244–5.
54. R. Paterson, 'The Fall of Fortress Singapore: Churchill's Role and the Conflicting Interpretations', *Sophia International Review*, vol. 30, 2008, p. 53.
55. Fennell, *Fighting the People's War*, p. 146.
56. Churchill, *The Grand Alliance*, p. 520; Gilbert, ed., *The Churchill Documents*, vol. 16, p. 660 (13 May 1941).
57. Butler, *Grand Strategy*, vol. II, Appendix IV.
58. Churchill, *The Grand Alliance*, p. 521.
59. Danchev, 'Dilly-Dally', pp. 27–8.
60. Alex Danchev, 'Dill', in John Keegan, ed., *Churchill's Generals*, London, Weidenfeld & Nicolson, 1991, p. 52.
61. David Reynolds, 'The Atlantic "Flop": British Foreign Policy and the Churchill–Roosevelt Meeting of August 1941', in Douglas Brinkley and David R. Facey-Crowther, eds., *The Atlantic Charter*, New York, St. Martin's Press, 1994, pp. 138–9.
62. C. Smith, *England's Last War Against France*, p. 173.
63. Brian P. Farrell, 'Yes, Prime Minister: Barbarossa, Whipcord, and the Basis of British Grand Strategy, Autumn 1941', *The Journal of Military History*, vol. 57, no. 4, 1993, p. 607.
64. Lyman, *Tobruk*, p. 186.
65. Lyman, *Tobruk*, p. 187.
66. Joly, *Take These Men*, pp. 143–4.
67. Joly, *Take These Men*, p. 145.
68. French, *Raising Churchill's Army*, pp. 215–16.
69. Playfair, *The Mediterranean and Middle East*, vol. 2, pp. 172–3.
70. Raugh, *Wavell in the Middle East*, pp. 242–3.
71. Initially a company of the DAK's 56th Short Range Reconnaissance Battalion.
72. Farrell, 'Yes, Prime Minister', p. 607.
73. Raugh, *Wavell in the Middle East*, pp. 237–8.

22: Taking the Gloves Off

1.   D. Sheridan, ed., *Among You Taking Notes: The Wartime Diary of Naomi Mitchison, 1939–1945*, London, Gollancz, 1985, p. 153 (22 June 1941).
2.   Mass Observation Diarist 5220, 22 June 1941.
3.   Mass Observation Diarist 5390, 23 June 1941.

4. Stebbing, *Diary of a Decade, 1939–50*, p. 87 (22 June 1941).

5. Beardmore, *Civilians at War*, p. 117 (24 June 1941).

6. Mass Observation File Report 848, *Public Opinion about Russia*, August 1941, p. 15.

7. M. Gilbert, ed., *The Churchill Documents*, vol. 16, p. 836 (22 June 1941).

8. Davison, ed., *The Complete Works of George Orwell: A Patriot After All, 1940–1941*, p. 517.

9. Colville, *The Fringes of Power*, p. 405 (22 June 1941).

10. Philip M. H. Bell, *John Bull and the Bear*, London, E. Arnold, 1990, p. 28.

11. P. M. H. Bell, *John Bull and the Bear*, pp. 38–9.

12. P. M. H. Bell, *John Bull and the Bear*, p. 36.

13. M. Kitchen, 'Winston Churchill and the Soviet Union during the Second World War', *The Historical Journal*, vol. 30, no. 2, 1987, p. 419.

14. Gilbert, ed., *The Churchill Documents*, vol. 16, p. 835 (22 June 1941).

15. Dilks, ed., *The Diaries of Sir Alexander Cadogan*, p. 390 (30 June 1941).

16. Danchev and Todman, *War Diaries 1939–1945: Field Marshal Lord Alanbrooke*, p. 166 (13 September 1940).

17. Hinsley, *British Intelligence in the Second World War*, vol. 1, p. 482.

18. Gilbert, ed., *The Churchill Documents*, vol. 16, p. 871 (29 June 1941).

19. Reynolds, *From Munich to Pearl Harbor*, p. 132.

20. Stebbing, *Diary of a Decade*, p. 84 (29 May 1941).

21. Reynolds, *The Creation of the Anglo-American Alliance*, p. 214.

22. Reynolds, 'The Atlantic "Flop"', p. 145.

23. Gilbert, ed., *The Churchill Documents*, vol. 16, p. 1125 (28 August 1941).

24. David Carlton, *Churchill and the Soviet Union*, Manchester, Manchester University Press, 2000, pp. 86–7; Roof, 'A Separate Peace?', p. 250.

25. Alexander Hill, 'British Lend-Lease Aid and the Soviet War Effort, June 1941–June 1942', *The Journal of Military History*, vol. 71, no. 3, 2007, p. 779.

26. Hill, 'British Lend-Lease Aid', p. 788.

27. Hill, 'British Lend-Lease Aid', p. 796.

28. Todman, *Britain's War: Into Battle, 1937–1941*, p. 692.

29. Roof, 'A Separate Peace?', p. 239n.

30. Nikolay A. Kozhanov, 'The Pretexts and Reasons for the Allied Invasion of Iran in 1941', *Iranian Studies*, vol. 45, no. 4, 2012, p. 494.

31. Richard A. Stewart, *Sunrise at Abadan*, New York, Praeger, 1988, p. 107.

32. Stewart, *Sunrise at Abadan*, p. 216.

33. Churchill, *The Grand Alliance*, p. 589.

34. Stewart, *Sunrise at Abadan*, p. 183.

35. Stephen M. Miner, *Between Churchill and Stalin: The Soviet Union, Great*

Britain, and the Origins of the Grand Alliance, Chapel Hill, NC, University of North Carolina Press, 1988, p. 156.

36. NA: CAB 66/19/45, Relations with Russia, 14 November 1941, p. 1; CAB 65/24/3, War Cabinet Conclusions, Confidential Annexes, 3 December 1941, p. 1.
37. Miner, *Between Churchill and Stalin*, p. 178.
38. Kitchen, 'Winston Churchill and the Soviet Union', p. 418.
39. Moorhouse, *The Devils' Alliance*.
40. Moorhouse, *The Devils' Alliance*, p. 93.
41. Moorhouse, *The Devils' Alliance*, p. 85.
42. Evelyn Waugh, *The Sword of Honour Trilogy*, Harmondsworth, Penguin, 1984, p. 594.
43. Carlton, *Churchill and the Soviet Union*, p. 72.
44. HC Deb 8 September 1942, vol. 83, col. 95.
45. Miner, *Between Churchill and Stalin*, p. 150.
46. Gilbert, ed., *The Churchill Documents*, vol. 16, p. 964 (20 July 1941).
47. Miner, *Between Churchill and Stalin*, pp. 157–8.
48. Gilbert, ed., *The Churchill Documents*, vol. 16, p. 841 (23 June 1941).
49. Farrell, 'Yes, Prime Minister', pp. 604–5.
50. R. Mackay, *Britain's Fleet Air Arm in World War II*, Atglen, Schiffer, 2005, p. 141.
51. Gilbert, ed., *The Churchill Documents*, vol. 16, p. 903 (7 July 1941).
52. Gilbert, ed., *The Churchill Documents*, vol. 16, p. 991 (28 July 1941).
53. Sheila Lawlor, 'Britain and the Russian Entry into the War', in Richard Langhorne, ed., *Diplomacy and Intelligence during the Second World War*, Cambridge, Cambridge University Press, 1985, p. 172.
54. Overy, *The Bombing War*, p. 266.
55. Denis Richards, *Portal of Hungerford*, London, Heinemann, 1977, p. 272 (emphasis in the original).
56. Richards, *Portal of Hungerford*, pp. 202–3.
57. Richards, *Portal of Hungerford*, p. 186.
58. Gilbert, ed., *The Churchill Documents*, vol. 16, p. 483 (12 April 1941).
59. Ken Delve, *Fighter Command 1936–1968*, Barnsley, Pen & Sword, 2007, p. 59.
60. Peter Caygill, *The Biggin Hill Wing, 1941*, Barnsley, Pen & Sword, 2008.
61. Gilbert, ed., *The Churchill Documents*, vol. 15, p. 493 (8 July 1940).
62. Gilbert, ed., *The Churchill Documents*, vol. 15, pp. 693–4 (20 August 1940).
63. Max Hastings, *Bomber Command*, London, Pan, 1979, pp. 83–6.
64. Webster and Frankland, *The Strategic Air Offensive against Germany 1939–1945*, vol. 1, p. 203.
65. Hastings, *Bomber Command*, p. 89.

66. Webster and Frankland, *The Strategic Air Offensive against Germany*, vol. 4, p. 440.
67. Webster and Frankland, *The Strategic Air Offensive against Germany*, vol. 1, p. 151.
68. Webster and Frankland, *The Strategic Air Offensive against Germany*, vol. 1, p. 159.
69. Webster and Frankland, *The Strategic Air Offensive against Germany*, vol. 1, p. 228.
70. Webster and Frankland, *The Strategic Air Offensive against Germany*, vol. 1, p. 163.
71. Hastings, *Bomber Command*, pp. 104, 84–5.
72. Overy, *The Bombing War*, pp. 267–8.
73. Gilbert, ed., *The Churchill Documents*, vol. 16, p. 1218 (15 September 1941).
74. Gilbert, ed., *The Churchill Documents*, vol. 15, p. 1027 (2 November 1940); Hastings, *Bomber Command*, p. 97.
75. Webster and Frankland, *The Strategic Air Offensive against Germany*, vol. 1, p. 161.
76. Hastings, *Bomber Command*, p. 96.
77. Overy, *The Bombing War*, p. 256.
78. Overy, *The Bombing War*, p. 260.
79. Overy, *The Bombing War*, p. 258.
80. Webster and Frankland, *The Strategic Air Offensive against Germany*, vol. 4, p. 190.
81. Webster and Frankland, *The Strategic Air Offensive against Germany*, vol. 4, p. 195.
82. Biddle, *Rhetoric and Reality in Air Warfare*, p. 189.
83. 'The Hague Rules of Air Warfare', *The World War I Document Archive*, https://wwi.lib.byu.edu/index.php/ The_Hague_Rules_of_Air_Warfare [accessed 13 February 2020].
84. Peter W. Gray, *The Leadership, Direction and Legitimacy of the RAF Bomber Offensive from Inception to 1945*, London, Bloomsbury Academic, 2012, pp. 137–8.
85. Gray, *The Leadership, Direction and Legitimacy of the RAF Bomber Offensive*, p. 138.
86. Biddle, *Rhetoric and Reality in Air Warfare*, p. 103.
87. Overy, *The Bombing War*, p. 250.
88. Hew Strachan, 'Strategic Bombing and the Question of Civilian Casualties up to 1945', in Jeremy Crang and Paul Addison, eds., *Firestorm: The Bombing of Dresden, 1945*, London, Pimlico, 2006.

89. Gray, *The Leadership, Direction and Legitimacy of the RAF Bomber Offensive*, p. 180.
90. Webster and Frankland, *The Strategic Air Offensive against Germany*, vol. 4, p. 113.
91. Overy, *The Bombing War*, p. 245.
92. Webster and Frankland, *The Strategic Air Offensive against Germany*, vol. 4, p. 129.
93. Martin Middlebrook and Chris Everitt, *The Bomber Command War Diaries*, London, Penguin, 1990, p. 111.
94. Webster and Frankland, *The Strategic Air Offensive against Germany*, vol. 4, p. 136.
95. Hastings, *Bomber Command*, p. 353.
96. Postan, *British War Production*, Appendix 4.
97. Middlebrook and Everitt, *The Bomber Command War Diaries*, p. 200.
98. Gilbert, ed., *The Churchill Documents*, vol. 16, p. 1270 (27 September 1941).
99. Richards, *Portal of Hungerford*, pp. 189–90.

23: March on to Better Days

1. O'Brien, *Civil Defence*, p. 428. Thanks to Daniel Jackson for details.
2. Middlebrook and Everitt, *The Bomber Command War Diaries*, p. 199.
3. NA: CAB 66/18/37, Weekly Résumé (no. 105) of the Naval, Military and Air Situation from 0700 August 28th to 0700 September 4th, 1941, 4 September 1941.
4. 'SC-42', *UBoat.net*, https://uboat.net/ops/convoys/convoys. php?convoy=SC-42 [accessed 13 February 2020].
5. HMS *Otus* (N-92), *U-boat.net*, https://uboat.net/allies/warships/ship/3399. html [accessed 13 February 2020]; 'Andrea Gritti', *Con la pella appesa a un Chiodo*, https://conlapelleappesaaunchiodo.blogspot.com/2013/10/andrea-gritti.html [accessed 13 February 2020].
6. NA: CAB 66/18/37, p. 6.
7. Colville, *The Fringes of Power*, p. 437 (5 September 1941).
8. Gilbert, ed., *The Churchill Documents*, vol. 16, p. 1150 (3 September 1941).
9. Gilbert, ed., *The Churchill Documents*, vol. 16, p. 1150 (3 September 1941).
10. Colville, *The Fringes of Power*, p. 436 (3 September 1941).
11. Crowson, *Facing Fascism*, p. 185.
12. Fry, *The Politics of Crisis*, pp. 142–3.
13. Roberts, *Eminent Churchillians*, pp. 141–2.
14. Roberts, *Eminent Churchillians*, p. 164.
15. Fry, *The Politics of Crisis*, p. 135.
16. Roberts, *The Holy Fox*, p. 209.

17. Ball, ed., *Parliament and Politics in the Age of Churchill and Attlee*, p. 180 (1 February 1940).
18. Ball, ed., *Parliament and Politics in the Age of Churchill and Attlee*, p. 197 (10 May 1940).
19. Ball, ed., *Parliament and Politics in the Age of Churchill and Attlee*, p. 207 (18 June 1940).
20. Ball, ed., *Parliament and Politics in the Age of Churchill and Attlee*, p. 213 (16 July 1940).
21. Roberts, *Eminent Churchillians*, p. 209.
22. HC Deb 7 May 1941, vol. 371, col. 880.
23. HC Deb 7 May 1941, vol. 371, cols. 945–6.
24. Nicolson, ed., *The Diaries and Letters of Harold Nicolson*, p. 164 (7 May 1941).
25. Mass Observation File Report 862, *Fourteenth Weekly Report*, September 1941, p. 1.
26. NA: INF 1/292, Home Intelligence Weekly Report no. 49, 10 September 1941.
27. Woolven, ed., *The London Diary of Anthony Heap, 1931–1945*, pp. 337–9 (Retrospect – 1940).
28. Gallup, ed., *The Gallup International Public Opinion Polls*, p. 49 (November 1941).
29. *Daily Express*, 3 September 1941, p. 2.
30. Mass Observation File Report 857, *Postwar Jobs*, September 1941, p. 1.
31. Last, *Nella Last's War*, p. 160 (2 September 1941).
32. *Times*, 1 July 1940, p. 8.
33. Roberts, *The Holy Fox*, p. 252.
34. Ball, ed., *Parliament and Politics in the Age of Churchill and Attlee*, pp. 214–15 (31 July 1940).
35. Ball, ed., *Parliament and Politics in the Age of Churchill and Attlee*, p. 229 (30 November 1940).
36. Ball, ed., *Parliament and Politics in the Age of Churchill and Attlee*, p. 260 (7 July 1941).
37. Davison, ed., *The Complete Works of George Orwell: All Propaganda Is Lies, 1941–1942*, London, Secker & Warburg, 2000, p. 23 (28 August 1941).
38. 'September 11, 1941: Fireside Chat 18', *Miller Center*, https://millercenter.org/the-presidency/presidential-speeches/september-11-1941-fireside-chat-18-greer-incident [accessed 13 February 2020].
39. Daniel Morgan and Bruce Taylor, *U-Boat Attack Logs*, Annapolis, MD, Naval Institute Press, 2012, p. 145.
40. Reynolds, *The Creation of the Anglo-American Alliance*, p. 240.
41. Noriko Kawamura, 'Emperor Hirohito and Japan's Decision to Go to War with the United States', *Diplomatic History*, vol. 31, no. 1, 2007, p. 61.

42. 'The MAUD Report, 1941', *Atomicarchive.com*, http://www.atomicarchive. com/Docs/Begin/MAUD.shtml [accessed 13 February 2020].

43. Gilbert, ed., *The Churchill Documents*, vol. 16, p. 1138 (30 August 1941).

44. Graham Farmelo, *Churchill's Bomb*, London, Faber & Faber, 2013, p. 190; M. Gowing, *Britain and Atomic Energy, 1939–1945*, London, Macmillan, 1964, p. 106.

BIBLIOGRAPHY

Archival Sources
Imperial War Museum, Documents Archive
Bombardment of the French Fleet at Oran, Misc. 21 (381)
Thames TV Interviews for a Documentary on the Blitz, 67/262/1
V. Bawtree, 91/5/1
S. Burr, 88/8/1
J. Garnham-Wright, 97/19/1
M. Morris, 80/38/1
B. A. Pond, 78/27/1

Imperial War Museum, Sound Archive
Charles Tinson, 15255
Desmond Woods, 23846

Liddell Hart Centre for Military Archives
Richard O'Connor papers

Mass Observation Archive
Diarist 5175
Diarist 5220
Diarist 5341
Diarist 5382
Diarist 5396
Diarist 5420
Diarist 5390
File Report A5, 'Expenditure of 1,380 Middle Class Households in 1938–39', January 1938
File Report A9, 'Social Attitudes to Margarine', December 1938
File Report 4, 'ARP Instructions', October 1939
File Report 63, 'Peace – Sylt', March 1940
File Report 99, 'Political Crisis Report', May 1940
File Report 135, 'Reactions to Internment of Mosley', May 1940

File Report 181, 'Capitulation Talk in Worktown', June 1940

File Report 251, 'Public Opinion about Mr. Chamberlain', June 1940

File Report 282, 'General Morale Report', June 1940

File Report 284, 'Survey of Public Opinion', June 1940

File Report 349, 'Stay Where You Are' leaflet, August 1940

File Report 408, 'Human Adjustments in Air Raids', September 1940

File Report 436, 'Shelter in London', October 1940

File Report 495, 'Coventry', November 1940

File Report 706, 'Liverpool', May 1941

File Report 844, 'Hull', August 1941

File Report 848, 'Public Opinion about Russia', August 1941

File Report 857, 'Post-War Jobs', September 1941

File Report 862, 'Fourteenth Weekly Report', September 1941

National Archives, Kew

CAB 23/94 Cabinet Conclusions, 30 August 1938

CAB 23/95 Cabinet Conclusions, 17 September 1938

CAB 23/98 Cabinet Conclusions, 18 March 1939

CAB 23/100 Cabinet Conclusions, 30 August 1939

CAB 23/100 Cabinet Conclusions, 1 September 1939

CAB 24/281 Sir Miles Lampson to Lord Halifax, 6 December 1938

CAB 24/287 IRA Outrages, 30 June 1939

CAB 65/2 War Cabinet Conclusions, 7 December 1939

CAB 65/5 War Cabinet Conclusions, 13 February 1940

CAB 65 7 War Cabinet Conclusions, 10 May 1940

CAB 65 7 War Cabinet Conclusions, 13 May 1940

CAB 65/7 War Cabsinet Conclusions, 27 May 1940

CAB 65/8 War Cabinet Conclusions, 5 July 1940

CAB 65/13 War Cabinet Conclusions, Confidential Annexes, 12 May 1940

CAB 65/13 War Cabinet Conclusions, Confidential Annexes, 15 May 1940

CAB 65/13 War Cabinet Conclusions, Confidential Annexes, 18 May 1940

CAB 65/13 War Cabinet Conclusions, Confidential Annexes, 26 May 1940

CAB 65/13 War Cabinet Conclusions, Confidential Annexes, 27 May 1940

CAB 65/24/3 War Cabinet Conclusions, Confidential Annexes, 3 December 1941

CAB 66/1/42 Note by the Chancellor of the Exchequer, 21 September 1939

CAB 66/1/44 Conversation with M. Daladier and General Gamelin, 21 September 1939

CAB 66/1/47 Minutes of 2nd Supreme War Council Meeting, 22 September 1939

CAB 66/2/40 Germany: Stocks and Supplies of Petroleum, 13 October 1939

CAB 66/3/12 Air Requirements for the Army, 3 November 1939

CAB 66/3/18 Chiefs of Staff on Air Policy, 11 November 1939

CAB 66/4/12 Norway – Iron Ore Traffic, 16 December 1939

CAB 66/6/39 French Government's Views on the Future Conduct of the War, 26 March 1940

CAB 66/7/30 Letter from the Commander-in-Chief, British Expeditionary Force, 11 April 1940

CAB 66/7/25 Review of the Strategical Situation, 4 May 1940

CAB 66/7/48 British Strategy in a Certain Eventuality, 25 May 1940

CAB 66/8/18 Resolutions of the 10th Meeting of the Supreme War Council, 31 May 1940

CAB 66/11/42 Future Strategy, 4 September 1940

CAB 66/13/43 Huyton Camp, 25 November 1940

CAB 66/15/26 Telegram from Commander-in-Chief, Middle East, to the War Office, 7 March 1941

CAB 66/18/37 Weekly Résumé (No. 105) of the Naval, Military and Air Situation from 0700, 28 August, to 0700, 4 September 1941

CAB 66/19/45 Relations with Russia, 14 November 1941

CAB 67/3/159 Scale of Public Opinion As Regards Civil Defence Measures, 20 December 1939

CAB 67/4/35 Survey of the National Resources, 30 January 1940

CAB 67/8/80 Air Raid Shelter Policy, 31 October 1940

CAB 67/9/44 Air Raids on London, September–November 1940, 5 May 1941

CAB 68/1/9 Economic Warfare, 1st Monthly Report, 12 September 1939

CAB 68/4/43 Economic Warfare, 5th Monthly Report, February 1940

CAB 106/223 Letter by Field Marshal Lord Ironside on relations with the French General Staff, 1940

CAB 106/253 'Crowded Hour', Personal Account of Action in France, by A. C. Geddes, 1940

CAB 106/273 Correspondence on Draft Official History, 1947–52

INF 1/264 Home Intelligence Daily Report no. 12, 30 May 1940

INF 1/264 Home Intelligence Daily Report no. 22, 11 June 1940

INF 1/264 Home Intelligence Daily Report no. 28, 18 June 1940

INF 1/264 Home Intelligence Daily Report no. 29, 19 June 1940

INF 1/264 Home Intelligence Daily Report no. 39, 2 July 1940

INF 1/264 Home Intelligence Daily Report no. 44, 8 July 1940

INF 1/264 Home Intelligence Daily Report no. 45, 9 July 1940

INF 1/264 Home Intelligence Daily Report no. 52, 17 July 1940

INF 1/264 Home Intelligence Daily Report no. 56, 23 July 1940

INF 1/264 Home Intelligence Daily Report no. 78, 17 August 1940

INF 1/264 Home Intelligence Daily Report no. 95, 9 September 1940

INF 1/264 Home Intelligence Daily Report no. 96, 10 September 1940
INF 1/264 Home Intelligence Daily Report no. 101, 16 September 1940
INF 1/264 Home Intelligence Daily Report no. 102, 17 September 1940
INF 1/292 Home Intelligence Weekly Report no. 49, 10 September 1941

Newspapers and Magazines
British Medical Journal
Daily Express
Daily Mail
Daily Mirror
Daily Telegraph
The New Yorker
The Spectator
Sunday Express
The Times
The Times Literary Supplement

Articles in Periodicals
Anthony Adamthwaite, 'The British Government and the Media, 1937–1938', *Journal of Contemporary History*, vol. 18, no. 2, 1983
Amy Bell, 'Landscapes of Fear: Wartime London, 1939–1945', *Journal of British Studies*, vol. 48, no. 1, 2009
Donald S. Birn, 'The League of Nations and Collective Security', *Journal of Contemporary History*, vol. 9, no. 3, 1974
D. W. Brogan, 'What Happened to France', *The Political Quarterly*, vol. 12, no. 1, 1941
John C. Cairns, 'A Nation of Shopkeepers in Search of a Suitable France: 1919–40', *The American Historical Review*, vol. 79, no. 3, 1974
Angus Calder, 'The Myth of 1940', *London Review of Books*, vol. 2, no. 20, 16 October 1980
Richard Carrier, 'Some Reflections on the Fighting Power of the Italian Army in North Africa, 1940–1943', *War in History*, vol. 22, no. 4, 2015
Jennifer Craig-Norton, 'Contesting the Kindertransport as a "Model" Refugee Response', *European Judaism*, vol. 50, no. 24, 2017
R. H. S. Crossman, 'Labour and Compulsory Military Service', *The Political Quarterly*, vol. 10, no. 3, 1939
N. J. Crowson, 'The Conservative Party and the Call for National Service, 1937–1939: Compulsion versus Voluntarism', *Contemporary British History*, vol. 9, no. 3, 1995
Alex Danchev, '"Dilly-Dally", or Having the Last Word: Field Marshal Sir John Dill

and Prime Minister Winston Churchill, *Journal of Contemporary History*, vol. 22, no. 1, 1987

Laura K. Donohue, 'Regulating Northern Ireland: The Special Powers Acts, 1922–1972', *The Historical Journal*, vol. 41, no. 4, 1998

John Ellison, '"The Legendary War and the Real One": *The Lord of the Rings* and the Climate of its Times', *Mallorn: The Journal of the Tolkien Society*, vol. 26, 1989

Bryce Evans, 'Fear and Loathing in Liverpool: The IRA's 1939 Bombing Campaign on Merseyside', *Transactions of the Lancashire and Cheshire Historical Society*, vol. 162, 2013

Brian P. Farrell, 'Yes, Prime Minister: Barbarossa, Whipcord, and the Basis of British Grand Strategy, Autumn 1941', *The Journal of Military History*, vol. 57, no. 4, 1993

Geoffrey Field, 'Nights Underground in Darkest London: The Blitz, 1940–1941', *International Labor and Working-Class History*, vol. 62, no. 3, 2002

David French, 'The Mechanization of the British Cavalry between the World Wars', *War in History*, vol. 10, no. 3, 2003

Edward Glover, 'Notes on the Psychological Effects of War Conditions', *International Journal of Psychoanalysis*, vol. 22, 1941

Julie V. Gottlieb, 'Neville Chamberlain's Umbrella: "Object" Lessons in the History of Appeasement', *Twentieth Century British History*, vol. 27, no. 3, 2016

Richard S. Grayson, 'Imperialism in Conservative Defence and Foreign Policy: Leo Amery and the Chamberlains, 1903–39', *The Journal of Imperial and Commonwealth History*, vol. 34, no. 4, 2006

Adrian Gregory, 'Peculiarities of the English? War, Violence, and Politics: 1900–1939', *Journal of Modern European History*, vol. 1, no. 12, 2003

Richard Griffiths, 'A Note on Mosley, the "Jewish War" and Conscientious Objection', *Journal of Contemporary History*, vol. 40, no. 4, 2005

A. C. Hepburn, 'The Belfast Riots of 1935', *Social History*, vol. 15, no. 1, 1990

Marianne Hicks, '"No War this Year": Selkirk Panton and the Editorial Policy of the *Daily Express*, 1938–39', *Media History*, vol. 14, no. 2, 2008

Alexander Hill, 'British Lend-Lease Aid and the Soviet War Effort, June 1941–June 1942', *The Journal of Military History*, vol. 71, no. 3, 2007

Brett Holman, '"Bomb Back, and Bomb Hard": Debating Reprisals during the Blitz', *Australian Journal of Politics & History*, vol. 58, no. 3, 2012

Jeffrey L. Hughes, 'The Origins of World War II in Europe: British Deterrence Failure and German Expansionism', *The Journal of Interdisciplinary History*, vol. 18, no. 4, 1988

Matthew Hughes, 'The Banality of Brutality: British Armed Forces and the Repression of the Arab Revolt in Palestine, 1936–39', *English Historical Review*, vol. 124, no. 507, 2009

Matthew Hughes, 'The Practice and Theory of British Counterinsurgency: The

Histories of the Atrocities at the Palestinian Villages of al-Bassa and Halhul, 1938–1939', *Small Wars & Insurgencies*, vol. 20, no. 3–4, 2009.

Edgar Jones, 'Public Panic and Morale: Second World War Civilian Responses Re-Examined in the Light of the Current Anti-Terrorist Campaign', *Journal of Risk Research*, vol. 9, no. 1, 2006

Edgar Jones et al., 'Civilian Morale during the Second World War: Responses to Air Raids Re-Examined', *Social History of Medicine*, vol. 17, no. 3, 2004

Noriko Kawamura, 'Emperor Hirohito and Japan's Decision to Go to War with the United States', *Diplomatic History*, vol. 31, no. 1, 2007

Martin Kitchen, 'Winston Churchill and the Soviet Union during the Second World War', *The Historical Journal*, vol. 30, no. 2, 1987

Nikolay A. Kozhanov, 'The Pretexts and Reasons for the Allied Invasion of Iran in 1941', *Iranian Studies*, vol. 45, no. 4, 2012

Tony Kushner, 'Truly, Madly, Deeply ... Nostalgically? Britain's On–Off Love Affair with Refugees, Past and Present', *Patterns of Prejudice*, vol. 52, no. 2–3, 2018

Richard M. Langsworth, 'Did Churchill Ever Admire Hitler?', *Finest Hour*, vol. 156, 2012

Jon Lawrence, 'Fascist Violence and the Politics of Public Order in Inter-War Britain: The Olympia Debate Revisited', *Historical Research*, vol. 76, no. 192, 2003

Jon Lawrence, 'Forging a Peaceable Kingdom: War, Violence, and Fear of Brutalization in Post–First World War Britain', *The Journal of Modern History*, vol. 75, no. 3, 2003

Frank Magee, '"Limited Liability"? Britain and the Treaty of Locarno', *Twentieth Century British History*, vol. 6, no. 1, 1995

Joseph A. Maiolo, 'The Admiralty and the Anglo-German Naval Agreement of 18 June 1935', *Diplomacy & Statecraft*, vol. 10, no. 1, 1999

Joseph A. Maiolo, 'Deception and Intelligence Failure: Anglo-German Preparations for U-boat Warfare in the 1930s', *Journal of Strategic Studies*, vol. 22, no. 4, 1999

Joseph S. Meisel, 'Air Raid Shelter Policy and its Critics in Britain before the Second World War', *Twentieth Century British History*, vol. 5, no. 3, 1994

Marc Milner, 'The Battle of the Atlantic', *Journal of Strategic Studies*, vol. 13, no. 1, 1990

Keith Neilson, 'The Defence Requirements Sub-Committee, British Strategic Foreign Policy, Neville Chamberlain and the Path to Appeasement', *English Historical Review*, vol. 118, no. 477, 2003

Jacob Norris, 'Repression and Rebellion: Britain's Response to the Arab Revolt in Palestine of 1936–39', *Journal of Imperial and Commonwealth History*, vol. 36, no. 1, 2008

Richard J. Overy, 'Hitler and Air Strategy', *Journal of Contemporary History*, vol. 15, no. 3, 1980

Richard J. Overy, 'Air Power and the Origins of Deterrence Theory before 1939', *Journal of Strategic Studies*, vol. 15, no. 1, 1992

Richard J. Overy, '"The Weak Link"? The Perception of the German Working Class by RAF Bomber Command, 1940–1945', *Labour History Review*, vol. 77, 2012

Robert Alexander Clarke Parker, 'British Rearmament 1936–9: Treasury, Trade Unions and Skilled Labour', *English Historical Review*, vol. 96, no. 379, 1981

Rab Paterson, 'The Fall of Fortress Singapore: Churchill's Role and the Conflicting Interpretations', *Sophia International Review*, vol. 30, 2008

G. C. Peden, 'The Burden of Imperial Defence and the Continental Commitment Reconsidered', *The Historical Journal*, vol. 27, no. 2, 1984

G. C. Peden, 'A Matter of Timing: The Economic Background to British Foreign Policy, 1937–1939', *History*, vol. 69, no. 225, 1984

Glyn Prysor, 'The "Fifth Column" and the British Experience of Retreat, 1940', *War in History*, vol. 12, no. 4, 2005

Samir Puri, 'The Role of Intelligence in Deciding the Battle of Britain', *Intelligence and National Security*, vol. 21, no. 3, 2006

David Reynolds, '1940: Fulcrum of the Twentieth Century?' *International Affairs*, vol. 66, no. 2, 1990

Abraham M. Roof, 'A Separate Peace? The Soviet Union and the Making of British Strategy in the Wake of "Barbarossa", June–September 1941', *The Journal of Slavic Military Studies*, vol. 22, no. 2, 2009

Raphael Samuel, 'Suburbs under Siege: The Middle Class Between the Wars, Part III', *New Socialist*, no. 11, May–June 1983

Max Schoenfeld, 'Winston Churchill as War Manager: The Battle of the Atlantic Committee, 1941', *Military Affairs*, vol. 52, no. 3, 1988

Nick Smart, 'Four Days in May: The Norway Debate and the Downfall of Neville Chamberlain', *Parliamentary History*, vol. 17, no. 2, 1998

C. T. Stannage, 'The Fulham By-Election, 25 October 1933', *The Historical Journal*, vol. 14, no. 1, 1971

G. Bruce Strang, '"The Worst of All Worlds": Oil Sanctions and Italy's Invasion of Abyssinia, 1935–1936', *Diplomacy and Statecraft*, vol. 19, no. 2, 2008

Selina Todd, 'Class, Experience, and Britain's Twentieth Century', *Social History*, vol. 39, no. 4, 2014

Charles Townshend, 'The First Intifada: Rebellion in Palestine, 1936–39', *History Today*, vol. 39, July 1989

P. E. Vernon, 'Psychological Effects of Air Raids', *Journal of Abnormal and Social Psychology*, vol. 36, 1941

Matthew Worley, 'What Was the New Party? Sir Oswald Mosley and Associated Responses to the "Crisis", 1931–1932', *History*, vol. 92, no. 1, 2007

Chapters of Books

Martin Alexander, 'Dunkirk in Military Operations, Myths, and Memories', in Robert Tombs and Emile Chabal, eds., *Britain and France in Two World Wars*, London, Bloomsbury, 2013

Sidney Aster, '"Guilty Men": The Case of Neville Chamberlain', in Robert Boyce and Esmonde M. Robertson, eds., *Paths to War: New Essays on the Origins of the Second World War*, London, Palgrave, 1989

John Baxendale, '"You and I – All of Us Ordinary People": Renegotiating "Britishness" in Wartime', in Nick Hayes and Jeff Hill, eds., *Millions Like Us? British Culture in the Second World War*, Liverpool, Liverpool University Press, 1999

Christopher M. Bell, 'The View from the Top: Winston Churchill, British Grand Strategy, and the Battle of the Atlantic', in Marcus Faulkner and Christopher M. Bell, eds., *Decision in the Atlantic*, Lexington, KY, Andarta Books, 2019

Philip M. H. Bell, '"Thank God for the French Army": Churchill, France, and an Alternative to Appeasement in the 1930s', in Christopher Baxter et al., eds., *Britain in Global Politics*, vol. 1: *From Gladstone to Churchill*, London, Palgrave Macmillan, 2013

Brian Bond, 'Preparing the Field Force, February 1939–May 1940', in Brian Bond and Michael Taylor, eds., *The Battle of France and Flanders, 1940: Sixty Years On*, London, Leo Cooper, 2001

John Buckley, 'The Air War in France', in Brian Bond and Michael Taylor, eds., *The Battle of France and Flanders, 1940: Sixty Years On*, London, Leo Cooper, 2001

John C. Cairns, 'The French View of Dunkirk', in Brian Bond and Michael Taylor, eds., *The Battle of France and Flanders, 1940: Sixty Years On*, London, Leo Cooper, 2001

Martin Ceadel, 'Interpreting East Fulham', in Chris Cook and John Ramsden, eds., *By-Elections in British Politics*, London, UCL Press, 1997

Sebastian Cox, 'A Comparative Analysis of RAF and Luftwaffe Intelligence in the Battle of Britain, 1940', in Michael Handel, ed., *Intelligence and Military Operations*, London, Cass, 1988

Jeremy A. Crang, 'The Defence of the Dunkirk Perimeter', in Brian Bond and Michael Taylor, eds., *The Battle of France and Flanders, 1940: Sixty Years On*, London, Leo Cooper, 2001

Hazel Croft, 'Rethinking Civilian Neuroses in the Second World War', in P. Leese et al., eds., *Traumatic Memories of the Second World War and After*, London, Palgrave, 2018

Alex Danchev, 'The Central Direction of War, 1940–41', in John Sweetman, ed., *Sword and Mace: Twentieth-Century Civil–Military Relations*, London, Brassey's, 1986

Alex Danchev, 'Dill', in John Keegan, ed., *Churchill's Generals*, London, Weidenfeld & Nicolson, 1991

John Ferris, 'Achieving Air Ascendancy: Challenge and Response in British Strategic Air Defence, 1915–40', in Sebastian Cox, ed., *Air Power History: Turning Points from Kitty Hawk to Kosovo*, London, Frank Cass, 2002

John Ferris and Evan Mawdsley, 'The War in the West, 1939–40: The Battle of Britain?', in John Ferris and Evan Mawdsley, eds., *The Cambridge History of the Second World War,* vol. 1: *Fighting the War*, Cambridge, Cambridge University Press, 2015

Robert Frank, 'The Second World War through French and British Eyes', in Robert Tombs and Emile Chabal, eds., *Britain and France in Two World Wars*, London, Bloomsbury, 2013

Karl-Heinz Frieser, 'The War in the West, 1939–1940: An Unplanned Blitzkrieg', in John Ferris and Evan Mawdsley, eds., *The Cambridge History of the Second World War,* vol. 1: *Fighting the War*, Cambridge, Cambridge University Press, 2015

W. R. Inge, 'Religion', in Hugh Kingsmill, ed., *The English Genius: A Survey of the English Achievement and Character*, London, Right Book Club, 1938

Douglas Johnson, 'Churchill and France', in Robert Blake and William Roger Louis, eds., *Churchill*, Oxford, Clarendon Press, 1996

Sheila Lawlor, 'Britain and the Russian Entry into the War', in Richard Langhorne, ed., *Diplomacy and Intelligence during the Second World War*, Cambridge, Cambridge University Press, 1985

Anthony Lentin, 'Lloyd George, Clemenceau, and the Elusive Anglo-French Guarantee Treaty, 1919', in Alan Sharp and Glyn Stone, eds., *Anglo-French Relations in the Twentieth Century*, London, Routledge, 2002

Tony Mason, '"Hunger ... Is a Very Good Thing': Britain in the 1930s', in Nick Tiratsoo, ed., *From Blitz to Blair: A New History of Britain since 1939*, London, Phoenix, 1998

Williamson Murray, 'British Grand Strategy 1933–1942', in Williamson Murray et al., eds., *The Shaping of Grand Strategy: Policy, Diplomacy, and War*, Cambridge, Cambridge University Press, 2011

Joseph Nevo, 'Palestinian-Arab Violent Activity during the 1930s', in Michael J. Cohen and Martin Kolinsky, eds., *Britain and the Middle East in the 1930s: Security Problems, 1935–39*, New York, St. Martin's Press, 1992

M. R. H. Piercy, 'The Manouevre That Saved the Field Force', in Brian Bond and Michael Taylor, eds., *The Battle of France and Flanders, 1940: Sixty Years On*, London, Leo Cooper, 2001

Henry Probert, 'Allied Land-Based Anti-Submarine Warfare', in Stephen Howarth and Derek Law, eds., *The Battle of the Atlantic 1939–1945*, London, Greenhill Books, 1994

Roland Quinault, 'Churchill and Democracy', in David Cannadine and Roland Quinault, eds., *Winston Churchill in the Twenty-First Century*, Cambridge, Cambridge University Press, 2005

David Reynolds, 'Churchill and the British "Decision" to Fight On in 1940', in Richard Langhorne, ed., *Diplomacy and Intelligence during the Second World War*, Cambridge, Cambridge University Press, 1985

David Reynolds, 'The Atlantic "Flop": British Foreign Policy and the Churchill–Roosevelt Meeting of August 1941', in Douglas Brinkley and David R. Facey-Crowther, eds., *The Atlantic Charter*, New York, St. Martin's Press, 1994

David Reynolds, 'Churchill and the Gathering Storm', in David Cannadine and Roland Quinault, eds., *Winston Churchill in the Twenty-First Century*, Cambridge, Cambridge University Press, 2005

Francis Robinson, 'The British Empire and the Muslim World', in William Roger Louis, ed., *The Oxford History of the British Empire*, vol. 4: *The Twentieth Century*, Oxford, Oxford University Press, 1999

Gerry Rubin, 'In the Highest Degree Ominous: Hitler's Threatened Invasion and the British War Zone Courts', in Katherine O'Donovan and Gerry Rubin, eds., *Human Rights and Legal History*, Oxford, Oxford University Press, 2000

Alan Sharp, 'Anglo-French Relations from Versailles to Locarno', in Alan Sharp and Glyn Stone, eds., *Anglo-French Relations in the Twentieth Century*, London, Routledge, 2002

Kevin Smith, '"Immobilized by Reason of Repair" and by the Choice "between Lithgow and Hitler"', in Marcus Faulkner and Christopher M. Bell, eds., *Decision in the Atlantic*, Lexington, KY, Andarta Books, 2019

Hew Strachan, 'Strategic Bombing and the Question of Civilian Casualties up to 1945', in Jeremy Crang and Paul Addison, eds., *Firestorm: The Bombing of Dresden, 1945*, London, Pimlico, 2006

Hew Strachan, 'The Territorial Army and National Defence', in Keith Neilson, ed., *The British Way in Warfare: Power and the International System, 1856–1956*, London, Routledge, 2016

Andrew Taylor, 'Speaking to Democracy: The Conservative Party and Mass Opinion from the 1920s to the 1950s', in Stuart Ball and Ian Holliday, eds., *Mass Conservatism: The Conservatives and the Public since the 1880s*, London, Frank Cass, 2002

Daniel Todman, 'Defining Deaths: Richard Titmuss's Problems of Social Policy and the Meaning of Britain's Second World War', in Nicholas Martin et al., eds., *Aftermath: Legacies and Memories of War in Europe, 1918–1945–1989*, London, Ashgate, 1989

D. C. Watt, 'Churchill and Appeasement', in Robert Blake and William Roger Louis, eds., *Churchill*, Oxford, Clarendon Press, 1996

Books

Paul Addison, *The Road to 1945: British Politics and the Second World War*, London, Pimlico, 1994

Air Ministry [Hilary Saunders], *The Battle of Britain*, London, HMSO, 1941

Richard. J. Aldrich and Rory Cormac, *The Black Door: Spies, Secret Intelligence and British Prime Ministers*, London, William Collins, 2016

Martin S. Alexander, *The Republic in Danger: General Maurice Gamelin and the Politics of French Defence, 1933–1940*, Cambridge, Cambridge University Press, 1992

Alan Allport, *Browned Off and Bloody-Minded: The British Soldier Goes to War, 1939–1945*, London, Yale University Press, 2015

L. S. Amery, *The Forward View*, London, Unwin, 1935

L. S. Amery, *My Political Life,* vol. 3: *The Unforgiving Years, 1929–1940*, London, Hutchinson, 1955

Verily Anderson, *Spam Tomorrow*, London, Rupert Hart-Davis, 1956

Christopher Andrew, *Defend the Realm: The Authorized History of MI5*, London, Allen Lane, 2009

Anglo-American Committee of Inquiry, *A Survey of Palestine,* vol. 2, Jerusalem, The Government Printer, 1946

Harry Arrigonie, *British Colonialism: 30 Years Serving Democracy or Hypocrisy?* Bideford, Lazarus Press, 1998

Douglas Arthur, *Desert Watch*, Bedale, Blaisdon, 2000

James Bailey, *The Sky Suspended*, London, Bloomsbury, 1964

Stuart Ball, ed., *Parliament and Politics in the Age of Churchill and Attlee: The Headlam Diaries, 1935–1951*, Cambridge, Cambridge University Press, 1999

Ernest Barker, ed., *The Character of England*, Oxford, Clarendon Press, 1947

John Barnes, ed., *The Empire at Bay: The Leo Amery Diaries, 1929–1945*, London, Hutchinson, 1988

Corelli Barnett, *The Collapse of British Power*, London, Eyre Methuen, 1972

Brian Barton, *Northern Ireland in the Second World War*, Belfast, Ulster Historical Foundation, 1995

Greg Baughen, *The RAF in the Battle of France and the Battle of Britain*, Stroud, Fonthill, 2016

Greg Baughen, *The Fairey Battle*, Stroud, Fonthill, 2017

J. Baxendale and C. Pawling, *Narrating the Thirties: A Decade in the Making, 1930 to the Present*, Basingstoke, Macmillan, 1996

George Beardmore, *Civilians at War*, London, John Murray, 1984

André Beaufre, *1940: The Fall of France*, New York, Knopf, 1968

Ian F. W. Beckett, *The Great War, 1914–1918*, London, Pearson, 2001

Catherine B. Behrens, *Merchant Shipping and the Demands of War*, London, HMSO, 1956

Amy Helen Bell, *London Was Ours*, London, I. B. Tauris, 2008

Philip M. H. Bell, *A Certain Eventuality: Britain and the Fall of France*, London, Saxon House, 1974

Philip M. H. Bell, *John Bull and the Bear*, London, E. Arnold, 1990

Philip M. H. Bell, *France and Britain, 1900–1940: Entente and Estrangement*, London, Longman, 1996

G. Harry Bennett, ed., *Roosevelt's Peacetime Administrations, 1933–41: A Documentary History*, Manchester, Manchester University Press, 2004

G. H. Bennett and R. Bennett, *Survivors: British Merchant Seamen in the Second World War*, London, Hambledon, 1999

Geoffrey Best, *Churchill and War*, London, Hambledon, 2005

Uri Bialer, *The Shadow of the Bomber: The Fear of Air Attack and British Politics, 1932–1939*, London, Royal Historical Society, 1980

Tami Davis Biddle, *Rhetoric and Reality in Air Warfare: The Evolution of British and American Ideas about Strategic Bombing, 1914–1945*, Princeton, NJ, Princeton University Press, 2002

Patrick Bishop, *Fighter Boys: The Battle of Britain, 1940*, New York, Viking, 2003

Brian Bond, ed., *Chief of Staff: The Diaries of Lieutenant-General Sir Henry Pownall*, vol. 1: *1933–1940*, London, Archon Books, 1973

Brian Bond, *British Military Policy between the Two World Wars*, Oxford, Oxford University Press, 1980

Brian Bond, *Britain, France, and Belgium, 1939–1940*, London, Brassey's, 1990

Joanna Bourke, *Fear: A Cultural History*, Berkeley, CA, Shoemaker & Hoard, 2007

Chaz Bowyer, *The Royal Air Force, 1939–1945*, Barnsley, Pen & Sword, 1996

Alec Brew, *The Turret Fighters: Defiant and Roc*, Marlborough, Crowood Press, 2002

Stephen Brooke, *Labour's War*, Oxford, Clarendon Press, 1992

Arthur Bryant, *The National Character*, London, Longman, 1934

Arthur Bryant, *English Saga*, London, Collins, 1940

Patrick Buckland, *The Factory of Grievances: Devolved Government in Northern Ireland, 1921–39*, Dublin, Gill and Macmillan, 1979

Stephen Bungay, *The Most Dangerous Enemy*, London, Aurum, 2010

James Ramsay Montagu Butler, *Grand Strategy*, vol. 2: *September 1939–June 1941*, London, HMSO, 1967

Angus Calder, *The People's War: Britain, 1939–1945*, London, Jonathan Cape, 1969

Angus Calder, *The Myth of the Blitz*, London, Pimlico, 1991

John Campbell, *The Iron Lady*, London, Vintage, 2008

Wilfred Campbell, *Sagas of Vaster Britain: Poems of the Race, the Empire and the Divinity of Man*, London, Hodder & Stoughton, 1914

David Cannadine, *The Rise and Fall of Class in Britain*, New York, Columbia University Press, 1999

David Cannadine, *The Decline and Fall of the British Aristocracy*, London, Penguin, 2005

Robert J. Caputi, *Neville Chamberlain and Appeasement: Fifty Years of Conflict*, Selinsgrove, PA, Susquehanna University Press, 1999

David Carlton, *Churchill and the Soviet Union*, Manchester, Manchester University Press, 2000

Humphrey Carpenter, *J. R. R. Tolkien: A Biography*, Boston, MA, Houghton Mifflin, 2000

Humphrey Carpenter, ed., *The Letters of J. R. R. Tolkien: A Selection*, Boston, MA, Houghton Mifflin, 2000

Bob Carruthers, *Hitler's Wartime Orders*, Barnsley, Pen & Sword, 2018

Richard Carswell, *The Fall of France in the Second World War: History and Memory*, London, Palgrave, 2019

'Cato', *Guilty Men*, London, Victor Gollancz, 1940

Peter Caygill, *The Biggin Hill Wing, 1941*, Barnsley, Pen & Sword, 2008

Martin Ceadel, *Pacifism in Britain, 1914–1945*, Oxford, Clarendon, 1980

John Charmley, *Chamberlain and the Lost Peace*, London, Macmillan, 1991

Thomas Childers, *The Third Reich: A History of Nazi Germany*, New York, Simon & Schuster, 2017

Winston S. Churchill, *The Second World War*, vol. 1: *The Gathering Storm*, New York, RosettaBooks, 2002

Winston S. Churchill, *The Second World War*, vol. 2: *Their Finest Hour*, New York, RosettaBooks, 2002

Winston S. Churchill, *The Second World War*, vol. 3: *The Grand Alliance*, New York, RosettaBooks, 2002

Anthony Clayton, *The British Empire as a Superpower, 1919–39*, Athens, GA, University of Georgia, 1986

Max Cohen, *What Nobody Told the Foreman*, London, Spalding & Levy, 1953

Michael J. Cohen, *Britain's Moment in Palestine: Retrospect and Perspectives, 1917–1948*, London, Routledge, 2014

Kim Coleman, *A History of Chemical Warfare*, New York, Palgrave, 2005

Basil Collier, *The Defence of the United Kingdom*, London, HMSO, 1957

Lizzie Collingham, *The Taste of War*, London, Allen Lane, 2011

John Rupert Colville, *Man of Valour: The Life of Field-Marshal the Viscount Gort*, London, Collins, 1972

John Rupert Colville, *Winston Churchill and His Inner Circle*, New York, Wyndham, 1981

John Rupert Colville, *The Fringes of Power*, London, Hodder & Stoughton, 1985

John Connell, *Wavell: Scholar and Soldier*, London, Collins, 1964

Mark Connelly, *We Can Take It! Britain and the Memory of the Second World War*, New York, Pearson Longman, 2004

Noël Coward, *Australia Visited*, London, Heinemann, 1940

Maurice Cowling, *The Impact of Hitler: British Politics and British Policy, 1933–1940*, Cambridge, Cambridge University Press, 1975

Travis L. Crosby, *The Impact of Civilian Evacuation in the Second World War*, London, Croom Helm, 1986

N. J. Crowson, *Facing Fascism: The Conservative Party and the European Dictators, 1935–1940*, London, Routledge, 1997

N. J. Crowson, *Britain and Europe: A Political History since 1918*, London, Routledge, 2010

Anthony J. Cumming, *The Battle for Britain: Interservice Rivalry between the Royal Air Force and Royal Navy, 1909–1940*, Annapolis, MD, Naval Institute Press, 2015

Alex Danchev and Daniel Todman, *War Diaries 1939–1945 Field Marshal Lord Alanbrooke*, Berkeley, CA, University of California Press, 2001

John Darwin, *The Empire Project the Rise and Fall of the British World-System, 1830–1970*, Cambridge, Cambridge University Press, 2011

Peter Davison, ed., *The Complete Works of George Orwell: Facing Unpleasant Facts, 1937–1939*, London, Secker & Warburg, 2000

Peter Davison, ed., *The Complete Works of George Orwell: A Patriot After All, 1940–1941*, London, Secker & Warburg, 2000

Peter Davison, ed., *The Complete Works of George Orwell: All Propaganda Is Lies, 1941–1942*, London, Secker & Warburg, 2000

Somerset de Chair, *The Impending Storm*, New York, Richard R. Smith, 1930

Anne de Courcy, *Diana Mosley*, London, Chatto & Windus, 2003

Harry Defries, *Conservative Party Attitudes to Jews, 1900–1950*, London, Frank Cass, 2001

Len Deighton, *Blood, Tears and Folly*, London, Cape, 1993

Ken Delve, *Fighter Command 1936–1968*, Barnsley, Pen & Sword, 2007

Richard Deveson, ed., *My Dearest Family: An Austrian Refugee's Letters to London from America, 1938–1945*, privately published, 2017

Peter Dewey, *War and Progress: Britain 1914–1945*, London, Longman, 1997

David Dilks, ed., *The Diaries of Sir Alexander Cadogan, O.M., 1938–1945*, London, Cassell, 1971

Directorate of Army Education, *The British Way and Purpose Consolidated Edition*, London, 1944

M. L. Dockrill, *British Establishment Perspectives on France, 1936–40*, New York, St. Martin's Press, 1999

Paul W. Doerr, *British Foreign Policy, 1919–1939*, Manchester, Manchester University Press, 1998

Douglas V. Duff, *Bailing with a Teaspoon*, London, John Long, 1953

David Dutton, *Austen Chamberlain: Gentleman in Politics*, Bolton, Ross Anderson, 1985

David Dutton, *Neville Chamberlain*, London, Arnold, 2000

James Dyrenforth et al., *Adolf in Blunderland*, London, Muller, 1939

David Edgerton, *Britain's War Machine: Weapons, Resources and Experts in the Second World War*, London, Penguin, 2011

David Edgerton, *The Rise and Fall of the British Nation*, London, Allen Lane, 2018

Lionel Ellis, *The War in France and Flanders, 1939–40*, London, HMSO, 1954

Peter Elphick, *Lifeline: The Merchant Navy at War, 1939–1945*, London, Chatham, 1999

Basil Embry, *Mission Completed*, London, Methuen, 1957

Clive Emsley, *Hard Men: The English and Violence since 1750*, London, Hambledon and London, 2005

Jonathan A. Epstein, *Belgium's Dilemma: The Formation of the Belgian Defense Policy, 1932–1940*, Leiden, Brill, 2014

Richard J. Evans, *The Third Reich in Power*, London, Penguin, 2006

K. D. Ewing and C. A. Gearty, *The Struggle for Civil Liberties: Political Freedom and the Rule of Law in Britain, 1914–1945*, Oxford, Oxford University Press, 2000

David Faber, *Speaking for England: Leo, Julian and John Amery, The Tragedy of a Political Family*, London, Free Press, 2005

Graham Farmelo, *Churchill's Bomb*, London, Faber & Faber, 2013

Jonathan Fennell, *Fighting the People's War*, Cambridge, Cambridge University Press, 2018

Geoffrey G. Field, *Blood, Sweat, and Toil: Remaking the British Working Class, 1939–1945*, Oxford, Oxford University Press, 2011

Patrick Benedict Finney, *Remembering the Road to World War Two: International History, National Identity, Collective Memory*, London, Routledge, 2011

Robert Fisk, *In Time of War: Ireland, Ulster and the Price of Neutrality, 1939–45*, London, Andre Deutsch, 1983

Constantine FitzGibbon, *The Blitz*, London, MacDonald, 1970

Peter Fleming, *Invasion 1940*, London, Rupert Hart-Davis, 1957

Robert Forczyk, *We March against England*, London, Osprey, 2016

Robert Forczyk, *Case Red*, London, Osprey, 2017

Robert F. Foster, *Modern Ireland, 1600–1972*, London, Penguin, 1989

Martin Francis, *The Flyer: British Culture and the Royal Air Force, 1939–1945*, Oxford, Oxford University Press, 2008

Norman L. R. Franks, *Valiant Wings: The Battle and Blenheim Squadrons over France, 1940*, London, William Kimber, 1988

Norman L. R. Franks, *RAF Fighter Command, 1936–1968*, Somerset, Patrick Stephens, 1992

Derek Fraser, *The Evolution of the British Welfare State*, London, Macmillan, 1973

David French, *Raising Churchill's Army*, Oxford, Oxford University Press, 2000

Graham Freudenberg, *Churchill and Australia*, Sydney, Macmillan, 2008

Karl-Heinz Frieser, *The Blitzkrieg Legend: The 1940 Campaign in the West*, Annapolis, MD, Naval Institute Press, 2005

G. K. Fry, *The Politics of Crisis: An Interpretation of British Politics*, Basingstoke, Palgrave, 2001

George H. Gallup, ed., *The Gallup International Public Opinion Polls: Great Britain 1937–1975*, vol. 1: *1937–1964*, New York, Random House, 1976

Juliet Gardiner, *The Blitz*, London, Harper Press, 2010

W. J. R. Gardner, *Decoding History: The Battle of the Atlantic and Ultra*, Basingstoke, Macmillan, 1999

Margaret Gaskin, *Blitz: The Story of December 29, 1940*, Orlando, FL, Harcourt, 2006

Azar Gat, *Fascist and Liberal Visions of War: Fuller, Liddell Hart, Douhet, and Other Modernists*, Oxford, Clarendon, 1998

N. H. Gibbs, *Grand Strategy*, vol. 1: *Rearmament Policy*, London, HMSO, 1976

Philip Gibbs, *Ordeal in England*, London, Heinemann, 1937

Martin Gilbert, *Finest Hour: Winston S. Churchill, 1939–1941*, London, Heinemann, 1983

Martin Gilbert, ed., *The Churchill Documents*, vol. 15: *Never Surrender, May 1940– December 1940*, Hillsdale, MI, Hillsdale College Press, 2011

Martin Gilbert, ed., *The Churchill Documents*, vol. 16: *The Ever-Widening War, 1941*, Hillsdale, MI, Hillsdale College Press, 2011

Michael Glover, *Invasion Scare 1940*, London, Leo Cooper, 1990

Julie V. Gottlieb, *'Guilty Women', Foreign Policy, and Appeasement in Inter-War Britain*, Basingstoke, Palgrave, 2015

Margaret Gowing, *Britain and Atomic Energy, 1939–1945*, London, Macmillan, 1964

Peter W. Gray, *The Leadership, Direction and Legitimacy of the RAF Bomber Offensive from Inception to 1945*, London, Bloomsbury Academic, 2012

Bernard Grey, *War Reporter*, London, Robert Hale, 1942

Eric Grove, *The Defeat of the Enemy Attack upon Shipping, 1939–1945*, Aldershot, Ashgate [for the Navy Records Society], 1998

J. B. S. Haldane, *ARP*, London, Gollancz, 1938

David Ian Hall, *Strategy for Victory: The Development of British Tactical Air Power, 1919–1943*, Westport, CT, Praeger, 2008

W. K. Hancock and M. M. Gowing, *The British War Economy*, London, HMSO, 1949

Victor Davis Hanson, *The Second World Wars: How the First Global Conflict was Fought and Won*, New York, Basic Books, 2017

Nicholas Harman, *Dunkirk: The Necessary Myth*, London, Hodder & Stoughton, 1980

Bernard Harris, *The Origins of the British Welfare State: Society, State, and Social Welfare in England and Wales, 1800–1945*, Basingstoke, Palgrave, 2004

J. P. Harris, *Men, Ideas, and Tanks*, Manchester, Manchester University Press, 1995

Tom Harrisson, *Living through the Blitz*, London, Collins, 1976

Tom Harrisson and Charles Madge, *War Begins at Home*, London, Chatto & Windus, 1940

Oliver Harvey, *The Diplomatic Diaries of Oliver Harvey, 1937–1940*, New York, St. Martin's Press, 1971

Max Hastings, *Bomber Command*, London, Pan, 1979

Thomas Hennessey, *A History of Northern Ireland*, New York, St. Martin's Press, 1997

F. H. Hinsley, *British Intelligence in the Second World War*, 5 vols, London, HMSO, 1979

James Lansdale Hodson, *Through the Dark Night*, London, Gollancz, 1941

James Lansdale Hodson, *Towards the Morning*, London, Gollancz, 1941

Bruce Hoffman, *Anonymous Soldiers: The Struggle for Israel, 1917–1947*, New York, Knopf, 2015

Quintin McGarel Hogg, *The Left Was Never Right*, London, Faber & Faber, 1945

James Holland, *The Rise of Germany, 1939–1941*, New York, Grove Atlantic, 2015

Brett Holman, *The Next War in the Air: Britain's Fear of the Bomber, 1908–1941*, Farnham, Ashgate, 2014

Alistair Horne, *To Lose a Battle*, London, Macmillan, 1969

Michael Howard, *The Continental Commitment: The Dilemma of British Defence Policy in the Era of the Two World Wars*, London, Temple Smith, 1972

Richard Hough and Denis Richards, *The Battle of Britain*, New York, Norton, 2008

Daniel Hucker, *Public Opinion and the End of Appeasement in Britain and France*, Farnham, Ashgate, 2011

Matthew Hughes, *Britain's Pacification of Palestine: The British Army, the Colonial State, and the Arab Revolt, 1936–1939*, Cambridge, Cambridge University Press, 2019

Talbot Imlay, *Facing the Second World War: Strategy, Politics, and Economics in Britain and France, 1938–1940*, Oxford, Oxford University Press, 2003

Alan Jackson, *The Middle Classes, 1900–1950*, Newton Abbott, Thomas, 1991

Julian Jackson, *The Fall of France: The Nazi Invasion of 1940*, Oxford, Oxford University Press, 2003

Lawrence James, *The Rise and Fall of the British Empire*, London, Little, Brown, 1994

Kevin Jefferys, *Politics and the People: A History of British Democracy since 1918*, London, Atlantic, 2007

Roy Jenkins, *The Chancellors*, London, Macmillan, 1998

Boris Johnson, *The Churchill Factor*, London, Riverhead, 2015

Ian Johnston and Ian Buxton, *The Battleship Builders: Constructing and Arming British Capital Ships*, Barnsley, Seaforth, 2013

Cyril Joly, *Take These Men*, London, Constable, 1953

John Jordan and Robert Dumas, *French Battleships, 1922–1956*, Barnsley, Seaforth Publishing, 2009

Hilda Kean, *The Great Cat and Dog Massacre*, Chicago, IL, University of Chicago Press, 2017

Hugh Kearny, *The British Isles: A History of Four Nations*, Cambridge, Cambridge University Press, 2006

Edward Keith-Roach, *Pasha of Jerusalem*, London, Palgrave Macmillan, 1994

Stephen Kelly, *Idle Hands, Clenched Fists: The Depression in a Shipyard Town*, Nottingham, Spokesman, 1987

Darren Kelsey, *Media, Myth, and Terrorism: A Discourse-Mythological Analysis of the 'Blitz Spirit' in British Newspaper Responses to the July 7th Bombings*, London, Palgrave, 2014

Greg Kennedy, *The Merchant Marine in International Affairs, 1850–1950*, London, Cass, 2000

Paul M. Kennedy, *Strategy and Diplomacy, 1870–1945: Eight Studies*, London, Fontana, 1984

Ian Kershaw, *Hitler, 1936–1945: Nemesis*, London, Penguin, 2000

Stephen King-Hall, *Our Own Times, 1913–1938*, London, Nicholson & Watson, 1938

M. W. Kirby, *Operational Research in War and Peace*, London, Imperial College Press, 2003

John Kiszely, *Anatomy of a Campaign: The British Fiasco in Norway, 1940*, Cambridge, Cambridge University Press, 2017

Miriam Kochan, *Britain's Internees in the Second World War*, London, Macmillan, 1983

Martin Kolinsky, *Britain's War in the Middle East: Strategy and Diplomacy, 1936–42*, Basingstoke, Macmillan, 1999

Ann Kramer, *Conscientious Objectors of the Second World War: Refusing to Fight*, Barnsley, Pen & Sword, 2013

Tony Kushner, *The Persistence of Prejudice: Antisemitism in British Society during the Second World War*, Manchester, Manchester University Press, 1989

Arthur Lane, *Empire Soldier*, Stockport, Nesa News Publishers, 2004

Tony Lane, *The Merchant Seamen's War*, Manchester, Manchester University Press, 1991

Nella Last, *Nella Last's War*, London, Profile, 2006

Joshua Levine, *The Secret History of the Blitz*, New York, Simon & Schuster, 2016

Bex Lewis, *Keep Calm and Carry On*, London, Imperial War Museum, 2017

Basil H. Liddell Hart, *The British Way in Warfare*, London, Faber & Faber, 1932

Basil H. Liddell Hart, *Europe in Arms*, London, Faber & Faber, 1937

Basil H. Liddell Hart, *The Defence of Britain*, London, Faber & Faber, 1939

James Loughlin, *Ulster Unionism and British National Identity since 1885*, London, Pinter, 1995

William Roger Louis, *In the Name of God, Go! Leo Amery and the British Empire in the Age of Churchill*, New York, W. W. Norton, 1992

John Lukacs, *Five Days in London, May 1940*, London, Yale University Press, 1990

Robert Lyman, *Tobruk: The Battle That Saved North Africa*, London, Macmillan, 2009

Thomas Babington Macaulay, *Speeches of Lord Macauley*, London, Longmans, 1877

Robert Mackay, *Half the Battle: Civilian Morale in Britain during the Second World War*, Manchester, Manchester University Press, 2002

Ron Mackay, *Britain's Fleet Air Arm in World War II*, Atglen, PA, Schiffer, 2005

S. P. MacKenzie, *The Home Guard*, Oxford, Oxford University Press, 1995

Roderick MacLeod, ed., *Time Unguarded: The Ironside Diaries, 1937–1940*, New York, McKay, 1963

Donald M. MacRaild, *The Irish Diaspora in Britain, 1750–1939*, London, Palgrave, 2011

Joseph Maiolo, *The Royal Navy and Nazi Germany, 1933–39*, London, Macmillan, 1998

Joseph Maiolo, *Cry Havoc: How the Arms Race Drove the World to War, 1931–1941*, New York, Basic Books, 2010

Patricia and Robert Malcolmson, eds., *A Free-Spirited Woman: The London Diaries of Gladys Langford, 1936–1940*, London, London Record Society, 2014

William Manchester, *The Last Lion: Winston Spencer Churchill: Alone, 1932–1940*, Boston, MA, Little, Brown, 1983.

Peter Mandler, The *English National Character,* New Haven, CT, Yale University Press, 2006

Francis K. Mason, *The British Fighter since 1912*, London, Putnam, 1992

Mass Observation, *Britain*, Harmondsworth, Penguin, 1939

Ernest R. May, *Strange Victory: Hitler's Conquest of France*, New York, Hill and Wang, 2000

Mark Mazower, *Hitler's Empire: Nazi Rule in Occupied Europe*, London, Penguin, 2009

David McGrory, *A History of Coventry*, Chichester, Phillimore, 2003

J. McKenna, *The IRA Bombing Campaign against Britain, 1939–1940*, Jefferson, NC, McFarland, 2016

B. J. C. McKercher, *Transition of Power: Britain's Loss of Global Preeminence to the United States, 1930–1945*, Cambridge, Cambridge University Press, 1998

Ross McKibbin, *The Ideologies of Class: Social Relations in Britain, 1880–1950*, Oxford, Clarendon, 1990

Ross McKibbin, *Classes and Cultures: England 1918–1951*, Oxford, Oxford University Press, 1998

Leo McKinstry, *Spitfire*, London, John Murray, 2007

Ian McLaine, *Ministry of Morale*, London, Allen & Unwin, 1979

Martin Middlebrook and Chris Everitt, *The Bomber Command War Diaries*, London, Penguin, 1990

Militärgeschichtliches Forschungsamt (Potsdam), *Germany and the Second World War*, 13 vols, Oxford, Clarendon, 1990

Stephen M. Miner, *Between Churchill and Stalin: The Soviet Union, Great Britain, and the Origins of the Grand Alliance*, Chapel Hill, NC, University of North Carolina Press, 1988

Roger Moorhouse, *The Devils' Alliance: Hitler's Pact with Stalin, 1939–1941*, New York, Basic Books, 2014

Daniel Morgan and Bruce Taylor, *U-Boat Attack Logs*, Annapolis, MD, Naval Institute Press, 2012

Kenneth O. Morgan, *Michael Foot: A Life*, London, Harper Press, 2007

Jan Morris, *Sound the Trumpets: An Imperial Retreat*, Harmondsworth, Penguin, 1982

Oswald Mosley, *A National Policy*, London, Macmillan, 1931

Mo Moulton, *Ireland and the Irish in Interwar England*, Cambridge, Cambridge University Press, 2014

Ronaldo Munck and Bill Rolston, *Belfast in the 1930s: An Oral History*, New York, St. Martin's Press, 1987

Venetia Murray, *Castle Howard: The Life and Times of a Stately Home*, London, Viking, 1994

Williamson Murray, *Strategy for Defeat: The Luftwaffe, 1933–1945*, Maxwell AFB, AL, Air University Press, 1982

Williamson Murray, *The Change in the European Balance of Power, 1938–1939: The Path to Ruin*, Princeton, NJ, Princeton University Press, 1984

Lewis Bernstein Namier, *Diplomatic Prelude, 1939–1939*, London, Macmillan, 1948

National Council for Civil Liberties, *Report of a Commission of Inquiry Appointed to Examine the Purpose and Effect of the Civil Authorities (Special Powers) Acts (Northern Ireland) 1922 & 1933*, London, NCCL, 1936

Tom Neil, *Gun Button to Fire*, London, William Kimber, 1987

Scott Newton, *Profits of Peace: The Political Economy of Anglo-German Appeasement*, Oxford, Clarendon, 1996

Harold Nicolson, *Why Britain Is at War*, Harmondsworth, Penguin, 1939

Nigel Nicolson, ed., *The Diaries and Letters of Harold Nicolson: The War Years, 1939–1945*, New York, Atheneum, 1966

Francis R. Nicosia, *Nazi Germany and the Arab World*, Cambridge, Cambridge University Press, 2014

Barbara Nixon, *Raiders Overhead: A Diary of the London Blitz*, Banbury, Gulliver, 1980

Terence O'Brien, *Civil Defence*, London, HMSO, 1955

David O'Donoghue, *The Devil's Deal: The IRA, Nazi Germany and the Double Life of Jim O'Donovan*, Dublin, New Island, 2010

Gordon Olive, *Spitfire Ace*, Stroud, Amberley, 2015

Vincent Orange, *Dowding of Fighter Command*, London, Grub Street, 2011

Vincent Orange, *Churchill and His Airmen*, London, Grub Street, 2012

Richard J. Overy, *The Road to War*, London, Macmillan, 1989

Richard J. Overy, *The Battle of Britain*, New York, W. W. Norton, 2002

Richard J. Overy, *The Morbid Age*, London, Penguin, 2010

Richard J. Overy, *The Bombing War: Europe, 1939–1945*, London, Penguin, 2014

Richard J. Overy, *The Birth of the RAF, 1918*, London, Allen Lane, 2018

Mollie Panter-Downes, *London War Notes, 1939–1945*, New York, Farrar, 1971

Robert Alexander Clarke Parker, *Chamberlain and Appeasement*, London, Macmillan, 1994

Robert Alexander Clarke Parker, *Churchill and Appeasement*, London, Macmillan, 2000

Ian Patterson, *Guernica and Total War*, London, Profile, 2008

Rachel Pistol, *Internment during the Second World War: A Comparative Study of Great Britain and the USA*, London, Bloomsbury, 2017

I. S. O. Playfair, *The Mediterranean and Middle East,* vol. 1: *The Early Successes against Italy, to May 1941*, London, HMSO, 1954

I. S. O. Playfair, *The Mediterranean and Middle East*, vol. 2: *The Germans Come to the Help of Their Ally, 1941*, London, HMSO, 1956

Douglas Porch, *The Path to Victory*, New York, Farrar, Straus and Giroux, 2004

Bernard Porter, *The Absent-Minded Imperialists: Empire, Society, and Culture in Britain*, Oxford, Oxford University Press, 2004

Bernard Porter, *The Lion's Share: A Short History of British Imperialism, 1850–2004*, London, Pearson, 2004

Michael Postan, *British War Production*, London, HMSO, 1952

J. B. Priestley, *English Journey*, London, Heinemann, 1934

J. B. Priestley, *Out of the People*, New York, Harper, 1941

J. B. Priestley, *Postscripts*, London, Heinemann, 1940

Robin Prior, *When Britain Saved the West: The Story of 1940*, London, Yale University Press, 2015

Roland Quinalt, *British Prime Ministers and Democracy*, London, Continuum, 2011

John Ramsden, *The Age of Balfour and Baldwin, 1902–1940*, London, Longman, 1978

Harold E. Raugh, *Wavell in the Middle East, 1939–1941*, Norman, OK, University of Oklahoma, 2013

John P. Ray, *The Night Blitz, 1940–1941*, London, Cassell, 1996

David Reynolds, *The Creation of the Anglo-American Alliance, 1937–41: A Study in Competitive Co-Operation*, London, Europa, 1981

David Reynolds, *From Munich to Pearl Harbor: Roosevelt's America and the Origins of the Second World War*, Chicago, IL, Ivan R. Dee, 2001

David Reynolds, *In Command of History: Churchill Fighting and Writing the Second World War*, London, Penguin, 2005

Denis Richards, *Portal of Hungerford*, London, Heinemann, 1977

Denis Richards and Hilary Aldan St George Saunders, *The Royal Air Force, 1939–1945*, 3 vols, London, HMSO, 1953

Thomas E. Ricks, *Churchill and Orwell*, London, Penguin, 2017

Andrew Roberts, *The Holy Fox: A Biography of Lord Halifax*, London, Weidenfeld & Nicolson, 1991

Andrew Roberts, *Eminent Churchillians*, London, Weidenfeld & Nicolson, 1994

Derek Robinson, *Invasion 1940*, London, Constable, 2005

Norman Rose, *Harold Nicolson*, London, Jonathan Cape, 2005

Stephen Roskill, *The War at Sea*, vol. 1: *The Defensive*, HMSO, 1954

Victor Rothwell, *Anthony Eden: A Political Biography, 1931–1957*, Manchester, Manchester University Press, 1992

B. Seebohm Rowntree, *Poverty and Progress: A Second Social Survey of York*, London, Longman, 1941

A. L. Rowse, *All Souls and Appeasement*, London, Macmillan, 1961

John Ruggiero, *Hitler's Enabler: Neville Chamberlain and the Origins of the Second World War*, Santa Barbara, CA, Praeger, 2015

Chris Ryder, *The RUC: A Force under Fire*, London, Mandarin, 1997

Arthur Salter, *Personality in Politics*, London, Faber & Faber, 1948

Charles Saumarez Smith, *The Building of Castle Howard*, London, Pimlico, 1997

Robert Seamer, *The Floating Inferno: The Story of the Loss of the Empress of Britain*, Wellingborough, Stephens, 1990

Tom Segev, *One Palestine, Complete: Jews and Arabs under the British Mandate*, New York, Metropolitan Books, 2000

Robert C. Self, ed., *The Neville Chamberlain Diary Letters*, vol. 4: *The Downing Street Years, 1934–1940*, Aldershot, Aldgate, 2005

Robert. C. Self, *Neville Chamberlain: A Biography*, Aldershot, Ashgate, 2006

Robert Paul Shay, *British Rearmament in the Thirties*, Princeton, NJ, Princeton University Press, 1977

Naomi Shepherd, *Ploughing Sand: British Rule in Palestine, 1917–1948*, London, John Murray, 1989

Dorothy Sheridan, ed., *Among You Taking Notes: The Wartime Diary of Naomi Mitchison, 1939–1945*, London, Gollancz, 1985

A. J. Sherman, *Island Refuge: Britain and Refugees from the Third Reich, 1933–1939*, London, Elek, 1973

A. J. Sherman, *Mandate Days: British Lives in Palestine, 1918–1948*, London, Thames and Hudson, 1997

T. A. Shippey, *J. R. R. Tolkien: Author of the Century*, Boston, MA, Houghton Mifflin, 2002

Brendan Simms, *Britain's Europe*, London, Allen Lane, 2016

Brendan Simms, *Hitler: A Global Biography*, New York, Basic Books, 2019

A. W. Brian Simpson, *In the Highest Degree Odious: Detention without Trial in Wartime Britain*, Oxford, Clarendon Press, 1992

William Simpson, *One of Our Pilots Is Safe*, London, Hamish Hamilton, 1942

Colin Sinnott, *The RAF and Aircraft Design, 1923–1939*, London, Frank Cass, 2001

Edward Smalley, *The British Expeditionary Force, 1939–40*, New York, Palgrave, 2015

Nick Smart, *Neville Chamberlain*, London, Routledge, 2009

Colin Smith, *England's Last War Against France: Fighting Vichy, 1940–1942*, London, Phoenix, 2010

Malcolm Smith, *British Air Strategy between the Wars*, Oxford, Clarendon, 1984

Malcolm Smith, *Britain and 1940: History, Myth, and Popular Memory*, London, Routledge, 2000

May Smith, *These Wonderful Rumours! A Young Schoolteacher's Wartime Diaries, 1939–1945*, London, Virago, 2012

Edward Louis Spears, *Assignment to Catastrophe*, vol. 1: *Prelude to Dunkirk, July 1939–May 1940*, London, Heinemann, 1954

Neil Stammers, *Civil Liberties in Britain during the Second World War*, London, Croom Helm, 1983

Andrew Staniforth, *The Routledge Companion to UK Counter-Terrorism*, Oxford, Routledge, 2013

Tom Stannage, *Baldwin Thwarts the Opposition: The British General Election of 1935*, London, Croom Helm, 1980

Peter Stansky, *The First Day of the Blitz*, London, Yale University Press, 2008

Nicholas Stargardt, *The German War: A Nation under Arms, 1939–45*, New York, Basic Books, 2015

Edward Stebbing, *Diary of a Decade, 1939–50*, Lewes, Book Guild, 1998

Andrew David Stedman, *Alternatives to Appeasement: Neville Chamberlain and Hitler's Germany*, London, I. B. Tauris, 2011

Zara Steiner, *The Lights That Failed: European International History, 1919–1933*, Oxford, Oxford University Press, 2005

Zara Steiner, *The Triumph of the Dark: European International History, 1933–1939*, Oxford, Oxford University Press, 2013

Graham Stewart, *Burying Caesar: The Churchill–Chamberlain Rivalry*, London, Weidenfield, 1999

Richard A. Stewart, *Sunrise at Abadan*, New York, Praeger, 1988

Margot Strickland, *Angela Thirkell: Portrait of a Lady Novelist*, London, Duckworth, 1977

A. J. P. Taylor, *Europe: Grandeur and Decline*, Harmondsworth, Penguin, 1961

Frederick Taylor, *Coventry: Thursday, 14th November 1940*, London, Bloomsbury, 2015

Rosemary Taylor and Christopher Lloyd, *The East End at War*, Stroud, Sutton, 2012

John Terraine, *The Right of the Line*, London, Hodder & Stoughton, 1985

John Terraine, *Business in Great Waters: The U-Boat Wars, 1916–1945*, London, Leo Cooper, 1989

Margaret Thatcher, *The Path to Power*, London, HarperCollins, 1995

Angela Thirkell, *Cheerfulness Breaks In*, New York, Knopf, 1941

Julian Thompson, *Dunkirk*, London, Sidgwick & Jackson, 2008

Neville Thompson, *The Anti-Appeasers: Conservative Opposition to Appeasement in the 1930s*, Oxford, Clarendon Press, 1971

Andrew Thorpe, *Britain in the 1930s: The Deceptive Decade*, Oxford, Blackwell, 1995

Richard M. Titmuss, *Problems of Social Policy*, London, HMSO, 1950

Daniel Todman, *Britain's War: Into Battle, 1937–1941*, London, Penguin, 2016

J. R. R. Tolkien, *The Fellowship of the Ring*, Boston, MA, Houghton Mifflin, 1994

Adam Tooze, *The Wages of Destruction: The Making and Breaking of the Nazi Economy*, New York, Penguin, 2008

E. S. Turner, *The Phoney War on the Home Front*, London, M. Joseph, 1961

Carel Willem M. van de Velde, *Narrative of a Journey through Syria and Palestine in 1851 and 1852*, Edinburgh and London, Blackwood, 1854

Meredith Veldman, *Margaret Thatcher: Shaping the New Conservatism*, New York, Oxford University Press, 2015

Peter Walters, *The Story of Coventry*, Stroud, The History Press, 2013

Wesley K. Wark, *The Ultimate Enemy: British Intelligence and Nazi Germany, 1933–1939*, Ithaca, NY, Cornell University Press, 2010

Kenneth Warren, *Steel, Ships and Men: Cammell Laird, 1824–1993*, Liverpool, Liverpool University Press, 1998

Bernard Wasserstein, *Britain and the Jews of Europe, 1939–1945*, London, Clarendon Press, 1979

Evelyn Waugh, *The Sword of Honour Trilogy*, Harmondsworth, Penguin, 1984

Charles Webster and Noble Frankland, *The Strategic Air Offensive against Germany 1939–1945*, 4 vols, London, HMSO, 1961

Richard Weight, *Patriots: National Identity in Britain, 1940–2000*, London, Macmillan, 2002

Gordon Williamson, *U-Boat Tactics in World War II*, Oxford, Osprey, 2010

Trevor Wilson, *The Myriad Faces of War: Britain and the Great War, 1914–1918*, Cambridge, Polity, 1986

Ian S. Wood, *Britain, Ireland and the Second World War*, Edinburgh, Edinburgh University Press, 2010

Richard Woodman, *The Real Cruel Sea: The Merchant Navy in the Battle of the Atlantic, 1939–1943*, London, John Murray, 2004

Guy Woodward, *Culture, Northern Ireland, and the Second World War*, Oxford, Oxford University Press, 2015

Robin Woolven, ed., *The London Diary of Anthony Heap, 1931–1945*, Woodbridge, Boydell & Brewer, 2017

Robert Wybrow, *Britain Speaks Out, 1937–87: A Social History as Seen through the Gallup Data*, Basingstoke, Macmillan, 1989

Ina Zweiniger-Bargielowska, *Austerity in Britain*, Oxford, Oxford University Press, 2002

Dissertations

Matthew Lee Powell, 'Army Co-Operation Command and Tactical Air Power Development in Britain, 1940–1943', PhD diss., University of Birmingham, 2013

Erin M. K. Weir, 'The Nazi Submarine Blockade: A Near Victory of Economic Warfare?', MA diss., University of Calgary, 2007

Lesley Whitworth, 'Men, Women, Shops, and "Little Shiny Homes": The Consuming of Coventry, 1930–1939', PhD diss., University of Warwick, 1997

Jane Cole Woods, '"To Blow and Burn England from Her Moorings": The Irish Republican Army and the English Bombing Campaign of 1939', PhD diss., University of Kentucky, 1995

Robin Woolven, 'Civil Defence in London, 1935–1945', PhD diss., King's College London, 2001

DVDs

BFI Film and Video Distribution, *Land of Promise: The British Documentary Movement, 1930–1950*, London, BFI Video, 2008

Web Sites

Con la pella appesa a un chiodo

https://conlapelleappesaaunchiodo.blogspot.com/2013/10/andrea-gritti.html [accessed 13 February 2020]

'Author Quotes: W. H. Lewis' First Impressions of Lord of the Rings'

M. Landers

https://mlanders.com/2014/03/16/author-quotes-w-h-lewis-first-impressions-of-lord-of-the-rings/ [accessed 6 February 2020]

'Cadillac: British Steam Tanker'

U-boat.net

https://uboat.net/allies/merchants/ship/796.html [accessed 27 January 2020]

'Coronation Avenue, Stoke Newington, in the Blitz'

BBC WW2 People's War

https://www.bbc.co.uk/history/ww2peopleswar/stories/26/a2090026.shtml [accessed 24 January 2020]

'Franklin Roosevelt's Press Conference, December 17, 1940'

Franklin D. Roosevelt Presidential Library and Museum

http://docs.fdrlibrary.marist.edu/odllpc2.html [accessed 25 January 2020]

'From Peace to War: Royal Air Force Rearmament Programme, 1934–1940'

The Spitfire Site

http://spitfiresite.com/2010/04/from-peace-to-war-royal-air-force-rearmament-programme-1934–1940.html [accessed 22 January 2020]

'Great Britain Shall Go Forward: Lord Halifax, Radio Address, 22 July, 1940'

World War II Resources

http://www.ibiblio.org/pha/policy/1940/1940-07-22a.html [accessed 22 January 2020]

'The Hague Rules of Air Warfare'

The World War I Document Archive
https://wwi.lib.byu.edu/index.php/The_Hague_Rules_of_Air_Warfare [accessed 13 February 2020]
'HMS *Otus* (N-92)'

U-boat.net
https://uboat.net/allies/warships/ship/3399.html [accessed 13 February 2020]
'How the Fairey Battle Won the War'

Hush-Kit
https://hushkit.net/2017/06/13/how-the-fairey-battle-won-the-war/ [accessed 11 January 2020]
'The Indispensable Man'

The Churchill Society of New Orleans
http://www.churchillsocietyneworleans.com/the-indispensable-man/ [accessed 15 January 2020]
'London Blitz 1940: The First Day's Bomb Attacks Listed in Full'

The Guardian Datablog
https://www.theguardian.com/news/datablog/2010/sep/06/london-blitz-bomb-map-september-7–1940 [accessed 24 January 2020]
'The Luftwaffe over Liverpool: Memories of a Wartime Childhood'

Commonweal
https://www.commonwealmagazine.org/luftwaffe-over-liverpool [accessed 24 January 2020]
'The MAUD Report, 1941'

Atomicarchive.com
http://www.atomicarchive.com/Docs/Begin/MAUD.shtml [accessed 13 February 2020]
'My Last Appeal to Great Britain: Adolf Hitler, Speech made to the Reichstag, 19 July, 1940'

World War II Resources
http://www.ibiblio.org/pha/policy/1940/1940–07–19b.html [accessed 22 January 2020]
'Not Forgotten', the 1939 IRA Bomb Attack'

Historic Coventry
http://www.historiccoventry.co.uk/articles/s-shaw.php [accessed 15 June 2016]
'Patrol Information for U-99, 25 July – 5 August, 1940'

U-boat.net
https://uboat.net/boats/patrols/patrol_4756.html [accessed 27 January 2020]
'Planned Dates for the Attack on the Western Front 1940'

Axis History Forum
https://forum.axishistory.com/viewtopic.php?t=159879 [accessed 9 January 2020]
'SC-42'

UBoat.net
https://uboat.net/ops/convoys/convoys.php?convoy=SC-42 [accessed 13 February 2020]
'September 11, 1941: Fireside Chat 18'

Miller Center
https://millercenter.org/the-presidency/presidential-speeches/september-11-1941-fireside-chat-18-greer-incident [accessed 13 February 2020]
'Ships Built by Cammell Laird'

Wirral Archives
https://www.wirral.gov.uk/sites/default/files/all/Libraries%20and%20archives/List%20of%20Cammell%20Laird%20Ships.pdf [accessed 1 January 2020]
'A View from the Motor Coach: J. B. Priestley's English Journey Scrapbook'

100 Objects from Special Collections at the University of Bradford
https://1000objectsbradford.wordpress.com/2011/11/16/a-view-from-the-motor-coach-j-b-priestleys-english-journey-scrapbook/ [accessed 19 December 2019]

ACKNOWLEDGEMENTS

The idea of writing a 'big book' about Britain and the Second World War has been something I have been thinking about for at least the last twenty years, but it was not until 2015 that I was in a position to pitch the idea to a major publisher. My thanks first of all should, then, go to my agent Andrew Gordon, who took the project on without hesitation and whose enthusiasm and good advice has been essential to the completion of *Britain at Bay*. I am extremely grateful to Cecily Gayford, Penny Daniel, Andrew Franklin, and all the team at Profile Books in the UK who have helped to turn a rough idea into a finished product. Wendy Strothman handled the North American rights with great skill, and Keith Goldsmith at Knopf has been a superb editor. Both Cecily and Keith read numerous drafts of the manuscript, and their editorial suggestions were instrumental in making it a far better book than I ever could have written by myself.

Gary Sheffield, Jonathan Fennell, Brett Holman, Richard Carswell and Andreas Biermann all read some or all of the drafted material and offered innumerable suggestions and corrections, many of which prevented me from making embarrassing mistakes of fact. I am very grateful for their kindness and expertise. All errors in the final work are, of course, mine and mine alone. I am also grateful to Jonathan Boff, Tara Finn, Ian Garner, Dan Jackson, Amy Milne-Smith, Stephen Moore, Andrew Newson, Lynsey Shaw Cobden, Chris Smith, Dan Todman, Victoria Taylor, Jonathan Ware and Duncan Weldon, among others, for offering research assistance, suggestions, advice or simply encouragement which proved invaluable along the way.

I am grateful to my employer, Syracuse University, and in particular to the Department of History in the Maxwell School of Citizenship and Public Affairs for making it possible for me to complete this book. I would like to thank in particular my colleagues, especially Susan Branson, Norman Kutcher and Junko Takeda for their patience and good humour in bearing with me during five sometimes testing years. I'd also like to thank SU's Interlibrary Loan Department, without which it would have been simply impossible to conduct the secondary source reading necessary for this project. Lydia Wasylenko, the History Department's outgoing library specialist, helped to obtain some fantastic resources for the university, including the Mass Observation Online archive, which proved invaluable.

Much of the primary source research for was conducted at the Imperial War Museum and the UK National Archives in London, and I am grateful to the staff there for their expert assistance. Thank you to those copyright holders who kindly permitted material to be reproduced here. All reasonable effort has been made to contact in advance those holding copyright over the original sources included in *Britain at Bay*; if for some reason anyone has been overlooked, please contact the publisher so this omission can be rectified in future editions.

I am grateful, as ever, for the enormous kindness and generosity extended to me by Tom and Moira Deveson while staying in London. Professor D'Maris Coffman of University College London has been my close friend since graduate school, and has remained a rock of good advice, help and comfort. I am thankful to my family in the UK, in particular to my sisters Carolyn and Susi, for their love and support. Lastly, I want to thank my wife Barbara and my children Thomas, Katharine and Lizzie, for being part of this adventure. As I write in May 2020, the five of us are in house-bound quarantine in circumstances that I could not have possibly imagined five years ago when I began this book. Many comparisons, most of them not very convincing, have been made between the Covid-19 pandemic emergency of this year and the home front experience of the Second World War. Specious analogies aside, there has been something about the way in which our lives have been turned upside down over the past few months to offer a glimpse, however slight, of what it must have felt like to be an ordinary observer of the great and unsettling drama of the 1940s. I will be forever grateful to my wife and children for making what has often been a bleak and soul-sapping few months bearable. It is because of them that I had the strength of will to finish *Britain at Bay*, and it is because of them that I now look forward with excitement to completing this history of the British at war in a second future volume.

INDEX